Cases in

# Commercial Real Estate Investing

### John McMahan

McMahan Real Estate Services LLC
San Francisco, California
*www.mcmahanrealestate.com*

# Cases in Commercial Real Estate Investing
By John McMahan

Published by:
**McMahan Real Estate Services LLC, San Francisco, California**
www.mcmahanrealestate.com

Copyright © 2005 by John McMahan

ISBN: 0-9770189-0-3

Library of Congress Control Number: 2005905081

Printed in the United States of America

All rights reserved. No part of this book may be reproduced or transmitted in any form or by any means, electronic or mechanical, including photocopying, recording or by any information storage and retrieval system, without prior written permission from the author.

For information, address McMahan Real Estate Services LLC
2905 Scott Street, San Francisco, CA 94123
info@mcmahanrealestate.com
(415) 775-1517

# Table of Contents

|  | Page |
|---|---|
| **Acknowledgements** | |
| **Foreword** – How to Prepare for Case Discussion | |
| **Introduction** – Chapter Summaries | 9 |

## Section I: Portfolio Management

| | | |
|---|---|---|
| Chapter 1: | NOTE ON INSTITUTIONAL REAL ESTATE INVESTMENT | 17 |
| Chapter 2: | ARIZONA BUILDING CORPORATION<br>*Role of Real Estate in a Mixed Asset Portfolio* | 37 |
| Chapter 3: | GLOBAL MANUFACTURING CORPORATION<br>*Portfolio Restructuring* | 51 |
| Chapter 4: | VALLEY ISLAND PUBLIC EMPLOYEES' RETIREMENT SYSTEM (VIPERS)<br>*Impact of Technology on Portfolio Strategy* | 73 |
| Chapter 5: | BARTON STATE TEACHERS' RETIREMENT SYSTEM (BarSTRS)<br>*Impact of "Return Compression" on Portfolio Strategy* | 105 |

## Section II: Asset Management

| | | |
|---|---|---|
| Chapter 6: | NOTE ON ASSET MANAGEMENT | 127 |
| Chapter 7: | NOVATO FAIR SHOPPING CENTER<br>*Tenant Restructuring* | 151 |
| Chapter 8: | LODESTAR, INC.<br>*Lease Negotiation* | 167 |
| | Case A: Jim Maroney | *167* |
| | Case B: Allison Bowers | *190* |
| Chapter 9: | CORPORATE REAL ESTATE | 207 |
| | Case A: Sprint Corporation<br>*Facilities Management Strategy* | *207* |
| | Case B: Jones Lang LaSalle<br>*Service Provider Strategy* | *216* |

| Chapter 10: | ASSET MANAGEMENT AND LEADERSHIP MINICASES | **229** |
|---|---|---|
| | Case A: Phillips, Roth, & Blair LLC | *229* |
| | Case B: TRUCOMM, Inc. | *231* |
| | Case C: Cherry Orchard Shopping Center | *233* |
| | Case D: Clarkson Development Company Inc. | *235* |
| | Case E: Monroe Real Estate Advisors, Inc. | *237* |
| | Case F: National Realty Trust, Inc. | *239* |
| | Case G: RealWorld.com, Inc. | *241* |

## Section III: Transaction Management

| Chapter 11: | NOTE ON PROPERTY ACQUISITION | **243** |
|---|---|---|
| Chapter 12: | HIGHTECHOFFICE, INC. A<br>*Project Acquisition* | **277** |
| Chapter 13: | HIGHTECHOFFICE, INC. B<br>*Acquisition Due Diligence* | **299** |
| Chapter 14: | SAN MARCOS INDUSTRIAL PARK A<br>*Project Acquisition* | **315** |
| Chapter 15: | SAN MARCOS INDUSTRIAL PARK B<br>*Property Disposition* | **329** |

## Section IV: Enterprise Management

| Chapter 16: | NOTE ON STRATEGIC MANAGEMENT | **343** |
|---|---|---|
| Chapter 17: | GENERAL GROWTH PROPERTIES, INC.<br>*Public vs. Private Markets* | **363** |
| Chapter 18: | WESTERN REAL ESTATE ADVISORS<br>*REIT Roll-Up* | **407** |
| Chapter 19: | HINES INTERESTS LP: EMERGING MARKETS REAL ESTATE FUND II<br>*Global Investing* | **429** |
| Chapter 20: | PACIFIC APARTMENT TRUST, INC.<br>*Enterprise Strategy and Governance* | **451** |

# Acknowledgements

First, I would like to thank Susanne Cannon, Director of Real Estate at DePaul University for giving me the initial idea to publish a real estate casebook.

I also would like to thank the following industry professionals for reviewing portions of the book dealing with their respective areas: Craig A. Severance, Founder & CEO, RealConnected, LLC (former head of acquisitions, AMB Property Corporation); Deirdre A. Kuring, Executive Vice President, BRE Properties, Inc.; Geoffrey Dohrmann, Chairman & CEO, Institutional Real Estate Inc.; Noel W. Nellis, Esq., Chair, Global Real Estate Practice, Orrick, Herrington & Sutcliffe LLP; Preston Sargent, Senior Vice President, Kennedy Associates Real Estate Counsel, Inc. All of these individuals are experienced players in their respective fields and contributed a current "real world" view of the material covered.

Jeannine Drew, the editor of my first book, *Property Development*, took time out of a busy schedule to edit portions of this book and, as usual, did an excellent job. I would also like to give a special thanks to Lena Sloan, who recently received a Masters Degree in International and Development Economics from the University of San Francisco, for her assistance in proofing the book and coordinating the printing process; as well as Richard Goodwin, of REGco. Design, for designing the cover; Lowell W. Hawkins who edited most of the cases; and my daughter, Vanessa, who helped organize the cases and was a steady, constructive critic throughout. In addition, Andrew Light, Dennis Williams, Espen Thoegersen, Janet Martinez, and Kevin Deeble provided research material and analytical support for certain cases.

I also am indebted to the many real estate academicians, research professionals, and industry leaders who have used and commented on my cases and other writing over the last several years: Blake Eagle, NCREIF; Bob Edelstein, UC Berkeley; David Ling, University of Florida; Doug Abbey, Stanford; Frank McDowell, BRE Properties, Inc.; Fred Halperin, NAREIM; Gail Haynes, PREA; Glenn Mueller, Colorado State; Hamid Moghadam, AMB Property Corporation; Gloria Schuck, MIT; Herve Kevenides, NYU; Jan deRoos, Cornell; Jeff Fisher, Indiana University; Jim Webb, Cleveland State; Joe Gyourko, Wharton; Ken Lusht, Penn State; Kent Wiegel, Washington Mutual; Kerry Vandell, Wisconsin; Lynne Sagalyn, Wharton: Mark Eppli, Marquette; Mike Grupe, NAREIT; Michael Young, RREEF; Peter Pike, PikeNet; Rick Peiser, Harvard; Ronald Rogers, University of South Carolina; Scott Urdang, Wharton; Steve Grenadier, Stanford; Steven Ott, University of North Carolina (Charlotte); Susanne Cannon, DePaul

University; Thomas Kinateder, Nuertingen University (Germany); Tim Riddiough, Wisconsin; Tom Bothen, University of Illinois (Chicago); Tom Thibodeau, University of Colorado; and Wylie Greig, RREEF.

Finally, I wish to express my gratitude to my wife of 32 years, Jacqueline, for her patience in enduring what is always a longer-than-expected writing process and to my children – Cathy, Jason, Justin, and Vanessa – for the challenges and pleasures they have provided their father over the years.

John McMahan

San Francisco

June, 2005

# FOREWORD

# How to Prepare for Case Discussion

The cases in this book were written with two objectives in mind: (1) to disseminate information about a subject and (2) to place the reader into a manager's role as a decision maker. The former objective is achieved through the introductory text in the first chapter of each section and throughout the case itself. The minicases also provide an opportunity to fine-tune the analytical and leadership skills often required of a manager of a private or public real estate enterprise.

The second, more difficult objective is to begin thinking like a professional real estate manager in dealing with a fundamental business decision that has to be made. This might be an acquisition manager dealing with a pending transaction, an asset manager trying to restructure the tenancies in a shopping center, a REIT manager trying to deal with tough new governance requirements, a pension fund manager worrying about restructuring an investment portfolio, or a manager faced with any of the myriad of other tactical and strategic decisions that are made every day in the world of commercial real estate investing.

Most of the cases in this book are based on real people making actual decisions, although, in certain cases, the names and circumstances have been disguised at the request of the people involved or to improve the learning potential of the case. Historical perspective is provided by the ten year span over which these cases occur, through one of the most challenging decades in US real estate history.

As a student, you can play an important role in the case learning process by preparing well for each case before you come to class. This is accomplished by reading the case in advance, doing whatever analytical work is required, focusing on the decision(s) that have to be made, making the decision, and being prepared to support your decision in what hopefully will be a spirited discussion among your peers. This is not unlike the real-world situation most real estate managers face when approaching a key management or board meeting.

A few suggestions on how to approach case preparation:

- ❑ Place yourself in the shoes of the protagonist in the case. What pressures is this individual under in terms of timing (always a problem), job responsibilities, professional and personal integrity, career aspirations, etc.? How do these pressures impact the decision that has to be made?

- ❑ Who are the other players in the case? What will be their views, and to what degree can they be expected to be supportive or in conflict with your position? How do you plan to deal with this situation?
- ❑ What are the alternative decisions that should be considered? What are the opportunities presented by making the right decision? Ramifications of making the wrong decision?
- ❑ What evidence is provided in the case to support your decision? How reliable is the factual data upon which it is based? Is the data unbiased?
- ❑ What are the alternatives to this decision? What are the arguments pro and con for these alternatives? Are you prepared to change your mind about your original decision?
- ❑ What did you learn from this case? How is the learning experience similar to other cases the class has discussed? How is it different?

Case learning is not easy, but it is a microcosm of what you will face in the real world of real estate management. The first step in an effective learning process is solid preparation before you come to class.

A few additional thoughts: The questions at the end of each chapter are meant to stimulate your thinking about the material covered in the case and to provide the foundation for making good decisions. They are not a substitute for thinking about the decisions you make. Also, the questions are meant to be illustrative and by no means represent all of the questions that the case suggests.

Case learning is meant to be a supplement and not an alternative to text and lectures, which provide the overall foundation of understanding required for good case discussion. Do not substitute preparation for cases for time you would have otherwise spent with your other course work. You need both to get the most out of your real estate educational experience.

Good luck and enjoy!

John McMahan

# INTRODUCTION

## Chapter Summaries

### Section I: Portfolio Management

#### Chapter 1: NOTE ON INSTITUTIONAL REAL ESTATE INVESTMENT

Discusses the post-war history of commercial real estate with a focus on how pension funds and REITs became a major force in commercial real estate investing. Explores major trends in the risk/return profile of real estate, the major institutional players in the current market, and strategic considerations in developing a real estate investment strategy.

#### Chapter 2: ARIZONA BUILDING CORPORATION (1993)[1]
*Role of Real Estate in a Mixed Asset Portfolio*

Marilyn Breadwell is a pension consultant working on her first consulting assignment for Arizona Building Corporation, a Phoenix-based construction products manufacturing company.

The case takes the student through each of the steps involved in establishing an investment strategy for a mixed asset portfolio, including determining the investment "efficient frontier," mean variance analysis, role of real estate in a mixed asset portfolio, selection of an optimum mix of asset classes, and matching asset risk with a pension fund's risk profile. Includes a view of the political dynamics of the various constituencies within a pension fund in setting investment policy.

#### Chapter 3: GLOBAL MANUFACTURING CORPORATION (1993)
*Portfolio Restructuring*

Bob McFee is the Manager of Real Estate for the pension fund of Global Manufacturing Corporation (GMC), which had been a pioneer in investing in real estate in the 1980s, although most of the investments have subsequently turned sour.

In 1990, Bob was brought in to workout the existing portfolio and recommend a strategy for a new direction. He soon discovered that he was dealing with basic portfolio issues, such as: What should be the target allocation for real estate? What should be the role of fixed income in real

---

[1] Dates in parenthesis refer to the approximate time when the case takes place.

estate? Securitized real estate? Where should investments be located? Which property types?

Introduces the concept of the "four quadrants" of real estate and explores using real estate investments to influence broader social objectives. Case also looks at international real estate as well as the desirability of "leveraging property investments." The case ends with a discussion of the problems of the successful integration of "old" and "new" portfolios.

## Chapter 4: VALLEY ISLAND PUBLIC EMPLOYEES' RETIREMENT SYSTEM (VIPERS) (2001)
### Impact of Technology on Portfolio Strategy

Mason Rourke is Director of Real Estate for a major Midwest pension fund with $3.2 billion in real estate. He has just been asked by his Chairman to prepare for a meeting of the Board in two weeks, which will be devoted primarily to the impact of technology on real estate.

Key factors to be evaluated are the impact of technology on property types, geographic areas, and overall portfolio return. Reviews development of the World Wide Web, new economy financing, e-business, and the collapse of the dot-com boom. Recommendation is expected on whether to restructure the portfolio and, if so, any changes that may be required in the real estate allocation.

## Chapter 5: BARTON STATE TEACHERS' RETIREMENT SYSTEM (BarSTRS) (2003)
### Impact of "Return Compression" on Portfolio Strategy

Eleanor Rigby is the Director of Real Estate for a major pension fund and is putting the final touches on the 2004 real estate investment strategy. The complexity of the analysis is compounded by market conditions in which real estate demand and prices are increasing at a time when real estate investment fundamentals are declining. Reviews various investment strategies including "core," "enhanced core," "value added," and "opportunity" investments. Also considers the role of various property types and geographical markets in setting a strategy as well as "constrained vs. commodity" markets.

# Section II: Asset Management

## Chapter 6: NOTE ON ASSET MANAGEMENT

A discussion of the evolution of asset management as an emerging force in the real estate investment industry. Explains the difference between asset management and property management. Reviews a new view of tenants as the "customer" and the proper focus of asset managers. Includes a review of the responsibilities of the asset manager and how his/her activities relate to other areas of management, such as acquisitions and financial reporting.

## Chapter 7: NOVATO FAIR SHOPPING CENTER (2002)
### *Tenant Restructuring*

Pamela Grant is the asset manager for Novato Fair, an older community center located in a market with rapidly expanding incomes and retail sales. She is currently responsible for developing a re-leasing strategy for three tenants whose leases expire in 2003. Case involves market analysis, tenant sales history, tenant lease rollover, comparable properties, anchor lease expansion, and relocating tenants to achieve greater overall center sales.

## Chapter 8: LODESTAR, INC. (2001)
### *Lease Negotiation*

Two cases for use in teaching lease negotiating strategies involving the leasing of 50% of a recently completed office building in a weak Dallas market. Prospective tenant is Lodestar, Inc., a high technology firm relocating from the San Francisco Bay Area.

These cases are often taught by dividing the class into two groups, each representing either Jim Maroney or Allison Bowers in the negotiations.

**Case A: JIM MARONEY** is Senior Vice President of Asset Management for Centaur Advisors, a Boston-based investment advisor, which has developed the building and is now attempting to secure its first tenant, Lodestar, Inc., a San Francisco-based energy firm moving to the Dallas metropolitan area.

Major landlord issues include impact of below-market anchor tenant lease on subsequent leasing activity; financing above-standard tenant improvements backed by tenant Letter of Credit; and subcontracting high speed telecommunications services to an outside service provider.

**Case B: ALLISON BOWERS** is the Vice President of Corporate Real Estate for Lodestar, Inc.

Major tenant issues include relocating a major facility to a new metropolitan area, using firm credit line to finance real estate improvements, and operating a high tech firm in a facility with telecommunications being provided by an outside service provider.

## Chapter 9: CORPORATE REAL ESTATE (2002)

### Case A: SPRINT CORPORATION
*Facilities Management Strategy*

Deals with problems of a major, rapidly growing telecommunications company in meeting its real estate operating requirements on an international basis. Chronicles the creation of management initiatives based on Cisco's "Net Ready" success factors of leadership, governance, technology and competency, in order to determine the extent to which technology can assist in solving some of the firm's growth problems.

Explores the working relationship between real estate and human resource functions, as well as the problems of servicing the needs of an organization operating in a "silo" structure.

### Case B: JONES LANG LASALLE
*Service Provider Strategy*

Case focuses on a major service provider's attempt to use new technology to better serve its clients and, in so doing, gain advantage in a highly competitive industry. Explores the use of technology to improve efficiency of real estate transactions, management of projects, lease administration, and to speed up property accounting procedures. Reviews several major initiatives being undertaken by service providers to pool resources in approaching the market (e. g., "Project Constellation").

## Chapter 10: ASSET MANAGEMENT AND LEADERSHIP MINICASES (Two Pages Each)

Seven minicases involving various challenges facing asset managers and other members of real estate management. The focus is on an analytical approach to problem solving.

**Case A: PHILLIPS, ROTH, & BLAIR LLC (1999)** Case deals with re-leasing of key tenant office space in a mid-rise Sunbelt office building. Involves balancing of rate, term, tenant finish, and parking spaces.

**Case B: TRUCOMM, INC. (2003)** Deals with the default of a build-to-suit tenant in a declining office market and efforts to reprice and negotiate a "blend and extend" solution.

## Case C: CHERRY ORCHARD SHOPPING CENTER (2005)

Focuses on the role of asset management in responding to an unsolicited offer to purchase an existing asset in the portfolio ("Hold/Sell Analysis").

## Case D: CLARKSON DEVELOPMENT COMPANY, INC. (2002)

Leadership case involving a construction supervisor for a Boston real estate development company.

## Case E: MONROE REAL ESTATE ADVISORS, INC. (2002)

Leadership case focusing on a CEO's handling a monthly management meeting.

## Case F: NATIONAL REALTY TRUST, INC. (2002)

Leadership case involving a district manager dealing with a subordinate's handling of rent delinquencies.

## Case G: REALWORLD.COM, INC. (2002)

Leadership case involving the head of a product development group in a weekly management meeting.

# Section III: Transaction Management

## Chapter 11: NOTE ON PROPERTY ACQUISITION

Discussion of the roles and steps involved in property acquisition. Focus is on understanding investor objectives; importance of investment strategy; deal sourcing; investment underwriting; investment risk analysis; role of the investment committee; negotiating agreements; physical, legal, and business due diligence; and waive and closing.

## Chapter 12: HIGHTECHOFFICE, INC. A (2002)
### *Property Acquisition*

Jeb Collins is head of acquisitions for HiTechOffice, Inc. (HiTech), which invests in office complexes tenanted by high technology firms. He is trying to finalize a Letter of Intent to purchase a $21.4 million office and research building in Dallas. Tenants include a major biotech firm relocating from the Bay Area, a service center for a national wireless firm, and a computer school.

Underwriting issues include a Letter of Credit backing over-standard improvements for the biotech firm, a telecomm access agreement, and the weak North Dallas office market. The market is of particular concern due to continuing levels of new construction and the increasing tendency of existing firms to sublease space.

## Chapter 13: HIGHTECHOFFICE, INC. B (2002)
### Acquisition Due Diligence

This case is based on HighTechOffice A. The case focuses on issues associated with property due diligence such as physical, legal, and business risks associated with the purchase. Also involves issues specific to the A case such as the Letter of Credit and the provision of technological services by an independent contractor.

## Chapter 14: SAN MARCOS INDUSTRIAL PARK A (2003)
### Project Acquisition

Beth Sawyer is an Investment Officer for an opportunity fund. She has been asked to analyze an Investment Memorandum they have received regarding a new industrial development in San Diego County, one of the fastest growing, most desirable real estate investment markets in the nation.

In developing her analysis, she needs to consider the San Diego market for industrial uses, the quality of the development, the functionality of the buildings, the mix of existing tenants, the market for the remaining space, and the ability to upgrade to office use in the future.

Based on her analysis, she must develop a bid price and a recommendation of whether to proceed or not. The case deals with investing in a period of increasing demand and prices for real estate at a time of declining market fundamentals.

## Chapter 15: SAN MARCOS INDUSTRIAL PARK B (2005)
### Property Disposition

This case is based on the disposition of one building in San Marcos Industrial Park to raise funds for investor distribution. The property disposition process is viewed from the seller's perspective and includes a discussion of each of the major steps in the property disposition process including targeting buyers, the broker selection process, listing agreements, disposition alternatives, confidentiality agreements, offering memoranda, purchase and sale agreements, due diligence, and the closing process.

# Section IV: Enterprise Management

## Chapter 16: NOTE ON STRATEGIC MANAGEMENT

Reviews the history of strategic management thinking and its application to real estate enterprises. Includes an overview of popular management strategies, such as Michael Porter's "five forces," Hamel and Prahalad's "core competencies," and Jack Welch's "rate of organizational change" and their application to real estate.

## Chapter 17: GENERAL GROWTH PROPERTIES, INC. (1998)
### Public vs. Private Markets

John Bucksbaum is EVP and CAO of General Growth Properties (GGP), a public Real Estate Investment Trust (REIT). He has asked his general managers to review trends affecting the firm and recommend possible changes in GGP's overall business strategy.

This case discusses how strategic capital market decisions can play a key role in building a small Midwestern store into one of the great retail success stories of the last century. Focuses on the decision to operate as a private or public company based on trends evolving in the retail marketplace and the capital markets. Discusses the importance of strategic mergers to accelerate corporate growth as well as the value of long-term relationships with key business partners.

The case also examines the changing nature of consumer shopping patterns, retail markets, the impact of technology on retail operations as well as the rise of "New REITs" and the importance of this vehicle in supporting large, national real estate operations.

## Chapter 18: WESTERN REAL ESTATE ADVISORS (1997)
### REIT Roll-Up

Camille Concilatore is the Director of Portfolio Management for Western Real Estate Advisors (Western), a highly successful office and industrial investment advisor. She is the member of management responsible for convincing Western's pension fund investors to approve a proposal to roll up Western's assets into a new REIT.

The case looks at tradeoffs in making a transition from both the advisor's and pension investor's points of view. Includes evaluation of possible changes in original proposal to make it more acceptable to pension investors.

## Chapter 19: HINES INTERESTS LP: EMERGING MARKETS REAL ESTATE FUND II (1999)
### Global Investing

Hasty Johnson is the Chief Financial Officer of Hines Interests LP, a worldwide real estate development and management firm. He is facing a General Partners meeting called to decide whether or not to proceed with a second Emerging Markets Real Estate Fund and, if so, how to position the fund in the marketplace.

The case focuses on the move of Hines Interests LP into the international real estate investing field. Looks at the problems (and attractions) of investing in emerging markets. Also reviews the "linkage" between foreign and domestic markets.

The case also examines the role of foreign governments in creating an attractive investment environment, as well as the importance of selecting the "right" local partner. Includes a review of investment vehicles, the importance of structuring equity ownership to meet different investor objectives, tax issues, and the importance of allocating returns to meet investor references. The issues surrounding the introduction of a second fund are also considered, including performance of the first fund, country selection, and equity investor positions.

## Chapter 20: PACIFIC APARTMENT TRUST, INC. (2005)
### Enterprise Strategy and Governance

This case focuses on largely successful efforts of a multifamily REIT to grow through strategic planning and the corporate governance challenges currently facing public real estate organizations. In 2004 the REIT finds itself in a position of having to divert considerable management resources to governance issues. This arises from Enron's collapse, other corporate misadventures, and the ensuing efforts of legislative and regulatory bodies to bring greater accountability and transparency to America's corporate world (Sarbanes-Oxley legislation, etc.).

Discusses how one real estate organization responded to this changing world, and the impact on the organization and its real estate operations. Looks at the corporation from the viewpoint of the Board, Senior Management, and operating personnel.

# 1
# NOTE ON INSTITUTIONAL REAL ESTATE INVESTMENT[1]

## BRIEF HISTORY

### *Life Insurance Companies: The First Institutional Real Estate Investors*

World War II was financed largely through debt sold by the US government to America's financial institutions, primarily life insurance companies. Following the war, as this debt matured, insurance companies utilized the proceeds to invest in real estate mortgages, attempting to satisfy the nation's pent up demand for real estate of all types.

In order to support this investment program, many insurance companies established regional offices to make and manage their mortgage and equity real estate investments. As described in greater detail in Chapter 6, this "on the ground" asset management infrastructure enabled them to become investment managers for other, more passive institutional investors, primarily pension funds.

### *Emergence of Pension Funds*

Pension funds were established in the 1950's by corporations such as General Motors, to supplement Social Security and attract and retain key employees. The investment objectives of these early pension funds were relatively modest – to preserve accumulated capital, achieve sufficient returns to meet

---

[1] Copyright ©2005 by John McMahan. All rights reserved.

beneficiary liabilities, and maintain sufficient liquidity to pay the funds' operating expenses.

**Pension Managers Avoid Real Estate:** Most pension fund managers avoided real estate equity investment on any scale until 1975.[2] This hesitancy was based primarily on concerns about the nonfungibility, market fragmentation, infrequent pricing, lack of an auction market, and general lack of information about the asset class. Many fund managers also believed that real estate favored taxable, rather than tax-exempt investors. As a result of these and other concerns, real estate was perceived to be riskier than financial investments such as stocks and bonds.[3]

**ERISA Sets New Investment Standards:** In 1974, Congress passed the Employment Retirement Income Security Act (ERISA). This legislation was directed primarily at preventing a repeat of pension abuses related to corporate bankruptcy (Studebaker) and union graft and corruption (Teamsters).

ERISA established tough new fiduciary standards for the management of pension plans. Henceforth, managers of pension fund capital were expected to:

- Discharge their duties solely in the interests of participants and beneficiaries.
- Demonstrate "prudence" in all investment decisions.
- Diversify plan investments to minimize the risks of large losses.

Penalties for violating ERISA standards became "personal and criminal" to drive home to individual trustees the serious consequences of violating the provisions of the new legislation. ERISA also established the obligation for pension sponsors to look at the total spectrum of investment opportunities. This opened up consideration of nonfinancial assets such as real estate.

**Inflation Provides the Final Push Toward Real Estate:** In 1975–79, double-digit inflation destroyed the values of many portfolios, as stocks proved not to be the inflation hedge advertised. In fact, inflation turned out to be a dual threat to pension funds: pension liabilities increased faster than normal as inflation pushed up wages and other costs, and investments supporting these liabilities posted lower real returns.

---

[2] Prior to this time, insurance companies and bank trust departments did invest pension capital in whole loan mortgages and net leased properties on a fully discretionary basis, using insured accounts.

[3] It should be noted that many of the pension decision makers had been trained in the management of financial assets and had little previous exposure to real estate as an investment.

As a result, the present value of future investment flows of many pension funds shifted from positive to negative. For the first time, "unfunded liabilities" became a major issue, forcing pension managers to consider investing at least a portion of their assets in inflation-resistant investments such as real estate.[4]

**Prudential Pioneers "Open-End" Real Estate Investment Funds:** Prudential established the Prudential Realty Income Separate Account (PRISA) in 1970 which, by 1975, was well positioned to take advantage of the pension community's dual challenges of complying with ERISA and dealing with the ravages of double-digit inflation.

PRISA was organized as a unit trust with an infinite life (i.e., "open-end"). In order to provide a measure of liquidity, Prudential allowed participants to withdraw their funds on a quarterly basis, in a manner similar to open-end mutual stock and bond funds. It wasn't long before many of the large insurance companies and commercial banks had similar open-end funds including AETNA, CIGNA, Travelers, John Hancock, Equitable, Metropolitan Life, First Chicago, Wachovia, and others.

**Pros and Cons of Open-End Funds:** As more insurance companies and commercial banks began sponsoring open-end funds, the merits and flaws of these new real estate investment vehicles became more apparent. On the plus side, they were generally large pools of capital, reflecting a diverse investor base in which small investors believed they could safely participate. Through the periodic withdrawal device, open-end funds also provided investors with a measure of liquidity.

Disadvantages included the fact that investors were buying and selling on appraised values rather than actual market transactions. Also, the "queue" to take investment capital out was not always viewed as being fair to all investors.[5] This could be a particular concern if the fund sponsor were forced to liquidate properties in order to meet redemption requests.

---

[4] In 1980, the Department of Labor (DOL) brought a major ERISA case against the Plumbers Union of Northern California and its principal leader, Joseph P. Mazzola. The case was decided in favor of the DOL, upheld on appeal, and ultimately established industry standards for real estate portfolio diversification. The author served as the portfolio diversification expert for the DOL.

[5] The problem wasn't so much the "queue" per se, but the way it was administered, namely on a first-in first-out rather than pro-rata basis. This forced pension managers to notify the fund sponsor of its desire to liquidate if others were doing so, creating somewhat of a "run on the bank" mentality.

**Emergence of Closed-End Funds:** Observing the success of financial institutions in attracting large sums of capital from pension funds, Coldwell Banker and several other large entrepreneurial real estate firms began sponsoring closed-end funds, which they believed were more reflective of the true nature of real estate as a relatively illiquid asset.[6]

The holding entity is a unit trust, but here the similarly to open-end funds ends. Closed-end funds have a finite life, usually ten years. Investor dollars are "called for" to fund properties as they are acquired. The investor establishes the maximum amount of capital they wish to invest in the fund and capital is drawn against this commitment until the maximum is reached. Closed-end funds also are more focused in terms of investment strategy, investing in properties of a particular type, in a certain geographical area, or which had other distinguishing characteristics.

There are several disadvantages of closed-end funds. They generally invest in smaller properties, there is less diversification within the funds, and fund sponsors are perceived to be under greater pressure to invest. They also are highly illiquid, with investors unable to reclaim cash until the fund is liquidated. A major concern was that liquidation might come at the wrong time in the real estate cycle, forcing investors to accept lower returns or, in some cases, a possible loss of capital value.[7]

**Qualified Plan Asset Manager (QPAM) Legislation:** In the early 1980's, Congress clarified ERISA requirements regarding the hiring of real estate managers.[8] The role of a Qualified Plan Asset Manager (QPAM) was established to allow plan sponsors to escape direct responsibility for the management of real estate assets in their portfolios.

To qualify, a manager had to (1) have the power to acquire, manage, and dispose of any real estate assets in its portfolio; (2) be registered as an investment advisor under the Investment Advisors Act of 1940 (or a bank or insurance company as defined by ERISA); and (3) acknowledge in writing that it was a fiduciary of the plan.[9] Not only did this legislation lessen the liability of plan sponsors for actions of its managers, but managers who qualified were given more flexibility in the management of portfolio assets,

---

[6] Coldwell Banker utilized a limited partnership format as the investment entity. Subsequent closed-end funds sponsored by RREEF, Heitman, LaSalle, and AEW used a group trust format, which was closer to being a true commingled fund.
[7] Although closed end funds didn't use appraisals for liquidation purposes, they were used in determining annual fees. This created what many investors viewed as a conflict of interest because the manger was perceived to be less interested in selling when portfolio assets were highly valued, as this would reduce the manager's fee income.
[8] The term "investment manager" is used generically throughout this book to include registered investment advisors, managers of Real Estate Investment Trusts (REITs), general partners, and any other individuals or firms who serve as a fiduciary to real estate investors.
[9] Natalie A. McKelvy, *Pension Fund Investments in Real Estate*, 1983.

particularly in terms of transaction approvals, management deployment, asset operating decisions, etc.

**Tax Reform Act of 1981 Leads to Excesses:** Meanwhile, the Tax Reform Act of 1981 had been quite favorable to taxable real estate investors. Features such as accelerated depreciation, investment tax credits, and real estate's exemption from the "basis rule" combined to attract a large amount of investment capital into increasingly fragile real estate schemes.

US investors were joined in the rush to real estate by foreign investors including the Japanese, who had few real estate opportunities at home and were under considerable pressure to take advantage of the dollar–yen spread to convert largely frozen US subsidiary earnings into hard assets.

**Tax Reform Act of 1986 Reduces the Role of Individual Investors:** The excesses of the 1981 Act were reversed in the Tax Reform Act of 1986, sharply reducing the attraction of real estate to taxable investors. This, in turn, reduced the role of the individual investor and opened up the field to institutional investors such as pension funds, insurance companies and (unfortunately, as it would turn out) thrifts.

**Disintermediation of Traditional Capital Markets Leads to Deregulation:** Merrill Lynch and other investment banks had introduced cash management or "money market" accounts in the late 1970's. These accounts paid investors a market rate of interest on their savings rather than the regulated rate paid by banks and thrifts. Over the next several years, money market accounts created a large disintermediation of capital from traditional savings institutions.

The banks and thrifts responded by lobbying successfully for a deregulation of banking, which would allow them to compete with the rapidly growing money market funds. One of the byproducts was the move of thrifts into commercial mortgage lending. Seemingly unconcerned with their lack of experience in this new field, thrifts began financing a wide variety of projects in various phases of development throughout the country. In many cases, these projects were in out-of-the-way locations that previously had not been the focus of real estate investment activity.

**Boom, Bust and Recovery:** As a result of changes in tax policy and financial institution deregulation, a major demand/supply disequilibrium began developing in the late 1980's. As might be expected, yields evaporated, values plummeted, and real estate became increasingly unattractive vis-à-vis financial assets.

By 1990, mortgage lending turned negative and a major credit crunch developed in real estate capital markets. This led to a virtual halt in the construction of new projects and a wave of mortgage foreclosures, ultimately leading to the bankruptcy of several major thrifts.

Congress established the Resolution Trust Corporation (RTC) in 1991 to take over properties serving as collateral for failed mortgages and sell them in the capital market to new investors, who purchased them at a substantial discount. These investors served as a valuable conduit in liquidating the RTC portfolio, which renewed Wall Street's interest in real estate.[10] Ultimately, defaulted properties ended up in stronger hands and a degree of equilibrium returned to real estate markets. Among many developers and investors, the watchword was now "stay alive 'til '95," when the markets were expected to recover.

## *Real Estate Investment Trusts (REITs)*

For most pension funds that had invested in real estate, the bloom was off the rose by the early 1990's. No wonder: the overall loss to pension real estate portfolios was significant, in some cases as much as 30%.

Several observers concluded that the problem was not real estate per se, but direct investment vehicles such as open- and closed-end funds. Thus began a move to securitize real estate equities in the form of Real Estate Investment Trusts (REITs), Real Estate Operating Companies (REOC's), and other public investment vehicles. The prevailing wisdom was that securitized instruments would minimize potential investor losses by providing proper management incentives, corporate governance, efficient markets, and the ability to exit investments fairly rapidly.

**Legal Structure of REITs:** REITs had been originally organized by Congress in 1960 as a means of allowing greater individual participation in real estate on a tax "pass-through" basis. The legal entity was a corporation or trust managed by a board of directors or trustees. Here the resemblance to other public companies ended, however, reflecting the special nature of REITs.

REITs are required to have at least 100 shareholders, no five of which could own more then 50% of the stock (the 5/50 rule).[11] REITs also must hold 75% of their assets in real estate equity, mortgages, shares in other REITs, cash, and certain other securities. Seventy-five percent (75%) of the income must consist of rents or mortgage interest payments. Ninety-five percent

---

[10] Many of these restructurings utilized mortgage pools, which led to rapid growth in the Commercial Mortgage Backed Securities (CMBS) industry.
[11] The original rule was modified to allow pension funds to invest by considering individual plan beneficiaries as REIT shareholders (the "look through" rule).

(95%) must be "passive" and 95% of taxable income must be distributed currently. REITs also cannot act as "dealers," must be integrated, and their shares must be transferable.

**Early REITs:** At first, most REITs were small, passive, and managed externally. There was little management ownership, analyst coverage, or market activity.

In the late 1960's, several financial institutions created new REITs as a vehicle to underwrite and fund mortgage loans that were too risky for their traditional portfolios. These were largely construction loans, often secured by speculative projects located in secondary markets.

Ultimately, REITs were the largest source of mortgage financing for the 1971–75 real estate boom. Most of these REITs collapsed in the mid 1970's, however, leading to a 75% loss in REIT market value. This gave REITs a negative image in the investment community for at least the next 10 years.

Largely as a result, REITs did not attract any significant new capital and, luckily, missed the real estate "bubble" of the 1980's. In the subsequent collapse of real estate markets at the end of the decade, all forms of capital for real estate evaporated. Developers and investors found themselves with highly leveraged properties, often built with short-term financing, and no source of refinancing. With interest rates falling and real estate at bargain basement prices, Wall Street saw an opportunity to arbitrage private and public markets.

**"New" REITs:** The Kimco offering in late 1991 was the first sign that REITs could play a major role in financing real estate and, more importantly, real estate operating companies. During 1991, eight REIT IPO's raised $808 million. A similar number were completed in 1992, raising $919 million.[12]

While this was meaningful investment activity, particularly in a capital-starved real estate market, 1993 proved to be a real turning point, with 75 equity IPO's raising $11.1 billion. Excluding placements of less than $50 million, 39 IPOs were completed raising $8.2 billion, approximately 14% of total IPO activity in the entire securities market for the year. More real estate capital was generated by these 39 IPOs than by any other source.[13]

Perhaps more significantly, the character of the 1993 IPOs was dramatically different. Most of the new REITs were organized as vertically integrated real estate operating companies specializing by property type. They were also significantly larger: ten equity REITs had market capitalization of over $500

---

[12] National Association of Real Estate Investment Trusts (NAREIT).
[13] NREIT, Ibid.

million (versus two at the end of 1991), and 40 had capitalization exceeding $200 million (versus 10 in 1991).[14]

Almost two-thirds of new REITs were structured as Umbrella Partnership REITs (UPREITs). Under this structure, the REIT and the original investors each owned an interest in an Operating Partnership (OP), an approach designed to reduce the tax impact on selling private investors.

Most of the 1993 IPOs were internally managed and in many cases, management had significant equity positions, thus minimizing conflicts and enhancing congruency of objectives with investors. Most of the management groups had spent their careers specializing in a particular property type and had effectively worked together as a team for many years, through at least one full real estate cycle (Exhibit 1).

### Exhibit 1
### "Old" vs. "New" REITS

| Old REITs | New REITs |
| --- | --- |
| 1960 – 1992 | 1992 – 1998 |
| Passive investments | Operating company |
| Externally administered | Self-administered |
| Institutional sponsors | Entrepreneur sponsors |
| Small mgmt. ownership | Large mgmt. ownership |
| Diversified portfolio | Focused portfolio |
| Small capital base | Larger capital base |
| Little analyst coverage | More analyst coverage |

At year-end 1993, the REIT market was thriving. The total market capitalization of all REITs increased to $31.6 billion. The 30 largest REITs represented $15.1 billion versus $8.6 billion at the beginning of the year.[15]

## Shift in Institutional Investment Strategy

As noted earlier, pension real estate investment strategies in the 1970's and 80's had focused on portfolio diversification and protecting investment returns from inflation. With the major downturn in real estate values in the late 1980's and early 90's, however, pension plans became less concerned with diversification and more interested in attempting to match risk and return. As a result, a portion of new investment dollars began shifting to higher yielding "opportunistic" investments, often sponsored by nontraditional managers, such as investment banking firms and developers.

---

[14] NAREIT, Ibid.
[15] NAREIT, op. cit.

Exhibit 2 illustrates the organization of real estate investment products along the risk/return curve

**Exhibit 2
Real Estate Investment Strategies**

While the definitions were not always consistent, most pension plans and investment managers viewed the various levels of risk and return somewhat as follows:

**Core:** Investments in office, industrial, retail, and apartment properties built with quality construction and located in major metropolitan areas of the United States. Leverage was generally not used, with most properties having a stabilized income stream at the time of purchase. Total investment return expectations were generally in the 8-10% range.

**Enhanced-Core:** Core-quality properties with some type of problem that needs to be "enhanced" before the properties can produce stabilized income at acceptable yield levels. This enhancement may take the form of redevelopment, re-tenanting, refinancing, or some other form of problem mitigation. This category also includes the development of new core properties, with the use of leverage to enhance returns. Investment return expectations varied, but were generally in the 10-12% range.

**Value-Added:** This category consists of properties that did not meet core quality standards, but which could add value to the overall portfolio. These investments generally involve a higher level of risk and included properties such as hotels, restaurants, entertainment complexes, factory outlets, and business showrooms. Often, these value-added investments also involved a higher level of financial leverage. Expected investment returns were generally in the 12-15% range.

**Opportunistic:** Investment situations which involved some form of value arbitrage arising from disequilibrium in the marketplace. The classic situation was the RTC marketing of deeply discounted properties in the mid-1990's, followed by the subsequent recovery of the real estate market, producing significantly above-average returns for those investors who participated.

Opportunities of this scale proved difficult to find in the latter part of the decade, requiring more of a niche approach. Opportunity programs often focused on land investment, infill development, foreign properties, and enterprise investment. Opportunistic investments usually involved higher levels of leverage, with most sponsors investing "side-by-side" with pension investors.[16] Total returns were sometimes in the 20%+ range, but most were less, generally 15-18% for domestic investments.[17]

## Renewed Interest in Real Estate "Cash Generators"

In the latter half of the 90's, as the Baby Boom generation began reaching retirement age, a growing number of pension plans were finding themselves in a negative cash flow position, with current beneficiary obligations exceeding current contributions and investment income. Many of these plans allocated new investment dollars to more cash-generating real estate investments, as the nation's economic boom and the cyclical recovery of real estate made these investments more attractive. Core and enhanced-core real estate began once again competing favorably for pension capital, due to their use as an inflation hedge, and to the relatively low yields available in the bond market.

By 2001, many pension funds found themselves with underallocations to real estate, and some began increasing their allocations. Real estate had finally become an accepted, and often highly desired, addition to the investment portfolios of pension funds.

## CURRENT SITUATION

As of 2003, the total value of US real estate assets was $4,716 billion. Of this total, approximately $2,471 billion (52.4%) was owned by financial institutions. Approximately 17.1% of this was equity ($423 billion); the balance was debt.[18]

---

[16] In many cases, sponsor returns are subordinated to pension investor returns until certain predetermined return thresholds are reached.
[17] Early opportunity funds were sponsored by Wall Street firms such as Morgan Stanley, as well as entrepreneurial mangers such as JMB, AEW, and Equity Financial.
[18] Source: *Emerging Trends in Real Estate 2004*, Rosen Consulting Group; Urban Land Institute; PricewaterhouseCoopers.

Exhibit 3 illustrates the breakdown of institutional equity real estate investment by investor in 2003. The largest share of equity real estate – 46.6% – was held by REITs, with $197.1 billion in assets. This represents an increase from 42.5% over the prior year.

**Exhibit 3
Institutional Real Estate Equity Investment
2003**

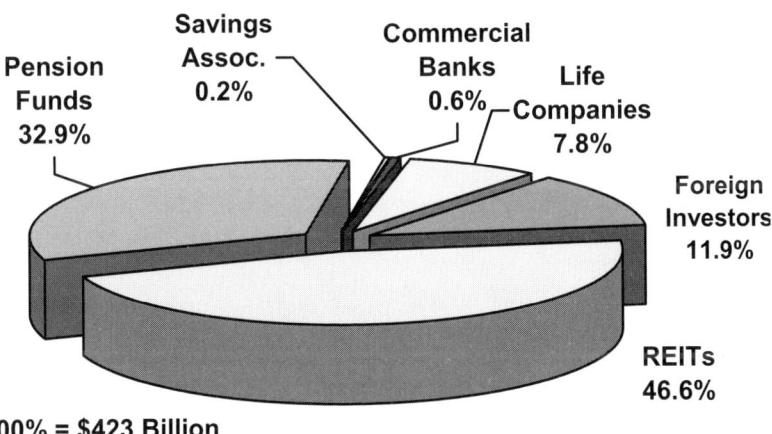

100% = $423 Billion

Source: *Emerging Trends in Real Estate 2004,* Rosen Consulting Group; Urban Land Institute; PricewaterhouseCoopers

Altogether, pension plans owned a total of $139.1 billion in real estate equity, or 32.9% of the total. This was down from 37% the prior year, primarily due to concerns about an overheated market, and a growing preference to invest through REIT vehicles rather than directly.

Today, most pension plans have a positive view of real estate as an investment class. Most plan trustees are aware of real estate's lower volatility, portfolio diversification benefits, and ability to generate cash flow. Unfortunately, real estate investment in the near term may be constrained due to the difficulty of increasing target allocations since it means lower allocations to other, more established, asset classes.

## *Major Pension Players*

The ten largest pension investors in real estate are outlined in Exhibit 4. Note that only one of the plans is sponsored by a corporation; the remainder are public employee plans. Three of the plans are located in California. These ten plans represent 44.9% of the funds supplied by the 200 largest funds investing in real estate equities.

### Exhibit 4
### Ten Largest Pension Investors in Real Estate
### 2004

| | | |
|---|---|---|
| 1. | California Public Employees | $11,900 million |
| 2. | California State Teachers | 5,275 |
| 3. | General Motors | 4,940 |
| 4. | New York State Teachers | 4,351 |
| 5. | Ohio State Teachers | 4,239 |
| 6. | Florida State Board | 4,005 |
| 7. | Washington State Board | 3,890 |
| 8. | Michigan Retirement | 3,260 |
| 9. | New York State Common | 3,186 |
| 10. | Los Angeles County Employees | <u>2,959</u> |
| | Total | 48,005 |

Source: Pensions & Investments January 24, 2005

Exhibit 5 shows the ten largest pension investors in REITs. Two are corporate plans; the rest are public plans. These ten plans represent 56.0% of the total capital supplied by the top 200 funds investing in REITs.

### Exhibit 5
### Ten Largest Pension Investors in REITs
### 2004

| | | |
|---|---|---|
| 1. | General Motors | $2,021 million |
| 2. | Florida State Board | 1,762 |
| 3. | IBM | 1,208 |
| 4. | New York State Teachers | 1,194 |
| 5. | Maryland State Retirement | 1,160 |
| 6. | Pennsylvania School Employees | 805 |
| 7. | California Public Employees | 751 |
| 8. | Ohio Public Employees | 653 |
| 9. | Texas County & District | 626 |
| 10. | Massachusetts PRIM | <u>624</u> |
| | Total | 10,804 |

Source: Pensions & Investments January 24, 2005

Exhibit 6 outlines the ten largest pension fund managers. Note that nine of the ten firms are now owned or controlled by financial institutions (including three foreign institutions) and one is a major corporation. Two of the firms were initially entrepreneurial companies but subsequently have been acquired by financial institutions. These 10 firms represent 56.2% of the total capital managed by the 50 largest firms.

### Exhibit 6
### Ten Largest Pension Real Estate Managers
### 2004

| | |
|---|---|
| 1. TIAA CREF | $37,173 million |
| 2. RREEF/DB Real Estate | 16,813 |
| 3. JP Morgan Fleming | 16,599 |
| 4. Principal Real Estate | 15,606 |
| 5. Prudential Real Estate | 13,136 |
| 6. Morgan Stanley Real Estate | 10,272 |
| 7. UBS Realty Investors | 8,760 |
| 8. ING Clarion/Real Estate | 8,752 |
| 9. General Motors Management | 8,570 |
| 10. INVESCO Real Estate | 8,318 |
| **Total** | **143,999** |

Source: Pensions & Investments December 27, 2004

## Other Alternatives

For pension funds that want to avoid the manager selection process, some real estate pension consultants (e.g., Townsend, Russell, PCA, and ORG) offer a "fund of funds" in which they will select investment managers and monitor their performance on behalf of pension fund clients. These vehicles are similar to those available to stock, bond, and mutual fund investors.

Investors also may invest in a fund of funds in which a fund is established comprised of individual investment funds. These funds give smaller investors an opportunity to obtain greater diversification while avoiding the individual manager selection process.

Some firms serve as secondary market players, providing liquidity to investors who need to exit existing investment programs. Examples include Landmark, Liquid Read Estate, and Wall Street Realty Capital.

## Target Allocations to Real Estate

Exhibit 7 highlights the percentage allocation to real estate by type of fund for the years 2000–2004. As the Exhibit indicates, the average allocation to real estate by all pension plans rose during this period, from 4.3% to 5.5%, an increase of 27.9%. The greatest increase was by union plans, up 40.4%. Public plans were next at 33.3%, followed by endowments and foundations

(20.9%) and corporate plans (3%). In terms of size, smaller plans (under $10 billion) increased 37.5%, and larger plans (under $10 billion) increased 8.2%.

**Exhibit 7
Allocation to Real Estate
Percentage of Total Portfolio
2000 - 2004**

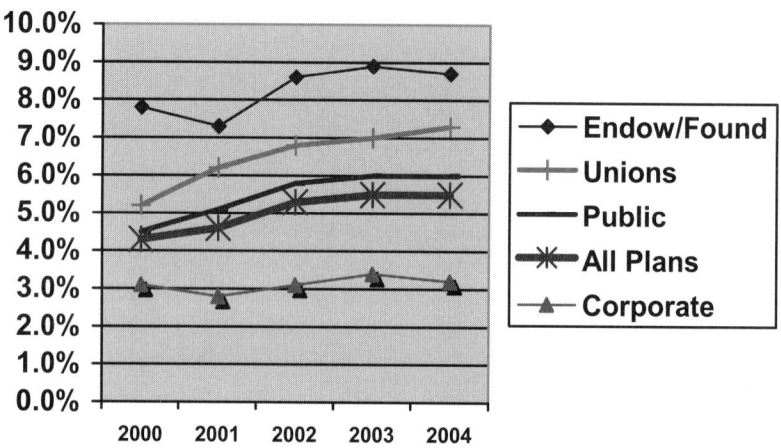

Source: Pension Real Estate Association; Standard & Poor's Money Market Directories

Since allocations are stated in percentages, increases in real estate must come from other asset classes. During the 2000-2004 period, most of the increase in real estate allocations came at the expense of bonds (down 6.8%), with a lower percentage decline in allocation to stocks (down 1.1%).

In terms of their ability to realize target allocations, 77.0% of the plans surveyed by PREA reported their actual allocation was less than target, 13.1% reported being on target (within .2%), and 9.8% said they were over target. Reasons given were (1) a lack of investment product in the marketplace that met their criteria and (2) Improvement in the stock market (which declined over the five years but increased in 2004).[19]

## Real Estate Investment Vehicles

Exhibit 8 breaks down real estate investment vehicles in 2004 by type of pension plan.

---

[19] Source: Pension Real Estate Association, op cit.

**Exhibit 8
Investment by Vehicle
2004**

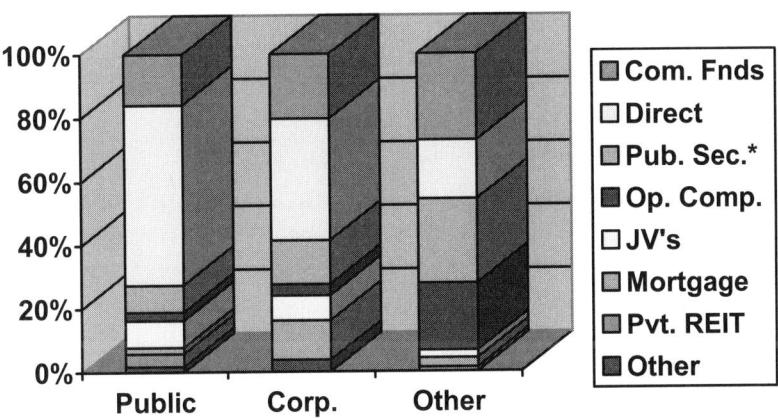

* REITs, REOCs, CMBS, Other

Source: Pension Real Estate Association, 2005

Note that commingled funds, direct investment, and public securities (mostly REITs) consistently comprise 75-80% of total pension real estate investment activity, regardless of the type of pension fund investor. Also, pension funds hold $18.9 billion in public REITs and $3.6 billion in private REITs. This combined total is the equivalent of 7.7% of total REIT assets as of February, 2005.[20]

The interest in pooled accounts has grown dramatically since 2000. There are several reasons for this: (1) Pooled accounts enable more efficient deployment of capital and enable investors to achieve portfolio diversification earlier; (2) Most brokers today won't allow an investment manager to enter the bidding process if the manager doesn't have discretion; and (3) Investors are committing the majority of new capital to opportunity funds and off-shore pooled investments, in order to share risks with other investors.

---

[20] Sources: Pension Real Estate Association and National Association of Real Estate Investment Trusts.

## Leverage

In general, pension fund investment portfolios are not as highly leveraged as the portfolios of private investors. Only 5.3% of pension portfolios allow greater than a 75% Loan to Value (LTV) ratio. Forty-three percent (43.9%) allow a 31-50% LTV ratio; 38.6% allow 51-75%, and 10.5% of portfolios allow a LTV of 11-30%.[21]

## Property Characteristics

**Geography:** The largest percentage of pension investments was in the West (36.4%), followed by the South (22.0%), East (27.8%), and Midwest (13.8%). Generally, corporate plans were more apt to hold investments in the East and Midwest, while public and other plans focused on investing in the West and South. Generally, there was not a large difference in geographical preference between smaller plans (under $25 billion) and those over $25 billion.[22]

**Property Type:** Office was the most popular type of property investment in pension portfolios (34.5%), followed by Apartments (20.4%), Retail (18.7%), Industrial/R&D (13.5%), and Hotels (3.5%).[23] The remaining 9.4% was primarily invested in land/timber, senior housing, mixed use, and self-storage facilities.

## Pension Investor Preferences

It is also interesting to note current pension fund attitudes towards various real estate investment products.[24]

**Direct Investment:** Direct investment in real estate is difficult for all but the largest pension plans (over $50 billion in assets) due to the greater difficulty in diversifying portfolios, the larger investment required, and higher administrative costs. For these reasons, while many of the largest pension funds may favor direct investment vehicles, a significant number consider commingled funds and real estate securities as attractive alternatives.

**Debt vs. Equity:** Most pension funds believe that commingled funds should concentrate on either debt or equity.

**Investment Risk:** About one half of pension plans surveyed utilize enhanced-core investment strategies. Of these, virtually all accept some development and lease-up risk. A large majority also accept second-tier markets and the use of acceptable leverage (50–65% LTV ratio) on individual

---

[21] Source: Pension Real Estate Association, op. cit.
[22] Pension Real Estate Association, op. cit.
[23] Source: Pension Real Estate Association, op. cit,
[24] Source: *Emerging Trends in Real Estate 2004*, op. cit.

properties and no more than 15-20% of the total real estate portfolio. About half accept a certain amount of geographical concentration.

**Preference Returns:** Most pension funds do not require a preferred investment return as a condition of investing.

**Quarterly Distributions:** The majority of pension funds require a quarterly cash distribution of income and sales proceeds. This may be linked to the negative cash flows that some plans are now experiencing.

**Withdrawals:** Some pension investors require a withdrawal provision providing for liquidation of their investment within 6 to 12 months of withdrawal.

## *Strategic Considerations*

Before an investment strategy can be finalized, pension funds consider (explicitly or implicitly) a series of strategic trade-offs. Exhibit 9 is a flow chart showing the strategic considerations involved in moving from a decision to invest in real estate to putting an investment program in place. The first question is the amount of funds that the pension fund wishes to commit to real estate. In today's investment environment, if the pension fund is not willing to commit $100 million to real estate, they are, for all practical purposes, restricted to a REIT portfolio or a pooled investment vehicle.

The decision then becomes what type of investment vehicle (or mix of vehicles) would be most appropriate – open-end funds, closed-end funds, or REITs.

Considerations in selecting an investment vehicle include:

**Liquidity:** REITs are the most liquid of the three vehicles, trading every business day. Most open-end funds allow redemptions quarterly. Closed-end funds vary in terms of redemption policies but generally are illiquid over the life of the fund.

**Risk Diversification within the Investment Vehicle:** REITs represent the smallest units and therefore can be easily diversified, even in modest portfolios. Open-end fund units are not as fungible as REITs, but it is possible to invest in more than one, depending upon the terms of the fund.

Some closed-end fund sponsors have multiple funds and may encourage investors to invest in more than one fund. The success of both open- and closed-end fund diversification depends heavily on the strength and depth of the investment manager and requires a higher level of diligence on the part of investors before making a final decision.[25]

## Exhibit 9
## Strategic Considerations

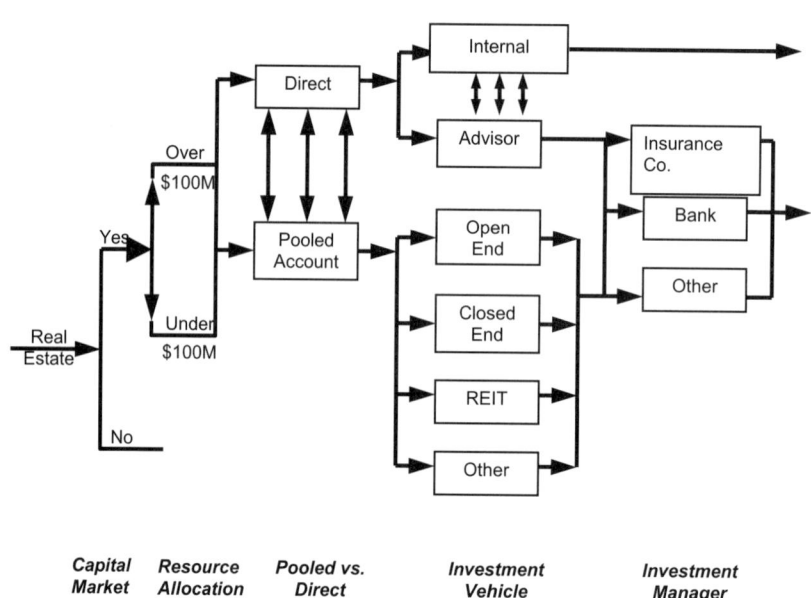

**Risk Diversification across Investment Vehicles:** Some institutional investors strive to diversify not only across investment vehicles but by investment managers as well. In many cases, these allocations are influenced by the need for liquidity. REITs provide virtually immediate liquidity, open-end funds provide medium term liquidity, and closed-end funds are considered to be longer term commitments which (hopefully) represent a trade-off between a lack of liquidity and higher returns.

**Investment Manager:** Once the fund type has been chosen, the next decision is which investment manager(s) to select to implement the investment program. Open-end funds are generally sponsored by large insurance companies, banks, or nonprofit organizations (e.g., AFL-CIO). Closed-end funds are usually sponsored by entrepreneurial firms, although some of them are now so large that they have almost become institutions in their own right. Also, as noted previously, many of the entrepreneurial firms have been acquired by financial institutions.

---

[25] It should be noted that this approach does not provide diversification by manager.

As also noted earlier, REITs are one of the few financial assets which have dedicated managers, that is, who only manage REIT investments. Some firms that sponsor closed- and open-end funds also have REIT management organizations, but these groups generally don't manage other financial assets.

The selection of a real estate investment manager generally involves a "beauty contest" between competing managers, based on criteria such as investment strategy, dedicated staff, and investment track record. Pension consultants can be major influencers as to the outcome of this process, as it is one of their roles to track the performance of real estate investment managers for their investor clients.

## Questions for Discussion

The following questions are designed to explore the major issues raised in this chapter.

1. What entities initially established US pension funds? What were their objectives? What are some of the reasons pension funds avoided investing in real estate until 1975?

2. Why was ERISA passed by Congress? What were some its key provisions? What role did it play in pension funds deciding to invest in real estate?

3. What impact did the inflation of the late 1970s have on pension funds deciding to invest in real estate? Why?

4. Describe the characteristics of open-end funds. Who generally sponsored these funds? What are their advantages? Disadvantages?

5. Describe the characteristics of closed-end funds. Who generally sponsored them? How do they differ from open-end fund? What are their advantages? Disadvantages?

6. What impact did the tax legislation of 1981 and 1986 have on US real estate markets? What was the impact on pension fund real estate portfolios? What was the role of the Resolution Trust Corporation (RTC)? What role did Wall Street play?

7. What are the requirements for a corporation to be treated for tax purposes as a Real Estate Investment Trust (REIT)?

8. What were the characteristics of the "new REITs" that emerged in the 1990's? How did they contrast with earlier REITs?

9. In the late 1980's and early 1990's, pension investors changed their strategy towards real estate investing. What was the nature of this shift, and how did it impact their investments in real estate?

10. Why did pension funds become interested once again in "core" investments in the late 1990's?

11. What are the trends in the percentage of funds that pension plans allocate to real estate? Why do these allocations change over time?

12. Describe the current attitudes of pension plan managers towards real estate investment vehicles? What is the prevailing attitude toward geographical location of assets? Property types?

13. What are the strategic steps in a pension fund implementing a real estate investment program? Describe investor considerations at each step.

Please use these questions as a guide and not a format or a reflection of all of the questions that need to be addressed by the case.

# 2

# ARIZONA BUILDING CORPORATION[1]

## Role of Real Estate in a Mixed Asset Portfolio

Marilyn pushed back in her chair, took off her glasses, and stared out the window. She had been working on an assignment for a new client, Arizona Building Corporation (ABC), and was trying to come up with the most appropriate asset mix for their pension portfolio. She had been completely absorbed with a tremendous amount of quantitative data and now was beginning to weigh some of the qualitative aspects of the problem and come to a final decision.

Marilyn Breadwell was a pension fund consultant for one of the nation's preeminent pension consulting firms. A graduate of one of the West's finest business schools, Marilyn had worked in a variety of financial positions before entering the pension consulting field two years earlier. The ABC account was the first time Marilyn had headed a consulting project team, and she saw it as an opportunity to solidify her rapid rise within the firm.

The project team had analyzed the projections of ABC's pension liabilities over the next 10 years and evaluated the ability of the current mix of assets to meet these liabilities. They had then run a series of projection models of various asset mixes that might be utilized instead of the current mix. Marilyn was now faced with selecting the most appropriate mix for ABC's pension plan and more specifically, with defining the role of real estate, if any, in the portfolio.

---

[1] This case was originally written by John McMahan in 1994 based on material prepared by Callan Associates, an international pension consulting firm. Copyright © John McMahan, 1994, 1996, 2004, all rights reserved.

## ABC Pension Plan Liabilities

ABC, headquartered in Phoenix, made a wide variety of manufactured products mostly for the highly cyclical commercial construction field. As of January 1, 1993, the firm had 2,578 employees in its pension plan with an annual payroll of $59 million. Retirement benefit payments in 1993 were $1.74 million dollars with an actuarial liability of $71 million.

Exhibit 1 illustrates the anticipated growth in the firm's pension plan membership. The active work force was expected to grow at a rate of 1% annually, reaching 2,072 members in the year 2003. At the beginning of the projection period, the average age of the work force was 41 years with an average of 10 years of service.

Based on anticipated demographic changes (e.g., separation, retirement, disabled, and death), the total plan membership was expected to increase at a rate of 3.8% annually, with inactive members increasing from 27% in 1993 to 44% in the year 2003.

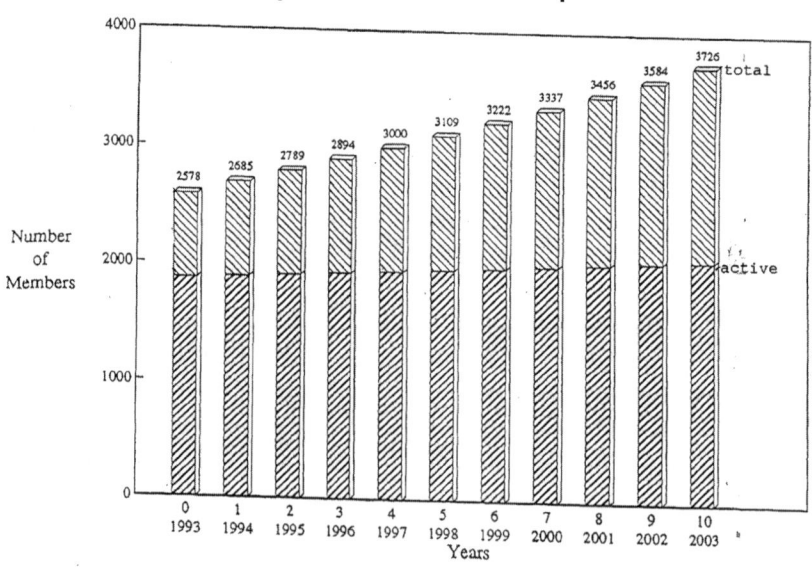

**Exhibit 1**
**Projected Plan Membership**

Exhibit 2 projects the growth in payroll (nominal dollars) over the ten year period. Annual pay increases were assumed to be 6.5% and with annual additions to the work force, the total payroll was expected to increase 8.6% per year.

## Exhibit 2
### Projected Payroll

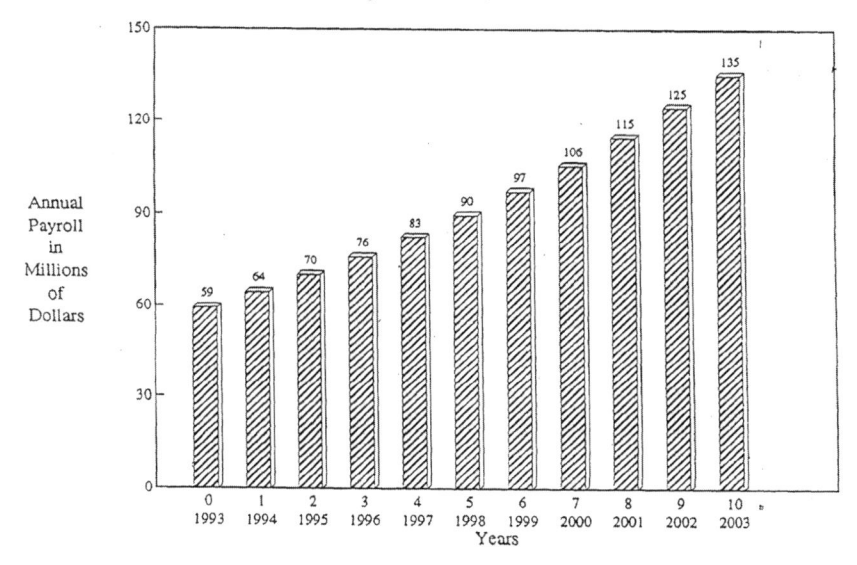

| Year | Annual Payroll (Millions of Dollars) |
|---|---|
| 1993 | 59 |
| 1994 | 64 |
| 1995 | 70 |
| 1996 | 76 |
| 1997 | 83 |
| 1998 | 90 |
| 1999 | 97 |
| 2000 | 106 |
| 2001 | 115 |
| 2002 | 125 |
| 2003 | 135 |

Exhibit 3 projects the amount of annual pension benefit payments that ABC would be expected to pay over the ten year period. Due to the increasing number of inactive members of the pension plan, annual benefits were expected to grow by about 16% per year.

## Exhibit 3
### Projected Benefit Payments

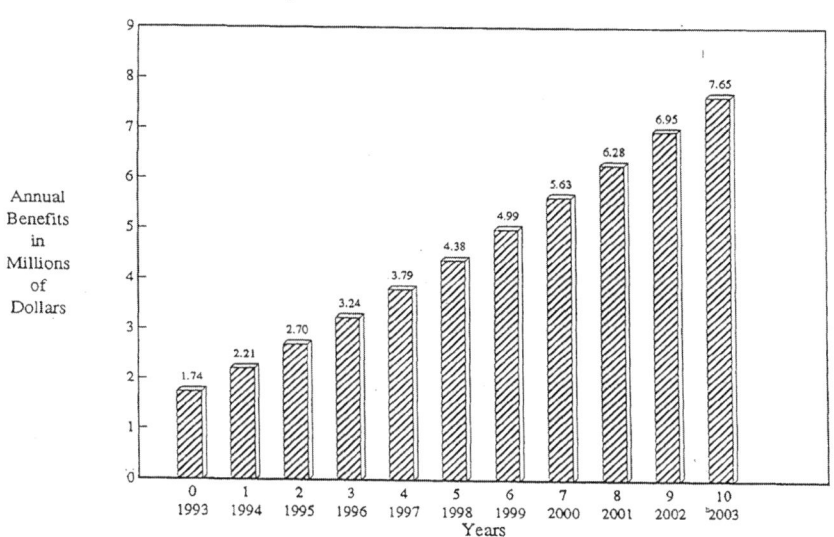

| Year | Annual Benefits (Millions of Dollars) |
|---|---|
| 1993 | 1.74 |
| 1994 | 2.21 |
| 1995 | 2.70 |
| 1996 | 3.24 |
| 1997 | 3.79 |
| 1998 | 4.38 |
| 1999 | 4.99 |
| 2000 | 5.63 |
| 2001 | 6.28 |
| 2002 | 6.95 |
| 2003 | 7.65 |

Exhibit 4 estimates the level of actuarial liabilities that the pension plan would have at the end of each year based on an 8.5% discount factor. The actuarial funding method used by the plan to value its liabilities is the Entry Age Normal funding method. Under this method, the actuarial funding target is the accrued liability, which is the present value of future benefit payments less the present value of future normal costs.

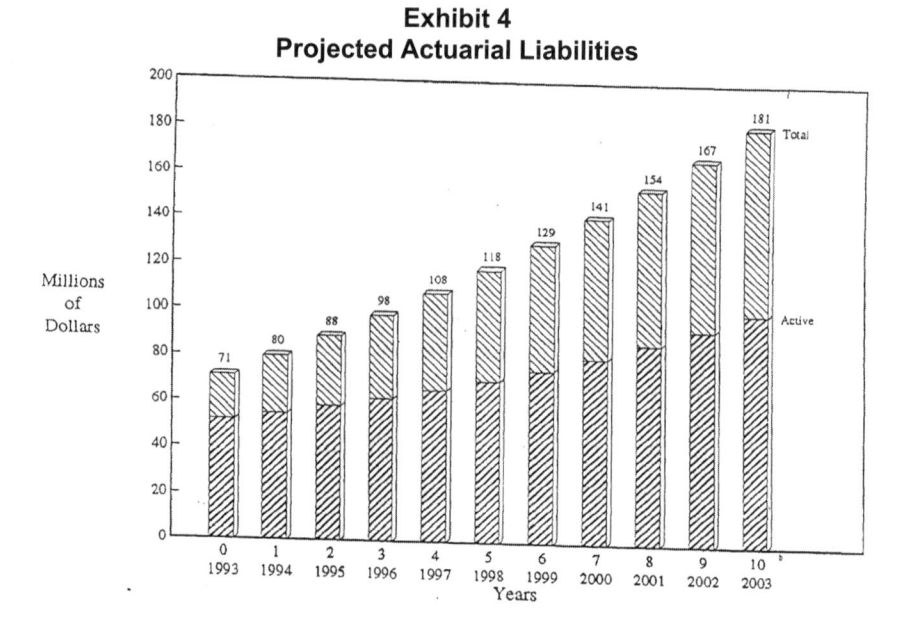

**Exhibit 4**
**Projected Actuarial Liabilities**

| Year | Total |
|------|-------|
| 1993 | 71 |
| 1994 | 80 |
| 1995 | 88 |
| 1996 | 98 |
| 1997 | 108 |
| 1998 | 118 |
| 1999 | 129 |
| 2000 | 141 |
| 2001 | 154 |
| 2002 | 167 |
| 2003 | 181 |

## Plan Assets

As of January 1, 1993, ABC's pension plan assets were invested in four principal asset categories: 45% in domestic equity, 35% in domestic fixed-income, 10% in international equity, and 10% in cash. No funds had been invested in real estate to date, although there was considerable pressure to do so.

Exhibit 5 illustrates the historical capital market return for major asset classes over 15 years ending December 31, 1992.

Exhibit 6 contains five year projections of the return and standard deviation (from the median) of each major asset class. These projections were based on a review of possible economic scenarios as well as an examination of the historical relationship between major economic and financial variables and of five year asset performance characteristics.

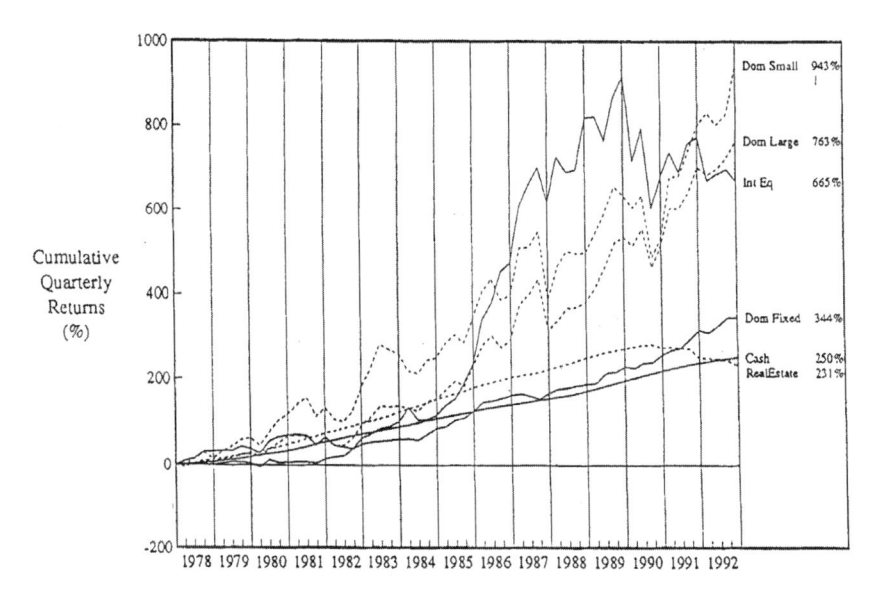

## Exhibit 5
## Cumulative Returns
## For Fifteen Years Ended December 31, 1992

[Chart showing cumulative quarterly returns (%) from 1978 to 1992 with final values: Dom Small 943%, Dom Large 763%, Int Eq 665%, Dom Fixed 344%, Cash 250%, RealEstate 231%]

## Exhibit 6
## Capital Market Projections (1993 – 2003)

| Asset Class | Proxy Index | Expected Annual Return | Expected Standard Deviation |
|---|---|---|---|
| Domestic Large Cap | S&P 500 Index | 10.00 | 16.60 |
| Domestic Small Cap | Callan Small Cap Index | 11.20 | 22.90 |
| International Equity | MSCI EAFE Index | 10.75 | 22.90 |
| Domestic Fixed | Lehman Bros Govt/Cap Bond | 6.85 | 6.40 |
| International Fixed | Salomon Bros Non-US Bond | 7.50 | 13.50 |
| Real Estate | Callan Composite | 7.90 | 19.00 |
| Private Placement | Callan Composite | 13.00 | 32.30 |
| Cash Equivalent | 90-Day Treasury Bills | 4.75 | 0.65 |
| Inflation | Consumer Price Index | 4.00 | 1.75 |

Asset mix combinations also took into consideration the historical interrelationships of performance characteristics between the various asset classes (Exhibit 7). This analysis involved searching for inequality relationships among the risks and correlations that indicate which risks and correlations have tended to be higher than others over time and over various cycles.

## Exhibit 7
### Correlation Between Asset Classes

|  | Dom LC | Dom SC | Int Eq | Dom Fx | Int Fx | Real Est | Priv Pl |
|---|---|---|---|---|---|---|---|
| Dom Lg Cap | 1.00 | | | | | | |
| Dom Sm Cap | .93 | 1.00 | | | | | |
| Intl Equity | .62 | .51 | 1.00 | | | | |
| Dom Fixed | .51 | .42 | .41 | 1.00 | | | |
| Int Fixed | .29 | .13 | .72 | .44 | 1.00 | | |
| Real Estate | .25 | .22 | .17 | .33 | .10 | 1.00 | |
| Priv Plac | .79 | .91 | .60 | .35 | .16 | .19 | 1.00 |
| Cash Equiv | -.15 | -.20 | -.27 | .11 | -.23 | .29 | -.20 |

As indicated in Exhibit 7, the correlation between asset classes can range from +1.0 to -1.0. A correlation of +1.0 means that the two asset category returns move in exactly the same manner or direction, and a correlation of -1.0 means that the returns move in exactly opposite directions.

While a single asset may be very risky, a portfolio of many assets will be much less risky. This occurs because some of the risks associated with individual assets will be partially offset by the different risks of other assets.

For this reason, a pension fund can diversify some of the risk of the individual asset classes by combining asset categories, which are less than perfectly correlated. As an example, a pension plan with a 50% investment in bonds and 50% investment in stocks will have an expected return, which is the average of the returns of the two asset classes, but will have a risk level lower than the average of the asset class risks. This reduced risk is due to low correlations between the price movement of stocks and bonds.

Exhibit 8 projects the median returns and standard deviations from the median for ABC's pension plan utilizing five asset mix alternatives. Asset mix #1 is the most conservative and has the lowest level of expected risk and return. Asset mix #5 is the most aggressive and has the highest expected risk and return.

The optimal combinations of assets form an "efficient frontier" of asset mix alternatives. Since investors are risk averse, asset mixes lying on the efficient frontier are preferred to asset mixes to the right of the efficient frontier. Exhibit 9 illustrates the efficient frontier for the five asset mix alternatives available to ABC's pension plan.

## Exhibit 8
## Asset Mix Alternatives

| Porfolio Component | Current Mix | Limits Min | Limits Max | Asset Mix Alternative 1 | 2 | 3 | 4 | 5 |
|---|---|---|---|---|---|---|---|---|
| Domestic Lg Cap | 45 | 20 | 70 | 20 | 20 | 26 | 37 | 44 |
| Domestic Sm Cap | 0 | 0 | 15 | 0 | 3 | 6 | 5 | 15 |
| International Equity | 10 | 0 | 15 | 0 | 6 | 12 | 15 | 15 |
| Domestice Fixed | 35 | 20 | 70 | 63 | 57 | 42 | 25 | 20 |
| International Fixed | 0 | 0 | 10 | 8 | 6 | 3 | 3 | 0 |
| Real Estate | 0 | 0 | 10 | 4 | 6 | 9 | 10 | 1 |
| Private Placement | 0 | 0 | 5 | 0 | 2 | 2 | 5 | 5 |
| Cash Equivalent | 10 | 0 | 5 | 5 | 0 | 0 | 0 | 0 |
| Totals (%) | 100 | | | 100 | 100 | 100 | 100 | 100 |
| Return (%) | 8.45 | | | 7.50 | 8.07 | 8.64 | 9.21 | 9.78 |
| Std Dev (%) | 10.41 | | | 7.29 | 8.81 | 10.63 | 12.65 | 15.00 |

## Exhibit 9
## Asset Mix Risk and Return

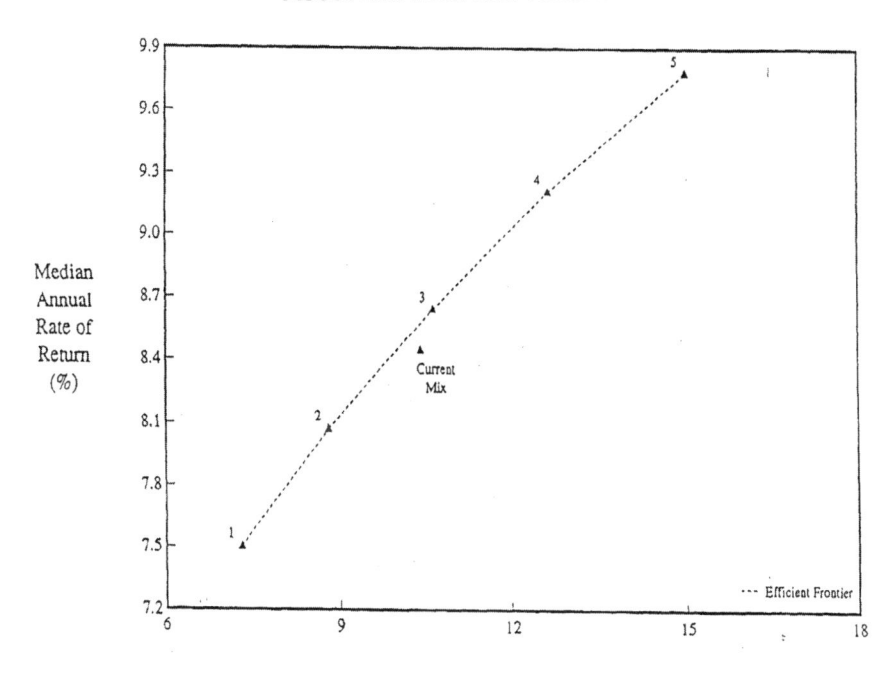

## Integrating Assets and Liabilities

Exhibit 10 projects the market value of ABC's plan assets under each of the asset mix scenarios and compares them to the plan's actuarial liability. This projection assumes that the rates of return are consistent year after year.

**Exhibit 10**
**Projected Market Value of Assets**

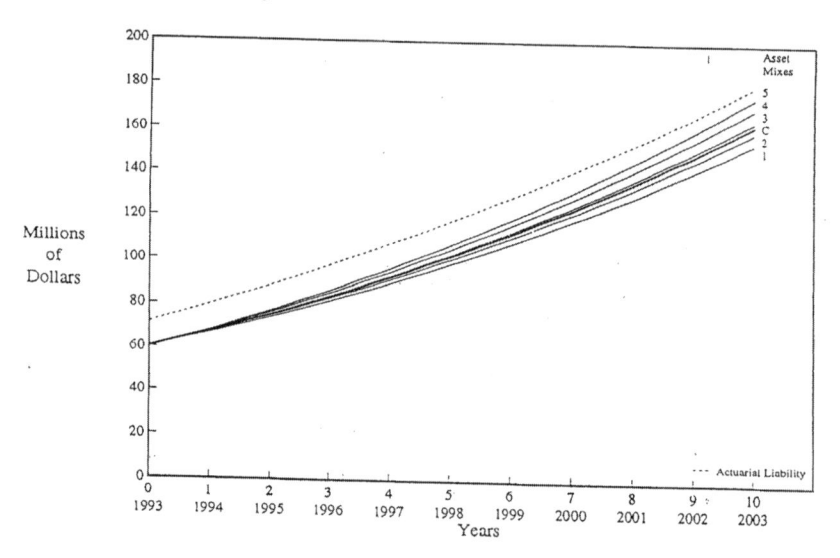

**Exhibit 11**
**Range of Market Value of Assets**

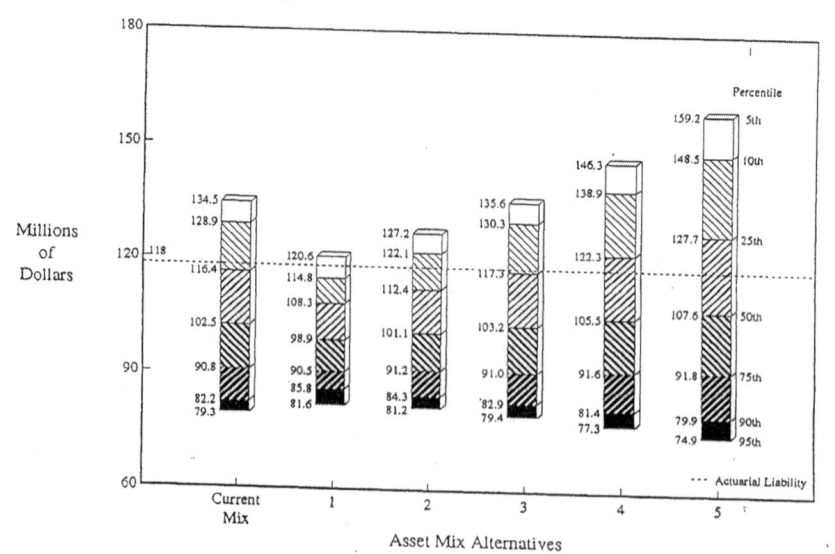

Exhibit 11 indicates the impact of the full range of returns on the projected market value of the plan's assets as of January 1998. The ranges of market values shown in this graph reflect the interaction between the actuarial liabilities, projected benefit payments, projected funding, and range of investment returns after five years. Exhibit 11 shows that employing a more aggressive asset mix alternative would result in a greater range of asset market values.

In terms of projected level of actuarial liabilities, Exhibit 11 indicates that the current asset mix and all of the asset mix alternatives appear to have less than a 50% probability of exceeding the projected actuarial liability by January 1998.

Exhibit 12 indicates that ABC's annual pension contributions as a percentage of pay would decline over a ten year period. This reduction is a result of ABC's payroll increasing at a faster rate than employer contributions. For the most conservative asset mix, average contributions are projected to be slightly over 6% of pay by the tenth year.

**Exhibit 12**
**Projected Contributions as Percentage of Pay**

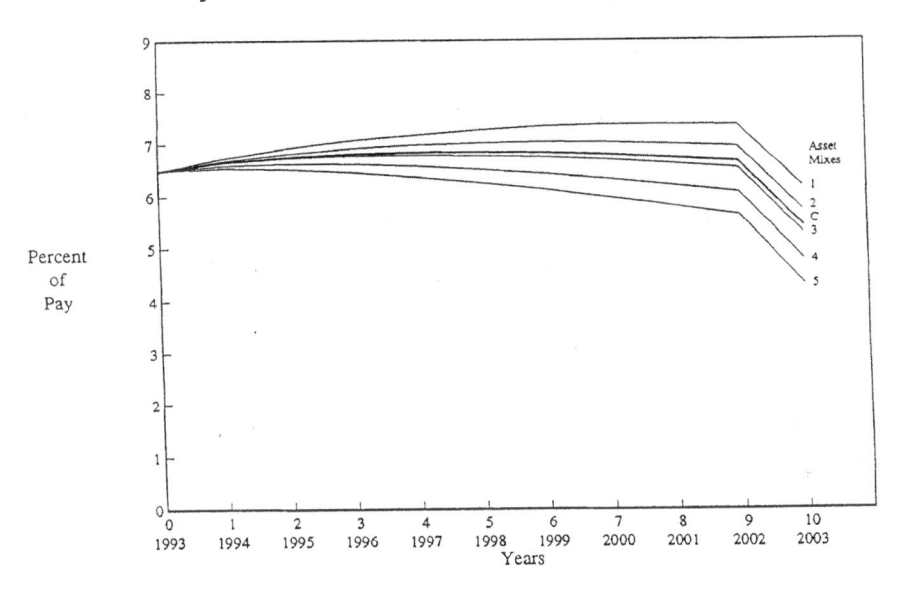

The range of actuarial surplus created under each of the asset mix alternatives is illustrated in Exhibit 13. A plan's actuarial surplus represents the actuarial value of plan assets in excess of plan liabilities. Actuarial surplus is a measure of the funded status of the plan, with a positive value representing an over funded plan and a negative value representing an underfunded plan.

## Exhibit 13
### Range of Actuarial Surplus

Millions of Dollars vs. Asset Mix Alternatives (Current Mix, 1, 2, 3, 4, 5)

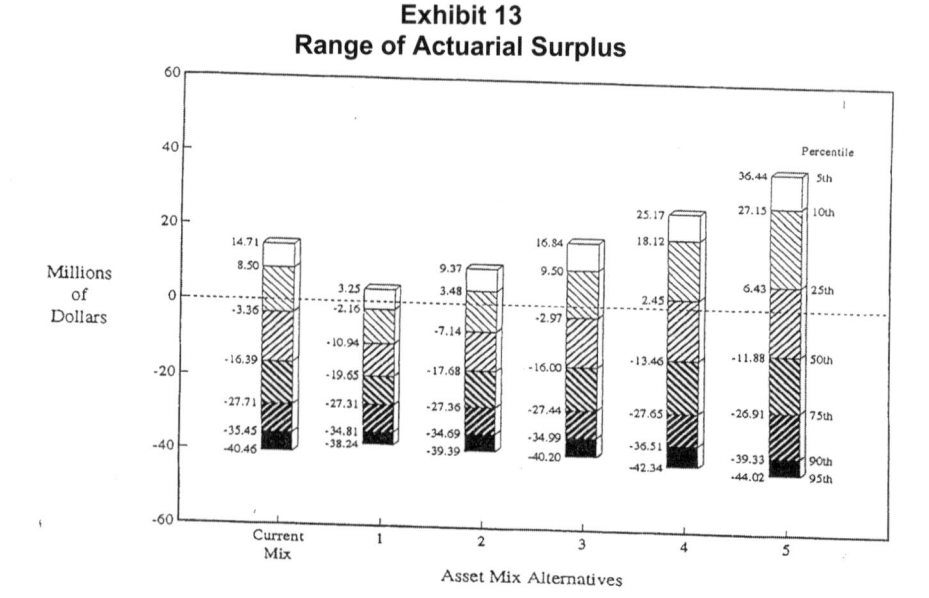

| Percentile | Current Mix | 1 | 2 | 3 | 4 | 5 |
|---|---|---|---|---|---|---|
| 5th | 14.71 | 3.25 | 16.84 | 9.50 | 25.17 | 36.44 |
| 10th | 8.50 | 3.48 | 9.37 | 2.45 | 18.12 | 27.15 |
| 25th | -3.36 | -2.16 | 3.48 | -2.97 | 6.43 | 6.43 |
| 50th | -16.39 | -10.94 | -7.14 | -16.00 | -13.46 | -11.88 |
| 75th | -27.71 | -19.65 | -17.68 | -27.44 | -27.65 | -26.91 |
| 90th | -35.45 | -27.31 | -27.36 | -34.99 | -36.51 | -39.33 |
| 95th | -40.46 | -34.81 | -34.69 | -40.20 | -42.34 | -44.02 |
|  |  | -38.24 | -39.39 |  |  |  |

Exhibit 14 projects the range of ultimate net cost to ABC for each of the asset mix alternatives through January 1998. Ultimate net costs reflect the interaction between the range of actuarial liabilities, market value of assets, and funding requirements.

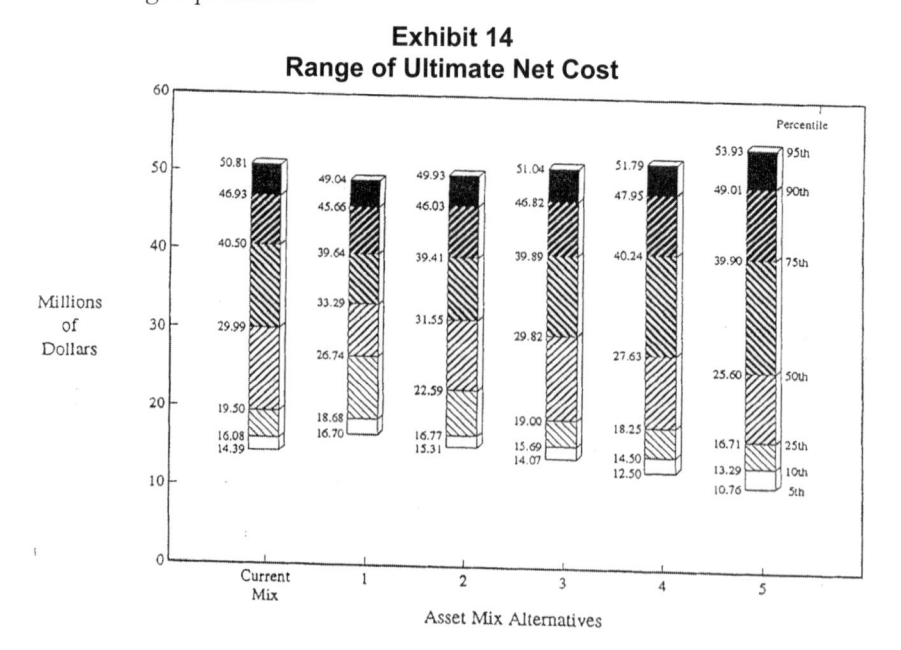

## Exhibit 14
### Range of Ultimate Net Cost

| Percentile | Current Mix | 1 | 2 | 3 | 4 | 5 |
|---|---|---|---|---|---|---|
| 95th | 50.81 | 49.04 | 49.93 | 51.04 | 51.79 | 53.93 |
| 90th | 46.93 | 45.66 | 46.03 | 46.82 | 47.95 | 49.01 |
| 75th | 40.50 | 39.64 | 39.41 | 39.89 | 40.24 | 39.90 |
| 50th | 29.99 | 33.29 | 31.55 | 29.82 | 27.63 | 25.60 |
|  |  | 26.74 | 22.59 |  |  |  |
| 25th | 19.50 | 18.68 | 16.77 | 19.00 | 18.25 | 16.71 |
| 10th | 16.08 | 16.70 | 15.31 | 15.69 | 14.50 | 13.29 |
| 5th | 14.39 |  |  | 14.07 | 12.50 | 10.76 |

## Selecting the Optimum Asset Mix

With an understanding of the dynamics of the interaction between the various asset mix alternatives, Marilyn's next step was to select the asset mix that would best suit the investment requirements of ABC's pension plan.

She knew that she could determine the level of risk versus reward for each alternative (measured in terms of Ultimate Net Cost) by using the median (50th percentile) values as the expected reward and by using the worst-case (95th percentile) as the level of risk that might be expected. With this approach, the current mix of ABC's portfolio could be compared to each asset mix, and then they could be compared to each other. Out of this process, one of the asset mixes could be selected as best meeting ABC's requirements.

## Role of Real Estate

Whereas Marilyn was familiar with the role of stocks and bonds in the pension portfolio, she felt less assured in dealing with real estate. She was well aware of the traditional reasons for including real estate in a mixed asset portfolio: (1) a closer approximation of the world stock of wealth; (2) a dampening of portfolio volatility due to an inverse correlation with stocks; and (3) providing an inflation hedge for the portfolio.

She had considerable concern, however, about the negative returns that real estate had experienced during the late 1980s and early 1990s and what this portended for the future. On one hand, if real estate really was inversely correlated with equities, as all of the research suggested, the relatively flat outlook for the stock market might suggest increased returns for real estate. On the other hand, the real estate market was still staggering, and there was little indication of robust recovery for at least two to three years.

Marilyn was also concerned with the inflation-hedge argument. Although real estate had been an outstanding inflation hedge in the past, she wasn't sure how good an inflation hedge real estate would be in a continuing overbuilt market environment. She was left, of course, with the "world wealth" argument, but this seemed to be too much of a "because it's there" argument to suit her analytical mind.

## The Decision-Making Environment

In terms of ABC management, Marilyn felt that the Chief Investment Officer (CIO) and the Chief Financial Officer (CFO) would be very concerned about any future shortfalls in funding. ABC had been underfunded for many years and had recently taken several charges against earnings to improve funding levels. These charges couldn't have come at a worse time as the building construction industry had been in the worst economic slump since the great depression. In fact, there was still bad blood between the CFO and the Chief Executive Officer (CEO) who hadn't been very pleased with the inability of the Treasury staff to generate sufficient investment earnings to meet projected pension liabilities.

As a result of the charges, the Retirement Committee of the Board had been shuffled, and there were two new outside directors on the Committee who had made it very clear that they expected the pension plan to be self-funding. Interestingly, one of these directors was a major Phoenix real estate investor who had recently argued for an expanded allocation to real estate. He was convinced that the real estate "bust" was over and that real estate would outperform financial assets over the next few years.

There were also several large institutional shareholders who viewed the underfunding charges as being the result of poor investment management and therefore unnecessary. One of the investors was so upset that it sold its stock and let it be known to the investment media why it was doing so. Unfortunately, the press had picked up the story two days prior to a board meeting where one of the agenda items was the CEO's new compensation package, which was closely tied to ABC's stock value. The stock had taken a large hit and not surprisingly, action on the CEO's compensation package was postponed and ended up being considerably less generous than recommended.

As a result of the many years of underfunding, ABC's retired employees had formed a Pension Action Committee (PAC) that met on several occasions with the Retirement Committee in what turned out to be very heated meetings. Although the PAC was pleased with the progress that had been made in increasing the plan's funding level, they were still pressing hard for 100% funding. The PAC was headed by Joe Thunderstorm, ABC's founder and long-time CEO, who seldom passed up an opportunity to be critical of the firm's current leadership. Unfortunately, this individual was very popular among ABC's retired employees and was still quite influential with older members of the Board.

In fact, Marilyn recalled that Thunderstorm had been instrumental in forcing the Retirement Committee to hire a new consultant, thus leading to the search that had resulted in Callan being selected. Competition for the contract had been extremely intense, and Callan's top management was ecstatic to have won. Marilyn knew that being selected to manage the account was a major vote of confidence in her personally and helped to justify her rapid rise in the firm, which in some cases was over more senior consultants.

Marilyn adjusted her glasses and returned to the numbers. She knew that she would have to answer both the quantitative as well as the qualitative aspects of the analysis if she was going to obtain approval of the Retirement Committee at its scheduled meeting in five days. Her boss had asked for a preliminary report the following day, and she knew she had to come to a decision and begin writing soon. No matter what, it was going to be a long night.

## Questions for Discussion

Questions that should be addressed in this case include:

1. What are the characteristics of US pension plans and how does their structure impact investment portfolio decisions?
2. How are ABC's pension decisions affected by the nature of its business?
3. How do ABC's pension asset and liabilities interact to impact portfolio investment decisions?
4. What is the mix of investment assets in the current portfolio? What will be the return/risk profile of these assets over the next 5 years if no changes are made in asset mix?
5. What is the "correlation" between various assets in portfolio combinations and why is it important in improving investment returns and/or reducing risk?
6. What is the range of asset mix alternatives open to ABC over the next eleven years (1993 – 2003)?
7. Based on the data presented in the case, which of the five asset mix alternatives should Marilyn recommend to ABC? Why?

Please use these questions as a guide and not a format or a reflection of all of the questions that need to be addressed by the case.

# 3

# GLOBAL MANUFACTURING CORPORATION[1]
## Portfolio Restructuring

It was late spring 1993. Bob McFee had a presentation to the Investment Committee of the Board of Directors of Global Manufacturing Corporation (GMC) in four days, and he still hadn't finalized the strategic plan for real estate.

Bob had joined GMC three years earlier as the Manager of Real Estate for the firm's pension fund. He had stepped into a difficult situation in which the real estate investment program had collapsed and the prior director resigned. Many of the properties in the real estate portfolio had developed serious problems, with investment performance dropping seriously below expectations.

Bob had been brought in to stem the hemorrhaging, work out the portfolio, and develop and implement a strategic plan for the operations going forward operations. The workout was largely complete, and Bob was now faced with presenting the Investment Committee with a strategic plan that he hoped would prevent many of the mistakes of the past and raise the portfolio contribution of real estate to acceptable levels in the future.

### GMC's Venture into Real Estate

GMC, a large manufacturing firm based in Cleveland, began investing in real estate in 1984 with an investment target of 5-15%. In 1986, the plan committed approximately $200 million to closed-end funds. One year later

---

[1] This case was prepared by John McMahan in 1995. Copyright © 1995 and 2004 by John McMahan, all rights reserved.

they expanded this commitment, invested an additional $600 million through separate accounts, and made their first international real estate investment in Canada.

In 1988, the plan diversified into higher risk investments such as "undervalued" assets and hotels. Mortgages and other non-core investments were also targeted for the portfolio. Almost $400 million was committed during 1988.

In 1989, the plan moved further up the real estate risk curve through investments with selected development partners and in specialty corporations. They also made their second international investment in the United Kingdom. By the end of the year, the real estate portfolio stood at over $1.3 billion. In order to further expand the portfolio, the upper end of the target range was expanded to 20%.

## *The Workout*

In 1990 it all came crashing down. Many of the higher risk investments went sour and the core portfolio was caught up in the general downturn in the real estate markets. New commitments to real estate were halted, the real estate director resigned, and a major workout period began.

In early 1991, Bob was hired to work out the problems of the portfolio and establish a strategic plan for moving forward. With an MBA from a major east coast university, Bob had over 20 years in real estate as a property manager, developer, and workout specialist. He had been through some difficult times and knew what it took to successfully work out a portfolio.

Bob began restaffing, hiring two seasoned real estate professionals and transferring a real estate attorney from another department in the corporation. Bob believed that he had assembled a very special team, with a diverse background and set of skills, that could oversee the workout and, once this was accomplished, begin implementing a new investment program that would contribute to the overall success of GMC's pension portfolio.

The initial phase of the workout took two long years. Sixteen properties were sold, four managers terminated, and several portfolios consolidated and realigned. In addition, a valuation and performance measurement policy was established in order to monitor the performance of the investments by standardizing the reporting of each manager.

As a result of the workout, the GMC portfolio was reduced to 51 properties with a "marked-to-market" value of approximately $1 billion. Approximately 30% of the portfolio was office, 36% retail, 6% industrial, and 6% apartments. The remaining 22% "other" category included hotels, trailer parks, mini warehouses, and other specialized investments. Exhibit 1

## Chapter 3 - Global Manufacturing Corporation                     -53-

compares the property type mix of the portfolio with properties comprising the Russell/NCREIF (R/N) Index.

The total annual return on the real estate portfolio since 1984 was 3.4%. Almost two thirds of the portfolio was located in 6 metropolitan areas: Toronto, Washington DC, Chicago, New York, Indianapolis, Los Angeles, and Montreal (Exhibit 2). Most of these were suburban properties, although there were a few regional malls and downtown office buildings. In terms of the development cycle, 81% were leased, 8% were in lease up, and 11% were in the development or rehab phase (Exhibit 3).

Bob and his staff had reviewed each of the properties and ascribed risk assessments indicating how much risk the staff believed each investment represented. Returns were then projected for each property over a 10 year period and then matched with the risk assessment to get an anticipated risk-adjusted return for the existing portfolio (Exhibit 4). Approximately 10% of the portfolio had returns of less than 5%, and 15% had a risk exposure exceeding 20%.

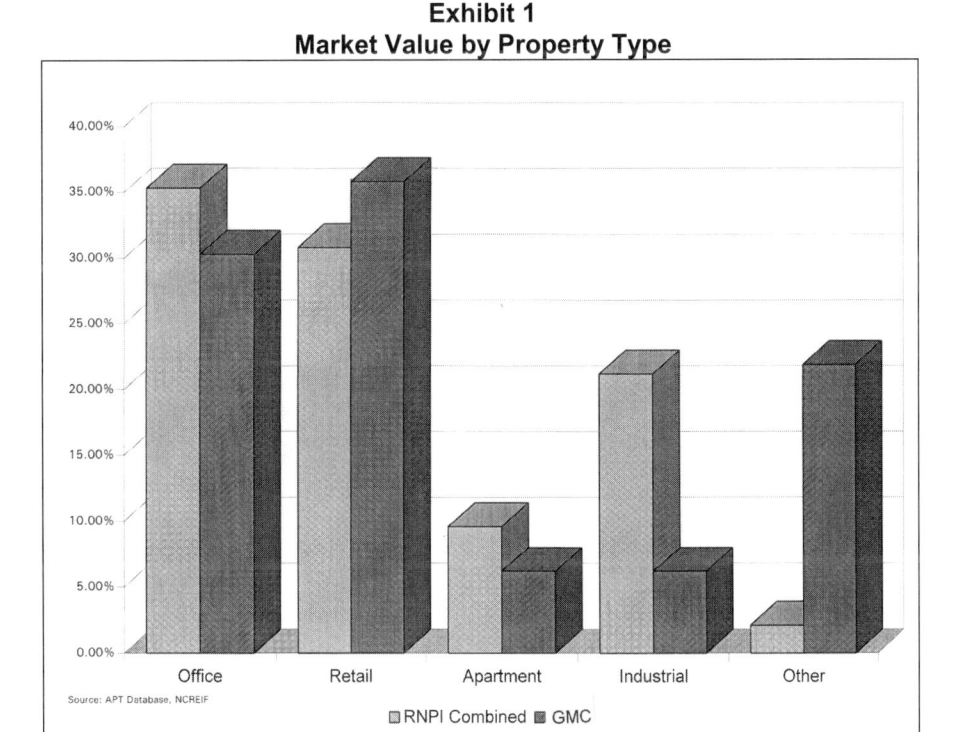

**Exhibit 1**
**Market Value by Property Type**

## Exhibit 2
## Top 15 MSAs by Net Market Value

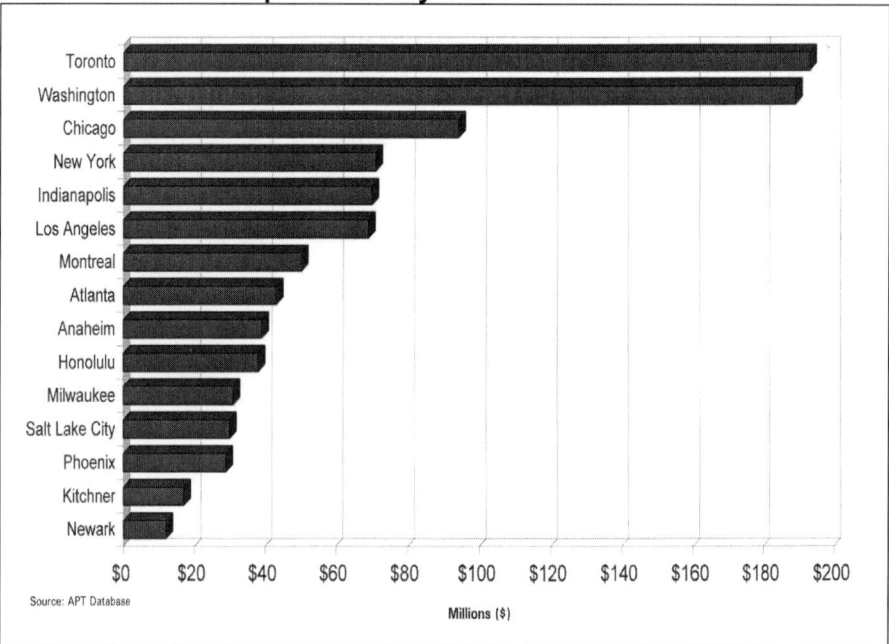

| MSA | Value |
|---|---|
| Toronto | ~$195M |
| Washington | ~$190M |
| Chicago | ~$95M |
| New York | ~$72M |
| Indianapolis | ~$70M |
| Los Angeles | ~$70M |
| Montreal | ~$52M |
| Atlanta | ~$45M |
| Anaheim | ~$40M |
| Honolulu | ~$40M |
| Milwaukee | ~$32M |
| Salt Lake City | ~$30M |
| Phoenix | ~$28M |
| Kitchner | ~$18M |
| Newark | ~$14M |

Source: APT Database
Millions ($)

## Exhibit 3
## Property Life Cycle, 1990-1992

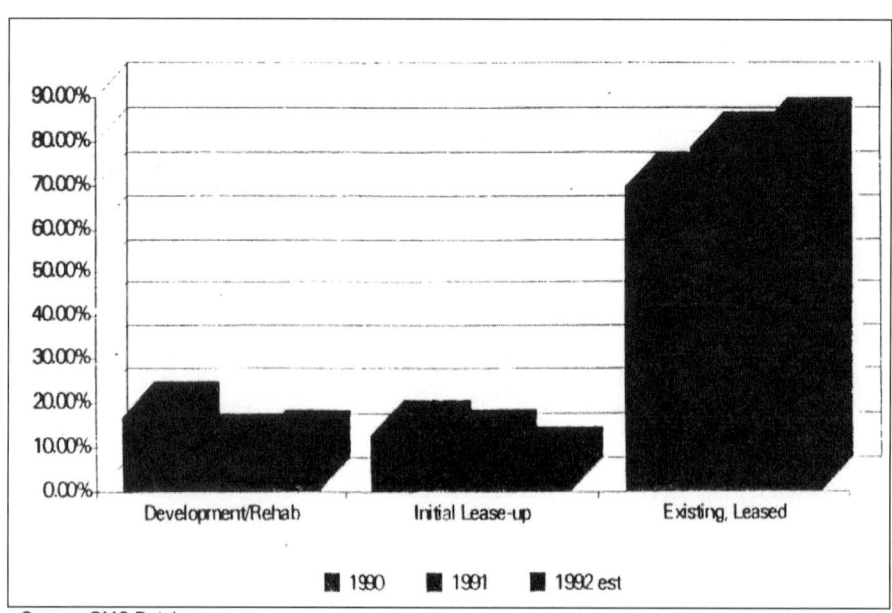

| Category | 1990 | 1991 | 1992 est |
|---|---|---|---|
| Development/Rehab | ~18% | ~15% | ~15% |
| Initial Lease-up | ~18% | ~15% | ~13% |
| Existing, Leased | ~70% | ~78% | ~88% |

Source: GMC Database

**Exhibit 4
GMC Real Estate Portfolio
Risk/Return Analysis**

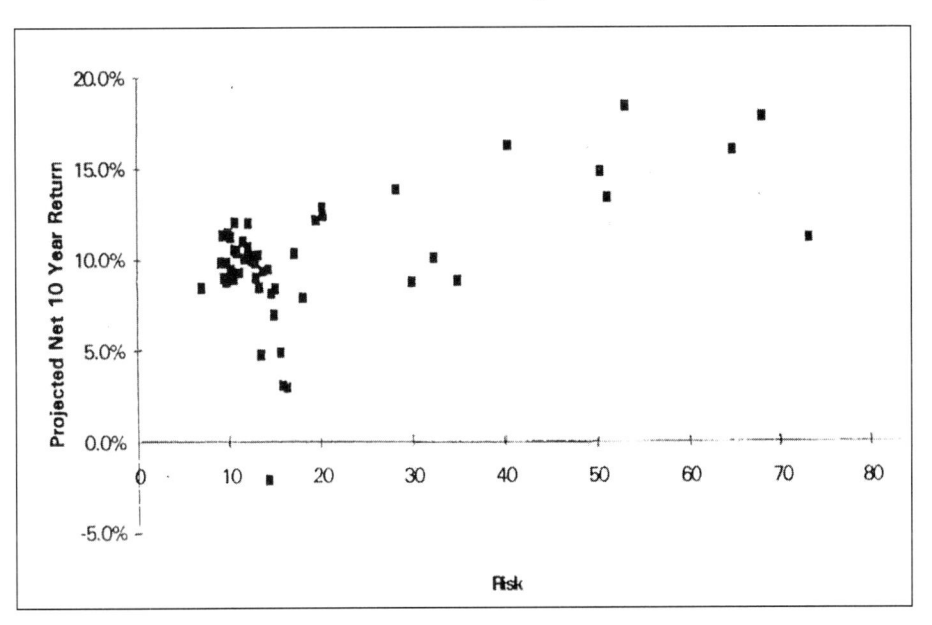

## The Strategic Plan

With the workout program moving along well, Bob and his staff began working on the strategic plan. A research study of mortgage investment was commissioned and extensive "brainstorming" meetings were held with a planning team of academics, managers, and consultants in order to determine the best way to proceed.

As a result of these meetings and extensive reading, Bob had a good command of the issues in developing a strategic plan but was still somewhat confused about the trade-offs and prioritization that transformed ideas and concepts into a plan that could be successfully implemented. There were several key questions that still remained to be answered:

1. **What Should Be The Target Allocation For Real Estate?** As of the end of 1992, the GMC pension fund portfolio held investments of approximately $12.2 billion. Despite heavy payments to an aging workforce, the portfolio was expected to grow at 4% annually over the next 10 years. At $1 billion, real estate represented 8.2% of GMC's total pension fund investment portfolio, an amount considerably greater than the average pension fund investment of 4%. It was less, however, than the 12% that

would be allocated on the basis of real estate assets as a percentage of all investable assets.

The strategic planning team had undertaken extensive modeling which indicated that based on expected returns, levels of risks, and correlation between asset classes, the allocation to real estate should be 15-20%. Bob felt comfortable with this allocation, as did some members of the planning team, but others pressed for a lower allocation at least until the existing portfolio had fully stabilized and the staff had demonstrated to the Investment Committee that real estate could perform to their expectations.

**2. *What Should Be The Overall Level of Portfolio Risk/Return?*** Bob knew that equity real estate was a highly cyclical asset class whose recent performance had been extremely disappointing not only in the GMC portfolio but throughout most of the pension community at large. Real estate would not be a desired asset, however, if one believed that its future performance would mirror its recent past.

This sentiment meant that the success of the strategic plan would have to be measured on the basis of competitive future returns. The problem was in estimating future returns based on historical data. Exhibit 5 contains data for the 1978-1992 period for real estate and other asset classes. Exhibit 6 projects the planning team's estimate of future performance over the next 10 years.

In terms of its position in the overall GMC investment portfolio, real estate was seen to have a low or even negative correlation with other major asset classes (Exhibit 7). In fact, the recent dismal performance of real estate occurred at a time when the stock and bond markets were experiencing new historical highs.

**Exhibit 5**
**Historical Asset Class Performance, 1978-1992**

|  | Total Return | Standard Deviation | Excess Return per Unit of Risk** |
|---|---|---|---|
| Real Estate--RNPI | 8.46% | 11.05%* | .050 |
| U.S. Stocks--S&P 500 | 15.83% | 15.62% | .507 |
| U.S. Bonds--LGCI | 10.43% | 8.77% | .287 |
| Foreign Stocks--EAFE | 15.75% | 19.60% | .400 |
| Foreign Bonds--FORBOND | 12.21% | 14.43% | .298 |
| 90 Day T-Bills--CASH | 7.91% | 1.29% | N/A |
| Inflation--CPI | 5.56% | 2.00% | N/A |

## Exhibit 6
### Expected Real Estate Performance, 1993-2002

|  | Total Return | Standard Deviation* | Excess return per Unit of Risk |
|---|---|---|---|
| Real Estate--RNPI | 10.50% | 11.05% | .543% |
| 90 Day T-Bills--CASH | 4.50% | 1.29% | N/A |
| Inflation--CPI | 3.50% | 2.00% | N/A |

*Assumes future standard deviations will be the same as in the period 1978-1992.

## Exhibit 7
### Asset Class Correlations, 1978-1992

|  | Real Estate | U.S. Stocks | U.S. Bonds | Foreign Stocks | Foreign Bonds | Inflation | T-Bills |
|---|---|---|---|---|---|---|---|
| Real Estate | 1.00 |  |  |  |  |  |  |
| U.S. Stocks | -.10 | 1.00 |  |  |  |  |  |
| U.S. Bonds | -.20 | .36 | 1.00 |  |  |  |  |
| Foreign Stocks | .04 | .65 | .35 | 1.00 |  |  |  |
| Foreign Bonds | -.15 | .13 | .55 | .56 | 1.00 |  |  |
| Inflation | .49 | -.14 | -.33 | -.25 | -.34 | 1.00 |  |
| T-Bills | .67 | -.16 | -.11 | -.22 | -.33 | .55 | 1.00 |

With real estate representing such a large and diverse market, investment opportunities could be found along a long risk/return curve. In essence, real estate "mirrored" the entire GMC investment portfolio (Exhibit 8). Bob liked to think about the opportunities as being four "quadrants" bridging both debt and equity investments in both private and public markets (Exhibit 9).

## Exhibit 8
## Real Estate Risk/Return vs. Corporate Securities

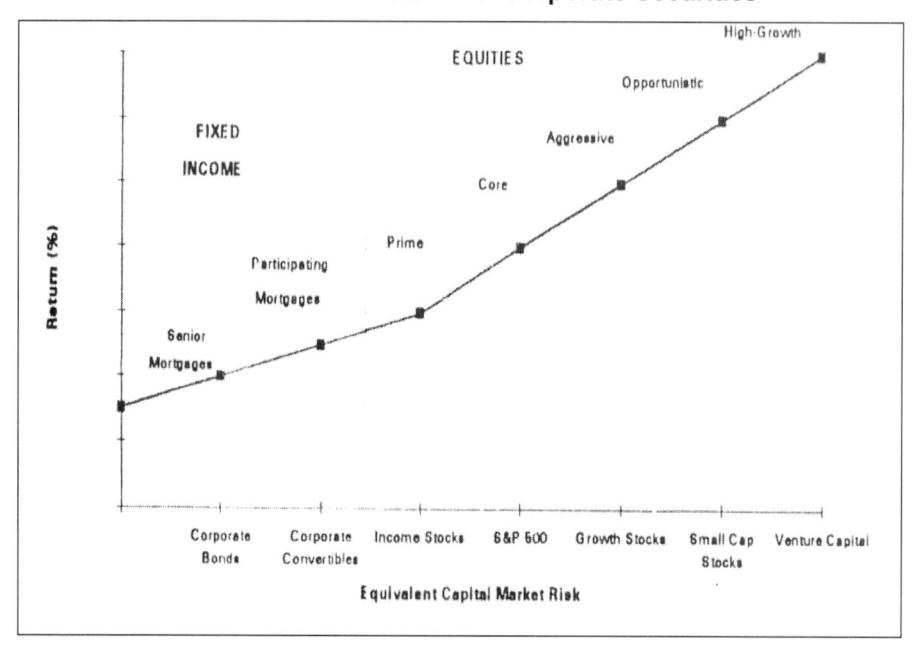

*Y-axis: Return (%)*
*X-axis: Equivalent Capital Market Risk*

X-axis labels: Corporate Bonds, Corporate Convertibles, Income Stocks, S&P 500, Growth Stocks, Small Cap Stocks, Venture Capital

Plot labels: EQUITIES, FIXED INCOME, High-Growth, Opportunistic, Aggressive, Core, Prime, Participating Mortgages, Senior Mortgages

## Exhibit 9
## Four Quadrants of Real Estate Finance

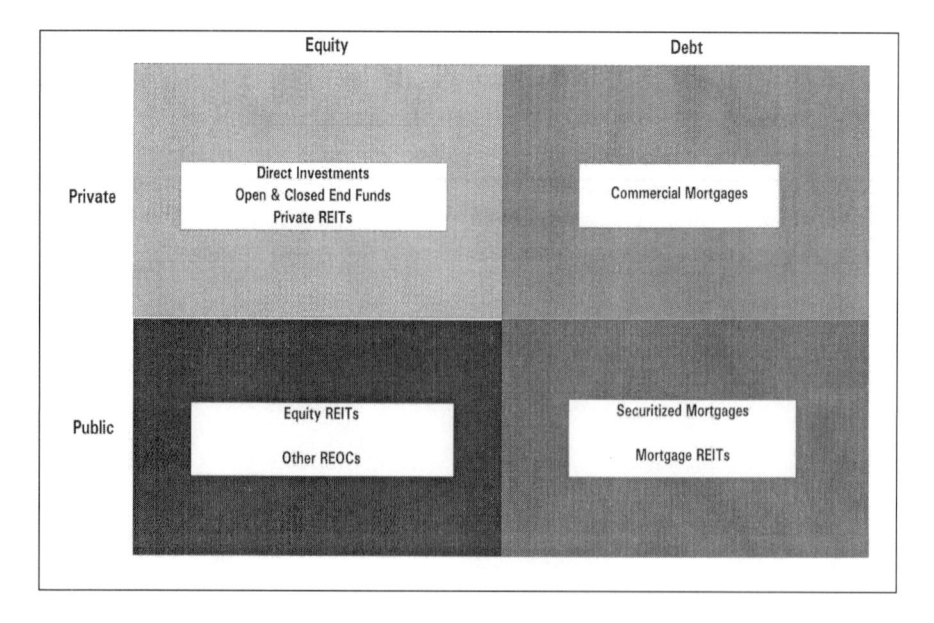

|  | Equity | Debt |
|---|---|---|
| Private | Direct Investments<br>Open & Closed End Funds<br>Private REITs | Commercial Mortgages |
| Public | Equity REITs<br>Other REOCs | Securitized Mortgages<br>Mortgage REITs |

With the large concentration in the existing portfolio at the higher end of the risk/return range and with many of the investments difficult to exit, several members of the planning team advocated risk-adverse investments, at least for the initial return to real estate investing. Others felt that existing market conditions reflected a "window of opportunity" that would only exist for a few years. They argued strongly that GMC should adopt a much more risk-oriented investment strategy in order to seize this once-in-a-lifetime opportunity to generate higher returns and restore confidence in real estate's ability to improve the performance of the overall portfolio.

**3. *What Is The Role Of Fixed Income Real Estate?*** For those members of the planning team advocating a risk-adverse strategy, fixed income real estate appeared to be a logical choice for initial portfolio expansion. There were also some compelling arguments in the marketplace.

At the end of 1992, the total value of the commercial and multi-family mortgage market in the US exceeded $1 trillion, which was only 35% smaller than the corporate bond market. Traditional fixed income investors such as insurance companies and banks had been withdrawing funds in an effort to scale back their real estate portfolios to meet new risk-based asset accounting requirements (Exhibit 10).

**Exhibit 10**
**Net Flow of Funds into Mortgages**

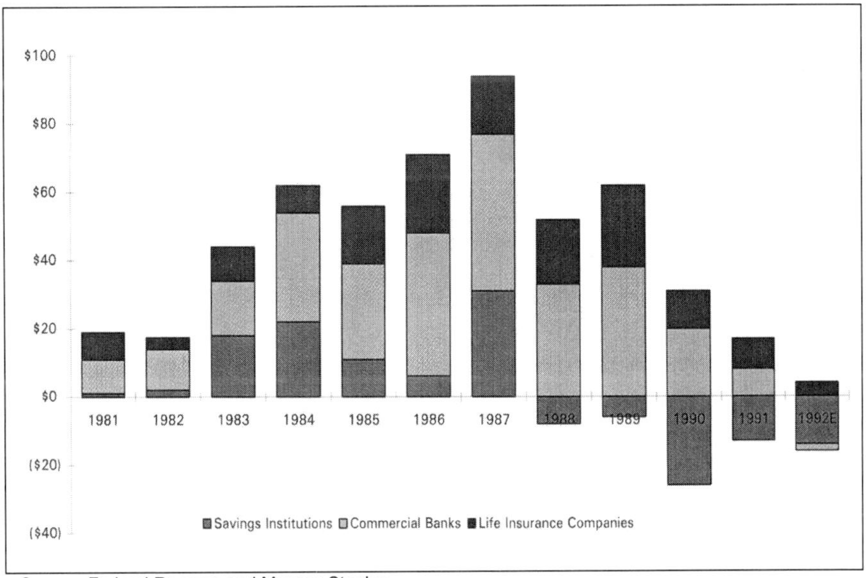

Source: Federal Reserve and Morgan Stanley

While there had been considerable interest on the part of pension funds in the multi-family mortgage market, there had not been much appetite for commercial mortgages. In Bob's estimation, this condition created a major opportunity.

Commercial mortgages were currently generating yields that were 200-250 basis points over equivalent treasuries. This figure compared quite favorably with the corporate bond spread of 100-150 basis points (Exhibit 11).

The supply side also appeared favorable for fixed income real estate investing. Non-residential construction had dropped to an extremely low level (Exhibit 12) and as indicated, traditional fixed income investors were continuing to withdraw from the market.

**Exhibit 11**
**Commercial Mortgage Spreads**

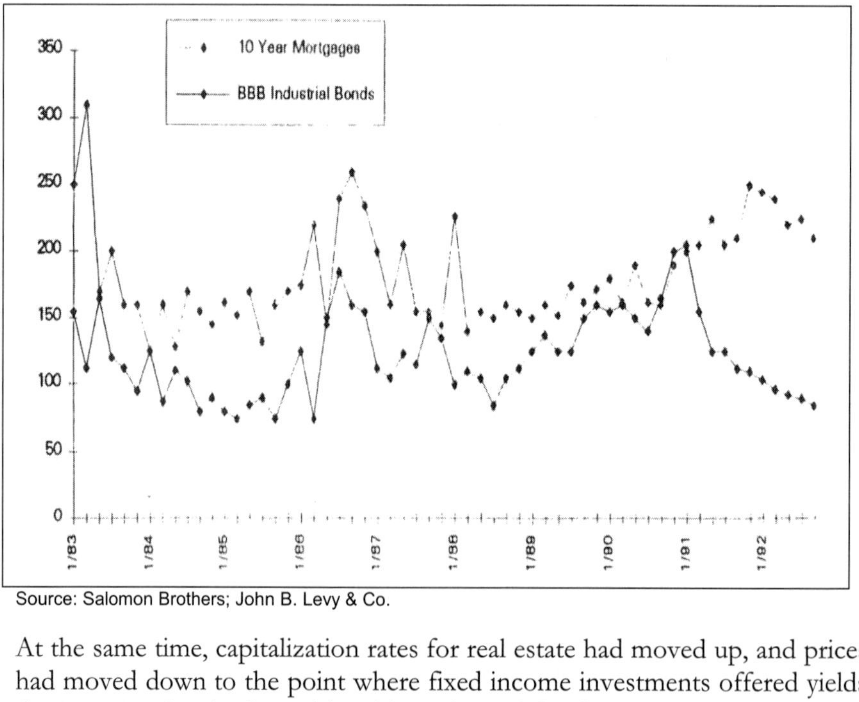

Source: Salomon Brothers; John B. Levy & Co.

At the same time, capitalization rates for real estate had moved up, and prices had moved down to the point where fixed income investments offered yields that compared quite favorably with equity and fixed income alternatives. Cap rates exceeded 90 day T-Bills by 600 basis points, 10 year T-Bonds by 200 basis points, and the S & P 500 earnings/price ratio by 400 basis points (Exhibit 13). Underwriting standards also appeared favorable. The combination of severely written down asset values and historically conservative loan to value ratios (40-50%) had created an equity "cushion" unparalleled since World War II. Debt coverage ratios were also at historically high levels.

**Exhibit 12**
**Aggregate Value of Non-residential Construction**

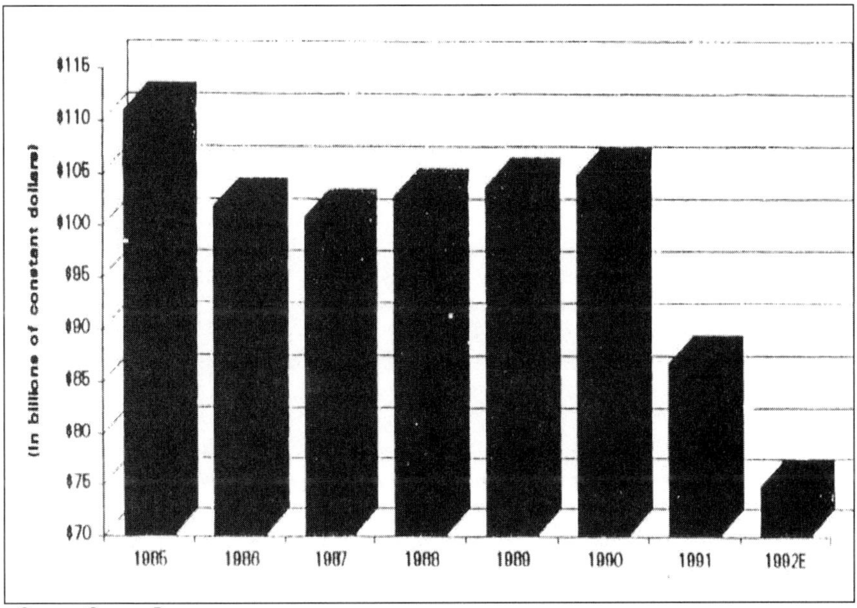

[Bar chart showing values in billions of constant dollars from 1985 to 1992E. Approximate values: 1985 ~$114, 1986 ~$102, 1987 ~$103, 1988 ~$105, 1989 ~$106, 1990 ~$107, 1991 ~$88, 1992E ~$75.]

Source: Census Bureau

Despite the attractiveness of fixed-income real estate, Bob knew that it would not be an easy sell to the Investment Committee, at least as part of the real estate program. Several members had previously expressed the view that if GMC's pension plan were to invest in real estate mortgages, it should be through their fixed income managers, not through the real estate staff.

However, Bob felt that he could counter this argument since the origination and management of commercial mortgages required a high level of real estate expertise. Even if the real estate staff did not originate the mortgages, it would still have to understand and sign off on the originations of others. The management of mortgage portfolios, in Bob's mind, definitely required real estate expertise, particularly if a loan got into trouble.

**Exhibit 13
Cap Rates**

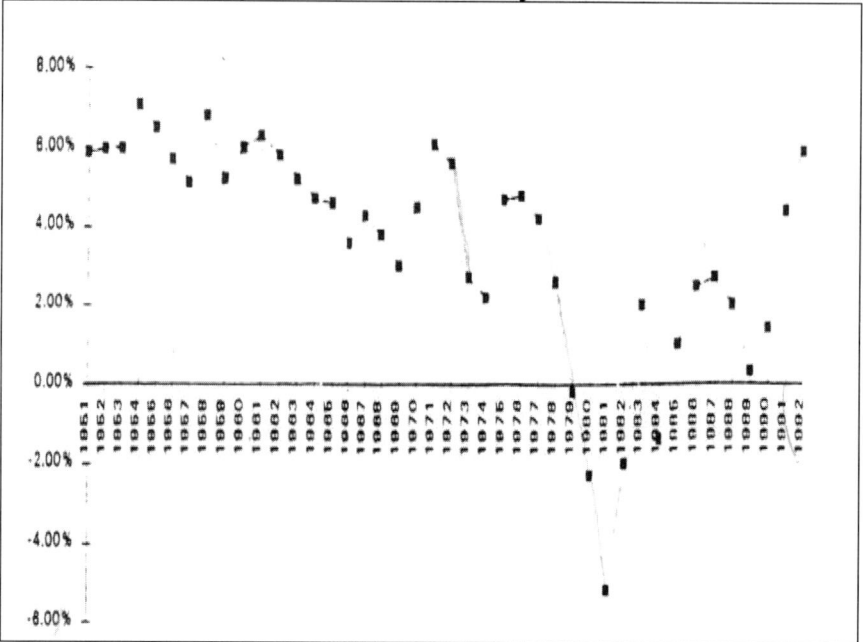

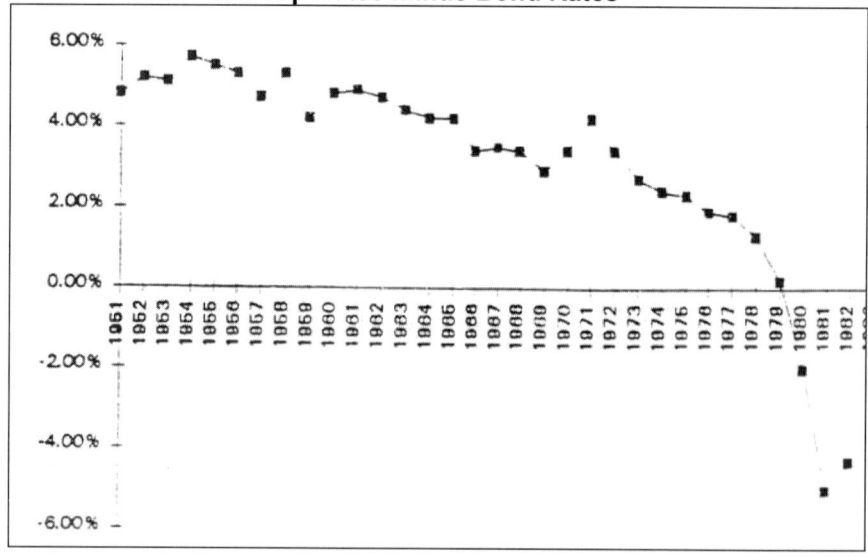

**Cap Rates minus Treasury Bill Rates**

**Cap Rates minus Bond Rates**

## Cap Rates minus Stock E/Ps

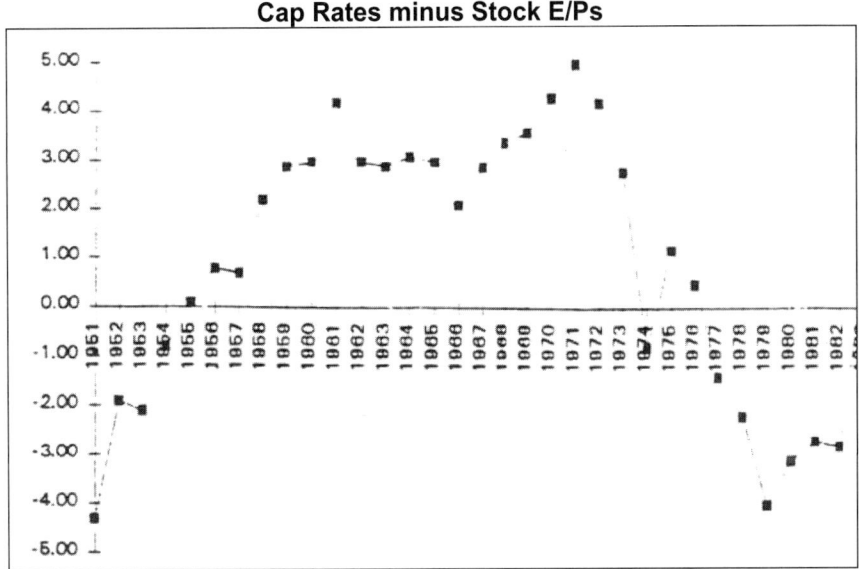

*[Chart showing data points from 1951 to 1982, with values ranging from approximately -5.00 to 5.00]*

Source: Quester Associates NREI

On the other hand, Bob mused, the rapid growth in securitized real state debt might influence the Investment Committee to prefer a securitized approach, in which case the program could clearly be handled by fixed income security managers.

### 4. What Is The Role Of Securitized Equity Real Estate?

Although not a new concept, real estate equity securitization was also gaining momentum as an alternative to the private ownership vehicles that had typified institutional real estate investments over the last 15 years.

The most prevalent form of equity securitization was Real Estate Investment Trusts (REITs), which had grown very rapidly since 1990 (Exhibit 14).

The level of new capital raised in 1992 was 25% higher than that of 1991 and was expected to increase another 50% in 1993.

One of the reasons for the growth in new REIT capital was the extent to which REITs had outperformed the private real estate market (Exhibit 15). The REIT index had also been a leading indicator of performance trends in the private real estate markets.

Although most of the new capital raised was from retail investors, pension funds were beginning to take more interest in REITs. They were attracted not only by the strong performance record and the inherent liquidity of publicly traded stocks, but also by the side-by-side investment by REIT managers and the high level of governance as a result of outside directors, government regulation, and an emerging investment analysis community.

**Exhibit 14
Public Equity REIT Capital Raised**

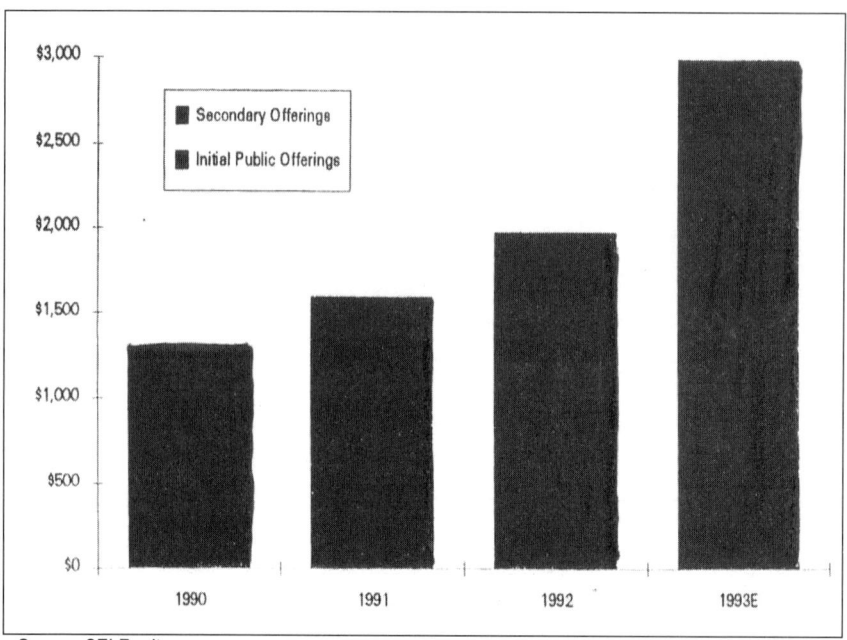

[Bar chart showing Secondary Offerings and Initial Public Offerings for years 1990, 1991, 1992, 1993E, with values rising from approximately $1,300 in 1990 to nearly $3,000 in 1993E]

Source: SEI Realty

Bob thought that this approach would be attractive to the Investment Committee but was concerned again with the issue of whether REIT investments would be managed by the real estate staff or equity managers. Several members of the Investment Committee viewed REITs as small cap stocks, to be managed by stock managers who specialized in this type of security.

**5. *Where Should the Investments be Located?*** As indicated in Exhibit 2, almost two thirds of GMC's existing real estate portfolio was located in 6 major metropolitan areas. There was a great deal of discussion by the planning team as to how portfolio diversification should proceed in the future. The existing portfolio had been largely diversified on a "naive" basis by property type and metropolitan area. It had also been influenced by where the investment managers were comfortable in operating.

## Exhibit 15
## Public vs. Private Real Estate Performance

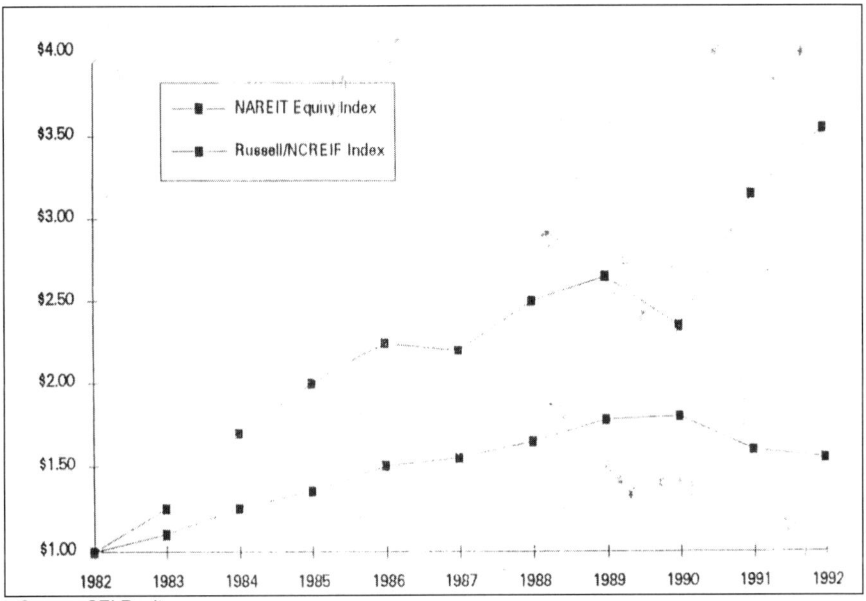

[Line chart showing NAREIT Equity Index and Russell/NCREIF Index from 1982 to 1992, with values ranging from $1.00 to approximately $3.50+]

Source: SEI Realty

Several analytical models were developed to show how a more scientific portfolio might look. A relatively simple approach would be to re-balance the portfolio towards the R/N portfolio (Exhibit 16). Several of the members of the team were critical of this approach, however, in light of the poor performance of the R/N portfolio, which was largely due to heavy concentrations in office investments.

## Exhibit 16
## Russell-NCREIF Property Index Composition

| PROPERTY TYPE | PERCENT |
|---|---|
| Office / R&D | 43 % |
| Retail | 26 % |
| Industrial / Wrhse | 18 % |
| Residential | 11 % |
| Other | 2 % |
| Source: Russell- NCREIF ||

Another approach would be to diversify the portfolio by economic region, an idea introduced by Salomon Brothers and based on Joel Garreau's book, *"The Nine Nations of North America"* (Exhibit 17). Still other members of the team wanted to utilize a "shift-share" approach, in which the portfolio would be re-balanced by individual metro areas and based upon the economic base relationship of each area to others in the portfolio (Exhibit 18). This approach would emphasize increased weightings towards metro areas that were strong in utilities/transportation, civilian high-tech/communications, and durable and non-durable goods manufacturing and decreased weightings in areas where finance & insurance, government services, defense, and tourism were concentrated.

**Exhibit 17**
**Salomon Brothers Eight-Region Segmentation**

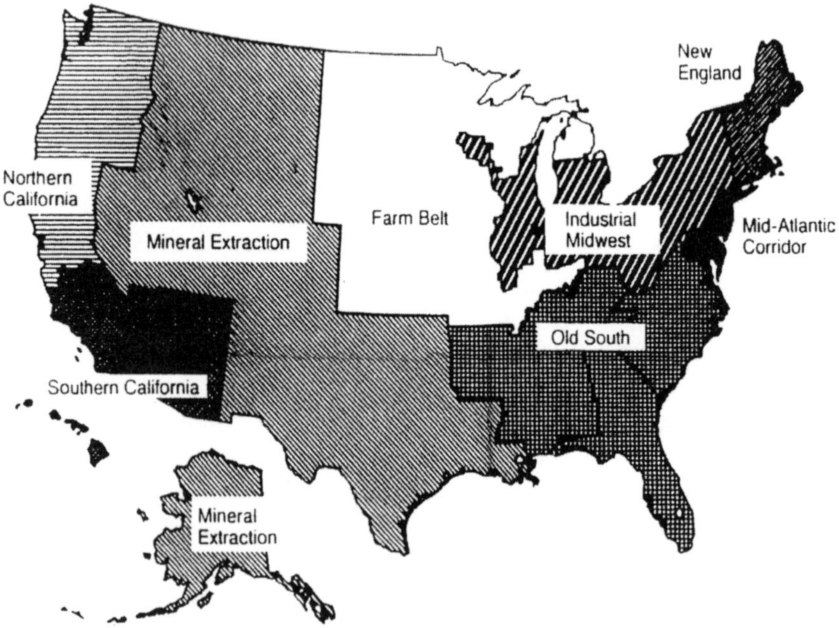

Source: Salomon Brothers

A small group within the planning committee wanted to do away with *any* diversification requirements for the portfolio and focus instead on achieving greater operating efficiencies by concentrating in a few key markets. In coming to this position, this group relied on a recent study which indicated that property returns were more dependent on internal factors such as leases and operating margins than portfolio diversification.

**6. What Property Types Should Be Emphasized?** In terms of property type diversification, Most members of the team felt that the GMC portfolio

## Chapter 3 - Global Manufacturing Corporation -67-

had enough special property types such as hotels, raw land, and mini-storage facilities for the time being and that the focus should be on some of the more traditional types that were under-represented in the existing portfolio, primarily apartments and industrial.

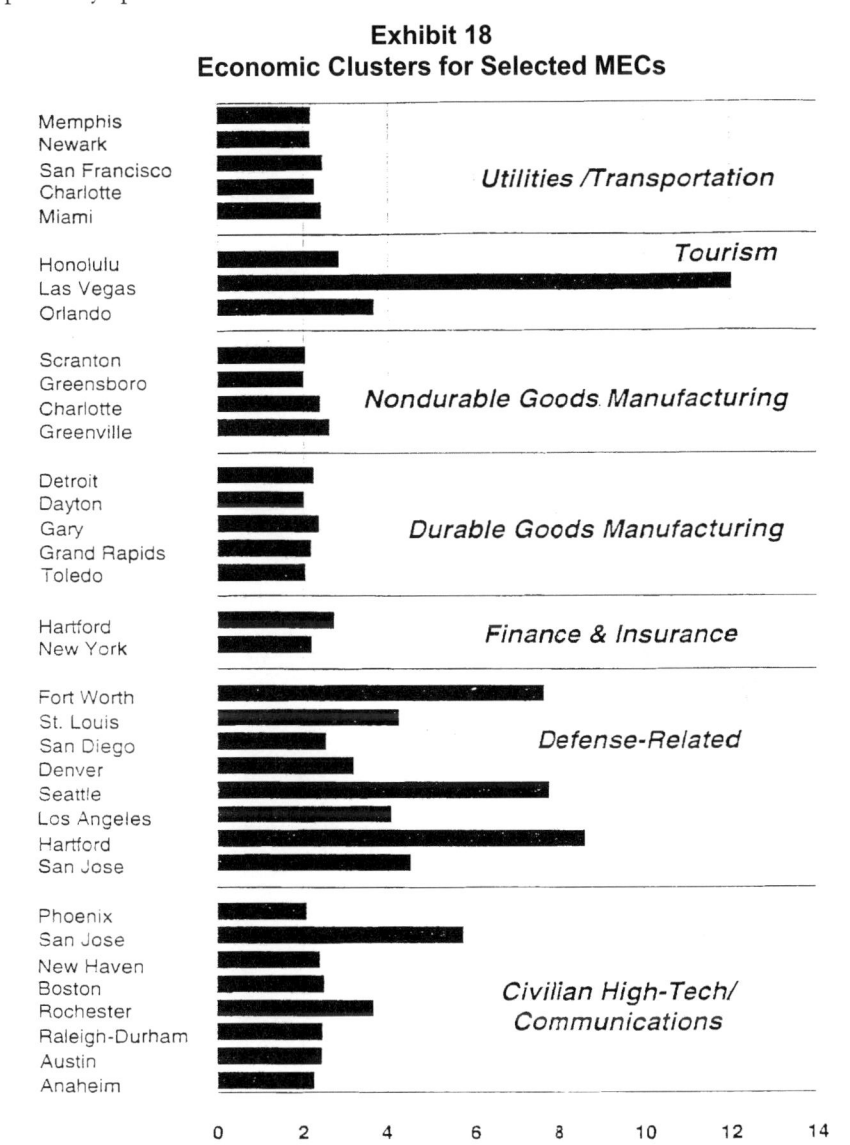

**Exhibit 18**
**Economic Clusters for Selected MECs**

|  |  |
|---|---|
| Memphis, Newark, San Francisco, Charlotte, Miami | Utilities/Transportation |
| Honolulu, Las Vegas, Orlando | Tourism |
| Scranton, Greensboro, Charlotte, Greenville | Nondurable Goods Manufacturing |
| Detroit, Dayton, Gary, Grand Rapids, Toledo | Durable Goods Manufacturing |
| Hartford, New York | Finance & Insurance |
| Fort Worth, St. Louis, San Diego, Denver, Seattle, Los Angeles, Hartford, San Jose | Defense-Related |
| Phoenix, San Jose, New Haven, Boston, Rochester, Raleigh-Durham, Austin, Anaheim | Civilian High-Tech/Communications |

*Location Quotient (Multiple of U.S. Concentration)*

Interestingly, a small group wanted to continue to emphasise office investments since the price discounting had been greatest in this category and the buying opportunities were very attractive. This was countered by the argument that the decline in office values was secular, reflecting a long term reduction in office demand. A few members of the team expressed a similar concern about retail.

Several argued that, whatever final diversification policy was developed, it should apply to all investments: equity and fixed income; public or private markets; and pooled or direct investment.

**7. What Should Be The Policy Towards International Real Estate Investment?** There was also considerable discussion regarding international real estate investments. GMC currently had investments in Canada and the UK. The fund's experience with these investments had been somewhat disappointing, however, and there were several members of the planning team who felt that the level of international investments should be reduced.

Other members of the team believed that the problems with existing international investments were primarily the result of the type of investment (office and retail) and the fact that it was made at the high end of the market cycle. They argued that the focus should be on more aggressive investments in advanced industrial countries and conservative investments in faster growing economics such as Asia and Latin America.

Still another group wanted to confine all international investments to a securitized format. The public real estate markets in many industrialized countries were much more advanced than the US and offered opportunities for growth with the ability to get out if the investment didn't pan out or changes in the country made investment less desirable.

**8. What Should Be GMC's Policy Regarding Social Investing?** Historically, GMC had never had a policy regarding social investing in real estate. Unlike public employee plans, GMC and other corporate pension plans did not have a large amount of pressure to consider investments that had objectives other than producing the highest risk-adjusted investment return for the beneficiaries of the plan. The only exception had been the plan's decision to sell its South African investments several years back as a protest against the government's policy of apartheid.

But times were changing. Several of the older industrial states where GMC had extensive operations were pressuring corporations to invest a portion of their pension plan portfolio in state and local bond issues, particularly those directed at inner city "opportunity zones". Some of the powerful unions that GMC dealt with were also discussing the possibility of pension fund investment in special pools that had been created to invest in union built properties across the nation. At the Federal level, the Department of Labor had let it be known that social investing by America's pension funds would be a top priority of the new administration.

In his reading on the subject, Bob had detected a much more practical approach by the new proponents of social investing. Most recognized that proposed investments must be in the economic interests of the plan's beneficiaries first and, only when that objective had been achieved, could social investing goals be considered. This was a major departure from previous calls for social investing where there had not even been lip service given to the fact that these investments might not be in the interests of the plan's beneficiaries.

Bob wasn't sure where he stood on the issue. While he had been very involved politically as a young college student he, like so many of his generation, had focused inwardly on his career during the last 20 years and had only recently become aware of some of the problems that were proposed to be addressed by social investing. He knew that the problems were real, however, and that maybe there was a leadership role for GMC's pension plan. The pressure from government and GMC's unions was certainly real and the firm's CEO had recently delivered a speech supporting corporate leadership for solving many of the nation's social ills.

On the other side, GMC was under increasing fire from institutional investors to improve the earnings of the corporation. Two of the new members of the Board of Directors had been literally "forced" on the corporation as a result of these lobbying efforts. Any shortfall in pension investment performance would have to be made up by charges to corporate earnings, something these new directors would certainly not like.

Regardless of the form it took Bob knew that he had to have a policy recommendation on social investing as an integral part of his strategic plan.

**9. What Should Be the Policy Regarding Leverage?** GMC's current real estate portfolio was 44% leveraged. Bob did not want to increase this level of leveraging, but he did want to have a policy spelling out under what conditions the portfolio could be leveraged and the amount and type of leveraging that should be employed. He was particularly concerned with new equity investments, especially since current market conditions created a positive yield spread.

Historically, GMC had leveraged individual investments, based on available financing and manager investment style. Bob wondered if it might not be better to leverage all or selected portions of the portfolio on a "pooled" basis to take advantage of cyclical swings in interest rates. While this approach would no doubt require cross-collateralization and cross-defaulting, GMC would have some flexibility to substitute assets in the pool if defaults occurred.

Bob knew that one objection that would be raised by the Investment Committee would be why the plan should borrow at all when it might become involved as a lender through the fixed income investment program. Bob wasn't sure which side of this issue he was on or if it was necessary to take a side but rather borrow when it was opportune and lend when the market moved in another direction.

**10. *How Do Strategic Differences Get Resolved?*** One of the immediate challenges that Bob faced was to resolve the differences within his planning team and integrate the new investment proposals with the existing portfolio.

One of the consultants to the planning team had developed a hypothetical model of GMC's real estate portfolio which included both existing investments and a recommended investment program (Exhibit 19). This model suggested that most of the new investment dollars be directed towards senior and participating mortgages. The equity portion of the portfolio would remain relatively intact except that an increasing portion would be in a securitized format such as REIT's. The overall target was to have 30% of the core equity real estate portfolio in a securitized form within 3 years.

This approach, of course, reflected the risk-adverse approach advocated by the consultant and embraced by many members of the planning team. There were others, however, who continued to push for a more aggressive investment program to take advantage of advantageous pricing in the marketplace. This group would emphasize stepped-up direct investment in office and hotel properties with little regard for geographical diversification. They would also utilize aggressive vehicles such as limited partnerships and joint ventures. Their rationale was that this type of approach would produce dramatically higher returns which would go a long way towards making the Investment Committee forget about the poor performance of the real estate portfolio in the past.

In terms of integrating the old and new portfolios, decisions had to be made regarding the further disposition of existing assets. One approach would be to sell off the underperforming and/or higher risk assets or perhaps to turn the development properties back to the development partner. Another approach would be to dispose of specific property types such as office or those properties contained in the "Other" category. Some members of the planning team advocated selling assets on a geographical basis to reduce concentration in certain markets or to get out of international direct investing entirely. One member of the team was against selling any of the assets in the existing portfolio because GMC would have to take such a beating on price.

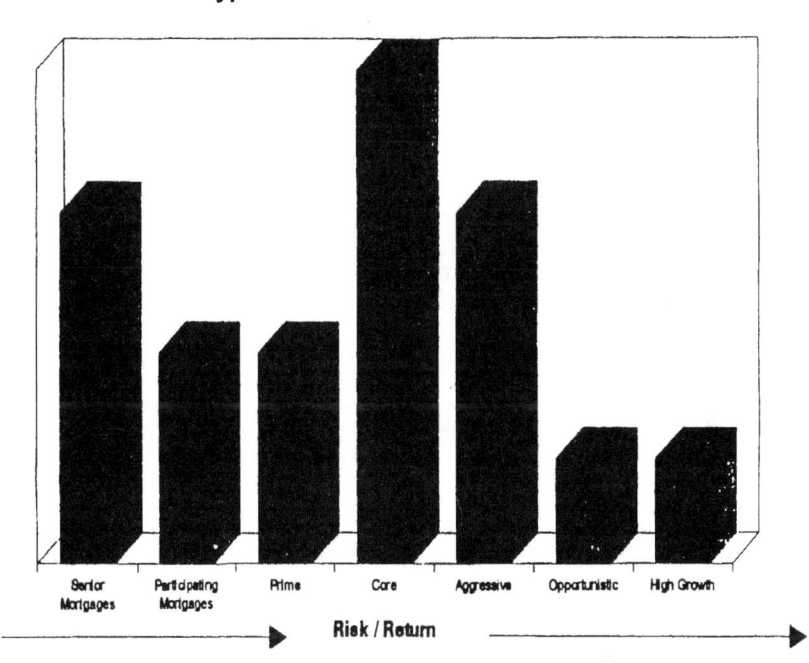

**Exhibit 19**
**Hypothetical Portfolio Distribution**

[Bar chart showing portfolio distribution across categories arranged by Risk/Return: Senior Mortgages, Participating Mortgages, Prime, Core, Aggressive, Opportunistic, High Growth]

**Risk / Return**

**11. *How Should The Strategic Plan Be Implemented?*** Another thorny issue was implementation. Bob believed that the immediate implementation focus had to be on completing the work out of the existing portfolio. He wanted to reduce the number of existing investments from 51 to 30 by the end of 1994, with a clearly articulated role for each investment. The size of the remaining investments would be in the $30-$80 range with most of them in the $50-$60 range.

Bob also wanted to reduce the number of outside managers from 13 to 6-8 over the same time period. This reduced number of managers would be responsible for 3-4 investments each, providing Bob's staff an opportunity to develop a close working relationship with each manager.

Most of the existing managers would be able to handle direct investments in apartments and industrial, but Bob knew that he would probably have to hire new managers for fixed income real estate and REITs as these were more specialized areas. This, of course, assumed that the Investment Committee didn't opt for having these areas handled by the plan's stock and bond managers. Bob wondered if it wouldn't be prudent to have an alternative plan for managing fixed income and REITs in-house by his staff.

One of the moves that Bob had insisted on during the workout phase was to have each property in the portfolio valued annually by an appraiser appointed by the plan and not the investment manager. Bob felt that this change had provided the staff with a more independent view of the value of each asset and removed a concern of the Investment Committee about manager conflict of interest. Going forward, Bob wondered if he shouldn't modify this policy to have appraisals every other year rather than annually. He also had to come up with a policy regarding the selection of appraisers. Several members of the planning team wanted to rotate the appraisers every few years.

In terms of timing, the planning team had come up with a three year implementation schedule; although Bob wasn't sure that it was realistic. On the one hand he wanted to have an aggressive implementation program, but he also wanted to be sure that he could meet the targeted schedule. He had built up a lot of credibility with the Investment Committee as a result of his work out efforts and didn't want to blow it on a failed implementation schedule.

As Bob pondered these questions, he once again reminded himself that he had only four days to wrap up his recommendations. With production lead times, this meant he had to have a final draft competed by the end of the next day. He knew that he had to have firm, creditable answers to all of the questions, as well as an identification of priorities and a realistic implementation program.

# 4

# VALLEY ISLAND PUBLIC EMPLOYEES' RETIREMENT SYSTEM[1]

## Impact of Technology on Portfolio Strategy

Mason Rourke let out a long sigh and leaned back in his chair. He had just hung up on a phone call from his Chairman, Andrew McCracken, who was requesting a change in the Agenda for the next Board meeting that was scheduled in two weeks on April 30, 2001. McCracken wanted to devote the entire meeting to real estate. He had recently attended a conference on the impact of high technology on real estate and was very concerned that their real estate portfolio was vulnerable to many of the negative impacts of technology and not well positioned to participate in the opportunities that technology might have to offer.

Mason was Director of Real Estate for The Valley Island Public Employees' Retirement System (VIPERS), a $47.4 billion plan with a widely diversified investment portfolio. Valley Island County, a once prosperous Midwestern manufacturing and agriculture center, had witnessed a steady loss of population over the last several years as younger people left for Chicago and other larger cities and the remaining population had become increasingly older. As an example, the average age of county employees was now 47, and VIPERS was facing a negative cash flow situation beginning in 2004.

---

[1] This case was prepared by John McMahan, Copyright © 2001, all rights reserved.

## VIPERS' Investment Portfolio

VIPERS' current portfolio diversification strategy called for 5% cash, 65% stocks, 20% bonds, and 10% real estate and other investments (Exhibit 1). The current stock investment strategy was growth (50%), yield (30%), and international (20%).

**Exhibit 1**
**Valley Island Public Employees' Retirement System**
**Investment Portfolio, June 30, 2000 (Millions)**

| Investment | Amount | Percentage | Target |
|---|---|---|---|
| Cash | $1,563.0 | 3.3% | 5.0% |
| Stocks | $32,684.2 | 69.0% | 65.0% |
| Bonds | $9,350.2 | 19.7% | 20.0% |
| Real Estate | $3,228.1 | 6.8% | 10.0% |
| Other | $543.9 | 1.1% | Inc. in RE |
| Total | $47,369.5 | 100.0% | 100.0% |

Approximately $3.2 billion of VIPERS' assets (6.8%) were invested in real estate and included core investments (55.2%), opportunistic investments (26.5%), and public REITS (18.3%) (Exhibit 2). Investment returns from the real estate portfolio had been declining over the last several years, a matter of increasing concern to the Board (Exhibit 3; Appendix A).

**Exhibit 2**
**Valley Island Public Employees' Retirement System**
**Real Estate Portfolio, June 30, 2000 (Millions)**

| Investment | Amount | Percentage | Target |
|---|---|---|---|
| Core Investments | $1,783.2 | 55.2% | 50.0% |
| Opportunistic | $854.4 | 26.5% | 25.0% |
| Public REITs | $590.5 | 18.3% | 25.0% |
| Total | $3,228.1 | 100.0% | 100.0% |

**Exhibit 3**
**Valley Island Public Employees' Retirement System**
**Real Estate Portfolio Investment Returns, June 30, 2000**

| Investment | 1 year | 3 years | 5 years |
|---|---|---|---|
| Core Real Estate | 9.1% | 10.3% | 9.2% |
| Opportunistic Real Estate | 6.4% | 13.4% | 19.3% |
| Public REITs | 15.5% | 4.7% | 9.3% |
| Weighted Average | 9.6% | 10.1% | 11.9% |

The core real estate portfolio was invested in office (21.0%), industrial (28.9%), retail (37.1%); and multifamily (13.0%) properties (Exhibit 4; Appendices B through E). The office portfolio was invested primarily in suburban properties across the nation as well as in an older CBD building in the Chicago area. The industrial portfolio was comprised largely of older warehouse properties located primarily in the Midwest and South. Retail properties included regional, community, and neighborhood centers, also located largely in the Midwest and South. Multifamily investments were largely garden apartment projects with several of the newer projects located in the East and West.

**Exhibit 4**
**Valley Island Public Employees' Retirement System**
**Core Real Estate Portfolio, June 30, 2000 (Millions)**

| Type | East | Midwest | South | West | Totals | Percent | Target |
|---|---|---|---|---|---|---|---|
| Office | $62.6 | $123.7 | $116.5 | $71.7 | $374.5 | 21.0% | 20.0% |
| Industrial | $68.4 | $195.3 | $171.2 | $80.3 | $515.2 | 28.9% | 30.0% |
| Retail | $97.5 | $250.2 | $210.3 | $103.7 | $661.7 | 37.1% | 35.0% |
| Multifamily | $32.4 | $61.5 | $66.1 | $71.8 | $231.8 | 13.0% | 15.0% |
| Total | $260.9 | $630.7 | $564.1 | $327.5 | $1,783.2 | 100.0% | 100.0% |
| Percent | 14.6% | 35.4% | 31.6% | 18.4% | 100.0% | | |
| Target | 20.0% | 30.0% | 25.0% | 25.0% | 100.0% | | |

The opportunistic portfolio of $854.4 million consisted of six separate opportunity funds with investments in the US, Europe, Asia, and South America. Strategies included leveraging, development, and mortgage investing (Exhibit 5). The public REIT portfolio consisted of investments in 76 different REITs across a wide variety of sectors (Exhibit 6).

**Exhibit 5**
**Valley Island Public Employees' Retirement System**
**Opportunistic Real Estate Portfolio, June 30, 2000 (Millions)**

| Fund | Date | Focus | Committed | Funded |
|---|---|---|---|---|
| A | Feb-94 | Loans | $150.7 | $150.7 |
| B | Jul-96 | Leverage | $135.4 | $135.4 |
| C | Apr-96 | Development | $149.3 | $149.3 |
| D | Apr-96 | Development | $110.8 | $110.8 |
| E | Sep-98 | Europe | $177.4 | $121.9 |
| F | Sep-98 | Asia/So.America | $130.8 | $93.0 |
| | Total | | $854.4 | $761.1 |

### Exhibit 6
### Valley Island Public Employees' Retirement System
### Public REIT Portfolio, June 30, 2000

| Sector | Investment (Millions) | No.REITs | % |
|---|---|---|---|
| Apartments | $37.8 | 13 | 6.4% |
| Community Centers | $123.6 | 14 | 20.9% |
| Diversified | $74.2 | 11 | 12.6% |
| Free Standing Retail | $84.8 | 5 | 14.4% |
| Industrial | $43.1 | 4 | 7.3% |
| Mfg. Homes | $15 | 2 | 2.5% |
| Mixed O-I | $37.3 | 3 | 6.3% |
| Office | $50.2 | 11 | 8.5% |
| Regional Malls | $61.1 | 6 | 10.3% |
| Self Storage | $15.9 | 2 | 2.7% |
| Specialty | $47.5 | 5 | 8.0% |
| Total | $590.5 | 76 | 100.0% |

The real estate portfolio was managed by 16 different managers who had been hired over a period from 1983 to 1999 (Exhibit 7). No manager had been fired. VIPERS utilized three different consultants over this period but had fired all of them.

## Mason's Memorandum

In order to brief the Board, McCracken has asked Mason to prepare a memorandum outlining the impact of technology on VIPERS' real estate portfolio with recommendations for changes in portfolio strategy to mitigate possible negative impacts and enhance investments in areas of opportunity.

In addition to possible changes in direct investments, McCracken wanted the Board to explore shifts in VIPERS' opportunistic and real estate security portfolios. The opportunistic portfolio had been somewhat of a "black box" for the Board for some time, and they weren't sure of the level of risk of these investments or of how vulnerable they might be to technology.

McCracken noted that several REITs had recently developed technology strategies that could possibly provide strategic market advantages and higher rates of share appreciation for VIPERS. Legislation also had become effective which permitted REITs to invest up to 25% of their capital base in new areas, one of which could be technology. McCracken had been pleased with VIPERS' REIT strategy, particularly the investment returns posted in 2000.

## Exhibit 7
### Valley Island Public Employees' Retirement System
### Investment Managers, June 30, 2000 (Millions)

| Manager | Year Hired | Amount Managed | Focus Core | Focus Opportunity | Focus REIT |
|---|---|---|---|---|---|
| 1 | 1983 | $457.3 | $457.3 | | |
| 2 | 1983 | 315.7 | 315.7 | | |
| 3 | 1983 | 106.4 | 106.4 | | |
| 4 | 1985 | 157.5 | 157.5 | | |
| 5 | 1985 | 143.9 | 143.9 | | |
| 6 | 1987 | 166.3 | 166.3 | | |
| 7 | 1987 | 121.6 | 121.6 | | |
| 8 | 1994 | 150.7 | | $150.7 | |
| 9 | 1996 | 135.4 | | 135.4 | |
| 10 | 1996 | 149.3 | | 149.3 | |
| 11 | 1996 | 110.8 | | 110.8 | |
| 12 | 1998 | 177.4 | | 177.4 | |
| 14 | 1998 | 130.8 | | 130.8 | |
| 13 | 1998 | 257.2 | | | $257.2 |
| 15 | 1999 | 288.8 | 157.3 | | 131.5 |
| 16 | 1999 | 359.0 | 157.2 | | 201.8 |
| | **Totals** | **$3,228.1** | **$1,783.2** | **$854.4** | **$590.5** |

The Chairman also was concerned about the softening economy and the impact that it might have on the portfolio and any possible restructuring efforts. Many of the manufacturing firms in Valley Island had already begun sizeable layoffs. The press was also full of stories about bankruptcies of dot-com companies and earnings estimate shortfalls by US companies across the entire economic spectrum.

In addition, McCracken was interested in Mason's recommendations regarding VIPERS' current stable of managers. McCracken felt that several of the managers weren't carrying their weight and that some consolidation might be in order. Such consolidation would also help ease the staff workload that had become worse since the cutback in hiring two years ago. He also wanted Mason to revisit the consultant issue and see if an outside review of their real estate strategy might help reverse the deterioration in investment returns and better position the fund for the future.

Mason saw an opportunity to discuss the major technology-related issues with the Board and, he hoped, to evolve a consensus on how best to proceed. Fortunately, Mason had been personally interested in the subject for some time and had been collecting research publications, articles, and other material that could provide a foundation for the memo.

In preparing his memo, Mason knew that he had to carefully balance his recommendations between a genuine concern about possible problems in the portfolio and the opportunities that technology investing could bring. He had learned the hard way that panicking the Board was almost as dangerous as underestimating a problem.

Unfortunately, the immediate problem was timing; in order for Mason to get the memo to the Board in sufficient time to meet the two week legal notification requirement, he would have to have it in the mail late the next day. He began reviewing the research material and outlining the structure of his memorandum.

## Understanding the New Economy

**Early Building Blocks:** In the mid-to-late 1990s, the United States experienced an unprecedented increase in economic growth, employment, and personal financial wealth. The building blocks for this phenomenon had been established several years earlier as a result of changes in public policy, the private business sector, and technology.

Public policy influences included the end of the Cold War, a worldwide reduction in trade barriers, deregulation of America's financial system, the Federal Reserve's close monitoring of monetary policy, and a federal fiscal policy focused on deficit reduction.

In the private sector, a major shift had also occurred in public perception. Often disdained in the 1960s and 1970s, business firms and people became "heroes" to the American public in the 1980s and 1990s, particularly those who chose to become entrepreneurs. Buoyed by an increasing willingness to accept investment risk, billions of dollars came out of personal savings and poured into the stock market, thus creating one of the biggest and longest bull markets in US history. The seemingly endless increases in market values created a growing feeling of personal wealth and helped to foster a consumer-spending boom.

**Role of Technology:** The growth in the stock market was based on a major expansion in corporate earnings, which was largely fueled by unprecedented increases in worker productivity. These increases emerged primarily as a result of a confluence of technological innovations, which had been in the development process for many years but finally came on stream in the 1990s.

The development and refinement of the personal computer provided individual employees with a powerful tool to do their jobs better. The continuing miniaturization of silicon chip technology not only reduced the cost and improved the performance of computers, but also allowed the imbedding of computer chips in virtually all types of machines, appliances, transportation vehicles, and other integral tools of American society.

Telecommunications technology also made major progress. The development and deployment of an extensive world wide satellite system made it possible to transmit wireless voice and data to virtually every corner of the globe almost instantaneously. With the dissolution of the Communist Empire, many newly freed countries found themselves with little existing telecommunications infrastructure and increasingly turned to emerging wireless technology as a relatively simple, broad-based solution.

Considerable technological progress also occurred in wire-based technology, particularly where fiber-optic cables were involved. Each of these technologies had its problems, however, as wireless transmission was often uncertain and wired transmission often had insufficient bandwidth to handle the load generated by the considerably faster data and voice generation systems.

Despite these problems, the public continued to flock to new telecommunication technologies: the number of worldwide wireless Internet users increased 187% in 2000, and the number of US DSL and cable-modem connections was up 88%[2] in the same year.

By 2000, the technology sector had become the largest sector of US Gross Domestic Product – larger than housing, automobiles, or food. By 2006, technology was expected to employ 50% of all US workers.[3] Investors also recognized the importance of intellectual property in determining value. In 1981, market value and book value were essentially the same; by 2000, market value was 4.2 times book value.[4]

**World Wide Web:** In the late 1990s, all of these seemingly independent technologies became increasingly integrated though the evolution of the Internet or "world wide web." The Internet was not entirely new; it had been originally introduced over 30 years ago as ARPAnet, a communication system established by the US Department of Defense and several major universities to enable their mainframes to communicate more efficiently. With the development of the desktop computer in the 1980s, Tim Berners-Lee's writing of new Worldwide Web software in the early 1990s, and the introduction of the web browser in 1994, the web subsequently established itself as a means of exchanging and sharing data between an almost unlimited numbers of users at very little cost.

---

[2] *The Industry Standard.*
[3] US Department of Commerce; includes hardware, software, and telecommunications.
[4] Arthur Andersen.

The web also allowed individuals and organizations to communicate instantaneously through electronic mail. Email has subsequently become so ubiquitous that it is now the preferred means of communication for a large part of the world.[5] While still primarily sent through the personal computer, email is increasingly finding applications in telephones, handheld personal organizers, and home appliances.

**E-Business:** Sensing an opportunity, American business began developing commercial applications for the web. These generally fell into one of two categories: B2C (business to consumer) and B2B (business to business).

>**B2C Market:** A wide range of B2C applications proliferated in the late 1990s and early 2000. Several of these were "portal" websites, which attempted to provide users convenient access to the myriad of offerings on the web and thereby collect advertising, transaction, and other revenue. Other applications focused on selling products such as books, computers, CDs, clothing, food, drugs, and even furniture to individual consumers. Still others targeted service areas such as stock brokerage, commercial banking, mortgage banking, travel, insurance, and real estate. A few connected individual buyers and sellers through auction based systems. In 2000, B2C commerce was $28 billion,[6] up 62% over 1999 but still less than 2% of total retail sales.

>During the 2000 holiday season, 63% of Internet users purchased online, vs. 47% in 1999. Forty-four percent were very satisfied with their purchases; only 1% was dissatisfied. Nine out of ten expected to make online purchases again in 2001. (Typically, Internet purchases represented 20% of all holiday purchasers in 2000; this figure was expected to rise to 30% in 2001).[7]

>**B2B Market:** While the B2C market received most of the media attention, the vast market for business firms to sell to each other represented a much more significant opportunity. Increasingly, business managers were learning that the web could dramatically reduce operating costs through higher employee productivity, the need for fewer employees, better inventory control, and more direct distribution channels, which could reduce or eliminate the need for a "middle person."

---

[5] In 2000, an average of 9.7 billion email messages were sent daily worldwide, up 64% over 1999. Source: *The Industry Standard*.
[6] US Department of Commerce.
[7] Knowledge Systems and Research, Inc.

Using an *"intranet,"* which linked far-flung employees to headquarters and to each other, firms were also able to expedite the day-to-day communications required to run their organizations more efficiently. Using an *"extranet,"* firms could communicate directly with outside vendors and suppliers in a similar fashion.

If fact, the web was revolutionizing the manufacturing process itself. Firms, being unable to fine-tune customer purchasing needs, have traditionally had to produce large amounts of inventory that doesn't always sell during the business year. This requirement not only increased inventory-holding costs but also resulted in heavy discounts as unsold inventory is liquidated. Utilizing the web, manufacturers now can permit the customer to design, order, and pay for the product that he or she wants, often before it goes into production.

The economic benefits of the web can be further enhanced by the use of auction-type "exchanges" to facilitate information flow between firms and to execute a transaction at the lowest possible price. As of early 2001, many industries such as autos, airplanes, energy, building materials, and others were in the process of organizing exchanges to tap this opportunity.

Recognizing the revolutionary aspects of this breakthrough, Jack Welch, CEO of General Electric, vowed to "transform GE into an Internet company." Many other major American manufactures are now moving in the same direction. In 2000, expenditures for B2B commerce were $213 billion, up 120% over 1999.[8] By 2010, one third of the world's B2B economy is expected to be online with one third of the B2B ecommerce to be auction based. Over ten thousand new B2B companies are expected to emerge over the next 10 years.[9]

**New Economy Financing:** Financing for the New Economy came largely from corporate investment in new technology, the NASDAQ exchange, and venture capital investment funds. The usual pattern was for venture firms to fund start up costs and then be taken out of most or all of their investment position by an IPO, usually offered on NASDAQ. With the public's insatiable thirst for new technology issues, there appeared to be an unlimited source of capital available to fuel the New Economy.

---

[8] *The Industry Standard* .
[9] IBM; Legg Mason; The Gartner Group.

In 2000, venture capital firms raised a record $92.3 billion, much of it from pension funds, for investment in Internet and other technology-related companies over the next three to five years.[10] This represented a 54% increase over the $60 billion raised the previous year but was down considerably in the fourth quarter, as concern developed over the economic value of Internet start-up companies.

**Dot-Coms to Dot-Bombs:** The financing nirvana began crumbling in early 2000. From a peak in the first quarter, the NASDAQ index declined over 34% by year-end.[11] Major technology firms were significantly depressed from previous highs and were continuing to report missed earnings projections into 2001. Several companies that were trading for less than $1 per share were under active consideration for de-listing; many were heading into bankruptcy. The B2C sector was particularly impacted. Firms that failed to achieve profitability had their market valuations slashed by as much as 95% between peaks in 1999 and 2001.

Several reasons were suggested for the collapse of so many B2C firms. The customer acquisition cost for web firms was $82 each vs. $38 for traditional stores and only $12 for catalogue operations.[12] Heavy reliance on advertising revenue placed many firms in a vulnerable position as website users became increasingly aggravated by the distraction of banner ads. Most B2C firms also failed to consider the very "local" nature of retailing with many customers feeling more comfortable in a physical store than becoming lost in the often confusing instructions of retail web sites. This was particularly important when it came to returning merchandise; web firms totally underestimated the percentage of sales that would be returned. Paco Underhill, an industry observer, put it very well:

> "At the end of the day, retailing is all about running details and making them perfect day in and day out."[13]

Lacking a take-out option, many venture firms began reevaluating their positions. The first step was to suspend future funding for start-up companies until they could get a better fix on when the company could expect to become profitable. Underwriting standards were tightened regarding additional capital, and new investments were largely deferred until the situation clarified. Many firms were urged or pushed to consolidate with other firms to preserve

---

[10] Venture Economics.
[11] Economy.com.
[12] Shop.org.
[13] *Business Week,* January 4, 2001.

remaining capital. Many that wouldn't or couldn't consolidate went bankrupt. By the second quarter of 2000, the pre-IPO evaluation of e-commerce start-ups had dropped 75%.[14]

Many of the venture firms concluded that surplus funds had encouraged unwise investments in questionable businesses. As a Director of Dell Ventures put it,

> "There were a lot of businesses getting funded that weren't really businesses at all. They were really just interesting features on a Web site."[15]

In retrospect, most observers agreed that the collapse of the dot.com financing bubble did not change the magnitude of the fundamental changes occurring in the world's way of doing business, nor did it alter the significant investment opportunities that these changes would offer investors over the longer term.

## *Impact of the New Economy on Real Estate*

In early 2001, America's real estate industry also was licking its wounds from the dot-com collapse. Many firms and industry organizations had committed significant resources to a wide variety of real estate applications ranging from new reporting and control systems to virtual markets for everything from the purchase of toilet paper to the sale of individual properties. While there was considerable disappointment, there were some real estate managers who believed that the whole experience had been a "flash in the pan" – mostly hype and exaggeration – and that that now, thankfully, they could return to the business of developing and managing their properties.

There were others, however, who viewed the dot-com collapse as a wake up call and that as fundamental structural changes began taking over, real estate would be altered irretrievably, perhaps more than other industries. Already, indications were that the construction management, mortgage banking, real estate brokerage, and property management sectors would never be the same.

Real estate investors were less concerned about real estate jobs than possible changes in the value of their real estate investment portfolios. Concurrently, many real estate entrepreneurs were looking for possible investment opportunities in changing consumer patterns that would affect the demand and supply for individual properties.

---

[14] *The Industry Standard.*
[15] San Francisco Chronicle, February 23, 2001.

**Impact on Property Types:** Concerns regarding the impact of the New Economy on real estate demand were based on a simple premise: the Internet involves activities conducted in cyberspace, which is non-physical, and real estate is based on activities conducted in buildings, which are physical. The logical extension appears to be:

> *Any activity that occurs in cyberspace is one that will not occur in physical space. If the overall level of real estate activity does not increase to offset losses, overall net demand for real estate will fall.*

Even if demand does not fall, the type of real estate utilized may be different or it may occur in a different location, thus rendering existing properties uneconomic. Most observers believed that the nature and magnitude of any impact would vary considerably by property type:

> **Retail:** The major impact on net physical demand appears to be in the retail sector. Although retail sales increased at three times the rate of inflation in the 1999-2000 period, the 2000 Christmas season was the worst since 1991, and indications were that sales would continue to slow as the economy began to cool and the impact of the stock market slide on personal wealth began to sink in.[16]
>
> Perhaps more ominously, over 200 million square feet of new retail space was started in both 1999 and 2000, often in markets that were already seriously over-stored. The nation now had 5.6 billion square feet of retail space, a historically high of 20 square feet per person.[17]
>
> At current sales levels, it would take approximately $50 billion in new retail sales to support this new space. Looking forward, an additional 35 new regional and super-regional shopping centers were scheduled to open by 2002, totaling 41 million square feet of retail space. This pace contrasts with 33.3 million that opened between 1997 and 1999.[18]
>
> In addition, several major national retailers including Montgomery Ward and Bradlees declared bankruptcy and put additional millions of square feet back on the market (Montgomery Ward alone owned more than 250 stores).[19] In related developments, Sears announced that it would close 83 of its specialty tire and hardware stores and

---

[16] Carl E. Steidtmann Ph.D., Skating on Thin Ice . . . And Breaking Through, *PriceWaterhouseCoopers*, January 15, 2001.
[17] *Business Week*, February 12, 2001.
[18] Peter P. Kozel, Retail Sector's Condition Expected to Deteriorate, *Real Estate Forum*, January, 2001.
[19] A deal was announced on March 28, 2001, whereby KIMCO and Target will buy the Montgomery Ward properties.

four of its mainline department stores; Office Depot would close 70 stores and cut back on expansion; the house wares retailer, Lechters, announced plans to close 166 stores. Additionally, Circuit City, Nordstrom and Gap all slowed planned expansions.[20]

While the collapse of the dot-coms involved many retail start-ups, there was still a 62% increase in Internet sales in 2000, which was mostly generated by established retailers who were now viewing the Internet as another channel of distribution along with physical stores and catalogue sales. Indications are that these "multi-channel" retailers will increasingly dominate retailing, leaving behind both the "pure play" web retail firms and retailers who considered the Internet no different than TV shopping.

The adjustment of retailers to the new technology doesn't necessarily mean that retail real estate is no longer threatened. As noted earlier, *every dollar of web based retail sales is a dollar not spent in a physical store.* The $28 billion in web-based retail sales in 2000 is the equivalent of 50-60 regional shopping centers!

Most observers believe that the ultimate impact on retail real estate will vary by the type of retail property and location. Power centers appear to be the most impacted due to the concentration of commodity goods most susceptible to web competition. Older regional and community centers also appear vulnerable, largely due to over-storing in many locations and weaker tenant mixes. First line regional centers and neighborhood centers appear to be least impacted.

**Industrial:** Industrial properties are expected to be impacted in a very different way than retail. While there may be some loss in overall net demand, the major impact will be a shift in the type and location of space demanded and the location of the demand.

This trend is due to the fact that the way in which American businesses use industrial space is going through major changes. During the last half of the twentieth century, the ratio of private inventories to final sales declined by 56.3%. In 1950, it took over $4 in goods in inventory to produce $1 in sales; by the end of the century, it took slightly more than $2.[21]

This dramatic change was the result of several technological and other advances that significantly altered the manufacturer-to-customer supply chain during the period. The development of the

---

[20] *Business Week*, op. cit.
[21] AMB Properties, Inc.

Interstate highway system in the 1950s increased the speed by which manufacturers could reach their customers. This change was followed by the "just in time" (JIT) method of scheduling production introduced by the Japanese and widely imitated by American industry. Next came the introduction of bar coding, which allowed manufacturers and suppliers to more closely monitor sales and inventory levels. The final factor was the introduction of the Internet, which provided firms with a centralized control point over their entire production-distribution-sales cycle. The recent emergence of online bidding through eMarkets will no doubt further accelerate these trends.

Competitive pressure to move goods faster to the consumer means 1) less space will be required to store inventories and 2) different types of buildings will be required to service modern business requirements.

These new buildings will vary from traditional industrial buildings in the following respects:

- Emphasis on repackaging and speed of transfer rather than storage
- Located adjacent to major transportation inter-modal nodes, in many cases "on the tarmac" at major airports
- Shape: longer, more linear; less square
- Height: less emphasis on high cubage for rack storage
- Items stored: smaller items; individually packaged
- Accommodations for transportation
    - More truck bays
    - Larger truck turning and storage areas
- Accommodations for communication
- At or near fiber-optic trunk lines
- Reliable power for computer operations
- Accommodations for higher employee densities
    - Air conditioning
    - Amenities
    - More employee parking

Most observers believe that the major negative impact will fall on older, usually smaller industrial buildings located on small land parcels where building modifications – even new construction – are usually difficult if not impossible. There is also a view that second tier industrial cities may be less attractive to industrial users who prefer to be closer to major transportation hubs located within or near large local markets.

**Office:** The impact on office space demand is more indirect in nature, as it is linked through the demand for employee space and workplace dynamics. While it is too early to tell, decline in office space demand will most likely occur in sectors that have been heavily disintermediated such as mortgage banking, travel, security sales, etc., but the problems appear to be more complex.

On the positive side, office related employment is a growing part of the economy with business profits increasingly driven by investment in intellectual capital where knowledge workers are a key ingredient of business success. In a tight labor market, the workplace environment is increasingly important in attracting and retaining key employees. The cost of losing employees is usually much greater than the cost of creating 150 square feet of office space. Rationally, firms *should* be concerned with maintaining and perhaps expanding their office space commitments.

In most industries, however, there has been a move in recent years to *reduce employee work areas* through open space plans and shared facility programs such as hoteling. This not only applies to engineers and technology personnel, but also to support employees and even senior management.[22]

While any one firm's space reduction efforts may not be important, the collective action of many firms increasing density at the same time could ultimately mean less net demand for office space. This may explain, in part, how the US was able to add so many new office jobs over the last several years without adding significant amounts of new office construction.[23]

One of the reasons employees appear willing to accept higher densities in their office environment is that they are, in most cases, spending less time there. With the mobility offered by the personal computer, cell phones, and e-mail, people are increasingly working in

---

[22] Average office space-per-employee declined from 220SF in 1992 to 193SF in 1999. Source: Prudential Real Estate Investors.
[23] The other explanation is the large overbuilding of office space in the 1980's and the subsequently high vacancy factors in most US markets into the 1990's.

other venues such as their homes, second homes, hotels, and airplanes. As some managers put it in a recent survey:

> "Five years ago the office was a pretty big part of my life; now it's just another place to go. I don't have to be here to get my work done."
>
> "People can work out of the office or in Timbuktu. It's never going back the way it was."
>
> "The empire of your own box isn't relevant anymore. Work is mobile – the cell phone, e-mail, and your computer. It's not just technology; it's a mindset – like casual clothes. What's going on is a convergence of life, work, and home."[24]

The drive to lower real estate costs also has led many corporate real estate managers to locate office functions in other property types, most notably industrial buildings. Industrial construction is not only cheaper, but facilities can be located closer to residential areas and designed in an "open space" manner, which allows more flexibility in creating and disbanding task force and project teams. Individual buildings also provide firm identification that may be lost in a multi-tenant building. Often located on fiber-optic trunk lines, these types of facilities are increasingly offering employers attractive alternatives to CBD high-rise and mid-rise suburban office space.[25]

**Multifamily Residential:** Most observers do not anticipate any serious negative impact on multifamily residential. On the contrary, there are indications that multifamily should enjoy strong tenant demand for the next decade. This expectation is due to the very large Echo Boom cohort (only slightly smaller than the boomers themselves) presently reaching maturity and the desire of many retiring boomers to have a more urban, hassle-free lifestyle. Apartments also should benefit from the high cost of ownership housing in many of the technology-oriented metro areas experiencing strong economic growth.

If anything, multifamily ownership could benefit from technology in terms of enhanced tenant services, more efficient coordination of maintenance operations, and lower costs of purchasing goods and services. These factors should help to reduce tenant turnover, maintain higher occupancy levels, and lower operating costs – all of which contribute to the investor's bottom line.

---

[24] Lend Lease Corporation, *Emerging Trends in Real Estate 2000*.
[25] Kennedy Associates of Seattle has reportedly developed over 30 industrial type facilities for the office use of major blue chip corporations in various cities around the country.

**Hotels:** The New Economy brings both good and bad news for hotel investors. The efficiency of the web should help improve hotel operating efficiencies, particularly in the areas of reservation management, employee deployment, and procurement. On the negative side, hotels can expect greater pricing pressure because of less demand from business travelers (more virtual meetings), more comparison-shopping by prospective guests, and the move of more hotels to a web auction format. More immediately, hotels can expect less revenue from telecommunications charges as guests increasingly call and pull down their emails through handheld wireless devices.

**Impact on Metro Areas:** Technology allows the dispersal of economic activity in a manner not possible before. Recognizing the importance of knowledge employees as a critical firm resource, business managers now are able to locate operations in areas attractive to key employees. With half of the work force expected to be in technology related industries by 2006, there is increasing importance on locating in areas with strong technology infrastructure (e.g., universities, training, etc.).

This trend is borne out in the metro area growth statistics. Between 1990 and 1997, 65% of the difference in annual metro area growth during this period could be traced to technology industry growth.[26] Exhibit 8 indicates the ranking of the top 25 metro areas of the technology-based economy – i.e. the percentage of national high tech output multiplied by the high tech output location quotient for each metro area. At an extreme, San Jose (Silicon Valley) is almost 24X more concentrated in technology output than the average US metro area. More common are ratios in the 3X to 7X range. Metro areas that rank high in technology output also may be areas that rank high in real estate investor preference and are also most attractive to graduating students entering the labor force.

---

[26] Milken Institute.

**Exhibit 8
High Tech Metro Areas
Ranked by Composite Index[27]
1998**

| Rank | City | Index |
|---|---|---|
| 1 | San Jose | 23.69 |
| 2 | Dallas | 7.06 |
| 3 | Los Angeles | 6.91 |
| 4 | Boston | 6.31 |
| 5 | Seattle | 5.19 |
| 6 | Washington, D.C. | 4.98 |
| 7 | Albuquerque | 3.75 |
| 8 | Chicago | 3.67 |
| 9 | New York | 3.46 |
| 10 | Atlanta | 3.40 |
| 11 | Middlesex, N.J. | 3.40 |
| 12 | Phoenix | 3.40 |
| 13 | Orange County | 2.59 |
| 14 | Oakland | 2.21 |
| 15 | Philadelphia | 2.19 |
| 16 | Rochester | 1.95 |
| 17 | San Diego | 1.93 |
| 18 | Raleigh Durham | 1.89 |
| 19 | Denver | 1.81 |
| 20 | Newark | 1.80 |
| 21 | Austin | 1.78 |
| 22 | San Francisco | 1.62 |
| 23 | Houston | 1.62 |
| 24 | Boise | 1.43 |
| 25 | New Haven/ Stamford | 1.33 |

Source: Milken Institute

There also are shifts occurring within metro areas. One trend is the reversal of the decline of the CBD in many American cities. Exhibit 9 compares the change in CBD population between 1970-90 and 1990-99. During this period, Denver, Phoenix, and Atlanta were able to reverse population losses from the 70s and 80s. Even cities with reportedly "dead" downtowns such as Dallas have been able to regain much of the loss. Cities with growth in the earlier period such as Cincinnati, Seattle, and Portland have made subsequent additional gains.

---

[27] Percentage of national high-tech real output multiplied by the high tech real output location quotient for each metro.

**Exhibit 9
CBD Population Change**

| CBD | 1970-90 | 1990-99 |
|---|---|---|
| Dallas | (50.0%) | 32.1% |
| Denver | (10.4%) | 28.7% |
| Cincinnati | 10.5% | 25.3% |
| Seattle | 12.8% | 25.0% |
| Portland, OR | 14.9% | 14.6% |
| Phoenix | (18.7%) | 11.3% |
| Atlanta | (5.6%) | 5.5% |

Source: University of Pennsylvania

Positive changes are also occurring in office employment in many CBDs with much of it in culturally attractive older office and industrial buildings. Exhibit 10 looks at the change in B&C CBD office space vacancy during the last half of the 1990s. High technology metros such as San Francisco, New York, and Seattle have reduced their vacancy levels to relatively low levels, and even cities like Houston and Baltimore have made impressive gains.

**Exhibit 10
Change in CBD Vacancies***

| CBD | 11/31/95 | 12/31/99 | %Change |
|---|---|---|---|
| NYC (Downtown) | 27.6% | 11.6% | -16.0% |
| Houston | 42.8% | 27.5% | -15.3% |
| Baltimore | 24.1% | 12.5% | -11.6% |
| San Francisco | 14.7% | 3.2% | -11.5% |
| Seattle | 9.2% | 3.3% | -5.9% |
| US Aggregate | 19.9% | 11.4% | -8.5% |

Source: Reis Reports                     *B&C Space

## Recommendations to the Board

As Mason began drawing together his conclusions and recommendations for the Board, he began going over the key points for each of the real estate investment portfolios.

**Core Real Estate Portfolio:** Mason was convinced that many of VIPERS' investments in the core portfolio were gong to be impacted negatively by technology. He was particularly concerned about the industrial buildings that the fund had owned for many years, most of which were situated on small parcels with limited truck access (Appendix C). He was also concerned about the metro areas where many of the properties were located: many medium-sized cities in the Midwest and South. Most of these areas did not have a strong technology infrastructure, and he wasn't sure how competitive they would be in the future.

On the positive side, the fund had industrial investments near airports in Chicago, Miami, and Los Angeles (San Bernardino) where inter-modal activity was increasing rapidly. He also recalled that they owned some land "on the tarmac" in Oakland and Seattle.

Retail also was a concern. Many of VIPERS' properties were older regional and community centers mostly located in the Midwest and South (Appendix D). In the East and West, VIPERS had focused on newer neighborhood centers in rapidly growing metro areas. VIPERS also owned some older regional centers in New York, Cleveland, Dallas, and Houston, which were not performing well largely due to high vacancy and weakening tenant credit. Fortunately, they had made a decision not to invest in power centers or freestanding buildings where a large part of the web impact was expected.

Much of VIPERS' office portfolio was relatively new, consisting of suburban office buildings in Washington DC, Chicago, Atlanta, Dallas, Phoenix, Sacramento, and San Diego (Appendix B). Many of the tenants were technology-oriented firms or call centers for Old Economy firms. Mason was particularly concerned about the call center tenants, however, because he had read that many large corporations were cutting back the number of call centers as they relied more and more on the web to handle customer interface.

Mason wasn't overly concerned about the multifamily investments in the East and West, as these were largely newer projects in major metro areas (Appendix E). If fact, he saw opportunities to take advantage of new technology to provide high speed access to tenants and perhaps develop some type of community portal for each unit. He was concerned, however, about the large number of older multifamily units located in the Midwest and South.

Mason began contemplating possible mitigation strategies that he could recommend to the Board. He thought that the older, smaller industrial buildings probably could be sold and that the funds could be redeployed to larger metro areas where inter-modal projects might be developed. He knew the Board was keen on industrial investment, and he saw this sell and buy strategy mainly as a repositioning within the sector.

Retail was a different story. Mason believed that as a result of competition from the web, overbuilding, and tenant credit weakness, VIPERS retail target should be reduced from its current level through disposition of the smaller properties located in older metro areas. Funds generated could then be available for expansion of the core multifamily sector or possibly into multifamily REITs.

He also thought that the Board should investigate converting some of the larger retail centers that weren't doing well into non-retail uses. His research had uncovered several examples of successful center conversions to office parks, "carrier" hotels[28], schools, and other uses. It was also conceivable that some of the centers with high vacancy should be razed and the land sold or used for other purposes such as multifamily.

Mason regarded the office sector as pretty stable and not requiring too much remedial action at this time. The exceptions were the call center operations, which he thought would require reworking into more traditional office building configurations. He also believed that some of the older properties in the Midwest and South would require a case-by-base review to see whether they should be kept or sold.

In addition to his review of property types, Mason was concerned with the general geographical mix of the core portfolio. He wondered if it wouldn't be worthwhile to review all of the metro areas where the fund had investments and determine which had the best outlook for future economic growth. While he was impressed with the growth statistics for technology-based metro areas, he was concerned with the meltdown of technology stocks and the impact this might have on the long-term growth of technology rich metro areas. Mason also liked the constrained growth markets but worried about the viability of these high cost, environmentally sensitive areas in a period of possible recession and rolling electricity blackouts. California was already paying a price for not building any electrical generation capacity for the past 12 years and a misdirected approach to deregulation.

---

[28] Buildings containing computers, routers and other infrastructure of the New Economy.

**Opportunistic Portfolio:** Mason wasn't sure how much, if any, of the fund's opportunistic investments were in projects that might be negatively impacted. He also wasn't sure whether VIPERS could get out of any of its investment, even if it wanted to. He wondered, however, if the Board shouldn't revisit the magnitude of its opportunistic investment position and determine whether these funds were meeting the overall goals of the investment program. This would be good timing as Funds A and B would be liquidating in 2001 and 2002, and the sponsors would be asking VIPERS if it wished to reinvest.

In terms of possible new investments, he noted a press release regarding a new $500 million Real Estate/Technology Fund that CalPERS had established with CBRichard Ellis (Exhibit 11). Mason thought this might be a good avenue to pursue, although he knew that VIPERS would have to have a significantly smaller exposure.

**Public REIT Portfolio:** While the Chairman was generally pleased with the fund's REIT investments in 2000, the sector had never really performed as well historically as the Board had anticipated. Mason reviewed the performance of each of the REIT sectors for 2000 (Exhibit 12) but wasn't quite sure what to recommend to the Board regarding changes in portfolios or managers.

In his research, Mason had come across an article on the new REIT Modernization Act (RMA), legislation that went into effect on January 1, 2001. This act allowed REITs to invest up to 20% of their total asset value in Taxable REIT Subsidiaries (TRS), which then could become involved in a wide range of business activities. Mason noted that some of the proposed investments had a technology orientation and wondered if this wasn't a way to gain indirect exposure to investment opportunities.

### Exhibit 11
### CalPERS Press Release, October 17, 2000

# Press Release

October 17, 2000
Contact: Brad Pacheco/Pat Macht
CalPERS Office of Public Affairs
(916) 326-3991

## CalPERS Selects CB Richard Ellis Investors To Run $500 Million Real Estate/Technology Fund

**SACRAMENTO, CA** - The California Public Employees' Retirement System (CalPERS) has selected CB Richard Ellis Investors, L.L.C. to manage the System's $500 million Joint Real Estate and Alternative Investment Management Technology Program.

Under the program, the Los Angeles, California-based global investment management company will make investments in real estate and real estate-related entities, and capitalize on opportunities created from the convergence of the technology and real estate industries.

CalPERS believes the convergence creates an opportunity for the System to invest in companies that develop real estate technology infrastructure and services, and in real estate assets expected to benefit from providing space or services to tenants in high growth sectors of the economy.

"CB Richard Ellis Investors has demonstrated experience investing in private equity, technology and real estate," said William D. Crist, President of CalPERS Board of Administration. "They have a global network of relationships with technology tenants and an understanding of technology real estate requirements that suits them well for this job."

CalPERS is expected to leverage its $9.3 billion real estate portfolio and network of contacts in the venture capital industry to generate a variety of investment opportunities for the new fund, including:

- Forming strategic alliances with and investing in emerging companies at the intersection of real estate and technology, such as telecommunications firms, online commercial property listing services, and energy management entities;
- Assembling real estate portfolios in technology markets such as Silicon Valley, Boston's Route 128 and Raleigh/Durham's Research Triangle that are likely to benefit from high growth industries; and
- Providing real estate solutions to high growth tenants as their strategic real estate partner and potential equity investor.

"This investment vehicle is a unique blend of asset classes that will help capture value for

## Exhibit 12
## Real Estate Related Technology Firms
## Companies Sorted by Target Sector/Market
## (Adjusted for Bankrupt/Consolidated Firms)

**Consortiums**
Constellation Real Technologies
Octane Office Technology Consortium

**Cross-Industry: Listings**
Cityfeet.com
CoStar Group
eSpace Connexions
LOCATION-net (retail)
LoopNet
Mr. OfficeSpace.com
OfficeGuide.com
OfficeSpace.com
PropertyFirst.com
PropertyRover
RealtyIQ.com
Storetrax.com (retail)
TenantMix (retail)
WebRealEstate.com

**Cross-Industry: Infrastructure/Telecom**
eLInk Communications
Everest Broadband Networks
Eziaz, Inc.
Gillette Global Network
Metromedia Fiber Network
MyShoppingCenter.com (retail)
nex-i.com
OnSite Access
UrbanMedia
Winstar Communications, Inc.
Wired Business
Wired Environments

Xbuilding.com
Grid Magazine
Commercial Real Estate Direct
New England/NY Real Estate Journal
NREI
RENTV.com

**Cross-Industry: Research Information**
AnySite Technologies
Claritas
F.W. Dodge / The McGraw-Hill Companies
Geonomics, Inc.
jobsite.com
Reis
SRC
Torto Wheaton Research
Trade Dimensions

**Cross-Industry: Marketing**
Access Technology Services (Imagemaker)
CirclesOnLine
iPIX
LASERtech Floorplans

**Cross-Industry: ASP/Software/Efficiency Tools**
AMSI
Bay Logics
Bricks-n-Bytes (SBK Technology, Inc.)
Building Extranet
Corrigo
CityWire.com / REOL Services
EggSystems.com
eMortgage Desk
ePropertyTax
Interactive Expert Systems
IntraLinks, Inc.
Protegic
RealPrompt
REApplications.com
RESoft, Inc.
RexOffice
ServiceChannel, Inc.
Tampa Bay Systems, LLC
UReal, Inc.
Visser Software Services, Inc.
VISTAInfo
WorkplaceIQ
Xceligent, Inc.

**Investment Sales Sector**
1031 Exhange.com
1031Properties.com
1031Xchange.com
AmeriQuotes.com
EProperty
PropertyAuction
PropertyID.com
RealCapitalMarkets.com

**Development/Building Sector**
Bricsnet
Buildfolio
Buildpoint
Buzzsaw
e-Builder
iScraper
Struxicon

| | |
|---|---|
| **Leasing/Transaction Sector**<br>Business Integration Group<br>DealMover.com<br>Lease Cost Solutions<br>ManagePath<br>MovePoint<br>MyContracts.com<br>NAI Directory<br>OfficeFinder<br>Office2Share.com<br>OfficeQuest.com<br>Peracon<br>RealCentric<br>Spacify.com<br>TenantWise<br>**Financing/Capital Markets Sector**<br>Capital Engine.com<br>CapitalThinking<br>C-Lender.com<br>DebtX.com<br>EquityCity<br>Equityhound<br>MortgageRamp.com<br>Property Capital<br>Redbricks<br>**Cross-Industry: News/Media**<br>@Property.com / DealMaker<br>GlobeSt.com<br>**Property Ownership/Management Sector**<br>AptBiz.com<br>AssetEye, Inc.<br>AvidXchange.com<br>Brickwire<br>BuildingLink.com<br>Buyers Access<br>Corrigo | ebuyxpress<br>Elevator News Network<br>FacilityPro.com<br>Forge Consultants, Inc.<br>Honeywell Portico<br>iBuilding<br>Landlord.com<br>LesConcierges<br>Management Reports International<br>manageStar.com<br>National Facilities Group<br>OpsXchange<br>OurBuilding.com<br>Peregrine Systems<br>Phatpipe<br>PowerBuyer Service<br>PropertyOps.com<br>Purchase Pro (AEC Connect)<br>RealPage<br>RealStandard.com (retail)<br>REManage<br>RentPort, Inc.<br>Service Channel, Inc.<br>SiteStuff<br>TenantDirect<br>TenantTools, Inc.<br>Touchcom, Inc. / One Facility.com<br>The REALM<br>Vectiv (retail)<br>VIPDesk.com<br>Virtual Premise<br>Workspeed<br>Works.com<br>Yardi Systems |

**Real Estate Cycle:** Mason was worried that whatever portfolio restructuring the Board undertook might be too late in light of the continuing softening in the economy. Employee layoffs had already begun spreading from the dot-com firms to traditional business sectors, thus reducing consumer confidence and beginning to affect spending decisions. He noted that in March America's jobless claims had risen to a five year high, up 46% from the previous year, and the University of Michigan' consumer sentiment index had dropped to its lowest level since 1993.[29] While the full impact of declining personal wealth was not yet fully known, it was already clear that many people were gearing up for a difficult time ahead.

---

[29] Wall Street Journal, April 13, 2001.

Although real estate demand and supply were in general equilibrium in most markets, there were indications that property investments might be impacted as well (Exhibit 13). Already, several property types and markets were beginning to soften as firms cut back on expansion plans and cancelled or delayed existing space commitments. Retailers, viewing the terrible Christmas season and slowing 2001 sales, were cutting back on new outlets and seeking ways to get out of existing leases. Even multifamily rents were softening in some of the hottest markets where the only direction for many years had seemed to be up.

Mason was concerned that the time might have passed to dispose of many older properties, particularly if they were becoming economically obsolete or were located in structurally declining markets. On the other hand, with the rapid growth in technology expected, most of these properties would probably be even more obsolete after the general economy had begun to grow again, and maybe it was best to take their licks now.

**Real Estate Allocation:** Mason also wasn't quite sure how to handle the real estate allocation issue. VIPERS' heavy commitment to growth stocks had resulted in a major decline in the value of its total portfolio, possibly reducing the amount of funds that would be available for real estate. Mason didn't believe that the Board would approve an increase in the current target allocation and was concerned that the unused allocation may also evaporate. Perhaps worse, property disposition proceeds generated by a portfolio restructuring might not be reallocated to real estate.

### Exhibit 13
### Public REITS
### Investment Performance by Property Sector, 2000

| Sector | Total Return | Dividend | Appreciation |
|---|---|---|---|
| Lodging/Resorts | 45.8% | 9.4% | 36.3% |
| Apartments | 35.5% | 6.5% | 29.0% |
| Office | 35.5% | 6.6% | 28.9% |
| Mixed O-I | 32.0% | 6.9% | 25.0% |
| Industrial | 28.6% | 6.7% | 21.9% |
| Health Care | 25.8% | 10.3% | 15.6% |
| Diversified | 24.1% | 7.0% | 17.1% |
| Regional Malls | 23.5% | 7.7% | 15.8% |
| Mfg. Homes | 20.9% | 6.5% | 14.5% |
| Community Centers | 15.1% | 8.5% | 6.6% |
| Self Storage | 14.7% | 5.3% | 9.4% |
| Free Standing Retail | 9.0% | 8.4% | 0.5% |
| Specialty | -31.6% | 7.6% | -39.2% |
| Equity REIT Index* | 26.4% | 7.2% | 19.1% |

Source: NAREIT  *Weighted by implied market capitalization

On the other hand, Mason observed that real estate was in a better position than previous downturns in the economy. Most property markets were in good shape and with the exception of retail, there was not an excessive amount of new construction in the pipeline. Real estate cash flows also were generally strong, an important factor with VIPERS facing negative cash flow in the next few years. Perhaps, he thought, he should make a case to the Board for an increase in the real estate allocation.

**Managers and Consultants:** Mason had believed for some time that VIPERS had too many real estate managers and that some of them were no longer effective in producing acceptable returns. He was particularly concerned with his ability to manage the process since the Board had cut back his staff to two professionals, one for the core portfolio and one for REITs and Opportunity Funds. This would become even more difficult if the Board decided to seek out technology-oriented investment opportunities that required special skills that his staff did not presently have.

The consultant issue was a ticklish one. Mason had enjoyed working with the last consultant and saw a continuing future need, particularly if the Board decided to restructure its real estate portfolio. He knew he had to be careful here, however, because McCracken didn't trust consultants, believing their fees to be a waste of money. Several of the other Board members, on the other hand, shared Mason's view that a good consultant could help them resolve many of the current issues facing the Board regarding its real estate portfolio.

As he began writing his memo, Mason knew that whatever he recommended would be controversial with some of the Board members, but he also knew that he simply had to be straightforward and provide them with a good understanding of the problems and opportunities represented by structural and cyclical change and with the most effective strategies for proceeding.

It was already 10:00 PM, and he knew it would be a long night. He just hoped that he could get the memo completed by morning, as he still had to finish and mail his tax return to avoid a late penalty. He also noted apprehensively that Friday was April 13.

## Appendix A
## Investment Indices

|  | 2000 | 3 Years | 5 Years | 10 Years |
|---|---|---|---|---|
| **NCREIF** | | | | |
| **Total** | | | | |
|    Income | 8.5% | 8.6% | 8.7% | 8.4% |
|    Appreciation | 3.3% | 4.4% | 3.8% | (0.0) |
|    Total | 12.0% | 13.2% | 12.8% | 6.7% |
| **Region** | | | | |
|    East | 12.7% | 13.7% | 13.0% | 6.4% |
|    Midwest | 8.4% | 10.8% | 10.5% | 6.2% |
|    South | 8.6% | 11.3% | 10.9% | 7.0% |
|    West | 15.6% | 15.3% | 15.0% | 7.2% |
| **Property Type** | | | | |
|    Apartment | 12.8% | 12.9% | 12.6% | 9.5% |
|    Hotel | 7.7% | 12.1% | NA | NA |
|    Industrial | 13.8% | 13.8% | 14.2% | 7.9% |
|    Office | 13.8% | 15.1% | 15.4% | 5.9% |
|    Retail | 7.7% | 10.0% | 8.7% | 5.3% |
| **NAREIT (Equity)** | 26.7% | 0.4% | 9.4% | 12.2% |
| **S&P 500** | -9.2% | 12.3% | 18.4% | 17.5% |
| **3 month Treasury** | 6.0% | 5.3% | 5.3% | 4.9% |
| **Consumer Price Index** | 3.4% | 2.6% | 2.5% | 2.7% |

## Appendix B
## Valley Island Public Employees' Retirement System
## Office Portfolio

| Property | Location | Value ($M) | Age | SF |
|---|---|---|---|---|
| | **East** | | | |
| 1 | Greenwich. CT | $31.4 | 12 | 221,751 |
| 2 | Tyson's Corner, VA | 20.7 | 4 | 97,458 |
| 3 | Wakefield, MA | 10.5 | 19 | 74,153 |
| | Subtotal | 62.6 | | 393,362 |
| | **Midwest** | | | |
| 4 | Chicago, IL | 60.7 | 18 | 428,672 |
| 5 | Chicago, IL | 32.5 | 3 | 153,013 |
| 6 | Cincinnati, OH | 10.3 | 5 | 48,493 |
| 7 | Columbus, OH | 7.6 | 12 | 53,672 |
| 8 | Minneapolis, MN | 12.6 | 19 | 88,983 |
| | Subtotal | 123.7 | | 772,834 |
| | **South** | | | |
| 9 | Atlanta, GA | 25.3 | 1 | 119,115 |
| 10 | Dallas, TX | 33.7 | 3 | 158,663 |
| 11 | Houston, TX | 46.2 | 17 | 326,271 |
| 12 | Orlando, FL | 11.3 | 14 | 79,802 |
| | Subtotal | 116.5 | | 683,851 |
| | **West** | | | |
| 13 | Denver, CO | 26.2 | 16 | 185,028 |
| 14 | Phoenix, AZ | 15.7 | 2 | 73,917 |
| 15 | Sacramento, CA | 13.5 | 4 | 63,559 |
| 16 | San Diego, CA | 16.3 | 2 | 76,742 |
| | Subtotal | 71.7 | | 399,247 |
| | **Total/Average** | 374.5 | 9.4 | 2,249,294 |

## Appendix C
## Valley Island Public Employees' Retirement System
## Industrial Portfolio

| Property | Location | Value ($M) | Age | SF |
|---|---|---|---|---|
| | **East** | | | |
| 1 | Baltimore, MD | $9.1 | 32 | 258,523 |
| 2 | Norwalk, CN | 11.3 | 27 | 321,023 |
| 3 | Providence, RI | 8.8 | 23 | 250,000 |
| 4 | Scranton, PA | 8.3 | 21 | 235,795 |
| 5 | Springfield, MA | 13.7 | 16 | 389,205 |
| 6 | Trenton, NJ | 17.2 | 18 | 488,636 |
| | Subtotal | 68.4 | | 1,943,182 |
| | **Midwest** | | | |
| 7 | Chicago, IL | 14.3 | 12 | 406,250 |
| 8 | Chicago, IL | 10.3 | 15 | 292,614 |
| 9 | Cleveland, OH | 15.9 | 12 | 451,705 |
| 10 | Cleveland, OH | 17.4 | 11 | 494,318 |
| 11 | Cleveland, OH | 19.4 | 12 | 551,136 |
| 12 | Cleveland, OH | 14.5 | 16 | 411,932 |
| 13 | Columbus, OH | 14.9 | 23 | 423,295 |
| 14 | Detroit, MI | 11.7 | 17 | 332,386 |
| 15 | Edina, MN | 4.7 | 19 | 133,523 |
| 16 | Elgin, IL | 11.9 | 16 | 338,068 |
| 17 | Gary, IN | 15.7 | 16 | 446,023 |
| 18 | Kansas City, MO | 11.3 | 12 | 321,023 |
| 19 | Minneapolis, MN | 19.3 | 16 | 548,295 |
| 20 | Sandusky, OH | 7.6 | 24 | 215,909 |
| 21 | Toledo, OH | 6.4 | 27 | 181,818 |
| | Subtotal | 195.3 | | 5,548,295 |
| | **South** | | | |
| 22 | Augusta, GA | 7.2 | 17 | 204,545 |
| 23 | Arlington, TX | 12.7 | 2 | 240,530 |
| 24 | Baton Rouge, LA | 17.7 | 27 | 502,841 |
| 25 | Biloxi, MS | 13.9 | 23 | 394,886 |
| 26 | Galveston, TX | 16.3 | 4 | 308,712 |
| 27 | Jacksonville, FL | 24.9 | 6 | 565,909 |
| 28 | Little Rock, AK | 9.1 | 25 | 258,523 |
| 29 | Miami, FL | 18.3 | 27 | 519,886 |
| 30 | Midland, TX | 18.3 | 4 | 346,591 |
| 31 | Odessa, TX | 16.9 | 6 | 384,091 |
| 32 | Oklahoma City, OK | 15.9 | 3 | 301,136 |
| | Subtotal | 171.2 | | 4,027,652 |
| 33 | Aurora, CO | 11.4 | 4 | 215,909 |
| 34 | El Cajon, CA | 9.7 | 13 | 275,568 |
| 35 | Oakland, CA | 13.2 | 12 | 187,500 |
| 36 | Phoenix, AZ | 9.3 | 3 | 176,136 |
| 37 | Sacramento, CA | 11.7 | 17 | 332,386 |
| 38 | San Bernardino, CA | 13.6 | 4 | 257,576 |
| 39 | Seattle, WA | 11.4 | 5 | 107,955 |
| | Subtotal | 80.3 | | 1,553,030 |
| | Total/Average | $515.2 | 15.1 | 13,072,159 |

## Appendix D
## Valley Island Public Employees' Retirement System
## Retail Portfolio

| Property | Location | Value ($M) | Age | SF | Type |
|---|---|---|---|---|---|
| | **East** | | | | |
| 1 | McLain, VA | $14.6 | 3 | 155,983 | N |
| 2 | Orlando, FL | 17.9 | 4 | 191,239 | N |
| 3 | Rye, NY | 65.0 | 17 | 1,041,667 | R |
| | Subtotal | 97.5 | | 1,388,889 | |
| | **Midwest** | | | | |
| 4 | Akron, OH | 24.6 | 23 | 394,231 | C |
| 5 | Ann Arbor, MI | 6.3 | 5 | 67,308 | N |
| 6 | Cincinnati, OH | 19.2 | 19 | 307,692 | C |
| 7 | Cleveland, OH | 101.3 | 27 | 1,623,397 | R |
| 8 | Duluth, MI | 12.1 | 19 | 193,910 | C |
| 9 | Edina, MI | 15.2 | 33 | 243,590 | C |
| 10 | Elgin, IL | 22.1 | 12 | 354,167 | C |
| 11 | Madison, WI | 13.5 | 28 | 216,346 | C |
| 12 | Shaker Heights, OH | 7.0 | 26 | 112,179 | N |
| 13 | Terre Haute, IN | 14.6 | 3 | 155,983 | C |
| 14 | Toledo, OH | 14.3 | 18 | 229,167 | C |
| | Subtotal | 250.2 | | 3,897,970 | |
| | **South** | | | | |
| 15 | Austin, TX | 22.5 | 3 | 240,385 | N |
| 16 | Birmingham, AL | 14.0 | 19 | 224,359 | C |
| 17 | Dallas, TX | 58.8 | 26 | 942,308 | R |
| 18 | Dallas, TX | 16.2 | 4 | 173,077 | N |
| 19 | Houston, TX | 61.6 | 29 | 987,179 | R |
| 20 | Jacksonville, FL | 11.2 | 23 | 179,487 | C |
| 21 | Midland, TX | 11.4 | 29 | 182,692 | C |
| 22 | Odessa, TX | 14.6 | 22 | 233,974 | C |
| | Subtotal | 210.3 | | 3,163,462 | |
| | **West** | | | | |
| 23 | Bakersfield, CA | 13.5 | 29 | 216,346 | C |
| 24 | Los Angeles, CA | 19.4 | 4 | 207,265 | N |
| 25 | Phoenix, AZ | 17.1 | 2 | 182,692 | N |
| 26 | Portland, OR | 12.2 | 23 | 195,513 | C |
| 27 | San Diego, CA | 21.2 | 3 | 226,496 | N |
| 28 | Seattle, WA | 20.3 | 16 | 325,321 | N |
| | Subtotal | 103.7 | | 1,353,632 | |
| | Total/Average | $661.7 | 16.8 | 9,803,953 | |

## Appendix E
## Valley Island Public Employees' Retirement System
## Multifamily Portfolio

| Property | Location | Value ($M) | Age | Units |
|---|---|---|---|---|
| | **East** | | | |
| 1 | Arlington, VA | $9.1 | 6 | 148 |
| 2 | Newton, MA | 12.3 | 7 | 200 |
| 3 | Princeton, NJ | 11.0 | 3 | 149 |
| | Subtotal | 32.4 | | 497 |
| | **Midwest** | | | |
| 4 | Columbus, OH | 11.7 | 17 | 238 |
| 5 | Columbus, OH | 14.3 | 12 | 290 |
| 6 | South Bend, IN | 10.3 | 15 | 209 |
| 7 | Miami, OH | 17.4 | 11 | 353 |
| 8 | Ann Arbor, MI | 7.8 | 27 | 158 |
| | Subtotal | 61.5 | | 1,249 |
| | **South** | | | |
| 9 | Atlanta, GA | 7.2 | 12 | 146 |
| 10 | Nashville, TN | 15.9 | 17 | 323 |
| 11 | Orlando, FL | 16.9 | 17 | 343 |
| 12 | Richardson, TX | 12.7 | 15 | 258 |
| 13 | San Antonio, TX | 13.4 | 18 | 272 |
| | Subtotal | 66.1 | | 1,343 |
| | **West** | | | |
| 14 | Bellevue, WA | 14.5 | 3 | 196 |
| 15 | Bolder, CA | 9.3 | 5 | 126 |
| 16 | Irvine, CA | 15.2 | 8 | 247 |
| 17 | Phoenix, AZ | 8.7 | 3 | 118 |
| 18 | Pleasanton, CA | 12.8 | 6 | 208 |
| 19 | Sacramento, CA | 11.3 | 12 | 230 |
| | Subtotal | 71.8 | | 1,125 |
| | **Total/Average** | **$231.8** | **11.3** | **4,213** |

## Questions for Discussion

Questions that should be addressed in this case include:

1. What are the characteristics of VIPERS' real estate portfolio as of April, 2001?

2. What impact (if any) has technology had on real estate to date? What impact will it have in the future? What implications does it have on VIPERS' portfolio restructuring efforts?

3. What has been the impact of technology on the growth and development of metropolitan areas? What implications does this have, if any, on VIPERS' real estate program?

4. What should Mason recommend to the Board regarding the restructuring of the real estate portfolio, as it relates to the following:

    - Allocation to real estate
    - Core Portfolio
    - Opportunistic Portfolio
    - Public Real Estate Securities

5. What should Mason recommend regarding managers and consultants?

Please use these questions as a guide and not a format or a reflection of all of the questions that need to be addressed by the case.

# 5

# BARTON STATE TEACHERS' RETIREMENT SYSTEM[1]

## Impact of "Return Compression" on Portfolio Strategy

Eleanor picked up the draft investment memorandum and began reviewing what her staff had written (starts on the third page (p. 107)). She knew that a big gap remaining were the final recommendations regarding the real estate strategy for 2004 and that it was her responsibility to make those final recommendations.

Eleanor Rigby was Director of Real Estate for the Barton State Teachers' Retirement System (BarSTRS). Eleanor had been with BarSTRS since graduating from college in 1984, working her way up from analyst to her recent appointment as Director of Real Estate.

BarSTRS was a $72.0 billion pension plan with a relatively old employee profile for a teachers' retirement system. Many of the plan beneficiaries were beginning to retire and it was anticipated that the plan would be cash flow negative by 2007.

BarSTRS had invested in real estate since 1993 and its real estate holdings currently represented slightly over 4.0% of the total portfolio.[2] The fund's experience with real estate had been quite good, averaging an overall unleveraged annual return of 11.3% since inception. This return was particularly attractive in light of the significant losses that the fund had experienced in the stock and bond markets over the past two years. In fact, there was strong support on the Board to raise the real estate allocation from

---

[1] This case was prepared by John McMahan and Espen Thoegersen. Copyright © John McMahan, 2003 and 2004, all rights reserved).
[2] BarSTRS' $2.9 billion in real estate investments included: industrial (29.4%); multifamily (23.8%); retail (19.7%); office (11.9%); and other (15.2%).

its present target level of 5.0%. Eleanor wasn't sure she wanted to recommend this, however, in light of some recent indications that the real estate market might be overheated, much like the stock market of the late 1990's.

She proceeded to read the draft investment memorandum to see if she could get any new insights that would help her come to a final recommendation.

**Barton State Teachers' Retirement System
Investment Memorandum
2004 Real Estate Strategy
(Draft)**

June 3, 2003

To:   Board of Trustees

From:   Eleanor Rigby
        Director of Real Estate

Re: 2004 Real Estate Investment Strategy

This investment memorandum outlines our recommended strategy for real estate investment in 2004. Since this is such a critical year for our plan, we have gone into much more detail than we normally would. Trends in institutional real estate investment activity are initially reviewed, followed by a discussion of the extent and nature of pension investment in real estate, a review of the current real estate market, and our recommendations for an investment strategy.

## *Institutional Real Estate Investment*

As of September 2002, the total US real estate investment universe was estimated at $4.63 trillion.[3] Institutional investors owned $2.24 trillion (48.4%) of the total universe, with the remaining $2.39 trillion (51.6%) held by non-institutional investors such as government agencies, corporations, and individual investors. Between 1995 and 2002, institutional investment in real estate increased from $1.2 trillion to $2.24 trillion, an average annual growth rate of 14.9%. Of the 2002 total, approximately $402.8 billion (18.0%) was in the form of equity real estate with the balance being debt at $1,841.4 billion (82.0%).

Exhibit 1 shows the major institutional real estate equity investors and their share of the market.

In addition to their direct investment holdings, pension funds own shares in Real Estate Investment Trusts (REITs), making them an even larger player in the institutional real estate equity market.

---

[3] Emerging Trends 2003: Rosen Consulting Group & Lend Lease Real Estate Investments.

### Exhibit 1
### Institutional Real Estate Equity Investors
### As of September, 2002

| Investors: | % |
|---|---|
| Real Estate Investment Trusts | 42.5 |
| Pension Funds | 36.9 |
| Foreign Investors | 11.6 |
| Life Insurance Companies | 8.0 |
| Commercial Banks | 0.6 |
| Savings Associations | 0.2 |
| Total | 100.0 |

Source: Emerging Trends in Real Estate 2003

## Pension Fund Investment in Real Estate

**Major Players:** As of 2002, public pension plans[4] comprised the largest group of pension real estate investors (72.2%), followed by corporate plans (21.2%), and Taft Hartley plans (6.6%). With the exception of General Motors, all of the top ten pension real estate investors are public plans.

### Exhibit 2
### Top 10 Pension Fund Real Estate Investors
### 2002

|  | Pension Fund | Real Estate Assets ($Billions) | Total Assets ($Billions) | % of Assets |
|---|---|---|---|---|
| 1 | CalPERS | $ 11.7 | $ 129.0 | 9.1% |
| 2 | CalSTRS | 5.1 | 88.0 | 5.8% |
| 3 | GM Corp. | 4.8 | 74.0 | 6.5% |
| 4 | STRS of Ohio | 4.6 | 42.0 | 11.0% |
| 5 | NYSTRS | 4.0 | 66.0 | 6.1% |
| 6 | State of Michigan Retirement System | 3.9 | 42.0 | 9.3% |
| 7 | Washington State Investment Board | 3.5 | 38.0 | 9.2% |
| 8 | NY State Common Retirement Fund | 3.4 | 96.0 | 3.5% |
| 9 | Florida State Board of Administration | 3.3 | 79.0 | 4.2% |
| 10 | PERS of Ohio | 3.1 | 45.0 | 6.9% |
|  | **Top 10 Total** | **47.4** |  | **6.8%** |

Source: Pensions & Investments (National Real Estate Investor)

---

[4] Based on numbers from the 2003 Money Market Directory.

**Attraction of Real Estate as an Investment:** According to the 2003 Plan Sponsor Survey[5] conducted by Institutional Real Estate, Inc. and Kingsley Associates, the positive sentiment among plan sponsors towards real estate is at an all-time high.

Given the turmoil experienced in the stock markets over the past three years and the tremendous losses that have occurred, it is easy to understand the relative attractiveness of real estate in the current market. Exhibit 3 demonstrates this clearly.

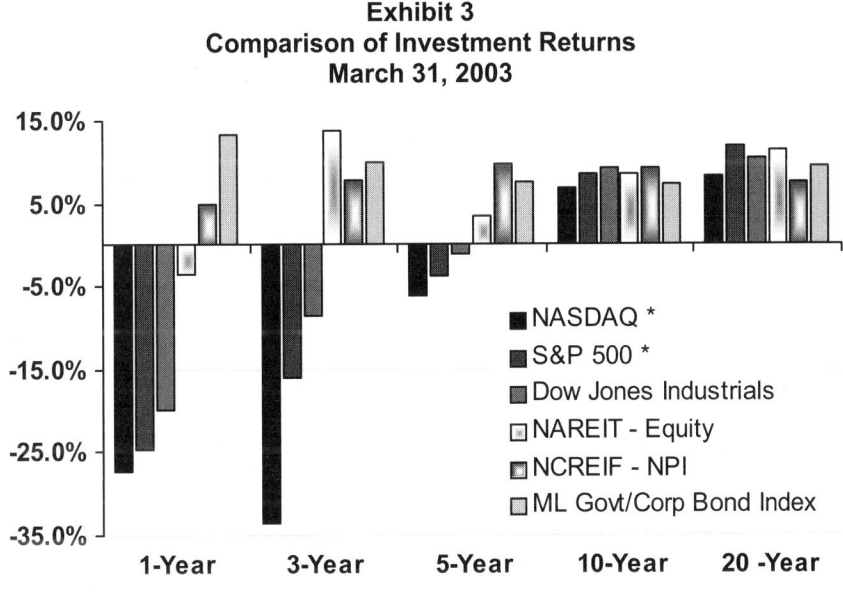

**Exhibit 3**
**Comparison of Investment Returns**
**March 31, 2003**

[Bar chart comparing NASDAQ*, S&P 500*, Dow Jones Industrials, NAREIT - Equity, NCREIF - NPI, and ML Govt/Corp Bond Index returns over 1-Year, 3-Year, 5-Year, 10-Year, and 20-Year periods.]

Source: NAREIT          * Price appreciation only

This favorable view of real estate is strengthened by the dismal outlook for other investment classes. Several observers expect returns in the stock and bond markets to be in the single digits over the next 10 years. As an example, Ron Kaiser of Bailard, Biehl, and Kaiser[6] expects total annual stock returns (S&P 500) to be 1.1% over the next 10 years, assuming a going-in price to earnings (P/E) ratio of 28X. Should the P/E ratio revert back to its historic high of 35X, however, stocks could return as much as 9.0% annually. On the other side, if P/E's fall to their previous lows of 8X, stocks would return a negative 1.4% annually over the next 10 years.

---

[5] Conducted by Institutional Real Estate Inc. and Kingsley Associates. Published January 2003.
[6] *Capital Market Returns*, February 24, 2003 by Ronald W. Kaiser (Bailard, Biehl & Kaiser, Inc.).

In contrast, Kaiser expects annual real estate returns to be 7.1% (assuming initial cap rate of 8.2%), ranging from a low of 5.3% (10.8% cap rate) to a high of 8.0% (8.0% cap rate).[7] Exhibit 4 summarizes Kaiser's expected 10-year annual return projections.

**Exhibit 4
Forecast Returns
Winter 2003**

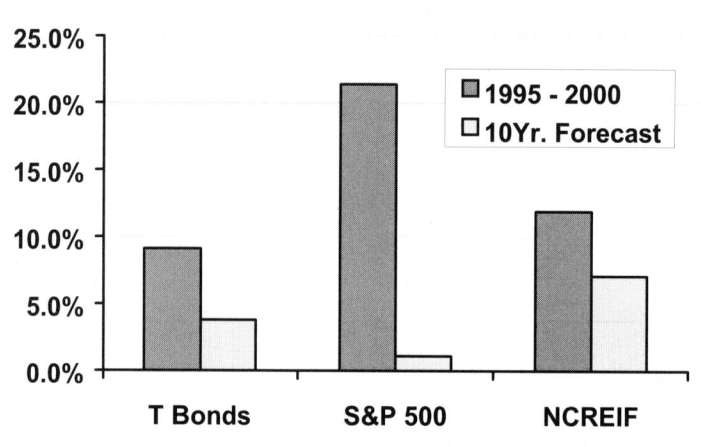

[Bar chart comparing 1995-2000 returns vs 10Yr. Forecast for T Bonds, S&P 500, and NCREIF]

Source: Ron Kaiser, Bailard, Biehl & Kaiser

To some extent, real estate is increasingly viewed as being "the best of the worst" investment alternative. This is particularly important to pension funds that are expected to be fully invested and yet are constrained in selecting between relatively few capital market alternatives. As a result of the continuing bear market, pension plans have lowered their investment return assumptions for all asset classes.

In addition, the survey indicates that pension plans have slowly started to reallocate some of their portfolio investment targets to reflect today's new investment environment.

One of the more interesting observations is that plan sponsors are no longer overallocated to real estate as a percentage of their total portfolios, as was the case in 2002. According to the survey, the 2003 underallocation to real estate was approximately $14.0 billion when applied across all plan sponsors.[8] In comparison, the over-allocation in 2002 represented $32.3 billion.

---

[7] Initial Cap Rates as of 1Q03 were: Industrial R&D, 9.5%; Industrial Warehouse, 8.7%; Multifamily, 8.1%; Office CBD, 8.9%; Office Suburban, 9.5%; Retail Mall, 8.8%; Retail Neighborhood, 8.9%; and Retail Power, 9.3%. Source: RERC Survey.
[8] Based on assets listed in the Money Market Directory.

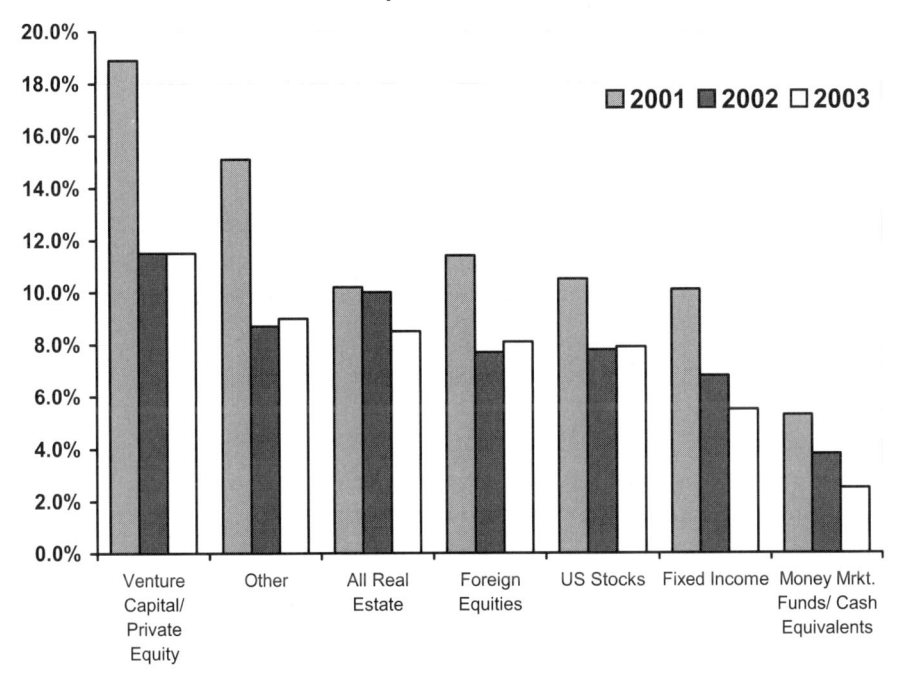

## Exhibit 5
## Plan Sponsor Return

Source: Institutional Real Estate, Inc., 2003 Plan Sponsor Survey

## Exhibit 6
## Plan Sponsor Investment Allocations
## 2003 vs. 2002

| Sector | 2003 Mean (%) Target | Actual | +/- | 2002 Mean (%) Target | Actual | +/- |
|---|---|---|---|---|---|---|
| Real Estate | 8.54 | 8.32 | (0.22) | 7.34 | 7.81 | 0.47 |
| US Stocks | 40.07 | 38.78 | (1.29) | 42.96 | 42.64 | (0.32) |
| Foreign Equities | 13.65 | 13.02 | (0.63) | 13.88 | 12.26 | (1.62) |
| Fixed Income | 27.58 | 29.23 | 1.65 | 26.64 | 28.81 | 2.17 |
| Venture Capital/Private Eq. | 5.50 | 4.78 | (0.72) | 4.97 | 3.71 | (1.26) |
| Money Mrkt. Funds/Cash Eq. | 0.87 | 1.78 | 0.91 | 1.17 | 1.82 | 0.65 |
| Other | 3.80 | 4.07 | 0.27 | 2.58 | 2.66 | 0.08 |

Source: Institutional Real Estate, Inc., 2003 Plan Sponsor Survey

Exhibit 7 represents pension plans' expected capital flows to investment managers in 2003 and the break down between the various types of real estate targeted.

**Exhibit 7**
**Expected Capital Flows To Investment Managers**

| Sector | Mean (%) 2001 | 2002 | 2003 |
|---|---|---|---|
| Private Equity (Core) | 44.0 | 34.1 | 39.4 |
| Private Equity (Value-Added) | 18.4 | 26.9 | 27.4 |
| Private Equity (Opportunistic) | 19.6 | 20.6 | 11.2 |
| Private Equity (Mixed) | -- | -- | 6.6 |
| Foreign Real Estate | 8.2 | 4.4 | 2.9 |
| REITs | 6.9 | 0.7 | 4.0 |
| Private Mortgages | 0.9 | 8.4 | 0.6 |
| CBMS | 1.8 | 0.9 | 0.7 |
| Other | 0.2 | 3.9 | 3.5 |
| TOTAL CAPITAL FLOWS (n) | $34.4Bn | $27.6Bn | $30.5Bn |

Source: Institutional Real Estate, Inc., 2003 Plan Sponsor Survey

The importance of cash generation to fund pension liabilities is illustrated by the fact that 43.4% of real estate investment capital in 2003 is directed at core direct investments and REITs, both historically known for consistent cash returns. In fact, the survey indicates that pension funds have increased their allocations towards these investments in 2003, at the same time as they have cut their allocations to opportunistic investments approximately in half. This further reflects pension funds' current appetite for income producing assets.

Many pension real estate investors also view their real estate investments as being a solid complement to the volatility of their stock and bond portfolios. This is largely due to the negative correlation between real estate and financial assets. In essence, many investors believe that adding real estate to a mixed-asset portfolio can reduce volatility and enhance overall portfolio returns.

Pension funds are also attracted to real estate because of the large cash component of the annual return, which helps in meeting funding obligations to their beneficiaries. In fact, the findings from the Plan Sponsor Survey indicated that real estate income now represents 17.3% of benefits paid.[9] As we know so well, these obligations have been growing over the last few years, largely due to the increased number of baby boomers reaching retirement age, and are expected to increase even more as their ranks swell over the next 10 years.

---

[9] Institutional Real Estate, Inc., 2003.

## Investment Strategies

In placing these funds, pension investors seek out one or more investment strategies, generally based on the level of risk and anticipated investment return. While these strategies are not always clearly defined, they usually break down as follows:

**Core:** Generally viewed as being investments in Class A office buildings, shopping centers, industrial, and apartment properties in major metropolitan areas. Anticipated investment returns: 8%-10%.[10] A large component of this return is in the form of cash.

**Enhanced Core:** Core investments requiring some form of remedial activity such as remodeling, re-tenanting, etc. Anticipated return level: 10%-12%.

**Value Added:** Investments requiring some form of higher risk activity in order to create value. Activities may involve development, leveraging (50%-60% of value), smaller metro areas, or more risky property types such as hotels, power centers, etc. Anticipated returns: 12%-15%.

**Opportunistic Investments:** Generally, no restriction on the location, age, or type of property. Investments may involve very high levels of leveraging (70% or more), mezzanine financing, and in some cases, entity investing. Often involves shorter holding periods (3-5 years). Anticipated returns: 15%-20%.[11]

**Investment Preferences:** Exhibits 8 and 9 indicate pension funds' ranking of property types and markets based on interviews conducted in late 2002. Apartments, industrial, and community shopping centers continued the popularity established in recent years. CBD office and full service hotels declined in popularity, largely as a result of reduced investment returns.

### Exhibit 8
### Property Type Preferences*
### 2003

| | |
|---|---|
| Apartments | 5.7 |
| Warehouse Industrial | 5.5 |
| Community Shopping Centers | 5.5 |
| CBD Office | 4.8 |
| R&D Industrial | 4.3 |
| Full Service Hotels | 4.3 |
| Regional Malls | 4.3 |
| Suburban Office | 4.2 |
| Power Centers | 3.8 |
| Limited Service Hotels | 3.3 |

*10.0 = "Excellent"; 0.0 = "Poor"
Source: Emerging Trends in Real Estate interviews, September 2002.

---

[10] Approximate return levels as of early 2003.
[11] Opportunity funds generally promised 20.0%+ returns until the recent economic downturn.

### Exhibit 9
### Market Area Preferences*
### 2003

| | |
|---|---|
| Washington DC | 6.7 |
| New York | 6.6 |
| Los Angeles | 6.3 |
| San Diego | 6.3 |
| Chicago | 5.9 |
| Boston | 5.9 |
| Miami | 5.6 |
| San Francisco | 5.3 |
| Seattle | 5.0 |
| Philadelphia | 4.9 |

* 10.0 = "Excellent"; 0.0 ="Poor"
Source: Emerging Trends in Real Estate interviews, September 2002

Perhaps the most striking feature of this survey is the fall in popularity of Boston and San Francisco, largely a result of major declines in their technology sectors.

It is interesting to note that all of the top 10 market areas are "constrained" markets in which real estate supply is restricted as an integral part of public policy. This is in direct contrast to "commodity markets" where the emphasis is on job formation, with real estate being viewed largely as a factor of production.[12] In commodity markets, real estate returns are often adversely impacted by the desire to keep down production costs, such as rent. This is accomplished by increasing levels of new construction, leading to higher vacancy factors and ultimately lower rents.

Exhibit 10 is based on a study by The Johnson-Souza Group of the same store Net Operating Income (NOI) of selected multifamily REITs between 1996 and 2001. The REITs are grouped into constrained and commodity categories, based on the geographical location of the majority of their portfolio. This study concludes that multifamily REITs operating in constrained markets have produced an annual return averaging approximately 500 basis points higher than REITs operating primarily in commodity markets. [13] As a result, many pension investors are restricting their investments to constrained market areas and, in essence, "red lining" commodity markets.

---

[12] Atlanta and Dallas are good examples of commodity markets.
[13] Note that this study is based on real estate returns, independent of stock values.

**Exhibit 10
Supply Constrained vs. Commodity Markets** [14]
**(REIT focus)**

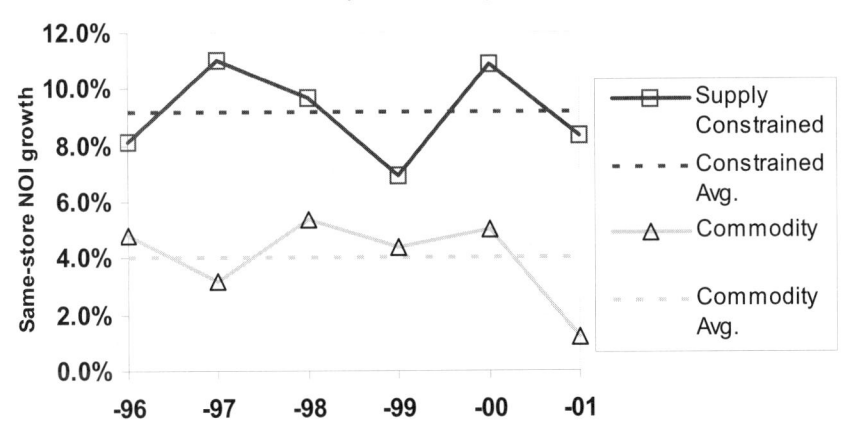

*(Chart showing Same-store NOI growth from -96 to -01, with series: Supply Constrained, Constrained Avg., Commodity, Commodity Avg.)*

Source: The Johnson-Souza Group

## Current Real Estate Market

**Vacancy Rates:** Largely as a result of the rapid decline in US jobs and the retrenchment of companies attempting to cope with the recession, office and industrial vacancy began increasing rapidly in 2000 and continued increasing well into 2003[15] (Exhibit 11 on page 116).

**Rental Rates:** Increasing vacancies began placing pressure on office rental rates almost immediately, and, to a lesser extent, industrial properties which tend to have fewer employees per square foot of space (Exhibit 12 on page 116).

**Investment Returns:** With increasing vacancies and declining rents, it wasn't long before investment returns began turning down in 2001 (Exhibit 13).

---

[14] Constrained market REITs include: AvalonBay, BRE Properties, Essex, and C.E.Smith. Commodity market REITs include: Camden, Gables, Post Properties, and Summit Properties.
[15] In 2001 and 2002, the US office market registered the lowest negative absorption in 15 years. (Source: Torto Wheaton Research, May 12, 2003)

**Exhibit 11**
**Vacancy Rates, 1989-2002**

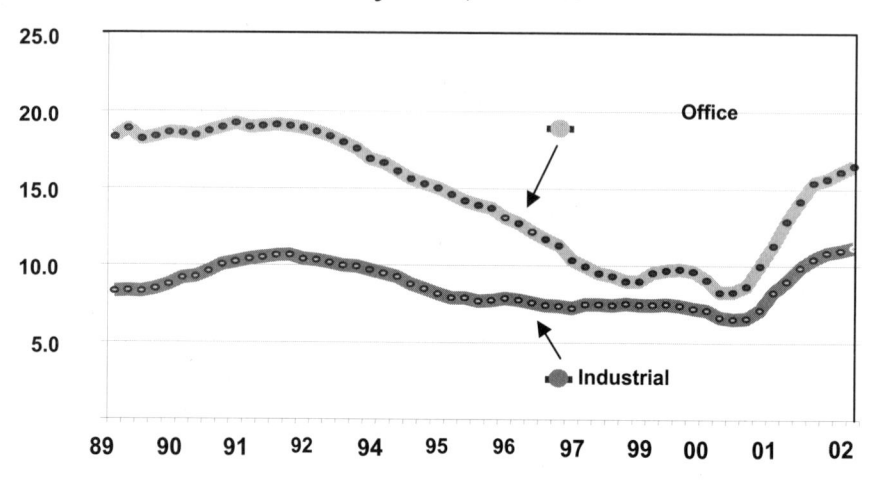

Source: Torto Wheaton Research, Kennedy Associates

**Exhibit 12**
**Percentage Change in Quarterly Rents**
**(1Q98-4Q02)**

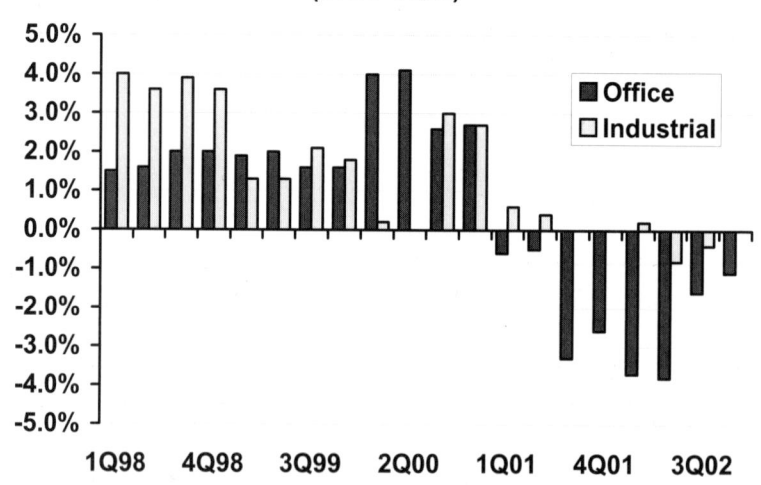

Source: Torto Wheaton Research, Kennedy Associates

**Exhibit 13**
**NCREIF Property Index Returns**
**(1Q93 – 4Q02)**

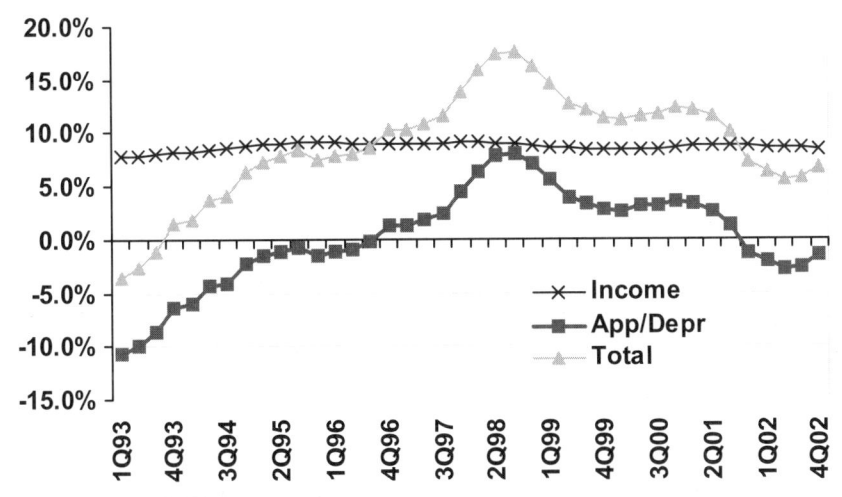

[Line chart showing Income, App/Depr, and Total returns from 1Q93 to 4Q02, with values ranging from -15.0% to 20.0%]

Source: RERC (NCREIF)

This decline in returns impacted all property types with the exception of retail (Exhibit 14).

**Exhibit 14**
**NCREIF Investment Returns**
**By Property Type**
**December 31, 2002**

| ANNUAL RETURNS (TOTAL) | | | | |
|---|---|---|---|---|
| Property Type | 1-Year | 3-Year | 10-Year | 20-Year |
| Retail | 13.7% | 9.4% | 7.8% | 8.8% |
| Multifamily | 8.8% | 10.4% | 11.4% | - |
| NPI Index | 6.8% | 8.7% | 9.3% | 7.7% |
| Industrial | 6.7% | 10.0% | 10.5% | 8.6% |
| Office | 2.8% | 7.6% | 9.1% | 6.0% |

Source: NCREIF

**New Construction:** Historically, negative changes in the real estate market have led to a decline in new construction. This was true in this cycle, but not until a significant amount of new space had been delivered to the markets. As outlined in Exhibit 15, industrial construction was the first property type to turn down in 1999, followed by hotels and office in 2001. However, new retail construction continued strong, preventing total construction from turning down until 2002.

**Exhibit 15**
**Value of Construction Put in Place**
(Current dollars)

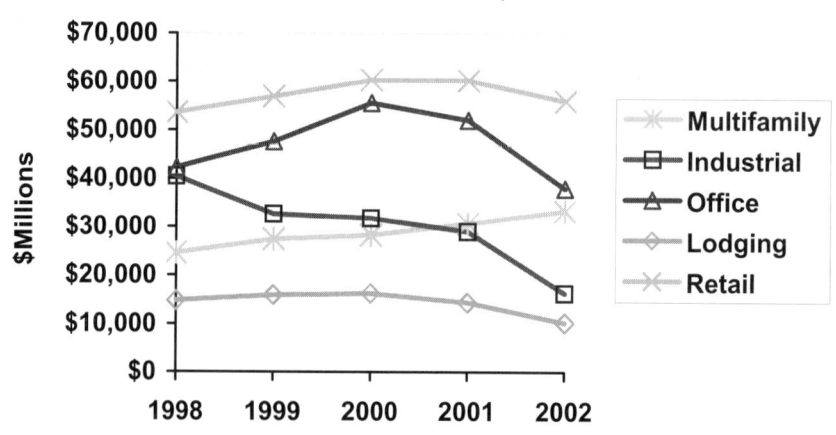

[Line chart showing $Millions from $0 to $70,000 for years 1998-2002, with series: Multifamily, Industrial, Office, Lodging, Retail]

Source: U.S. Census Bureau

**Property Prices:** In the past, property prices usually have turned down as fundamentals weaken. This was not the case in 2002, however, as prices increased seemingly independent of the underlying fundamentals (Exhibit 16).

**Exhibit 16**
**Quarterly Change in Property Prices**
4Q00-3Q02

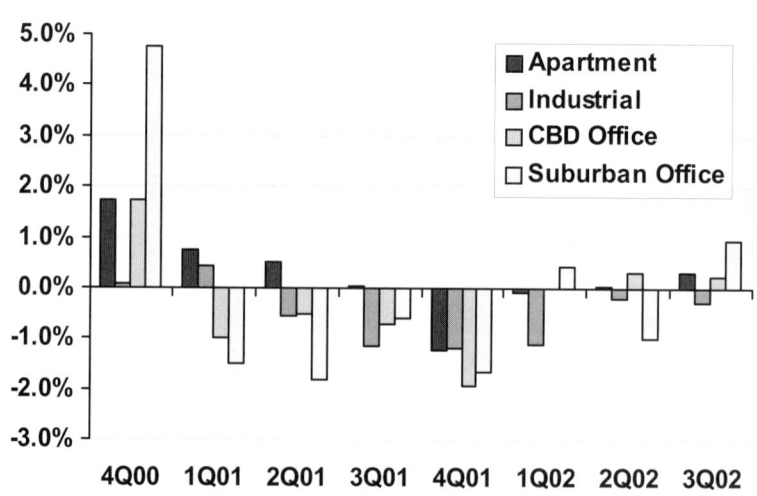

[Bar chart showing quarterly changes from -3.0% to 5.0% for 4Q00 through 3Q02, with series: Apartment, Industrial, CBD Office, Suburban Office]

Source: National Real Estate Index; Kennedy Associates

**Cap Rates:** The increases in office prices resulted in a decline in capitalization rates, almost the opposite effect that normally accompanies a decline in market fundamentals (Exhibit 17).

**Exhibit 17
CBD Office Cap Rates
(1985-2002)**

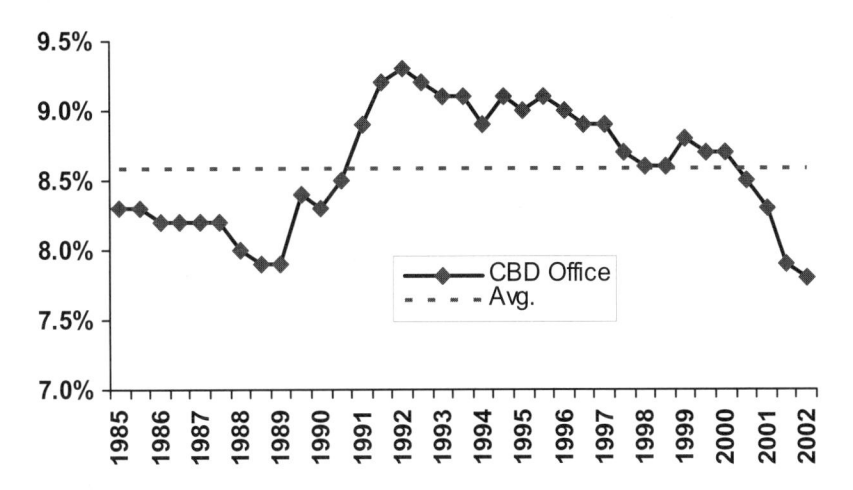

Source: National Real Estate Index; Kennedy Associates

**Disconnect Between Prices and Fundamentals:** The upward movement of prices has resulted in a divergence between prices and fundamentals, particularly in the case of CBD office buildings (Exhibit 18).

**Exhibit 18
Price and Rent Are Diverging
(1985-2002)**

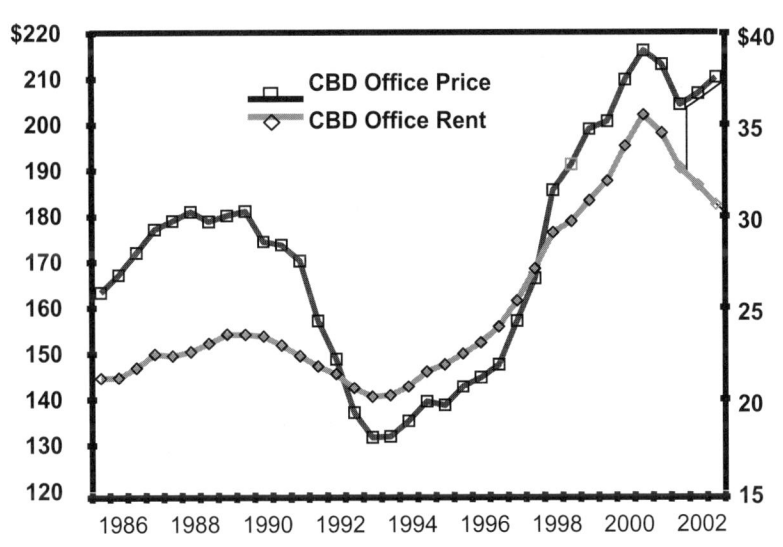

Source: Kennedy Associates

**Pension Investment Activity:** Exhibit 19 indicates the level of pension investment in equity real estate by property type. Note that investment in most property types increased in 2002, with the exception of apartment and industrial, further indicating the strong motivation towards real estate investment as the best of the available capital market alternatives.

**Exhibit 19**
**Pension Equity Investment in Real Estate**
**Annual**

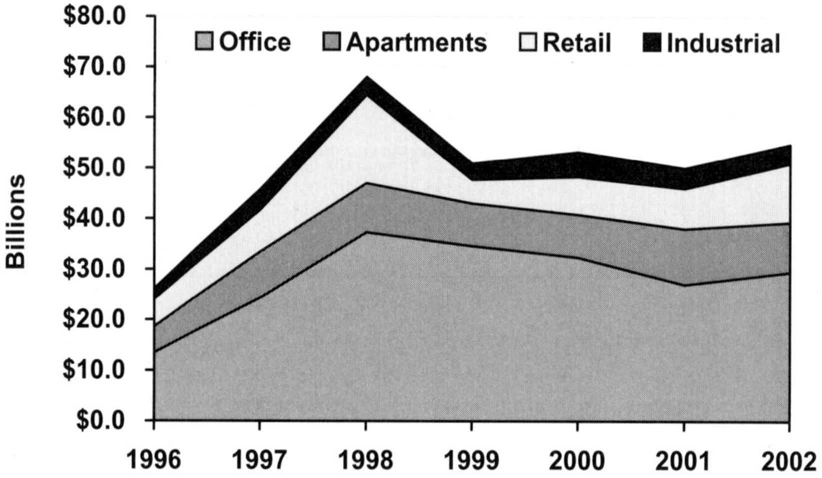

Source: Institutional Real Estate, Inc.; Kennedy Associates

**Foreign Investors:** Pension funds were not the only investors driving up prices in 2002. After exiting the US real estate markets in the late 1990s, largely due to the sliding value of the Euro and the strong dollar, German capital is once again flooding into US real estate markets.

The Germans' return is largely the result of a weakened dollar and a stabilized Euro, making US property investment attractive. In addition, Germany's Fourth Financial Market Promotion Act, a sweeping new financial services act, went into effect on July 1, 2002. This new law enables German open-end funds to increase their investments in US commercial properties and also allows German commercial banks to widen their activities in the US.

Further, German investors have lower return expectations than their US counterparts. As a result, they find US property yields more attractive than what is currently available in Europe and are willing to pay up for US investments. Combined with their willingness to hang on to an asset longer to make the numbers work, Germans now have emerged as aggressive bidders for trophy properties in selected markets across the US. According to

Real Capital Analytics, Germans alone acquired approximately $4 billion worth of US real estate in 2002.[16]

As for foreign real estate investors in general, they fell short of their 2002 investment goals according to the results of a recent survey conducted by the Association of Foreign Investors in Real Estate (AFIRE).[17] Seventy nine percent (79.0%) of the survey respondents, owning a combined $70 billion of US real estate assets, indicated that it was either "somewhat" or "very difficult" to find attractive real estate investment opportunities during the past year. This may be the reason these investors failed to meet their targeted US investment allocations for 2002. In addition, respondents stated that they were concerned about weakening market fundamentals.

That said, the respondents remained extremely positive about US real estate, ranking it number one in offering the "most stable and secure real estate investments; the best opportunity for capital appreciation; and the best risk-adjusted return potential." In total, they indicated that they plan to increase their US real estate investments to a total of $11.1 billion this year vs. $9.2 billion in 2002. Germans are expected to count for the lion's share of these investments.

As for the most attractive property markets, the respondents' preferences were Washington, D.C., New York, Los Angeles, Chicago, and San Francisco, in that order. The most favored property types were Multifamily, Industrial/R&D, Office, Retail, and Hotels, also in order of preference.

**1031 Exchanges:** Another major source of investment capital in 2002 came from sellers of real estate attempting to avoid capital gains taxes through 1031 exchanges. These investors not only benefited from enhanced proceeds from their selling property but could pay 20% - 25% more for their exchange property and still be ahead of having to pay the tax.

**Future Outlook:** Despite current problems, some encouraging signs in the real estate market appear to be emerging, particularly in the bell-weather industrial sector. Many industrial metrics are turning positive and it is entirely possible that 2003 could be the first year in some time to see positive industrial net absorption.

While industrial properties should be the first to benefit from the economic recovery, retail and apartments are positioned to follow. Office markets are presently the weakest and should be the last property type to recover, most likely in the second quarter of 2004. This is due to new office construction and sublease space overhang as well as the general market clearing process as

---

[16] WSJ.com - *Real Estate Journal,* April 16, 2003.
[17] 2002 AFIRE Foreign Investment Survey.

leases turn. Job loss is still a problem in many cities, perhaps extending the point of recovery even further.

**Exhibit 21**
**Industrial Metrics Are Turning Positive**

|  | 2001 | Projected 2002 | Projected 2003 | Trend |
|---|---|---|---|---|
| **Completions (MSF)** | 232M | 115M | 90M | ▼ |
| **Vacancy Rate** | 9.9% | 11.0% | 10.2% | ▼ |
| **Net Absorption** | -155M | -20M | 166M | ▲ |
| **Job Growth (% Chg)** | 0.2% | -0.8% | 0.7% | ▲ |
| **Imports (% Chg)** | -2.9% | 3.4% | 6.2% | ▲ |
| **Retail Sales (% Chg)** | 3.6% | 3.2% | 4.3% | ▲ |
| **Industrial Production (%Chg)** | -3.7% | -0.3% | 3.3% | ▲ |

Source: RREEF Research

**Exhibit 22**
**Timing of Market Recoveries**

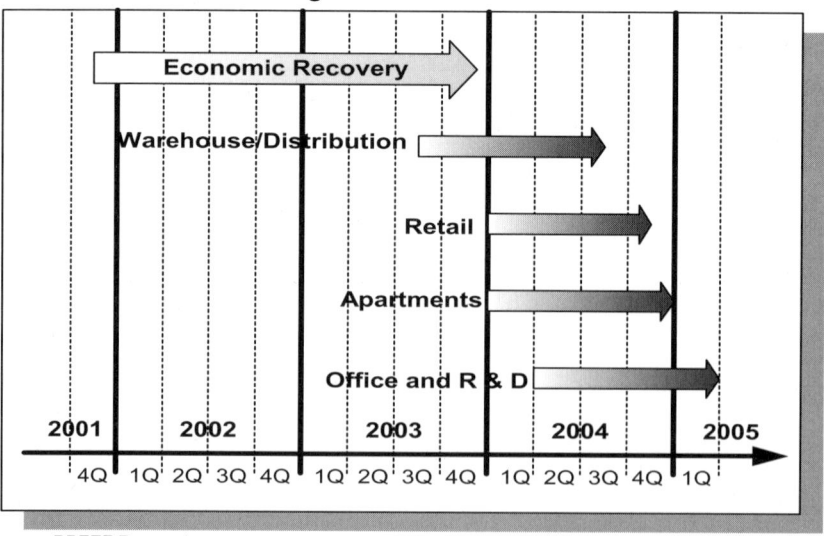

Source: RREEF Research

**Office Market Recovery:** Since office is the sector in which we are most underinvested and our top new investment priority, it would be beneficial to look at it a little more closely. In terms of geography, the only office markets that are expected to recover in 2003 are New York and the District of Columbia (Exhibit 23). Most other markets should show signs of recovery in 2004, with hard-hit markets (mostly technology) recovering in 2005 or later.

### Exhibit 23
### Projected Recovery of US Office Markets

| 2003<br>Early Recovery | 2004<br>National Average | Late 2005+<br>Late Recovery |
|---|---|---|
| District of Columbia<br>New York | Boston<br>Chicago<br>Ft. Lauderdale<br>Houston<br>Los Angeles<br>Miami<br>No. New Jersey<br>Oakland/East Bay<br>Orange County<br>Phoenix<br>Portland<br>Tampa<br>Raleigh<br>San Diego<br>St. Louis | Atlanta<br>Austin<br>Dallas<br>Denver<br>Minneapolis<br>No. Virginia<br>Orlando<br>Philadelphia<br>San Francisco<br>San Jose<br>Seattle |

Source: RREEF Research

Here are some of the problems. At year-end 2002, national office vacancy stood at 16.1%, almost twice the level of the market at the end of 2000. Only two markets -- New York and Tucson -- had vacancy rates less than 10.0%. National CBD vacancy stood at 12.7%, with suburban vacancy at 18.1%. In some of the tech sub-markets in Boston, Dallas, and Seattle, vacancies were almost 30.0%.[18]

Sublease space continues to contribute to the high vacancy levels, with 123 MSF of sublease space available at year-end 2002, up from 107 MSF at the same period in 2001. On the positive side, the amount of sublease space fell in 2Q02, but only slightly.[19]

With increased vacancies, rent levels have fallen and are expected to drop an additional 20.0% this year.[20] In some markets, the decline is even greater as landlords have begun making substantial rent reductions and non-rental concessions in light of continuing economic uncertainty and minimal tenant leasing activity. In order to retain good tenants, some landlords are taking the initiative to propose mid-term rental reductions in exchange for other non-

---

[18] *RREEF Research*, December 2002.
[19] *RREEF Research*, ibid.
[20] *RREEF Research,* op. cit.

rental tenant concessions (e.g., longer lease terms; less desirable space; increased percentage rents in retail properties, etc.).

Torto Wheaton Research (TWR) projects that the increase in office vacancy will begin to moderate in 2003 with rents beginning to rise in 2004 and 2005. TWR comments further: "In a typical property, with leases rolling to market at an average pace, the sliding market conditions will place downward pressure on NOI streams as the bubble of the late 1990s is moved off of rent rolls."[21]

The big question overhanging the office market is the outlook for jobs. Layoffs still continue and few firms are hiring. As a result, net absorption of office space continues to be negative. While this situation should begin turning around in 2003, the recovery still will be very fragile.

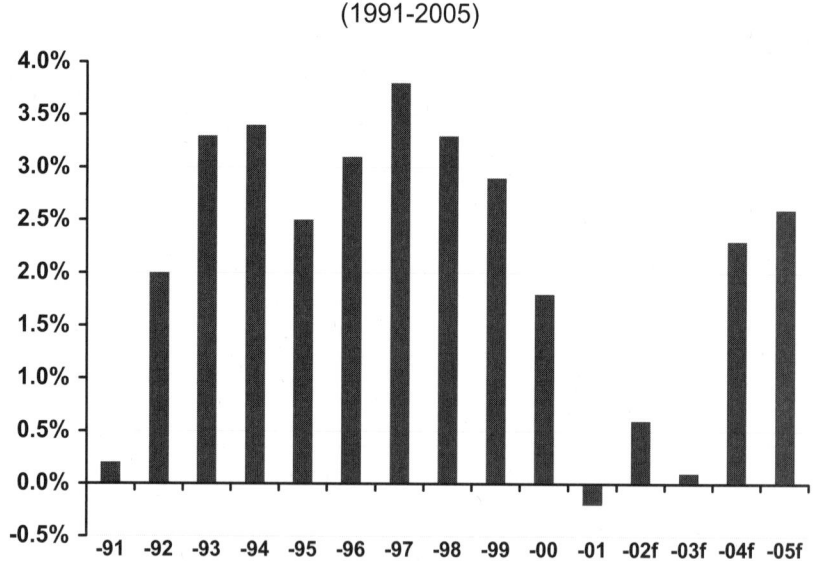

**Exhibit 24**
**Annual Office Employment Growth**
(1991-2005)

Source: Bureau of Labor Statistics; Rosen Consulting Group

**Investor Expectations:** In interviews in late 2002, institutional office investors stated that they expect office investments to average a 11.4% gain in value over the next five years or 2.3% annually.[22] Coupled with a cash yield of 7.0%-8.0%, total returns are expected to be in the 9.3%-10.3% range. While these expectations are considerably less than the experience of the late 1990's when office properties appreciated 14.8% annually,[23] they still may be

---

[21] *TWR About Real Estate*, Volume 4, Number 4, February 3, 2003.
[22] *Emerging Trends 2003*, Lend Lease.
[23] Torto Wheaton, Op. Cit.

inconsistent with the realities of the marketplace and the price levels at which properties are currently trading. Throughout the history of the Torto Wheaton Research Office Property reports, the average annual appreciation in office values has been only 0.86%.[24]

Some investors, notably Germans and other foreign investors, are taking a different approach -- not expecting much appreciation at all. Instead, they are buying "bankable" income streams in Class A buildings that they believe will produce "bondlike" returns even with the possibility of continuing weak market fundamentals. With a positive interest spread of 200-500 bp over historically low interest rates, these investors believe they are "bridging" any downturn that might occur during the next few years and financing it on very attractive terms.[25]

There is another factor that should be considered. One of the outgrowths of the corporate scandals of the last few years is a new FASB law that requires corporations to discontinue the use of synthetic leases on approximately $100 billion in operating properties. The firms have three options: (1) bringing values to the balance sheet and take an earnings loss, (2) renegotiate the loan terms, or (3) converting them to sale/leasebacks. Since most operating corporations don't want to tie up capital in real estate and lenders will have to put in more capital to make loan transactions work, it is anticipated that many firms will take the sale/leaseback route. This could generate even more buying opportunities for "bondlike" investors, perhaps priced more attractively than those currently on the market.

## *Recommendations*

With all of this market uncertainty, this is probably the most difficult real estate strategy memo we have ever written. The issues we must deal with include:

- ☐ 2004 real estate capital allocation
- ☐ Risk level allocation (e.g., core, valued added, opportunistic)
- ☐ Property type allocations
- ☐ Geographic market preferences
- ☐ Anticipated investment returns by property type

**Real Estate Allocation:** We recommend that… (Eleanor, it's all yours from here)

---

[24] TWR Viewpoint, January 23, 2003.
[25] In 1990, 6.0% cap rates were 200 bp less than the Treasury rate.

### Continued from page 2 (p.106):

Eleanor put down the draft memo and began to collect her thoughts about how to approach the recommendations. She was well aware of the desire of some Board members to increase the real estate allocation, but was concerned about the overheated real estate market and the impact of the investment return issue on future asset values and returns.

Her major concern was that, as the economy improves, ten-year treasury yields could rise from the current 4.0% range to a more normal trading range of 6.0% or so. If spreads over treasuries remain the same as they have over the last decade, cap rates could increase to the 8.0%-9.0% range. If this happens, properties purchased at currently low cap rates would experience a near-term loss in market value. This would require a mark-to-market write down to reflect this change in value. Asset depreciation would then cut into cash yields rather than enhancing them and BarSTRS overall investment returns would suffer. She also was concerned about the pressure on cash yields as a result of a slow economic recovery and having to make substantial rent concessions as leases turn.

She cancelled her dinner plans, ordered a pizza and diet Pepsi, and began struggling with her final recommendations. She knew it would be another all-nighter.

## *Questions for Discussion:*

Questions that should be addressed in this case include:

1. What should be BarSTRS 2004 real estate capital allocation?
2. What should be the level of allocation to each level of risk (e.g., core, value added, opportunistic)?
3. What should be the Plan's property type allocations?
4. Should there be a geographic market preference? If so, which markets should be selected and why?
5. What is the current market situation in real estate? How should it influence (if at all) BarSTRS strategic plan?
6. What should be the timing of implementing the new investment initiatives?

Please use these questions as a guide and not a format or a reflection of all of the questions that need to be addressed by the case.

# 6

# NOTE ON ASSET MANAGEMENT[1]

## Brief History[2]

The role of the asset manager has evolved over the last 50 years, as real estate has moved from individual to institutional ownership and from the management of a few buildings in a single market to large portfolios of properties, often located in dispersed geographical markets.

**Banks and Insurance Companies:** Among the first active institutional investors in real estate were banks and, more importantly, insurance companies. In the early 1950's, insurance companies began investing proceeds from the liquidation of government bonds acquired during World War II.

A problem quickly emerged: Most of the insurance companies were located in the northeast, while most of the available investment properties were in the rapidly growing areas of the south and west. To diversify their real estate portfolios geographically (which they desired to do), life insurers would need to acquire knowledge of multiple markets.

Insurance companies could meet the local requirements of leasing and property management through outsourcing. However, it became increasingly essential to the growth and successful operation of their rapidly expanding investment programs to employ experienced, well trained real estate professionals in an oversight capacity.

---

[1] Copyright ©2005 by John McMahan. All rights reserved.
[2] This history is covered in greater detail in Chapter 1.

Consequently, insurance companies began to dedicate resources to meet this requirement. These resources, in the form of specific employees operating out of regional offices, were expected to manage the local service firms (property managers, leasing brokers, transaction brokers, etc.) in each of the local markets, as well as translate operating data generated by the properties into a format that was consistent with the company's method of reporting and overall strategic investment objectives. Most importantly, these regional asset managers were expected to provide leadership, and to integrate the strategic objectives of the home office with the realities of multiple real estate markets.

**Pension Funds:** The Employee Retirement Income Security Act (ERISA) was passed in 1974 to regulate the investment of pension fund capital. This legislation segregated pension "plan assets" from sponsor assets and established stringent legal requirements and penalties for firms and individuals involved in managing plan assets.[3]

Prior to ERISA, pension funds usually did not invest plan assets in real estate, and when they did, they pursued "bondlike" investments (e.g., single tenant properties and mortgages). After ERISA's passage, it was clear that pension plan portfolios were *expected to be diversified* across the entire spectrum of investment assets, including real estate.

**Open-End Funds:** In the mid- to late 1970's, insurance companies, led by Prudential and several other insurance companies and banks established "open-end" pooled funds to invest pension capital in real estate. The concept was to allow pension investors to freely invest in and withdraw their capital from (if they desired) these commingled/pooled funds on a quarterly basis, similar to stock and bond mutual funds.

The pension plans liked these new funds, and in very few years they became billion dollar investment operations. To manage these operations, it was only natural that the insurance company sponsors would turn to the managers of their internally owned assets, and the asset management structures they had created for their own portfolios.

**Closed-End Funds:** In the late 1970's and early 1980's, entrepreneurial firms joined in investing pension capital destined for real estate. The entrepreneurial firms largely utilized finite-life closed end funds, in which assets were held for a predetermined time before returning capital to the pension investors. This provided investment managers with more control over the implementation of the investment strategy of the fund during the holding period. This also led to

---

[3] ERISA legislation came as a result of the collapse of the Studebaker Corporation pension plan as well as the criminal behavior of several union pension plans, most notably the Teamsters. As a result, penalties for violating many ERISA provisions became personal and criminal

the development of a more aggressive approach to the management of assets, expanding the role of the asset manager.

**REITs:** Real Estate Investment Trusts (REITs) were established in 1960, but for most of their first 35 years were largely passive investment vehicles, in which management of the REIT properties was usually outsourced to outside investment advisors.

In the mid 1990's, a series of new REITs was organized, largely from development firms that took advantage of the opportunity to recapitalize their companies by going public. Most of firms had highly leveraged real estate portfolios and had run into problems in the late 1980's and early 1990's and were in need of a major cash infusion.

These "new" REITs were quite different from the traditional ones. The new REITs were vertically integrated organizations, generally specializing in a single property type and, sometimes, a specific geographic region. As a result, asset management and property management were usually handled internally, and REIT asset managers were highly focused and involved in the day-to-day operations of the properties in the portfolio.

**Opportunity Funds:** The mid 1990's also witnessed the introduction of opportunity funds. These funds amassed substantial sums of institutional and individual capital in a pooled format, to seek higher investment returns than those obtained through traditional "core" investment strategies. Initially sponsored by Wall Street investment banking firms, the management of opportunity funds ultimately spread to include entrepreneurial firms offering a wide variety of investment strategies and financial structures.

Opportunity funds initially outsourced most of their real estate management functions, often working with local operating partners who were responsible for both originating and managing investment assets. In recent years, many opportunity funds, recognizing the need for better control of the investment process, began developing internal management capabilities in both transactional and asset management.

## *Today's Asset Manager*

The Institute of Real Estate Management (IREM) defines asset management as "[a] system that directs and measures the performance of asset groups (in this case, real estate assets) and produces a flow of information needed by ownership to make investment decisions."

IREM goes on to outline how the modern asset manager is involved in the investment process:

*"Prior to ownership, the asset manager participates in the acquisition and/or development process, to ensure long-term asset performance in accordance with the investor's objectives. During the holding period, the asset manager directs, measures, and changes asset performance as appropriate. To attain the end of maximizing the value of real estate investments, the asset manger is involved in the process of enhancing value during operations and recommending disposition at the appropriate time."*

The modern real estate asset manager is a multidisciplined, highly trained real estate professional who is expected not only to manage investment assets during the investment holding period, but also to be an integral part of the acquisition and disposition processes. Quite simply, the asset manager has evolved into a business manager responsible for a portfolio of real estate assets.

The professionalism of today's asset manager is also a reflection of the much higher fiduciary standards required to manage real estate investment programs in today's complex and highly litigious business environment. The asset manager must deal with much more varied levels and frequency of financial reporting on both the property and portfolio level. This is largely due to the drive to bring greater transparency to the management and ownership of real estate assets.

## *Asset vs. Property Management*

Many people confuse asset management with property management. Property management is the day-to-day management of individual properties, generally involving responsibility for custodial services, maintenance, supply procurement, lease administration, and property level accounting. Property management services can be provided by third party property management firms, affiliated property management organizations, or as an internal management function, best exemplified by the approach taken by many REITs.

Property management is a vital function at the heart of a successful real estate investment program, but it is only one activity in a broad range of asset manager responsibilities. The much broader scope of management responsibility of the asset manager usually encompasses the following functions:

- ❏ Tenant relationships
- ❏ Business planning and budgeting
- ❏ Supervision of property management services
- ❏ Property and portfolio level financial reporting

- Project management (construction of tenant space)
- Risk management
- Leasing oversight
- Financing/refinancing
- Hold/sell analyses
- Assistance with investor relations
- Portfolio rebalancing recommendations

Although not a direct responsibility, the asset manager is also a major participant in both the acquisition and disposition process of portfolio assets.

Another difference between asset and property managers is their background. Unlike many property managers, most asset managers are college graduates, with many having advanced degrees. Some have come up through the ranks of property management, but most have accounting, finance, development, or transaction management backgrounds.

In today's world, asset management is almost always an internal function of an investment management firm, whereas property management can be internally or externally provided, depending upon the property type/location or senior management's view of the most effective delivery system for property management services.

## Asset Manager's Role in Property Acquisition

The modern day asset manager is often a vital link between the acquisition of real estate assets and the successful management of these assets over the investment holding period.

**Deal Sourcing:** Even before an asset has been acquired, the asset manager is integrally involved in the investment process. The asset manager assists the acquisition team by continually monitoring markets, the success (failure) of competitive projects, and, most importantly, the future space needs of existing tenants in the investment manager's portfolio(s).

Tenants within the portfolio of properties and in the general market can be a valuable source of new acquisition leads. Understanding tenants' space requirements can lead to potential build-to-suit opportunities and/or the identification of leasing candidates for buildings that are being marketed without tenants.

The asset manager also should be in continual contact with other members of the real estate community, who may be able to provide valuable leads to potential acquisitions. This includes leasing brokers (both project and tenant representatives), mortgage bankers, construction loan officers, title company employees, appraisers, and market research professionals.

**Deal Screening:** The asset manager usually has a good grasp of the trends and issues in the markets in which the investment manager operates. More importantly, it's a view established over a period of time as opposed to the "heat of the moment" of an individual deal. With this market knowledge, the asset manager can offer a clear perspective as to how a particular investment prospect fits into the overall fabric of the local market.

Being in the market over a period of time also gives the asset manager a good perspective of the physical characteristics of a building and how attractive/unattractive it may be to tenants in the local market. This knowledge becomes more important as the sourcing process broadens and new markets are targeted for possible investments.

The asset manager also may be more sensitive to the interrelationships between tenants, and can help to avoid a situation in which economic "linking" accelerates the collapse of a tenant base during a declining market. These considerations become particularly important in buildings in which one or a few tenants represent the major portion of the projected rental cash flow from the investment.

Finally, the asset manager may be better prepared to evaluate the quality of the building's existing property management and spot opportunities to enhance cash flow through new management initiatives. These initiatives may involve physical changes in the building (which may require additional capital outlays) or ways in which the building is maintained (e.g., more frequent cleaning, parking enhancements, common area and restroom upgrades, additional amenities, improved lighting, better security, etc.).

A question might be: "Why not use local brokers to accomplish these objectives rather than tying up the valuable time of an asset manager?" While a broker can provide important insights on related transactions and current market pricing, brokers don't always understand the critical ingredients in the successful management of a building, or the importance of longer-term economic and market forces. They also may not have an understanding of the investment manager's culture, or the strategic investment objectives of its investors. Furthermore, brokers' compensation is based on the success of a transaction, rather than the longer-term success of a property investment.

**Preliminary Underwriting:** If the property survives preliminary screening and a site visit, it is time for the Acquisition Team to consider it as a prospective acquisition and begin a preliminary underwriting of its investment potential.

During this process, the asset manager serves as an "on call" resource supplying information such as local market knowledge/data, building operating characteristics/costs, and lease terms.

**Investment Committees:** The asset manager's perspective also can be a vital ingredient in the evaluation of a proposed investment by the firm's investment committee. When coupled with the pricing and deal structuring perspective of the acquisition team, the investment committee can gain both a short and longer-term understanding of the proposed transaction.

**Investment Agreement Negotiations:** Depending upon the nature of the proposed transaction, the asset manager also may be asked to provide information/data for the preparation of the Letter of Intent (LOI) and the Purchase and Sale ("P&S") Agreement.

**Due Diligence:** The asset manager has a vital role in the due diligence process. At the beginning of due diligence, there may be some critical questions raised in the preliminary underwriting that need to be evaluated in more detail. Some of these may be market-related, such as evaluating competitive projects more extensively, or analyzing longer-term micro and macro economic factors that may impact demand issues in the local market.

During the due diligence process, the buyer is usually permitted to interview a representative of each tenant. A member of the asset management team, preferably the individual who will be assigned to manage the building, conducts these interviews.

Utilizing the asset manager to conduct the tenant interview can help to provide a foundation for a strong landlord-tenant relationship. This is reinforced significantly if, after the transaction is closed, the asset manager calls on each of the tenants with a checklist and timetable to correct problems mentioned during the interview.

In all of these areas, the asset manager brings skills and resources to the acquisition team necessary in determining whether to proceed with the transaction or to require modifications in the deal to bring it more in line with investor objectives.

**Final Underwriting:** In some cases, the terms of the P&S Agreement can be renegotiated to compensate the buyer for problems unearthed by the due diligence process. This compensation might be in the form of a lower price; a holdback of a portion of purchase funds until a problem can be corrected; a guarantee or warranty by the seller; or some other modification of the transaction. The asset manager can be a valuable resource for the acquisition team in these negotiations.

**Waive and Closing:** The asset manager assigned to the property should become familiar with the closing statement as soon as deposits have been waived. The closing statement is prepared by the title company from the perspective of both the buyer and seller. The closing statement details the purchase price, loans that are paid off (seller) or originated (buyer) as well as transaction costs, such as title and escrow fees, loan fees, and legal fees. The closing statement contains many of the opening entries in the books of account for the new property(ies) for which the asset manager will become responsible.

## Transition to Asset Management

A smooth and efficient transition of property from the seller to the buyer will appear seamless to the tenants and provide an excellent opportunity for a strong first impression of the investment manager as the new owner. There are several steps in a successful ownership transition:

**Acquisition Report:** All of the information collected in the due diligence and analytical processes are contained in the acquisition report, which is the investment manager's official record of the transaction.

As noted in Chapter 1, this report provides the background data and blueprint necessary to achieve a successful transition. In addition, the document provides the foundation for the asset manager's first year business plan.

Specific information from the Acquisition Report that the asset manager should know includes:

- ❏ Purchase price (both generally and on a dollars-per-square-foot basis)
- ❏ Projected holding period
- ❏ Space absorption projections, if applicable
- ❏ ARGUS/Excel model assumptions (suite by suite)
  - Lease rate
  - Annual increases
  - Term
  - Commission cost
  - Tenant improvement cost
  - Lease start dates
  - Concessions
  - Options
  - Special provisions
  - Expense "stop" (if applicable)

- Exit price and dollars per square foot

**Investment Partnership Agreement:** If the investment is held by a limited partnership, the asset manager should make certain that he/she understands the nature of the agreement and how it might affect ongoing management operations.

Specific information that the asset manager should know from this agreement includes:

- Structure of any debt on or to be placed on the property
- Background of all partners
    - Name
    - Amount invested
    - Real estate investment policy (written statement, if available)
    - Real estate strategy (written statement, if available)
- Distributions to limited partners during projected holding period
- Nominal dollars to investors
- Projected percentage return to investors

**Title-Holding Entity:** A title holding entity was established prior to close. The asset manager should review the incorporation documents in order to determine the state in which the new entity is domiciled and understand the powers/limitations that the entity possesses.

**ERISA and EBIT Issues:** If investing for or with a pension fund, ERISA[4] and Unrelated Business Taxable Income (UBIT) issues may have been identified in the due diligence process. The asset manager should fully understand these issues and be certain to manage the property in such a way that they do not become future problems.

**Property Accounting:** Information from the acquisition report and the closing statement provide many of the opening entries for the investment's property account. Bank accounts for the new holding entity also should be established prior to close. The asset manager should discuss these issues with accounting personnel and be certain that he/she fully understands how the bank accounts will be handled.

**Cash Management Procedures:** If an investment partner (e.g., pension fund) requires a lockbox for tenant rental payments, care must be taken that

---

[4] An example of an ERISA-related issue would be a situation in which selection of a property is tied to hiring members of the pension fund to construct or manage the project (union plans). Another example would be having a tenant in a property which is closely linked to the plan sponsor (corporate or public plans).

sufficient time is allowed to handle situations that might place the pension fund in danger of violating ERISA or other statutes.

**Mitigation Action Plan:** The final underwriting report may include a list of mitigation steps for various risks uncovered. If so, the asset manager is usually responsible for mitigating all risks that are assumed by the buyer, and immediately should prepare an action plan to accomplish this objective.

**Meet with Tenants:** Once the asset manager fully understands all aspects of the operation of the property, he/she is ready for kick-off meetings with the existing tenants. Prior to the meetings, the asset manager should review the lease abstract, the tenant's estoppels, and the tenant acquisition interview to be certain that he/she is aware of the tenant's existing rights and obligations, as well as the tenant's attitude towards the building and its prior management. If there are complaints from tenants, the asset manager should have an action plan to remedy them. If a need for additional space was mentioned in the interview, the asset manager should be prepared to discuss in detail the nature and magnitude of these needs.

## *Investment Holding Period*

The asset manager has direct responsibility for the performance of each property in his/her portfolio during the investment holding period.

**Tenant Relations:** One of the major changes in asset management best practices over the last several years has been the evolving view of the tenant (legal term) as a user of real estate "space" to being a "customer" (business term) of real estate "services." This is much more than merely a change in terminology; it represents a change in attitude on the part of the industry toward recognizing the tenant as fundamental to the ultimate success of a property and the true source of income and cash flow for the investment.

This makes good sense, because real estate is the "residual" of other business activities. If the building is not serving the specific needs of the customer (tenant), ultimately the customer will be lost to competing projects.

If the tenant is a major regional or national corporation, in which the leasing approval process is centralized, a negative experience with one property owner (asset management company) can adversely affect decisions regarding other buildings owned or managed by the same firm. Since customers also talk to each other through personal relationships and trade organizations, this may result in the loss of new customers and, over time, adversely affect the image of the building(s) in the business community. This directly reflects on the reputation of the investment manager as an owner and operator of commercial buildings.

This shift in perspective was accelerated by the dot-com and telecom implosion, and related recession that began in mid-2000, and the impact and reaction to the events of September 11, 2001. In addition, the consolidation of ownership in the industry has placed greater emphasis on the use of branding to build strong customer allegiance, which can often make a difference in tenant retention during economic downturns.

One of the best ways to enhance an investment manager's "brand" is through a customer-centric service orientation and high-level client relations. Steps in this process include:

**Tenant's Business:** Maintaining good personal relations with the building's customers (tenants) is one of the most important responsibilities of the asset manager. The editor of *Rent & Retain* magazine, as an example, maintains that roughly two-thirds of tenants are lost through a lack of personal contact.[5] As a result, more and more property owners are focusing on customer relations as a way to enhance the bottom line.

A first step in better understanding your customer is to acquire a thorough knowledge of the customer's business. In new acquisitions, this information generally is provided by the tenant interview, which ideally is conducted by the asset manager who will be assigned the property if it is acquired. This knowledge can be enhanced by an exploration of the firm's website, news releases, and, if the customer is a public company, public filings, and analyst reports.

For buildings that have been in the portfolio for some time, it may be necessary to resurvey the customer base. Each of these interviews should be personal and not done by mail, email, or telephone.[6] This allows the customer to expand on the questions and/or bring up issues that were not considered when the questionnaire was originally formulated. It also helps to build a direct personal relationship between the customer and the asset manager.

Key questions that need to be addressed include:

- What is the customer's core business(s)?
- What are the firm's major products/services?
- Who are their major competitors?
- How are they organized?
- Who are the key members of management?

---

[5] *Journal of Property Management*, September 1, 2002.

[6] In the case of an office tenant, the interview should be with the head of business operations. If the tenant is a large firm, this will most likely be the divisional head based in the subject office. In a smaller firm, it may be the CEO, COO, or CFO. Be sure that it's a person with knowledge of the firm's business operation.

**Tenant's Financial Condition:** Many landlords only check their customer's financial status when the original lease is negotiated, at the time of subsequent renegotiations, or when rent is in default. Unfortunately, problems may arise in the intervening period that may lead the tenant to look elsewhere for new space when the lease renewal comes up or, worse, declare bankruptcy along the way. By keeping in touch with the Company's customers on a regular basis, the asset manager will have a better idea of the current financial health of the tenant.[7]

Important information to update includes:

- Revenue growth trends
- Expense trends
- Overall profitability
- Receivable aging
- Quick ratios
- Vendor credit experience
- Credit ratings (if any)
- Available cash resources

It is also helpful to understand how susceptible the tenant firm is to cyclical and/or seasonal change.

**Tenant's Management of Real Estate Facilities:** Another important consideration is to understand how the tenant manages its operating properties. Key questions to be answered include:

- What is the firm's strategy/policies regarding the use of real estate?
- How are corporate real estate decisions made?
- What other facilities do they have in the area? Other cities?
- How does the subject building fit into the tenant's overall business and real estate strategy/policies?

**Tenant's View of the Building and its Management:** The final step is to gain the tenant's perspective on the subject building and its management. Areas of concern include:

- What is the tenant's view of the subject building (likes/dislikes)?
  - Tenant space
  - Parking

---

[7] Many leases have covenants requiring the submission of periodic financial statements, but they are not always enforced.

- Operating equipment (HVAC, plumbing, electricity, elevators, etc.)
❑ What is their view of the management of the building?
- Building management
- Janitorial
- Security
- Billing and collections
❑ What is the tenant's views on, and reaction to, the leasing process?

With this base of knowledge, the asset manager can begin building personal relationships with each of the tenants, fully cognizant of their operating characteristics, policy towards real estate, and overall economic health. In order to maintain credibility, building-related problems identified in the interview(s) must be dealt with as soon as possible following the interview. The resolution of the complaint(s) provides another opportunity to expand the personal relationship with the tenant while, at the same time, demonstrating that the investment manager cares about its customers.

## Lease Renewals

A recent survey of a 12 million square foot office portfolio with a 6 percent rollover indicated that $900,000 per year could be added to the bottom line for every 10 percent of expiring space that was renewed rather than re-tenanted.[8]

Renewal negotiations are even more critical during economic downturns, when additional space is coming on the market and rents are falling. This has been aggravated in recent years by rent spikes that left many tenants paying severally over-market rents. It's important, therefore, to assess each customer's situation and have a strategy for dealing with each challenge before it becomes an irremediable problem.

**Market Conditions:** All lease renewal strategies are subject to market conditions in the months leading up to lease expiration/termination. If vacancies are low and rents rising, the asset manager is in a position to maintain or raise rents, extend the term of the lease, renegotiate terms of the lease to be more favorable to the landlord, or, in some cases, all of the above. This is also a good time to explore an expansion of current space, either in the same building or another in the investment manager's investment portfolio, as long as no conflicts exist.

On the other side, the customer (tenant) is faced with a decision of paying increased rent in the future versus the near term costs of relocating, both in

---

[8] *Journal of Property Management*, Ibid.

terms of monetary costs such as the build-out of new space as well as the cost of staff downtime. Generally, every attempt should be made to treat customers fairly and attempt to retain not only their tenancy but their good will as well.

Over the last twenty years, landlord-favorable markets have occurred infrequently in the United States and often in limited locations. More typical is the situation of increasing vacancies, stable or falling rents, and intense competition for new tenants. Under these market conditions, the importance of maintaining good customer relations is paramount. It is equally important, however, to make certain that the tenant is worth keeping.

**Rights of the Parties:** The next step is to determine the rights of the parties. The following questions should be addressed:

- What are the notification requirements in the lease?
- Does the customer have an option to renew? If so, what are the renewal terms and conditions?
- Is the option renewal rent at "market" or a stipulated amount?
- Is the renewal conditioned on maintaining certain financial benchmarks?

**Tenant's Financial Condition:** By remaining current on the customer's financial condition, the asset manager should have a good understanding as to the current financial strength of the tenant firm as well as whether or not it is going to survive in the longer term. If there is no renewal option, or the option requires meeting certain financial conditions that are unlikely to be met, it's best to know this as early as possible so that marketing efforts to other prospective tenants can begin.

Based on this assessment, the asset manager has several alternatives:

- **Lease Renewal:** The simplest action is to renew the lease under its existing terms and conditions. If there is a renewal option, with no minimal financial requirements, there is also the possibility of a negotiated termination of the lease, which may turn out to be better for all concerned.
- **Lease Expansion:** If the customer's business operation is expanding and its financial statements are healthy, the renewing customer may be a good candidate for more space in the building, or a move to another portfolio asset.
- **Lease Termination:** In most cases, if a tenant's financial condition is tenuous, it's preferable to ask the tenant to leave at the end of the lease term rather than renew the lease, with the prospects of bankruptcy during the renewal period.

- **Reduction in Rent:** In situations where the option rent is over-market, the solution usually involves a negotiated rate at economics that approximate market. In these situations, the financial advantage to the landlord of keeping good tenants is apparent (compared to losing the tenant and having to go through the re-leasing process).
- **"Blend and Extend":** In user markets that have more space than there are tenants to fill it, and where rents are trending down, often it is in the best interest of the landlord to approach tenants well before the expiration of their lease, to offer a reduction in the scheduled rent in exchange for an early renewal and extension of the lease. This strategy helps the landlord to stabilize cash flow, albeit at a reduced level.
- **Reduction in Space:** Another alternative is a reduction in space. By keeping current regarding the customer's business operations and financial condition, the asset manager should have a reasonably good idea of whether an offer to reduce space is appropriate.
- **Relocation:** The tenant also can be relocated to less expensive space in the building.

In all situations, the asset manager should openly discuss the situation, well in advance of lease termination. Although circumstances will be different in each case, a good guideline is to begin these discussions six to twelve months in advance of the lease termination date.

## *New Leases*

**Internal Candidates:** When a new project is developed or an existing customer decides (or is asked) to leave a building, the re-leasing process begins. The first step is to find out if the vacant space can be leased to any of the existing customers. In the case of less-than-full floor space, adjacent customers may be good prospects for expansion. The availability of full floor space may open up an opportunity for less-than-full floor customers to expand, or for existing full floor customers to relocate to more attractive space (better views, more convenient access, etc.).

If it is not possible for customers to relocate within the building, there may be customers in other properties operated by the investment manager that might wish to relocate to the vacant space. Again, be aware that client/capital conflicts must be cleared first. The asset manager should continually be on the lookout for relocating tenants within the same market area to properties operated by the investment manager.

Even if tenants contacted do not want the space, the fact that the investment manager demonstrates an interest in meeting their continuing space requirements strengthens the relationship, and reinforces the customer's view of the investment manager as being a service-oriented "business partner" rather than merely a landlord. This also demonstrates the importance of the asset management team maintaining contact with its customers on a continuing basis, in order to know the current status of the tenant's business operation and its ongoing space requirements well in advance of lease expiration.

**External Candidates:** If there are no internal candidates, the vacating space goes on the market through the local brokerage community. The investment manager maintains continuing relations with leasing brokers and tenant representatives in each local market.

While the leasing team is responsible for generating external candidates, the asset manager should take the lead once a prospective customer has been identified.

It is at this stage that the asset manager begins the process of getting to know its customers -- developing information about the firm, its business operation, and how the customer manages and utilizes its their real estate operating facilities.

The asset manager also is expected to have a full understanding of all of the characteristics of the current rental market, competing properties, and the economics underlying the available space to be leased, including:

- **Market**
  - Size of market
  - Overall vacancy
  - Nature of the market vacancies
  - Absorption (by quarter)
  - Competitive projects under development
  - New construction planned
- **Competition (top five competing buildings)**
  - Space available
  - Location in the competitive properties of all available space
  - Lease expirations
  - Comparable lease transaction terms
- **Lease Terms**
  - Term
  - Rental rate
  - Concessions

- Tenant finish allowance
- Leasing commission
- Options

The asset manager must clearly convey to other members of the listing team his/her expectations for leasing the space. This is accomplished through consistent (weekly) project meetings (preferably in the vacant space) with an updated Leasing Status Report, also prepared weekly.

**Deal Approval Sheet:** The deal approval sheet is the final step in the closing of the lease transaction. This sheet compares the proposed lease transaction to the lease economics projected for the space and explains reasons for any substantive variations.

## Building Operations

The asset manager is responsible for the day-to-day operation of the building, including:

- Custodial
- Maintenance (building and grounds)
- Security
- Procurement

These duties are typically delegated to an experienced property manager-- either an employee of the investment management firm or a third-party service provider.

The property manager (internal or external) is a direct report to the asset manager on all matters related to operation of the building. In managing this relationship, the asset manager is generally responsible for:

- Approval of the annual budget
- Review/action in connection with major items identified in each monthly operating report from the property manager
- Implementation of the customer surveys
- Attendance at major tenant meetings
- Managing lease delinquencies and renewals

## Construction Management

The property manager is responsible for management of all on-site construction activities, including building repairs/improvements and customer space build-outs. Larger firms may have an employee who specializes in construction management, who also would report to the asset manager on any projects in his/her asset portfolio.

**Building Repair/Improvements:** While the property manager has lead responsibility for building repairs and improvements, the asset manager should remain abreast of progress on these activities so he/she can answer questions posed by tenants about issues such as scope of the project, current status, and anticipated completion date.

**Customer Space Build-outs:** The asset manager takes a greater role in customer space build-outs, since he/she is responsible for maintaining good customer relations, and there generally are reasons for ongoing tenant interface. This includes attendance at meetings with the space planner as well as ongoing discussions with the customer, with a view toward possible re-leasing of the space at some point in the future.

**New Building Development:** The asset manager is responsible for having general knowledge of new development projects and recent acquisitions in market areas where portfolio assets are located.

## Familiarity with Key Documents

The asset manager works closely with the property manager and the accounting department in maintaining accounting records for each property. This requires that the asset manager be fully aware of several key documents and reports underlying the investment process, including:

**Original Underwriting:** In order to manage a building successfully, it is important that the asset manager fully understand the original underwriting assumptions, including:

- Purchase price (total and per square foot)
- Exit price (total and per square foot)
- Projected holding period
- Absorption period
- Distributions during the holding period
- Lender requirements
- Amount of debt
- Equity investors
- Amount invested
- Percent return during absorption period
- Nominal dollars to investors

**Loan Agreement:** The asset manager also should understand all of the essential elements of loan documentation and terms for each asset in their portfolio. Key components include:

- Interest rate spread over the London Inter-Bank Overnight Rate (LIBOR)
- Loan term
- Breakdown between interest and principal amortization
- Renewal fee
- Required Loan to Value (LTV) ratio
- Required Debt Service Coverage Ratio (DSCR) ratio
- Conditions of default by both borrower and lender
- Reserve requirements (if any)
- Lender participation
- Property tax and insurance impounds (if any)

**Schedule of Distributions:** In limited partnership situations, the asset manager should also understand the projected underwriting distributions, when they are supposed to occur, and the allocations to each investor. The schedule of distributions is included in each property's annual budget.

## *Letters of Credit:*

**Property/Portfolio Analysis:** Periodically or upon special request, the asset manager is responsible for preparation of the following analytical reports:

**Cash Flow Analysis:** The original ARGUS/Excel suite-by-suite projections should be updated by the asset manager each quarter. Key elements that will require updating include:

- Lease rate(s)
- Annual rent increases
- Term
- Commission cost
- Suite improvement costs
- Lease start date
- Vacancy
- Expenses
- Inflation
- Financing terms

These updates are then compared to the original underwriting, in order to determine the effects of any reduction in rental income and/or acceleration of operating costs on project cash flow.

**Discounted Cash Flow Analysis (DCF):** Utilizing the assumptions of the annual cash flow analysis, the asset manager should develop a current estimate of the value of the property derived from a DCF, based on the property's business plan. The discount factor utilized in the analysis is the investor's target return, or in the case of investment partnerships, the return stated in the original partnership agreement.

**Annual Business Plan:** An important part of the asset management process is the development and annual review of a business plan for each property in the investment portfolio(s). The property annual business plan describes where the property stands in terms of the original investment underwriting, and the actions that will be taken by the asset manager during the year to enhance and position the property in the marketplace.

In developing the annual business plan, the asset manager reviews and possibly revises the original pro forma cash flow analysis to take into consideration recent events as well as new management initiatives that will be undertaken in the future.

**Responding to Unsolicited Offers ("Hold/Sell Analysis"):** In addition to monitoring the progress of a property in relation to the original investment underwriting, the asset manager also must be prepared to respond to unsolicited offers for individual properties in the portfolio. This requires a systematic process by which these offers can be evaluated against the original investment strategy and against the current annual business plan. The DCF value analysis provides a simple benchmark against which unsolicited offers can be evaluated.

In order to be considered, an all-cash offer should be at least equal to the estimate of the projected NPV of the property. This is based on the concept that cash in hand today is worth more than cash in the future, which is dependent upon the realization of a series of assumptions in the DCF analysis.[9]

In some circumstance, an outside buyer might be willing to pay more for the property than this minimum requirement. Specifically, the property may bring a higher price if:

---

[9] The investment manager also needs to review whether or not a replacement property can be acquired on *more* favorable terms.

- The potential buyer has a more optimistic view of the future opportunities for the property than the investment advisor does.
- The buyer is willing to accept a lower investment return.
- The buyer has a non-investment use for the property that results in a higher valuation. An example would be a company (perhaps an existing tenant) that wants to use the property as a headquarters building for its operations, or a buyer that is considering an adaptive reuse (e.g., converting office to condominiums or hotel) that is a higher and better use in the current market.
- The buyer has tax objectives that permit paying a higher price.

Regardless of the reason, the investment manager is faced with a decision that has to be made and justified to its investors. In reaching this decision, it should be established that:

- The investor has held the property for a sufficiently long period (generally, at least one year) to be able to evaluate its future potential.
- The NPV analysis is reasonably current.
- Other properties in the portfolio are not materially dependent upon the subject property.
- The offer does not require conditions adverse to the investment manager or its investors.
- All of the investors have acknowledged that they are willing to accept a return earlier than originally projected.[10]
- In the case of taxable investors, the investment manager has established the tax status of the property and whether or not investor(s) wish to undertake a Section 1031 ("like kind") Tax Deferred Exchange.

If the situation meets these additional criteria, then the sale is submitted to the investment committee for approval.

## *Financial Reporting*

The asset manager works closely with the internal and external accountants in preparing periodic financial reports for portfolio investors. The asset manager is directly responsible for a quarterly review of the assets under his/her

---

[10] This should have been established in the investment agreement, or subsequently acknowledged via the written consent of all investors.

management, which then becomes an important supplement to financial reports to the investors.

From time to time, the asset manager may be asked to prepare specialized reports on an asset or group of assets under his/her management.

## Investor Relations

The asset manager also may be asked to participate in meetings with investor partners, or in marketing presentations to prospective investors.

## Role in Asset Dispositions

As with the acquisition of assets, the asset manager is a vital link between the management of assets and their successful disposition.

**Role of an "Exit Strategy":** During the acquisition process, certain assumptions were made with respect to how and when a property would be sold, and at what price. Collectively, these assumptions are known as the "exit strategy."

The exit strategy is considered one of the most important elements of the investment process, because a property sale often represents the liquidity event all of the investors contemplate to achieve the projected returns.

Therefore, it is essential that an exit strategy be formulated and thoroughly understood by the investment advisor and the investors at the initiation of the investment process.

**Investment Committee:** If a property has achieved its exit strategy assumptions (or, in the case of an unsolicited offer, meets the criteria outlined previously), the analysis is presented to the investment committee along with a recommendation for disposition.

The investment committee then proceeds to weigh all of the factors and implications involved in the sale of the property and vote on a course of action.

**Premarketing Activities:** Once a property has been approved for sale by the investment committee, premarketing activities are initiated. Proper planning and execution of the premarketing activities help ensure a smooth and timely disposition process. A well-planned, carefully orchestrated disposition strategy is a direct reflection of the professionalism and industry perception of the investment manager.

**Broker Selection:** In most cases, targeted buyers are accessed through the real estate brokerage community. Although "off market," "principal to principal" transactions may occur, they are rare.

More importantly, the investment manager has a fiduciary responsibility to its shareholders and investment partners to do broad marketing and expose the property to as many potential buyers as possible, and may assume some degree of liability by not doing so. Therefore, most investment managers utilize the brokerage community to market their properties.

## Questions for Discussion

The following questions are designed to explore the major issues introduced in this chapter.

1. What are the major differences between an asset manager and a property manager? How are their roles complementary?
2. What are the responsibilities of an asset manager in the property acquisition process? Disposition process?
3. What are the key steps in a smooth transition of assets from acquisition to asset management?
4. What are the key elements of the acquisition report that the asset manager should be aware of in order to perform his/her asset management duties effectively?
5. What are some of the reasons for viewing the tenant as a "customer"?
6. What should the asset manager know about each of his/her tenants, and why?
7. What are the key steps the asset manager should take in renewing leases with existing tenants that are identified as "keepers"? How should those that are not be handled?
8. How should the asset manager approach possible internal candidates for new leases? External candidates?
9. How should the asset manager and the property manager work together in terms of building operations? Suite construction?
10. How does the asset manager work with the property accountant?
11. What is the role of the asset manager in responding to unsolicited offers?
12. What are some of the analytical procedures that the asset manager can utilize to keep on top of assets in his/her portfolio?

Please use these questions as a guide and not a format or a reflection of all of the questions that need to be addressed by the case.

# 7

# NOVATO FAIR SHOPPING CENTER[1]

## Tenant Restructuring

In spring 2002, Pamela Grant was reviewing the file on the Novato Fair Shopping Center, one of the properties in her portfolio of 12 retail properties. Pamela was an asset manager for Left Coast Advisors (LCA), an investment advisor to major pension funds, with 9 years of experience as an asset manager specializing in neighborhood and community shopping centers.

Pamela's current concern was developing a re-leasing strategy for three tenants whose leases expired in 2003. LCA's asset management policy was to take the initiative in lease renewals rather than waiting for the tenant to make a decision, which often came too late to change direction if it were a tenant that LCA wanted to keep.

This policy called for preparation of a detailed re-leasing strategy at least 12 months before the date of lease expiration. The asset manager was expected to recommend retaining, relocating, or replacing the tenant and present an action plan for implementing the recommendation.

In the case of Novato Fair, two of the leases would expire in April 2003 and one in October. The tenant of greatest concern was Rite Aid, a large national drug store chain which had experienced considerable financial problems in recent years and was closing outlets in many older centers in the Bay Area. Another national chain with a 2003 lease expiration was Radio Shack, which

---

[1]This case was prepared by John McMahan based on teaching materials developed by Dennis M. Williams, Senior Director, Northmarq Capital, Inc for his mortgage banking class at the University of San Francisco. Copyright © John McMahan, 2002 and 2004, all rights reserved.

also was reevaluating outlet locations as leases matured. The final turning tenant was Holiday Cleaners, a local dry cleaning operation.

Pamela had been out to the property on several occasions recently, as well as preparing a detailed review of competing centers. She was expected to have her recommendations completed by the end of the day and be prepared to support them at the second quarter asset review meeting the following day.

## Novato Fair

Novato Fair was a neighborhood shopping center located in the City of Novato in Marin County, north of San Francisco. The Center was originally developed in 1969 and has since undergone four renovations, but it still looked somewhat rundown. (See Exhibits 1 and 2 as well as Appendix B). LCA had purchased the property for $12,600,000 in 1994 at a price discount due to environmental contamination from a dry cleaning facility. LCA had subsequently cleaned up the contamination and replaced the dry cleaning operator.

Chapter 7 - Novato Fair Shopping Center     -153-

**Exhibit 1
Site Plan**

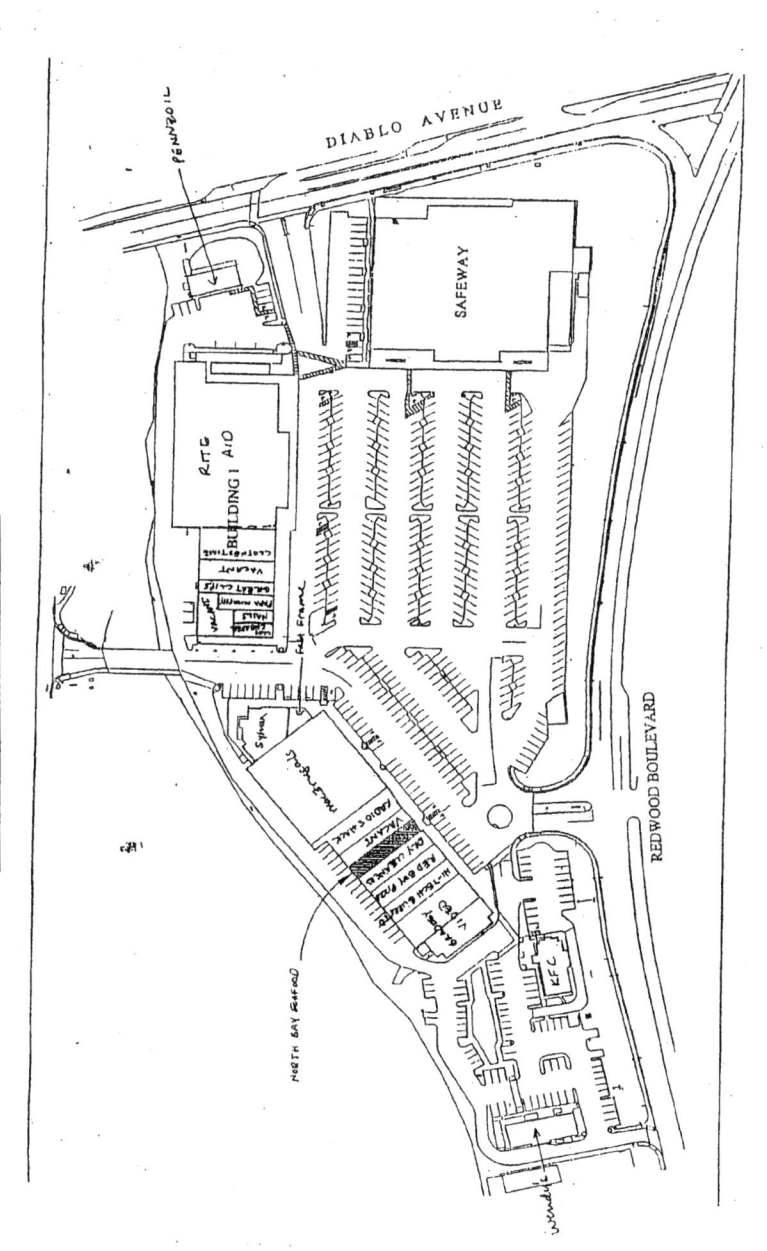

## Exhibit 2
## Property Description

| | |
|---|---|
| **Site** | 11.3 Acres (492,228 sq. ft.) |

**Net Rentable Area**

| Space | Sq. Ft. |
|---|---|
| Safeway | 51,199 |
| Rite Aid | 25,276 |
| MacFrugal's | 15,708 |
| Pennzoil Pad | 1,586 |
| Wendy's Pad | 2,450 |
| KFC Pad | 2,617 |
| In-Line Shops | 35,633 |
| Total | 134,469 |

| | |
|---|---|
| **Parking** | 530 Spaces |
| **Year Built** | 1969- Northern and Southern Retail Shops |
| | 1983- Safeway |
| | 1988- Wendy's |
| | 1989- KFC Restaurant |
| | 1990- Pennzoil |
| **Foundation** | Concrete slab over spread footings |
| **Construction** | Single-story tilt-up concrete structures, utilizing plywood roof decking, glue laminated wood girders and wood columns. Pad buildings are typical 2x4 wood-frame constructions. |
| **Roof** | Built-up asphalt systems with flood coat, gravel or mineral surfacing depending on location. |
| **HVAC:** | AC provided by roof-mounted packaged systems and split systems. Heat provided by the same packaged system. |
| **Plumbing Systems** | Plumbing systems are copper. |
| **Fire** | Wet-type fire protection systems. |
| **Interior Lighting** | Primarily fluorescent, per tenant specifications. |
| **Floor Coverings** | Primarily asphalt tile, per tenant specifications. |

## City of Novato

The City of Novato is located in Marin County, 29 miles north of San Francisco. Novato is 43 square miles in size with a population of 53,000. Incorporated on January 20, 1960, the city enacted local building laws that have helped the city maintain 3,500 acres of open space and parks. The low population density in Novato had resulted in a rural small town atmosphere which, when combined with the close proximity to the employment centers of San Francisco and Oakland, created a highly desirable place to live.

According to Jill Hill's June 2001 Real Estate Guide for Marin County, the median price for a house in Novato was $454,786. As of January 2001, the California Department of Finance reported the apartment occupancy rate for Novato at approximately 92%.

Novato historically has had a low unemployment rate. As of September 2001, there were 27,730 employed residents in the city, and the unemployment rate was 2.5%, which compared favorably to the state level of 5.2%.

## Marin Retail Market

Since 1980, the Marin retail market had experienced rapid increases in per capita income which had been largely responsible for the strong growth in retail sales. Marin County had over $2.9 billion in taxable retail sales during 2000 according to the Center for Continuing Study of the California Economy. This volume is expected to increase 23% by 2010.

The City of Novato's annual retail sales in 1999 were estimated at approximately $463.2 million, up 4.18% from the prior year's amount of $443.8 million. Novato Fair's annual retail sales accounted for 10% of the City's total sales. Since 1989, retail sales in the city had increased an average of 6.29% per year, a rate nearly double that of Marin County at 3.76%. Since this survey, Novato's rate of retail growth had consistently increased, roughly paralleling Marin County over the same period.

## Competition

As of the second quarter of 2001, Marin County contained approximately 6.12 million square feet of retail inventory with a vacancy rate of 3.2%. The total retail base for the City of Novato is 1.4 million square feet and has a vacancy of 2.8% (See Appendix A).

Retail shop rents in the County have remained relatively stable, ranging from $1.50-$3.00/sf/mo (NNN) even through the recession of the early 1990s. Regional mall space commands rents at the high end of this rental range while neighborhood shopping center rents are generally at the lower end (See Exhibits 6 - 8).

The supply of retail properties had remained relatively constant over the years. New construction was limited considerably by the stringent development controls imposed by county and city governments. Adjusting to the changes in county demographics, a number of existing centers had undergone renovations to capture the rapidly growing segment of upscale consumers.

Novato Fair was located near several other neighborhood and community centers. The most comparable retail centers included: Downtown Novato Center, Vintage Oaks at Novato, Nave Center, San Marin Plaza, The Square Shopping Center, and Tresch-Triangle Shopping Center. Nave Center and Downtown Novato Center were located within a one-mile radius of Novato Fair and were considered the most direct competition for Novato Fair.

## *First Tenant Repositioning*

In 2001, Pamela completed her first tenant repositioning of the property. This involved creating 4,050 SF of new space for Safeway's operation and leasing 5,220 SF of space to four new in-line tenants: Fast Frame, Cigarettes Cheaper, Gateway Nails, and Sylvan Learning Center.[2] This space was created from the move out of Clothestime (4,050 SF) and the use of 1,170 SF of then-vacant space. Exhibit 9 is a revised pro forma operating statement based on the repositioning.

## *New Tenant Repositioning Recommendation*

As Pamela pored over the figures for what seemed to be an eternity, she had mixed feelings about her recommendations. She knew she would have to come to a conclusion quickly and begin preparing her report if she were going to be prepared for the asset review meeting the following day. She also made a resolution to stop drinking double-strength cafe lattés and chewing on her third pen in a week.

---

[2] As is common with most retail leases, the LCA had the right to relocate in-line tenants, at its own expense.

## Chapter 7 - Novato Fair Shopping Center -157-

### Exhibit 3
### Rent Roll

| | Tenant | Sq.Ft. | Lease Comm. | Lease Expir. | Base Rent/SF | Annual Rent | Comments |
|---|---|---|---|---|---|---|---|
| Anchors: | Safeway | 51,199 | Sep-02 | May-28 | $0.33 | 200,188 | |
| | Rite Aid | 25,276 | Oct-83 | Oct-03 | $0.35 | 107,625 | |
| | MacFrugal's | 15,708 | Sep-94 | Jan-10 | $0.70 | 132,831 | |
| | **Total Anchors** | **92,183** | | | **$0.40** | **440,644** | |
| Pads: | Pennzoil | 1,586 | Oct-90 | Oct-10 | $2.73 | 51,894 | |
| | Wendy's | 2,450 | Jun-88 | May-08 | $1.95 | 57,246 | 6/03:$2.38 |
| | KFC | 2,617 | Jul-89 | Aug-09 | $1.95 | 61,377 | 8/02: $1.95; 8/03: $2.02; 8/03: $2.08; 8/04: $2.08; 8/07:2.28; 8/08: $2.35 |
| | **Total Pad** | **6,653** | | | **$2.14** | **170,517** | 8/05: $2.15; 8/06: $2.21; |
| In-line: | Bradley Video | 7,050 | Feb-00 | Jan-09 | $1.54 | 130,073 | |
| | North Bay Seafood | 3,000 | Jul-86 | Mar-06 | $2.31 | 83,025 | |
| | Radio Shack | 2,850 | Nov-91 | Apr-03 | $2.39 | 81,795 | |
| | Holiday Cleaners | 2,113 | May-95 | Apr-03 | $1.66 | 41,996 | 5/02: $1.65 |
| | Red Boy Pizza | 1,847 | Dec-97 | Dec-05 | $1.41 | 31,340 | |
| | High Tech Burrito | 1,400 | May-00 | Jun-05 | $2.79 | 46,863 | |
| | Great Clips | 1,340 | Feb-98 | Feb-05 | $1.88 | 30,307 | 2/02: $1.91; 2/03: $1.99 |
| | Papa Murphy's Pizza | 1,080 | Dec-97 | Nov-04 | $1.94 | 25,080 | |
| | Fast Frame | 900 | May-99 | Apr-05 | $2.66 | 28,770 | 4/03: $2.68; 5/03: $2.75; 5/04: $2.84 |
| | Cigarettes Cheaper | 770 | Mar-00 | Mar-05 | $2.31 | 21,316 | 3/05:$2.50 |
| | Gateway Nails | 750 | Apr-00 | Apr-05 | $2.13 | 19,188 | 4/02/: $2.16;4/03: $2.25; 4/04: $2.34 |
| | Sylvan Learning Center | 2,800 | Mar-99 | Mar-04 | $1.70 | 57,195 | *Tenant has vacated, but is still paying rent.* |
| | **Total In-line** | **25,900** | | | **$1.92** | **596,948** | |
| | Vacant Shops | 9,733 | | | $2.15 | 251,111 | |
| | **Total In-line** | **35,633** | | | **$1.98** | **848,059** | |
| | **Gross Income** | **134,469** | | | **$0.90** | **1,459,220** | |
| | Total Shops Leases | 124,736 | 93% | | | | |
| | Shops to be Leased | 9,733 | 7% | | | | |
| | | **134,469** | | | | | |

## Exhibit 4 – Tenant Sales History

| Tenant | Sq. Ft. | Yrs. In Bus. | # of Stores | 1998 Annual Sales | 1998 Sales/SF | 1999 Annual Sales | 1999 Sales/SF | 2000 Annual Sales | 2000 Sales/SF | 2001 5-Mo. YTD | 2001 Change of Sales |
|---|---|---|---|---|---|---|---|---|---|---|---|
| **Anchors** | | | | | | | | | | | |
| Safeway | 42,799 | 74 | 1,650 | 26,963,000 | $630 | 28,162,000 | $658 | 29,830,944 | $697 | N/A | N/A |
| Rite Aid | 25,276 | 38 | 3,800 | 5,182,000 | $205 | 5,182,000 | $205 | 5,180,170 | $205 | N/A | N/A |
| MacFrugal's | 15,708 | 12 | 1,200 | 2,215,000 | $141 | 2,498,000 | $159 | 2,601,994 | $166 | N/A | N/A |
| **Total Anchors** | **83,783** | | | **34,360,000** | **$410** | **35,842,000** | **$428** | **37,613,108** | **$449** | – | – |
| **Pads** | | | | | | | | | | | |
| Pennzoil | 1,586 | 111 | 3,000 | 882,000 | $556 | 923,000 | $582 | 958,768 | $605 | 425,585 | 11.39% |
| Wendy's | 2,450 | 36 | 5,500 | 688,000 | $281 | 730,000 | $298 | 658,812 | $269 | 285,008 | -0.43% |
| KFC | 2,617 | 50 | 300 | 877,000 | $335 | 924,000 | $353 | 956,435 | $365 | 419,151 | 11.24% |
| **Total Pads** | **6,653** | | | **2,447,000** | **$368** | **2,577,000** | **$387** | **2,574,015** | **$387** | **1,129,744** | **8.62%** |
| Bradley Video | 7,050 | 12 | 10 | 860,000 | $122 | 860,000 | $122 | 879,193 | $125 | 392,888 | 5.02% |
| Clothestime | 4,050 | 26 | 276 | 421,000 | $104 | 429,000 | $106 | 407,921 | $101 | N/A | – |
| North Bay Seafood (1) | 3,000 | 11 | 1 | 225,000 | $75 | 250,314 | $83 | 261,523 | $87 | 62,718 | -1.66% |
| Radio Shack | 2,850 | 79 | 7,100 | 650,000 | $228 | 707,078 | $248 | 842,738 | $296 | 314,601 | -8.30% |
| Holiday Cleaners | 2,113 | 15 | 161 | 70,000 | $33 | 50,844 | $24 | 69,021 | $33 | 31,482 | 15.30% |
| Red Boy Pizza (2) | 1,847 | 2 | 11 | 235,000 | $127 | 340,000 | $184 | 382,158 | $207 | 25,225 | 4.84% |
| High Tech Burrito (2) | 1,400 | 16 | 15 | 763,000 | $545 | 777,000 | $555 | 714,066 | $510 | 227,647 | -5.82% |
| Great Clip | 1,340 | 18 | 1,301 | 158,000 | $118 | 180,000 | $134 | 169,933 | $127 | 62,482 | -11.32% |
| Papa Murphy's Pizza | 1,080 | 20 | 360 | 355,000 | $329 | 382,000 | $354 | 353,100 | $327 | 70,330 | -9.85% |
| **Total In-Line** | **24,730** | | | **3,737,000** | **$151** | **3,976,236** | **$161** | **4,079,653** | **$165** | **1,287,373** | **-2.31%** |
| **Total In-Place** | **115,166** | | | | | | | | | | |

(1) These are 3-mo. YTD numbers.  (2) These are 4-mo. YTD numbers.

## Exhibit 5
## Tenant Lease Rollover

| Tenant | Lease Exp. | Sq.Ft. | % of Total | Annual Rent | % of Total |
|---|---|---|---|---|---|
| **2001** | | | | | |
| Shops To Be Leased | - | 9,733 | | 251,111 | |
| **Total 2001** | | **9,733** | **7.2%** | **251,111** | **18.2%** |
| **2003** | | | | | |
| Radio Shack | Apr-03 | 2,850 | | 81,795 | |
| Holiday Cleaners | Apr-03 | 2,113 | | 41,996 | |
| Rite Aid | Oct-03 | 25,276 | | 107,625 | |
| **Total 2003** | | **30,239** | **22.5%** | **231,416** | **16.8%** |
| **2004** | | | | | |
| Sylvan Learning Center | Mar-04 | 2,800 | | 57,195 | |
| Papa Murphy's Pizza | Nov-04 | 1,080 | | 25,080 | |
| **Total 2004** | | **3,880** | **2.9%** | **82,275** | **6.0%** |
| **2005** | | | | | |
| Great Clips | Feb-05 | 1,340 | | 30,307 | |
| Cigarettes Cheaper | Mar-05 | 770 | | 21,316 | |
| Gateway Nails | Apr-05 | 750 | | 19,188 | |
| Fast Frame | Apr-05 | 900 | | 28,770 | |
| High Tech Burrito | Jun-05 | 1,400 | | 46,863 | |
| Red Boy Pizza | Dec-05 | 1,847 | | 31,340 | |
| **Total 2005** | | **7,007** | **5.2%** | **177,784** | **12.9%** |
| **2006** | | | | | |
| North Bay Seafood | Mar-06 | 3,000 | | 83,025 | |
| **Total 2006** | | **3,000** | **2.2%** | **83,025** | **6.0%** |
| **2008** | | | | | |
| Wendy's | May-08 | 2,450 | | 57,246 | |
| **Total 2008** | | **2,450** | **1.8%** | **57,246** | **4.2%** |
| **2009** | | | | | |
| Bradley Video | Jan-09 | 7,050 | | 130,073 | |
| KFC | Aug-09 | 2,617 | | 61,377 | |
| **Total 2009** | | **9,667** | **7.2%** | **191,450** | **13.9%** |
| **2010** | | | | | |
| MacFrugal's | Jan-10 | 15,708 | | 132,831 | |
| Pennzoil | Oct-10 | 1,586 | | 51,894 | |
| **Total 2010** | | **17,294** | **12.9%** | **184,724** | **13.4%** |
| **2028** | | | | | |
| Safeway | May-28 | 51,199 | | 200,188 | |
| **Total 2028** | | **51,199** | **38.1%** | **200,188** | **14.5%** |
| **Grand Total** | | **134,469** | **100.0%** | **1,376,195** | **100.0%** |

## Exhibit 6
## Comparable Properties

| | Name/Location | Sale Date | NRA (SF) | Year Built | Sale Price | Price/ SF | Cap Rate | Occ. | |
|---|---|---|---|---|---|---|---|---|---|
| 1 | Fiesta Plaza Shopping Center 2001-2035 Novato Blvd. Novato, CA | Aug-01 | 46,562 | 1964 | $5,125,000 | $110 | 8.46% | 95% | Small neighborhood center with Salvation Army thrift store as the main tenant. Some upper level office |
| 2 | Linda Mar Shopping Center 1215-1430 Linda Mar Blvd. Pacifica, CA | Jun-01 | 168,480 | 1989 | $21,084,250 | $125 | 8.67% | 85% | Community center anchored by Safeway, Rite Aid and Ross Dress for Less. |
| 3 | The Square Shopping Center 18615 Sonoma Highway Sonoma, CA | Apr-01 | 78,272 | 1975 | $7,585,000 | $97 | 9.50% | 95% | Neighborhood center anchored by Long's Drugs. |
| 4 | Broadway Point Broadway & Mt. Diablo Blvd. Walnut Creek, CA Buyer: UBS; Seller: Wilson, Meany | Jan-01 | 81,435 | 1998 | $24,805,000 | $305 | 7.75% | 100% | Anchored by Eddie Bauer, Williams Sonoma, Pottery Barn, and others. Superior to the subject in terms of location and tenant mix. |
| 5 | Quinto Village 18736-18860 Cox Ave. Saratoga, CA (Santa Clara Co.) | Jan-01 | 80,579 | 1951/ 1990 | $12,710,000 | $158 | 8.60% | 100% | a 26,000 sq. ft. grocer. This center has a superior location in The Silicon Valley, and is located just south of Saratoga Ave. and east of Hwy85. Location, appeal, and tenant mix is superior to the subject. |
| 6 | Union Square Marketplace One Union Square Union City, CA | Jan-01 | 189,445 | 1990 | $27,162,500 | $143 | 8.75% | 98% | Neighborhood shopping center, located approx. 60 miles south of the subject. The anchor tenant is Gene Quito Market, Anchor tenants are Safeway and Rite Aid. |
| 7 | Warm Springs Plaza 44645-46547 Mission Blvd. Fremont, CA | Dec-00 | 121,481 | 1986 | $26,855,000 | $221 | 8.20% | 100% | Neighborhood center anchored by Albertson's and Long's Drugs. |
| 8 | Powell Street Plaza SEC Shellmound St. & Christie Emeryville, CA (Alameda Co.) | In Contract | 165,549 | 1988 | $44,075,000 | $266 | 8.32% | 100% | This is a listing of a Community/lifestyle center located approx. 60 miles southeast of the subject. The center is located near a major freeway (HW 80) and just over the Bay Bridge from San Francisco. The center is anchored by Circuit City, Trader Joe's, and Ross Dress for Less, and New York Fabrics. Constructed in 1988 it is in good overall condition. This is a good comparable given the tenant mix and a proximity to the freeway. |

## Exhibit 7
## Anchor Rent Comparables

| | Tenant/Address | Built/Renov | Anchor | Leased SF | Lease Start Date | Term (Yrs) | In-line Shop Rent/SF | Expense | Comparison to Subject |
|---|---|---|---|---|---|---|---|---|---|
| 1 | Saratoga Plaza Saratoga Ave. @ Hwy. 280 Saratoga, CA | 1975 | Lion Foods | 33,300 | May-00 | 20 | $1.03 | NNN | Second-generation anchor tenant suite, formerly occupied by Albertson's. Step rent adjustments every 5th year. |
| 2 | Marina Shopping Center 10118 Bandley Drive Saratoga, CA | 1979 | Marina Foods | 31,416 | Jul-01 | 25 | $1.05 | NNN | Second-generation anchor tenant suite, formerly occupied by Railey's. Rental rates are flat over the term. |
| 3 | Best Buy 1840 Fitzgerald Drive Pinole, CA | 2000 | Best Buy | 46,217 | Jan-00 | 20 | $1.39 | NNN | Freestanding retail warehouse building in Contra Costa County. Located in developing retail hub just off Hwy. 80. Annual 3% CPI increases. |
| 4 | Burlington Coat Factory 3111 W. Rohnert Park Expry. Rohnert Park, Ca | 1985 | Burlington Coat Factory | 85,340 | Apr-99 | 10 | $0.51 | NNN | Second-generation retail bldg., formerly occupied by Kmart. The tenant refurbished the building at it's own cost. Rent is flat for the term. |
| 5 | Ravenswood Shopping Center East Bayshore Road at Pulgas Ave. East Palo Alto, CA | 2000 | Best Buy | 45,000 | Feb-01 | 25 | $2.31 | NNN | Located in new Power Center. Co-Anchored with Home Depot and Circuit City. Freestanding bldg. 3% annual increases. |

(1) In-place rent after Safeway expansion.

## Exhibit 8
## In-Line Store Rent Comparables

| | Tenant/Address | Built/ Renov. | Anchors | Total SF | Occup. | Start Date | Term (Yrs) | Leased SF | Shop Rent/SF | Comparison to Subject |
|---|---|---|---|---|---|---|---|---|---|---|
| 1 | Triangle Center 1559 South Novato Blvd. Novato, CA | 1963 | Dance Studio | 41,200 | 100% | Nov-00 | 3 | 1,600 | $1.04 | Annual CPI increases. This is a Strip Center with local tenants. Inferior to the subject. |
| 2 | San Marin Plaza NWC San Andreas & San Marin Novato, CA | 1984 | Apple Market | 70,375 | 84% | Jan-01 | 5 | 1,500 | $1.28 | Annual CPI increases. This is a neighborhood center with local tenant mix. Inferior tenant mix to the subject. Six vacancies. |
| 3 | Nave Shopping Center 1535 South Novato Blvd. Novato, CA | 1970 | Bell Market US Post Office | 110,500 | 93% | Feb-01 | 5 | 1,500 | $1.18 | Annual CPI increases. Older neighborhood center anchored by Bell Market. |
| 4 | Downtown Novato Center SWC 7th and Grant Ave. Novato, CA | | Albertson's Long's Drugs Best Buy | 160,000 | 99% | Jun-01 | 5 | 4,500 | $1.79 | Annual CPI increases. Older community center in downtown Novato. |
| 5 | Vintage Oaks at Novato SEC Rowland Blvd. at Hwy 101 Novato, CA | 1992 | Costo Macy's Furn. Target | 580,341 | 97% | May-01 | 5 | 1,030 | $2.31 | Annual CPI increases. Regional Center with superior appeal and tenant mix. Several new leases in mid to late 2000. |
| 6 | The Square Shopping Center 18615 Sonoma Highway Sonoma, CA | 1974 | Bell Market Long's Drugs | 78,272 | 93% | Dec-01 | 5 | 1,600 | $1.38 | Older neighborhood center anchored by Bell Market and Long's Drugs. Inferior overall to the subject. |

## Exhibit 9
## Pro Forma – Safeway Expansion

| | | | | | | | |
|---|---|---|---|---|---|---|---|
| **Potential Gross Income** | | | | | | | $1,923,403 |
| _Rental Income_ | | | | | | | |
| Major Anchors | 92,183 | sf @ | $0.40 | /sf | 440,644 | | |
| Pads | 6,653 | sf @ | $2.14 | /sf | 170,517 | | |
| Shops Leased | 25,900 | sf @ | $1.92 | /sf | 596,948 | | |
| Vacant Shops | 9,733 | sf @ | $2.15 | /sf | 251,111 | | |
| **Total Rental Inc.** | **134,469** | **sf @** | **$0.90** | **/sf** | **1,459,220** | | |
| _Reimbursements_ | | | | | | | |
| Anchor Exp. Recoveries | | | $0.29 | /sf | 315,644 | | |
| Non Anchor Exp. Recoveries | | | $0.24 | /sf | 148,539 | | |
| **Total** | **134,469** | **sf @** | **$1.19** | **/sf** | **1,923,403** | | |
| **Vacancy @** | 5.5% | 1 | | | | | 79,900 |
| **Effective Income** | | | | | | | **$1,843,503** |
| **Expenses** | | | | | | | **$571,500** |
| | | | $/sf | | Total | | |
| Operating Expenses | | | $3.74 | | 503,100 | | |
| Management @ | 3.0% | | $0.41 | | 55,000 | | |
| Replacement Reserve @ | | | $0.10 | | 13,400 | | |
| **Total Expenses** | | | **$4.15** | | **571,500** | | |
| **Net Operating Income** | | | | | | | **$1,272,000** |

| | _Vacancy (none on_ | % |
|---|---|---|
| 1 | _reimbursements)_ | Vac. |
| | Safeway | 0.0% |
| | Rite Aid / McFrugal's | 5.0% |
| | Pads | 5.0% |
| | In-line Shops | 7.0% |
| | **Weighted Total** | **5.5%** |

## Appendix A
## Marin Real Estate Market

Marin County Vacancy Estimates - Second Quarter, 2001          back

View Previous Vacancy Report

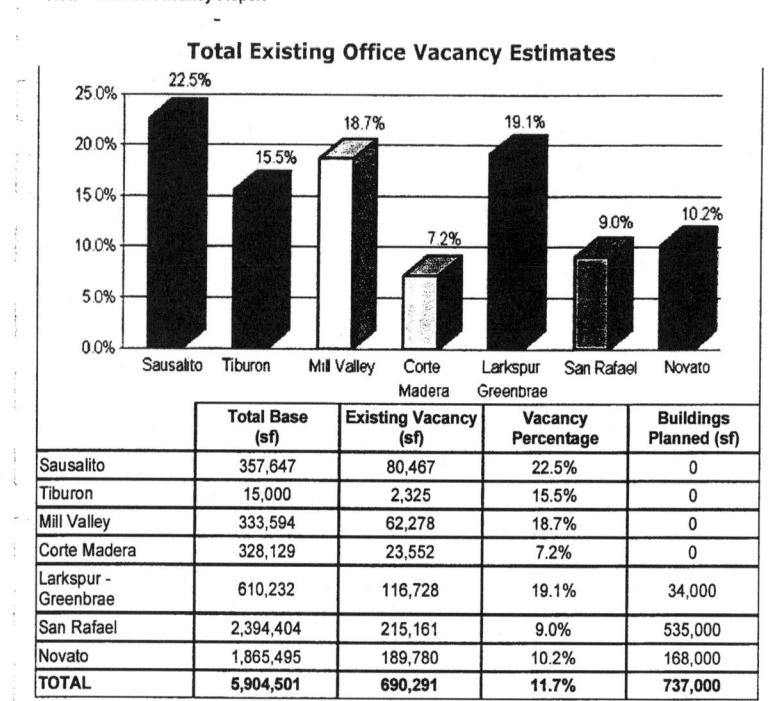

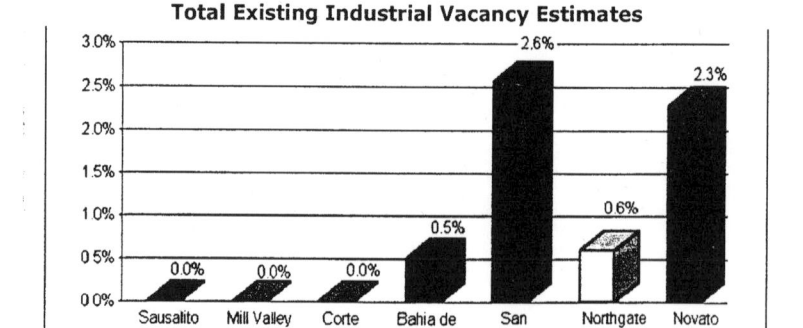

### Total Existing Office Vacancy Estimates

- Sausalito: 22.5%
- Tiburon: 15.5%
- Mill Valley: 18.7%
- Corte Madera: 7.2%
- Larkspur Greenbrae: 19.1%
- San Rafael: 9.0%
- Novato: 10.2%

|  | Total Base (sf) | Existing Vacancy (sf) | Vacancy Percentage | Buildings Planned (sf) |
|---|---|---|---|---|
| Sausalito | 357,647 | 80,467 | 22.5% | 0 |
| Tiburon | 15,000 | 2,325 | 15.5% | 0 |
| Mill Valley | 333,594 | 62,278 | 18.7% | 0 |
| Corte Madera | 328,129 | 23,552 | 7.2% | 0 |
| Larkspur - Greenbrae | 610,232 | 116,728 | 19.1% | 34,000 |
| San Rafael | 2,394,404 | 215,161 | 9.0% | 535,000 |
| Novato | 1,865,495 | 189,780 | 10.2% | 168,000 |
| **TOTAL** | **5,904,501** | **690,291** | **11.7%** | **737,000** |

### Total Existing Industrial Vacancy Estimates

- Sausalito: 0.0%
- Mill Valley: 0.0%
- Corte Madera: 0.0%
- Bahia de Rafael: 0.5%
- San Rafael: 2.6%
- Northgate: 0.6%
- Novato: 2.3%

http://www.keegancoppin.com/research/vacancy/2001/marin_2001_2nd.htm

## Appendix B
## Market Report

| | Total Base (sf) | Existing Vacancy (sf) | Vacancy Percentage | Buildings Planned (sf) |
|---|---|---|---|---|
| Sausalito | 455,000 | 0 | 0.0% | 0 |
| Mill Valley | - 126,000 | 0 | 0.0% | 0 |
| Corte Madera | 313,500 | 0 | 0.0% | 0 |
| Bahia de Rafael | 698,000 | 3,500 | 0.5% | 0 |
| San Rafael | 2,575,000 | 66,033 | 2.6% | 0 |
| Northgate | 516,188 | 3,100 | 0.6% | 0 |
| Novato | 1,778,659 | 40,634 | 2.3% | 0 |
| TOTAL | 6,462,347 | 113,267 | 1.8% | 0 |

### Total Existing Retail Vacancy Estimates

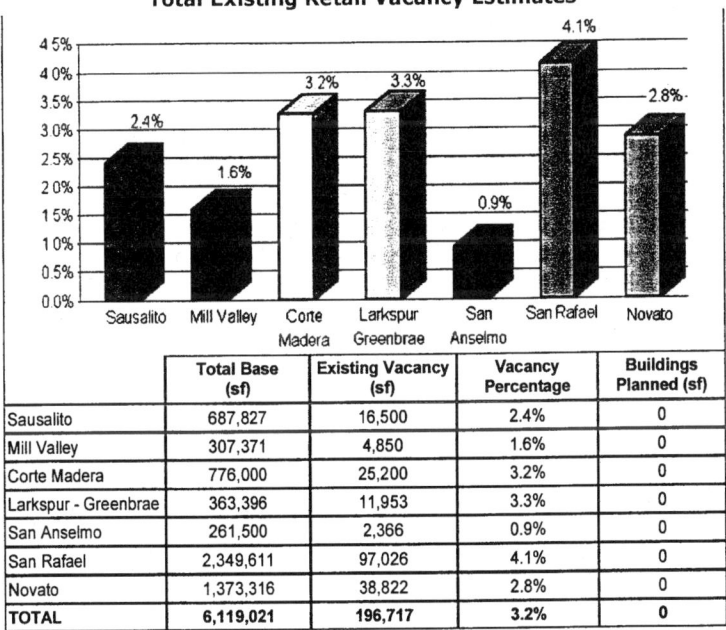

Sausalito: 2.4%
Mill Valley: 1.6%
Corte Madera: 3.2%
Larkspur Greenbrae: 3.3%
San Anselmo: 0.9%
San Rafael: 4.1%
Novato: 2.8%

| | Total Base (sf) | Existing Vacancy (sf) | Vacancy Percentage | Buildings Planned (sf) |
|---|---|---|---|---|
| Sausalito | 687,827 | 16,500 | 2.4% | 0 |
| Mill Valley | 307,371 | 4,850 | 1.6% | 0 |
| Corte Madera | 776,000 | 25,200 | 3.2% | 0 |
| Larkspur - Greenbrae | 363,396 | 11,953 | 3.3% | 0 |
| San Anselmo | 261,500 | 2,366 | 0.9% | 0 |
| San Rafael | 2,349,611 | 97,026 | 4.1% | 0 |
| Novato | 1,373,316 | 38,822 | 2.8% | 0 |
| TOTAL | 6,119,021 | 196,717 | 3.2% | 0 |

Copyright © by Keegan & Coppin Company, Inc., all rights reserved. Text, graphics, and HTML code are protected.

http://www.keegancoppin.com/research/vacancy/2001/marin_2001_2nd.htm

## Questions for Discussion

Questions that should be addressed in this case include:

1. What is unique about the Marin County retail market?
2. What is the general impact of "constrained growth" public policies on retail development and operations?
3. How does Novato compare to other Marin County communities as an attractive location for retail?
4. Why are neighborhood shopping centers attractive as a real estate investment? What are the drawbacks?
5. What are the specific attractions of Novato Fair? Drawbacks?
6. Did Left Coast Associates (LCA) "buy right" in acquiring Novato Fair? Why?
7. Why are tenants slow to move out of centers like Novato Fair?
8. What was the strategy behind the First Tenant Repositioning (Safeway, et. al.)? Do you think it was a good move on the part of LCA? Why?
9. What should Pamela recommend in terms of the New Repositioning? Why?

Please use these questions as a guide and not a format or a reflection of all of the questions that need to be addressed by the case.

# 8

# LODESTAR, INC.[1]

## Lease Negotiation

## Case A: JIM MARONEY

In June, 2001, Jim Maroney was in his Boston office, putting the final touches on a leasing package for Lodestar, Inc., a prospective major tenant for the Plano Office Center, a new office project that had recently been completed by his firm, Centaur Advisors (Centaur).

Allison Bowers, Lodestar's Director of Real Estate, was due in his office that afternoon to finalize a lease term sheet. If they could reach agreement on the lease terms, Jim planned to take it to Centaur's Investment Committee at their weekly meeting in two days. If the Investment Committee approved the terms, a formal lease could be negotiated with the firm to take over approximately half of the space in what was still an empty office building.

Lodestar was a six-year-old high technology firm that had survived the dot-com meltdown of the past 12 months. The firm was based in the San Francisco Bay Area but wished to relocate to Dallas to reduce operating costs and assure reliable energy availability. The firm was considering occupying 50% of the building on a 10-year lease with a rental adjustment to market at the end of the fifth year.

While he was very supportive of the leasing proposal, Jim was concerned about certain aspects of the lease, particularly the special nature of the tenant

---

[1] This case was prepared by John McMahan in 2002. Copyright © 2002 and 2004 all rights reserved.

improvements, which would have to be financed by Centaur. Jim had asked for a Letter of Credit (LC) supporting the above-standard improvements to which Lodestar had agreed. Jim was worried, however, about the terms of the LC and whether Centaur was really protected against a sizeable cost that they would probably not be able to recover if Lodestar defaulted on its lease.

Jim also was worried about the overall office market in Dallas and, frankly, nationally, as a result of the economic downturn into which the nation seemed to be sinking. The weak market had forced him to offer a rent lower than the $19.00 per square foot asking rate for the ground floor, which probably meant that the rest of the building would lease at less than pro forma as well.

## Centaur Advisors

Jim was Senior Vice President of Asset Management for Centaur Advisors, a Boston-based investment advisor. Centaur was formed in 1988 to provide real estate investment advisory services for pension plans, endowment funds, and foundations. The firm had grown over the years to the point where, by 2001, it managed over $3.0 billion in client assets, consisting of 110 properties in 22 markets across the county. Centaur's investments included office buildings, warehouses, "flex" R&D buildings, shopping centers, hotels, and apartments. Historically, the firm had overweighted to suburban office and industrial buildings and by the summer of 2001, these properties comprised over half of Centaur's portfolio.

Centaur's investment strategy was to focus on newly developed properties located in growth markets that had a lower cost advantage at the time of acquisition or development. The firm generally invested through joint venture arrangements with local developers. In terms of investment performance, Centaur had outperformed the NCREIF index over the prior three years.[2]

## High Technology Office Program

One of the reasons for Centaur's superior investment performance was a series of successful high technology suburban office buildings developed for its clients. The projects, almost all of which were located in rapidly growing markets, were essentially industrial buildings that had been designed in such a way as to make them attractive to office users. The key ingredients in this strategy were:

- Rapidly growing market

---

[2] National Council of Real Estate Investment Fiduciaries.

- High profile suburban location
- Located near a fiber-optic service line
- Two-story design
- Abundant parking
- Cost effective rents (lower than Class A rates)
- Open plan designed for flexible interior office layout
- Minimal core areas

The markets were selected based on Centaur's ongoing research as well as continuing discussions with a series of local developers who Centaur relied upon to generate new projects within their target markets. Suburban locations were preferred not only because of lower land costs but also because of their proximity to quality residential and shopping areas. Parking was provided at a ratio of five stalls per 1,000 sq. ft and ideally in such a manner that would surround the building so that tenants and their employees could have rapid access to their spaces. This intent was reinforced by having multiple entrances to the buildings.

A key ingredient in the success of the program was having large open work areas with an absence of columns. This space configuration allowed tenants to arrange and rearrange their space as various projects teams were organized and disbanded. It also permitted employers to increase employee densities, thereby lowering rent-per-employee costs.[3] Centaur found that the combination of lower rents and higher employee densities was a powerful tool in attracting high quality tenants. Interestingly, many of Centaur's tenants were not dot-com firms but rather "old economy" Fortune 500 companies.

Another key was the availability of fiber-optic trunk service at or near the building site. Most tenants required at least T-1 capacity on a 24/7 basis. To date, Centaur had provided this capability internally but was facing increasing pressure from tenants and investors to contract with outside firms to install and maintain the service.

The employees of most of the firms in the high-technology program were generation X-ers in their 20s and 30s. The open space design generally appealed to the "open" organizational structure that many X-ers preferred. In most of the buildings, there was a common area containing several campus-type amenities such as a snack bar, nap room, laundry pick-up, and in some of the larger projects, a concierge to handle personal tasks for the employees.

---

[3] This lower ratio was generally a goal of most employers. The average space per employee dropped from 220 sq. ft in 1992 to 193 sq. ft in 1999 (Source: Building Owners and Managers Association).

Depending upon the investment objectives of the client, the projects would be sold within a 3-5 year period. Three projects had been sold to date with IRRs of 21.0%, 26.5%, and 40.4% annually[4].

The Plano Office Center, located in the Dallas/Fort Worth metro area, was designed to be just such a project.

## The Dallas/Fort Worth Metropolitan Area

With 5 million people, Dallas/Fort Worth was the fifth largest metropolitan area in the U.S. and the largest in the State of Texas. Almost one million residents arrived after 1990, resulting in a 23.5% increase for this period. Population was expected to increase another 12% by 2005. Dallas' median household income was the highest in Texas ($51,516) but considerably lower than other major metro areas in the Nation.

Dallas/Fort Worth's economic structure had several overriding characteristics that strongly influenced its short and long-term growth rates. A well-diversified economy minimized market risk against a downturn in any particular industry. Most of the principal industries comprising Dallas' economic base were well positioned for expansion over the next several years. The metro area was a major transportation hub and scored high in terms of energy availability and reliability, a factor of growing concern to prospective tenants. Finally, Dallas/Fort Worth was governed by a strong pro-business philosophy at both the local and state level.

## The Dallas/Fort Worth Office Market

In large measure, the Dallas/Fort Worth office market reflected the area's strong pro-growth and pro-jobs philosophy. The objective of these policies was to keep land costs and building rents low so that the area continued to be attractive to new firms and existing firms didn't leave. A very general plan, relatively lenient zoning restrictions, largely non-union labor, and an expedited entitlement process helped to accomplish this objective.

The result of these policies was an office market with relatively low rents and high vacancy rates. This situation also encouraged a considerable amount of shifting between office nodes as new product become available, often at lower costs. Several institutional investors believed that this type of policy implicitly favored real estate speculators at the expense of long-term investors. As a result, some refused to invest in this type of market.

Exhibit 1 outlines the Dallas office market as of March 31, 2001. During the first quarter, the market continued a relatively high level of net absorption

---

[4] Centaur targeted a minimum financial return of 15.0% annually on its development projects.

largely due to tenants occupying new space upon completion of construction. The net positive gain, however, masked some major shifts between submarkets. As an example, the older LBJ Freeway market had net negative absorption of 569,100 sq. ft as tenants relocated in anticipation of a five level interchange. In addition, the Dallas CBD, which had been slower to recover for many years, benefited from space expansions by existing tenants.

The vacancy rate of 15.5% was down from 17.4% during the first quarter of 2000. Class A office space also improved from 11.3% during the last quarter of 2000 to 10.8% as of March 31, 2001. In terms of rent, Class A space averaged $22.85, Class B averaged $18.18, and Class C averaged $14.20 per square foot.[5] A survey of metro area real estate professionals during the first quarter indicated expected going-in cap rates of 8.8% and anticipated IRRs of 11.6%.[6]

Because of the increasing levels of sublease space coming back on the market, tenants appeared able to drive better deals. On the other hand, landlords were getting tougher on lease terms, including asking for Letters of Credit and getting a larger percentage of the rent paid up front.[7]

Metro area new office construction in 2000 was 4.1 million sq. ft, which was down considerably from the 11.3 million in 1999. Of the 969,023 sq. ft of space delivered during the first quarter of 2001, 35% was preleased and occupied. As of March 31, 2001, 4.7 million sq. ft of new space was under construction, which involved 36 office projects, 21 of which were located in the Far North Dallas and Richardson/Plano submarkets. Approximately 17.2% of this space was preleased.

## *Far North Dallas Submarket*

Far North Dallas is located to the west of the Dallas North Tollway (Exhibit 2). This submarket has led the metro area office market in both speculative construction and absorption for the last three years. In 2000, Far North Dallas absorbed just under 2.4 million sq. ft, which represented over one third of the metro area total. Absorption was split almost evenly between Class A and B buildings. Demand was particularly strong in the build-to-suit market, with new facilities developed for Pizza Inn, Inc., Lacerte Software Corporation, Computer Associates, Ericsson, and Freddie Mac. At year end the vacancy rate was 11.8%.

The pace slowed in the first quarter of 2001 with a net gain of 316,700 sq. ft (Exhibit 1). Looking forward, 58% of the 3.5 million in new metro-wide

---

[5] Plano Office Center would be classified as a Class B building.
[6] Real Estate Research Corporation, *Investment Survey*, 1Q, 2001.
[7] Sublease space is included in March 31, 2001 numbers (Exhibit 1).

office construction for delivery in 2001 will be in this submarket, with 11% currently preleased. An additional 835,000 sq. ft is under construction for delivery in 2002.[8]

## Richardson Plano Submarket

Located to the east of the Dallas North Tollway, this submarket had been almost as active as Far North Dallas. Absorption for the year was 1,567,200 sq. ft with rental rates increasing 5.9%. At year's end, vacancy was 6.3%. Major new facilities announced during the year included Cisco for 1.5 million sq. ft, Fujitsu Network Communications, Inc., which plans to add 3,000 employees to its Richardson headquarters, and Sanmina Corporation, which expects to develop a 750,000 sq. ft campus facility.

First quarter 2001 demand was down with only 136,900 sq. ft being absorbed. An additional 973,800 sq. ft was still under construction with 9% preleased.

## Plano Office Center

The Plano Office Center was located on a 12-acre parcel located on the western side of the Dallas North Tollway north of the Dallas CBD (Exhibit 2). There was a considerable amount of office building activity in the area with the worldwide headquarters of JC Penney and Frito-Lay north of the site and Dallas Air Park, a major private office and industrial park developed by Ross Perot, Jr., to the south. New residential subdivisions were located to the west of the site.

The Plano Office Center had been planned as a two-story office building similar to others successfully developed by Centaur as part of its high technology program (Exhibit 3). The building's leaseable area was 160,000 sq. ft, which could be split into four 40,000 sq. ft increments. The plan called for 800 parking spaces surrounding the building with multiple pedestrian access points into the building.

Exhibit 4 outlines construction costs for the project. The land purchase had closed on June 20, 2000, and construction was completed approximately ten months later. Land costs were $4,200,000 with construction and other development costs of $15,676,400 million. The project was built under a guaranteed maximum contract by Phleger-Jones, a national developer that Centaur had worked with previously.

---

[8] Kennedy Wilson Research, *Office Market Overview*, 1Q, 2001.

Exhibit 5 outlines pro forma Net Operating Income (NOI) for the project. Gross rents were scheduled to average $18.50 per sq. ft with Net Operating Income (NOI) expected to be $2,377,500, once the project was stabilized.

Although several prospects had toured the building, there had been no leases signed to date. Lodestar was the first prospective tenant that had reached the draft term sheet stage.

## *Negotiations with Lodestar*

While Jim was preparing the lease package, the phone rang, and it was Janet Burch, one of the head leasing agents for Phleger-Jones, calling from their San Francisco office to check on the Lodestar situation. In April, Janet had introduced Lodestar and Centaur, and the two firms had been discussing the Plano Office Center for the last two months. The result of the discussions was a draft term sheet, which was the focus of Jim and Allison's meeting at 3:00 PM that afternoon. (Exhibit 6).

The biggest hurdle to overcome in the negotiations was that Lodestar wanted a special allowance for additional tenant improvements (TI) of approximately $12.00 per sq. ft. This special allowance would be used largely to create "clean rooms" for their lab operations. Since Lodestar was not a rated credit, the Term Sheet required that Lodestar secure an LC for the additional TIs. The LC would be reduced 10% each year that the lease was in force. In addition, Lodestar would pay an annual "bonus rent" equal to 10% of the funds advanced by Centaur in connection with the special allowance. (Exhibits 7 & 8).

Jim also had required that Loadstar purchase high-speed telecommunications access from Building Access Inc., a Boston based telecom service firm. Centaur planned to use the Plano Office Building as a test installation prior to the roll out of a program to subcontract high speed access to the rest of Centaur's office portfolio across the nation.

## *Telecom Access Agreement*

For some time, Centaur had been under considerable tenant pressure to provide a higher level of telecommunications services. Jim had reviewed the qualifications of several service providers and had selected a Boston firm, Building Access, Inc., to provide the service nationally. The firm had been highly recommended by Centaur's Information Technology officer, Allan Debrowski. Centaur's construction VP also had cleared the system with Phleger-Jones for use in the Plano Office Center as a test case.

Given the importance of the decision, Jim had asked to see one of Building Access' multitenant installations under construction before giving final approval. Subsequently, he visited a building site on Route 128 where Business Access had a roof antenna installation under construction. Allan was already there and greeted him as he stepped out of his car.

Allan introduced Jim to Joe Adams, a representative of Building Access. The three men began a tour of the site. Joe described how the fiber-optic lines entered the building, were connected to a telephone closet on each floor, and were then distributed to tenants in the building. Allan asked some technical questions and seemed to be satisfied with the responses that Joe provided.

At the end of the tour, Jim and Allan caucused and decided to proceed with the test installation at the Plano Office Center. Jim then found Joe and asked if he could get a sample Access Agreement over to Centaur's office so that it could be reviewed and forwarded to Lodestar, the first prospective tenant for the building. Joe said that that he would email a summary of the terms in a typical agreement as soon as he returned to his office (Exhibit 9).

## Getting Ready for the Meeting with Allison

As he began his final preparation for the meeting with Allison, Jim couldn't help but think, how much more appealing Centaur's investment package would be to their pension client with a signed ten-year lease for 50% of the space, even at less than pro forma rental levels. In fact, Plano Office Center was the first building in their high technology program that had been completed without at least one tenant in place.

He was concerned, however, with the highly specialized nature of the extra TIs that were a condition of the deal. While he realized that Centaur would ultimately recapture their investment, he worried that if Lodestar defaulted, Centaur might end up with specialized clean rooms that would be difficult to rent to a new tenant. The Letter of Credit, therefore, took on additional significance in his decision. Jim reviewed once again the sample LC documents forwarded by Allison, and remembered that they were similar to ones he had used in the past.

The Access Agreement, however, was new to Jim. He knew that their pension client would be impressed that Centaur was outsourcing the technical services since they had always questioned the advisor about performing services that were not one of their real estate core competencies.

The agreement called for an advance payment of $150,000 by Centaur, which would be refunded as each tenant was signed up. If a tenant didn't sign up, however, Centaur would be stuck paying for the unused capacity. Jim also was concerned with how prospective tenants might view the arrangement and whether this might limit their market for tenants who had specialized requirements or arrangements with other service providers. Finally, Jim wondered what impact, if any, the access agreement might have on the future sale of the building.

As the afternoon wore on, Jim also had a gnawing feeling about the deteriorating Dallas office market. His friend at lunch had given him a copy of a Torto-Wheaton report that suggested problems in the office market might not be limited just to Dallas (Exhibit 10).

But as Jim thought more about it, the positive aspects of the deal tempered his concerns. Dallas was one of the most attractive markets to corporations such as Lodestar who were fleeing high operating costs and power shortages in other metro areas. In fact, Lodestar might represent the beginning of high tech firms leaving the Bay Area, Boston, New York, and other high cost areas for lower cost operating environments and more dependable sources of energy. Lower housing costs were an additional advantage that Dallas enjoyed.

Jim also noted that the building concept that Centaur had developed for the high technology program had been a highly successful product – tenants loved it, the returns were exceptional, and Centaur's investors were very pleased, particularly the pension fund to which the investment had been allocated.

His thoughts were shattered by a louder than normal ringing of his phone. It was Allison in the lobby for their 3:00 PM meeting.

### Exhibit 1
### Dallas/Fort Worth Multitenant Office Market

**First Quarter, 2001**

|  | Rentable* | Absorbed* | Vacancy | Average Rent |
|---|---|---|---|---|
| **Dallas CBD** | 31,832.7 | 222.8 | 24.9% | $18.29 |
| **LBJ Freeway** | 21,062.3 | (569.1) | 17.9% | $20.41 |
| **Far North Dallas** | 20,908.9 | 316.7 | 11.0% | $22.98 |
| **Las Colinas** | 20,152.8 | (51.1) | 12.8% | $22.88 |
| **Central Expwy** | 11,352.9 | (48.0) | 15.3% | $19.89 |
| **Mid-Cities** | 10,699.9 | (4.5) | 10.8% | $17.22 |
| **Ft. Worth CBD** | 9,869.3 | (7.8) | 15.8% | $15.68 |
| **Richardson/Plano** | 9,660.4 | 136.9 | 8.3% | $20.04 |
| **Stemmons Frwy.** | 8,785.8 | 74.4 | 16.0% | $16.83 |
| **Turtle Creek** | 8,524.4 | 2.6 | 9.4% | $22.99 |
| **Other** | 17,342.1 | 127.0 | 16.8% | $19.80 |
| **Totals/average** | 170,191.5 | 199.9 | 15.5% | $19.76 |

Source: CB Richard Ellis * Thousands

**Exhibit 2
Area Map**

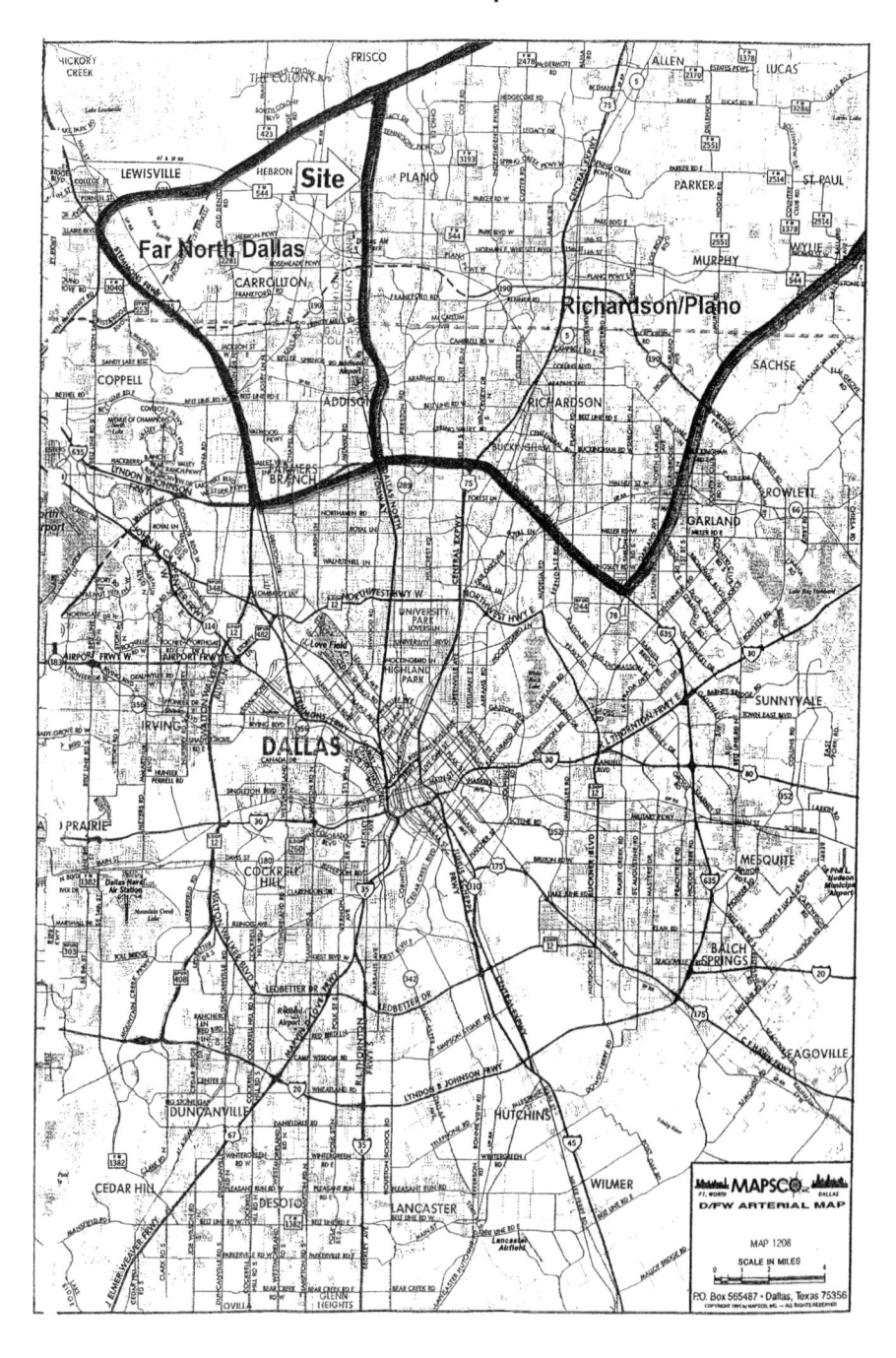

*Chapter 8 - Lodestar, Inc. Case A: Jim Maroney*  -177-

**Exhibit 3
Site Plan**

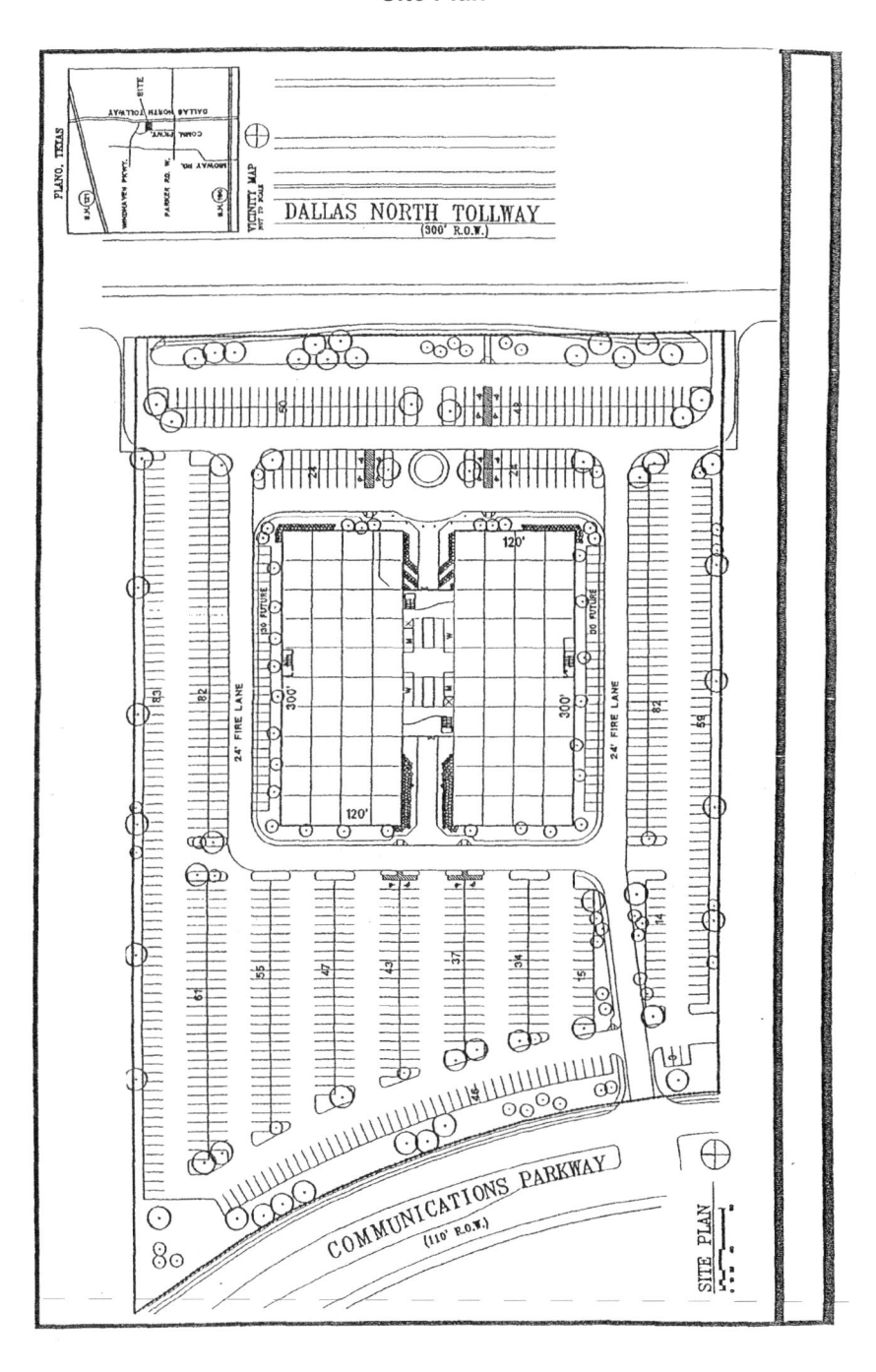

## Exhibit 4
## Plano Office Center Construction Budget

**Land** $4,200,000

**Hard Costs**
| | | |
|---|---:|---:|
| Shell construction | 5,580,900 | |
| Tenant finish | 3,100,500 | |
| HVAC, deck insulation, drop ceiling, and lights | 1,756,950 | |
| Lobby walls | 930,150 | |
| Ditch drainage and roadway extension | 325,000 | |
| Landscaping/Irrigation | 265,600 | 11,959,100 |

**Soft Costs**
| | | |
|---|---:|---:|
| Commissions | 1,906,600 | |
| Development fee | 485,000 | |
| Title/survey reserve at sale and purchase | 205,800 | |
| Interim capital fee | 197,600 | |
| Shell architecture | 183,500 | |
| Tenant finish architecture | 103,400 | |
| Land taxes | 59,000 | |
| Construction testing | 41,000 | |
| Engineering | 39,000 | |
| Legal | 32,500 | |
| Architecture reimbursements | 13,000 | |
| Construction consultant | 13,000 | |
| Marketing | 10,000 | |
| Environmental report | 8,000 | |
| Miscellaneous | 6,500 | |
| Contingency | 413,400 | 3,717,300 |

**Total construction costs** 19,876,400

## Exhibit 5
## Plano Office Center
## Pro Forma Income
## 2002

| Revenue | SF | Rent/SF | Annual |
|---|---|---|---|
| Suite A (Ground) | 40,000 | $19.00 | $760,000 |
| Suite B (Ground) | 40,000 | 19.00 | 760,000 |
| Suite C (Second) | 40,000 | 18.00 | 720,000 |
| Suite D (Second) | 40,000 | 18.00 | 720,000 |
| Total | 160,000 | 18.50 | 2,960,000 |

**Vacancy Allowance (5%)**      148,000

**Effective Gross Revenue**      2,812,000

| Operating Expense | Gross | Reimbursed | Net |
|---|---|---|---|
| Property Taxes | 413,500 | | 413,500 |
| Insurance | 21,000 | | 21,000 |
| CAM* | 395,000 | 395,000 | -0- |
| Total | 829,500 | 395,000 | 434,500 |

**Net Operating Income**      2,377,500

\* Common Area Maintenance

## Exhibit 6
## Proposed Term Sheet (Draft)

| | |
|---|---|
| **Lessor:** | Centaur Advisors |
| **Lessee:** | Lodestar, Inc. |
| **Building:** | Plano Office Center |
| **Address:** | 8600 Dallas North Tollway |
| **City:** | Plano, TX |
| **Suites:** | A & B (ground floor) |
| **Square Footage:** | 80,000 SF |
| **Use:** | Manufacturing of microcircuit boards and other computer peripherals for medical field |
| **Tenant Finish:** | Open plan; concrete and tile floor; paint. |
| **Parking:** | 400 dedicated spaces |
| **Term:** | 10 years |
| **Rent:** | $18.50 PSF annually; adjustment to market at end of 5th year |
| **Utilities:** | Tenant pays electricity |
| **Common Area Maintenance:** | Tenant reimburses pro-rated share |
| **Taxes and insurance:** | Tenant pays prorate share of increases beyond first year |
| **Telecommunications:** | Serviced by Building Access, Inc. |
| **Options to Renew:** | One for 5 years at market |
| **Signage Rights** | To be negotiated. |
| **Special Features:** | $12.00 per square foot tenant finish allowance for above-standard improvements; backed by letter of credit from bank acceptable to lesser; additional annual payment to lesser of bonus rent equal to 10% of total allowance. |

## Exhibit 7
## Example of Letter of Credit

Date of Issue: June 1, 2001

Our Irrevocable Standby Credit:
Date of Expiry: June 30, 2001
Place of Expiry: At our above counters.

Applicant:
XYZ Tenant, Inc.

Beneficiary:
ABC Owner, Inc.

Amount: USD $2,500,000.00

We hereby establish in your favor this credit available with Bank, at AnyTown, CA by payment of your draft(s) at sight drawn on Bank accompanied by:

1. Your signed and dated statement worded as follows:

> "The undersigned, an authorized representative of ABC Owner, Inc., hereby certifies that XYZ Tenant, Inc. has defaulted under the lease agreement dated July 1, 2000 between ABC Owner, Inc. and XYZ Tenant, Inc. regarding security deposit."

Partial drawings are permitted. (More than one draft may be drawn and presented under the Letter of Credit.)

This Letter of Credit is transferable and may be successively transferred but only to a single transferee whom you shall have advised us in your instrument of transfer is the assignee under and in connection with and as part of your assignment of your interest in the Lease between you and XYZ Tenant, Inc. for the premises located at 100 Main Street, AnyTown, California 99999. Any such transfer may be effected only through ourselves (all bank fees to be charged to Applicant) and upon presentation to us at our above-specified office of a duly executed instrument of transfer in the form of Exhibit A attached hereto together with the original of this Letter of Credit and payment of by ABC Owner, Inc. of our transfer fee in the amount of ¼% of the amount of this Letter of Credit. Any transfer of this Letter of Credit may not change the place of expiration of this Letter of Credit from our above-specified office. Each transfer shall be evidenced by our endorsement on the reverse of the original of this Letter of Credit, and we shall deliver the original of this Letter of Credit so endorsed to the transferee.

This Letter of Credit expires at our above address on June 30, 2001 but will be automatically extended, without written amendment, in each succeeding calendar year, up to but not beyond June 30, 2005, unless we have sent written notice to you at your above address that we elect not to renew this Letter of Credit beyond the date specified in such notice, which date will be June 30, 2001 or any subsequent June 30 but not beyond June 30, 2005 at least forty-five (45) calendar days after the date we send you such notice. Notice of non-renewal shall be deemed received by you four (4) business days after the date such notice is deposited in the U.S. mail, postage prepaid

That payment is to be made by transfer to an account with us or at another bank, we and/or such other bank may rely on an account number specified in such instructions even if the number identifies a person or entity different from the intended payee.

Documents must be presented to us no later than 5:00p.m.

Draft(s) must indicate the number and date of this credit.

Each draft presented hereunder must be accompanied by this original credit for our endorsement thereon of the amount of such draft.

Documents must be forwarded to us via courier in one parcel and may be mailed to Bank, operation group, Northern California, 525 Main Street, 25th Floor, AnyTown, CA 99999.

This credit is subject to the uniform customs and practice for documentary credits (1993 revision), international chamber of commerce, publication number 500, and engages us in accordance with the terms thereof.

Yours Truly,

Bank

## Exhibit 8

## Example of Letter of Credit Lease Provision

6. <u>Security</u>

    6.1    <u>Security Deposit</u>. Contemporaneously with the execution of this Lease, Tenant shall pay to Landlord the Security Deposit, which shall be held by Landlord to secure Tenant's performance of its obligations under this Lease. The Security Deposit is not an advance payment of Rent or a measure or limit of Landlord's damages upon an Event of Default (defined in Section 17). Landlord may, from time to time and without prejudice to any other remedy, use all or a part of the Security Deposit to perform any obligation Tenant fails to perform hereunder. Following any such application of the Security Deposit, Tenant shall pay to Landlord on demand the amount so applied in order to restore the Security Deposit to its original amount. Provided that Tenant has performed all of its obligations hereunder, Landlord shall, within thirty (30) days after the Term ends, return to Tenant the portion of the Security Deposit which was not applied to satisfy Tenant's obligations. The Security Deposit may be commingled with other funds, and no interest shall be paid thereon. If Landlord transfers its interest in the Premises and the transferee assumes Landlord's obligations under this Lease, then Landlord may assign the Security Deposit to the transferee and Landlord thereafter shall have no further liability for the return of the Security Deposit.

    6.2    <u>Letter of Credit</u>. In lieu of the Security Deposit referenced above, concurrently with Tenant's execution of this Lease. Tenant may deliver to Landlord an irrevocable letter of credit as hereinafter described (the "<u>Letter of Credit</u>"). The Letter of Credit shall (i) be an irrevocable standby letter of credit, (ii) name Landlord as beneficiary, (iii) be payable on sight draft accompanied only by Landlord's certification that it is entitled to payment thereon because an Event of Default under the Lease has occurred, (iv) be for an initial term of at least twelve (12) months and, subject to the terms set forth below, shall be renewed thereafter no later than thirty (30) days prior to any expiration date thereof so that the Letter of Credit remains in effect during the entire period ending thirty (30) days after the expiration of the initial Term and any renewal term of this Lease, (v) assure payment in the total amount of $8,122,274.95, and (vi) be otherwise in form reasonably acceptable to Landlord. If Tenant fails timely to renew its Letter of Credit, then Landlord shall have the right to draw thereon, and retain the amounts so drawn as the Security Deposit. The following provisions shall govern the parties' rights and obligations with respect to the Letter of Credit:

        6.2.1    Landlord shall be entitled to recourse against the Letter of Credit to recover any loss or damage it may suffer as a result of any breach or default by Tenant under this Lease. Partial and multiple draws shall be permitted under the Letter of Credit. After any such draw, Tenant shall pay to Landlord on demand the amount so drawn to be held as part of the Security Deposit.

    6.2.2    Provided an Event of Default has not occurred during the twelve (12) month period prior to each reduction and Tenant's financial condition as of the date of each reduction, in Landlord's reasonable judgment, is equal to or better than its financial condition as of the Commencement Date, Landlord shall reduce the required amount of the Letter of Credit as follows:

| Lease Month | Letter of Credit Amount |
| --- | --- |
| 1 – 12 | $8,122,275.00 |
| 13 – 24 | $7,445,419.00 |
| 25 – 36 | $6,768,562.00 |
| 37 – 48 | $6,091,706.00 |
| 49 – 60 | $5,414,850.00 |
| 61 – 73 | $4,737,994.00 |
| 73 – 85 | $4,061,137.00 |
| 85 – 97 | $3,384,281.00 |
| 97 – 109 | $2,707,425.00 |
| 109 – 120 | $2,030,569.00 |

Without limitation, Tenant may satisfy the financial condition requirement set forth above if, as of the date of each scheduled reduction, Tenant can provide evidence reasonably acceptable to Landlord that Tenant then has cash or cash equivalents on hand in an amount equal to or greater than the total of the next twelve (12) months of Basic Rent coming due under this Lease. Subject to the above, Tenant's failure to keep the Letter of Credit in effect during the entire initial term of the Lease, or Tenant's failure to furnish written evidence to Landlord of the yearly renewal of the Letter of Credit, shall be an Event of Default hereunder.

    6.2.3    Tenant shall pay, as Additional Rent under this Lease, any and all costs or fees charged in connection with the Letter of Credit that arise due to: (i) Landlord's sale or transfer of all or a portion of the Building; or (ii) the addition, deletion or modification of any beneficiaries under the Letter of Credit.

**Exhibit 9**
**SUMMARY OF KEY PROVISIONS**
**TELECOMMUNICATIONS SERVICES AGREEMENT**

**Parties to Agreement**

Property Owner: Centaur Advisors, Inc.

Service Provider: Building Access, Inc.

**Services Provided Tenants**

Local, intraLATA toll (or local toll), long distance, high-speed data, internet, video/cable television, cable Internet and other lawful services and applications that Service Provider may provide now or in the future.

Service Provider holds all right and title to the services and retains the right, in its sole discretion, to control, add to, delete, and/or change such services.

Service Provider has the right, but not the obligation, to market and contract with Tenants for the provision of any or all of the Services on an individual subscriber basis, independent of Owner.

Orders for service(s) shall be solely between Service Provider and individual Tenants. Service Provider retains the right to terminate such service(s) to Tenants who fail to abide by the terms and conditions of service contracts.

**Installation of Services**

Property Owner provides Service Provider with a non-exclusive easement on, over, under, within, and through the Premises (both land and improvements) as necessary or desirable for: Service Provider to provide services to tenants.

Within this easement, Service Provider has the right to construct and install and use any cabling, wiring, power supplies, risers, conduits, distribution wiring and facilities, cross-connect facilities and/or distribution frames (collectively referred to as "Facilities"), and any rights of way and entrance facilities within and into the building, as necessary or useful, for the provision of services to the Tenants, whether owned, installed, controlled or maintained by Service Provider or not.

Service Provider has the right to install on the roof of any building on the Premises an antenna or other equipment, as necessary or desirable for the provision of services to the Tenants, together with any wiring or cabling from the antenna to the rest of the facilities.

Property Owner is not responsible for installation charges, monthly subscription rates, equipment deposits, or other charges for subscribers' service(s).

**Charges for Services**

Service Provider is responsible for collection of charges, billing, accounting, and other services related to subscriber accounts.

Owner is not responsible for installation charges, monthly subscription rates, equipment deposits, or other charges for subscribers' service(s).

## Term of Agreement

Agreement becomes effective on the date of the agreement and continues as so long as Service Provider or Agent may provide the Services, not to exceed ____*_ years from the date of this Agreement. Thereafter, the Agreement is automatically renewed for consecutive terms of ____*_ years each, unless written notice of termination is given by either party.

## Termination

This Agreement may be terminated prior to expiration of its term:

(a) by either party in the event of material breach of this Agreement after 30 days' written notice, unless the other party cures or commences to cure such breach during such 30-day period and diligently proceeds with such cure; or

(b) by Service Provider upon at least 60 days' written notice if Service Provider is unable, or it becomes impracticable, to continue distribution of any one or more of the Services due to any law, rule, regulation, judgment, contract with third party or other reason beyond the reasonable control of Service Provider.

Upon termination of this Agreement and any other legally enforceable rights of access to provide Services, Service Provider shall, at its sole option, have an additional ninety (90) days to remove or abandon part or all of the Facilities, in its sole discretion.

## Assignment/Successors

Benefits and obligations of Agreement run with the land and will inure to and are binding upon the successors, assigns, heirs, and personal representatives of Service Provider and Owner during the Term hereof.

## Subordination Rights

Agreement is subordinate to all leases, mortgages, and/or deed of trust which may now or hereafter affect the Premises, and to all renewals, modifications, consolidations, replacements and extensions thereof.

Service Provider's obligation to subordinate this Agreement to any present or future mortgage, deed of trust or lease is subject to and contingent upon satisfaction of such mortgagee's, trustee's or lessor's obligation to recognize and not disturb Service Provider's rights and obligations under this Agreement.

## Sale of Property

Easement runs with the land and binds Owner, and each and every subsequent owner thereof, for the term of this agreement

Owner makes assumption of the Agreement a condition of any sale, transfer or assignment of the property.

* Negotiated

## Exhibit 10
## Torto Wheaton Report, May 4, 2001

**TORTO WHEATON RESEARCH ANNOUNCES OFFICE ABSORPTION NEGATIVE FOR FIRST TIME IN RECORDED HISTORY AS DEMAND SLOWS --**
Torto Wheaton Research's view on longer-term prospect still favorable.

BOSTON, MA -- Friday, May 4, 2001 -- Torto Wheaton research announced that Office demand dramatically slowed in the 1st quarter of 2001. Net absorption in the 53 markets (72 MSA's) that the firm tracks was down from a positive 19.9 million square feet in the 4th quarter of 2000 to a negative 16.9 million in the 1st quarter. There has never been a period of negative net absorption in the sum of the markets, even during the recession of the early 1990s.

Torto Wheaton Research's analysis indicates that there were two components to the falloff in net absorption. The first is the sublease space that has reentered the market with the failure of high-tech firms. Beyond this sublease space, however, demand has shut down. Were it not for the sublease space net absorption would have come in at roughly 3 million square feet in the 1st quarter. While 3 million square feet of positive net absorption, sans sublease, certainly is better than a negative 16.9 million, it is an extremely weak 1st quarter.

Although these are dramatic and significant numbers, the 1st quarter results do not change Torto Wheaton Research's view on longer-term trends. Torto Wheaton Research's forecast for 2001 has net absorption at about 50 percent of last year's level, rising vacancy rates and a falling rate of rent growth.

*Table 1. Breakdown of Vacancy Changes by Location Type, 1st Quarter 2001*

|  | Metropolitan | Downtown | Suburban |
|---|---|---|---|
| # of Markets with Vacancy Increases | 41 | 29 | 41 |
| # of Markets with Vacancy Decreases | 11 | 15 | 11 |
| Total Number of Markets | 53 | 46 | 53 |
| # of Markets by Range of Vacancy Increases |  |  |  |
| 300 basis points plus | 4 | 4 | 6 |
| 200 to 299 basis points | 7 | 6 | 8 |
| 100 to 199 basis points | 14 | 6 | 13 |
| Vacancy Rates, Sum of Markets | 9.5 | 7.7 | 10.6 |

Across 28 of the 53 market areas (72 MSAs) that Torto Wheaton Research reports upon showed negative net absorption. As demonstrated in Table 2 below, the negative results are widespread.

*Table 2. Markets with Negative Net Absorption in the 1st Quarter*

| | | |
|---|---|---|
| Austin | Long Island | San Francisco |
| Boston | Los Angeles | San Jose |
| Chicago | Miami | Seattle |
| Cleveland | New York | Stamford |
| Denver | Northern New Jersey | Tampa |
| Fresno | Oakland | Washington, D.C. |
| Hartford | Orange County | Westchester |
| Houston | Phoenix | Wilmington, DE |
| Indianapolis | Portland | |
| Kansas City | San Diego | |

According to Torto Wheaton Research positive news to be taken out of the 1st quarter numbers includes two issues. The reasons for negative net absorption could reverse quickly. It is commonly believed that the tech bust must end somewhere. Some reports have tech company bankruptcies peaking in February. Second, if other companies are indeed "frozen" by uncertainty, then the resolution of that uncertainty through interest rate cuts or a clear signal as to a bottom to the economic situation would result in net absorption proceeding forward as before.

It also may be the case that in today's more efficient real estate leasing market, tenants are waiting for some relief to the high rents. Torto Wheaton Research's data on asking rents are showing stability across markets with only San Francisco and Honolulu declining more than 5 percent over the 1st quarter. Landlords may be seeing decreased effective rents through other adjustments. The fact that most have not been forced to adjust their marquee numbers is an indication of the healthy state that the markets were in before the 1st quarter. Landlords also may not wish to give up some of the lofty rent levels too early, especially since most markets are still tight.

About Torto Wheaton Research
Boston-based Torto Wheaton Research is the premier provider of commercial real estate forecasting, analysis and consulting services for office, industrial, retail, multi-family and hotel property types. The firm provides unrivaled market knowledge through a full suite of research products and specializes in commercial real estate risk management through strategic debt and equity consulting. Highly sophisticated and reliable forecasting models, and proven analytical expertise, have earned the company international recognition. Torto Wheaton Research is on the web at www.tortowheatonresearch.com.

Home
© Torto Wheaton Research

## Chapter 8 - Lodestar, Inc. Case A: Jim Maroney -189-

## *Questions for Discussion*

Questions that should be addressed in this case include:

1. Calculate the 10 year IRR of the Lodestar lease. Does this IRR meet Centaur's minimum financial return objectives?
2. What other factors should Centaur's management committee consider in addition to minimum financial return objectives?
3. What are the negatives of proceeding?
4. Based on the above analysis, what are Centaur's key interests in the Lodestar negotiation? Priorities?
5. What are Lodestar's interests in these negotiations?
6. What are Lodestar's alternatives to executing a lease with Centaur?
7. What are the areas of the negotiations in which the interest of the parties converge? Diverge?
8. What changes should Jim expect Allison to propose in the draft term sheet (Exhibit 6)? What should be his response? Why?

Please use these questions as a guide and not a format or a reflection of all of the questions that need to be addressed by the case.

# Case B: ALLISON BOWERS

In June 2001, Allison Bowers was in a taxi heading from Logan Airport to a 3:00 PM negotiating session with Jim Maroney, the Senior Vice President of Asset Management for Centaur Advisors (Centaur). Centaur was an investment advisor to pension plans and the developer of the Plano Office Center, a recently completed Dallas office project, which Lodestar was interested in leasing.

## *Lodestar, Inc.*

Allison was Vice President of Corporate Real Estate for Lodestar, Inc. (Lodestar), a six-year old high technology firm started by two University of California engineering professors. The firm specialized in the development of microcircuit boards for medical research computers. Lodestar had patented three new products, one of which had become successful almost overnight and was now being adopted in rapidly growing volume by hospitals throughout the nation.

Lodestar had turned profitable in 1998 and remained so ever since. Largely because of the success of this product, the firm had grown rapidly and reached 310 employees by early 2001. Operations were located in facilities in several older buildings in Berkeley and Oakland, California. Lodestar's management had considered consolidating their various locations into a single building but had been discouraged by the high costs of renting new facilities in the Bay Area and by their employees' difficulty in finding affordable housing within a reasonable commute.

Allison, an experienced real estate facility manager, had been hired in 2000 with the immediate assignment of finding a new location somewhere in Northern California where Lodestar could find reasonable rents and affordable housing for its employees. After interviews with key Lodestar managers, Allison developed the following criteria sheet to aid her in the search:

- 70,000 sq. ft with options for future expansion
- Suburban location
- Close to affordable residential areas
- One or two-story design
- Fiber-optic service line within 100 yards
- Parking of at least 6 stalls per 1,000 sq. ft
- Open plan with flexible interior office layout

- High visibility from freeway or major arterial
- Below market rents, if possible.

After a few months of searching, Allison had narrowed down potential sites to the Sacramento area.

In early 2001, the search was dramatically altered by California's energy crisis and the prospect of rolling blackouts over the coming summer months. Lodestar used large amounts of electricity in the manufacturing process and insisted on a 100% reliable supply. The prospect of possibly losing their consistent flow of energy now shifted the search not only out of the Bay Area but out of California as well.

## *The Dallas/Fort Worth Metropolitan Area*

After several weeks of searching across the nation, Allison had zeroed in on the Dallas/Fort Worth metropolitan area as the best location for Lodestar's new headquarters. With 5 million people, Dallas/Fort Worth was the fifth largest metropolitan area in the U.S. and the largest in the State of Texas.

Dallas/Fort Worth's socioeconomic structure had several important characteristics that appealed to Allison. The metro area was a major transportation hub and scored high in terms of energy availability and reliability. The area's labor force was highly trained and largely non-union. Reasonably priced housing was available in close proximity to attractively priced, largely new office facilities. More relaxed zoning laws made it attractive to firms like Lodestar with large complex laboratory operations. Property taxes were low, and the area's strong pro-business philosophy insured that they would stay that way.

In large measure, the Dallas/Fort Worth office market reflected the area's strong pro-growth and pro-jobs philosophy. The objective of these policies was to keep land costs and building rents low so that the area continued to be attractive to new firms and existing firms didn't leave. A very general plan, relatively lenient zoning restrictions, largely non-union labor, and an expedited entitlement process helped to accomplish this objective. The result of these policies was an office market with lots of leasing activity, but large amounts of vacant space, relatively low rents, and high tenant turnover.

## *Richardson/Plano Area*

The area within the Dallas/Fort Worth market that she liked the best was the Richardson/Plano area. Located to the east of the Dallas North Tollway, this area was the second most active office market in the Dallas/Fort Worth metro area in 2000. (Exhibit 1) Absorption for the year was 1,567,200 sq. ft, and growth in rental rates increasing 5.9%. At year's end, vacancy was 6.3%.

Major new facilities announced during the year included Cisco for 1.5 million sq. ft, Fujitsu Network Communications, Inc., which plans to add 3,000 employees to its Richardson headquarters, and Sanmina Corporation, which expects to develop a 750,000 campus facility.

Demand slowed in the first quarter 2001, however, with only 136,900 sq. ft being absorbed. The vacancy rate increased to 8.3% with average rents of $20.05 per sq. ft. An additional 973,800 sq. ft was still under construction with 9% preleased.

## *Plano Office Center*

Within the Richardson/Plano area, Allison had looked at several buildings and selected the largely completed Plano Office Center as her first choice. The Plano Office Center was situated on a 12-acre parcel located on the western side of the Dallas North Tollway, (Exhibit 2). There was a considerable amount of office building activity in the area with the worldwide headquarters of JC Penney and Frito-Lay north of the site and Dallas Air Park, a major private office and industrial park developed by Ross Perot, Jr., to the south. New residential subdivisions were located primarily to the west of the site.

The Plano Office Center was a two-story office building similar to many others developed by Centaur (Exhibit 3). The building's leaseable area was 160,000 sq. ft, which could be split into four 40,000 sq. ft increments. The plan called for 800 parking spaces surrounding the building with multiple pedestrian access points.

In touring the building, Allison was particularly attracted to the large open work areas with an absence of columns. This space configuration would allow Lodestar to arrange and rearrange their space as various projects teams were organized and disbanded. It also would permit higher employee densities, thereby lowering rent-per-employee costs.[9]

Most of Lodestar's employees were generation X-ers in their 20s and 30s. Plano Center had several campus-type amenities which Allison thought would appeal to their eclectic work style. These conveniences included a snack bar, nap room, laundry pick-up, and a concierge to handle personal tasks for tenant employees. Another attraction was the availability of fiber-optic trunk service to the building.

After completing the tour, Allison reviewed her criteria sheet and concluded that the property met most of Lodestar's requirements. She then did some

---

[9] This lower ratio is a goal of most employers. The average space per employee dropped from 220 sq. ft in 1992 to 193 sq. ft in 1999 (Source: Building Owners and Managers Association)

web research on Centaur and discovered that the firm had been formed in 1988 to provide real estate investment advisory services for pension plans, endowment funds, and foundations.

Centaur had grown over the years to the point where, by 2001, it managed over $3.0 billion in client assets, which consisted of 110 properties in 22 markets across the county. Centaur was best known for developing and managing newly developed office and industrial buildings located in markets that would appeal to firms seeking lower operating costs and an abundant reliable energy supply. Sounded much like Lodestar's situation, Allison thought.

## Meeting with Senior Management

Allison returned to San Francisco and went over her findings with Lodestar's senior management. At first there was some resistance to moving to Dallas, but as Allison laid out the facts, the decision became more and more attractive. Dallas had not only lower costs and more reliable energy supplies but also a large pool of talented, technically trained people with the skills that Lodestar required. The presence of excellent graduate programs in engineering at Dallas universities meant not only that there would be a pool of potential employees but also transferred employees could keep up on their continuing education requirements.

In addition, the nearby housing was generally of good quality and significantly less expensive than in the Bay Area. Most of the communities in North Dallas had good public school systems and a wide variety of community activities.

Allison discussed the lease terms with her colleagues and while the asking rent of $19.00 per square foot looked quite reasonable, particularly when compared to the Bay Area, they all knew that this was for traditional office/R&D space and not the highly sophisticated clean rooms and other facilities that Lodestar required. Allison had done some calculations and determined that they would need an average of at least $12.00 per square foot in tenant finish allowance to meet their requirements.

Allison also made the management group aware of the weak office market currently existing in the Dallas/Fort Worth area and emphasized that they may be able to get some additional rental concessions, particularly since they would be the first tenant in the building, taking half of the space.

After extensive discussions, the senior management team decided to make a counteroffer of $18.00 per square foot for a ten year lease subject to receiving $12.00 per square foot in tenant finish allowance to cover their above-standard tenant finish.

## Lease Negotiations

Allison contacted Jim Maroney, the head of Centaur's asset management group to review Lodestar's proposed counteroffer. After listening to Allison, he indicated that their offering rent of $19.00 was pretty much market, but they would be willing to consider a lower offer provided they could work out the other terms of the rental agreement.

Jim was troubled, however, by the $12.00 per square foot in tenant finish allowance that Allison was asking. He then inquired if Lodestar was a public firm. Allison said no but that they were quite profitable and that she would be glad to forward current financial statements.

Jim made a mental note that a strong financial statement would not be enough for him to secure an approval for the above-standard tenant allowance from his Investment Committee. He thought for a moment and then asked Allison if Lodestar would be willing to post a Letter of Credit (LC) from their bank to guarantee the tenant finish work. Allison told him she would have to check with their bank and get back to him.

After hanging up, Allison called Heather Conglin, Lodestar's contact at their bank, and asked what the terms would be for an LC that would meet Centaur's requirements. Heather replied that their current policy was a 1% placement fee and an annual charge of 1% of the outstanding balance. Allison then asked for a copy of a sample LC agreement which Heather emailed to her immediately (Exhibits 4 & 5). She reviewed the sample agreements and then forwarded them on to Jim.

The next day Jim called and said that the form of the LC was acceptable and they were willing to discuss a lower rent, but that he needed two additional concessions: (1) Lodestar would pay an annual bonus rent above the base rent equal to 10% of the $12.00 above-standard tenant finish allowance, and (2) the lease would require a mid-term rental adjustment to market at the end of the fifth year. Allison said that she would have to get approval from her management committee and she couldn't guarantee acceptance of these additional terms.

They left it that Jim would draft a term sheet summarizing their negotiations to date, including the two new points that he had introduced, and get it to Allison for approval by her management committee.

The next morning, Allison received a draft Term Sheet from Jim along the lines they had been discussing (Exhibit 6). Allison was pleased to see that Jim had pegged the rental rent at $18.50 per sq. ft, considerably under the listing rate and competitive with current market comparables.

Jim suggested that Allison come back to their offices in Boston to complete the negotiations. She replied that this could probably be arranged since she was going to be in New York the following week and could take the shuttle up to Boston, have their meeting, and then return directly to the Bay Area. Actually, she was pleased to have a personal meeting with Jim because she didn't want to go back to her management committee without a firm deal. She also found that face-to-face meetings were the best way to reach final agreement in any negotiating environment.

Jim then said that he had an additional disclosure to make: Centaur had made a decision to outsource their telecomm services to Building Access, Inc., a reputable Boston firm that had similar installations throughout the country. This would be a test case for Centaur and if it worked, they would consider expanding the contract to most if not all of their other properties. Allison asked if Jim could send her a summary of the proposed agreement, and he faxed it to her immediately (Exhibit 7).

The next week Allison was on the shuttle from New York to Boston and began reviewing again the pluses and minuses of the proposed deal with Centaur. She thought that Centaur's rental rate proposal was fair and that their agreement to provide the additional tenant finish allowance was a key positive element in the transaction.

She was more concerned with the LC that Centaur was requiring and wondered if there was any way this requirement could be waived. While the bank was willing to provide the LC, they intended to include it in the maximum limit of Lodestar's overall credit facility. While this sounded benign, Allison knew that Lodestar needed all of its credit facility to continue growing.

As to the mid-term rent adjustment, Allison thought this could cut either way in light of the highly overbuilt Dallas office market and the amount of new construction still coming on line. She was mulling over a "cap" on this adjustment, however, just in case the market suddenly hardened and rents went up rapidly. She thought that a cap in the 15-20% range would probably be fair.

She was also somewhat concerned with the parking allocation of 400 spaces which was considerably less than the 480 they were seeking. This concern was tempered by the fact that Lodestar was leasing one half of the building and getting one half of the available parking stalls, so maybe it was a fair proposal after all. She certainly didn't want to fight with subsequent tenants over parking as the result of Lodestar getting a higher than pro rata initial allocation.

Finally, Allison was skeptical of the decision to outsource the telecommunications services. Telecommunications are a critical function for most tenants, particularly those involved in highly secure technology operations. Her concerns were heightened as more and more telecom companies came under financial pressure with many slipping into bankruptcy.

She decided she would try to press Centaur to install and operate the system itself so that Lodestar could be assured that the service would not be interrupted or tied up in lengthy litigation. Failing that, she at least wanted to get a clause in the access agreement to substitute their own provider if they were dissatisfied with the service provided by Building Access.

As the plane touched down, Allison knew she had her work cut out for her if she was going to be able to bring the lease negotiations to a successful conclusion. She got into the taxi and headed for her 3:00 PM meeting with Jim.

## Exhibit 1
## Dallas/Fort Worth Multitenant Office Market
### First Quarter, 2001

|  | Rentable* | Absorbed* | Vacancy | Average Rent |
|---|---|---|---|---|
| Dallas CBD | 31,832.7 | 222.8 | 24.9% | $18.29 |
| LBJ Freeway | 21,062.3 | (569.1) | 17.9% | $20.41 |
| Far North Dallas | 20,908.9 | 316.7 | 11.0% | $22.98 |
| Las Colinas | 20,152.8 | (51.1) | 12.8% | $22.88 |
| Central Expressway | 11,352.9 | (48.0) | 15.3% | $19.89 |
| Mid-Cities | 10,699.9 | (4.5) | 10.8% | $17.22 |
| Ft. Worth CBD | 9,869.3 | (7.8) | 15.8% | $15.68 |
| Richardson/Plano | 9,660.4 | 136.9 | 8.3% | $20.04 |
| Stemmons Frwy. | 8,785.8 | 74.4 | 16.0% | $16.83 |
| Uptown/turtle Creek | 8,524.4 | 2.6 | 9.4% | $22.99 |
| Other | 17,342.1 | 127.0 | 16.8% | $19.80 |
| Totals/average | 170,191.5 | 199.9 | 15.5% | $19.76 |

Source: CB Richard Ellis    *Thousands

Exhibit 2
Area Map

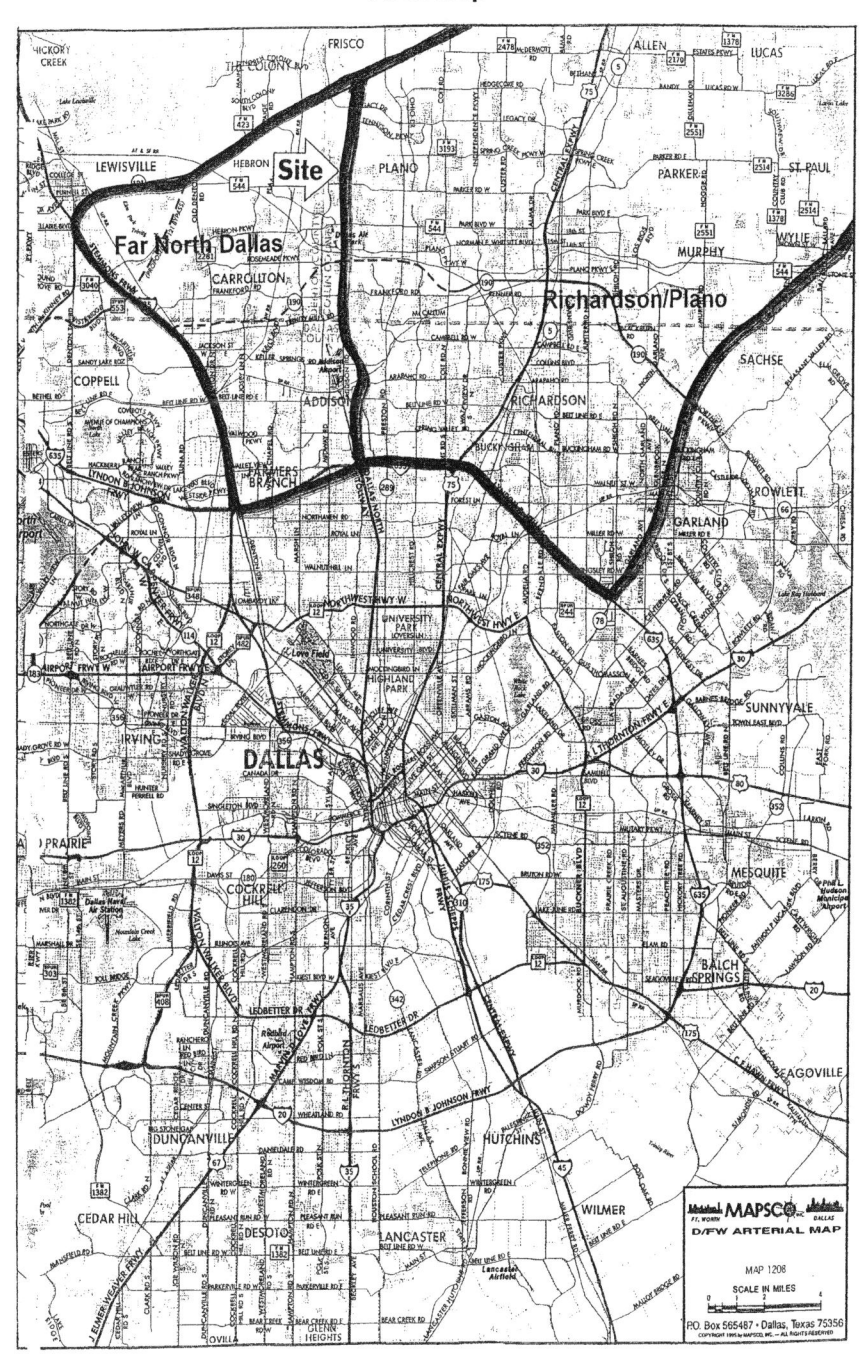

*Asset Management*

**Exhibit 3
Site Plan**

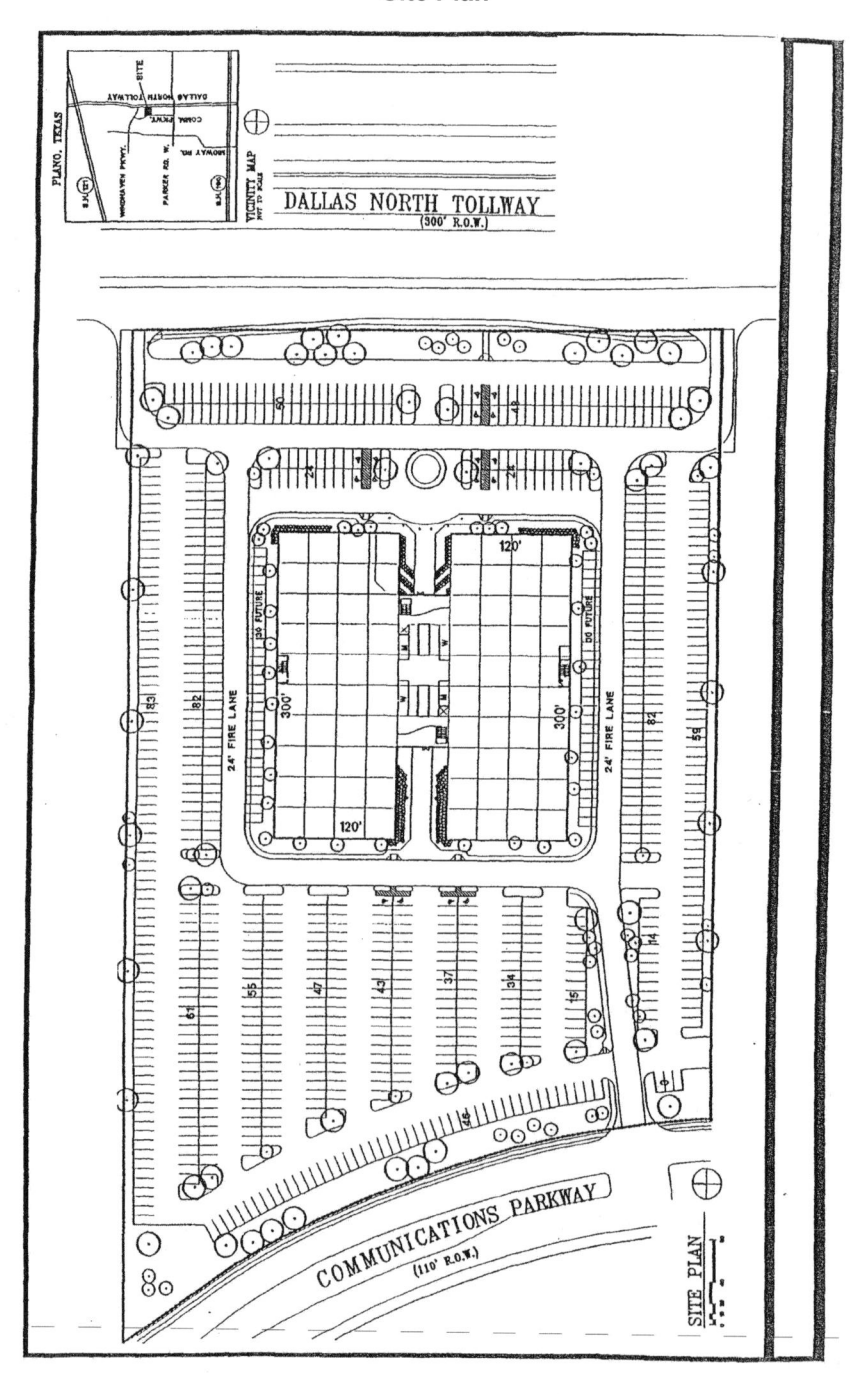

## Exhibit 4
## Example of Letter of Credit

Date of Issue: June 1, 2001

Our Irrevocable Standby Credit:
Date of Expiry: June 30, 2001
Place of Expiry: At our above counters.

Applicant:
XYZ Tenant, Inc.

Beneficiary:
ABC Owner, Inc.

Amount: USD $2,500,000.00

We hereby establish in your favor this credit available with Bank, at AnyTown, CA by payment of your draft(s) at sight drawn on Bank accompanied by:

1. Your signed and dated statement worded as follows:

"The undersigned, an authorized representative of ABC Owner, Inc., hereby certifies that XYZ Tenant, Inc. has defaulted under the lease agreement dated July 1, 2000 between ABC Owner, Inc. and XYZ Tenant, Inc. regarding security deposit."

Partial drawings are permitted. (More than one draft may be drawn and presented under the Letter of Credit.)

This Letter of Credit is transferable and may be successively transferred but only to a single transferee whom you shall have advised us in your instrument of transfer is the assignee under and in connection with and as part of your assignment of your interest in the Lease between you and XYZ Tenant, Inc. for the premises located at 100 Main Street, AnyTown, California 99999. Any such transfer may be effected only through ourselves (all bank fees to be charged to Applicant) and upon presentation to us at our above-specified office of a duly executed instrument of transfer in the form of Exhibit A attached hereto together with the original of this Letter of Credit and payment of by ABC Owner, Inc. of our transfer fee in the amount of ¼% of the amount of this Letter of Credit. Any transfer of this Letter of Credit may not change the place of expiration of this Letter of Credit from our above-specified office. Each transfer shall be evidenced by our endorsement on the reverse of the original of this Letter of Credit, and we shall deliver the original of this Letter of Credit so endorsed to the transferee.

This Letter of Credit expires at our above address on June 30, 2001 but will be automatically extended, without written amendment, in each succeeding calendar year, up to but not beyond June 30, 2005, unless we have sent written notice to you at your above address that we elect not to renew this Letter of Credit beyond the date specified in such notice, which date will be June 30, 2001 or any subsequent June 30 but not beyond June 30, 2005 at least forty-five (45) calendar days after the date we send you such notice. Notice of non-renewal shall be deemed received by you four (4) business days after the date such notice is deposited in the U.S. mail, postage prepaid

That payment is to be made by transfer to an account with us or at another bank, we and/or such other bank may rely on an account number specified in such instructions even if the number identifies a person or entity different from the intended payee.

Documents must be presented to us no later than 5:00p.m.

Draft(s) must indicate the number and date of this credit.

Each draft presented hereunder must be accompanied by this original credit for our endorsement thereon of the amount of such draft.

Documents must be forwarded to us via courier in one parcel and may be mailed to Bank, operation group, Northern California, 525 Main Street, 25th Floor, AnyTown, CA 99999.

This credit is subject to the uniform customs and practice for documentary credits (1993 revision), international chamber of commerce, publication number 500, and engages us in accordance with the terms thereof.

Yours Truly,

Bank

## Exhibit 5
## Example of Letter of Credit Lease Provision

6. <u>Security</u>

    6.1    <u>Security Deposit</u>. Contemporaneously with the execution of this Lease, Tenant shall pay to Landlord the Security Deposit, which shall be held by Landlord to secure Tenant's performance of its obligations under this Lease. The Security Deposit is not an advance payment of Rent or a measure or limit of Landlord's damages upon an Event of Default (defined in Section 17). Landlord may, from time to time and without prejudice to any other remedy, use all or a part of the Security Deposit to perform any obligation Tenant fails to perform hereunder. Following any such application of the Security Deposit, Tenant shall pay to Landlord on demand the amount so applied in order to restore the Security Deposit to its original amount. Provided that Tenant has performed all of its obligations hereunder, Landlord shall, within thirty (30) days after the Term ends, return to Tenant the portion of the Security Deposit which was not applied to satisfy Tenant's obligations. The Security Deposit may be commingled with other funds, and no interest shall be paid thereon. If Landlord transfers its interest in the Premises and the transferee assumes Landlord's obligations under this Lease, then Landlord may assign the Security Deposit to the transferee and Landlord thereafter shall have no further liability for the return of the Security Deposit.

    6.2    <u>Letter of Credit</u>. In lieu of the Security Deposit referenced above, concurrently with Tenant's execution of this Lease. Tenant may deliver to Landlord an irrevocable letter of credit as hereinafter described (the "<u>Letter of Credit</u>"). The Letter of Credit shall (i) be an irrevocable standby letter of credit, (ii) name Landlord as beneficiary, (iii) be payable on sight draft accompanied only by Landlord's certification that it is entitled to payment thereon because an Event of Default under the Lease has occurred, (iv) be for an initial term of at least twelve (12) months and, subject to the terms set forth below, shall be renewed thereafter no later than thirty (30) days prior to any expiration date thereof so that the Letter of Credit remains in effect during the entire period ending thirty (30) days after the expiration of the initial Term and any renewal term of this Lease, (v) assure payment in the total amount of $8,122,274.95, and (vi) be otherwise in form reasonably acceptable to Landlord. If Tenant fails timely to renew its Letter of Credit, then Landlord shall have the right to draw thereon, and retain the amounts so drawn as the Security Deposit. The following provisions shall govern the parties' rights and obligations with respect to the Letter of Credit:

        6.2.1    Landlord shall be entitled to recourse against the Letter of Credit to recover any loss or damage it may suffer as a result of any breach or default by Tenant under this Lease. Partial and multiple draws shall be permitted under the Letter of Credit. After any such draw,

Tenant shall pay to Landlord on demand the amount so drawn to be held as part of the Security Deposit.

6.2.2 Provided an Event of Default has not occurred during the twelve (12) month period prior to each reduction and Tenant's financial condition as of the date of each reduction, in Landlord's reasonable judgment, is equal to or better than its financial condition as of the Commencement Date, Landlord shall reduce the required amount of the Letter of Credit as follows:

| Lease Month | Letter of Credit Amount |
| --- | --- |
| 1 – 12 | $8,122,275.00 |
| 13 – 24 | $7,445,419.00 |
| 25 – 36 | $6,768,562.00 |
| 37 – 48 | $6,091,706.00 |
| 49 – 60 | $5,414,850.00 |
| 61 – 73 | $4,737,994.00 |
| 73 – 85 | $4,061,137.00 |
| 85 – 97 | $3,384,281.00 |
| 97 – 109 | $2,707,425.00 |
| 109 – 120 | $2,030,569.00 |

Without limitation, Tenant may satisfy the financial condition requirement set forth above if, as of the date of each scheduled reduction, Tenant can provide evidence reasonably acceptable to Landlord that Tenant then has cash or cash equivalents on hand in an amount equal to or greater than the total of the next twelve (12) months of Basic Rent coming due under this Lease. Subject to the above, Tenant's failure to keep the Letter of Credit in effect during the entire initial term of the Lease, or Tenant's failure to furnish written evidence to Landlord of the yearly renewal of the Letter of Credit, shall be an Event of Default hereunder.

6.2.3 Tenant shall pay, as Additional Rent under this Lease, any and all costs or fees charged in connection with the Letter of Credit that arise due to: (i) Landlord's sale or transfer of all or a portion of the Building; or (ii) the addition, deletion or modification of any beneficiaries under the Letter of Credit.

## Exhibit 6
## Proposed Term Sheet (Draft)

| | |
|---|---|
| **Lessor:** | Centaur Advisors |
| **Lessee:** | Lodestar, Inc. |
| **Building:** | Plano Office Center |
| **Address:** | 8600 Dallas Tollway |
| **City:** | Plano, TX |
| **Suites:** | A & B (ground floor) |
| **Square Footage:** | 80,000 SF |
| **Use:** | Manufacturing of microcircuit boards and other computer peripherals for medical field |
| **Tenant Finish:** | Open plan; concrete and tile floor; paint. |
| **Parking:** | 400 dedicated spaces |
| **Term:** | 10 years |
| **Rent:** | $18.50 per sq. ft annually; adjustment to market at end of 5th year |
| **Utilities:** | Tenant pays electricity |
| **Common Area Maintenance:** | Tenant reimburses pro rata share |
| **Taxes and Insurance:** | Tenant pays pro rata share of increases beyond first year |
| **Telecommunications:** | Serviced by Building Access, Inc. |
| **Options to Renew:** | One for 5 years at market |
| **Signage Rights:** | To be negotiated |
| **Special Features:** | $12.00 per square foot tenant finish allowance for above-standard improvements; backed by letter of credit from bank acceptable to lessor; additional annual payment to lessor of bonus rent equal to 10% of total allowance. |

**Exhibit 7**
**SUMMARY OF KEY PROVISIONS**
**TELECOMMUNICATIONS SERVICES AGREEMENT**

### Parties to Agreement

Property Owner: Centaur Advisors, Inc.

Service Provider: Building Access, Inc.

### Services Provided Tenants

Local, intraLATA toll (or local toll), long distance, high-speed data, internet, video/cable television, cable Internet and other lawful services and applications that Service Provider may provide now or in the future.

Service Provider holds all right and title to the services and retains the right, in its sole discretion, to control, add to, delete, and/or change such services.

Service Provider has the right, but not the obligation, to market and contract with Tenants for the provision of any or all of the Services on an individual subscriber basis, independent of Owner.

Orders for service(s) shall be solely between Service Provider and individual Tenants. Service Provider retains the right to terminate such service(s) to Tenants who fail to abide by the terms and conditions of service contracts.

### Installation of Services

Property Owner provides Service Provider with a non-exclusive easement on, over, under, within, and through the Premises (both land and improvements) as necessary or desirable for: Service Provider to provide services to tenants.

Within this easement, Service Provider has the right to construct and install and use any cabling, wiring, power supplies, risers, conduits, distribution wiring and facilities, cross-connect facilities and/or distribution frames (collectively referred to as "Facilities"), and any rights of way and entrance facilities within and into the building, as necessary or useful, for the provision of services to the Tenants, whether owned, installed, controlled or maintained by Service Provider or not.

Service Provider has the right to install on the roof of any building on the Premises an antenna or other equipment, as necessary or desirable for the provision of services to the Tenants, together with any wiring or cabling from the antenna to the rest of the facilities.

Property Owner is not responsible for installation charges, monthly subscription rates, equipment deposits, or other charges for subscribers' service(s).

### Charges for Services

Service Provider is responsible for collection of charges, billing, accounting, and other services related to subscriber accounts.

Owner is not responsible for installation charges, monthly subscription rates, equipment deposits, or other charges for subscribers' service(s).

**Term of Agreement**

Agreement becomes effective on the date of the agreement and continues as so long as Service Provider or Agent may provide the Services, not to exceed ____* years from the date of this Agreement. Thereafter, the Agreement is automatically renewed for consecutive terms of ____* years each, unless written notice of termination is given by either party.

**Termination**

This Agreement may be terminated prior to expiration of its term:

(a) by either party in the event of material breach of this Agreement after 30 days' written notice, unless the other party cures or commences to cure such breach during such 30-day period and diligently proceeds with such cure; or

(b) by Service Provider upon at least 60 days' written notice if Service Provider is unable, or it becomes impracticable, to continue distribution of any one or more of the Services due to any law, rule, regulation, judgment, contract with third party or other reason beyond the reasonable control of Service Provider.

Upon termination of this Agreement and any other legally enforceable rights of access to provide Services, Service Provider shall, at its sole option, have an additional ninety (90) days to remove or abandon part or all of the Facilities, in its sole discretion.

**Assignment/Successors**

Benefits and obligations of Agreement run with the land and will inure to and are binding upon the successors, assigns, heirs, and personal representatives of Service Provider and Owner during the Term hereof.

**Subordination Rights**

Agreement is subordinate to all leases, mortgages, and/or deed of trust which may now or hereafter affect the Premises, and to all renewals, modifications, consolidations, replacements and extensions thereof.

Service Provider's obligation to subordinate this Agreement to any present or future mortgage, deed of trust or lease is subject to and contingent upon satisfaction of such mortgagee's, trustee's or lessor's obligation to recognize and not disturb Service Provider's rights and obligations under this Agreement.

**Sale of Property**

Easement runs with the land and binds Owner, and each and every subsequent owner thereof, for the term of this agreement

Owner makes assumption of the Agreement a condition of any sale, transfer or assignment of the property.

* Negotiated

## Questions for Discussion

Questions that should be addressed in this case include:

1. What are some of the attractions to Lodestar of the Dallas/Fort Worth Metro Area? Of the Far North Dallas/Richardson Plano submarket? Of the Plano Office Center?

2. How well does the Plano Office Center match up with Allison's criteria for the location of a new facility? How important are the shortfalls as compared with the advantages?

3. What are Lodestar's interests in these negotiations? What are their alternatives?

4. What are Centaur's interests in these negotiations? What are their alternatives?

5. What are the areas of the negotiations where the interests of the parties converge? Diverge?

6. What can Lodestar trade-off and what would be the concession(s) that Centaur should be asked to make?

7. What modifications, if any, should Allison propose in the Draft Term Sheet (Exhibit 6)?

Please use these questions as a guide and not a format or a reflection of all of the questions that need to be addressed by the case.

# 9

# CORPORATE REAL ESTATE

## Case A: SPRINT CORPORATION[1]

Sprint Corporation (Sprint) is a Kansas City based global communications company serving more than 26 million business and residential customers in more than 70 countries. With 80,000 employees, the firm is a major user of a wide variety of real estate facilities throughout the world.

Sprint is widely recognized for developing, engineering and deploying state-of-the-art network technologies, including America's first nationwide all-digital, fiber-optic network (FON Division). Sprint also operates the largest all digital, nationwide wireless network in the US, serving 15.8 million subscribers (PCS Division). Nearly 100% of Sprint's customers are served by digital switching technology, which provides a platform for a whole portfolio of network-based voice, video, and data services.

### Management Strategy

In November 2000, Sprint announced a series of key strategic initiatives to build its wireless business into a major world-class service provider and to transform its wired service into a data-centric operation.[2] This would be achieved by:

---

[1] This case was prepared by John McMahan for the 2002 PikeNetForum in New York City. Copyright © 2002 and 2004, John McMahan, all rights reserved.
[2] Company Web Site, April 21, 2002.

- **Wireless Operations:** Investment to increase Sprint's US wireless network to third-generation capability. This would result in up to a doubling of voice capacity nationwide and would dramatically increase data speeds. The upgrade would also allow Sprint to improve spectrum efficiency, which should lead to improved operating margins.

- **Wired Operations:** Growth in wired-based products and services. This would primarily come from leveraging the company's Tier 1 Internet backbone. This should help to expand transport capabilities, web hosting, value-added services (such as managed network services and applications), and global IP services.

## *Financial Performance*

Each Sprint Division trades separately and both have come under the same financial pressures affecting the entire telecommunications industry: a combination of intense competition and the general slowdown in the overall economy.

**FON Division:** Sprint's FON division outperformed the S&P 500 through most of 2001 but ended the year announcing a fourth quarter loss of $578 million. The Division came under additional pressure in early February as a result of the bankruptcy of Global Crossings Ltd., a major customer of FON. Concerns also were developing about the debt structure of the telecommunications industry largely because of short-term debt pressure on Quest Communications International. Most analysts did not expect FON to be affected largely because it was not involved in similar accounting issues and seemed to have sufficient debt capacity. The FON Division had been downgraded by Fitch Ratings, however, and was under review by Moody's and Standard & Poors.[3]

While revenue and net income were down in the first quarter of 2002, financial performance appeared to be stabilizing. Chairman and Chief Executive, William T. Esrey stated:

> "This quarter, the FON Group demonstrated its resilience in the face of a challenging marketplace. In our local operations, we continue to aggressively manage costs, improve operating profits and sell our services in value-adding bundles."[4]

---

[3] Dow Jones Business News, February 19, 2002.
[4] Company press release, April 15, 2002.

**PCS Division:** Sprint's PCS Division had incurred a loss of $328 million in the fourth quarter of 2001 and announced in mid-February that it was closing five of its thirteen call centers and laying off 3,000 people, approximately 9% of its workforce.[5] On a positive note, PCS announced a few days later a new technological breakthrough – an easy-to-use software solution that would allow Sprint customers to access corporate e-mail, calendar, company directory, and personal contacts without having to synchronize when they returned to the office. Best of all, the customer's computer did not have to remain connected to the network for the solution to work.[6]

PCS financial performance in the first quarter of 2002 also appeared to be stabilizing. Revenue had soared 41% as average monthly revenue per user climbed to $60. Sprint PCS continued to add new subscribers. EBITDA more than doubled from the same quarter in 2001.

PCS continued to prepare for the launch of its third-generation wireless service (3G) in summer 2002. Mr. Esrey noted that:

> "3G offers greater speeds and the applications that business and consumers need on a wide array of devices. With new data services such as e-mail and photo attachments, 3G will allow Sprint customers to stay connected with a broad range of applications."[7]

Regarding Sprint as a whole, Mr. Esrey said:

> "Despite a challenging economy, we are seeing improvements in our traditional wireline business and continue to deliver outstanding results. Nevertheless, we remain focused on improving the efficiency of our operations enterprise wide."[8]

## Sprint Real Estate

Sprint Real Estate (SRE) was responsible for managing a worldwide inventory of real property assets and services supporting the company's operating and growth requirements. Assets included retail stores in most major cities; office facilities in Kansas City, regional, and international locations; transmission and maintenance facilities in numerous locations; and warehouse facilities throughout the world.

---

[5] Company press release, February 15, 2002.
[6] Company press release, February 20, 2002.
[7] Company Press Release, April 15, 2002.
[8] ibid.

SRE services included leasing/developing/disposing of real property facilities, lease administration, payment of property occupancy costs, and providing building security services.

While human resources (HR) was not a direct management responsibility of SRE, they had a close working relationship with the HR group in making certain that the physical work environment was conducive to the highest level of employee morale and work efficiency. SRE also interfaced on a continuing basis with the financial reporting group in terms of ongoing real property operations, cost control initiatives, and cash management.

As with the real estate groups of most US corporations, SRE viewed the line of business units (LOB) of the company as its major customers. The heads of these units had the option of utilizing local non-Sprint real estate resources, which were generally viewed by SRE as being non-standardized, duplicative, slower in execution, and of generally higher cost to the corporation. As a result, the SRE group sought to provide "integrated, innovative, cost-effective, and profitable services for the business enterprise" and by so doing, become the "sole provider of real property services" to each of the firm's business units.[9]

As an example, in providing space for the PCS division, SRE had to deal with the fast-moving world of technological product development and deployment. With the objective of achieving early market share penetration, the roll out of new products often required significant new physical infrastructure and facilities.

Some of these facilities came through the acquisition of existing firms, a portion was leased in local real estate markets, and in some cases, others involved new building development. There also was pressure on SRE to consider the reuse of existing Sprint facilities that were no longer required for their originally intended use. Unfortunately, this strategy often required more time to execute and/or involved getting mired in corporate red tape.

In all cases, the pressure on SRE to keep up with product deployment was intense. No one wanted a lack of real estate to become a bottleneck in the race to market. In some instances, this reaction resulted in higher acquisition, development, and operating costs, which in turn, required greater financial resources if the effort was to be successful. In some cases, this situation was further complicated by business strategy decisions such as combining office and warehousing in the same building.

If the new product turned out to be unsuccessful, SRE was faced with the job of unwinding Sprint's real estate commitments. Solving this problem

---

[9] Source: Sprint Internal Document.

could involve selling the facilities, re-leasing to new tenants, or transferring employees from other Sprint operations. Again, these solutions might involve higher costs and/or sublease revenue shortfalls, which could put additional strain on corporate financial resources.

Unlike most high growth technology firms, Sprint was faced with the additional uncertainty of operating within the constraints of the government laws and policies that regulate the telecommunications industry. Even if a product were successful in the marketplace, there was always the possibility that a required license might not be obtained in a timely fashion or the merger of a competitor could lead to changes in regulatory requirements.

There also was the issue of how facility costs should be allocated within the corporation. Should they be charged to the independent business unit that is utilizing the facility or to "Mother Sprint" as an overall corporate allocation? This issue became particularly critical in situations where facility costs were considerably higher than budgeted due to the pressures for rapid product deployment.

Operating within this environment of market, regulatory, physical, and corporate constraints, SRE management knew that they had to develop a clear understanding of what they could and couldn't do.

## *Project "Evolution"*

SRE management believed that a major key to improving their ability to deliver for their LOB clients was the development and integration of a web-based real property information system. Beginning in 1996, Sprint corporate management sought to become "net ready" through a series of firm-wide technology based initiatives that provided the foundation for such a system.

In November 2000, management committed to the vision of transforming SRE operations through the development of a more robust end-to-end, automated, and web-enabled business model. Based on Cisco's "Net Ready" success factors of leadership, governance, technology, and competency, Project Evolution ("Evolution") was launched.

The project addressed five key areas:[10]

- **Information Management:** Through Evolution, SRE sought to improve the timeliness and accuracy of information and intelligence needed to support better decision-making.

- **Streamline Processes:** Another objective was to streamline SRE's management processes. Targeted processes included space

---
[10] Company Internal Document.

forecasting; facility planning; moving, adding, or changing operating facilities; project management; accounting; and tracking company real property assets.

- **Initiative Prioritization and Selection:** By establishing priorities, SRE expected to communicate clear guidelines and insure better coordination of all Sprint property activities.

- **Accountability Metrics:** In order to establish greater employee and business group accountability, accurate and timely metrics would be required. These metrics would help to better align operations and support overall enterprise objectives.

- **Organizational Alignment:** Finally, Evolution was expected to better align the real estate function in terms of customer focus, communication, and efficient operations.

The plan was to implement Project Evolution in three phases.

## Phase 1.0

Phase 1.0 began in early April 2001 with the formation of a project team and selection of a consulting partner, Deloitte & Touche. Interviews with SRE associates, customers and process partners were conducted and several areas of immediate improvement were identified. These areas included streamlining processes, improving customer touch points, and strengthening SRE's strategic positioning within Sprint. A roadmap was developed that outlined two major imperatives:

1. Focus on six core areas for initial process improvements.
2. Identify key opportunities for SRE to focus its migration to a web-enabled business model.

Between May and October, six SRE teams focused on improving existing processes, standardizing data, developing better performance metrics, and establishing a better understanding of the firm's real property assets.

On October 11, 2001, the teams presented their Phase 1.0 recommendations to the whole group in order to understand better each team's approach and to identify areas of synergy within SRE and other process partners within the corporation. At this meeting, near-term implementation targets (Phase 1.5) were identified as well as longer-term (Phase 2.0) visions and recommendations.

## Phase 1.5: Near-Term Implementation

Phase 1.5 was kicked off in July 2001. It addressed the first imperative on the strategic roadmap, namely to develop a future vision of six core areas and to identify and develop process improvement opportunities, which could be implemented independent of major technology investments. The six areas targeted were:

| Target | Team |
|---|---|
| 1. Lease Administration | (Project Habitat) |
| 2. Data Standardization | (Project DNA) |
| 3. Resource Management | (Project Globalization) |
| 4. Project Management | (Project Lifecycle) |
| 5. Facilities Services/MACs | (Project Ecosystem) |
| 6. Performance Metrics | (Project Biometrics) |

Six teams comprised of cross-functional SRE managers and supported by director-level sponsors completed detailed process maps and implementation plans.

In addition to the Phase 1.5 process teams, an analysis was begun in mid-December 2001 to develop an overall IT strategy that would integrate and align with the business plans and strategy of both Sprint CRE and the Sprint Enterprise as a whole. This strategy addressed the following areas:

- Architecture
- Applications
- Data
- Operations

Between October and March, the SRE team focused on Phase 1.5 implementation. This resulted in several key accomplishments:

- A **Project Initiation Form** was developed which will allow 250 CRE customers (LOBs) to being initiating projects electronically.
- A **High Level Project Cost Template** was rolled out for use in discussing cost and budget issues with the business units finance organization.
- **Livelink** was selected and implemented as the corporate wide repository to access business documentation. In addition, significant progress was made in reducing the number of signatures required to obtain fiscal approval of real estate projects.

- A **Project Tracking Tool** was developed as a module in SEGIS and rolled out for immediate use. Approximately 45 SRE associates were trained in the use of this tool in late February
- In March, SRE rolled out a **Financial Tracking Tool** for use in coordinating activities with corporate finance managers.
- **Vendor Sourcing** strategies are being developed to validate selection of service providers.

## *Phase 2.0 Longer Term Visions and Recommendations*

Phase 2.0 was designed to address both the recommendations from the IT Strategy analysis and the second imperative of the strategic roadmap from Phase 1.0. Three major opportunities were identified:

- Project / Financial Management
- Self Service
- Robust integration of IT Infrastructure

A key aspect of IT strategy was a focus on "end-to-end" core real estate processes. SRE managers indicated that they wanted to manage the real estate business from an end-to-end process perspective to help eliminate the silos of information and reduce process hand-offs. This quickly became a key core component of the IT strategy

## *Issues and Challenges*

As of mid-April, SRE managers faced several challenges in the implementation of Project Evolution:

- As noted, SRE managers operate in a functional organizational "silos" with limited knowledge of the other processes required to deliver a complete real estate product (e.g., fully equipped office space). In the Evolution world of the future, people will be asked to be accountable for end-to-end processes that cover the entire real estate life cycle. The challenge will be to "migrate" solutions to support this fundamental change in organizational focus.
- New technical functionality will be required to meet the new business needs required by the changing organization. At the same time, SRE managers must ensure that they are leveraging existing technology investment as much as possible.
- In addition to changes in technology, enhanced leadership capabilities will be required to migrate to a new CRE business model based upon an end-to-end process view.

- Measurable accountability will have to be assigned to one person for each process function.
- Decisions involving project management, financial management, and self-service real estate operations will be critical in the success of the implementation effort.
- Decisions pertaining to integration of current user applications supporting the vision of Project Evolution and the selection of new solutions to address future Evolution process requirements must be made.
- Decisions pertaining to the managing the business based upon a "balanced scorecard" of measurements must be made.

Most, if not all, of the SRE managers knew that they had their work cut out for them if they were going to be successful in utilizing technology to fundamentally change the way real estate was managed within the corporation. If they could pull it off, SRE would move a long way towards achieving its goal of becoming "a valued partner by delivering innovative and competitive solutions" and by so doing, becoming the "sole provider of real property services" to Sprint's operating divisions.

## *Questions for Discussion*

Questions that should be addressed in this case include:

1. At the time of the case, what is Sprint's overall corporate strategy?
2. How does this affect Sprint's real estate group (SRE) and its operations?
3. What specific challenges does SRE face in dealing with Sprint's real estate?
4. What is SRE's relationship with the company's financial services group? With the HR group?
5. What is "Project Evolution" all about?
6. How was "Project Evolution" implemented?
7. As of mid April, 2002, what are some of the major issues and challenges facing SRE?

Please use these questions as a guide and not a format or a reflection of all of the questions that need to be addressed by the case.

# Case B: JONES LANG LASALLE[11]

Jones Lang LaSalle is a leading real estate services and investment management firm operating across more than 100 markets on five continents. The firm was created through the merger of LaSalle Partners, a U.S.-based real estate services and investment management firm, and Jones Lang Wootton, a British-based provider of global real estate services.

Jones Lang LaSalle offers comprehensive, integrated expertise, including investment, advisory, corporate, and management services on local, regional and global levels. Clients include real estate owners, occupiers and investors. The firm is also an industry leader in property and corporate facility management services with a global portfolio of approximately 725 million square feet under management.

LaSalle Investment Management, a member of the Jones Lang LaSalle group, has a global portfolio of more than $22 billion under management and is one of the world's largest real estate investment managers.

## Real Estate Services Sector

Jones Lang LaSalle operates in the highly competitive public real estate service sector, which includes investment banks, pension fund advisory firms and consulting firms as well as traditional real estate service providers such as Trammell Crow Company and Insignia Financial Group, Inc. Jones Lang LaSalle also competes with several national private firms such as CB Richard Ellis[12], Cushman and Wakefield, Transwestern, Staubach, Studley and a wide range of smaller companies.

In the last few years, the sector has been under significant profit pressure, largely due to a combination of several factors:

- Highly competitive market environment
- Cyclical nature of real estate earnings
- Dependency upon contingent income (i.e., brokerage commissions)
- Lack of growth in reported earnings
- Record of earnings "surprises" during the past few years
- Structural problems in absorbing global acquisitions

---

[11] This case was prepared by John McMahan for the 2002 PikeNetForum in New York City. Copyright © John McMahan 2002 and 2004, all rights reserved.
[12] Company press release, February 5, 2002.

- Downturn in global economies
- Downturn in the real estate economy

## *Management Strategy*

Jones Lang LaSalle places great emphasis on deepening and expanding client relationships to increase stable revenues derived from corporate strategic alliances, investor services, and investment advisory income. Success is measured by the firm's number of strategic alliances, square footage under leasing and management contracts, and growth in LaSalle Investment Management's assets under management.

In the services area, Jones Lang LaSalle's strategy is to become the "trusted real estate advisor" for global corporations. This includes not only traditional real estate services such as property management, facility management, project development, tenant representation, leasing and investment transactions, but also relatively new offerings such as data centers, mail and parcel delivery, security, employee feeding and company transportation.

Jones Lang LaSalle's service delivery is best described by its "Client Service Model."

> "Our mission is to deliver exceptional strategic, fully integrated global services and solutions for real estate owners, occupiers and investors."

## *Financial Performance*

The firm's initial public offering occurred in late 1997, and the stock subsequently traded below its IPO price until recently. For the fiscal year ending December 31, 2001, Jones Lang LaSalle announced adjusted net income of $40.5 million or $1.31 per diluted share.[13] This was in line with First Call consensus estimates and matched the firm's record 2000 performance. For the last half of 2001 and in early 2002, Jones Lang LaSalle's stock price traded above the S&P 500 average, contrasting favorably with Trammell Crow and Insignia, both of which traded at or below the average.[14]

In announcing 2001 results, Chris Peacock, Chief Executive Officer, stated:

> "This performance shows that our business model is flexible enough to perform well even in a very difficult and demanding year. All of our segments experienced lower revenues for the year as difficult economic conditions

---

[13] Company press release, February 5, 2002.
[14] Charles Schwab, March 1, 2002.

translated into a significant slowdown in transaction activity."[15]

Peacock attributed this performance to the firm's business strategy:

"We believe we have an unparalleled integrated global platform, the industry's best professionals, and clear strategic focus on core competencies and technology leadership. This combination has led to a strong backlog of business for the year and further expansion of our client base with major global engagements such as Microsoft and Rockwell Automation."

In terms of the future, he went on to say:

"We are continuing our focus on containing discretionary costs following the successful implementation of our global restructuring program but are investing appropriately in strategic business areas of the firm that offer the strongest future growth potential. As a result, our 2002 plan, although assuming flat revenues, anticipates that we will grow our comparable earnings per share by seven to 10 percent year on year."

In 2002, Jones Lang LaSalle announced a new contract with Motorola to provide worldwide real estate services, reflecting the firm's increasing presence as a major global service provider.

On March 14, 2002, Moody's Investor Services upgraded Jones Lang LaSalle's senior unsecured debt from Ba2 to Ba1. In supporting the upgrade, Moody's cited the firm's material improvement in credit fundamentals, relatively stable operating results and slightly improved margins in a challenging environment. This came largely as a result of a debt reduction of $100 million over the prior two years.[16]

## *The Commercial Real Estate Market*

The U.S. commercial real estate market represents approximately $5.0 trillion in assets, 45 percent of which is institutionally owned. Within the institutional market, $373 billion (18.2 percent) represents equity investments, 77.9 percent of which is owned by pension funds and Real Estate Investment

---

[15] Company press release, op.cit.
[16] Company Press Release, March 14, 2002.

Trusts (REITs). Properties include retail, office, industrial and multifamily investments.[17]

A large service sector exists to buy, sell, and manage these properties. Players include brokers, property and facility managers, financial service specialists, contractors, and other service providers such as lawyers, title insurance, and appraisal firms. Total annual revenues generated by the commercial real estate service sector are estimated to exceed $35 billion annually. The largest service sector, real estate brokerage, generates $12.8 billion annually, of which $7.6 billion represents leasing commissions and $5.2 billion in investment sales commissions.[18] Commission income is divided relatively evenly across each of the four major property types.

The real estate market is characterized by a large number of relatively small transactions that are very labor-intensive both in terms of time and data collection and storage. Information and documentation often are not standardized, and a plethora of state and local jurisdictions further complicate matters.

## *Role of Technology*

Emerging technology is expected to improve the efficiency of real estate transactions in a variety of ways:

- Provide a broader market of potential buyers or sellers (tenants or buildings)
- Provide more information in a timely fashion to make better decisions
- Provide greater transaction transparency
- Reduce transaction time
- Reduce transaction costs
- In some cases eliminate the service provider altogether (i.e., principal to principal)
- Improve reporting and process control

It is anticipated that most of these benefits will initially accrue to the principals involved in the transactions. While service providers will not be eliminated from the market, their role and value proposition with real estate

---

[17] Source: Rosen Consulting Group, Lend Lease Real Estate Investments, as of September 15, 2001.
[18] *Octane: Knowledge and Transaction Platform*, Jones Lang LaSalle, May 2001.

principals are expected to change dramatically. Brokers are most likely to become either:

- Advisors who add significant value through expert advice and insight, or

- Process facilitators who guide transactions using web-based tools

In either case, brokers will be expected to do more work in less time and probably for lower individual transaction fees. In anticipation of this trend, most U.S. brokerage firms, either individually or in collaboration with other firms, are developing more efficient transaction models. Most of these models are based on aggregating buyers and sellers through a common web-based platform that offers aggregated information (listing and availability), standardized documents, established processes, instantaneous messaging and event logs, and contract management (lease administration). Such a platform is expected to facilitate market information, negotiations and firm/personal relationships.[19]

## Use of Technology

Jones Lang LaSalle prides itself on client service and the use of best in class technology. With a focus on delivering solutions and developing integrated platforms, it has been innovative in working together with other members of the real estate services industry to build applications through Project Octane. Below is a description of Jones Lang LaSalle's technology value proposition, including involvement in Project Octane.

**Project Octane:** In March 2000, Jones Lang LaSalle, CB Richard Ellis, and Trammell Crow announced the formation of Project Octane (Octane), an alliance to develop comprehensive online services platforms, including e-procurement, data integration and transaction services for the real estate industry. The partners in Octane had completed a combined 47,000 sales and lease transactions in 1999, and as of Fall 2000, they managed more than 1.5 billion square feet of properties in the United States. Insignia Financial Group joined Octane as an equal partner on September 21, 2000.

The transaction services platform to be developed was intended to be a hardware and software application service provider offering an Internet-based marketplace, communication, collaboration, and process management vehicle for the benefit of the entire commercial real estate industry.

During the next year, the Octane members made several investments in real estate-related technology efforts. The largest of these was $30 million in

---

[19] Jones Lang LaSalle, ibid.

SiteStuff.com, an e-procurement firm. The concept was to have Octane's members purchase property management and maintenance, repair, and operations (MOR) products through SiteStuff. According to an Octane spokesman:

> "Our goal has always been to provide a reliable and advanced information-sharing mechanism that aggregates best-of-class information for the benefit of the entire commercial real estate industry."[20]

The alliance also became a combined partner in a broadly based consortium called Constellation Real Technologies. Constellation had been established to:

> "... form, incubate and sponsor real estate-related Internet, e-commerce and telecommunications enterprises; acquire interest in existing "best of breed" companies on a synergistic basis; and act as an opportunistic consolidator across property sectors in the emerging real estate technology area."[21]

The other partners in Constellation were AMB Property Corporation, Equity Office Properties Trust, Equity Residential Properties Trust, KB Home, Simon Property Group, Spieker Properties, JP Morgan Partners and Morgan Stanley.

**WorkplaceIQ:** On June 13, 2001, Octane announced the selection of WorkplaceIQ as its Application Service Provider (ASP) for the Transaction Management Services platform. Established in 1991, the firm is headquartered in Waltham, Massachusetts, with technology development facilities in Tel Aviv, Israel and a predominately European-weighted customer base.

For more than a year, WorkplaceIQ had been developing a corporate solution technology that would ultimately become the foundation for Octane's transaction platform. Octane's spokesman, said:

> "WorkplaceIQ is the perfect choice to provide the key technology components for the exchange's transaction platform – they have developed the most advanced software technology in the industry."

---

[20] Buildings.com, August, 2001.
[21] Company press release, June 18, 2001.

> For its part of the bargain, WorkplaceIQ received an immediate base of transactions to use in developing its platform.[22] John Fleming, the firm's CEO, said:

> "The Octane exchange will provide an industry knowledge base that aggregates and integrates real estate information, promotes best practices, and fosters tenant, landlord and broker collaboration on a new level."[23]

In order to fund the transaction, Octane members agreed to invest $2.5 million each in WorkplaceIQ and pay approximately $1 million a year in technology-licensing fees. For its part, WorkplaceIQ raised an additional $3 million in new capital from investors in its original financing round.[24]

**Withdrawal from Constellation Funding:** Octane soon announced that it was withdrawing from further funding obligations in Constellation, but that it would retain its initial investment. At the same time, eight new firms joined Constellation, bringing the total capital to $150 million.[25]

**Concept of Octane Questioned:** By Fall 2001, several of the high-profile real estate e-commerce sites targeting the leasing sector began to fail. These included Zethus, which burned through $15 million of Goldman Sachs' money; RealCentric, a tenant-oriented online business that lasted only 18 months; and Cubitz, which targeted the "do-it-yourself" tenant market and failed to move beyond its first round of financing.

With these failed efforts, the concept of Octane also came under scrutiny. Eileen Circo, writing in *Development Magazine Online* magazine, asked several penetrating questions:

> "Naysayers are quick to argue that the complex risk parameters and dollar size of most real estate transactions make virtual trading on the Internet impractical. Then why on earth would the top commercial real estate service providers sink valuable resources into this endeavor, especially at a time when the changing economic tide is likely to hinder prosperity in 2001? What are the Octane/WorkplaceIQ members really trying to accomplish?

---

[22] In 2000, Project Octane's member firms managed approximately 30 percent of the office deals in the United States over $20 million. Source: Wall Street Journal, June 13, 2001.
[23] Company press release, June 4, 2001.
[24] WorkplaceIQ raised $8 million in Series A funding in November 1999 from Genesis Partners, Cedar Fund, CLAC Ltd., Israel Infinity Fund and Vertex Investments.
[25] The new partners included Archstone Communities Trust, AvalonBayCommunities, Camden Property Trust, The Macerich Company, Taubman Centers, Inc., Starwood Hotels & Resorts Worldwide, Stichting Pensioenfonds ABP, and Teachers Insurance and Annuity Association.

Why would they want to cannibalize their own fee business? Are there analogies for success with a commercial-real-estate-wide platform in other industries? Can competitors really join together in industry-wide collaboration?"

Ms. Circo went on to conclude:

"... the success or failure of an industry-wide trading platform will rest with the collective efforts of the four Octane service providers to penetrate internally, provide incentives for their brokers, and set an enviable model of transaction behavior for their peers. It's not about lowering fees; it's all about delivering greater speed and market information accuracy to an ever-demanding client base."[26]

Six months later, Finn Johnson, Vice President of eBusiness at NAI, in Hightstown, New Jersey, was quoted in the March issue of *Real Estate Forum*:[27]

" ... consortiums are not going to work because you've got very fierce competitors trying to band together to produce a result and, in the final analysis, each has to decide for itself what it's going to do."

In the same issue, Victor S. Voinovich Sr., Chairman of Cleveland-based Interactive Decisions Support, said:

"Every firm in Octane has a different way of doing business ... (this creates) a massive problem with all those big players, getting them to agree on how to do business. The idea of a consortium is good, but Octane will soon outlive its usefulness except maybe as a think tank."

Joseph B. Rubin, a partner and director of real estate e-business for Ernst & Young, concluded:

"The (e-business) solutions that are working today, in lending or brokerage, are those that focus on the back office. It's not in-your-face stuff, or even stuff the customer will see. It's the guts of your business, all focused on cost reduction and process efficiency. The expectation that all transactions will get done entirely via the Internet, though, is not realistic."

---

[26] Development Magazine Online, fall, 2001. Ms. Circo is the former Managing Director of PikeNet.
[27] Joseph Dobrian, "E-Tools Still Fall Short", *Real Estate Forum*, March 2002.

This type of criticism is indicative of the sentiment among many industry players who forecasted that Project Octane would not be alive today. Yet, Project Octane recently celebrated its second anniversary and continues its steadfast commitment to deliver on its collaborative mandate.

## Integrated Information Platform

Jones Lang LaSalle believes that the use of technology and strategic solutions differentiates it in the marketplace. Technology in and of itself is not the key, but integrating sustainable, scalable applications with leading edge process is what benefits clients. To meet this objective, Jones Lang LaSalle delivers to its clients a comprehensive integrated solution known as the Integrated Information Platform (IIP). While Octane offerings are a small part of its overall technology initiatives, the IIP is the platform where new, integrated applications are regularly rolled out to better serve clients. The use of this platform was acknowledged in *Forbes* magazine's Best of the Web feature as the only real estate services company to partner with. The IIP is Jones Lang LaSalle's technology platform and utilizes many applications, tool sets, and a common web services-based development and integration methodology. Jones Lang LaSalle continually re-evaluates and enhances its integrated information platform to support all of its global real estate services. The platform is composed of three key elements:

- Web portal/knowledge management
- Business information warehouse
- Production systems (including Octane)

Jones Lang LaSalle's philosophy is that each element provides a vital function within the platform and ultimately will be fully integrated with the others through web services technologies.

## Web Portal

This Internet-based portal provides the gateway into the world of information that Jones Lang LaSalle provides to its clients. The site offers online, real-time access to each client's transactions and project, property and portfolio information. Information is displayed using web capsules containing information culled from internal and external sources via Microsoft's .NET technology. Examples of information that can be accessed include:

- Executive summary information
- Portfolio information

- Portfolio/property performance
- Benchmarks
- Project status
- Research and market information
- Financial and operating reports
- Best practices
- Discussion forums
- Access to production systems
- Links to other sites

Through security authentication, designated users can be assigned to various levels of access rights to submit and retrieve information. To date, Jones Lang LaSalle has implemented more than 50 client extranet sites worldwide.

## *Business Information Services*

Jones Lang LaSalle's business information warehouse populates capsules within the web portal with real estate operations and portfolio information. Clients and account team personnel can view data at various levels of detail and from multiple vantage points. Information can be displayed graphically or in table format from the portfolio level down to the detailed transaction level. Jones Lang LaSalle believes that this allows users to better understand and analyze business trends and benchmark performance across a portfolio, geographic region or other areas for comparative purposes.

## *Production Systems*

The final element is a series of vendor-based and custom-developed solutions linked through Jones Lang LaSalle's business information warehouse using standard technology tools to aid in analysis and consolidation. Choices between package solutions and those that are custom-developed by Jones Lang LaSalle are based on how they match the firm's best-in-class business process requirements.

Systems currently available through Jones Lang LaSalle's web portal include:

**Lease Administration:** Jones Lang LaSalle uses its internally developed lease administration tool, CredoNet, to enable clients to monitor and receives reports on their property portfolios. CredoNet allows the user to drill down to detailed data on individual properties. The system also allows for benchmarking of key property cost data across the portfolio. CredoNet received the IDRC Global innovator's Award for Corporate Real Estate.

**Transactions Management:** Working with Octane members, Jones Lang LaSalle will co-design and use WorkplaceIQ as its transactions management system. This tool allows Jones Lang LaSalle to build work processes that are specific to the needs of each client and transaction type. The system supports a collaborative database and secure environment that facilitate managing portfolio contracts, vendors, and operations.

**Project Management:** MAGNET® PTS project tracking system is used to support project management activities. The system maintains all project management activities including scope, schedule and budget. It also allows the user to track vendors and employee time charges as well as milestone completion.

**Property Management and Accounting:** Jones Lang LaSalle utilizes JDEdwards for this production function. JDEdwards integrates all aspects of operations with financials including real-time balance inquiry, the ability to track an unlimited number of sub-ledgers, and custom alternative client chart of account reporting. Electronic purchase order entry, routing, and approval also are available. All JDEdwards reports can be downloaded to other applications through simple user tools and viewed on a real-time basis through Jones Lang LaSalle's web portal.

**Call Center:** The vendors for call center activity and facility management are Clarify eFrontOffice and ClearHelpDesk™. This tool integrates, consolidates and routes every customer touch point including telephone, fax, mail and e-mail. Clarity provides the vehicle to assign, route, and track service requests.

**E-Procurement:** Working with Octane members, Jones Lang LaSalle uses SiteStuff as its e-procurement tool. SiteStuff provide online review and approval of invoices and automated entry into the Jones Lang LaSalle payables system. SiteStuff also provides an interface for field personnel purchasing MRO goods. Jones Lang LaSalle has found that through volume aggregation, total costs for these goods have been reduced by 10 to 20 percent per transaction.

## *Issues and Challenges*

Jones Lang LaSalle has more than 300 dedicated IT professionals in the firm working on this and other technology-related programs. To support this level of activity, the firm dedicates 10 percent of its annual revenue to investments in advanced hardware, software, and network and telecommunication systems.

Despite its strong commitment to technology, Jones Lang LaSalle is still faced with many challenges in the months and years to come. The major challenge is to complete the overall strategy and achieve a fully integrated program. This effort requires a determination by management to drive standards throughout the firm so that the strategy is fully embraced by Jones Lang LaSalle's employees and supported by various vendors. It also means a firm-wide commitment to product and service innovation as well as continuous investment in technology research and development. Finally, it involves the continuing support of Jones Lang LaSalle's existing clients and the willingness of new clients to try innovative approaches to solving old problems. To meet this challenge, Jones Lang LaSalle commits its operating and capital resources, but more important, it focuses project teams on innovation, integration, and change management, which is the most critical component. Through dedicated change managers, Jones Lang LaSalle looks to address shifts in behavior to further the effectiveness of technology.

While this may appear to be a Herculean task, most observers believe it is the only way that Jones Lang LaSalle can achieve its goal of becoming the "trusted real estate advisor" for global corporations.

## Questions for Discussion

Questions that should be addressed in this case include:

1. How would you describe the commercial real estate market?
2. What is the role of the real estate services sector? Why is it so competitive? What is the impact of this highly competitive environment on a public company such as JLL?
3. What is JLL's strategy to be a successful firm in this environment? How have they implemented this strategy to date?
4. What is the role of technology in implementing such a strategy?
5. How would you describe JLL's approach to establishing a technology platform?
6. How viable are Project Octane, Constellation, WorkplaceIQ and other cooperative attempts to develop an industry wide technology platform?
7. How would you describe JLL's approach to establishing an Integrated Information Platform (IPP)? Do you think it will be successful?
8. What are the challenges facing JLL moving forward with the IPP program? Are they realistic? Do you think they can be achieved?

Please use these questions as a guide and not a format or a reflection of all of the questions that need to be addressed by the case.

# 10
# ASSET MANAGEMENT AND LEADERSHIP MINICASES

# Case A: PHILLIPS, ROTH, & BLAIR, LLC[1]

You are the asset manager for the Waterside Building (Waterside), a high-quality office building located in Ft. Lauderdale, FL. The building is 12 floors in height and located next to the Inland Waterway. It has sweeping views of the surrounding residential and commercial areas and, in the near distance, the Atlantic Ocean.

The City of Ft. Lauderdale prides itself on its quality of life and is very particular about entitlements for new buildings. As a result, it generally takes 3 to 5 years to secure a building permit and only then after lengthy hearings and public debate.

Waterside, built in 1989 at the bottom of the real estate "depression," is considered one of the prestige office buildings in the Ft. Lauderdale area. Although the building took three years to lease up, it generally has remained fully leased ever since.

One of the major tenants in the building, Phillips, Roth, & Blair, LLC (Phillips) occupies a total of 40,000 SF on the 11th and 12th floors. Phillips, an old line, prestigious law firm, was one of the early tenants in the building. Their original annual rent was $9.50 PSF on a full service basis. It is now

---

[1] Copyright © John McMahan 2003 and 2004, all rights reserved.

1999, and Phillips" lease is up for renewal in 6 months. As a result of inflation adjustments, their current rent is $15.37 PSF. This includes the use of 40 reserved parking spaces, which are currently leasing at $150 per month per space.

Jim Morrison is Phillips' representative for building related matters. Jim was one of the founding partners when the firm was formed in 1969. He was selected for this role because of his professional practice, which is primarily real estate law, and also because he personally owns several retail and office buildings in southern Florida.

The office market in Ft. Lauderdale presently has a 3.1% vacancy rate vs. a 9.7% overall vacancy rate in the greater Miami area. This tight market primarily is due to the large number of high technology companies that have come into the area over the last five years. Most of these organizations are software firms that can operate out of either industrial or traditional office buildings. At the present time, 40% of Waterside is leased to high-tech firms.

The average office rent in Ft. Lauderdale for space similar to the Phillips' suites is $18.50 PSF annually. Most new leases are for five years with an option for renewal at market. Waterside's annual operating costs average $9.20 PSF.

On Tuesday, you meet with Jim to discuss the renewal of the Phillips' lease. He hands you a letter in which the firm is asking for a five-year renewal at $17.00 PSF. They also are asking for several major space upgrades including new carpeting, hardwood floors, wood paneling, painting, lighting, the relocation of several partitions, and ten new parking spaces. You thank Jim for his letter and tell him you will get back to him in a week or so.

The next day you meet with the building's architect and go over the suite upgrades that Jim is requesting. The architect takes some notes and calls you back the following day and tells you that the upgrades will cost approximately $35.00 PSF.

You then call the local bank that handles the building, and the loan officer indicates that you could probably finance up to 50.0% of the improvements at 8.0%, fully amortized over the lease term (24.34 annual constant for five years and 14.56 for ten years).

Finally, you stop by the parking operator's office. He says that he can free up the parking spaces, but that they will have to come out of public spaces, which currently generate average revenue of $15.00 per day per stall. He reminds you that 65% of this revenue goes to the building ownership.

**Assignment:** What lease renewal terms should you propose to Jim? (Assume that the targeted equity return is 12.0 %.)

# Case B: TRUCOMM, INC.[1]

Your firm is in the business of developing and acquiring office and industrial buildings in major US metro areas. While most of your activities have involved suburban space, from time-to-time, you have developed projects within urban areas. Most of this activity occurred in conjunction with the high-technology boom between 1997 and 2001.

One of these developments is a build-to-suit project for TruComm, Inc., a medium sized telecommunications company headquartered in Denver, CO. The project is located in the South of Market area of downtown San Francisco and is intended to be the regional center for TruComm's west coast and Asia operations.

In January of 2001, your firm entered into a lease with TruComm on the following terms:

| | |
|---|---|
| Building: | 100,000 SF (leasable) |
| Term: | 10 years |
| Lease Date: | January 13, 2001 |
| Occupancy: | January 1, 2003 |
| Rent: | $60.00 PSF per annum (years 1 - 5); $70.00 PSF per annum (years 6 - 10) |
| Expenses: | Landlord pays all operating expenses (estimated at $20.00 PSF; assumed to increase 2.0% annually) |
| TIs: | Landlord provides an $80.00 PSF turnkey build-out upon lease commencement |

Based on the signed lease, your firm began construction on the project on March 1, 2001. Total development costs are expected to be approximately $42,550,000. Your take-out loan commitment is for $25,530,000 (60% LTV) with a twenty-year amortization at 8.0% interest (Constant = 10.04). Construction is proceeding according to schedule, and you are confident that you can meet the January 1, 2003 move-in date and achieve the 12.0% IRR hurdle rate for projects of this type.

On January 4, 2002, TruComm's facility manager calls to inform you that due to extreme cutbacks in operation, they will not be able to occupy the space upon completion. They therefore are requesting a proposal from you as to what it would cost them to buy out their lease.

---

[1] Copyright © John McMahan, 2003 and 2004, all rights reserved.

Their request could not have come at a worse time. The San Francisco office market is probably the most devastated major metro area in the country, largely due to the economic collapse of the technology sector. This is particularly true in the South of Market area.

In checking with your local broker, she informs you that under current market conditions, you could probably get $40.00 PSF for the first five years with a $5.00 PSF increase at the beginning of year six. This is based on full-service operating expenses of $17.50 PSF in the first year of operations, increasing 2.0% annually over the remainder of the lease. She estimates that if she started immediately, it would take 6 months to have a tenant under lease on these terms. Although you don't ask, she reminds you that her leasing commission for a new tenant would be her standard 3.0% of the base rent over the base lease period. Her commission for a renewal of an existing tenant would be 1.0%.

You then call your project foreman and inquire as to the status of construction. He replies that the building shell is largely complete, but that the TI installation has not yet begun. He indicates that some of the TI materials have been delivered, but he is generally confident that additional shipments can be cancelled and the space successfully modified to a new tenant's requirements. He notes that TruComm's TI requirements were quite specialized and that for a normal tenant in the current market, the finish could probably be completed for about $45.00 PSF.

You ask if the building can be modified for multitenant use and he responds that, unfortunately, the design of the building was based on TruComm's specific requirements, and the building is too far along in construction to modify successfully for multitenant occupancy.

You then call the assigned property manager for the project and she informs you that for most tenants in the market place, the cost of property management runs about $17.50 PSF.

Finally, you call your mortgage broker and inquire if, in light of changes in the mortgage market, you can get a lower interest rate on the take-out loan commitment. Your mortgage broker replies that he could probably get an LTV of 65% at a 6.0% interest rate amortized over 20 years (Constant = 8.60). In addition, you would have to pay a 1.0% loan commitment fee.

**Assignment:** Calculate the buy-out cost of the lease. (Assume that the leasing broker finds a tenant that executes a five-year lease and renews in year six, according to the above-mentioned terms.)

# Case C: CHERRY ORCHARD SHOPPING CENTER[1]

It is 2005 and you are an asset manager with a shopping center REIT which specializes in rapidly growing urban areas located in the Western United States. The firm has been expanding rapidly and has a reputation in the marketplace for shrewd investment decisions and innovative asset management. This has resulted in strong earnings growth and a steady increase in the value of the Company's stock.

You have just received an email from your firm's VP of Acquisitions regarding a $50 million offer for the Cherry Orchard Shopping Center, which you manage. This is a 600,000 SF community shopping center located in Phoenix, Arizona, one of the fastest growing metropolitan areas in the nation. The city has a policy of keeping land costs relatively low in order to attract new firms which will employ local residents. This is accomplished by pro-business economic policies and relatively relaxed zoning requirements.

The center was built in 1996 and is anchored by a large home improvement chain store and a major regional food chain, which occupies half of the space. The remaining 300,000 SF is made up of upscale in-line shops (60%) and free-standing retail pad operations (40%). The land under the pads is owned by the center, but the buildings were built and are currently owned by the tenants, who pay ground lease payments, plus percentage rents on all sales.

Your firm purchased the center in 2001 for a price of $35 million from the original developer. Since then, you have invested approximately $11 million in extensive capital improvements and currently value the center at $46 million. The current annual net operating income (NOI) from the center is approximately $3 million, of which $2 million is from base rents and $1 million from overage rents.

You are currently projecting that NOI will grow at an annual rate of 3% over the next ten years. One member of your firm's investment committee is more bullish about the investment's prospects, expecting a 5% annual growth rate. You do not anticipate any additional capital expenditures during this ten-year period, other then normal annual budgeted items or those reimbursed by tenants. Nor do you anticipate any major capital improvements during the period.

---

[1] Copyright © John McMahan, 2005, all rights reserved.

Your firm has a target internal rate of return (IRR) of 12% annually, although there is considerable pressure from the investment committee to lower this rate to 10%, in light of the decline in cap rates and the limited acquisition opportunities in the marketplace.

**Assignment:** In the email, the Acquisition VP is asking for your recommendation regarding the following alternatives: (1) accept the offer, (2) reject the offer, or (3) propose a counteroffer with a specific price. She requests that, no matter what your recommendation, you support it with a quantitative analysis. And, incidentally, she wants your recommendation to appear on her desk by the end of the day. It is now 2:00 PM.

# Case D: CLARKSON DEVELOPMENT COMPANY, INC.[1]

Ed Mathews is a Boston-based Construction Manager for Clarkson Development Company, a major developer of high-rise office buildings in the Northeast. Ed has been with the firm for 18 years, starting out as a steel worker and then rising through successive positions with the firm as a foreman, superintendent, assistant manger, and finally manager.

With the financial assistance of the firm, he studied engineering at a local university, and received his structural engineering degree nine years ago. He is very proud of the fact that he has supervised the building of 6 high rise buildings on time and within budget and, perhaps more important to Ed, without a major accident.

In his non-working hours, Ed is heavily involved with the Roxbury Boys' and Girls' Club where he serves on the Board and is responsible for overseeing construction of the new club facility.

\*\*\*

It's a bright, fall Wednesday, and Ed is making his rounds on the Seagate Building, a new 25-story building in downtown Boston that Clarkson has under construction. He first encounters John Wynsinksi, the concrete foreman who is overseeing a major pour for the parking garage.

**John:** "Morning Ed, how does the pour look to you?"

**Ed:** "Looks OK, but Key-Riest, is it going slow. You're already four days behind and starting to get in the way of the steel delivery trucks."

**John:** "Well, we've really been striving for a quality pour, and it's just taken longer."

**Ed:** "I'm just as keen on quality as you are but this is ridiculous. You know how important this job is to the firm. Let's get back on schedule by next week. I want a full report on Tuesday."

Ed then moves on to the construction elevator and begins the ascent with Nick Rawlins, the elevator operator.

**Ed:** "Are you sure you've got the right clutch on this thing? It seems to me that it's slipping too much."

---

[1] Copyright © John McMahan 2002 and 2004, all rights reserved.

**Nick:** "Yeah, maybe you're right. I've got an idea of what the problem is and how we can fix it."

**Ed:** "You're not paid to solve problems. Your job is to make sure that the elevator runs safely; the engineers are the ones to solve any design problems. I'll mention it to them when I get back to the trailer."

**Nick:** "But I think I might be able to help."

Ed says nothing during the rest of the trip. He gets out on the 3rd floor and walks over to Bill who is supervising the installation of the steel floor decking. While he waits for Bill to finish talking to one of his crew, Ed looks carefully at the decking that has been installed.

**Bill:** "Morning Ed. What'd you think of the Red Sox game last night? Really a close game, eh?"

**Ed:** "That was quite a game, but I'm more concerned with the way you're connecting the decking to the girders; it just doesn't look right. Are you sure it conforms to the working drawings?"

**Bill:** "Yeah, come have a look."

Ed goes over to a portion of the decking that is completed and looks over the drawings.

**Ed:** "Well, I guess it conforms, but it still doesn't look right. I'll discuss it with the architect when I get back to the trailer."

**Bill:** "Well, if we're going to change anything, we'd better get going soon. Why didn't you say something when we were on the second floor?"

**Ed:** "I should have. I just can't catch everything."

Ed then turns around abruptly and heads back to the elevator.

On the descent, neither he nor Nick speaks.

# Case E: MONROE REAL ESTATE ADVISORS, INC.[1]

Nancy Bliss is CEO of Monroe Real Estate Advisors, Inc., a $2 billion pension real estate advisor based in Chicago. Nancy oversees a staff of 75 real estate professionals including specialists in property acquisition and disposition, asset management, marketing, finance, and research.

In addition to her work with Monroe, Nancy is heavily involved in charity and civic affairs in the greater Chicago area and is a close acquaintance of many major business and political figures.

\* \* \*

Monroe's monthly management meeting has been in progress for an hour.

**Nancy:** "Harry, what's happening on the new business front?"

**Harry:** "We're doing well with our new fund but starting to see a slowdown in separate account activity, which, of course, is our core business."

**Nancy:** "Why do you think this is happening?"

**Harry:** "I think the major reason is that the public pension funds are having a hard time competing for the employees necessary to manage the more intensive separate account programs."

**Nancy:** "Well, what do you plan to do?"

**Harry:** "Shift our marketing efforts to concentrate on the large public plans that still favor separate accounts."

**Nancy:** "Maybe there is a shift in the market that we should be sensitive to. Did you consider the development of another fund?"

**Harry:** "What do you think should be the focus of a new fund?"

**Nancy:** "I don't know. That's for you to come up with."

**Harry:** "I really don't have the resources to work on a new fund."

**Nancy:** "Well, then hire or borrow them."

**Ester** (research director)**:** "I think I can loan you one of our research analysts to work on trends in the marketplace that might indicate a niche that we should pursue."

---

[1] Copyright © John McMahan 2002 and 2004, all rights reserved.

**Allan** (acquisitions director): "I can also make some calls to the markets that we're working in to see what's hot."

**Nancy:** "Very well then, it's decided. Harry will form a task force to study the development of a new fund. The other members of the task force will be Ester and Allan, supported by one of Ester's research analysts. Plan to report back at our next monthly meeting. Any questions?"

There are no questions.

**Nancy:** "Let's move on. Since you mentioned the problems facing pension funds in finding good employees, are we having any similar problems hiring in the current marketplace?"

A chorus of moans and sighs of resignation fill the room.

**Nancy:** "Well, I can see that we're having problems. Can anyone be more specific?"

**Allan:** "We're just losing a lot of middle management people to other firms, both in and outside the real estate industry. We simply can't compete compensation-wise."

**Valorie** (asset management director): "We're also not able to compete for MBAs any more, at least not for those from the top schools. The graduates are more interested in either the higher salary they can get with consulting and investment banking firms or the upside potential with the dot.coms."

**Nancy:** "Well, do you have any solutions?"

No one speaks immediately.

**Nancy:** "Well, I want you to come up with some ideas for us to consider at our next meeting. Valorie will lead the effort."

Nancy looks at her watch.

**Nancy:** "Uh, unfortunately, I have to leave for a lunch with the Mayor. Good-bye everyone; see you next month."

The management group leaves. Nancy makes a quick phone call and then leaves the room herself.

# Case F: NATIONAL REALTY TRUST, INC.[1]

Phyllis Brown is a district manager for National Realty Trust, Inc., a major Real Estate Investment Trust (REIT) focusing on office buildings in the western United States. Prior to joining Western, Phyllis was a fifth grade school teacher for 6 years.

Phyllis manages 18 building managers located in three metro markets. The team is young and relatively inexperienced.

\* \* \*

Phyllis is currently meeting with Sue Wilson, who manages 11 properties - mostly suburban office buildings. The purpose of the meeting is to review Sue's portfolio.

Sue has recently been missing work periodically because of her 3-year-old son's illness but now seems to be back full-time.

**Phyllis:** "Glad to see you back at work. How is your son doing?

**Sue:** "Much better, thank you. I really appreciate the support that you and the other members of our team have given me over the last few weeks."

**Phyllis:** "Well, we want to make sure that your home and business lives are reasonably balanced. Goodness knows, we have asked you to work long hours on occasion, and your work has generally been first rate. It's the least we can do to help.

Now, let's talk about your properties. I've reviewed your performance numbers and am very concerned about the build up in rent delinquencies. It's clear that you have to step up your collection efforts. "

**Sue**: "Hmm. Maybe I should send out copies of the lease provisions to the slow payers reminding them of the terms of their leases. We have tough leases; this should get some results!"

**Phyllis:** "Well, the lease is certainly tough, and we need to inform the tenants of their legal obligations. I am concerned, however, that most of these tenants have been with us for some time, and many of the leases will turn over in the next year. We are in an increasingly softening rental market, and our competitors are stepping up their calls on our building owners. I certainly have lost my share of tenants *and* building owners because I didn't

---

[1] Copyright © John McMahan 2002 and 2004, all rights reserved.

handle a situation like this sensitively. We have to be very careful how we handle this.

Perhaps, a letter from you reminding them of the lease provisions would probably be more effective, followed by a personal call from you. What do you think?"

**Sue:** "Sounds like a good idea."

**Phyllis:** "We have to move fast, though, so please email me a draft tomorrow. We can then get on the phone to discuss any possible changes and how you should handle the follow-up calls. I want to be kept closely informed on this issue.

That's the major item on my agenda. Anything else that you want to discuss?"

**Sue:** "Well, I've been having some difficulty with the new reporting system that we installed last month. I just don't seem to get all of the changes."

**Phyllis:** "Don't be concerned. Others are having similar difficulties. You're a fast learner, and I'm confident you can get it with a little help. I'm putting together a training session next week that should help everyone understand it better. We can then follow up on any questions you still have at our next progress meeting. I would also want to hear what you thought of the session.

Well, I have to run. Sue, please keep me posted on your son's progress, and let me know if there is anything else we can do to help. "

**Sue:** "Will do. Talk to you tomorrow."

# Case G: REALWORLD.COM, INC.[1]

Will Murray heads a new product development group for RealWorld.com, a B2B firm developing a six-module, integrated management system for real estate applications. The firm started three years ago and is now establishing itself as an emerging force in the industry.

Will received a computer science degree (cum laude) with an MBA from a well-known west coast university, where he also taught remedial math part-time to help pay his tuition. Before joining the RealWorld team, he worked with a global management consulting firm installing web-based financial and control systems. Will has written several well-received papers for professional magazines regarding programming for e-commerce and other computer business applications.

\* \* \*

Will is currently conducting his weekly meeting with his staff.

**Will:** "Good morning everyone. Hope you all enjoyed the party the other night. Let's give Jim a big hand for putting up with us! (Applause)

Well, let's get going. Mary, where do we stand on the property management module?"

**Mary** (programmer): "It's running OK, but we're running into problems with the algorithms. We just can't seem to get them working right."

**Will:** "Did you look at that MIT paper that I suggested?"

**Mary:** "Yes, but it didn't seem to help. The approach they propose just doesn't seem to give us the reliability that we need."

**Will:** "Dave (programmer), maybe you could work with Mary on this. You've had a lot of experience with this type of thing, and we need to get the algorithms right before we can go much further with this module."

**Dave**: "I'd be glad to help."

**Will:** "Is that OK Mary?"

**Mary:** "Sure, I need all of the ideas that I can get."

**Will:** "Kathy (marketing), Liz (quality control), maybe you two should sit in too. I don't want to design a module that won't work in the marketplace."

**Kathy:** "Glad to."

---

[1] Copyright © John McMahan 2002 and 2004, all rights reserved.

**Liz:** "Sure, but can you give us a better idea of what you want us to accomplish?"

**Will:** "I think that you and the others can figure out what we need to break through. Thanks for your help. Keep me informed of your progress."

The meeting disbands. After the meeting, Will takes Mary aside.

**Will:** Mary, I hope you don't feel that I'm picking on you, but we just have to meet the January completion date for this module. The project management module is now signed off on, but we have to have the property management module before a final roll out date can be established.

**Mary:** "I know, but I'm just not sure that I'm up to the task. You know that these "cutting edge" algorithms have always been a problem for me."

**Will:** "I know, but I have confidence that you can handle it. You have one of the best mathematical minds that I know and have always come through when we needed it. Tell you what, why don't we go back to my office and review some of the basic concepts and see if they are any areas in which I can help before your meeting with the others. I used to teach this stuff, but I'm a little rusty too."

**Mary:** "Sounds good. Let's go."

# 11
# NOTE ON PROPERTY ACQUISITION[1]

As noted in Chapter 1, in the last several years, commercial real estate investment in the United States has become dominated by financial institutions, primarily pension funds. These investors are fiduciaries to their various constituents and, as such, concerned that their investment managers[2] follow "best practice" standards in order to avoid lawsuits or other adverse consequences once the transaction has been completed. It also helps to minimize expensive mistakes in pricing (e.g., higher capital costs) which investors ultimately pay for in diminished returns.[3]

As a result, most commercial real estate transactions require a "due diligence" evaluation on the part of the investor in order to decide whether or not to finalize the investment process. Generally, the acquiring investor undertakes these evaluations in a relatively short period of time (30-60 days) in an atmosphere of extreme pressure. Participants attempt to be as certain as possible that they have considered all aspects of the property, both positive and negative.

Assurances are usually required that those aspects of property ownership that are considered negative can be mitigated in some fashion, either before or

---

[1] Copyright ©2005 by John McMahan. All rights reserved.
[2] As noted in Chapter 1, the term "investment manager" includes registered investment advisors, managers of Real Estate Investment Trusts (REITs), general partners, and any other individuals or firms who serve as a fiduciary to real estate investors.
[3] Under the Employees Retirement Insurance Act (ERISA) of 1974, the board members and staff, as well as their investment managers have "personal, criminal" liability for their decisions and actions related to the pension plan.

after closing of the transaction. Having such a strategy *prior to close* is an important factor in the acquisition process.

This chapter explores the best practices associated with the acquisition process, focusing on the purchase of institutional grade commercial properties by professional investors.

## UNDERSTANDING INVESTOR OBJECTIVES

**Focused Investment Strategy:** As with most business situations, not all real estate investors have the same investment objectives. In the case of individual investors, as an example, older investors may be more interested in the level of cash flow, while younger investors may be more concerned with potential appreciation in the value of properties in their portfolio.

Individual properties also may serve different roles at different phases in their ownership cycle. As an example, a parcel of land may serve portfolio appreciation objectives in the early years of ownership and then be transformed into a cash generator at some point in the investment cycle through the development process.

Institutional investors attempt to mirror the interests of their constituents. Pension funds with an older participant profile may be more interested in investments which generate cash flow to pay retirement benefits while those with younger participants may desire investments which are expected to demonstrate greater appreciation in value, but pay little cash.

These differing investor objectives are managed by having focused investment strategies which carefully match the nature of the assets with the interests of the investor(s). Large investment managers may have a variety of investment products in which investors self-select the product which matches their investment interests. Smaller firms are faced with a more difficult problem of matching investors with available opportunities which may mean a more limited approach to the market and even turning down investment opportunities which are otherwise attractive.

Institutional investors also are multiasset investors, with investments in stocks, bonds, real estate, venture capital, etc. In multiasset portfolios, real estate often serves a purpose beyond its traditional role. As an example, institutional investors may want to include real estate investments in their portfolios because they complement other assets (such as stocks) in terms of investment return, cash generation, volatility, and risk.

In order to maintain market creditability (and continue to receive investment opportunities), it is important for the investment manager to have a clear statement to the marketplace as to the type of investment properties currently desired and to be willing to only pursue investments which reflect investor interests.

**Risk Diversification:** The need to have a focused investment program is balanced by the need to diversify risks within each investment portfolio.

Real estate is quite different than stocks, bonds, and other financial investments which can be bought and sold readily to balance and rebalance portfolio risk. Financial investments also have the advantage that they can be purchased in small increments so an investment portfolio can be diversified almost regardless of how little investment capital is involved.

Real estate portfolios are diversified by spreading potential risk by not concentrating investments in a single property type, geographical submarket, tenant business, or ownership vehicle. Since most portfolios are built "one property at a time," an individual portfolio may not be diversified until several properties have been acquired. This places an obligation on the investment manager to be conscious of the portfolio risks that are being assumed as properties are being added to the portfolio and to be certain that the overall direction of the investment activities are moving towards portfolio diversification rather than concentration.[4]

**Institutional Partnerships:** From time to time, investment managers may invest in partnership with financial institutions (e.g., pension funds, endowments, foundations, insurance companies, etc.) and, in some instances, with wealthy private investors.

The preferred vehicle for investing with outside partners is through joint-venture investment partnerships which are focused on an investment strategy that will be attractive to both investors and the owners of the operating company, who are usually the general partners in the investment partnership. In most cases, the financial partner will be investing the majority of funds required and may receive preferences in the sequencing of investment returns.

## IMPORTANCE OF INVESTMENT STRATEGY

Investors select investment advisors and partner with operating companies because they believe the investment strategy being employed is consistent with their overall investment objectives and that the advisor/partner can find, acquire, manage, and dispose of properties that fulfill their investment needs. In the case of investment partnerships, this strategic approach to real estate

---

[4] The exception would be pension funds with large real estate portfolios who engage an investment manager to "focus" on a single property type, geographical area, or investment strategy. In this situation, the pension plan is taking the diversification risk. This fact should be clearly acknowledged by both parties in the investment plan and management contract.

investing is encapsulated in the joint-venture agreement and other investment documents that comprise the contract between the parties.

It is therefore important that operating companies fully understand the strategic objectives of each of their investment products and continually keep in mind how assets under management continue to meet or diverge from stated investment objectives.

## PROPERTY ACQUISITION PROCESS

Exhibit 1 illustrates graphically the steps in the property acquisition process. Unfortunately, all of this must be accomplished within a relatively short period of time and often in competition with other active buyers in the marketplace, some with greater resources than others. This situation can be compounded when the investment manager is involved in multiple investment opportunities simultaneously. This means that, to be successful in sourcing superior investments, the investment manager must seek continually to build strong relationships with key players in the targeted real estate markets *before* pursuing specific transactions.

Real estate is very much a people business in which individuals help people whom they like, trust and know can perform. Often the strength of personal and firm relationships gives one buyer an advantage over another in discovering an investment opportunity or helps to ease the way in a difficult negotiating situation. It is also a major way to develop repeat business for the investment manager, with all of the efficiencies that this can represent.

### *Phase 1.0: Investment Search*

The major sources of investment opportunities are:

**Property Owners:** The decision to sell a property and whom to sell it to ultimately rests with the property owner. In today's world, however, property owners are often financial institutions or corporations where final decisions are made or approved by top executives and/or committees and it is not always possible to single out an individual as the "key" decision maker. It is important, therefore, to identify people that will heavily influence the decision to sell.

In the case of investment properties owned by investment advisors or REITs, the key "influencer" is often the asset or property manager responsible for managing the property.

If a corporation is the owner, there usually will be a person in the corporate real estate department responsible for managing the property. In some cases, this person will be situated in the headquarters or regional office of the corporation, which is often located in another city.

Chapter 11 - Note on Property Acquisition -247-

**Exhibit 1**
**Property Acquisition Process**

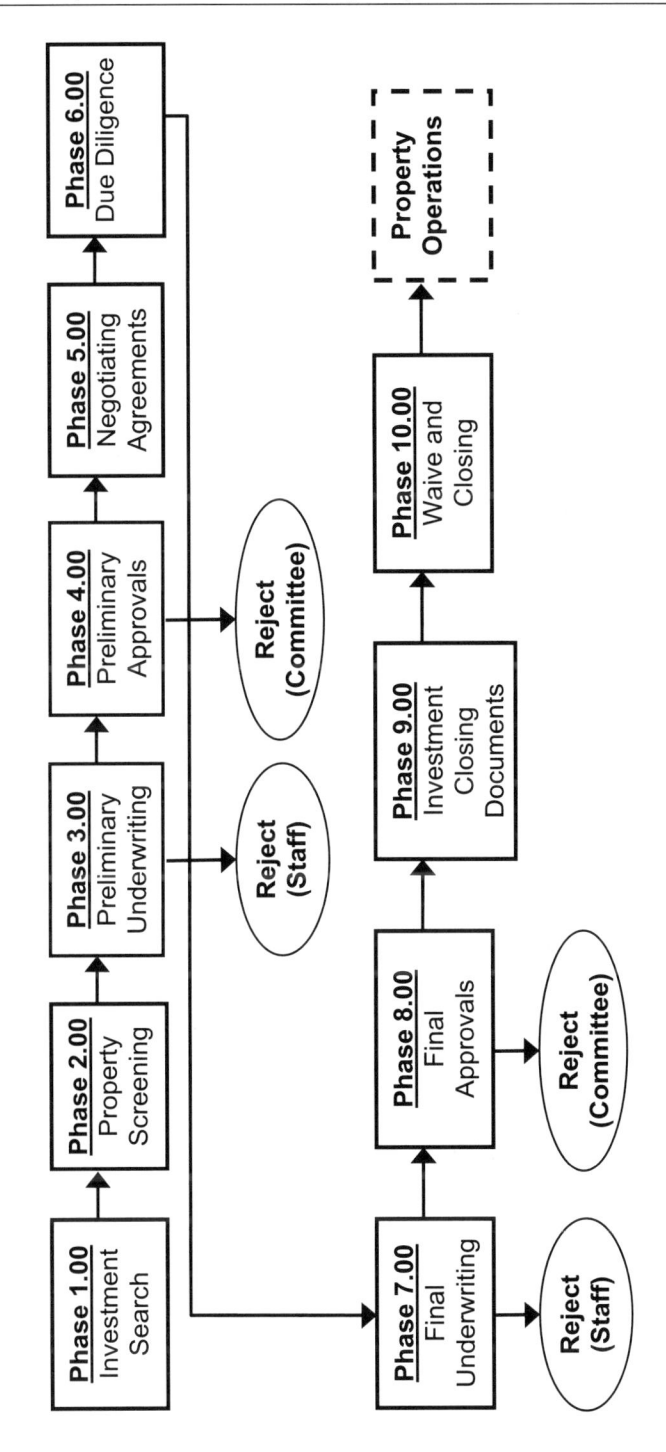

Phase 1.00 Investment Search → Phase 2.00 Property Screening → Phase 3.00 Preliminary Underwriting → Phase 4.00 Preliminary Approvals → Phase 5.00 Negotiating Agreements → Phase 6.00 Due Diligence → Phase 7.00 Final Underwriting → Phase 8.00 Final Approvals → Phase 9.00 Investment Closing Documents → Phase 10.00 Waive and Closing → Property Operations

Reject branches:
- Phase 3.00 → Reject (Staff)
- Phase 4.00 → Reject (Committee)
- Phase 7.00 → Reject (Staff)
- Phase 8.00 → Reject (Committee)

In these situations, individuals employed by the local third-party property or facility management firm may have a greater influence on the sales decision. In some cases, this person may be an employee of the same brokerage firm that has the sales listing agreement.

Acquisitions from developers may be quite different since many presell properties under construction or upon completion. In these situations, it is important to have a continuing relationship with the development managers and keep abreast of the schedule of future building completions. In some cases, this may create an opportunity to tie up a property while under construction, subject to final approval of due diligence and closing upon completion.

Maintaining relationships with property owners who are not actively marketing their properties also may provide a good source of potential acquisitions. In some instances, a property owner might prefer to forego an active marketing process and avoid unwanted publicity or additional cost. These property owners usually prefer to sell in a highly personalized, yet strictly confidential manner.

A property owner who has confidence in an investment manager's ability to perform and keep the terms of the transaction confidential can be very valuable. By purchasing property in this manner, the acquirer foregoes a highly competitive multibidder sales process, in effect controlling the acquisition process without interference from other prospective buyers.

**Brokers:** Relationships with brokers also are important in the success of an acquisition program. A listing broker who has been retained by a seller to market a property typically has considerable influence over the ultimate sales decision. A tenant representative or leasing broker also may be valuable in uncovering a property that will be coming on the market in the near future.

Since brokers usually are paid a "performance based" commission, they are particularly interested in the ability of a company to consummate a transaction successfully. Brokers also are interested in the reputation of such companies in respecting and supporting brokers and not trying to make the broker's commission the final "squeeze" in the negotiating process.

Effective investment managers are proud of their ability to close transactions successfully and efficiently. It is therefore important to bring this record of accomplishment to the attention of brokers whenever the opportunity arises.

**Tenants:** Tenants in an investment manager's existing portfolio can be a valuable source of new acquisition leads. Understanding a tenant's expansion needs and potential can lead to potential build-to-suit opportunities and/or leasing candidates for buildings that are being marketed without tenants.

A good way to find out more about tenant requirements is to stay in close contact with Asset Manager(s) responsible for the properties in the investment manager's portfolio(s). Maintaining such a dialogue may result in a "home grown" tenant, ultimately leading to a potential acquisition.

**Others:** Long-term private owners of older properties are often good leads for possible sale. These individuals can be accessed directly or through their professional advisors (e.g., accountants, attorneys, trust banks, estate planners, etc.)

Other members of the real estate community that may be able to provide leads to potential acquisitions include lending institutions, mortgage bankers, construction loan managers, title company employees, appraisers, market research professionals, etc.

**Summary:** the keys to successful property sourcing are to (1) identify players in organizations who might influence property sales decisions and (2) build personal relationships that may lead to a competitive advantage over other potential buyers.[5]

This can be accomplished by (3) knowing their objectives, both professionally and personally, and (4) building confidence that the investment manager can analyze and close a transaction in an expeditious manner at a competitive price.

## Phase 2.0: Property Screening

The screening process compares potential acquisitions against criteria "screens" to determine which submissions best measure up to a set of pre-established investment criteria. This process assists the investment managers in continuing to focus on acquiring properties that are consistent with the firm's investment strategy(ies).

It does not do any good to acquire properties that do not meet investment objectives regardless of how good the "deal" may be from a classic real estate point of view. It's even worse to compound the problem by trying to rationalize the investment criteria to fit the characteristics of the property.

An investment manager also has limited resources and pursuing one opportunity may keep the firm from pursuing another. This is not only a waste of time and money, but may lead to "opportunity costs" that ultimately can be much greater.

---

[5] In situations where competitive marketing is unavoidable, good relationships should insure that the investment manager at least will be allowed to compete for the property when it comes to market.

**Investment Criteria Sheet:** Investment Criteria Sheets are established by the Investment Committee.[6] Generally, these criteria are derived from the investment objectives of the firm's investors as expressed in various investment documents. Examples of investment criteria include geographical markets, property type(s), parcel size, building size and age, tenant mix and credit quality, lease turn characteristics, funds required, projected investor return, stage of entitlement, and property-specific risks to be avoided.[7]

Investment criteria for each investment program are then distributed to property owners, the brokerage community, and others who might influence a sales decision. In some cases, receipt of the investment criteria, coupled with a successful execution reputation, may lead to a decision to sell properties without marketing them extensively.

**Offering Memorandum:** Properties generally are offered for sale by means of an Offering Memorandum (OM). While the minimum level of information in the OM may change over time, it usually consists of the Metropolitan Statistical Area (MSA), property location (street address), property type (e.g., office, retail, industrial, multifamily, etc.), property size (SF), photos of the property, key tenants (by SF, if available), price, and the contact person for the transaction

**Submission Log:** Once the Investment Criteria Sheet has been distributed to prospective leads, OM's should begin arriving. Submissions may arrive in a variety of formats (e.g., email, fax, telephone, letter, etc.) and should be logged on a temporary basis as long as the minimum amount of information is a part of the OM and the property is not logged by another person or firm.

Once this information is received, the submission is registered temporarily (date and time stamped) and held for 48 hours pending receipt of additional information, which generally includes a rent roll, property financial statement (preferably for last two years), and the proposed purchase terms.

Following receipt of this additional information, the registration is complete and the submitting broker or principal is acknowledged as the procuring agent(s) for the transaction, should it occur.[8]

---

[6] Throughout this book, the term "investment committee" is used to represent a formal or informal group of the firm's owners and/or managers who establish and monitor the firms investment policy.

[7] In addition to property criteria, some investment managers include the "rules of engagement" under which they operate. As an example, the investment manager may accept submittals from non-listing brokers provided they include a letter signed by the listing broker acknowledging the relationship and indicating the terms of the commission split between the two firms.

[8] Brokers are then "protected" for a period (generally 2-3 months) provided they keep in touch and notify the buyer of any change in status of the property.

This log-in process is necessary in order to avoid broker disputes over potential commissions that can delay the acquisition process and may result in time wasting and possibly adverse litigation for the investment manager[9]

**Preliminary Screening:** As properties are submitted or uncovered through the investment manager's proactive initiatives, the immediate task is to quickly develop the facts about the property in order to compare it to the Investment Criteria Screen. This is generally a two or three page Underwriting Analysis in either Excel or Argus.

In many cases, the prospective buyer may not have all of the information necessary to make effective comparisons and must immediately take steps to get the required information from the broker, owner, or other submission source.

The objective is to eliminate properties that, for one reason or another, do not meet the criteria screen before a lot of time is spent on a site visit and/or further analytical work. Too often, a lot of time is burned off chasing deals that will ultimately prove unsuitable for the manager's investors.

**Preliminary Site Visit:** In some cases, the investment manager will have tracked a property before it comes to market and have a good idea of its location, key tenants, building quality, surrounding land uses, and market area.

If the property is unfamiliar, a quick site visit will be necessary to establish a "visceral" understanding of the property's features. This visit can be undertaken by a member of the acquisition or asset management team, depending upon individual availability.[10]

An external survey is generally sufficient, although gaining access to the building (if security permits) can often provide a better understanding of the features of the property (e.g., floor plan, design features, tenant diversity, building maintenance, etc.). It also is important to drive the neighborhood to review surrounding land uses, competing properties, etc. If possible, it is desirable to take photographs or videos of the property and the surrounding area.

## Phase 3.0: Preliminary Underwriting

If the property survives initial screening and a site visit, it is time to consider it as a prospective acquisition and begin a preliminary underwriting of its

---

[9] Ideally, the log-in process is entered on a data base rather than an excel or word program. This not only expedites the review but makes it easier to allocate deal reviews among the acquisition team, retrieve data on deals marked as good "comps", and auto-generate rejection letters.
[10] In certain situations, a trusted local contact may be utilized.

investment potential. This effort does not replace a rigorous Due Diligence process (discussed later) but rather allows for a preliminary understanding of the target asset to determine if an offer is warranted.

In the interests of time, the information and data submitted by the seller are deemed to be reasonably accurate, subject to final verification through the due diligence process. If fact, one of the roles of the Preliminary Underwriting is to identify risk issues that *must* be addressed during the Due Diligence phase.

**Preliminary Title Report:** One of the first steps is to order a preliminary title report from the local office of a national title company. This report will pinpoint the general history of the property's ownership and any liens that have been placed by other parties. A lien or other encumbrances may indicate parties who might have a claim to a security interest in the title.

A review of the preliminary title report also may indicate additional title research that needs to be undertaken in the Due Diligence phase.

**Preliminary Market Analysis:** A preliminary understanding of specific market conditions is a vital component of the Preliminary Underwriting, as it is necessary to understand how a potential acquisition property competes within its market area. To do so, it is important to identify which properties compete directly or indirectly with the subject property and what level of competition they represent.

New supply coming into a market has the potential to have a disruptive effect on market conditions. This makes it important, therefore, to identify other sites where new building construction is likely to occur, to the extent possible. An understanding as to whether and when these sites may be developed also can be helpful in better understanding the dynamics of the overall market.

**Metro Area Analysis:** The purpose of the metro area analysis is to develop a general understanding of socioeconomic trends that may affect the economic health of targeted sub markets in which the firm is active and in which prospective property acquisitions are located.

The metropolitan boundaries of most urban areas are well defined by governmental agencies, particularly the US Census Bureau, local planning agencies, and private market research firms. In order to study past trends and project future growth patterns, data should be collected on an annual basis over a 5 to 10 year period.

This data should be maintained for all metro areas in which the investment manager is operating or plans to operate in the future. It should be continually updated so that it is immediately available for due diligence and other purposes. State and national data in each of the categories also should be assessable for comparative purposes.

**Submarket Data:** Data on targeted submarkets is more difficult to generate but often more meaningful in understanding demand and supply trends and overall market conditions. In most metro areas, public agencies and private firms such as brokers maintain data by generally acceptable submarket definitions. In other words, these are the market areas that buyers/sellers and landlord/tenants would recognize as having relatively similar characteristics.

**Competitive Survey:** Within the submarket, specific buildings will compete directly with the subject property for tenants. It is important, therefore, to have an understanding of the competitive advantages/disadvantages of existing properties as well as new ones that are in the development pipeline. Important factors to consider include property location, accessibility, infrastructure, building(s) size and configuration, key tenants, and a ranking of the property vis-à-vis the potential acquisition property.

**Cash Flow Analysis:** This task consists of a pro-forma cash flow analysis (usually an Argus or Excel model) and forms the backbone of the preliminary underwriting of the investment opportunity. The analysis forecasts anticipated revenue and expenses over an anticipated holding period, generally 10 years. It incorporates items such as existing tenant sales, tenant lease obligations, and other leasing and market assumptions as well as anticipated expenses from property operations and tenant improvements, leasing commissions, and capital expenditures to determine net cash flow on an annual basis.

In the final year of the analysis, the property is assumed to be sold for cash in the subsequent year. The collective net cash flows over the holding period are then compared to the acquisition costs of the property to determine whether the investment will meet investor return expectations.[11]

The Pro-forma cash flow analysis[12] also can be utilized to establish the sensitivity of returns to various assumptions such as space vacancy, operating costs, financing, sales price, changes in market rents, tenant sales (retail), exit cap rates, tenant turnover costs, and other critical factors influencing investment return.

This information will prove valuable in the Letter of Intent negotiations as well as establishing which of the underlying assumptions need to be tested in greater depth during the Due Diligence phase. In the case of investment partnerships, the analysis can be expanded to include distribution flows to be certain that investment partners will receive targeted returns

---

[11] Usually expressed as an Internal Note of Return (IRR) or Net Present Value (NPV).
[12] This term and others used in this book may vary from time to time.

**Investment Risk Analysis:** Based on the information generated by the Cash Flow Analysis and other preliminary due diligence activities, a summary of the risks associated with the investment are outlined as well as anticipated mitigation steps to reduce or eliminate potential risks. The magnitude of each risk and its potential negative impact on the success of the investment will be tested in the Due Diligence phase, as well as the probabilities of success of planned mitigation measures.

## Phase 4.0: Preliminary Approvals

**Due Diligence Budget:** A Due Diligence Budget is suggested for each potential acquisition including anticipated internal time and costs as well as direct payments to third party contractors and the services they will provide. The Due Diligence Budget is usually approved by an officer or partner of the investment manager before any costs are incurred. The officer/partner also must approve any diligence contractors not on the approved list.

**Acquisition Timeline:** A timeline is recommended for most acquisitions. The Acquisition Timeline details critical events during the acquisition process. Acquisition Timelines are entered in the investment manager's main computer calendar so that interested parties can be aware of critical dates, possible conflicts in scheduling, the flow of cash deposits, etc. Timelines are recognized to be somewhat flexible and subject to change as circumstances warrant and provided the change is approved by both the buyer and seller.

**Investment Committee**: As previously noted, the Investment Committee is usually comprised of the senior officers or partners of the investment management firm. These individuals usually have many years of experience in all of the major disciplines required to successfully invest in real estate.

The purpose of the Investment Committee is to govern the investment practices and procedures of the investment manager to assure investors their interests are being protected and enhanced at all times. This generally includes approval of property acquisitions, dispositions, debt encumbrances, asset management business plans and budgets, significant property improvements, investment restructurings, due diligence budgets and contractors, and other major property and portfolio decisions.

The Investment Committee also is responsible for monitoring markets and trends in the real estate industry in order to establish and modify firm's investment policies as well as provide leadership regarding new investment programs to be developed for investor consideration.

Each member of the Investment Committee usually has a single vote on any action item. Generally, a majority of members must approve a transaction involving the acquisition or disposition of any property in investment portfolios. Some investment managers require a super majority or even unanimous approval in order to proceed with certain transactions.

Most Investment Committees are "on call" to meet at least once a month to review potential transactions and at least once a quarter to monitor the performance of the firm's investment portfolio.[13]

The Acquisition Information Summary and related detailed analytical material developed is transmitted to the Investment Committee for a decision as to whether or not to pursue the recommended investment opportunity. Employees involved in the preparation and evaluation of the opportunity are expected to be available to explain and defend their recommendations, as well as discuss future courses of action if the investment is approved or requires further evaluation.

## *Phase 5.0: Negotiating Agreements*

Once an investment opportunity has received preliminary approval from the Investment Committee, the next step is to attempt to negotiate a series of written agreements with the seller. This includes traditional contracts such the Purchase and Sale Agreement as well as more informal agreements such a Letter of Intent that establish business guidelines for reaching agreement on key issues prior to entering into legally binding contracts.

**Letter of Intent:**[14] A Letter of Intent (LOI) is used by the potential buyer to make an offer on a potential property acquisition. The LOI is a nonlegal term sheet that sets forth certain basic business parameters regarding a potential acquisition. In essence, this document "sets up" the negotiating process.[15] An LOI is usually executed by a Partner or Senior Manager of the investment manager.

While neither party is bound by an LOI, the concise document is critical in serving to reduce confusion and provide clarity about the business terms of an acquisition before legal documents are negotiated. In nonbidding situations, the LOI serves to temporarily remove the property from market competition and focuses the attention of the seller on the firm offering the LOI as the potential "buyer" of the property.

---

[13] Most investment committees meet at least twice on each acquisition: 1) to approve the due diligence budget and (2) to approve or reject the deal at the end of the due diligence process.
[14] The LOI is a "business" document and should not be prepared by an attorney or indicate an attorney as the contact. It's a good idea, however, to have the format of a standard LOI reviewed by an attorney.
[15] If possible, it's a good idea to have a statement in the LOI to the effect that "pricing is based on information supplied by the seller and the buyer reserves the right to adjust the price if the information proves incorrect in diligence.

The LOI also serves as a roadmap of the business terms of the agreement for attorneys subsequently involved in preparing the Purchase and Sale Agreement. It generally excludes attorneys from the negotiations until the respective representatives of each firm can reach agreement on its fundamental business terms.

**Purchase and Sale Agreement:** Once an LOI has been negotiated and executed by the business people, a Purchase and Sale Agreement (P&S Agreement) is negotiated by attorneys representing each side (or multiple sides, if more then one buyer is involved or external financing required). The P&S Agreement translates the business terms of the LOI into a binding and legally enforceable contract between the parties.

In addition to the terms outlined in the LOI, the P&S Agreement contains legal representations by the seller regarding the condition and legal status of the property and the fact that all documents and other materials will be provided to the buyer and are, to the seller's knowledge, complete and accurate. Other standard provisions include the timing and conditions of the due diligence review, rights to assign interests, default provisions, and casualty and condemnation clauses.

In some cases, buyers are able to negotiate certain warranties from the seller regarding the physical quality of the property and the performance of equipment such as HVAC, electrical, plumbing, and other critical systems. A big issue usually is the length of the warranty period, which has tended to shorten in the last several years.

Closing documents (e.g., bill of sale, warranty or grant deed, assignment of contracts, assignments of leases, etc.) are often negotiated at this time and attached as exhibits to the P&S Agreement. The purpose is to avoid panic negotiations just before closing which can be detrimental, usually to the buyer.

The P&S Agreement usually can only be executed on behalf of the investment manager by a senior office or partner of the firm.

**Earnest Money Deposit (EMD)**[16]: Today, most real estate transactions utilize an escrow to collect and disburse documents, funds, and other items required by the P&S Agreement. Funds can be either in the form of cash or a Letter of Credit (LOC) from a financial institution. If earnest money funds are not delivered into escrow by the date specified in the P&S Agreement, the buyer may be in default under the contract. It is important, therefore, to arrange for the transfer of funds well in advance of the specified date.

---

[16] In some situations, the EMD may be incorporated directly into the P&S Agreement.

If the deposit is in the form of an LOC, it is important to monitor the expiration date carefully to make sure it does not expire if the due diligence period is extended. If cash is utilized, the escrow holder should be given investment instructions to make sure that the deposit is earning interest.

In a competitive bid situation, the seller uses a more formal approach, utilizing two additional agreements to indicate the process.

**Confidentiality Agreement:** Once the proposed investment opportunity has been approved on a preliminary basis by the Investment Committee, the next task may be (if required by the seller) to execute a Confidentially Agreement (C/A) with the seller of the property(ies).[17] The C/A is a legally binding agreement in which a buyer promises not to disclose confidential information concerning a potential investment to anyone other than those directly involved with the specific acquisition.

The content of a C/A varies, but in all cases should be taken seriously by those involved as most agreements provide for damages, which can be severe. A C/A is usually executed by a member of the Investment Committee.

**Offering Memorandum:** Once a C/A has been submitted to a seller, confidential information about a potential acquisition may be released in the form of an Offering Memorandum (O/M). The O/M is a marketing package typically prepared by the seller or the listing broker who has been retained as the exclusive agent to market the property. The O/M typically includes an executive summary, property description, market analysis, pro-forma cash flow, rent roll, operating history, photographs, and maps.

Once a Purchase and Sale Agreement (P&S Agreement) has been negotiated and executed by the parties, the initial cash deposit is posted and the due diligence process begins.[18]

---

[17] Depending upon timing, the C/A and O/M may have been approved prior to the Management Investment Committee approving the transaction.
[18] In some cases, the due diligence period is tied to an events such as execution of the LOI (beginning) and receipt of all due diligence information required to conduct due diligence.

## Phase 6.0: Due Diligence

From a fiduciary liability perspective, due diligence is the most critical period in the acquisition process and one which requires the utmost attention of everyone involved.

This legal exposure is compounded by the fact that the time allowed for due diligence is relatively short (usually 30-60 days) and receipt and evaluation of due diligence materials requires the simultaneous involvement of a variety of technical specialists. In some cases, there may be additional pressure to approve the transaction due to a "backup buyer" waiting in the wings.

As a result, due diligence activities must be intensively managed by those engaged in the process.

**Role of Due Diligence:** The major objective of due diligence is to identify, quantify, and resolve important issues regarding the property(ies). If problems become evident, a strategy must be developed to mitigate any significant negative aspects which might adversely affect the investment. *It is not enough to discover problems; there also have to be solutions.* If there are no solutions, or they are inadequate, then the transaction should be terminated.

The due diligence process also involves verifying previously disclosed information and testing the assumptions which formed the basis of the cash flow analysis presented to the Investment Committee. It also may involve discovering new information from in-depth investigations that the seller would not permit until he/she knew that the terms of the transaction were legally binding, subject to satisfactory completion of buyer due diligence.

**Managing the Process:** Exhibit 2 discusses the due diligence process in terms of physical, legal and business activities. Most due diligence activities are performed by independent, third-party contractors. Potential problem areas may be analyzed by different contractors, requiring a final reconciliation by the due diligence team.

In some cases, the terms of the P&S Agreement can be negotiated to compensate the buyer for problems unearthed by the due diligence process. This might be in the form of a lower price, a holdback of a portion of purchase funds until a problem can be corrected, a guarantee or warranty by the seller, or some other provision in the P&S Agreement. Changes in the P&S Agreement obviously require approval of the seller so it becomes entirely a negotiated situation.

If the problems are relatively minor, the buyer may decide to "waive" the deposit and proceed to close the transaction. If the buyer waives, the deposit becomes non-refundable and a closing occurs shortly thereafter.

*Chapter 11 - Note on Property Acquisition* **-259-**

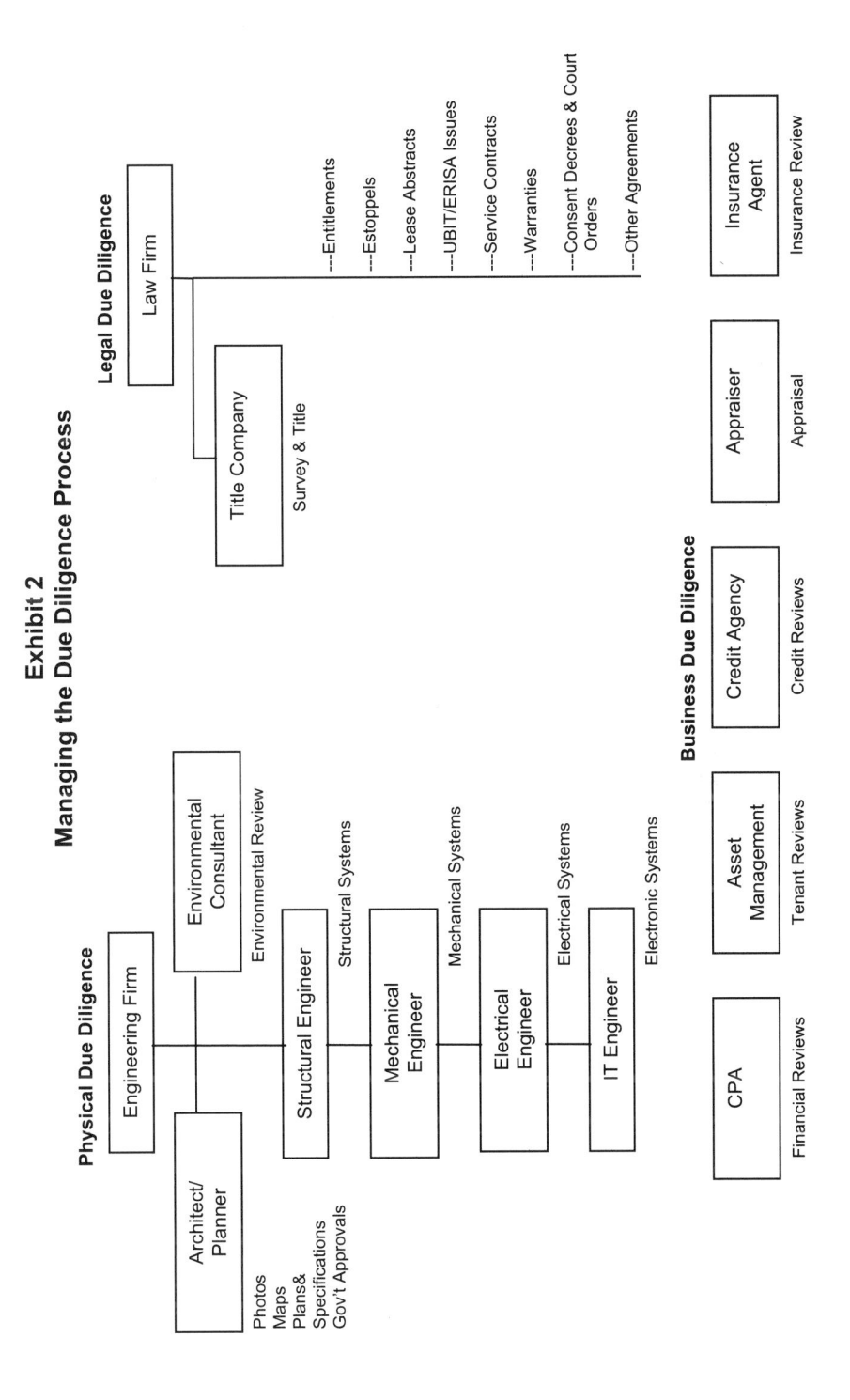

## Exhibit 2
## Managing the Due Diligence Process

### Physical Due Diligence

- **Architect/Planner**
  - Photos
  - Maps
  - Plans & Specifications
  - Gov't Approvals
- **Engineering Firm**
  - **Environmental Consultant** — Environmental Review
  - **Structural Engineer** — Structural Systems
  - **Mechanical Engineer** — Mechanical Systems
  - **Electrical Engineer** — Electrical Systems
  - **IT Engineer** — Electronic Systems

### Legal Due Diligence

- **Law Firm**
  - Entitlements
  - Estoppels
  - Lease Abstracts
  - UBIT/ERISA Issues
  - Service Contracts
  - Warranties
  - Consent Decrees & Court Orders
  - Other Agreements
- **Title Company** — Survey & Title

### Business Due Diligence

- **CPA** — Financial Reviews
- **Asset Management** — Tenant Reviews
- **Credit Agency** — Credit Reviews
- **Appraiser** — Appraisal
- **Insurance Agent** — Insurance Review

**Selecting Contractors:** It is particularly important that *independent, third party contractors retained by the buyer* be utilized for the technical portion of the due diligence process. While engineering, environmental, and other reports prepared by seller contractors can be utilized as historic information and points of reference, these reports should be reviewed and validated by the buyer's contractors, utilizing their own independent testing procedures.[19]

**Contractor Coordination:** In order to reduce the number of individual contractors, it is common to have a master contractor (usually an architectural or engineering firm) with more specialized firms serving as sub-contractors.[20] This also helps to put the total physical situation in perspective as well as reduce professional fees. Some professional firms specialize exclusively in performing due diligence activities.

**Budget and Timeline Update:** Once the due diligence contracts are in place it is timely to update the due diligence budget and acquisition timeline in order to reflect the specific delivery dates and costs of contracted work.

**Check List:** In order to ensure that the acquisition team performs all of the due diligence tasks that follow, a due diligence check list should be completed for each potential acquisition. Exhibit 3 is a representative due diligence check list.

## *Physical Due Diligence*

In the sections that follow, the most commonly used contractors are identified in parenthesis following the task that is to be performed.[21]

**Photos (architect/planner):** Property photos should include not only the subject property but surrounding land uses as well. Be particularly alert to power lines, pooled water, parking congestion, etc. The seller may have photos of the building under construction, which may prove helpful to the engineering contractors.

Aerial photos are helpful in describing the neighborhood and relationship of the property to major arterials, freeways, residential districts, etc. Historic aerial photos can be utilized in spotting previous uses of the property that might influence the environmental analysis (such as farms with underground gasoline storage tanks).

---

[19] Time permitting, it might be wise to bid out the diligence work. Sometimes significant savings can be obtained without compromising work quality.
[20] The master contractor may perform some of the specialized tasks directly.
[21] Investment manager litigation often centers around due diligence activities, with major emphasis on the "process" that is followed by the investment manager. It is critical, therefore, to make certain that the Company's due diligence process is systematic, well documented, and managed carefully.

## Exhibit 3
## Due Diligence Checklist

| Review Code | | | |
|---|---|---|---|
| A | Appraiser | I | Insurance Agent |
| AF | Acquiring Firm | L | Lawyer |
| AP | Architect Planner | ME | Mechanical Engr. |
| C | Consultant | NE | Environmental Engr. |
| CA | Credit Agency | S | Seller |
| EE | Electrical Engineer | SE | Structural Engr. |
| G | Government | T | Title Company |

| | Source | Review | √ |
|---|---|---|---|
| **Physical Due Diligence** | | | |
|   Photos | | | |
|     Property | S | AP/SE/NE | |
|     Aerial | S | AP/SE/NE | |
|   Maps | | | |
|     Metro area | S/G | AP/EE | |
|     Submarket | S/G | AP/EE | |
|   Plans and Specifications | | | |
|     Land use and circulation | S | AP/SE | |
|     Site plans | S | AP/SE | |
|     Building plans & specs | S | AP/SE | |
|     Tenant floor plans | S | AP/SE | |
|     Construction documents | S | AP/SE | |
|   Reports | | | |
|     Phase I Environmental | S | NE | |
|     Phase II Environmental | S | NE | |
|   Governmental Approvals | | | |
|     Building permits | S | AP/L | |
|     Zoning | S | AP/L | |
|     Zoning variances | S | AP/L | |
|     Certificates of occupancy | S | AP/L | |
|     Licenses | S | AP/L | |
|   Warranties | | | |
|     Roof | S | | |
|     HVAC | S | | |
|     Paving | S | | |
|   Service Contracts | S | | |
|   Existing Condition Survey | S | | |
|   Structural systems | | | |
|     Foundation | | SE | |
|     Load bearing | | SE | |
|     Exterior building shell | | SE | |
|     Floor system | | SE | |
|     Roofing system | | SE | |
|     Seismic | | SE/NE | |
|   Mechanical systems | | | |
|     Plumbing | | ME | |
|     HVAC | | ME | |
|     Vertical transportation | | ME | |
|   Electrical systems | | | |
|     Main system | | EE | |
|     Emergency power | | EE | |

- Electronic systems
    - Fiber-optic capacity — EE
    - Raised floors — EE
    - Phone demarcation — EE
    - Phone & server closets — EE
- **Repair History** — S
- **Environmental review**
    - Hazardous substances
        - Asbestos — NE
        - Radon gas — NE
        - Lead paint — NE
        - Sick building syndrome — NE
    - Soil conditions
        - Geological — NE/SE
        - Hydro geological — NE
    - Protected biological systems — NE
    - Catastrophic risk exposure
        - Flood Hazard Zone — NE
        - Flooding Hazard — NE
        - Fire Hazard — NE
        - Wildland — NE
        - Earthquake — NE
        - Seismic Hazard Zone — NE

# Legal Due Diligence
- Survey
    - Physical boundaries — L/T/S
    - Easements — L/T/S
    - Encroachments — L/T/S
    - CC&R's — L/T/S
    - Rights of way — L/T/S
    - Zoning violations — L/T/AP
- Title
    - Form of ownership — L/T
    - ALTA Title Insurance — L/T
    - Assignment of project — L/T
- Escrow
    - Buyer's Closing Statement — AC
    - Supplemental Instructions — AC
    - Amendments to Close — AC
- Entitlements
    - Zoning — AP/L/S
    - Zoning variances — AP/L/S
    - Building codes — AP/L/S
    - Utility permits — AP/L/S
    - Special District Permits — AP/L/S
    - Local Improvement Districts — AP/L/S
- Tenant Estoppels Certificates
    - Location of space — L/AF
    - Size of space (SF) — L/AF
    - Parking spaces — L/AF
    - Term of lease — L/AF
    - Starting date — L/AF
    - Rent — L/AF
    - Expense recovery — L/AF
    - Tenant options — L/AF
- Lease Abstracts — L/AF

| | | |
|---|---|---|
| Service Contracts | L | ☐ |
| Warranties | L | ☐ |
| Consent decrees and court orders | L | |
| Assignment of Project Documents | L/AC | ☐ |
| UBIT/ERISA Issues | L | |
| Tax Withholding | L/AC | |
| 1031 Status | L/AC | |
| **Business Due Diligence** | | |
| Market analysis | AF/C | ☐ |
| Financial analysis | AF | |
| Tenant interviews | L/AF | |
| Tenant Financial Review | AF | |
| Tenant Credit Review | AF/CA | |
| Appraisal (Optional) | L/AF/A | |
| Insurance review | | |
|     Existing coverage | L/AF/I | ☐ |
|     New coverage | L/AF/I | |

**Maps (architect/planner):** Maps are generally collected during the preliminary underwriting process. There may be some specialized maps, however, that need to be located in order to round out a picture of the property and the surrounding neighborhood. As an example, there may be specialized maps such as demographic, income, households, business taxes paid, etc. that may be helpful in updating the market analysis.

Local, state, and federal government agencies are usually the best sources for maps. City planners also should be interviewed regarding neighborhood characteristics, problem areas, future public works projects, public finances, etc.

**Plans and Specifications (architect/planner):** Plans and specifications of the property should include a land use and circulation plan, site plans, as-built building plans and specifications (if available), tenant floor plans, and construction documents (new buildings).

**Governmental Approvals (architect/planner):** Copies should be obtained of government approval documents including building permits, zoning, zoning variances, certificates of occupancy (CO), licenses, Americans with Disabilities (ADA) compliance reports, and safety infractions (e.g., fire sprinkler pressure, inadequate traffic signing, etc.).

Interviews should be held with local planning and zoning professionals to ascertain their views on existing problems with public infrastructure serving the subject site (e.g., roads, sewers, flood control, schools, public safety, etc.) as well as the status and funding of plans for these in the future.

**Structural Systems (structural engineer):** The key structural elements of the building(s) requiring analysis include the foundation, load bearing walls, exterior building shell, floor system, roofing system, and any specialized seismic considerations.

If deficiencies are discovered, the structural system analysis allows the buyer to seek a credit from the seller for any deficiencies that were not disclosed when the parties agreed to the purchase price. If the deficiencies were disclosed, the analysis provides a budgeted amount to correct the problem following close of escrow.

Common structural problems encountered include cracks in the foundation, roofing that needs full or partial replacement, or certain structural elements that do not meet current building codes. There also may be deterioration of the building shell.

**Mechanical Systems (mechanical engineer):** The mechanical engineer reviews the building in terms of three major areas: (1) Plumbing (e.g. tenant areas, sprinklers, etc.); (2) Heating, Ventilation, and Air Conditioning (HVAC)[22]; and (3) Vertical transportation (freight elevators, escalators, etc.).

A building's HVAC system is generally the major source of mechanical deficiencies. Typical problems include too much or too little heat/air between seasons and/or between different locations in the building(s). If the capacity of the system is sufficient, then the issue may be one of balancing the distribution of air. In addition to the mechanical engineer's calculations this is also a good area to explore in the tenant interviews (discussed below).

**Electrical Systems (electrical engineer):** Electrical systems that generally require analysis are the main power system and, if applicable, the emergency power system. It is also important to check lighting in exterior common areas, parking, and pedestrian walkways.

**Electronic Systems (IT engineer):** As more and more buildings utilize built-in electronic transmission systems, Information Technology (IT) becomes an increasingly important item of due diligence review. Areas of particular concern include fiber-optic cabling capacity, availability and flexibility of raised floor distribution systems, location of phone demarcation points[23], location of phone and server closets, etc.

Service contracts should be reviewed in cases where the electronic distribution system is controlled by an independent service provider

**Environmental Review (environmental consultant(s)):** The environmental review is one of the most critical elements of the due diligence process. An undetected environmental problem may exceed the purchase price of the property, imposing a huge remediation liability on the investment

---

[22] May also be undertaken by an HVAC contractor.
[23] Location where the phone service enters the building(s).

manager and possibly its investment partners. For practical purposes, it's wise to assume that the investment manager will pay for its' due diligence mistakes "one way or the other."[24]

Lenders also are highly sensitive to a property's environmental condition and may not finance a property if they are dissatisfied with the environmental review. For all concerned, this step in the due diligence process requires a high level of care to make certain that unwarranted and unknown environmental liabilities are not unwittingly assumed. It is critical, therefore, for those involved to thoroughly understand the following steps involved in the environmental review process.

**Phase I:** All acquisitions require a Phase I Environmental Analysis ("Phase I"). The Phase I examines historic property use as well as that of the surrounding area, identifying possible on-site or off-site environmental problems.

Depending upon the age of the building, the Phase I analysis may identify asbestos containing materials that may be present as well as possible soil or ground water contamination.

Additional areas of concern include investigation for the presence of radon gas, lead paint, mold, and sick building syndrome. In situations involving new construction in open land areas, the review also may include an examination of the impact of the project on protected biological systems. Flood and seismic risks also should be examined in areas prone to these calamities.

**Phase II:** If the Phase I analysis indicates that possible problems exist, the environmental consultant usually recommends that further investigation be conducted pursuant to a Phase II Environmental Analysis ("Phase II") which usually involves on-site testing, providing a higher level of analysis and accuracy from which to draw more precise conclusions.[25]

A Phase II negative finding does not necessarily disqualify a property from being purchased, provided adequate remediation measures have been adopted. The costs of remediation measures are usually an obligation of the seller. In terms of scheduling, a Phase II analysis usually requires a contract extension of the due diligence period.

---

[24] If the remedial costs are absorbed into the project, the investor's return is less, reflecting on the investment manager and possibly influencing the firm's ability to receive additional capital allocations. Worse, if the investor gets sued you can be sure that a named party (and most likely the payer of any damages) will be the investment manager and/or its insurance company.

[25] The LOI is a "business" document and should not be prepared by an attorney or indicate an attorney as the contact. It's a good idea, however, to have the format of a standard LOI reviewed by an attorney.

**Environmental Insurance:** In addition to conducting an Environmental Review, some buyers purchase environmental insurance coverage. Environmental insurance is another tool that mitigates environmental risk to the investment manager and its investors.

An environmental insurance policy usually covers costs associated with environmental cleanup when ordered by a governmental authority. Environmental insurance coverage also can be extended to lenders, who may accept this coverage in lieu of a recourse guarantee for environmental protection. In some situations, environmental insurance may be assigned to successors in interest.

## Legal Due Diligence

The second major area of Due Diligence concerns the myriad of legal considerations involved in a property acquisition. Generally this due diligence is undertaken by a single law firm, aided by legal research resources and the assistance of an experienced title company. The law firm also should have a background in hazard liability and environmental law in order to interpret the legal considerations of any pertinent physical due diligence findings.

**Survey and Title Review:** A survey depicts not only the physical boundaries and dimensions of the improvements, but also certain other legal rights including easements, encroachments, covenants, and rights of way.

From a due diligence perspective, the survey and title review are to:

- ❏ Determine that the title description shown on the survey is the same as that shown in the title report.
- ❏ Confirm exactly what real property is being acquired.
- ❏ Establish all easements and/or encroachments affecting the use of the property (some, if not all, of these may have been established in the preliminary title report).

Once the subject property's survey and title situation is understood, there may be several steps that need to be requested of the seller to "clean up" the title situation prior to close.

Perhaps the most important concern is to see if there are any liens that should be discharged and released or CC&R violations that need to be cleared up. It is also important to determine if there are any zoning violations. Finally, are there any easements or encroachments, which, if activated, would materially affect real estate operation on the property. An example would be the need to tear up a floor slab to repair underground utilities running under a building.

Since these actions will require negotiation and execution prior to close, discussions with the seller's counsel should begin as soon as possible.

**Entitlements:** Most properties are located in political jurisdictions that limit the use of the property by the owner. Through the legal process, these jurisdictions establish the uses of a property to which an owner is "entitled". Common entitlements include zoning variances, building codes, utility permits, Special District permits, and Local Improvement Districts (LID).

Entitlement due diligence consists of a review of the applicable zoning ordinances affecting the subject property and that of the surrounding area. Discussions also should be held with the local planning, zoning, and building departments to understand any contemplated changes that might affect the entitled status of the property.

The main purpose of this review is to determine (1) whether the property complies with the applicable zoning ordinances and building codes, including setback, parking[26], height, and coverage limitations (FAR)[27], and (2) whether there have been any zoning or building code violations, particularly any life/safety violations. The review also usually analyzes the consequences of a "nonconforming structure" being destroyed or damaged by a casualty event.

**Tenant Estoppels Certificates:** Tenant Estoppels Certificates (estoppels) are documents that verify certain lease information. Tenants are required in most leases to execute estoppels.[28] In general, it is the seller's responsibility to circulate and retrieve the estoppels. Timing is critical as the estoppels process may take several weeks to complete.

Estoppels allow the buyer to rely on certain lease facts that may have been critical in the original decision to purchase the property. Estoppels also usually surface any conflicts or misunderstandings between the landlord and the tenants.

Once Estoppels have been received by the buyer, they should be compared with the lease abstracts developed by the attorneys. Any changes or discrepancies should be noted.

**Lease Abstracts:** Concurrently with the estoppels process, the legal contractor should summarize the key elements of each of the tenant leases. Attorneys who are familiar with leasing issues and their structure generally develop abstracts that accurately and succinctly set forth the obligations of

---

[26] As an example, the zoning ordinance may require more parking than is currently provided on the property.
[27] Floor Area Ratio.
[28] Estoppels forms may be negotiated in conjunction with the P&S Agreement.

each tenant. The lease abstract generally covers the same information as is in the estoppels.[29]

The results of the lease abstract are then compared to the pro forma rent roll and financial analysis furnished by the seller as well as the executed tenant estoppels to determine any inconsistencies.

**UBIT/ERISA Issues:** If one or more of the equity investors are financial institutions, there may be Unrelated Business Income Tax (UBIT) or Employee's Retirement Income Security Act (ERISA) issues that need to be considered.

Any of these may possibly trigger undesirable consequences for pension fund investors, including possible loss of tax-exempt status or violation of ERISA regulations. It is important, therefore, that the due diligence attorney and tax accountant review all legal documents for possible UBIT and/or ERISA problems.

**Service Contracts:** P&S Agreements usually stipulate that the buyer has the right to assume or reject contracts for services such as trash removal, fire alarm monitoring, building security, landscaping, and janitorial services. Many of these contracts contain clauses that the buyer may find unacceptable such as nonmarket rates, poor service response, or use of outdated equipment. In addition, the buyer may simply want to use another service provider that he/she is using in other buildings in their portfolio.

As a result, the terms of the service contracts need to be reviewed during the Due Diligence phase. If the buyer does not like the terms of the contract(s) or wishes to change a service provider, they can do so after close, provided the contracts are cancelable in 30 days.[30] If they are not cancelable, the buyer should attempt to have them canceled by the seller or set aside holdbacks to cover the possible cost of liquidated damages.

**Warranties:** Attorneys also should review warranties and guaranties to make certain they are transferable to the buyer. If the contracts require transfer fees, these should be arranged by the seller before close. The closing documents should identify service contracts that the buyer wishes to retain and warranties that he/she wishes transferred.

**Consent Decrees and Court Orders:** While not common in most real estate transactions, the legal research should include consent decrees and/or court orders that might affect the property.

---

[29] Some investment managers attach a copy of the abstract to the estoppels certificate and get the tenant to confirm that their understanding is that these are the terms of the lease and that no breaches have occurred.

[30] Contracts not cancelable in 30 days may constitute ERISA violations.

**Other Agreements:** Other agreements that should be included in the legal due diligence include partnership and joint venture agreements, agreements requiring third party consent, and broker/finder contracts.

## Business Due Diligence

In addition to Physical and Legal Due Diligence, there may be other areas of due diligence that should be pursued.

**Financial Review (CPA firm):** A financial review confirms the historic operating and other financial statements of the property's operation. The financial audit provides a third party independent validation of the assumptions used in the Cash Flow Analysis, which is relied upon by the Management Investment Committee, investment partners, and possible lenders.

**Credit Review (credit agency/consultant):** Rental projections are only as good as the tenant's ability/willingness to pay. While not always completely reliable, a credit analysis can be helpful in establishing the future reliability of a tenant's attitudes towards its business obligations.

A preliminary indication can be gained through an internet survey of easily accessible sources such as Hoover's, S&P, D&B, or via a Bloomberg account. This analysis may indicate a more intense review of certain tenants who represent a high percentage of the anticipated cash flow and/or are identified in the preliminary analysis as having credit problems. This generally requires the services of a credit agency or a consultant specializing in credit analysis. Any credit problems flagged at this stage should be discussed thoroughly with the tenant during the tenant interview.[31]

**Tenant Interviews (asset management staff):** During the Due Diligence process, the buyer is usually permitted to interview a representative of each tenant. The tenant interview should be conducted by a member of the investment manager's asset management team, preferably the individual who will be assigned the property if the acquisition proceeds.[32]

Utilizing an asset manager to conduct the interview can provide a good beginning for a solid landlord-tenant relationship. This is reinforced if, after

---

[31] It also may be useful to analyze the SIC mix of tenants on the proposed property's future cash flow to establish increased vulnerability to a single industry or business group. This should then be compared with a continuing analysis of the investment fund/investor portfolio to track industry concentration trends on a broader scale.
[32] Some investment managers schedule the tenant interview considerably in advance to be certain that the right person is available for the interview. This is often accompanied by some promo material describing the new owner of the property (if the acquisition closes) as well as the tenant questionnaire so that the tenant representative is aware of the substance of the interview in advance of the meeting.

the transaction is closed, the Asset Manager calls on each of the tenants with a checklist and timetable to correct the problems mentioned during the interview.

**Appraisal:** An appraisal may be necessary if lender financing is to be utilized to close the transaction. Many lenders require an appraisal before they will approve a loan.[33]

**Insurance Review:** Review by an insurance company, agent, or consultant regarding the adequacy of existing coverage and unique problems the property may encounter in obtaining adequate coverage.

## Phase 7.0: Final Underwriting

As noted, the assumptions and conclusions of the Preliminary Underwriting should be continually updated over the life of the Due Diligence period. There are several tasks that need to be completed prior to the final Investment Committee decision to proceed with the investment.

**Reconciling Due Diligence Findings:** As the results of Due Diligence activities begin arriving, the acquisition team should begin reconciling the findings of the various contractors with each other and with the Preliminary Underwriting that was utilized to gain Preliminary Approval of the transaction by the Investment Committee.

One of the objectives of the Due Diligence process is to approach certain critical issues from several independent directions. As an example, the property's entitlements are reviewed by the architectural contractor, the legal consultant, and, if utilized, an Appraiser. Further, seismic risk exposure may be reviewed by both the structural engineer and the environmental consultant.

Problems with the building's electrical, mechanical, and electronic systems are covered by the engineering consultants, the legal consultants, and the tenant interviews. Critical factors in tenant leases are reviewed by the legal consultant, the tenant interviews, and, if utilized, an appraiser.

The findings of each of these contractors must be compared to each other to see if there are any significant differences in facts or opinions. If so, a member of the acquisition team must contact each of the involved parties and satisfactorily resolve any differences.

This seeming duplication of effort is an attempt to get several perspectives on major potential problem areas. It is usually the problems that haven't been identified by previous owners that prove to be the most expensive to mitigate

---

[33] Appraisers who value the property differently than the agreed-to price may be required to justify why it was not a market transaction.

following close. It is much better to know these costs in advance and have the seller bear (share) in the cost of resolution. The ultimate operating and capital savings generally will more than compensate for the small increments in professional fees.

Next, the reconciled due diligence findings need to be matched with the Preliminary Underwriting presented to the Investment Committee. In many cases discrepancies arise from misstated or inaccurate facts contained in the seller's offering memorandum. In other words, new information becomes available through the Due Diligence process, which was unknown to the seller or if known, not disclosed.

A memo is prepared for the Investment Committee outlining the material changes that have occurred since the Preliminary Underwriting. Sensitivity analysis should be performed to see what the impact is, if any, of these changes on the Cash Flow Projections and the ultimate success of the investment.

**Final Risk Underwriting:** Each of the major risks associated with the proposed investment is then matched with the proposed underwriting mitigation.

Mitigation costs are usually estimated by the due diligence contractor. These costs are then summarized and, depending upon their magnitude, discussed with the seller. Generally, minor costs are traded off if the seller accepts responsibility for the major items. This is often the case since, in most cases, the seller will have to pay these costs in the event of another buyer and "a buyer in hand may be worth more than one in the bush."

In most cases, the terms of the P&S Agreement can be altered to compensate the buyer for problems unearthed by the Due Diligence process. This might take the form of a lower price; a holdback of a portion of purchase funds until a problem can be corrected; a guarantee or warranty by the seller; or some other alteration in the agreement. Obviously, changes in the P&S Agreement require approval of the seller so it is entirely a negotiated situation.

Obviously, it is a critical negotiation, particularly if the mitigation costs are significant. If too much is demanded, the buyer risks (1) losing the transaction or (2) being forced to perform and absorb all of the costs after close.

If the problem(s) is relatively minor, the buyer may decide to "waive" the deposit and proceed to close the transaction. If the buyer waives, the deposit becomes nonrefundable and a closing occurs shortly thereafter (usually within 30 days).

**Final Cash Flow Analysis:** Based on the decisions reached in the Final Risk Underwriting, the Pro-forma cash flow analysis, which has been continually updated throughout the acquisition process, is now put into final form. Sensitivity and attribution analysis continue in order to give the Investment Committee the "what if" parameters necessary for a final decision.

## Phase 8.0: Final Approvals

With all of the information provided by the Final Underwriting, the Investment Committee is ready to make a decision regarding whether to proceed with the acquisition. This decision is usually a choice between three outcomes:

1. Approve the transaction as originally negotiated with the seller.
2. Approve the transaction with some final conditions imposed by the Investment Committee, subject to seller approval.[34]
3. Reject the transaction

Outcomes #1 and #3 are relatively straightforward. If the transaction is approved, the buyer waives its rights to the earnest money deposit and it proceeds to close. If the transaction is rejected, the earnest money deposit is returned, the amount of the pursuit costs are tallied, and the "lessons learned" from the experience hopefully applied to a future transaction.

Outcome #2 is more complex. If the conditions are relatively minor, the seller will most likely approve and proceed to close. If the conditions are significant, the seller may question the wisdom of agreeing to the changes. A lot will depend upon whether there are "back up" buyers waiting in the wings to step into the original buyer's position. Usually, the Investment Committee is aware of the level of competition and will proceed cautiously in making major last minute changes in the deal.

There also may be broader considerations such as whether future seller dispositions will be brought to the investment manager's attention if it has a reputation for changing the deal at the last minute. Given that the real estate investment community is relatively small and close-knit, it is also possible that the investment manager may be taken off potential buyer lists by other firms as well.

Finally, it may have been a long time since a transaction has been made in the particular fund/partnership slated to receive the acquisition. As a result, some

---

[34] In most cases, having the conditions come from the Investment Committee rather than the acquisition team improves the chances of seller agreement.

of the investors may be putting pressure on the investment manager to "make a deal" as quickly as possible.[35]

Clearly, the Investment Committee is ultimately responsible for the fiduciary behavior of the investment manager and facing tough decisions is part of their overall governance responsibilities. This is why the Committee must have the full support of all employees in reaching well-reasoned decisions, based on the best possible information available, and in a timely fashion.

## Phase 9.0: Investment Closing Documents

Once the Management Investment Committee approves the final transaction and the seller agrees, a series of legal documents are finalized.

**Financing Memorandum:** The Financing Memorandum is required for all transactions involving debt financing utilized as a part of the closing process. The document permits lenders to quickly review a potential acquisition and prepare a non-binding term sheet which details the terms and conditions of their loan. The financing memorandum generally includes a property description, pro-forma cash flow, market analysis, and lease comparables.

**Investor Memorandum:** Many acquisitions require an Investor Memorandum. If the investment manager does not have full discretion to invest, this document allows investment partners to review a potential acquisition to determine if an investment is warranted. The Investor Memorandum includes the same basic items as the Financing Memorandum as well as any management comments regarding possible areas of risk mitigation uncovered in due diligence and a final investment return analysis.

**Acquisition Report:** All of the information collected during the Due Diligence and analytical processes is now complied and included in the Acquisition Report, which is the official record of the transaction.[36] In addition, this document provides the foundation for the Asset Manager's first year business plan.

**Title Holding Entity:** The new title holding entity also has to be thought out carefully. In order to reduce liability exposure, most institutional investors insist on having a single entity established for each asset in order to reduce liability exposure. In the case of pension funds, this holding entity is usually a Limited Liability Corporation (LLC) or a 501C(25) corporation, which is limited to holding real estate assets exclusively.

---

[35] Interestingly, these may be the same investors who sue the Company for fiduciary neglect a few years later.
[36] The Acquisition Report should reflect all work performed by the acquisition team and its contractors.

Care must be taken to be sure that the new entity is enabled to transact business in the state in which the property is located. These organizational documents must be delivered to the title company in order to establish the buyer's "existence and authority."

Bank accounts for the new holding entity also should be established in advance. Some states require an owner to hold security deposits in a separate account in order to avoid commingling funds with property operations. In other situations, investors may require a lockbox for tenants' rental payments. Care must be taken that sufficient time is allowed to handle these situations, which might place pension fund investors in danger of violating ERISA or other statutes.[37]

## Phase 10.0: Waive and Closing

Waiving contingencies and putting the cash deposit at risk of forfeiture is usually prohibited without the prior expressed approval of the Investment Committee. It also may be a policy of the Investment Manager that all Due Diligence has been completed and there are no outstanding items whatsoever before a transaction can close. In acquisitions involving financing prior to close, there must be a binding commitment from a lender to provide acceptable financing.

The waiver should be considered the final and definitive moment in which all things which can be known or discovered about the acquisition have occurred. Therefore, the closing process becomes more of an administrative procedure whereby funds are placed into escrow and the title of the property passes to the buyer.

The closing process is generally divided into the following categories:

**Pro-Rations:** Pro-rations involve the apportionment of property revenues and expenses consistent with the time period in which they are earned or incurred. Information derived from the pro-rations is in turn incorporated into the Closing Statement.

**Closing Statement:** The Closing Statement is a "sources and uses" statement prepared by the Title Company from the perspective of both the buyer and seller.

The Closing Statement details the purchase price, loans which are paid off (seller) or originated (buyer) and transaction costs such as title and escrow fees, loan fees, legal fees, etc. Prior to closing, a Closing Statement must be

---

[37] Investment funds are generally prohibited from entering into 1031 transactions and reverse exchanges.

approved by both the buyer and the seller. Usually, a Closing Statement can only be approved by the Investment Committee or its representative.

**Transition to Asset Management:** It is important to effect a smooth and efficient transition of the new investment from seller to buyer. A smooth transition will appear seamless to the tenants and provides an excellent opportunity for a strong first impression by the new owner.

## *Questions for Discussion*

Questions that should be addressed in this case include:

1. How can an investment manager structure investment programs to meet varying investor objectives?
2. What are some of the major sources of new real estate investments? How is each of them accessed by the investment manager?
3. What are the five steps in "screening" potential real estate investments?
4. What are some of the potential risks that need to be identified in the investment underwriting? How are they underwritten?
5. What are the steps in developing a cash flow analysis of a prospective investment? How is the sensitivity of input assumptions tested?
6. Why is it important to budget due diligence costs associated with evaluation of a prospective investment? Development of an acquisition timeline?
7. What is the role of the Investment Committee? Who are the individuals usually on such a committee? How often do they meet? What level of positive voting is required to move forward with an offer?
8. What are the seller's objectives in using a Confidentiality Agreement? An offering memorandum?
9. What are the buyer's objectives in using a Letter of Intent (LOI) rather than a final contract?
10. If both buyer and seller agree on the terms of an LOI, what is the next agreement in the process? Who negotiates it?
11. What is the role in an acquisition transaction played by an Ernest Money Deposit (EMD)? What form does it usually take?

12. What is the purpose of the due diligence process? Who does it protect?
13. Who are the players in the due diligence process? How is it managed?
14. What is the difference between a Phase I and a Phase II environmental study? Why is it important?
15. What are the major issues covered by the legal due diligence work? The business due diligence?
16. How are the various risks uncovered by the due diligence process reconciled by the acquisition team?
17. How are potential mitigation costs negotiated with the seller?
18. What alternatives does the Investment Committee have in granting final approval of the transaction?
19. What are the investment documents? What role does each of them play in successively closing the transaction?
20. What are the 3 major steps in the closing process? What role does each play?

Please use these questions as a guide and not a format or a reflection of all of the questions that need to be addressed by this case.

# 12

# HIGHTECHOFFICE, INC.[1]

## Case A: Property Acquisition

In September, 2002, Jeb Collins was sitting at his computer in a hotel room in Boston trying to finalize a Letter of Intent (LOI) to purchase the Plano Office Center (Center) in Dallas, TX. He was scheduled to deliver the LOI the next morning to Donna Bull, the asset manager of the Center. Donna worked for Centaur Advisors Inc. (Centaur), a Boston based investment advisory firm, which had originally developed the Center.

Jeb was the head of acquisitions for HiTechOffice, Inc. (HiTech), a $600 million Real Estate Investment Trust (REIT) based in Arlington, VA, which specialized in office complexes tenanted by high technology firms. The REIT had been organized in 2000 to take advantage of real estate investment opportunities in the hard hit and rapidly contracting high technology sector. The firm had grown rapidly over the first eighteen months, but as a result of the continuing economic difficulties of high technology firms, it was finding it increasingly difficult to uncover new investment opportunities supported by economically strong tenants.

While Jeb was enthusiastic about the Center investment, he was concerned about certain aspects of the deal, particularly the special nature of the tenant improvements servicing fifty percent of the space. He was also worried about an access agreement to provide telecommunications services to the building. Finally, Jeb was concerned whether his underwriting compensated sufficiently for the soft Dallas office market.

---

[1] This case was prepared by John McMahan in 2002. Copyright © 2002 and 2004 by John McMahan, all rights reserved.

## Centaur Advisors

Centaur had been formed in 1988 to provide real estate investment advisory services for pension plans, endowment funds, and foundations. The firm had grown over the years to the point where, by the fall of 2002, it managed $3.7 billion in client assets, which consisted of 123 properties in 24 markets across the county. Centaur's investments included office buildings, warehouses, "flex" R&D buildings, shopping centers, hotels, and apartments. Historically, the firm had overweighted toward suburban office and industrial buildings and by the fall of 2002, these properties comprised almost 60% of Centaur's portfolio.

Centaur's investment strategy was to focus on newly developed properties located in growth markets, which had a lower cost advantage at the time of acquisition or development. The firm generally invested through joint venture arrangements with local developers. In terms of investment performance, Centaur had produced returns averaging 15.8% annually for the prior five years, a considerably higher return than the NCREIF[2] index for the same period. This performance was largely the result of a policy of selling investments to other investors once the buildings had become fully leased.

The projects, located in rapidly growing markets, were essentially industrial buildings that had been designed in such a way as to make them attractive to office users. The key ingredients in Centaur's strategy were:

- Rapidly growing market
- High profile suburban location
- Located near a fiber-optic service line
- Two-story design
- Abundant parking
- Cost effective rents (lower than Class A rates)
- Open plan designed for flexible interior office layout
- Minimal core areas

Markets were selected based on Centaur's ongoing research as well as continuing discussion with a series of local developers who Centaur relied upon to generate new projects within its target markets. Highly visible suburban locations were preferred not only because of lower land costs but also their proximity to affordable residential and shopping areas. Parking was

---

[2] National Council of Real Estate Investment Fiduciaries.

provided at a ratio of five stalls per 1,000 sq. ft and, ideally, in such a manner as to surround the building so that tenants and their employees could have rapid access to their space. This aim was reinforced by having multiple entrances to the buildings.

A key ingredient in the success of the program was having large, open work areas with an absence of columns. This space configuration allowed tenants to arrange and rearrange their space as various project teams were organized and disbanded. It also permitted employers to increase employee densities, thereby lowering rent-per-employee costs.[3] Centaur found that the combination of lower rents and higher employee densities was a powerful tool in attracting high quality tenants. Interestingly, many of Centaur's tenants were not dot-com firms but rather "old economy" Fortune 500 companies.

Another key was the availability of fiber-optic trunk service at or near the building site. Most tenants required at least T-1 capacity on a 24/7 basis. Historically, Centaur had provided this capability internally but had acceded to pressure from tenants and clients to contract with outside firms to install and maintain the service. The Center was the first building in Centaur's portfolio to outsource telecommunications services.

The employees of most of the firms leasing space in the high-technology program were generation Xers in their 20s and 30s. The open space design generally appealed to the "open" organizational structure that many Xers prefer. In some of the buildings, there was a common area containing several campus-type amenities such as a snack bar, nap room, laundry pick-up, and in the larger projects, a concierge to handle personal tasks for the employees.

## *Dallas/Fort Worth Metropolitan Area*

With 5.2 million people, Dallas/Fort Worth is the fifth largest metropolitan area in the US and the largest in the State of Texas. Over one million residents arrived after 1990, which resulted in a 21.3% growth rate for this period. Population was expected to increase another 11% by 2005. The median household income in Dallas was the highest in Texas ($52,131) but was considerably lower than in other major metro areas.

Dallas/Fort Worth's economic structure had several overriding characteristics that strongly influenced both its short- and long-term growth rates. A well-diversified economy minimized market risk against a downturn in any particular industry. In addition, most of the principal industries comprising Dallas' economic base were well positioned for expansion over the next several years. The metro area also was a major transportation hub and scored

---

[3] This was a goal of most employers. The average space per employee dropped from 220 S.F. in 1992 to 193 S.F. in 1999 (Source: Building Owners and Managers Association).

high in terms of energy availability and reliability, a factor of growing concern to prospective tenants. Finally, Dallas/Fort Worth was governed by a strong pro-business philosophy at both the local and state level.

## The Dallas/Fort Worth Office Market

In large measure, the Dallas/Fort Worth office market reflected the area's strong pro-growth and pro-jobs philosophy. The objective of these policies was to keep land costs and building rents low so that the area continued to be attractive to new firms and existing firms didn't leave. A very general plan, relatively lenient zoning restrictions, largely non-union labor, and an expedited entitlement process helped to accomplish this objective.

The result of these policies was a market with relatively low rents and high vacancy rates. This situation also encouraged a considerable amount of shifting between office nodes as new product became available often at lower costs. Several institutional investors believed that this type of policy implicitly favored real estate speculators at the expense of long-term investors. As a result, some refused to invest in this type of market.

Exhibit 1 outlines the Dallas office market as of March 31, 2002.[4] During the first quarter, the market continued a relatively high level of negative absorption largely because of continuing construction of space in an already soft office market.

---

[4] Note that the data source In Exhibit 1 is different than in Exhibit 1 in Chapter 8, as well as the geographical areas covered.

## Exhibit 1
## Plano Office Center
## Dallas Multitenant Office Market
## March 31, 2002

| Submarket | Rentable* | Absorbed* | Vacancy | Average Rent |
|---|---|---|---|---|
| Dallas CBD | 29,995.2 | (287.5) | 28.6% | $19.80 |
| LBJ Freeway | 21,786.5 | (295.3) | 24.3% | $20.00 |
| Far North Dallas | 25,320.1 | (123.7) | 27.9% | $22.20 |
| Las Colinas | 23,205.3 | (296.4) | 23.7% | $21.60 |
| Central Expressway | 11,199.7 | 44.5 | 19.7% | $19.70 |
| N.DallasPreston | 3,671.2 | (100.0) | 13.6% | $22.80 |
| Southwest Dallas | 1,275.6 | (10.9) | 24.2% | $13.50 |
| Richardson/Plano | 14,758.4 | (206.0) | 25.1% | $20.40 |
| Stemmons Frwy. | 9,405.3 | (29.7) | 24.2% | $19.90 |
| Uptown/Turtle Creek | 8,771.7 | (99.3) | 16.8% | $23.90 |
| Lewisville/Denton | 1,944.6 | 82.3 | 33.1% | $13.50 |
| Totals/Average | 154,977.4 | (1,290.4) | 24.6% | $20.70 |

* Thousands

Source: The Real Estate Center at Texas A&M University

The Dallas office market continued to deteriorate in the first quarter of 2002. Market absorption turned negative, largely as a result of the continued addition of new space to the market, despite an increase in average vacancy to 24.6% from 16.2% at the end of 2000. This situation was aggravated by a large shadow market created by the contraction of firms and increased subleasing activity.

As a result, average rental rates declined to $20.70 from an average of $21.71 at the end of 2000. The greatest percentage rental declines occurred in the Las Colinas (-9.7%), Uptown/Turtle Creek (-8.9%), and Dallas CBD (-8.7%) submarkets. The only submarket to experience a positive increase was the Stemmons Freeway area where average rents were up 21.9%. The total Dallas average market rent was off 4.7% since the end of 2000.

Because of these market conditions, tenants appeared able to drive better deals. On the other hand, landlords were getting tougher on lease terms, including asking for Letters of Credit and getting a larger percentage of the rent paid up front.

**Far North Dallas Submarket:** The Far North Dallas was located to the west of the Dallas North Tollway. This submarket had historically led the metro area office market in both speculative construction and absorption. In the first quarter of 2002, however, the submarket experienced negative absorption of 123,712 sq. ft, representing 9.6% of the total negative absorption in the Dallas market for the quarter.

This dramatic shift in absorption was primarily the result of the fact that 58% of the 3.5 million of new metro office construction for delivery in 2001 was centered in this submarket, of which only 11% of was preleased. An additional 835,000 sq. ft was still under construction for delivery in 2002.[5]

**Richardson Plano Submarket:** Located to the east of the Dallas Tollway, this submarket had been almost as active in terms of office space activity as Far North Dallas. Office absorption for 2001 was 1,567,200 sq. ft with rental rates increasing 5.9%. At year's end, vacancy was 6.3%. During the first quarter of 2002, absorption turned negative reaching 205,962 for the quarter (16.0% of the total Dallas market).

Major new facilities announced included Fujitsu's development of a 41 acre "Technology Business Complex with 18 new office and technology buildings; Nortel's development of a 150,000 sq. ft headquarters building as part of an 725,000 sq. ft complex; and a 100,000 sq. ft complex for WorldCom corporation.

## Plano Office Center

The Plano Office Center (Center) consisted of a two-story office building located on the western side of the Dallas North Tollway approximately 22 miles north of the Dallas CBD (Exhibit 2).

The land purchase had closed on June 20, 2000, with construction completed approximately a year later. The project had been built under a guaranteed maximum contract by Phleger-Jones, a national developer that Centaur had worked with previously. The building's leasable area was 160,000 sq. ft, which had been split into four 40,000 sq. ft increments (Exhibit 3).

The Center was located near the worldwide headquarters of J.C. Penney and Frito-Lay as well as the Dallas Air Park, a major private office and industrial park developed by Ross Perot, Jr., to the south. New residential subdivisions were located to the west of the site.

---

[5] Source: Kennedy Wilson Research.

Chapter 12 - HighTechOffice A          -283-

**Exhibit 2**
**Area Map**

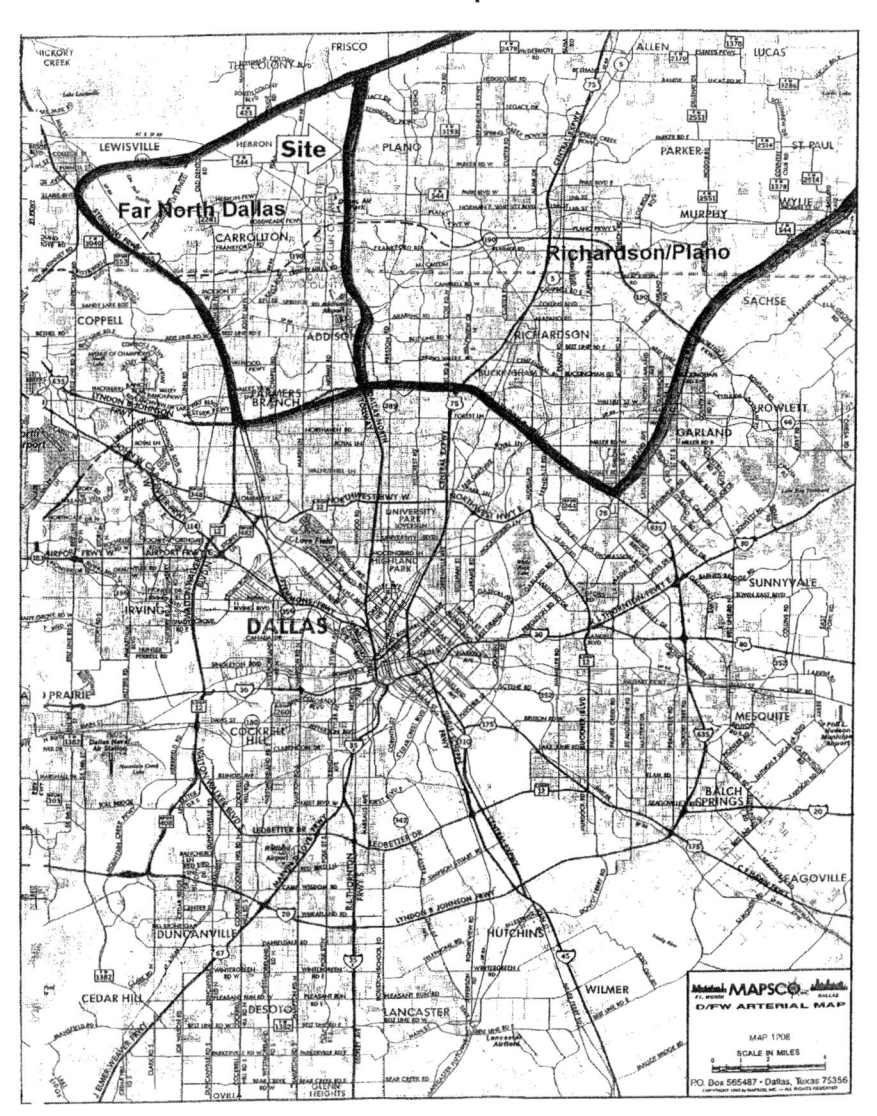

## Exhibit 3
## Site Plan

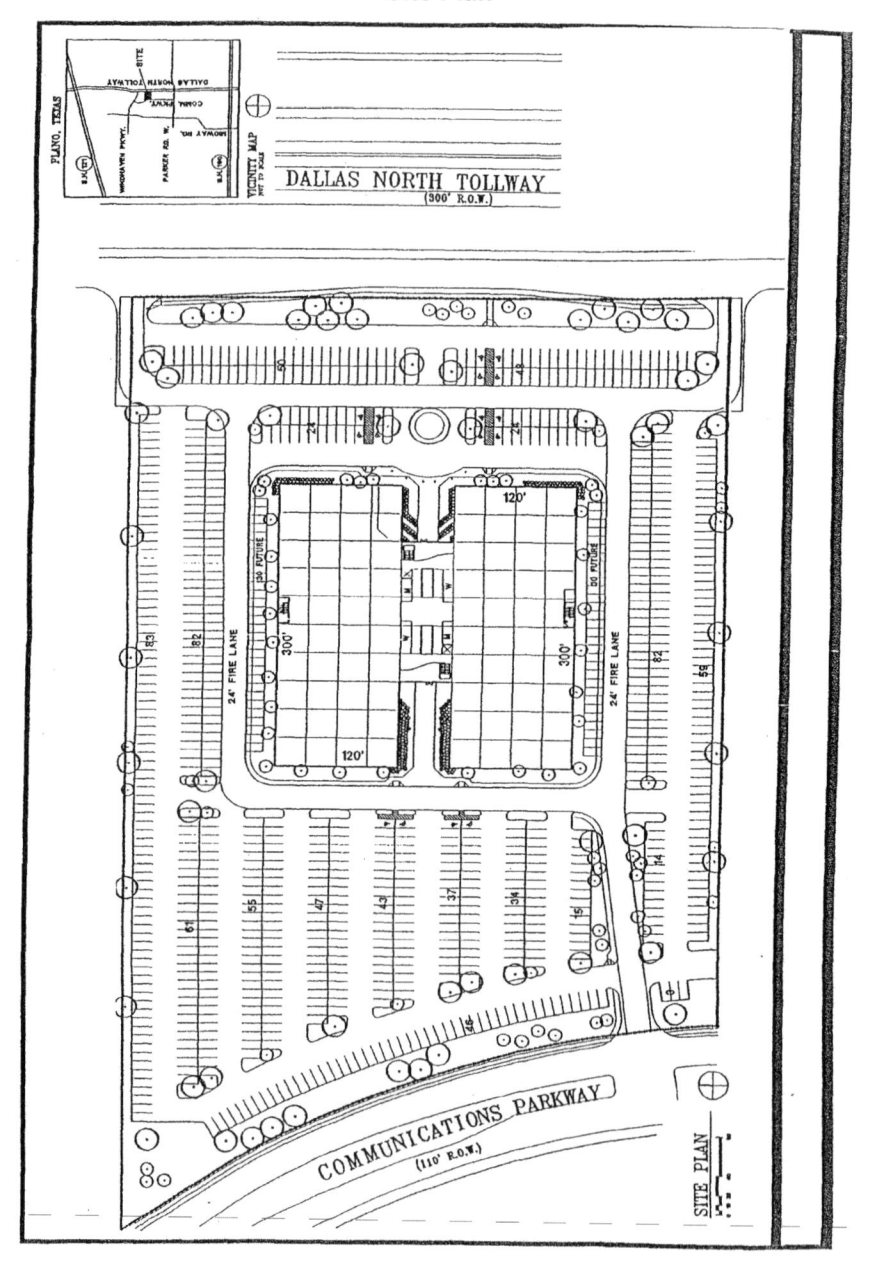

## Tenants

The Center was 100% leased to three tenants:

**Lodestar, Inc (Lodestar):** Lodestar was a seven-year old biotechnology firm that had survived the dot-com meltdown of technology firms over the past 18 months. The firm had been based in the San Francisco Bay Area but had relocated to Dallas to reduce operating costs and assure reliable energy availability. Lodestar currently had approximately 225 employees in 80,000 sq. ft on the ground floor of the Center.

Lodestar had a 10 year lease at $18.50 per sq. ft with a fifth year rental adjustment to market. In addition, Centaur had agreed to provide non-standard tenant improvements of approximately $12.00 per sq. ft for which Lodestar was willing to pay full cost reimbursement plus 10% amortized over 10 years. This allowance was used to create "clean rooms" for their lab work.

Although Lodestar had a BBB-credit rating, Centaur required the tenant to secure a Letter of Credit (LOC) to collateralize the cost of the additional TIs. The LOC was reduced 10% each year over the period of the lease.

Lodestar paid electricity and telecom charges directly as well as pro rata share (50%) of CAM changes and any increases in property taxes and insurance.

**American Telecom (American):** American was a Fortune 500 corporation involved in providing both wired and wireless communication services to several Southwestern states. American leased 40,000 sq. ft on the second floor of the western half of the Center for a call center and local service support facility. The call center was one of three in the United States supporting new product development primarily in the wireless division. The local service team was involved in repairing and servicing American's products in the Dallas/Ft. Worth metro area. American currently had approximately 310 employees employed in the facility.

American had a five-year lease at a rent of $16.50 per sq. ft with an option to renew at market. The lease called for American paying directly the electricity and telecom costs as well as reimbursing the landlord for 25% of annual CAM charges and 25% of any increases in property taxes and insurance.

**Computer Training Associates (Associates):** The second floor of the eastern half of the Center was leased to Associates, a privately owned Dallas firm involved in training computer application specialists. Associates offered introductory and advanced computer training as well as certification in specialized product installation such as Microsoft, Oracle, Cisco, JD Edwards, and other major software/hardware firms. The firm had been in existence for seven years and was considered the top computer-training firm in the metro area. Associates had 17 employees at the facility and an average student load of 125-150 students per day. Although Associates had no credit rating, it had an excellent history of meeting its obligations and strong banking relationships.

Associates had a five-year lease at a rate of $19.00 per sq. ft with an option to renew at market. The tenant paid all electricity and telecom costs directly as well as 25% of annual CAM charges and 25% of any increases in property taxes and insurance.

## HiTech's Offer

Exhibit 4 outlines Jeb's analysis of the pricing situation. Gross rents averaged $18.13 per sq. ft with $105,600 in additional income provided by the amortization of Lodestar's above standard improvements and the 10% bonus rent charges. Operating costs averaged approximately $4.54 per sq. ft (As noted, electricity and telecom were paid directly by the tenants as well as 25% of annual CAM charges and 25% of increases in property taxes and insurance over the first year).

**Exhibit 4**
**Plano Office Center**
**Pro Forma Pricing Analysis**

| Gross Revenue | | | | |
|---|---|---|---|---|
| Tenant | sq. ft | Rate/sq. ft | Rent | Revenue |
| Lodestar | 80,000 | $18.50 | $1,480,000 | $1,480,000 |
| American | 40,000 | 16.50 | 660,000 | 660,000 |
| Associates | 40,000 | 19.00 | 760,000 | 760,000 |
| Total | 160,000 | 18.13 | | 2,900,000 |
| Less: Vacancy and Bad Debt Allowance (10.0%) | | | | (290,000) |
| Effective Gross Revenue | | | | 2,610,000 |
| Operating Expenses | | | | |
| Property Taxes | | | 425,000 | |
| Insurance | | | 44,000 | 469,000 |
| TI Reimbursement and 10% bonus rent | | | | 105,600 |
| Net Operating Income | | | | 2,246,600 |
| Pro Forma Cap Rate | | | | 10.5% |
| Pro Forma Pricing | | | | 21,400,000 |

In developing his recommendation, Jeb had accepted the Lodestar TI reimbursement and bonus rent as operating revenue, relying primarily on the back-up collateral of the LOC. He was concerned, however, that his 10% vacancy allowance might be low in light of the soft Dallas office market and the fact that half of the Center's space would turn in five years.

Based on his analysis, Jeb estimated that the deal met the minimum investment hurdle rates that the firm required.[6] He therefore recommended to the Investment Committee that the building be purchased at a 10.5% cap rate or $21,400,000, which would be approximately $600,000 less than the $22,000,000 offering price. After extensive, often heated debate, HiTech's Investment Committee approved Jeb's recommendation.

Although he was concerned with the soft office market, Jeb continued to be very impressed with the positive aspects of the deal. Dallas was one of the fastest growing markets in the country. Corporations such as Lodestar were fleeing high operating costs and power shortages in other metro areas. In fact, Lodestar might just be the beginning of a trend in which high tech firms leave the Bay Area, Boston, New York, and other high cost areas for lower cost operating environments and more dependable sources of energy.

The Center's tenants were all related to high-technology and were therefore consistent with HiTech's strategic objectives. Although only American Telecom had a strong credit rating, generally they were all financially strong firms.

Jeb was concerned, however, with the highly specialized nature of the extra TIs that were a condition of the Lodestar lease. If Lodestar defaulted, HiTech might end up with specialized clean rooms that would be difficult to rent to a new tenant. The letter of credit, therefore, would take on additional significance in due diligence (Exhibit 5). Jeb reviewed the LOC again (as well as the relevant language in each of the tenant's leases), and the documents seemed to be similar to ones he had seen in the past.

Jeb also reviewed once again the telecom access agreement (Exhibit 6) and while he was less familiar with this type of agreement, he thought it seemed adequate. He still had a gnawing feeling, however, about unwinding the agreement if the service provider, BuildingAccess, Inc., had financial problems.

He thought there probably were other things to worry about, but his brain was already reeling from thinking about the transaction, and he wanted to get some sleep. He had been under considerable personal strain over the last several months as his recommendations were being scrutinized more

---

[6] HiTech's current rule of thumb was to pay no less than a 10.0% cap rate in commodity markets such as Dallas.

carefully than normal, since several of his recent transactions had not performed well, and he was under significant pressure to improve his batting average. In fact, Max Brodsky, HiTech's CEO, had recently mentioned to Jeb how impressed he was with Jerry Masters, the head of acquisition for one of HiTEch's major competitors, who was considered one of the top deal makers in the country.

Jeb looked again at the LOI in his computer (Exhibit 7) and wondered if he should make any final changes to give him more negotiating leverage. He was concerned, however, that one of their major competitors was rumored to be submitting an LOI as well, and he might lose the deal if he tightened the terms too much.

## Exhibit 5A
### Example of Letter of Credit

Date of Issue: June 1, 2000     Our Irrevocable Standby Credit:

Date of Expiry: June 30, 2001
Place of Expiry: At our above counters.

Applicant:
XYZ Tenant, Inc.

Beneficiary:
ABC Owner, Inc.

Amount: USD $2,500,000.00

We hereby establish in your favor this credit available with Bank, at AnyTown, CA by payment of your draft(s) at sight drawn on Bank accompanied by:

1.     Your signed and dated statement worded as follows:

"The undersigned, an authorized representative of ABC Owner, Inc., hereby certifies that XYZ Tenant, Inc. has defaulted under the lease agreement dated July 1, 2000 between ABC Owner, Inc. and XYZ Tenant, Inc. regarding security deposit."

Partial drawings are permitted. (More than one draft may be drawn and presented under the Letter of Credit.)

This Letter of Credit is transferable and may be successively transferred but only to a single transferee whom you shall have advised us in your instrument of transfer is the assignee under and in connection with and as part of your assignment of your interest in the Lease between you and

XYZ Tenant, Inc. for the premises located at 100 Main Street, AnyTown, California 99999. Any such transfer may be effected only through ourselves (all bank fees to be charged to Applicant) and upon presentation to us at our above-specified office of a duly executed instrument of transfer in the form of Exhibit A attached hereto together with the original of this Letter of Credit and payment of by ABC Owner, Inc. of our transfer fee in the amount of ¼% of the amount of this Letter of Credit. Any transfer of this Letter of Credit may not change the place of expiration of this Letter of Credit from our above-specified office. Each transfer shall be evidenced by our endorsement on the reverse of the original of this Letter of Credit, and we shall deliver the original of this Letter of Credit so endorsed to the transferee.

This Letter of Credit expires at our above address on June 30, 2001 but will be automatically extended, without written amendment, in each succeeding calendar year, up to but not beyond June 30, 2005, unless we have sent written notice to you at your above address that we elect not to renew this Letter of Credit beyond the date specified in such notice, which date will be June 30, 2001 or any subsequent June 30 but not beyond June 30, 2005 at least forty-five (45) calendar days after the date we send you such notice. Notice of non-renewal shall be deemed received by you four (4) business days after the date such notice is deposited in the U.S. mail, postage prepaid.

That payment is to be made by transfer to an account with us or at another bank, we and/or such other bank may rely on an account number specified in such instructions even if the number identifies a person or entity different from the intended payee.

Documents must be presented to us no later than 5:00p.m.

Draft(s) must indicate the number and date of this credit.

Each draft presented hereunder must be accompanied by this original credit for our endorsement thereon of the amount of such draft.

Documents must be forwarded to us via courier in one parcel and may be mailed to Bank, operation group, Northern California, 525 Main Street, 25th Floor, AnyTown, CA 99999.

This credit is subject to the uniform customs and practice for documentary credits (1993 revision), international chamber of commerce, publication number 500, and engages us in accordance with the terms thereof.

Yours Truly

Bank

## Exhibit 5B
## Example of Letter of Credit Lease Provision

6. Security

6.1 Security Deposit. Contemporaneously with the execution of this Lease, Tenant shall pay to Landlord the Security Deposit, which shall be held by Landlord to secure Tenant's performance of its obligations under this Lease. The Security Deposit is not an advance payment of Rent or a measure or limit of Landlord's damages upon an Event of Default (defined in Section 17). Landlord may, from time to time and without prejudice to any other remedy, use all or a part of the Security Deposit to perform any obligation Tenant fails to perform hereunder. Following any such application of the Security Deposit, Tenant shall pay to Landlord on demand the amount so applied in order to restore the Security Deposit to its original amount. Provided that Tenant has performed all of its obligations hereunder, Landlord shall, within thirty (30) days after the Term ends, return to Tenant the portion of the Security Deposit which was not applied to satisfy Tenant's obligations. The Security Deposit may be commingled with other funds, and no interest shall be paid thereon. If Landlord transfers its interest in the Premises and the transferee assumes Landlord's obligations under this Lease, then Landlord may assign the Security Deposit to the transferee and Landlord thereafter shall have no further liability for the return of the Security Deposit.

6.2 Letter of Credit. In lieu of the Security Deposit referenced above, concurrently with Tenant's execution of this Lease. Tenant may deliver to Landlord an irrevocable letter of credit as hereinafter described (the "Letter of Credit"). The Letter of Credit shall (i) be an irrevocable standby letter of credit, (ii) name Landlord as beneficiary, (iii) be payable on sight draft accompanied only by Landlord's certification that it is entitled to payment thereon because an Event of Default under the Lease has occurred, (iv) be for an initial term of at least twelve (12) months and, subject to the terms set forth below, shall be renewed thereafter no later than thirty (30) days prior to any expiration date thereof so that the Letter of Credit remains in effect during the entire period ending thirty (30) days after the expiration of the initial Term and any renewal term of this Lease, (v) assure payment in the total amount of $8,122,274.95, and (vi) be otherwise in form reasonably acceptable to Landlord. If Tenant fails timely to renew its Letter of Credit, then Landlord shall have the right to draw thereon, and retain the amounts so drawn as the Security Deposit. The following provisions shall govern the parties' rights and obligations with respect to the Letter of Credit:

6.2.1 Landlord shall be entitled to recourse against the Letter of Credit to recover any loss or damage it may suffer as a result of any breach or default by Tenant under this Lease. Partial and multiple draws shall be permitted under the Letter of Credit. After any such draw,

Tenant shall pay to Landlord on demand the amount so drawn to be held as part of the Security Deposit.

6.2.2 Provided an Event of Default has not occurred during the twelve (12) month period prior to each reduction and Tenant's financial condition as of the date of each reduction, in Landlord's reasonable judgment, is equal to or better than its financial condition as of the Commencement Date, Landlord shall reduce the required amount of the Letter of Credit as follows:

| Lease Month | Letter of Credit Amount |
|---|---|
| 1 – 12 | $8,122,275.00 |
| 13 – 24 | $7,445,419.00 |
| 25 – 36 | $6,768,562.00 |
| 37 – 48 | $6,091,706.00 |
| 49 – 60 | $5,414,850.00 |
| 61 – 73 | $4,737,994.00 |
| 73 – 85 | $4,061,137.00 |
| 85 – 97 | $3,384,281.00 |
| 97 – 109 | $2,707,425.00 |
| 109 – 120 | $2,030,569.00 |

Without limitation, Tenant may satisfy the financial condition requirement set forth above if, as of the date of each scheduled reduction, Tenant can provide evidence reasonably acceptable to Landlord that Tenant then has cash or cash equivalents on hand in an amount equal to or greater than the total of the next twelve (12) months of Basic Rent coming due under this Lease. Subject to the above, Tenant's failure to keep the Letter of Credit in effect during the entire initial term of the Lease, or Tenant's failure to furnish written evidence to Landlord of the yearly renewal of the Letter of Credit, shall be an Event of Default hereunder.

6.2.3 Tenant shall pay, as Additional Rent under this Lease, any and all costs or fees charged in connection with the Letter of Credit that arise due to: (i) Landlord's sale or transfer of all or a portion of the Building; or (ii) the addition, deletion or modification of any beneficiaries under the Letter of Credit.

# Exhibit 6
# SUMMARY OF KEY PROVISIONS
# TELECOMMUNICATIONS SERVICES AGREEMENT

**Parties to Agreement**

Property Owner: Centaur Advisors, Inc.

Service Provider: Building Access, Inc.

**Services Provided Tenants**

Local, intraLATA toll (or local toll), long distance, high-speed data, internet, video/cable television, cable Internet and other lawful services and applications that Service Provider may provide now or in the future.

Service Provider holds all right and title to the services and retains the right, in its sole discretion, to control, add to, delete, and/or change such services.

Service Provider has the right, but not the obligation, to market and contract with Tenants for the provision of any or all of the Services on an individual subscriber basis, independent of Owner.

Orders for service(s) shall be solely between Service Provider and individual Tenants. Service Provider retains the right to terminate such service(s) to Tenants who fail to abide by the terms and conditions of service contracts.

**Installation of Services**

Property Owner provides Service Provider with a non-exclusive easement on, over, under, within, and through the Premises (both land and improvements) as necessary or desirable for: Service Provider to provide services to tenants.

Within this easement, Service Provider has the right to construct and install and use any cabling, wiring, power supplies, risers, conduits, distribution wiring and facilities, cross-connect facilities and/or distribution frames (collectively referred to as "Facilities"), and any rights of way and entrance facilities within and into the building, as necessary or useful, for the provision of services to the Tenants, whether owned, installed, controlled or maintained by Service Provider or not.

Service Provider has the right to install on the roof of any building on the Premises an antenna or other equipment, as necessary or desirable for the provision of services to the Tenants, together with any wiring or cabling from the antenna to the rest of the facilities.

Property Owner is not responsible for installation charges, monthly subscription rates, equipment deposits, or other charges for subscribers' service(s).

**Charges for Services**

Service Provider is responsible for collection of charges, billing, accounting, and other services related to subscriber accounts.

Owner is not responsible for installation charges, monthly subscription rates, equipment deposits, or other charges for subscribers' service(s).

**Term of Agreement**

Agreement becomes effective on the date of the agreement and continues as so long as Service Provider or Agent may provide the Services, not to exceed __*__ years from the date of this Agreement. Thereafter, the Agreement is automatically renewed for consecutive terms of __*__ years each, unless written notice of termination is given by either party.

**Termination**

This Agreement may be terminated prior to expiration of its term:

(a) by either party in the event of material breach of this Agreement after 30 days' written notice, unless the other party cures or commences to cure such breach during such 30-day period and diligently proceeds with such cure; or

(b) by Service Provider upon at least 60 days' written notice if Service Provider is unable, or it becomes impracticable, to continue distribution of any one or more of the Services due to any law, rule, regulation, judgment, contract with third party or other reason beyond the reasonable control of Service Provider.

Upon termination of this Agreement and any other legally enforceable rights of access to provide Services, Service Provider shall, at its sole option, have an additional ninety (90) days to remove or abandon part or all of the Facilities, in its sole discretion.

**Assignment/Successors**

Benefits and obligations of Agreement run with the land and will inure to and are binding upon the successors, assigns, heirs, and personal representatives of Service Provider and Owner during the Term hereof.

**Subordination Rights**

Agreement is subordinate to all leases, mortgages, and/or deed of trust which may now or hereafter affect the Premises, and to all renewals, modifications, consolidations, replacements and extensions thereof.

Service Provider's obligation to subordinate this Agreement to any present or future mortgage, deed of trust or lease is subject to and contingent upon satisfaction of such mortgagee's, trustee's or lessor's obligation to recognize and not disturb Service Provider's rights and obligations under this Agreement.

**Sale of Property**

Easement runs with the land and binds Owner, and each and every subsequent owner thereof, for the term of this agreement.

Owner makes assumption of the Agreement a condition of any sale, transfer or assignment of the property.

* Negotiated

## Exhibit 7
## Letter of Intent

### HITECHOFFICE, INC.
*A Real Estate Investment Trust*
507 Huntigton Ave.
Alexandria, VA 22303
(571) 432 7610
(571) 432 7612 (Fax)
www.hitechoffice.com

May 14, 2002

Ms. Donna Bull
Vice President, Asset Management
Centaur Advisors, Inc.
114 Commonwealth Avenue
Boston, MA 05789

Dear Ms. Bull:

This letter will outline the basic terms and conditions of our proposal that HiTechOffice, Inc., a Real Estate Investment Trust domiciled in Delaware ("Buyer"), shall purchase from an entity affiliated with or advised by Centaur Advisors, Inc. ("Seller") the property described below (the "Property").

The general terms and conditions of this proposal are as follows:

1. **Property:** A fee simple interest in Plano Office Center, containing approximately 160,000 SF located on 12 acres of land in the City of Plano, TX, and including all personal property and trade names associated with the Property.

2. **Purchase price:** Sixteen million, five hundred thousand ($16,500,000), payable in cash at closing.

3. **Purchase Agreement:** The transaction is subject to the negotiation and execution of an agreement of purchase and sale (the "Purchase Agreement"), in form and substance satisfactory to both parties, setting forth all of the obligations of the parties. Buyer shall prepare the Purchase Agreement and submit it to Seller for approval.

4. **Conditions to Closing:** The Purchase Agreement shall provide that Buyer's obligation to consummate the acquisition of the Property shall be subject to the satisfaction of the following conditions, as well as additional conditions to be negotiated in the Purchase Agreement. Buyer shall have thirty (30) business days after full execution of the Purchase Agreement (the "Review Period") to determine in its sole discretion whether to proceed with the acquisition and shall so notify Seller prior to the expiration of the Review Period. Otherwise, the Purchase Agreement shall terminate without liability

on the part of Buyer or Seller. Seller shall provide Buyer true and correct copies of all pertinent documents regarding the Property outlined below, after signing this letter.

a) **Leases:** Review and approval by Buyer of all terms, conditions, and forms of the existing leases affecting the Property.

b) **Title:** Buyer's review and approval of title to the Property. Seller shall deliver to Buyer within ten (10) business days of Seller's execution hereof an ALTA owner's extended coverage preliminary title report, together with all exceptions referenced therein, covering the Property. Fee simple title to the Property shall be vested in Seller, and shall be good and marketable, and shall be free and clear of all existing liens and encumbrances, except as may be approved in writing by Buyer. Buyer expressly reserves the right to require Seller to discharge prior to closing such liens and encumbrances as Buyer may designate. A title company or companies acceptable to Buyer shall issue an ALTA Owner's Form B (amended 10/7/70) title insurance policy, or such other form as Buyer may elect, insuring title, where appropriate, in Buyer or Buyer's nominee which policy shall contain such endorsements, coinsurance, and reinsurance provisions as Buyer may require.

c) **Survey:** Buyer's review and approval of a current ALTA survey of the Property certified by a duly licensed surveyor or surveyors showing all physical conditions affecting the property sufficient for deletion of the survey exception from the required title insurance policy and otherwise acceptable to Buyer. Seller shall provide said survey at Seller's cost.

d) **Financial Information:** Buyer's review, verification and approval of the income and expenses relating to the ownership and operation of the Property.

e) **Tenant Financials:** Buyer's approval of the tenant's financial condition, and ability to fulfill the terms and conditions of their lease.

f) **Existing Encumbrances, Service Contracts, and Other Agreements and Reports:** Buyer review and approval of all documents evidencing or securing the existing encumbrances, all service contracts, certificates of occupancy, permits, environmental, subdivision or zoning documents, insurance policies, warranties, any other agreements, reports, studies, inspections or investigations of the Property, and any other contracts or documents of significance to the Property.

g) **Engineer/Architect's Reports:** Engineers and/or architects selected by Buyer shall inspect the Property and issue reports satisfactory in all respects to Buyer. Said reports will be obtained by Buyer and be at Buyer's sole cost.

h) **Physical Conditions:** Buyer's review and approval of the physical condition of the Property, including, without limitation, of all improvements located thereon and the operative systems of all such improvements and the confirmation that the Property does not contain any asbestos containing material or hazardous materials.

i) **Compliance with Laws:** Buyer's review and approval of evidence satisfactory to Buyer and its legal counsel that the property complies with all applicable zoning, subdivision, land use, redevelopment, energy, environmental, building and other governmental requirements applicable to the use, maintenance and occupancy of the Property.

j) **Condemnation:** Satisfactory confirmation that no condemnation proceeding is threatened or commenced with respect to the Property.

k) **Legal Review:** Approval by Buyer and its legal counsel of all documentation with regard to all leases, contracts, service agreements, closing documentation, title, certificates of occupancy and all other legal matters related to the Property and its acquisition by Buyer.

l) **Property Tax Bills:** Buyer's review and approval of the most recently available tax bills respecting the Property.

m) **Litigation List:** Buyer's review and approval of all actions, suits, and legal or administrative proceedings affecting the Property.

5. **Closing:** On or before fifteen (15) days following the expiration of the Review Period.

6. **Closing Costs:** Transfer taxes, CLTA title insurance premiums, premiums for endorsements and recording free shall be paid by Seller. All other closing costs shall be divided between Buyer and Seller according to local custom. All costs with regard to prepayment of the existing loan(s), if any, shall be paid by Seller.

7. **Prorations:** All income and expenses and other customarily prorated items shall be prorated as of the date of closing.

8. **Exclusive:** Seller agrees to withdraw the Property from the market until the execution of the Purchase Agreement or negotiations are otherwise terminated, during which time Seller agrees not to offer the Property or an interest therein for sale to any other party and to cease all negotiations for the Sale of the Property.

9. **Brokerage Fee:** Buyer has not dealt with any broker or finder in connection with this proposed transaction except Phleger-Jones Realty, Inc. In the Purchase Agreement, Buyer shall indemnify and hold Seller harmless from and against any and all claims, losses, costs, damages, liabilities for expenses, including, without limitation, reasonable attorneys" fees, arising out of the claim to a commission by any party which claim is based on the actions of Buyer. In the Purchase Agreement, except as provided in the preceding sentence, Seller shall indemnify and hold Buyer harmless from and against

3

any and all claims, losses, costs, damages, liabilities, and expenses, including, without limitation, reasonable attorneys' fees, resulting from a claim by any other party that such party is entitled to a commission as a result of the transaction contemplated hereby. Seller is responsible for payment of a broker's fee to _____.

10. **Ernest Money Deposit:** Within three (3) business days after the execution of the Purchase Agreement, Buyer shall deposit cash or procure the issuance of a Letter of Credit in the amount of One Hundred Sixty Five Thousand Dollars ($165,000). The Deposit shall be delivered to a mutually acceptable title company with any interest earned accruing to Buyer and shall be fully refundable to Buyer through the Review Period. If, after the Review Period, Buyer elects to proceed with the transaction, the Letter of Credit Deposit will be replaced with cash and become non-refundable as liquidated damages. If closing shall not occur for any reason other than a breach by Buyer, then the Earnest Money Deposit shall be returned to Buyer with any accrued interest.

This letter is not intended as, and does not constitute, a binding agreement by any party, nor an agreement by any party to enter into a binding agreement, but is merely intended to specify some of the proposed terms and conditions of the transaction contemplated herein. Neither party may claim any legal rights against the other by reason of the signing of this letter of intent or by taking any action in reliance thereon.

Each party hereto fully understands that no party shall have any legal obligations to the other, or with respect to the proposed transaction unless and until all of the terms and conditions of the proposed transaction have been negotiated and agreed to by all parties and set forth in a definitive agreement which has been signed by and delivered to all parties. The only legal obligations, which any party shall have, shall be those contained in such signed and delivered definitive agreement referred to above.

We look forward to working with you towards a closing of this transaction. If you wish to proceed, please have the Seller indicate acceptance of the foregoing by signing the enclosed copy of this letter in the space provided and returning it to me.

If a signed copy of this letter is not returned by May 22, 2002, it shall expire and become void.

Sincerely yours,

**HIGHTECHOFFICE, INC.**


John "Jeb" Collins
Director of Acquisitions

## Questions for Discussion

Questions that should be addressed in this case include:

1. In general terms, what are the positive and negative features of this investment?

2. What is the current and future status of the Dallas/Fort Worth office market, and in particular of the Far North Dallas and Richardson/Plano submarkets?

3. What are the strengths/weaknesses of the three tenants in the building?

4. How should Jeb underwrite the above-standard tenant improvements in the Lodestar lease?

5. How important is the high speed telecommunication access agreement with BuildingAccess, Inc.? How should Jeb handle the situation?

6. What changes would you make, if any, in Jeb's draft LOI (Exhibit 7)? Why? What would be the impact on projected return?

Please use these questions as a guide and not a format or a reflection of all of the questions that need to be addressed by the case.

# 13

# HIGHTECHOFFICE, INC.[1]
## Case B: Acquisition Due Diligence

On the evening of October 4th, 2002, Jeb Collins was sitting at his computer in his office in Boston, trying to finalize a memo to Manny Gonzales, the head of his due diligence group regarding the purchase of the Plano Office Center in Dallas, Texas.

Jeb was the head of acquisitions for HiTechOffice, Inc. (HiTech), a $600 million Real Estate Investment Trust (REIT) based in Arlington, VA, which specialized in office complexes tenanted by high technology firms.

The REIT had been organized in 2000 to take advantage of real estate investment opportunities in the hard-hit and rapidly contracting high technology sector. The firm had grown rapidly over the first eighteen months, but as a result of the continuing economic difficulties of high technology firms, was finding it increasingly difficult to uncover new investment opportunities supported by economically strong tenants.

Manny was a graduate of an upstate New York engineering school and had been involved in the construction of commercial real estate buildings prior to joining HiTech in 1995. He was initially involved in the development side of the firm that preceded HiTech before it became a REIT in 2000.

Jeb had been able to negotiate a letter of intent with Donna Bull, VP of Centaur Advisors, Inc. (Centaur) a Boston based investment advisory firm and the developers and owners of the property. After some heavy

---

[1] This case was prepared by John McMahan in 2005. Copyright © 2005 by John McMahan, all rights reserved.

negotiation, a Purchase and Sale Agreement (P&S) was concluded between the parties which gave Manny and his due diligence team until October 30th to complete its due diligence work, with a targeted closing date of November 14th.

## HiTech's Due Diligence Strategy

In the reorganization in anticipation of becoming a REIT, the senior management of HiTech decided to get out of the development business and focus exclusively on acquiring fully or partially leased properties. The logic was that taking the financial and leasing risk was a lot less dangerous than being in the development business. Also, there were a lot of contractors willing to assume the construction risk, many for costs not much more than their internal costs and, in any event, HiTech's investors were paying them for making good financing and tenant decisions, not building buildings.

From the start, it had been HiTech's belief that the major objective of due diligence was to uncover worst-case problems and, if discovered, develop a strategy to mitigate any significant negative aspects which might adversely affect the investment. Manny often reminded his group that *it is not enough to discover problems; there also have to be solutions.* If there are no solutions, or they are inadequate, then the transaction should be terminated.

Manny had always tried to reinforce with his team that due diligence was probably the most critical part of the acquisition process and one which required the utmost attention of everyone involved.

This legal exposure was compounded by the fact that the time allowed for due diligence was becoming shorter (sometimes 30 days or less) and receipt and evaluation of due diligence materials required the coordination of a variety of technical specialists. Increasingly, there also was additional pressure from the seller to approve the transaction due to a "backup buyer" waiting in the wings.

In some cases, the terms of the P&S Agreement could be negotiated to compensate the buyer for problems unearthed by the due diligence process. This might be in the form of a lower price, a holdback of a portion of purchase funds until a problem can be corrected, a guarantee or warranty by the seller, or some other provision in the P&S Agreement. Changes in the P&S Agreement obviously required approval of the seller so it became entirely a negotiated situation.

If the problems were relatively minor, HiTech might decide to "waive" the deposit and proceed to close the transaction. Most P&S agreements state that, if the buyer waives, the deposit becomes nonrefundable and a closing occurs shortly thereafter (usually 10-15 days).

The concept of a dedicated due diligence group was based on the belief that the time of acquisition "deal people" was better utilized concentrating on finding and negotiating deals than being responsible for the due diligence process. It was also believed that an experienced due diligence team would do a better job of uncovering possible risks that, if not mitigated, could be potentially costly to HiTech and its shareholders. With his engineering training and experience in development, Manny was the logical person to head up the new due diligence group.

## *Physical Due Diligence*

The most time-challenged steps of the due diligence process were those associated with the physical quality of the building and the land on which it was located. HiTech's policy was that most of its physical due diligence activities were performed by independent, third party contractors. Potential problem areas may be analyzed by different contractors, however, requiring a final reconciliation by the due diligence team.

The reason for HiTech's approach to physical due diligence was based on a concern that the results be "litigation proof," that is, that they use every reasonable effort to find out what the problems with the property might be, what mitigation steps were required, and what the costs would be of those mitigation steps. Jeb and other members of management had seen too many instances of a manager being sued by its investors for not being sufficiently thorough in the diligence process or by not retaining qualified independent professional assistance.

**Selecting Contractors:** HiTech senior management insisted that its due diligence team always utilize independent, *third party contractors retained by the firm* for the physical portion of the due diligence process. While engineering, environmental, and other reports prepared by seller contractors might be utilized as historic information and points of reference, these reports had to be reviewed and validated by HiTech's independent contractors, utilizing their own testing procedures.

The spectrum of due diligence contractors utilized by HiTech on any give acquisition might include one or more of the following:[2]

- ❑ Architect/planner
- ❑ Civil engineer
- ❑ Structural engineer
- ❑ Mechanical engineer
- ❑ Electrical engineer

---

[2] A single contractor might be responsible for more than one due diligence task.

- Information Technology (IT) engineer
- Environmental consultant
- Soil condition consultant
- Geological consultant
- Hydro geological consultant
- Hazardous substance consultant (e.g., asbestos, PC's, mold, radon gas, lead paint, sick building syndrome, etc.)
- Protected biological systems consultant
- Flood risk exposure consultant
- Seismic risk exposure consultant
- Other contractors that might be utilized included: building security consultants, insurance agents, surveyors, zoning specialists, etc.

In order to reduce the number of physical contractors, Hi Tech usually employed a master contractor (usually an architectural or engineering firm) with more specialized firms serving as subcontractors.[3] This also helped to put the total physical situation in perspective as well as reduce professional fees. Manny had found that several professional firms specialized exclusively in performing this role.

In performing its due diligence activities, HiTech's due diligence team focused on several types of materials and documents that, due to the extreme time pressures, usually had been previously prepared:[4]

**Photos (architect/planner):** Property photos generally included not only the subject property but surrounding land uses as well. The Due Diligence Team was particularly alert to power lines, pooled water, parking congestion, etc. The team also asked the seller to provide (if available) photos of the building(s) under construction, which might prove helpful to the engineering contractors.

Aerial photos were also helpful in describing the neighborhood and relationship of the property to major arterials, freeways, residential districts, etc. Historic aerial photos were utilized to spot previous uses of the property that might influence the environmental analysis.

**Maps (architect/planner):** Maps were generally collected during preliminary underwriting. There may be some specialized maps, however, that need to be located in order to round out a picture of the property and the surrounding neighborhood. As an example, there may be specialized maps such as

---

[3] The master contractor may perform some of the specialized tasks directly.
[4] The sub-contractor responsible for collecting and analyzing the materials and documents is shown in parenthesis.

demographic, income, households, business taxes paid, etc. that may be helpful in updating the market analysis.

Manny found that local, state, and federal government agencies were usually the best sources for maps. City planners also could be interviewed regarding neighborhood characteristics, problem areas, future public works projects, public finances, etc.

**Plans and Specifications (architect/planner):** Plans and specifications of the property generally included the land use and circulation plan, site plans, as-built building plans and specifications (if available), tenant floor plans, and construction documents in the case of new buildings.

**Governmental Approvals (architect/planner):** Copies were usually obtained of the following government approval documents: building permits; property zoning; zoning variances; certificates of occupancy (CO); licenses; Americans with Disabilities (ADA) compliance reports; and reports on previous safety infractions (e.g., fire sprinkler pressure, inadequate traffic signing, etc.).

**Structural Systems (structural engineer):** The key structural elements of the building(s) requiring analysis usually included: foundation; load bearing walls; exterior building shell; floor system; roofing system; and seismic reinforcing.

Common structural problems encountered include cracks in the foundation, roofing that required full or partial replacement, or certain structural elements that do not meet current building codes. There also may be deterioration in the building shell.

If deficiencies were uncovered, HiTech would seek a credit from the seller for any deficiencies that were not disclosed when the parties agreed to the purchase price. If the deficiencies were disclosed, the analysis provided a budgeted amount to correct the problem following close of escrow.

**Mechanical Systems (mechanical engineer):** The mechanical engineer reviewed the building(s) in terms of three major areas: (1) plumbing (e.g., tenant areas, sprinklers, etc.); (2) heating, ventilation, and air conditioning (HVAC) (may also be undertaken by an HVAC contractor), and (3) Vertical transportation (elevators, escalators, etc.).

Manny found that a building's HVAC system was generally the major source of mechanical deficiencies. Typical problems included too much or too little heat/air between seasons and/or between different locations in the building(s). If the capacity of the system were sufficient, the issue might be one of balancing the distribution of air. In addition to the mechanical engineer's calculations, he believed this was also a good area to explore in the tenant interviews in order to ascertain the actual user's perspective.

**Electrical Systems (electrical engineer):** Electrical systems that generally require analysis are the main power system and, if applicable, the emergency power system. The diligence team also had found out the hard way to perform a nighttime check of the lighting of exterior common areas, parking, and pedestrian walkways.

**Electronic Systems (IT engineer):** Manny had discovered that, as more and more buildings utilize built-in electronic transmission systems, Information Technology (IT) had become an increasingly important item of due diligence review. Areas of particular concern included fiber-optic cabling capacity, availability and flexibility of raised floor distribution systems, location of phone demarcation points (location where phone service comes into the building), location of phone and server closets, etc.

The Team also reviewed service contracts in cases where the electronic distribution system was controlled by an independent service provider.

**Environmental Review (environmental consultant(s)):** Like most due diligence professionals, the HiTech team believed the environmental review was one of the most critical elements of the due diligence process. The costs of fixing an undetected environmental problem could well exceed the purchase price of the property as well as impose a huge remediation liability on the investment manager and its investors. From experience, Manny had learned that it was wise to assume that the investment manager paid for its' due diligence mistakes one way or the other.

Manny also knew that lenders were highly sensitive to a property's environmental condition and may not finance a property if they were dissatisfied with the environmental review. For all concerned, this step in the due diligence process required a high level of care to make certain that unwarranted and unknown environmental liabilities were not unwittingly assumed.

All acquisitions therefore required a Phase I Environmental Analysis ("Phase I") which examined historic property use as well as that of the surrounding area, identifying possible on-site or off-site environmental problems.

Depending upon the age of the building, the Phase I analysis might identify asbestos-containing materials that could be present as well as possible soil or ground water contamination.

Additional areas of concern included investigation for the presence of radon gas, lead paint, mold, and sick building syndrome. In situations involving new construction in open land areas, the review might also include an examination of the impact of the project on protected biological systems. Flood and seismic risks also were examined in areas prone to these calamities.

If the Phase I analysis indicated that possible problems existed, the environmental consultant usually recommended that further investigation be conducted pursuant to a Phase II Environmental Analysis ("Phase II"). This usually involved on-site testing, providing a higher level of analysis and accuracy from which to draw more precise conclusions.

A Phase II negative finding did not necessarily disqualify a property from being purchased, provided adequate remediation measures could be adopted. The costs of remediation measures were usually an obligation of the seller. In terms of scheduling, a Phase II analysis usually required a legal extension of the due diligence period.

Manny had heard that an investment manager could be found negligent if a transaction were closed without ordering a Phase II evaluation when recommended by the Phase I environmental consultant.

**Environmental Insurance:** In addition to conducting an Environmental Review, it was HiTech's policy to secure environmental insurance coverage on most of its property acquisitions. An environmental insurance policy usually covers costs associated with environmental cleanup when ordered by a governmental authority. Environmental insurance coverage also could be extended to lenders, who may accept this coverage in lieu of a recourse guarantee for environmental protection.

## *Legal Due Diligence*

The second major area of due diligence dealt with the myriad of legal considerations involved in property acquisition. Generally this due diligence was undertaken by a single law firm, aided by legal research resources and the assistance of an experienced title company. The law firm usually had a background in hazard liability and environmental law in order to interpret the legal considerations of any pertinent physical due diligence findings.

Other consultants involved in the legal due diligence process might include: a Certified Public Accountant; document review specialist; lease abstract specialist; and/or a title consultant.

The major areas undertaken by the law firm and/or these specialists included:

**Survey and Title:** A survey depicts not only the physical boundaries and dimensions of the improvements, but also certain other legal rights including easements, encroachments, covenants, and rights of way. From a due diligence perspective, the survey and title review attempt to:

- ❏ Determine that the title description shown on the survey is the same as that shown in the title report.
- ❏ Confirm exactly what real property HiTech was acquiring.
- ❏ Establish all easements and/or encroachments affecting the use of the property (some, if not all, of these may have been established in the preliminary title report).

Manny believed that one of the most important concerns was to see if there were any liens that should be discharged or CC&R[5] violations that needed to be cleared up. It was also important to determine if there were any zoning violations.

Finally, the team needed to establish if there were any easements or encroachments, which, if activated, could materially affect operation of a property. An example would be the need to tear up a floor slab to repair underground utilities running under a building.

Since these actions required negotiation and execution prior to close, discussions with the seller's counsel were initiated as soon as possible.

**Entitlements:** Most properties are located in political jurisdictions that limit the use of the property by the owner. Through the legal process, these jurisdictions establish over time the uses of a property to which an owner is "entitled." Common entitlements include: zoning; zoning variances; building codes; utility permits; Special District permits; and Local Improvement Districts (LID).

Entitlement due diligence consisted of a review of the applicable zoning ordinances affecting the subject property and that of the surrounding area. Discussions also were held with the local planning, zoning, and building departments to understand any contemplated changes that might affect the future entitlements associated with the property.

The main purpose of this review was to determine (1) whether the property complied with the applicable zoning ordinances and building codes, including setback, parking,[6] height, and coverage limitations (FAR)[7] and (2) whether there have been any zoning or building code violations, particularly any life/safety violations. The review also may analyze the consequences of a "nonconforming structure" being destroyed or damaged by a casualty event.

During the due diligence process, attempts also were made to obtain from the local jurisdiction the Certificate of Occupancy for the building as well as

---

[5] Covenants, conditions, and restrictions.
[6] As an example, the zoning ordinance may require more parking than is currently provided on the property.
[7] Floor Area Ratio

any letters regarding compliance (or noncompliance) with zoning and/or building code ordinances.

Although HiTech could not officially rely on these documents, they provided an added measure of assurance that no major land use/zoning issues existed.

**Tenant Estoppels Certificates:** Tenant Estoppels Certificates (estoppels) are documents that verify certain lease information. Tenants were required in most leases to execute estoppels.[8] In general, it was the seller's responsibility to circulate and retrieve the estoppels and the process could take several weeks to complete.

Items usually covered in the estoppels included: location of space; size of space (SF); dedicated parking spaces; terms of the tenant's lease (e.g., lease term; starting date; base rent; any escalations; percentage rent; security deposit; method and timing of expense recovery; calculation of pro-rata share of expenses; options to renew; options on other space; lease termination, etc.).

Items that also might be covered by estoppels included: option to purchase the property; outstanding improvement allowances due tenant; subleasing arrangements; any known tenant or landlord defaults under the lease; side letters or other documents beyond the lease; ability of landlord to relocate in-line tenants (retail); and tenant's comments and complaints.

The use of estoppels allowed HiTech to rely on certain lease facts that may have been critical in the original decision to purchase the property. Manny found that estoppels also usually surfaced most conflicts or misunderstandings between the selling landlord and the tenant.

Once estoppels have been received by the buyer, they are usually compared with lease abstracts (discussed below) with any changes or discrepancies noted.

**Lease Abstracts:** Concurrently with the estoppels process, the legal contractor is summarizing the key elements of each of the tenant leases. Attorneys who are familiar with leasing issues and their structure generally develop abstracts that accurately and succinctly set forth the obligations of each tenant. The lease abstract generally covers much of the information in the estoppels.[9]

The results of the lease abstract are then compared to the pro forma rent roll and financial analysis furnished by the seller as well as the executed tenant estoppels to determine any inconsistencies.

---

[8] Estoppels forms were usually negotiated in the P&S Agreement.
[9] Lease abstract services are increasingly being outsourced to India and other foreign countries where the costs are considerably lower.

**UBIT/ERISA Issues:** If one or more of the equity investors are pension funds or other financial institutions, there may be Unrelated Business Income Tax (UBIT) or Employee's Retirement Income Security Act (ERISA) issues that need to be considered. Examples include: an affiliate of one of the pension fund investors is also a tenant in the building(s); future earn-outs of leveraged properties; parking income; cable television contract, etc.

Any of these might trigger undesirable consequences for pension fund investors, including possible loss of tax-exempt status or violation of ERISA regulations. It is important, therefore, that the due diligence attorney and tax accountant review all legal documents for possible UBIT and/or ERISA problems.

**Service Contracts:** P&S Agreements usually stipulate that the buyer has the right to assume or reject contracts for services such as trash removal, fire alarm monitoring, building security, landscaping, and janitorial services. Manny had found that many of these contracts contain clauses that are unacceptable to HiTech such as nonmarket rates, poor service response, or use of outdated equipment. In addition, Manny wanted the option to use another service provider, generally one that the firm was using in other buildings in their portfolio.

If the due diligence team did not like the terms of the contract(s) or wished to change a service provider, they could do so after close, provided the contracts were cancelable in 30 days.[10] If they are not cancelable, Manny made certain they were canceled by the seller or set aside holdbacks to cover the possible cost of liquidated damages.

**Warranties:** The attorneys also reviewed warranties and guaranties to make certain they were transferable to HiTech. If the contracts required transfer fees, it was important to have these paid by the seller before close. It was HiTech policy to have the closing documents identify service contracts that the firm wished to retain and warranties that it wished transferred.

**Consent Decrees and Court Orders:** While not common in most real estate transactions, Manny found it a good idea to conduct the necessary legal research to be certain to include consent decrees and/or court orders that might affect the property.

**Other Agreements:** Other agreements that might be included in the legal due diligence were partnership and joint venture agreements, agreements requiring third party consent, and broker/finder agreements.

---

[10] Service contracts not cancelable in 30 days also might constitute ERISA violations.

## Business Due Diligence

In addition to Physical and Legal Due Diligence, there were business-related areas of due diligence that HiTech often pursued.

**Financial Review (CPA firm):** A financial review confirmed the historic property operating statements and other financial statements of the property's operation. The financial audit provided a third party independent validation of the assumptions used in the pro-forma cash flow analysis, which was relied upon by the Investment Committee, shareholders, investment analysts, and lenders (if mortgage financing is involved).

**Tenant Interviews (asset management staff):** During the due diligence process, HiTech was usually permitted to interview a representative of each tenant. The tenant interview was usually conducted by a member of HiTech's asset management team, preferably the individual who would be assigned the property if the acquisition proceeded.

This interview is designed to accomplish the following: provide an introduction to HiTech as the new landlord; understand the background of interviewee; tenant's business operations and organizational structure (e.g., sole proprietor, corporation, subsidiary of public company, etc.); major competitors; customer profile; future outlook; profitability (general view); tenant's current use of the space (tour); establish tenant's current view of the building and space (e.g., parking, circulation, operating equipment (e.g., HVAC, plumbing, electricity, public space, etc.)); tenant's complaints about the management of the building (e.g., janitorial, security, billing/collections, marketing and promotion, etc.); and estimate tenant's anticipated future space needs.

Utilizing HiTech's asset management staff to conduct the interview usually provided a good beginning for a solid landlord-tenant relationship. This was reinforced if, after the transaction were closed, the asset manager assigned to the property called on each of the tenants with a checklist and timetable to correct problems mentioned during the interview.

**Appraisal:** An appraisal may be necessary if lender financing is to be utilized to close the transaction. Many lenders require an appraisal before they will even approve a loan.

**Insurance Review:** Review by an insurance company, agent, or consultant regarding the adequacy of existing coverage and unique problems the property may encounter in obtaining adequate coverage.

## Final Underwriting and Closing

Although the assumptions and conclusions of HiTech's preliminary underwriting were continually updated over the life of the due diligence period, there were several tasks that needed to be completed prior to the final decision to proceed.

**Reconciling Due Diligence Findings:** As the results of due diligence activities began arriving, HiTech's due diligence team began reconciling the findings of the various contractors with each other and with the preliminary underwriting that was utilized to gain preliminary approval by the Investment Committee.

One of the objectives of the due diligence process is to approach certain critical issues from several independent directions. As an example, the property's entitlements might be reviewed by the architectural contractor, the legal consultant, and, if utilized, an appraiser. Further, seismic risk exposure might be reviewed by both the structural engineer and the environmental consultant.

Problems with the building's electrical, mechanical, and electronic systems are covered by engineering consultants, legal consultants, and the tenant interviews. Critical factors in tenant leases are reviewed by the legal consultant, the tenant interviews, and, if utilized, the appraiser.

The findings of each of these contractors were compared to each other to see if there are any significant differences in facts or opinions. If so, the acquisition team must contact each of the involved parties and resolve any major differences.

This seeming duplication of effort was an attempt to get several perspectives on potential problem areas. It was usually the problems that hadn't been identified that proved to be the most expensive to mitigate following close. Manny believed it was much better to know these costs in advance and have the seller bear (share) in the cost of resolution. The ultimate operating and capital savings generally more than compensated for the relatively small increments in professional fees.

Next, the reconciled due diligence findings were matched with the preliminary underwriting presented to the Investment Committee. In some cases, discrepancies arise from misstated or inaccurate facts contained in the seller's offering memorandum. In other words, new information becomes available through the due diligence process, which was unknown to the seller or if known, not disclosed.

A memo is then prepared for the Investment Committee outlining the material changes that have occurred since the preliminary underwriting.

Sensitivity analysis was often performed to see what the impact is, if any, of these changes on the pro-forma cash flow projections and the ultimate success of the investment.

**Final Risk Underwriting:** Each of the major risks associated with the proposed investment is then matched with the proposed underwriting mitigation. An example might be:

|  | Risk | Mitigation |
|---|---|---|
| Physical: | Soil contamination | - Removal and replacement |
|  |  | - Monitor |
|  | Ground water contamination | - Pumping |
|  |  | - Monitor |
|  | Asbestos | - Removal |
|  |  | - Encapsulation |
|  | Seismic | - Seismic upgrade |
|  |  | - Insurance |
|  | Structural system | - Repair |
|  | Mechanical system | - Repair/Replace |
|  | Electrical system | - Repair |
|  | Electronic system | - Repair/Replace |
|  | Parking and circulation | - Redraw documents |
| Legal: | Title imperfection | - Title insurance |
|  | Lease | - Renegotiate (if possible) |

Mitigation costs were usually estimated by the due diligence contractor. These costs were then summarized and, depending upon their magnitude, discussed with the seller. Generally, minor costs were traded off if the seller accepted responsibility for the major items. This was often the case since, in most situations, the seller would have to pay these costs in the event of another buyer and "a bird in hand (HiTech) may be worth more than one in the bush (another buyer)."

In many cases, the terms of the P&S Agreement were altered to compensate HiTech for problems unearthed by the due diligence process. This might take the form of a lower price; a holdback of a portion of purchase funds until a problem could be corrected; a guarantee or warranty by the seller; or some other alteration in the P&S Agreement. Obviously, changes in the agreement required approval of the seller so it was entirely a negotiated solution.

This can be a critical negotiation, particularly if the mitigation costs are significant. If too much is demanded, the buyer risks (1) losing the transaction or (2) being forced to perform and absorb the costs after closing.

If the problems are relatively minor, the buyer may decide to "waive" the deposit and proceed to close the transaction. If the buyer waives, the deposit becomes nonrefundable and a closing occurs shortly thereafter (usually within 30 days).

**Final Cash Flow Analysis:** Based on the decisions reached in the final risk underwriting, the pro-forma cash flow analysis, which had been continually updated throughout the acquisition process, was now put into final form. Sensitivity and attribution analysis continued, however, in order to give the Investment Committee the "what if" parameters necessary for a final decision.

## Jeb's Due Diligence Memo

As Jeb wrapped up his memo to the due diligence team, he had a continuing concern about the special nature of the tenant improvements involving fifty percent of the space. He noted that it would be important to not only have the engineers check the reusability of the improvements but to have the lawyers advise as to whether HiTech could get out of the bank agreement (or at least had any leverage to modify it) if Lodestar defaulted.

He was also worried about the Building Access agreement to provide telecommunications services to the building. Although the agreement had been in place for a little over a year and the tenants appeared to be satisfied, he added a note to have the attorneys review the agreement closely to see if Building Access could be replaced if the situation changed. He also noted in his memo that the tenants be asked to comment confidentially on the quality and cost of the telecommunication services that Building Access was providing.

In terms of physical due diligence, Jeb added to his memo that he wanted to review the parking situation. He had noticed on his visits that the parking lot was always full during and for an hour or two after working hours. This was most likely due to the mix of tenants which had high employee densities and used the facility very intensively. The situation was compounded by the classes sponsored by Computer Training Associates which used their space even more intensively than the other tenants. Jeb had heard that they were shifting more of their classes to evening formats, but this needed to be confirmed in the tenant interviews.

While some of the parking problems appeared manageable, he noted that the structural engineer needed to give a preliminary opinion about the feasibility of decking portions of the parking area to provide additional parking spaces. This, of course would add to the cost of the acquisition and HiTech would have to provide interim parking for employees during the construction period.

As an alternative to decking, with the employee downtime involved, Jeb asked the due diligence team to check with owners of nearby vacant properties to see if additional land could be acquired and at what cost.

Finally, Jeb was concerned whether his underwriting compensated sufficiently for the soft Dallas office market. He wasn't sure, however, what he could do about it in diligence other than provide higher contingencies and a longer period to realize projected returns. He certainly had to level with the Investment Committee about the deteriorating market conditions, although HiTech was protected for at least four years by the three existing leases, assuming they did not default. Whoops! This meant that the tenant interviews, particularly the credit assessment, had to be more thorough than usual. He made another and final note in the memo, reviewed it once again, and emailed it on to Manny and his team. He then shut off his computer and went home. As he was leaving, he glanced at his watch – it was after midnight.

## Questions for Discussion

Questions that should be addressed in this case include:

1. What due you think of HiTech's approach of utilizing a separate group for its due diligence team (as opposed to having in done by the acquisition staff)? To what extent, if at all, is this approach influenced by their overall corporate growth strategy?

2. What does Jeb mean that the due diligence process should be "litigation proof"? How does he attempt to accomplish this in his approach to the due diligence process? What do you think of this approach? Why?

3. HiTech always uses a master contractor in its approach to due diligence? What are the advantages and disadvantages to this approach?

4. Why is the environmental review such a big deal in the due diligence process? What are the ramifications of having the wrong data or in making the wrong decision based on good data?

5. Which elements of the legal due diligence could be outsourced to another country (such as India)? Why are firms doing this?

6. How should service contracts by handled during the due diligence process? Why?

7. Why are tenant interviews important to the decision of whether or not to proceed with an acquisition? Who should conduct them? Why?

8. When would an appraisal be a part of the diligence process? Who should pay for it?

9. Who is responsible for reconciling due diligence findings? Why?

10. How are risks mitigated in the due diligence process? Who conducts the analysis? Why is it important?

11. What are examples of adjustments that can be made to have the Seller pay for the cost of mitigating property problems identified during the due diligence process? What if he or she refuses to agree?

12. Discuss the additional due diligence steps that Jeb is outlining in his memo to the due diligence team? Are there any additional ways to answer his questions other than what he has proposed? Are there any other concerns that you believe should be covered by the due diligence team.

13. Do you believe HiTech should proceed and close the investment as presently negotiated? If so, how do you rationalize the issues raised by Jeb in his memo? If not, what changes would have to be made by the seller in the P&S agreement for you to recommend the investment? Why would the seller make these changes?

Please use these questions as a guide and not a format or a reflection of all of the questions that need to be addressed by this case.

# 14

# SAN MARCOS INDUSTRIAL PARK[1]

## Case A: Project Acquisition

It was a beautiful spring day in San Francisco in 2003, and Beth Sawyer was getting ready to go out for a long walk along the Embarcadero.

As she glanced back at her computer screen to turn it off, she couldn't believe the email she had just received from her boss, Jim Culver, the founder and CEO of Western Investment Partners, LLC. He was on a business trip and had let her know in no uncertain terms that she had to complete her analysis of an investment memorandum they had received earlier in the week and email him back her conclusions by the end of the day. If the investment looked attractive, she would also have to come up with a price and terms for the offer and the projected return that investors might realize.

Beth was an investment analyst for Western, an opportunity fund that specialized in commercial real estate investments in high growth areas in California and other West Coast states. The offering Jim had asked her to review involved a new industrial park in San Diego County, one of the fastest growing, most desirable real estate investment markets in the nation.

The questions that Jim raised in his email were:

1. How strong is the demand for industrial space in Northern San Diego County?

2. What is the quality of the project's location, land use plan and building design?

---

[1] This case was prepared by John McMahan in 2003. Copyright 2003 and 2004 by John McMahan.

3. How strong are the tenants? Do they represent a good mix of business operations?

4. How successful will the San Marcos project be in capturing its share of future demand?

5. What is the market for the unleased space?

6. The buildings have been designed to upgrade to office uses in the future. How realistic is this assumption?

7. If they decided to proceed, what should be the pricing of the offer, bearing in mind that many investors in the current market place are prepared to make very aggressive bids and Western could probably expect stiff competition?

The reason for the speedup of the analysis was that Jim was going to be meeting with one of their major investors the following morning and wanted to discuss the investment, provided Beth believed they should proceed with an offer. The investor, who was new to the Fund, had been critical of the slowness with which Western had invested its capital since the raise had been completed over nine months ago.

In fact, Western had yet to make their first investment in the fund which was significantly behind the investment pace of their previous funds. Jim blamed this on the current real estate market where investors were willing to pay historically high prices for properties despite the weakening of real estate fundamentals. Some of these investors were Germans and other foreigners who were willing to accept much lower returns than American real estate investors. Jim couldn't blame it all on foreigners, however, since some of his more traditional domestic competitors had been sharpening their pencils as well.

Beth sighed and turned back to her computer. She knew she had her work cut out for her and how dependent Jim and the firm were on her ability to reach a sound recommendation. The walk along the Embarcadero would just have to wait.

\* \* \*

# Confidential Investment Offering Memorandum

San Marcos Industrial Park

May 15, 2003

This offering memorandum describes a prospective industrial park investment in San Diego, California.

## *San Diego*

With more than 1.25 million people, San Diego is the seventh largest city in the US and the second largest in California. The metropolitan area ranks 17th in the country. San Diego has been able to generate significant job growth at a time of national economic turmoil largely as a result of a highly diversified labor force, progressive local government, premier educational institutions, a variety of recreational opportunities, and a beautiful physical setting. No wonder Forbes magazine recently ranked San Diego as the "best place in the country to do business."

San Diego's economy is highly diversified across several industries – medical research, biotechnology, communications, defense/military industry, manufacturing, tourism, education, international trade, commercial shipbuilding and repair, and the expanding Port of San Diego.

Real estate investment values in San Diego have continued to increase not only due to strong tenant demand but also the limited amount of land available for development. This is because of physical constraints to the west (Pacific Ocean), north (Camp Pendleton Marine Corps base), east (mountains), and south (Mexico) as well as high quality development and building standards. San Diego's freeway system is also one of the finest in the nation.

## *Industrial Market*

Exhibit 1 shows a map of San Diego County.[2] Approximately 139 million square feet of industrial space currently exists in the County (Exhibit 2). The South County, San Marcos/Vista, and Miramar Road areas represent the greatest concentrations of industrial space.

From 1996 to 2001, San Diego County absorbed an average of approximately 4.6 million square feet of industrial space each year (Exhibit 3). As a result of the general economic downturn, annual absorption began declining in 1999 and was only 300,000 square feet in 2002. This year, however, absorption appears to be off to a more positive start.

---

[2] Exhibits are at the end of this case.

Exhibit 4 indicates the current vacancy rate[3] in each of the industrial submarkets in the County. Rancho Bernardo/Scripps Ranch, Carlsbad, South County, and San Marcos/Vista all have vacancy rates higher than the County average. Exhibit 5 illustrates land prices in selected industrial submarkets. Generally, land in the North County is priced higher than land in the South County and the outer districts of the North County (Oceanside, San Marcos/Vista, and Escondido). Industrial construction costs generally track with land topography, nearness to the ocean, and local building codes (Exhibit 6). Rents tend to track with land prices, construction costs, age of buildings in area, access to transportation, and quality of development (Exhibit 7).

## *The Property*

San Marcos Industrial Park (San Marcos) is a 45-acre industrial park located in North San Diego County near the City of San Marcos (see Exhibit 1). The property is located adjacent to US Highway 15, providing access to metropolitan San Diego and Mexico as well as the entire Southern California market. High quality housing of all types and prices is located within 20 minutes of the site. The Pacific Ocean is approximately 15 minutes away. One of the finest scientific/technical institutions in the nation, the University of California, San Diego, is located approximately 20 minutes south and west of the site. Downtown San Diego is approximately 30 minutes away.

San Marcos is master planned to be a state-of-the-art corporate complex with modern buildings, streets, landscaped areas, and a high-speed underground fiber optic communications network (Exhibit 8). Some buildings have coverage ratios as low as 29.1% with an overall ratio of 40.7%.

Inside, clear heights range from 24 to 38 feet. Dock high buildings have column spacing 50' X 60' feet or better. The depths of the single loaded buildings range from 180' to 205'. Aesthetic features include bull-nose panel crowns, balconies, aggregate sidewalks, bollards, teak benches, flagpoles, Viracon glass, and corporate landscaping. The buildings have sprinkler systems that are either ESFR or ESFR ready.[4] All of the buildings in Phase I and II are complete or scheduled for completion later this year.

The park provides ample opportunities to transition to a higher percentage of office uses as leases turn. All of the buildings are designed to be flexible, able to accommodate distribution, office, R&D, and higher-end flex uses. The larger buildings have four primary office locations, each with individual identity. Several buildings have first and second story knock-out panels to

---

[3] As of the end of first quarter 2003.
[4] Early Suppression Fast Response.

accommodate future windows. Mezzanine space can be added to the entire front elevations of each building. Loading dock and truck turning/storage areas can be converted to additional parking, bringing the parking ratio in a number of buildings to 4 cars per 1000 square feet.

## *Tenants*

Approximately 65% of the project is leased to an array of high quality domestic and international tenants (see Exhibit 9). Of the leases signed to date, there are no expirations until 2006 when approximately 31% of the space rolls over, followed by 15% and 54% in the subsequent years. It is anticipated that approximately 80% of the tenants will renew when their leases expire. All leases require six months notice to vacate. Tenants occupying over 100,000 require 12 months.

Major tenants are described below:

**International Express (105,409 SF):** This tenant is one of the largest package delivery companies in the world, transporting more than 11 million packages each business day. International's supply chain solutions combine logistics, financial services, international trade management, custom brokerage, supply chain management, e-commerce solutions, global freight, and mail services. The firm is currently ranked among the top 100 companies in the Fortune 500 index.

International uses approximately one third of its space for offices and the remainder for its distribution operations.

**Fine Leather Manufacturing (67,403 SF):** Fine Leather is one of the world's largest manufacturers of albums and folios sold to the professional photographic trade. The firm utilizes its facility to manufacture and distribute to its customers in over 30 nations worldwide. Approximately 60.0% of the space is used for manufacturing, 25.0% for distribution, and 15.0% for office.

**Sonora Export USA (59,760 SF):** One of Mexico's largest import-export companies, Sonora has been in business for over 40 years. This facility serves its export business in the 11 states in the Western United States. Approximately 20.0% of this tenant's space is office.

**Audio Specialty Corporation (57,405 SF):** Audio Specialty makes a variety of audio products including home stereo speakers, automobile sound systems, aviation headsets, and professional loudspeakers. This is an office and technical support facility serving the Southern California market.

**Cougar Air Express (43,879 SF):** Cougar is a freight-forwarding firm serving the Asian market. The firm has more than 1,500 employees in 146 offices throughout the world (including 12 in mainland China). This facility serves the Western US and Mexico. Approximately 25.0% is used for office.

**Japan Distributions USA (37,325 SF):** This firm is one of the largest Japanese export-import firms. The facility serves its customers in the Western United States. Approximately one third of the space is fitted out as offices.

## Expenses and Financing

Exhibit 10 outlines the annual operating expenses for the project that are borne by the landlord, with all other expenses paid directly or reimbursed by the tenant. Exhibit 11 indicates the leasing and capital costs as leases turn. Exhibit 12 contains pertinent information regarding the financing currently on the property. (Note: We have financial sources who have indicated an interest in refinancing the entire offering on the following terms: 65.0% LTV, 6.0% interest, 10 year term, 30 year amortization, and 1.0% financing fee.).

## Offering

This offering is being presented to principals only and is subject to a confidential registration process. It is anticipated that acquisition proposals will be made subject to a date-certain call for offers, which the marketing team will establish and then notify prospective investors. It is anticipated that the call for offers will occur within the next 60 days. All property and market tours will be scheduled with and directed by the marketing team. Minimum bid: $80,000,000.

If you wish to register interest in the offering or have questions, please contact Joseph Clark at 212-632-9703.

*Chapter 14 - San Marcos Industrial Park A* -321-

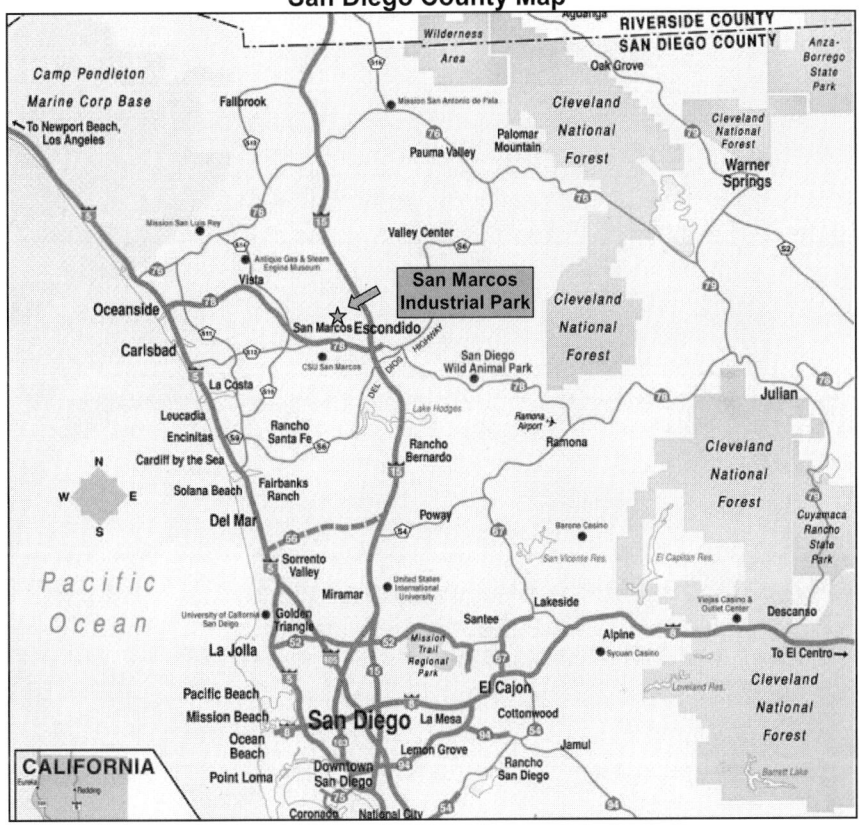

## Exhibit 1
## San Marcos Industrial Park
## San Diego County Map

### Exhibit 2
### San Marcos Industrial Park
### San Diego County Industrial Market
### March 31, 2003

| Location | MSF |
| --- | --- |
| South County | 23.9 |
| San Marcos/Vista | 16.2 |
| Miramar Road | 14.0 |
| Kearny Mesa | 12.4 |
| Central Industrial | 12.0 |
| Misc. | 10.8 |
| El Cajon/Miss Grg./La Mesa | 8.7 |
| Carlsbad | 8.5 |
| Escondido | 7.0 |
| Sorrento Mesa | 7.0 |
| RBernardo/ScrippsRanch | 7.0 |
| Poway | 6.0 |
| Oceanside | 5.5 |
| Total County | 139.0 |

### Exhibit 3
### San Marcos Industrial Park
### San Diego County Industrial Absorption
### (Annual)

| Year | MSF |
| --- | --- |
| 1996 | 4.8 |
| 1997 | 5.1 |
| 1998 | 6.2 |
| 1999 | 5.5 |
| 2000 | 3.8 |
| 2001 | 2.2 |
| 2002 | 0.3 |
| 2003 | 1.2 |
| **1996-2001 Average** | **4.6** |

### Exhibit 4
### San Marcos Industrial Park
### San Diego County Industrial Vacancy
### March 31, 2003

| Location | Vacancy |
|---|---|
| R. Bernardo/Scripps | 13.2% |
| Carlsbad | 9.0% |
| South Co. | 8.2% |
| SMarcos/Vista | 7.2% |
| **Total County** | **5.6%** |
| Poway | 5.5% |
| Oceanside | 5.4% |
| Sorrento M. | 5.3% |
| Miramar Road | 5.2% |
| Escondido | 4.0% |
| Kearny Mesa | 3.0% |
| El Cajon/Miss.Go.,/La Mesa | 2.7% |
| Central Ind.l | 2.2% |
| Misc. | 2.2% |

### Exhibit 5
### San Marcos Industrial Park
### San Diego County Land Prices – Selected Submarkets
### March 31, 2003

| Location | Price/SF |
|---|---|
| Sorrento Mesa | $ 24.85 |
| Kearny Mesa | 23.73 |
| Rancho Bernardo Ranch | 20.50 |
| Miramar Road | 16.30 |
| Poway | 14.95 |
| Carlsbad | 14.90 |
| El Cajon/Mission Gorge/La Mesa | 14.63 |
| Oceanside | 10.90 |
| San Marcos/Vista | 10.30 |
| Escondido | 10.30 |

## Exhibit 6
### San Marcos Industrial Park
### San Diego County Industrial Construction Costs – Selected Submarkets
### March 31, 2003

| Location | Price/SF |
|---|---|
| Sorrento Mesa | $105.00 |
| Kearny Mesa | 101.00 |
| RanchoBernardo/Scripps | 97.00 |
| Miramar Road | 83.00 |
| Carlsbad | 75.00 |
| Poway | 72.00 |
| Oceanside | 58.00 |
| Escondido | 57.00 |
| S.Marcos/Vista | 54.00 |
| El Cajon/MissG/La Mesa | 50.00 |

## Exhibit 7
### San Marcos Industrial Park
### San Diego County Industrial Rents
### March 31, 2003

| Location | Monthly* | Annual* |
|---|---|---|
| Sorrento Mesa | $ 0.99 | $ 11.88 |
| Kearny Mesa | 0.98 | 11.76 |
| Misc. | 0.97 | 11.64 |
| Miramar Road | 0.86 | 10.32 |
| Carlsbad | 0.83 | 9.96 |
| Rancho Bernardo/Scripps Ranch | 0.81 | 9.72 |
| Poway | 0.81 | 9.72 |
| **San Diego County** | **0.81** | **9.72** |
| Escondido | 0.80 | 9.60 |
| Central Industrial | 0.77 | 9.24 |
| San Marcos/Vista | 0.74 | 8.88 |
| El Cajon/Mission Gorge/La Mesa | 0.73 | 8.76 |
| South County | 0.68 | 8.16 |
| Oceanside | 0.68 | 8.16 |

*Average NNN rental rate

Chapter 14 - San Marcos Industrial Park A    -325-

# Exhibit 8
## San Marcos Industrial Park
## Site Plan

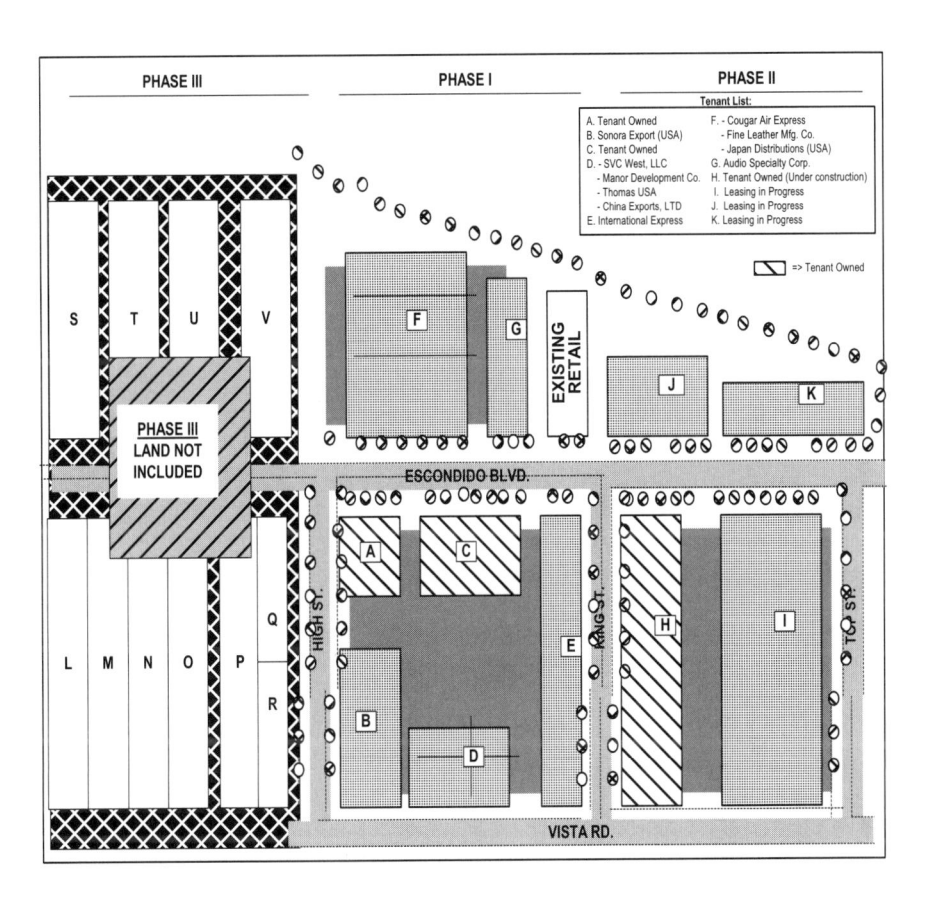

**Tenant List:**

A. Tenant Owned
B. Sonora Export (USA)
C. Tenant Owned
D. - SVC West, LLC
 - Manor Development Co.
 - Thomas USA
 - China Exports, LTD
E. International Express
F. - Cougar Air Express
 - Fine Leather Mfg. Co.
 - Japan Distributions (USA)
G. Audio Specialty Corp.
H. Tenant Owned (Under construction)
I. Leasing in Progress
J. Leasing in Progress
K. Leasing in Progress

▱ => Tenant Owned

PHASE III
PHASE I
PHASE II

PHASE III LAND NOT INCLUDED

EXISTING RETAIL

ESCONDIDO BLVD.
VISTA RD.
HIGH ST.
KING ST.
TC ST.

## Exhibit 9
## Marcos Industrial Park
## Building and Tenant Overview

| Bldg | Ste. | Tenant | Acres | RSF | Coverage | Lease Term Begin | Lease Term End | Rent PSF | Annual Revenue |
|---|---|---|---|---|---|---|---|---|---|
| A | | Tenant qwned | | | | | | | |
| B | | Sonor Export (USA) | 3.5 | 59,760 | 39.1% | 07/22/02 | 08/21/07 | $7.28 | $435,053 |
| C | | Tenant owned | | | | | | | |
| D | 100 | SVC West, LLC | | 14,789 | | 06/01/01 | 05/31/06 | 13.80 | 204,088 |
|   | 200 | Manor Development Co. | | 15,421 | | 06/01/01 | 09/30/06 | 13.88 | 214,043 |
|   | 300 | Thomas USA | | 13,344, | | 11/23/01 | 11/30/06 | 14.96 | 199,626 |
|   | 400 | China Exports, LTD | | 18,990 | | 11/15/01 | 11/15/06 | 12.75 | 242,123 |
|   |   | Subtotals | 3.4 | 62,544 | 42.6% | | | | 859,880 |
| E |   | International Express | 4.3 | 105,409 | 56.3% | 06/01/01 | 09/30/06 | 13.80 | 1,454,644 |
| F | 100 | Cougar Air Express | | 43,879 | | 09/01/01 | 08/31/06 | 7.12 | 312,418 |
|   | 200 | Fine Leather Mfg. Co | | 67,403 | | 07/10/03 | 03/31/08 | 6.49 | 437,445 |
|   | 400 | Japan Distributors (USA) | | 37,325 | | 02/01/02 | 12/31/06 | 6.43 | 240,000 |
|   |   | Subtotals | 7.9 | 148,607 | 43.2% | | | | 989,864 |
| G | 300 | Audio Specialty Corp. | 4.5 | 57,405 | 29.1% | 02/01/02 | 01/31/07 | 6.65 | 381,743 |
| H | | Tenant Owned (Under construction) | | | | | | | |
| I | | Leasing in Progress | 7.4 | 147,342 | 45.7% | 01/01/04 | 12/31/08 | 6.75 | 994,559 |
| J | | Leasing in Progress | 7.6 | 110,403 | 33.5% | 01/01/04 | 12/31/08 | 6.75 | 745,220 |
| K | | Leasing in Progress | 6.4 | 106,210 | 37.8% | 01/01/04 | 12/01/08 | 6.75 | 716,918 |
| | Totals/Average | | 45.0 | 797,680 | 40.7% | | | 8.25 | 6,577,881 |

### Exhibit 10
### San Marcos Industrial Park
### Annual Operating Expenses*

| Expense | $/sq. ft | Property Total |
|---|---|---|
| Utilities | $ 0.07 | $ 55,838 |
| Property Taxes | 0.47 | 374,910 |
| G&A | 0.12 | 95,722 |
| Management Fee | 0.17 | 135,606 |
| Insurance | 0.13 | 103,698 |
| Misc. | 0.07 | 55,838 |
| Repairs & Maintenance | 0.10 | 79,768 |
| Reserves | 0.15 | 119,652 |
| Total | 1.28 | 1,021,030 |

* Estimated 2004

### Exhibit 11
### San Marcos Industrial Park
### Leasing and Capital Cost Assumptions

| | |
|---|---|
| **Renewal probability** | 80.0% |
| **Leasing commissions** | 5.0% |
| **Annual CPI escalation** | 3.0% |
| **Standard Tenant Improvements** | $ 0.50 |
| **Average lease term** | 5 years |
| **Average downtime to build out** | 4 months |

## Exhibit 12
## San Marcos Industrial Park
## Existing Loans

|  | Phase I | Phase II |
|---|---|---|
| **Note Date** | 2/22/02 | 1/13/03 |
| **Maturity Date** | 2/28/12 | 1/31/13 |
| **Lender** | Independent Life | Maryland Life |
| **Portfolio Loan** | Yes | Yes |
| **Borrower** | San Marcos Industrial Park, Ltd. | San Marcos Industrial Park, Ltd. |
| **Initial Principal** | $17,573,740 | $20,313,902 |
| **6/1/03 Balance** | $17,222,265 | $20,313,902 |
| **Note Rate** | 7.2% | 6.0% |
| **Annual Constant** | 8.15% | 7.20% |
| **Annual Payment** | $1,432,260 | $1,462,601 |
| **Monthly Payment** | $119,355 | $121,883 |
| **Amortization** | 30 years | 30 years |
| **Prepayment Lockout** | open | 1/13/03 - 1/12/06 |
| **Yield Maintenance Period** | Comparable term treasuries, plus 50 BP | Comparable term treasuries, plus 50 BP |
| **Replacement Reserves** | None | $18,000/year, collected and available |

# 15

# SAN MARCOS INDUSTRIAL PARK[1]

## Case B: Property Disposition

It was a beautiful spring day in San Francisco in 2005, and Beth Sawyer was getting ready to go out for a long walk along the Embarcadero, when the phone rang. It was Beth's boss, Jim Culver, the founder and CEO of Western Investment Partners, LLC (Western). Jim said he was under a lot of pressure to deliver some cash to the investors in the fund that held San Marcos Industrial Park. He told her he wanted to sell one of the buildings in the project, to generate this cash and to demonstrate progress on the implementation of their investment strategy.

The San Marcos property, located in San Diego, had been purchased by Western in 2003 and had turned out to be a good investment for the firm. All of the unleased space had subsequently been leased, often at higher than pro forma rents. Western's reports to the investors had been very laudatory regarding the success of the investment, so it was only logical that, two years later, investors would like to begin seeing some return of principal.

The location of the property is illustrated in Exhibit 1; Exhibit 2 is a plot plan for the project.

---

[1] Copyright© 2005 by John McMahan, all rights reserved.

**Exhibit 1
Location Map**

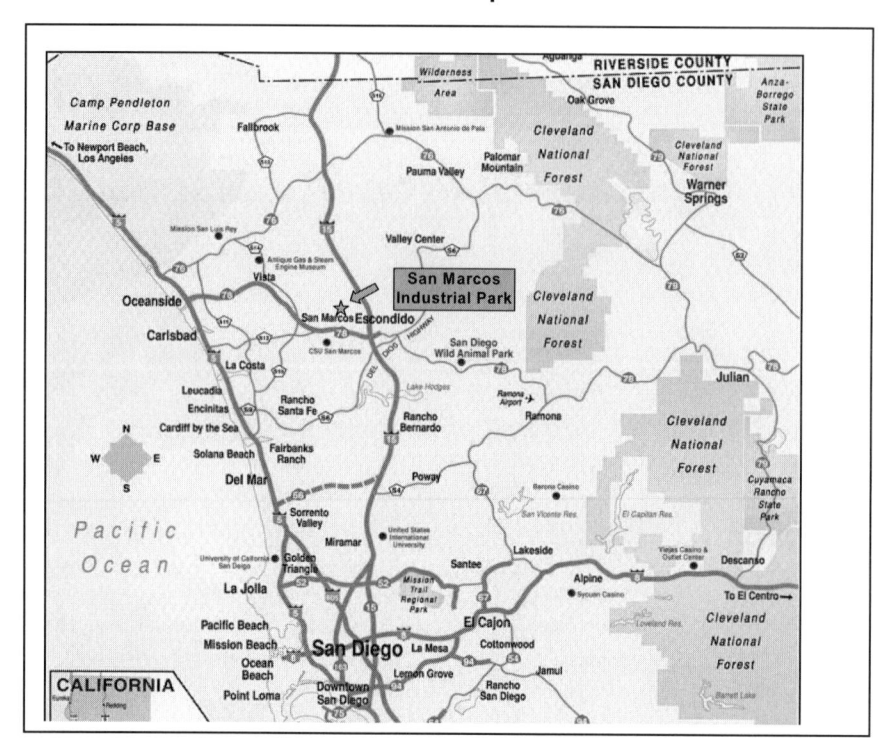

*Chapter 15 - San Marcos Industrial Park B*  -331-

## Exhibit 2
## San Marcos Industrial Park
## Plot Plan

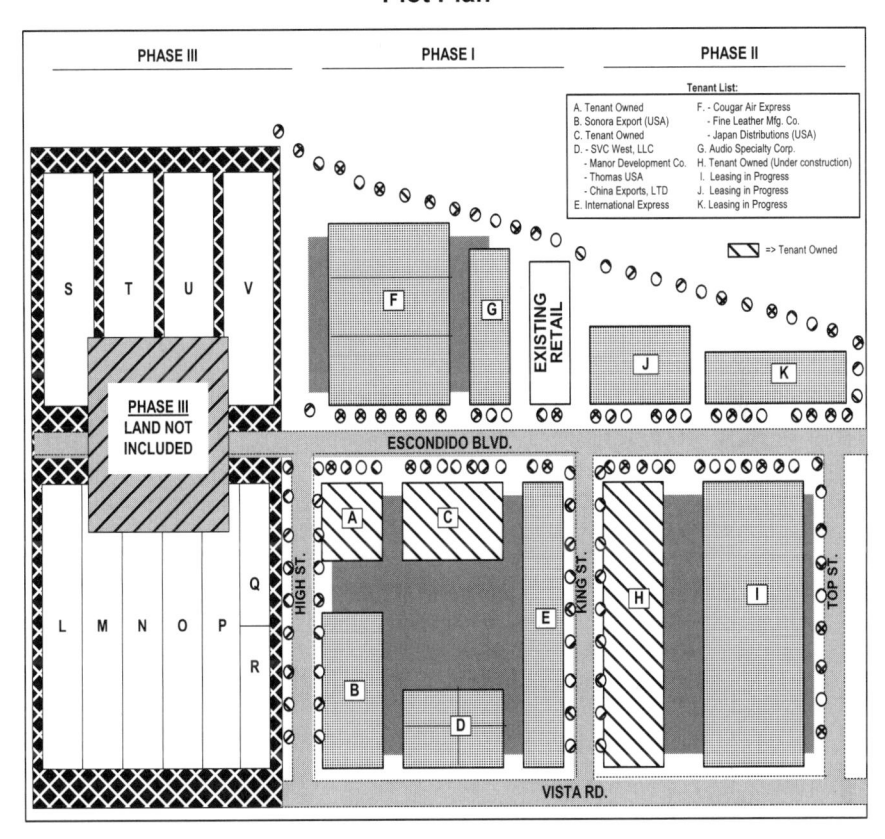

**Tenant List:**

- A. Tenant Owned
- B. Sonora Export (USA)
- C. Tenant Owned
- D. - SVC West, LLC
  - Manor Development Co.
  - Thomas USA
  - China Exports, LTD
- E. International Express
- F. - Cougar Air Express
  - Fine Leather Mfg. Co.
  - Japan Distributions (USA)
- G. Audio Specialty Corp.
- H. Tenant Owned (Under construction)
- I. Leasing in Progress
- J. Leasing in Progress
- K. Leasing in Progress

=> Tenant Owned

PHASE III — LAND NOT INCLUDED

ESCONDIDO BLVD.
HIGH ST.
KING ST.
TOP ST.
VISTA RD.

Jim told Beth that he wanted to sell the 148,204 sq. ft Building F, since Western's asset management team had been able to accelerate the tenant's 2006 lease renewals, all at respectable increases. The cost to the investors had been six months reduced rent (50%), which would burn off January 1, 2006 when the tenants began their new leases. The three tenants were:

**Cougar Air Express:** This tenant was a freight forwarding operation which used its space to service the needs of customers in Southern California. The firm leased 43,879 sq. ft in Building F and recently renewed its lease for another five years, beginning in early 2006, for $9.00 per sq. ft.

**Fine Leather Mfg. Co.:** This leather goods design and production firm specializes in high-end ladies purses, belts, wallets, and other upscale leather products. The company buys finished leather in large quantities, then uses its leased space to fabricate leather products which are distributed throughout the nation. The company had a seven-year lease at $9.75 per sq. ft.

**Japan Distributions (USA):** This firm imports finished goods from Japan, warehouses them in Building F, then distributes them throughout the nation. The firm leases 37,325 sq. ft and has agreed to a 10-year lease at $8.25 per sq. ft.

In their telephone conversation, Jim asked Beth to prepare a marketing plan that would be ready when he returned to San Francisco two days later. In the plan, he wanted Beth to identify the most likely buyers and how they should be accessed, and to outline the process Western should use in selecting a broker. He also asked her to draft an Offering Memorandum (OM) for his review.

## *Targeting Buyers*

Since San Marcos was a high quality project, Beth anticipated that Building F should be marketed primarily to institutional investors that have similar investment quality standards but are more risk adverse and usually willing to accept lower investment returns (pay a higher price). In essence, Western could arbitrage the capitalized value of the spread in investment returns as payment for its efforts in reducing investment risk through property repositioning.

Beth knew that institutional investors were typically represented by professional investment advisors who were responsible for acquiring properties for their clients' or shareholder's portfolios. Other sources of institutional capital were Real Estate Investment Trusts (REITs), Real Estate Operating Companies (REOCs), and private operating companies. These institutional buyers were generally professional in their approach, but they weighed factors such as building quality, tenant, mix, longer term project potential, and other factors in arriving at a price they were willing to pay.

Beth largely discounted the interests of partnerships representing High Net Worth (HNW) investors, as these partnerships were usually unwilling to pay a "retail" price but were interested in buying "wholesale," as Western had.

**Targeted Geographical Areas:** Beth also thought that the property's San Diego location would be very attractive to institutional investors, which usually have certain criteria for metropolitan areas in which try to focus their real estate investment activity.

Factors influencing their preferences/exclusions generally include:

- Public policy regarding the real estate entitlement process (e.g., most institutional investors generally prefer metro areas where the supply of retail real estate is constrained).
- Rate of economic growth (employment, new company formation, patents issued, etc.)
- Well-functioning physical infrastructure (e.g., highways and utilities).

Beth anticipated that San Diego would easily meet these preferred criteria.

**Property Criteria:** Beth also knew that institutional investors had property-related investment criteria. Again, she thought the San Marcos project would measure up very well in terms of planning and building quality. In particular, she believed that the ability to gradually upgrade the use of the building to office uses in the future would be an attractive feature for institutional investors.

**Tenant Criteria:** In some cases, criteria related to the property's tenants are factored into the investment decision, including:

- Tenant mix
- Tenant credit quality
- Lease rollover schedule

Here, Beth thought, the story was somewhat mixed. While the lease rollover schedule was now staggered as a result of Western's releasing efforts, the tenants were all involved in foreign trade, and their credit ratings were good, but not great. The exception was Japan Distributions USA, which had a strong credit rating but the Japanese parent had refused to sign directly or guarantee the lease, leaving the US subsidiary as the sole credit on the lease.

## Broker Selection

Beth planned to access targeted buyers through the real estate brokerage community. Although "principal to principal" transactions may occur, in her experience, they were rare. More importantly, Western had a fiduciary responsibility to its investors to expose the property to as extensive a market as possible and might assume some degree of liability (and face some potentially angry investors) by not doing so.

**Exclusive Representation:** Western would have to decide early on whether to work with a single brokerage firm on an exclusive basis, or to have an "open listing" This decision was usually a function of:

- The current market for investment properties
- The difficulty/ease of property disposition in the current market environment
- The availability of qualified brokerage firms serving the market in which the property is located
- Western's experience with specific brokerage firms or individuals

The real estate market was currently very frothy, with more investors than available properties in the market. As a result, Beth believed the property would have no problems being sold at a pretty good price. There were also several quality brokerage firms in California with whom Western had good relations. Beth knew she would have no problem developing a short list of qualified firms, most of which Western had dealt with in the past.

Selecting the right firm would be a larger problem. Beth began making a list of selection criteria related to experience in the institutional real estate market:

- Years of experience
- Professionalism and maturity of the proposed marketing team
- Number and value of recent disposition transactions with targeted buyers involving similar properties
- Number and value of recent acquisition transactions (not necessarily similar properties)
- Quality of market presentation (submittals to institutional buyers require similar skills and resources)

She also believed the selected firm should be familiar with the San Diego market. Key evaluation criteria included:

- Years involved in the market
- Scope and quality of market data
- Number of recent transactions completed similar to the San Marcos property
- Confidential reference checks
- Number and location of current listings for similar transactions
- Number and location of anticipated listings that might be competitive

Beth decided on a nonexclusive listing, due to the frothy nature of the market and her desire to maintain good relations with all of the quality brokers in the marketplace.

## Listing Agreement

After selecting a brokerage firm, the next step would be to enter into a Listing Agreement, a formal contract appointing the broker as the agent with the exclusive right to market the San Marcos property. The Listing Agreement generally contains the following provisions:

- Empowers the broker to market the property for a specified period
- Specifically sets forth the fee(s) to be paid to the broker upon consummation of a sale
- Identifies "excluded parties" -- potential purchasers who, if they ultimately buy the property, are excluded in determining the broker's fee arrangement[2]
- Establishes a schedule for the reporting of broker activity
- Outlines the method of handling seller-agent disputes
- Prescribes attorney's fees
- Provides for an extension of the term of the agreement, if applicable

Beth also knew that Western usually negotiated to have several specific points added to the Listing Agreement, including:

- Specific potential buyers to be marketed
- Minimum deposit required

---

[2] In some cases, the broker receives a reduced fee.

- Identification of seller financing that might be made available
- Role of the broker in assisting in the due diligence process

Beth also knew that Western would want a Confidentiality Agreement from any potential investors, prior to sending them a marketing package for the San Marcos property.

## Disposition format

Beth also had to decide whether to use a competitive bidding approach for the property or rely on a negotiated sale with a prospective buyer after the most likely candidate had been identified. Following are descriptions of the two approaches:

**Competitive Bidding:** The competitive bidding process is utilized primarily in the case of a portfolio sale or the disposition of a large "landmark" property. When this approach is utilized, the OM is distributed to prospective buyers, usually for a period of 30 days. During this period, the broker contacts each of the prospective buyers to answer questions, determine the prospect's level of interest, and solicit offers. At the end of this period, a "call for offers" is relayed to prospective buyers who, if they are interested in bidding, must properly indicate their interest.

**Negotiated Sale:** The nonbidding, negotiated approach to property disposition is used primarily for the sale of small and medium-sized properties on a one-off basis. Compared to simultaneous bidding, a more informal process is utilized, with the broker serving more as a "finder" or, in some cases, representing the potential buyer. The OM also is less formal and is distributed to a larger group of potential buyers. Interested buyers submit offers at their own discretion, and the offers are reviewed by Western and/or the broker as they are received.

Beth was undecided about the disposition method to be used. While Western would generally utilize a negotiated sale for a property of the size and type of San Carlos, she wondered if the current strong market might be able to support a competitive bid approach instead. Since Western would be marketing other properties in the project in the future, this approach would have the added advantage of showing the project to prospective buyers that might be interested in a subsequent offering as well.

Beth decided to wait for Jim to return to get his views before finalizing an approach.

## Confidentiality Agreement (C/A)

Prior to receiving a sales package for the disposition property, a prospective buyer executes a confidentiality agreement (CA). This protects the seller against misuse of certain sensitive information concerning the property, which a competitor might be able to use to Western's disadvantage. This includes information such as tenant lease terms, property operating data, and information about the disposing owner entity. In executing a CA, the prospective buyer agrees to use this sensitive information exclusively to evaluate a potential purchase of the disposition property.

Beth decided to use the standard CA agreement that Western used for other dispositions, modified to include the specifics of the San Marcos property.

## Offering Memorandum (O/M)

Assuming that she and Jim might make the decision to pursue a competitive bidding approach, Beth began preparing an OM on the property. The key elements included:

**Executive Summary:** The Executive Summary presents the disposition property's attributes in a concise manner, to allow for a quick and easy understanding of the proposed transaction.

**Disclaimer:** A disclaimer is a clause(s) that puts a potential buyer on notice that he/she is purchasing the disposition property on an "as is" and "where is" basis. Furthermore, the Company states that it makes no representations or warranties whatsoever as to the accuracy or completeness of the information presented in the OM. It is up to the buyer to undertake and pay for the due diligence necessary to support the final purchase decision. Beth decided to use Western's standard disclaimer statement.

**Property Location and Description:** The location of the disposition property is established with maps, along with a brief description of the property. She planned to use the location and plot plan exhibits Western had used in its due diligence report (Exhibits 1 and 2).

**Market Analysis:** This document is an analysis of current and historical market conditions, including factors such as:

- ❑ Space absorption (demand)
- ❑ New construction (supply)
- ❑ Market rental rates
- ❑ Recent property sales (comps)
- ❑ Recent leasing activity (comps)

Since information from the market analysis might be utilized by the buyer to support underwriting assumptions, Beth decided to have the broker(s) selected prepare the analysis, in order to avoid Western having direct responsibility for the data utilized.

**Sales Underwriting:** The sales underwriting is generally prepared by the seller and usually includes the property's projected cash flow. This information is used by a prospective buyer to establish the price he/she is willing to pay for the property. Since the buyer will be verifying the underlying assumptions of the underwriting during due diligence, it is critical that this information be as accurate as possible. If it is not, the buyer might have an opportunity to adjust the price offered.

Beth wrote an email to the San Marcos project manager and requested that he prepare the necessary underwriting numbers.

**Letter of Intent (LOI):** Most offers are in the form of a Letter of Intent (LOI). The LOI generally establishes a deadline for the acceptance of the offer. Western could either respond to a given LOI or let the proposal acceptance period lapse. Competing offers would be compared, and Western could ask for re-submittals by interested parties and then pursue the one that appears most attractive.

Beth wanted to make certain the each firm submitting an offer included certain minimum information, so that competing offers could be compared. She decided to include in the OM the following additional information requirements:

- Offering price and expirations
- Conditions, if any
- Amount and timing of cash deposits
- Terms regarding the assumption of existing debt (if utilized)
- Description and timing of due diligence documents to be provided by Western
- Critical points when documents and/or actions have to be completed and/or approved by each party
- Length of due diligence and closing periods
- Names of real estate brokers and finders who are exclusively entitled to a commission or finder's fee

If Western decided to use a competitive bidding approach, the LOIs from the various bidders would be incorporated into a Sales Summary. At this point, a meeting would be held with the listing broker to determine the best strategy and next steps. Depending on the offers received, it may be appropriate to select a buyer or consider an additional round of bidding.

In a negotiated approach, the Company would enter into LOI negotiations with the buyer submitting the most attractive offer. The most attractive offer may not be the dollar highest bid, but could be based on other attributes, such as a buyer's track record of closing acquisitions with a minimum of problems and in a timely fashion.

**Purchase and Sale Agreement (P&S):** Once an LOI has been negotiated and executed by the business managers, a P&S Agreement can be negotiated by attorneys representing the buyer and Western. The P&S Agreement translates the business terms of the LOI into a binding and legally enforceable contract between the parties.

In addition to the terms outlined in the LOI, the P&S Agreement contains legal representations by the seller regarding the condition and legal status of the property, and notes that all documents and other materials will be provided to the buyer and are, to the seller's knowledge, complete and accurate. Other standard provisions include the timing and conditions of the due diligence review, assignable rights, default provisions, and casualty and condemnation clauses.

Closing documents (e.g., bill of sale, warranty or grant deed, assignment of contracts, assignments of leases) should also be negotiated at this time and attached as exhibits to the P&S Agreement. This is important in order to prevent panic negotiations immediately prior to closing.

Beth decided not to include a copy of Western's typical P&S agreement, as she didn't want to get into a legal hassle with prospective buyers before a winning candidate had been identified. After that candidate was identified, she would have the legal documents sent to the buyer by Western's attorney.

**Earnest Money Deposit:** Today, most real estate transactions utilize a third party escrow service to collect and disburse documents, funds, and other items required by the P&S Agreement. Beth wanted to let prospective buyers know that funds could be either in the form of cash or a Letter of Credit (LC) from a financial institution.

**Diligence Documents Provided:** Beth also wanted prospective buyers know which documents Western would provide as soon as a P&S

Agreement had been executed and the initial cash deposit posted.[3] These documents include:

- Property survey
- Copies of third party reports (usually updated)
- Historical environmental reports
- Phase I environmental reports
- Environmental and Physical/Structural Survey
- Rent roll
- Copies of all leases
- Historical operating statements

The prospective buyer will need to inspect the property in person and with his/her third party contractors. The buyer also may wish to interview some or all of the tenants. Beth knew that she would have to coordinate these inspections and interviews with Western's Asset Manager responsible for the property, in order to ensure a smooth and efficient process and minimum amount of tenant disruption.

## *Property Reports*

Beth also included in the bid package a Phase I Environmental Report and the report of a structural engineer that Western had employed during the due diligence period in 2003 when it purchased the property. Beth tried to remember if there were any other diligence reports that should be included, or if any of the reports needed updating. She concluded that she had covered the bases and that the prospective buyer should be responsible for ordering any updates since Western's acquisition of the property. [4]

As she began finalizing the OM, Beth made a last-minute check on the accuracy of the information she had assembled so far. She knew that, to assure a smooth and efficient sales process, it was critical that all information in the OM be accurate. It is not the broker's responsibility to make sure that the property information is accurate; the broker relies on receiving accurate information about a property from the seller. Therefore, Western must ensure that any information released to the broker has been thoroughly

---

[3] Western had a company policy of not releasing certain information to a prospective buyer, including: (1) information related to the existing debt, and (2) information related to Western's ownership, investment structure, or profit participation regarding the subject property.

[4] It should be noted that, in order to meet fiduciary standards, institutional buyers will generally order their own reports from their own contractors. They then will use these reports in conjunction with the seller's reports to reach a final underwriting decision.

verified.[5] Both Western and the broker(s) also must be certain that each of the qualified potential buyers receives identical information.

Beth began work on the marketing plan and the draft OM. She knew she would have to postpone her walk on the Embarcadero for a day or so. Instead, she poured a cup of coffee and reached into her desk drawer for another *Krispy Kreme* doughnut.

---

[5] A complete record should be kept of the supporting data, in the event of a subsequent legal dispute with the actual buyer or a potential buyer not selected.

## Questions for Discussion

The following questions are designed to explore the major issues raised in this case study.

1. Why did Jim select Building F for disposition at this time? What are the strengths and weaknesses of the three tenants in Building F? What do you think of Jim's strategy to sell this particular building and why?

2. Why did Beth select institutional investors as the target buyers for the project? What do you think of her strategy and why?

3. What are the three reasons Beth believed the San Marcos project would be attractive to potential institutional buyers? Do you agree with her reasoning?

4. Why is Beth recommending utilizing a broker in the disposition process? What do you think of her criteria for selecting a broker? How important is local market knowledge? Why?

5. What are the key elements of the listing agreement with the selected broker, both general and specific? Why are these elements important, from Western's point of view?

6. Do you think Western should use a negotiated sale or a competitive bidding process? What are the pros and cons of each approach?

7. What should Western's position be regarding representations and warranties regarding the property? Which of these, if any, should be included in the OM?

8. What do you think of including LOI and due diligence elements in the OM to prospective buyers? Do you think this might reduce Western's negotiating leverage? If so, why?

9. Is there anything else that Beth should include in her marketing plan? If so, what and why?

Please use these questions as a guide and not a format or a reflection of all of the questions that need to be addressed by this case.

# 16

# NOTE ON STRATEGIC MANAGEMENT[1]

The concept of strategic management has been studied for over 50 years. During this period, management consultants and business school faculty have helped firms[2] to develop and implement wide-ranging strategic plans, to the point where strategic management is now widely accepted in America's general business community.

Strategic management involves positioning a firm in the marketplace through 1) strategic planning and 2) plan implementation. Strategic management may involve changing a firm's relationship with its customers, competitors, employees, shareholders, and/or other stakeholders. It could represent a change in the total organization or some of its business lines or products/services. It might involve merging or dissolving the firm itself.

The strategic planning process provides the roadmap for strategic management and lays the groundwork for the action steps to follow.

## The Strategic Planning Environment

Strategic planning is essentially thinking in the future – about the world, the nation, the business environment – and how a firm can best compete in the markets in which it chooses to operate. Strategic planning also involves anticipating the impact of major trends in the drivers of change (e.g.,

---

[1] This note was prepared by John McMahan in 1998 and 2005. Copyright © 1998 and 2005 by John McMahan. All rights reserved.
[2] Recognizing that obvious differences exist, the discussion in this chapter applies to many nonprofit and governmental organizations as well.

technology, deregulation, changing customer needs). Since no vision of the future is 100% correct, planning usually focuses on a "most likely" scenario while attempting to minimize the risk and maximize the rewards of alternative scenarios.

## Industry Factors Influencing Strategic Planning

Characteristics of the firm's industry may influence the strategic planning process. Firms in *emerging industries* (those growing faster than the overall economy) must deal with rapidly changing market characteristics, a high degree of technological innovation, shorter product cycles, and the emergence of new (often, unforeseen) competitors. The strategic planning process for these firms, by necessity, must consider a shorter time horizon and afford much higher levels of implementation flexibility.

The strategy of firms in *growth industries* (growing at the same rate as the overall economy) often focuses on a single or a few products/services. Although this strategy can lead to a strong competitive advantage, the firm is vulnerable to major shifts in its markets as a result of lifestyle changes, product substitution, and other forces. This is a particularly dangerous position for a firm during times of economic turmoil, when changes in strategy (e.g., new product development) may be difficult.

Firms in *mature industries* (growing more slowly than the overall economy, or declining) have a different set of problems. Their markets may be declining, with surplus capacity leading to thinner margins and intense levels of competition. Here the focus of strategic planning is usually on maintaining market share and increasing margins by reducing costs, or eliminating competition through consolidation. The time horizon is usually longer, with implementation less likely to be imperiled by unforeseen events.

The distribution of market share in a given industry may prove critical to the planning process. Firms in *fragmented industries*, in which no firm has a significant market share, may wish to adopt a strategy of expanding market share through the acquisition of other firms. Firms in *concentrated industries*, in which one or a few firms command a significant share, may be stifled in their attempts to increase market share, and the best strategic decision may be to leave the industry.

The relationship between the firm and its external environment also influences the strategic planning process. Firms that are *externally dependent*—on customers, suppliers, government, unions, etc.—have fewer strategic options and less flexibility in implementing their strategic plans.

The degree to which new firms can enter the marketplace also may have an impact on the planning process. Firms in industries with significant *barriers to entry* (e.g., large economies of scale, product differentiation, capital requirements, access to distribution channels, government policy) may focus their strategic planning efforts around maintaining or expanding these barriers. Firms in industries with few barriers may wish to discourage entry through branding, government regulation, or by other means.

## Influence of Firm's State of Evolution

A firm's planning environment is also influenced by its own stage of evolution. New, smaller firms are in an *entrepreneurial mode* in which a few owner/managers make most of the decisions, including strategic decisions. Medium-sized firms are usually in an *adaptive mode*. In these firms, strategic decisions are more closely linked to the existing strategy. Larger firms with multiple business lines are most apt to be in a formal *planning mode*. Strategic decisions are made through a comprehensive, formal process, which considers totally new initiatives. These larger firms can take more of a *portfolio approach* to planning, viewing each of the firm's business lines as one element in a total portfolio.

Planning may also be affected by the *company culture*—the set of important assumptions shared by members of the firm—and the *company self-concept*—how the firm thinks about itself. The culture may be explicit or implicit, shaped by the business environment of the firm's industry, the prior experience of employees in other firms, professional relationships, community standards, and the experiences that the employees share in their everyday work environment within the firm.

## Strategic Postures

In undertaking strategic planning, firms can adopt a variety of different postures regarding what they hope to achieve from the planning process. The posture chosen will depend on the position of the firm within its marketplace.

**Shape the Future:** This is the posture of the "market maker"— a firm with sufficient market share or resources, which, if successful, can largely dictate the rules of the game. The market maker is usually an *early entrant* or *pioneer* in the marketplace.

**Adapt to the Future:** Adapting is the posture of the "market taker"— a firm with insufficient market share or resources to dominate a market, but which can and will be a significant player.

**Reserve the Right to Play:** This is the posture of a *late entrant*—a firm that chooses to wait to enter a market until the players and outcomes are better defined but which strives to keep abreast of key elements of entry (e.g., research, technology, distribution channels, etc.).

## Working Assumptions

Strategic planning is based on several key assumptions:

- The strategic direction of business firms is at the heart of wealth creation.
- Most firms are in competition.
- The selection and implementation of strategic choices will heavily influence the success or failure of firms.
- Strategic choices must be integrated, reinforcing one another.
- Implementation of the strategic plan must be monitored frequently, with results measured against objectives on a continuing basis.
- The future is fluid, so the plan must be flexible enough to allow shifts in direction if circumstances change.

## Strategic Choices

At the heart of the planning process is the selection and integration of "strategic choices." What are the strategic choices that management[3] can make through the strategic planning process? The first set of choices relates to the objectives that the firm is trying to achieve:

> **Selection of Goals:** What goals does the company seek to achieve? What is the mission of the firm?

> **Market Positioning:** Where is the firm currently? Where should it be positioned in order to achieve its goals? How does it get there?

There are also choices related to changes in the scope and nature of the firm as a result of repositioning:

> **Selection of Products and Services:** What products/services should the firm offer in order to fulfill its obligations to its customers? How profitable are each of the firm's product/service lines, and to what extent do they interact to support the firm's mission and achievement of its goals?

> **Level of Scope and Scale:** How large should the firm be to operate efficiently? What are the tradeoffs in reaching this level, and how can they be overcome/mitigated?

---

[3] For the purposes of discussion, "management" is defined as including the Board of Directors, the Chief Executive Officer, and the members of senior management (e.g. CFO, COO, Director of Strategic Planning, and heads of the major operating units).

**Degree of Diversity:** How specialized should the firm be? What is the appropriate balance between corporate focus and risk diversification?

**Organizational Structure:** How should the firm be organized to best achieve its goals and fulfill the objectives of the strategic plan?

Finally, there are questions related to implementation: How will the strategic plan be executed and managed? How will results be measured?

## Targets of Strategic Planning

Strategic planning is directed at three major groups:

**Customers:** Existing and prospective buyers of the firm's products/services as well as other firms in the distribution system (e.g., wholesalers, distributors, retailers).

**Competitors:** Existing competitors, new entrants, and substitute products.

**Suppliers:** Other firms providing raw materials, labor, capital, services, etc.

## Potential Successful Outcomes

If successful, the strategic planning process should help companies to achieve the following outcomes:

**Differentiated Product/Service:** Effective strategic planning enables the firm to create sufficient differences in its products/services, improving the firm's image and increasing customer loyalty. If the plan is successful, it enables the firm to achieve higher margins and/or market share.

**Improved Efficiency:** Through effective strategic planning, firms can improve efficiencies in production, distribution, infrastructure, and capital costs, which should result in lower costs and/or higher value to customers.

**Greater Innovation/Focus:** Utilizes greater levels of specialization/ technology to secure higher margins, creates higher *switching costs* (customer's costs of changing suppliers) making it more difficult for competitors to enter/expand into the firm's markets.

## The Strategic Planning Process

The strategic planning process, in its simplest terms, can be reduced to three fundamental questions:

1) Where are we today? What does the future hold?

2) What position in the marketplace will add the greatest value to the firm's customers, employees, and shareholders?

3) What actions do we take to achieve that position?

To put it even more simply: Where are we now? Where do we want to go? How do we get there?

Entire professional competencies and theoretical constructs have grown up around answering each of these questions. The subject is too complex to address in detail here, but we can introduce some of the concepts involved in answering the questions and illustrate how they fit into the strategic planning process.

## Current and Future Situation

The first step in the strategic planning process is to assess the current position of the firm ("where are we now?"). The research process, to be valuable, must be fair, accurate, and, above all, objective in its approach as well as in the interpretation and dissemination of its findings. This is not always an easy task since a wide variety of stakeholders—board members, management, employees, shareholders, suppliers, financiers, etc.—may not like the answers that are forthcoming and may use the material to promote personal agendas that may not be in the best interests of the firm.

A minimum threshold of success is the ability of a firm to *operate effectively* over the long term in a highly competitive world. Operating effectively means providing the customer with better performance by creating greater value, or by delivering comparable value at a lower cost.

**Developing the Value Proposition:** A critical element in developing operational effectiveness is a thorough understanding of and identification with the increasingly demanding customer. Finding out who the customer really is and isolating the customer's needs, resources, and buying/use preferences is absolutely essential to a successful firm's operation. Based on this understanding, a firm develops the mix of products and services that it will offer each customer, the prices that it will charge, and the terms by which it will perform its obligations to the customer. This is the *value proposition* that defines the relationship between the firm and its customers.

**Core Competencies:** In order to fulfill its value proposition, a firm develops certain *competencies*. Hamel and Prahalad define a "competence" as "a bundle of skills and technologies rather than a single discrete skill or technology," representing "the sum of learning across individual skill sets and individual organizational units."[4] In other words, competency is a methodology for doing the things that the firm is "good at."

Unfortunately, firms often spend vast sums of management time and money developing competencies that are largely irrelevant to the customer in making "buy" decisions and developing long-term relationships. Part of this mismatch may be due to customers not being aware of their own needs but, more likely, it is the result of firms proceeding to build competencies without fully understanding whether those competencies will fulfill the value proposition.

Therefore, it's important to focus on *core competencies* that are essential to the successful operation of the firm in fulfilling its value proposition to its customers. To be considered a core competency, the bundle of skills must make an important contribution to the value of the firm as perceived by the customer. In other words, it must satisfy the value proposition equation.

Core competency also must be "competitively unique" within the industry, although not necessarily unique to one firm. Finally, a core competency should be "extendable" to new products and services in the future, enhancing its value over time through continued development and use.

**Determining Which Competencies are "Core":** How does a firm determine which competencies should be considered "core" and avoid a customer/competency mismatch? The answer is to *talk to the customer on an ongoing basis*. As simple as this sounds, it's amazing how many times strategic decisions are made without sufficiently understanding the person or organization making the buy decision, and what's important to them. Gaining this understanding requires more than a one-time customer survey or market research study. Such research is necessary but not sufficient. What is required is *customer intimacy*—an in-depth understanding of, and relationship with, those who purchase the firm's products and services.

**Building Customer Intimacy:** To build customer intimacy, the firm must establish a continuing dialogue with its existing and potential customers. The goal of the dialogue is to clarify known needs, identify unmet needs, and better understand attitudes toward the firm's current and potential service or product offerings.

The first step in this process is to establish *customer knowledge:* Who are the customers, and what are their requirements? It is also important to know the depth of the customer base, and how its size and activity patterns will change in the future. Is it vulnerable to new technology or business patterns? Is it vulnerable to demographic forces or lifestyle change?

---

[4] Gary Hamel & C.K. Prahalad, *Competing for the Future*, Harvard Business School Press, 1994.

If a firm has a heterogeneous customer base, certain customers may perceive some but not all of the core competencies that the firm possesses. This forces the firm to segment its markets and focus its efforts on building core competencies that meet the needs of the majority of its customers, and/or to determine that smaller customer groups will grow sufficiently to support the maintenance of each competency. Without this *market segmentation*, the firm is diluting its efforts by building competencies that are not economically viable.

Establishing and maintaining customer intimacy is a multifaceted undertaking involving continuing surveys, in-depth discussions with key customers, continuous debriefing of sales personnel, and attending the customer's professional and trade functions to hear and talk about issues and concerns.

This effort cannot be completely delegated. Senior management must be involved on a personal basis in establishing ongoing relationships with key customers and potential customers. This demonstrates to customers that senior management is concerned with their well-being. It also establishes a leadership model within the organization and eliminates any "noise" that might come from those with a personal stake in the outcome.

Technology can aid in implementing the process of building customer intimacy. By helping to define and track consumers, technology enables management to gather information from sales force and other personnel who interact with customers in order to monitor customers' attitudes towards the firm and its products/services. Technology also can help establish customer intimacy at the level of the individual, by allowing managers to respond more rapidly to problem situations with greater knowledge of the customer and his/her historical relationship with the firm.

**Competency Convergence:** Over time, customers' perceptions of the importance of specific core competencies can change. Competitors may adopt similar bundles of skills and technology to the point where there is a *competency convergence*, with no one firm having a strategic advantage. In fact, a core competency may become an industry standard by which all firms are measured. From the customers' viewpoint, this is expected.

**Benchmarking the Competition:** Defining the nature of the competition is closely related to and intertwined with understanding the customer. Who are the existing competitors, and how does the firm compare in the minds and actions of the customer? Who are the likely new competitors, and how will they change the competitive environment? How can the firm take industry leadership in defining and establishing a new *competitive space* in which it can be dominant?

Meaningful continuing analysis of the customer and the competition requires establishment of a *benchmarking* process, by which data produced from the interview/analytical process can be continuously compared to a standard. The standard used might be the average of the competitive universe in order to gain an idea of the firm's general market position. It is more useful to determine who the industry leaders are, and in terms of what they are doing. It may be even more enlightening to benchmark against other industries whose processes are more advanced. When complete, benchmarking establishes a set of *"best practices"* against which the activities of the firm can be compared and measured.

The costs of developing and analyzing meaningful benchmark data and best practices can be high. The cost of not doing so, however, means managing in a vacuum, which ultimately may be the most costly decision of all. One thing is clear: the process of benchmarking must be continuous and iterative.

The research process involves a high degree of interaction between the work elements, with findings in one area prompting additional research in another. Research should identify the optimal market position for the firm as well as the competitive advantages that it has or can establish. From this process, an understanding of a series of alternative courses of action begins to emerge.

## Formulating a Strategy

The next step is to begin consolidating courses of action into alternative strategies. This *strategic issue analysis* contrasts the company profile with its external environment to identify a range of possible strategic alternatives. Particular attention should be given to *critical success factors*—those areas in which high performance by the firm could result in an improved *competitive position*. After the strategic alternatives are identified, they are screened against the firm's mission statement to determine which strategic alternatives are consistent with the firm's overall goals and objectives. These alternative growth strategies can be either externally or internally focused.

**Externally Focused Strategies:** Strategic alternatives that focus on external growth are generally directed at moving the firm to a more optimal competitive position, with a focus on revenue enhancement. That might involve introducing new products/services, differentiating existing products/services, improving product distribution systems (*outbound logistics*), divesting existing operating units, or acquiring new operating units, among other actions. Since competitive marketplaces are seldom calm, the analysis of alternative growth strategies should also consider the potential *competitive reaction* to each alternative.

Often a growth strategy involves a choice between integrating horizontally or vertically. *Horizontal integration* expands the firm through acquisition or internal growth without significantly changing its stage in the production/marketing processes. This strategy is utilized to enter new geographical markets or eliminate competition in existing markets. *Vertical integration*, on the other hand, involves adding functions forward or backward in the production/marketing process. *Forward integration*, a form of vertical integration, could move the firm closer to the customer, thereby improving market share and potentially reducing costs to the point of sale. Acquiring a distributor is one example of forward integration.

**Internally Focused Strategies:** Internally focused growth strategies are usually associated with improving internal operations by lowering production costs, improving procurement policies (*inbound logistics*), or improving the firm's overall work environment. This may involve such initiatives as reorganizing the structure of the firm, re-engineering the way the firm undertakes certain activities, outsourcing non-core functions, or recapitalizing the balance sheet. It may also involve external actions, such as a merger or the acquisition of another firm. *Backward integration*, such as acquiring a supplier, could reduce costs to the consumer and/or improve product/service quality.

Growth strategies also may reflect the presence or absence of synergies between consolidating firms. *Concentric diversification* reflects a strategy of acquiring firms which are similar to, and synergistic with, the acquiring firm in terms of markets, products, and/or technology. *Conglomerate diversification* is a strategy of acquiring firms for investment purposes only, with little or no anticipated synergy with the acquired firm.

Highly specialized firms are faced with the decision of whether to diversify or focus their operations even more. Diversification usually reduces the risk of a business being affected by a major adverse event (e.g., product replacement, market area deterioration, loss of key executives) but it may also lead to a decline in the firm's major business activity. Given this choice, firms may decide it is better to "harden the silo" by developing a *defensible niche* in which margins improve and future competitive entry is made more difficult.

For large firms, a *grand strategy* evolves, which rationalizes and guides the *functional strategies* for each business unit with broader company objectives. This is a parallel process, with corporate planning focusing on top-down strategic issues and business unit managers working with bottom-up, operating issues.

In most cases, a change in strategic direction will involve some change in the structure of the organization, from fine-tuning an already smoothly-functioning organization to radically restructuring all aspects of the firm's operation. Whatever changes are made, it's critical for the organizational structure to be consistent with, and supportive of, the strategic plan.

**Dealing with Resource Constraints:** In the course of evaluating strategic alternatives management will reject alternatives that are unfeasible or not of sufficient economic value to the firm. The process of eliminating alternatives, while important, must be undertaken with some caution. Too often, strategic planning focuses on what a firm *can't do* rather than what it *must do* to gain a competitive advantage. It is certainly necessary to consider existing resources, particularly core competencies, but these should be viewed as a foundation, not a limitation. When a manager says, "Let's be realistic," it usually means that the *stretch thinking* essential to creative strategic planning has not been applied. (If it's the boss who says it, the firm is in real trouble!)

Effective strategic planning first establishes what the firm must do to establish competitive advantage, and then concerns itself with the resources required to achieve the goal. It may turn out that the firm will, in fact, be limited by its resources, but this assumption should be put to the most rigorous test imaginable. Well managed, creative firms are usually able to come up with the necessary resources, once they know what is required to achieve their strategic goals.

**Valuation of Strategic Alternatives:** As alternative strategies emerge, it is important to test them quantitatively against the baseline standards established during the current business evaluation research previously discussed. This testing may utilize *activity ratios* such as asset turnover, sales to fixed assets, return on assets (ROA), return on investment (ROI), and Economic Value Added (EVA) ©. Each alternative should enhance shareholder value and/or reduce downside risk when compared to the current strategic plan. If it does not, it should be rejected or modified to generate higher value. In some cases, the firm might continue to consider a strategic alternative with certain desirable nonquantifiable characteristics, but the costs of doing so must be fully understood.

As previously noted, strategic positioning means performing different activities than the competition or performing the same activities in a different way, requiring that strategic tradeoffs be made. Selecting a strategic alternative from multiple viable options will limit what a company can do, because no firm can be all things to all people. This increases risk because the selected alternative may turn out to be wrong and, once this is discovered, it might be too late to go back and take a different route. But making the "right" strategic decision(s) is what good management and industry leadership are all about, and if a correct strategic direction is chosen, it can distance the firm from its competitors and insure successful corporate growth and long-term profitability. The right decisions don't have to be optimal; they just have to be better than the competitor's decisions.

## Developing the Strategic Plan

Once each of the strategic alternatives has been tested, management can begin the process of selecting desirable alternatives and formulating the final strategic plan. The plan should first state the *company goals* that management expects to attain through implementation of the strategic plan. Next, these goals should be translated into *measurable objectives*, projected over a multiyear period. Measurable objectives might include improvement in market share, profitability, return on investment, technology leadership, productivity improvements, employee relations, and public responsibility, among others. In the early years of a firm, goal measurement should be tied to specific accomplishments in specific time periods (*annual goals*). Finally, *company policies* should be formulated, reflecting broad guidelines which will influence the thinking, decisions, and actions of managers and subordinates as the strategic plan is implemented.

There are several possible strategies for a firm to consider:

**Elimination of Non-Core Activities:** In order to force management to focus on establishing and maintaining core competencies, the strategic plan can identify and reduce or eliminate non-core activities by divesting or outsourcing them to other organizations. It's tough enough for management to make critical decisions on the things that really matter without having to concentrate resources on those that are important but not essential. In many cases, management discovers that the non-core activities weren't needed in the first place or can be performed better and less expensively by others.

**Maintaining/Reorienting Core Competencies:** Dealing with customers' changing perceptions of core competencies requires ongoing strategic planning and out-of-the-box thinking on the part of senior management. Given the high volatility of most markets and the rapid rate of industry change, maintenance and improvement of core competencies can be almost as difficult as establishing them in the first place.

Management must have the ability to deal with changing reality, to face hard facts about customers, the effectiveness of the firm's products and services, and the strength and nature of the competition.

**Establishing and/or Enhancing Competitive Advantage:** If the firm is already operating effectively, it should pursue a strategy of differentiating itself from the competition, through its products, services, or processes in order to gain a strategic advantage.

Once a firm is operating effectively, the next and most crucial step is to differentiate itself by adding value through products and services that give it a *strategic advantage* over the competition.[5] A firm's long-term profitability will depend, in large measure, upon the degree to which this strategic positioning can be achieved and sustained over time.

As opposed to operational effectiveness, which involves performing the same activities better, faster, or cheaper than the competition, competitive advantage requires performing different activities than the competition, or performing the same activities in a different way. This often requires management to make strategic tradeoffs — for example, between higher value and lower cost, products offered, and customers served. Making these choices requires a high degree of personal and organizational discipline and integrity, clear lines of communication, and a willingness to say "no."[6]

Firms may establish competitive advantage in a highly focused niche or across a broad range of products and services, depending upon size, resources, established market position, and level of operating effectiveness.

In pursuing a strategy to establish or enhance competitive advantage, the goal should be to achieve a strong, sustainable advantage. Weak competitive advantages result in contestable positions, whether the scope of the advantage is narrow or broad. For firms attempting a broad reach, moderate competitive advantages will allow the firm to participate in rivalry with other major firms but not establish clear-cut industry domination. Niche firms with a moderate level of competitive advantage will be able to participate in one-off matches with other firms of comparable advantage. <u>It is only strong, sustainable competitive advantages that will lead to defensible niches or, for the firm with broad scope, industry domination.</u>

Competitive advantage can be established without developing core competencies, it can be built on competencies, or it can be achieved by creating an entirely new strategic initiative.

**Independent of Core Competency:** Some companies can gain strategic competitive advantage *without* developing core competencies, through legal control of monopolies such as patents or zoning); a market position resulting from a relationship with another firm (e.g., franchise or licensing agreement); or through an image inherited from years of market share dominance (e.g., strong historical brand identity).

**Building on Existing Core Competencies:** More commonly, and of much more importance to most firms, is utilizing existing core competencies to build strategic competitive advantage. Judging the sustainability of competitive advantages arising out of core competencies is not easy. As

---

[5] Michael E. Porter, *What is Strategy?*, Harvard Business Review, November-December, 1996.
[6] Porter, Ibid.

previously noted, customer perceptions of what is expected from firms can change over time. Competitors also may improve their core competencies to the point where there is little differentiation between firms.

It's generally a good idea to assume that, in today's highly competitive world, most strategic advantages arising from existing core competencies will not be sustainable over extended periods of time unless they are redirected or combined with an entirely new strategic initiative.

As Michael Porter has noted, operational effectiveness is necessary but is not strategy. Porter argues that a firm can "outperform rivals only if it can establish a difference that it can preserve."

**Establishing New Initiatives:** Due to the time required to develop a competitive advantage, the rate of change in most industries, and corresponding competitor moves, it is often necessary to *leapfrog* the existing competitive environment. This may help the firm to establish entirely new competitive space in which it is not only a leader but establishes most, if not all, of the standards by which all firms will be measured.

As previously noted, leapfrogging the competition requires a stretch in thinking about the future, not only in terms of customer preferences but also in terms of the firm's resources. In essence, new initiatives require the firm to say "If we started from scratch, what would we do?" rather than be constrained by available resources.

## *Assets and Infrastructure*

Each strategic alternative carries with it certain asset and infrastructure requirements. In some cases, the decision will be to reduce or eliminate assets and/or infrastructure — for example, to sell or lease real estate or outsourcing non-core competencies of the firm. More likely, new resources will be required to implement an alternative, as in the addition of plants, employees, and/or new technology.

## *Implementation of the Strategic Plan*

To be successful, a strategic plan must become an integral part of a firm's daily operations and culture. This is often the most difficult aspect of the strategic management process.

**Institutionalization:** Institutionalizing the plan—translating it into short-term action guidelines for all employees—is one of the most difficult challenges facing management. Not surprisingly, this is where many strategic plans fail. The process of institutionalizing strategy requires the integration of a firm's structure, culture, leadership, and employee reward system. The seeds for success or failure may be sown in the planning process itself. A plan that is based on extensive management participation is more apt to receive the buy-in necessary for successful implementation.

**Organizational Structure:** Creating an organizational structure to support a strategic plan is a formidable problem. While firms may formulate a resourceful plan for their future, there is no single model for developing an organizational structure to successfully achieve the objectives of such plans. In many cases, the plan is forced onto an existing organizational structure, which may or may not be appropriate.

For many years American business primarily relied on *functional* organizational structures. The functional structure stresses improving productivity by encouraging specialization by functions (e.g., marketing, production, financial reporting). This structure can pose significant problems, however, which become even more apparent in a highly competitive environment.

By focusing internally, the customer is given less attention, and numerous layers of costly middle management are created, increasing overhead and requiring higher levels of revenue to break even. It is also extremely difficult to establish responsibility for the success or failure of specific products or service lines.

As a result, over the years several alternative organizational structures have emerged. The *matrix* structure delegates power to independent operating units, which then rely on centralized corporate facilities for functional support. Another approach is the *flat* organization, in which many middle management functions are eliminated. While this may reduce overhead and allow for more rapid decision making, information and communications are still largely centralized.

More recently, some firms have experimented with other forms of organization which are even less hierarchical in structure. Utilizing a *networked* structure, a firm is divided into units which operate independently of each other but within a framework that is consistent with broader corporate goals and objectives. Data and information are widely shared, largely through a telecommunication system linking all of the units to each other and to the corporate support group.

Unfortunately, the networked approach offers little opportunity to benefit from economies of scale and may lead to considerable duplication. It tends to work best in situations where local presence is critical and yet national information flow is needed to support local operations.

With a *virtual* organization, the firm performs internally only its core competencies (perhaps just marketing), while outsourcing all other activities (potentially including all production activities). Similar to the networked firm, heavy reliance is placed on a state-of-the-art telecommunication system linking individual units. The virtual organization also operates within an overall corporate strategic support structure, although there may be no formal corporate headquarters. This organizational structure is helpful in situations where being small helps in building customer intimacy, yet rapid access to other resources is required to perform larger tasks.

Some firms are also linking together a series of *work teams*, each dedicated to developing and marketing one or more new products and services. Team members can be employees or external contractors. The important thing is for team members to have the necessary complementary skills to bring the new idea to market or determine that it is infeasible to do so. The life of any work team varies, depending upon the complexity of the task and the degree of market success.

The work team approach represents the most focused attack on aligning work skills and motivation with customer requirements. The bad news is that this approach may require periodic, often wrenching, shifts in the organization and may be quite costly, as a result of resource duplication.

Each of these approaches to organizing the work effort has its advantages and drawbacks. Firms will have to experiment with various mixes and blends until the right combination is discovered, the one that works best for their markets, core competencies, and company culture. The most important concern is that the organizational approach follows, and is complementary with, the strategic goals that the firm has set. Any attempt to implement a new strategic initiative within an inappropriate structure is doomed to fail from the start.

**Transition:** A key element in making a final determination regarding strategic direction is the way in which the firm chooses to grow or *migrate* to its desired market position. Usually, there are three choices: grow internally, consolidate with another firm, or partner with another firm.

> **1. Grow Internally:** Most firms rely on internal resources to implement their strategic plan. This technique works well for firms that already have strong market share and significant resources. The advantage is that this approach is less disruptive to the firm's internal organization and, as a result, may be more lasting as it is implemented. Disadvantages include the potential for the wrong person to be placed in a critical role; possible delays in implementation; and the possibility that insufficient organizational change will be achieved.
>
> **2. Consolidate with Another Firm:** While getting bigger through consolidation is not an end in itself, mergers and acquisitions *do* have a place if they are well thought-out and accomplish one or more key objectives of a broader strategic plan focused on attaining competitive advantage. In fact, when the dust settles, it may be that the merged firm is

not significantly larger than before, but better positioned to serve its customer base.

The objectives for consolidation may vary, depending upon the strategic plan. One goal may be to gain access to geographical markets not presently served. Another may be to add one or more product/service lines that will enhance the firm's value proposition with the existing customer base. Still another may be to seek additional customers, spreading the same service/product mix over a larger base. In some cases, firms consolidate in order to obtain or enhance a strong management team.

Not all mergers are successful, particularly transactions involving weak firms. Without the resources to be an acquiring firm, the weak firm is truly adrift on the competitive seas. If it does nothing, it runs the risk of being scooped up by another firm and effectively dismantled for its remaining asset value. Needless to say, not too many managers are interested in this outcome, so they often seek another weak firm as a merger partner, so that management prerogatives can be preserved, at least temporarily. Usually, the result is simply a larger weak firm, perhaps with more problems than the individual firms faced prior to the merger.

**3. Partner with Another Firm:** *Strategic alliances* between firms (*partnering*) is gaining momentum, as firms seek to achieve strategic objectives without surrendering (or, in some cases, even sharing) operating control.

Partnering can take many forms. Firms may wish to expand into geographical markets or product/service lines where a single firm is dominant but doesn't wish to consolidate. Two or more firms may wish to enter a new, uncharted market in which no one firm by itself has the resources required to succeed. Desiring to round out a product/service mix, a large firm might want to enter a highly specialized market where only small, boutique firms can operate successfully.

To be successful, such alliances must achieve an important strategic objective for both (all) firms. In some cases, the objectives may be different but complementary. It's important to clearly lay out in writing the goals of both firms, and how the alliance will further these objectives. The plan should also establish how the alliance will operate on a day-to-day basis, including a clear indication of management responsibilities and financial arrangements.

Although often underestimated, successful alliances require a lot of management involvement. It is generally a sound idea for each (all) of the firms to dedicate (or hire) a senior manager to be responsible for the activities of the alliance. These individuals must be able to work well together if the alliance is to succeed. Progress should be measured on a periodic basis, including benchmarking data similar to what management receives from their internal operations. Customer response to alliances may be negative and could require a change in direction or even termination.

It should be noted that a broad-based strategy might involve more than one implementation technique.

## *Monitoring*

An ongoing *control and evaluation system* is important in order to assess the success of the repositioning effort and to establish a change in strategic direction, if required. *Milestone reviews* are established on the basis of time, critical events, or the use of a predetermined amount of resources. Properly defined goals and performance measurement tools, such as the *balanced scorecard*, can keep management apprised of the strategy's success or failure on an ongoing basis.

## *Maintaining Flexibility*

In an increasingly complex and rapidly changing business environment, it is critical that the strategic plan be continually reviewed to assess its continuing relevance. A *premise control system* can be used to systematically determine if the premises on which a strategy is based are still valid. *Contingency plans* can be developed, to be activated if certain *trigger points* are reached (e.g., a competitor takes a predicted action). During both planning and implementation, *game theory* can be useful in predicting the impact of certain changes on major premises, and in making changes to the strategy as new information (e.g., a competitor's response to your actions) becomes available.

## *Summary*

To summarize, operating effectiveness means having the requisite skills necessary to provide a successful value proposition to customers.

The successful firm's approach to providing value to customers and enhancing value over time is to develop and maintain a number of core competencies. Each core competency represents a bundle of skills and technology which transcend any one product or service, and in fact, provide a platform for launching successful new products and services. Generally, the goal is to produce valued products and services as efficiently as possible.

In order to maintain and expand their core competencies, successful companies will continually benchmark their performance against that of the competition and perform to best practice levels for their industry. In order to concentrate firm resources on establishing and maintaining core competencies, non-core activities should be eliminated or outsourced to others.

In today's highly competitive world, achieving operating effectiveness is equivalent to putting up the "table stakes" necessary to stay in the game. In fact, as more firms build core competencies, the competitive advantage enjoyed by early pioneers in an industry may largely evaporate.

To achieve the "winning hand" of long-term profitability, a firm must establish sustainable competitive advantage. Competitive advantage may be based on an extension and redirection of existing core competencies or created entirely from whole cloth, based on a reading of future trends and customer preferences.

Choosing among strategic alternatives requires an assessment of the assets and infrastructure required to implement the alternatives. It may involve trade-offs between objectives as well as pose substantial risk to the firm.

A key consideration in the ultimate success of any strategic plan is implementation. The first, and often most critical, implementation issue is the organizational structure that the firm will utilize, and its compatibility with the strategic plan. Transition plans are also important, involving consideration of a variety of techniques, including internal growth, consolidation, and/or partnering with other firms. Implementation must also involve some form of continual monitoring to determine the extent to which the repositioning effort is succeeding and if it is not, whether a change in direction would be desirable. Above all, the implementation process must be flexible and responsive to changes in major premises upon which the plan is based.

While by no means perfect, strategic plans may be the best (and perhaps only) approach to realizing a firm's growth objectives and, in some cases, ensuring its economic survival.

## *Questions for Discussion*

The following questions are designed to explore the major issues introduced in this chapter.

1. How does the firm's industry influence the strategic planning process? What is the impact of the firm's stage in the evolutionary cycle?

2. What are the three postures that a firm can take when embarking on the strategic planning process?

3. Describe some of the key assumptions underlying strategic planning.

4. What are the three major groups at which strategic planning is directed?

5. Describe three major outcomes of successful strategic planning.

6. What are three fundamental questions that strategic planning attempts to address?

7. Define the following concepts related to strategic planning:
    a. "Effective" operations
    b. Value proposition
    c. Core competencies
    d. Customer "intimacy"
    e. Competitive space

8. What is the difference between internally and externally oriented strategic alternatives?

9. How should a firm deal with resource constraints in terms of its strategic planning efforts?

10. What quantitative measures can be used to value strategic planning alternatives?

11. How can strategic plans be successfully implemented, in terms of the following:
    a. Organization
    b. Transition
    c. Possible partnerships

12. How can the progress of strategic plan implementation be monitored?

# 17

# GENERAL GROWTH PROPERTIES, INC.[1]

## Public vs. Private Markets

John Bucksbaum pushed harder on the pedals as he climbed the long hill. It was a beautiful spring Sunday in 1998, and he was trying to better his time over a familiar course but continued to be distracted by thoughts from work, something he swore he wouldn't allow to happen. He returned home and after putting away his bicycle and showering, sat down to collect his thoughts and see if he couldn't come to some conclusions before Monday's meeting with his key managers.

John was EVP and Chief Administrative Officer of General Growth Properties, Inc., a public Real Estate Investment Trust (REIT) based in Chicago. He was the third generation of a family of Midwestern retailers who had built a small grocery store near Des Moines into a $5.6 billion public company that was the second largest owner and operator of regional shopping centers in the U.S.

General Growth had been a pioneer throughout this period in virtually all aspects of regional center development and operation. The Bucksbaums had also been involved in a variety of ownership vehicles – corporations, partnerships, REITs – on both a private and public basis, and were considered leaders and innovators in the shopping center industry.

---

[1] This case was prepared by John McMahan in 1998. All material in the case is deemed to be factual except for the circumstances of the management meeting and its consideration of various strategic alternatives, which was added to provide an educational context. Copyright © 1998 and 2004 by John McMahan, all rights reserved.

John had been concerned for some time with many of the trends affecting real estate in general and retail REITs in particular. He had asked his senior managers to be prepared to spend the better part of Monday discussing these trends and looking at various alternatives available to the firm. From this discussion, he would draft a report to Matthew Bucksbaum, the firm's CEO and his father, with recommendations regarding possible changes in General Growth's business strategy.

As he savored an Evian, John began reminiscing about the rich and colorful history of his family and recalling the events that had led up to tomorrow's meeting (Exhibit 1).

## The Early Years

Matthew Bucksbaum was discharged from the Army in 1946 and returned to his boyhood home in Marshalltown, Iowa, approximately 50 miles from Des Moines. He and his brothers, Martin and Maurice, joined their father in the operation of a 6,000 square foot (SF) super market. In 1949, Matthew graduated from college and rejoined the family business. The Bucksbaums then proceeded to expand their grocery business.

**Exhibit 1**
**General Growth Properties**
**Company History**

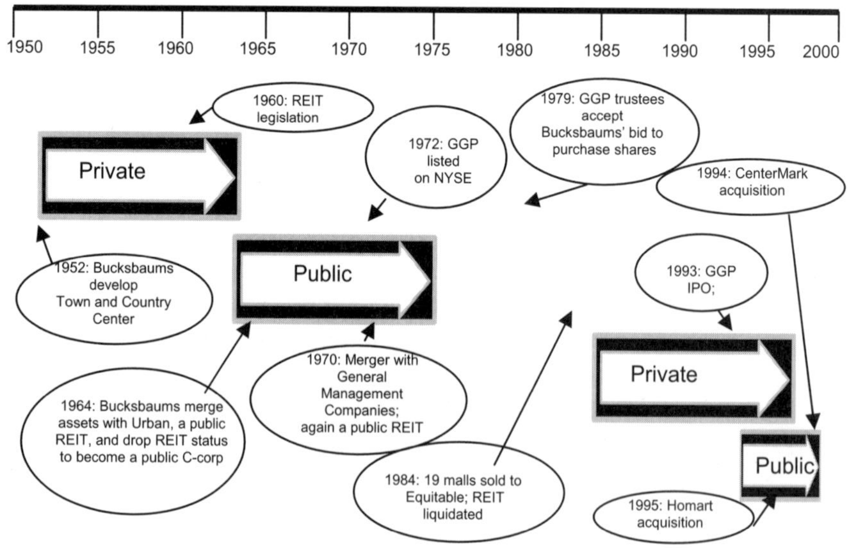

Timeline (1950–2000) events:
- 1952: Bucksbaums develop Town and Country Center
- 1960: REIT legislation
- 1964: Bucksbaums merge assets with Urban, a public REIT, and drop REIT status to become a public C-corp
- 1970: Merger with General Management Companies; again a public REIT
- 1972: GGP listed on NYSE
- 1979: GGP trustees accept Bucksbaums' bid to purchase shares
- 1984: 19 malls sold to Equitable; REIT liquidated
- 1993: GGP IPO
- 1994: CenterMark acquisition
- 1995: Homart acquisition

Phases: Private → Public → Private → Public

Source: General Growth Properties, Inc.

**Emergence of Shopping Centers:** Although the concept of a unified shopping complex first appeared in the early twentieth century, shopping centers really rose to prominence after World War II. Post-war growth of suburban populations and increased use of the automobile created demand for convenient, one-stop retail facilities outside of traditional and often congested urban centers.

Most of the projects built in the 1950s were strip centers catering to new suburban housing developments. A few were more innovative, offering enclosed pedestrian space, multiple levels, and full-line branches of downtown department stores as anchor tenants. Advances in shopping center design, tenant mix, and merchandising led to standard methods of project planning and recognition of the shopping center as a distinct land use and property type.[2]

**Town and Country Center:** The Bucksbaums were active leaders in this historical process. In 1952, the family began their evolution from retailer to retail developer when they became involved in the Town and Country Center, a well located 15-acre shopping center in Cedar Rapids, Iowa. The center was to be a neighborhood center anchored by the Bucksbaums' "CashWay" supermarket. It was becoming increasingly clear, however, that the original developer was not going to be able to proceed.

The developer proposed to sell the ground under the center to the Bucksbaums. Matthew recalled that they talked to an officer of Greenbaum Mortgage who advised "first get leases from national chains, and then we will help you find the money to build the project."[3]

The Bucksbaums improved on this formula by leasing the ground to an investor group, further leveraging the transaction. Additional stores were leased to W. T. Grant, Kinney Shoes, and F.W. Woolworth. They then secured a loan from Mass Mutual for $1 million at 4 1/8% for 30 years.

Construction of the project wasn't so easy. Costs exceed budget, and the Bucksbaums were placed under considerable financial pressure. Fortunately, Mass Mutual increased the mortgage to $1.2 million for another eighth of a point, and the center was completed and leased, thus creating the first community center in Iowa. Later, in assessing their mistakes, the Bucksbaums concluded that the center had a lot of "dead space" in the form of basements and second floor offices and it was essential that in the future, they focus on space that could be readily and efficiently leased.

---

[2] Urban Land Institute.
[3] All quotes attributed to individuals are based on interviews with General Growth management.

**Duck Creek Plaza:** In 1954, the family had sold their grocery stores to the Nash Finch Companies and became full time retail investor/developers. They moved to Bettendorf, another town near Des Moines, to build Duck Creek Plaza, an open mall anchored by Younkers Department Stores, a public company and one of Iowa's leading retailers. This would be the Bucksbaums' first shopping mall.

Over the next few years, the family developed a series of retail properties in Iowa, Illinois and Indiana, which were mostly downtown or shopping district commercial buildings under long term lease to the F. W. Woolworth Company and others.

During this period the Bucksbaums sharpened their business strategy and determined how it might be best achieved. They concluded that their major goal was *to maximize return on a real estate investment through the active development and management of new income producing properties*. They decided to concentrate on middle markets where they would have less competition.

To accomplish this strategy, the Bucksbaums believed they needed to control all aspects of day-to-day operations including land acquisition, planning and design, construction, leasing, and property management. Since all of these activities were interrelated and, to a large extent symbiotic, they believed their operations would require common, interwoven ownership of both investment and management entities.

**The REIT is Born:** In 1960, Congress passed the Real Estate Investment Trust Act creating a passive investment vehicle with certain tax avoidance features which its sponsors hoped would encourage long term investment in real estate by individual taxable investors.

REITs could be either investment trusts or 401C corporations managed by a board of directors or trustees. The majority of directors/trustees had to be independent of REIT management. Favorable tax treatment was obtained by annually electing REIT status, provided the firm met the following conditions:

- Have at least 100 shareholders. Five individuals could not own more than 50% of the stock (5/50 rule). [4]

- Seventy-five percent of assets must be in real estate equity, mortgages, REIT shares, or cash.

- Seventy-five percent of income must come from rents or mortgage interest.

---

[4] Congress subsequently passed legislation allowing the IRS to "look through" the pension fund structure and treat plan beneficiaries as individual shareholders. This effectively exempts pension funds from the 5/50 rule.

- No more than thirty percent of operating income can come from the sale of properties held less than 4 years.[5]
- Ninety-five percent of taxable income must be paid out annually.

While not a "pass through" vehicle such as traditional limited partnerships, REITs largely avoided taxation at the entity level by paying dividends on 95% of their net income, provided they qualified annually as a REIT. Shareholders then paid individual income taxes on that portion of the dividends which represented taxable income.

Most REITs in the early sixties were not internally managed and even in these cases, management did not participate extensively in stock ownership. There was little market activity and not much coverage from the financial community.

## Operating as a Public Company

By the mid-1960s, there were 7,600 shopping centers in the United States, some of which were large, enclosed, and temperature-controlled "regional malls."[6] These facilities drew customers from a broader market area by offering as many as three or four full-line department stores in addition to other retail categories -- a diverse selection previously available only in downtown retail areas. Enclosed malls were so popular and successful that by the latter half of the 1960s, many older open malls were being expanded and converted to the enclosed format.

**Decision to Go Public:** In 1964, the Bucksbaums made a decision to go public by merging their real estate interests with Urban America Real Estate Trust (Urban), which owned the assets and development rights to River Hills, a multiuse urban renewal project in Des Moines.

The Bucksbaums exchanged all of the capital stock in five Iowa Corporations for 300,000 shares of Urban's common stock, thus creating General Management Corporation (GMC). Shareholders in Urban received 6% Convertible Subordinated Debentures due in 1984. The $3 million offering was a best-effort, intrastate offering, which would subsequently trade over-the-counter on regional exchanges. A local underwriter – Iowa Underwriters, Inc. – handled the transaction.

Becoming a public corporation was not easy for the Bucksbaums, who had thus far financed the growth of their company with institutional project financing. A major factor in their success had been the close control of the entire development/management process. Their corporate culture was highly

---
[5] Congress subsequently passed legislation liberalizing this provision.
[6] International Council of Shopping Centers.

entrepreneurial with a strong emphasis on the ability to make rapid decisions. While they were concerned with the inevitable conflicts of interest that arose in a successful real estate operation, they decided that it was critical to their success that the entrepreneurial culture be maintained in the public company, disclosing any possible conflicts as they arose.

**Building an Organization:** The new company emerged with a mixed bag of assets including the Wakonda and College Square shopping centers, apartments, office buildings, and several development parcels. Six hundred thousand dollars were used to retire bank indebtedness with the remaining proceeds available for future development activity.

Matthew remembered Urban as a "public company with shareholders but with no one to lead it." This, of course, was exactly what the Bucksbaums intended to do. Martin and Matthew became the principal executive officers of the new company and embarked on an expansion program with a specialized development team capable of designing, building, leasing, and managing its own properties. GMC dropped its REIT status and operated as a "C" corporation. The availability of extensive Net Operating Losses (NOL) could shield shareholders from taxation for several years and the Bucksbaums believed that at the time, they needed the operating flexibility of a non-REIT format.

During this period, GMC became a regional shopping center developer/owner, largely as a result of a close working relationship with Younkers Department Store and Northwestern Mutual Life Insurance Company. Younkers, who had been an original investor in GMC, became a tenant in five GMC properties; Northwestern Mutual became a preferred lender on the firm's development projects.

**Merger with General Growth Properties**: In 1970, with NOL tax shelter running out, the Bucksbaums determined that it would be advantageous to its shareholders for the firm to elect REIT status though a merger with General Growth, a Des Moines based public REIT. In addition, the Bucksbaums organized the General Growth Management Companies (Management Companies) to acquire the assets of GMC that could not be owned by a REIT and entered into agreements for the management and operating services that a REIT could not perform for itself. As a part of the transaction, Maurice Bucksbaum sold his interests to Martin and Matthew and ceased to be an owner of the corporation. Piper, Jaffray & Hopwood, a Minneapolis investment banking firm, handled this transaction.

Over the next two years, the company increased the amount of leasable retail space from 2,186,000 to 3,746,000 square feet. Net Operating Income (NOI) increased from $2.0 to $2.8 million, and net income rose from $.43 to $.55

per share. The price of the stock increased from $6.75 to a high of $27.75. (See Exhibits 2 and 3 for a breakdown of operating data.)

**Exhibit 2
General Growth Properties
Leasable Space, 1965-72**

**(Thousands of SF)**

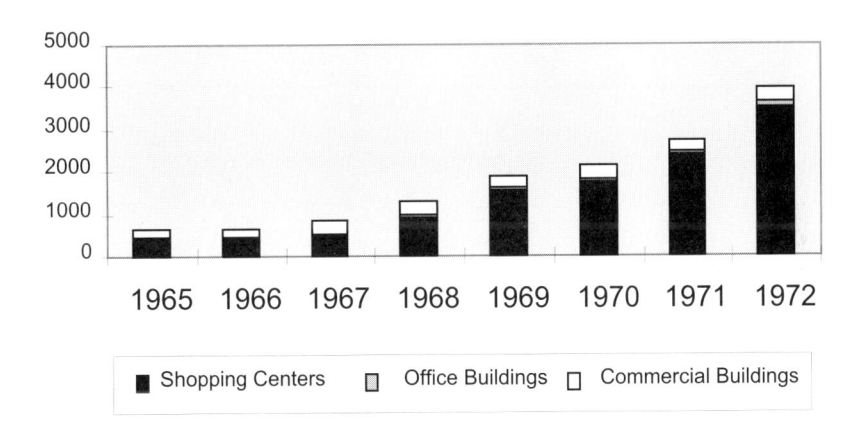

| Year | Total (approx.) |
|------|-----------------|
| 1965 | ~500 |
| 1966 | ~500 |
| 1967 | ~600 |
| 1968 | ~1300 |
| 1969 | ~1900 |
| 1970 | ~2200 |
| 1971 | ~2800 |
| 1972 | ~4000 |

■ Shopping Centers  ▫ Office Buildings  ▫ Commercial Buildings

Source: General Growth Properties, Inc.

**Continued Growth of Regional Centers:** By 1972 the number of shopping centers in the United States had risen to 13,174.[7] As competition among retail properties intensified, new formulas were promoted to attract customers. In addition to retail stores, developers also explored "mixed-use" opportunities, combining retail with other property types such as hotel, office, or residential.

Competition within the industry also encouraged tenant mixes that catered to consumers of a particular income bracket. Many centers situated near an affluent neighborhood became "fashion centers" with high-end department stores surrounded by small boutique shops. Other centers replaced their traditional anchor tenants with discount department stores in order to better compete on price. These centers often included hardware, home improvement, and drug stores that had traditionally operated from freestanding buildings.

---

[7] International Council of Shopping Centers.

## Exhibit 3
### General Growth Properties, 1972

**Real Estate Investments**
- Office Buildings 5%
- Motels 13%
- Commercial Buildings 3%
- Shopping Centers 57%
- Apartments 22%

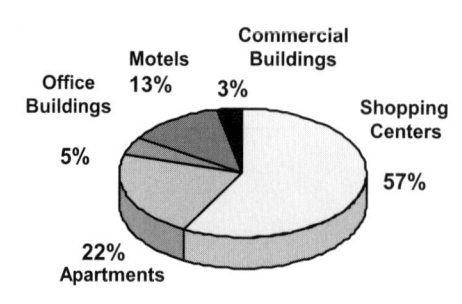

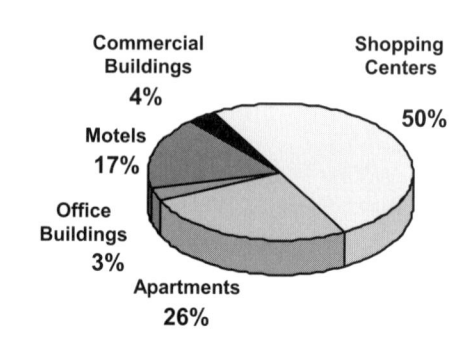

**Real Estate Revenues**
- Commercial Buildings 4%
- Shopping Centers 50%
- Motels 17%
- Office Buildings 3%
- Apartments 26%

**Net Income from Real Estate**
- Commercial Buildings 1%
- Shopping Centers 50%
- Motels 42%
- Office Buildings 4%
- Apartments 3%

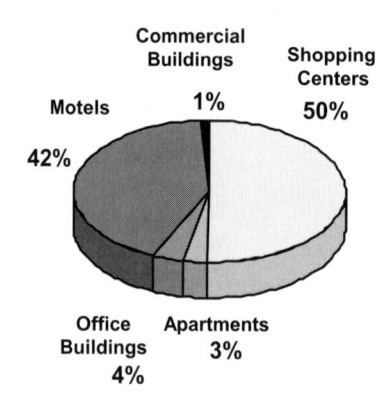

**Cash Flow from Real Estate**
- Commercial Buildings 0%
- Shopping Centers 54%
- Motels 35%
- Office Buildings 4%
- Apartments 7%

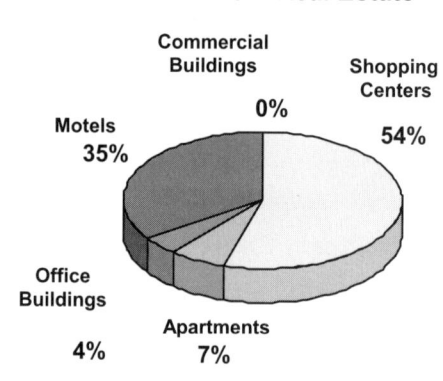

Source: General Growth Properties, Inc.

**Secondary Offering:** In 1972, the Bucksbaums decided to tap the secondary market in order to provide a broader source of capital for the continued growth of the firm. Approximately $21 million was raised, which, after paying down debt, generated a little over $11 million for expanded operations. Piper, Jaffray, and Hopwood, believing that they needed additional market clout, called in Goldman Sachs to lead the underwriting.

Following the offering, the company applied for listing of its shares on the New York Stock Exchange, and changed its name to General Growth Properties, Inc. (General Growth).

**REIT Market Disaster:** In the late 1960s, Wall Street had begun shifting the emphasis of REIT Initial Public Offerings (IPO) from long-term equity investments to short-term mortgage investments, largely in the form of construction loans. Mortgage REITs were the largest single source of capital funding for the 1971-75 real estate "boom," largely borrowing short and lending long in order to arbitrage the yield curve. This bubble collapsed in the mid-seventies and REITs became tarred with a negative image that they would not overcome for almost 20 years. Not all of this was investor perception – REIT *market values had declined by two thirds from their 1972 highs.*

## Operating as a Private Company

**The Decision to Go Private:** The REIT market collapse reduced investors' interest in REITs and while not devastating to General Growth, placed downward pressure on the company's share price.

The Bucksbaums decided that the timing might be propitious to take the company private again. Matthew recalled that "cap rates were going down, and the public market didn't seem to recognize the increase in underlying values. Since this was before the wide-spread use of Funds From Operations (FFO), investors seemed to have difficulty focusing on cash flow rather than net income."

On December 1, 1978, the Bucksbaums offered to purchase the equity interest of the trust for $28 per share. After some negotiation, the Bucksbaums and the Trustees entered into a merger agreement on April 6, 1979, to merge at a price of $30 per share. Goldman Sachs advised the Trust on the fairness of the transaction.

**Hostile Offer:** On June 1, 1979, Marathon U.S. Holdings, Inc., the U.S. real estate affiliate of Canadian Pacific Investments, Ltd., submitted a hostile cash offer of $35 per share. Although the Marathon offer was relatively free of conditions, Marathon was unable to secure a release from Aetna Life and Casualty (Aetna), who held mortgages on ten of the Trust's properties.

On July 16, 1979, the Bucksbaums made a cash merger proposal at $35.50 per share, which was immediately accepted by the Trustees. Noting that this price was higher than the shares had ever traded and was 50% over the last closing price prior to the announcement of the Bucksbaums' original proposal, Goldman Sachs determined that it was a "fair" price.

The Bucksbaums originally had planned to sell the 10 Aetna-financed shopping centers to the insurance company after the merger transaction closed. The sale was accelerated to consummate prior to close of the merger transaction and was approved by the Trustees on September 17, 1979.

**Class Action Suit:** On September 28, 1979, a class action suit was filed against the Trust and the Bucksbaums for failing to adequately consider the Marathon proposal. The suit sought to enjoin the Aetna transaction.

The class action suit was ultimately settled and in early 1980, Aetna Life and Casualty paid General Growth $265 million for 10 malls with over 4 million square feet of retail space. Four years later, the Company sold an additional 19 malls to Equitable for $800 million, which was the equivalent of $42 per share.[8]

Although many of these properties continued to be operated by the management company, the REIT shrunk to little more than a shell, and by 1985 its stock had ceased trading.

**Rebuilding the Company:** The next year Martin and Matthew formed a new company, General Growth Companies, Inc. (GGC). As a result of high interest rates, capital was scarce and if available, very expensive. Also, as a result of overbuilding, development risks were increasing significantly. The Bucksbaums also watched with interest as institutions, particularly pension funds, took an increasing interest in direct real estate investment.

In 1989, Equitable suggested that GGC purchase the Center Companies, a property management firm which operated an extensive portfolio of the insurance company's properties. Center Companies had failed as a developer and as Matthew recalled, the people at Equitable were certain that the Bucksbaums "could do a lot for this company."

With GGC's purchase of the Center Companies, the Bucksbaums' management company, General Growth Management (GGM), became the second largest manager of shopping center facilities in the United States. In addition to its management operations, GGC was actively developing shopping centers and by 1993 had accumulated a portfolio of 21 properties.

In 1990, in order to provide access to capital and diversify risk, GGC formed a development partnership with the IBM pension fund, Wells Fargo Bank, and The Frank Russell Company. The new partnership established a revolving line of credit for the development of new properties. Each project had to meet rigorous criteria established by the partnership committee but once approved, GGC had wide latitude to proceed with the project.

The relationship with Wells Fargo turned out to be beneficial to both firms. When Wells Fargo was under intense scrutiny by Federal regulators in the late 1980s, GGC voluntarily accelerated payment of loans in order to assist the bank in meeting higher capital requirements.

---

[8] General Growth Properties, Inc.

## Changing Retail Patterns

While the Bucksbaums continued to grow their private company, major shifts were occurring in the retail industry. Driven by technological innovation and America's ever-changing buying habits, this evolution spawned a dynamic market for retail space in which the appearance of new properties consistently eroded the profitability of older ones.

**The Over-storing of America**: The 1980s witnessed an unprecedented "boom" in shopping center construction with more than 16,000 completed during the decade.[9] Although the majority of these new projects were small neighborhood centers, shoppers were increasingly drawn to the wider selection of stores offered by large "super regional" centers (larger than 800,000 SF).

Annual increases in the supply of retail space, which included new construction and renovation of older space, reached an all time high in 1985, decreased until 1988, and then peaked again at 230 million square feet in 1989.[10] After a 30% drop during the recession of 1991, new supply rose steadily to 260 million square feet in 1995. By 1996 there were approximately 20 feet of retail space per capita in the United States, twice the level of the early 1970s.[11]

**New Threats:** This "boom" in retail space, together with changing American lifestyle preferences and evolution in the economics of retail distribution, created serious challenges for the shopping center industry. Fundamentally, retail tenants were changing how they used space. The trend toward dual income households and longer working hours increased the premium that consumers placed on the convenience of fast, one-stop shopping for products that were competitively priced. Retailers responded by seeking larger spaces, offering greater inventory selection, and pursuing aggressive pricing policies.

Developers countered by creating "power" centers and freestanding big box warehouse stores which competed directly with shopping centers. In the early 1990s, large freestanding retail construction averaged 79 million square feet per year – more than double the average in the 1980s.[12]

Evidence suggested that the new discount stores captured market share directly from department stores. From 1987 to 1994, traditional department stores' share of merchandise, apparel, and furniture sales fell from over 21%

---

[9] International Council of Shopping Centers.
[10] Anthony Downs, "The Painful Evolution of Today's Retail Markets", The Brookings Institution.
[11] Downs, ibid.
[12] International Council of Shopping Centers.

to approximately 15% while large discount department stores' market share grew from around 16% to about 21%.[13]

This trend had the greatest impact on smaller commercial centers (less than 400,000 SF), which could not efficiently offer the selection of newer retail formats. In 1986, both smaller commercial centers and super regional malls posted approximately $190 in inflation adjusted sales per square foot.[14] By 1994, however, smaller centers' sales had fallen to about $158, and large malls' sales had risen to approximately $198 (see Appendix A-1 for general shopping center statistics). Many existing facilities were becoming obsolete.

**The Impact of Technology:** The shift of retail operations to power centers and free standing buildings was facilitated by advances in retail-related technologies. Inventory management innovations such as bar-coding and on-line measurement systems allowed retailers to reduce off-shelf inventory. Retailers, therefore, required less space for the storage of goods and were able to commit more space to merchandising. This trend benefited retailers at both ends of the size spectrum: larger stores could carry a wider variety of goods and smaller, more specialized stores could be located closer to the markets they served. The result was that both large and small retailers sought spaces that were frequently not compatible with existing shopping center facilities.

## REITs Change As Well

**The "New REITs":** Largely as a result of the debacle of the 1970s, REITs missed the real estate "bubble" of the 1980s. In the subsequent collapse of the real estate markets at the end of the decade, all forms of capital for real estate evaporated. Developers and investors found themselves with highly leveraged properties, often built with short-term financing, and no source of refinancing. With interest rates falling and real estate yields rising, Wall Street saw an opportunity to arbitrage private and public markets. (See Appendices A-2 and A-3)

The Kimco offering in late 1991 was the first sign that REITs could play a major role in financing real estate and, more importantly, real estate operating companies. During 1991, eight IPOs involving REITs raised $808 million. A similar number were completed in 1992, raising $919 million.[15]

While this was meaningful investment activity, particularly in a capital-starved real estate market, 1993 proved to be a real turning point – 75 equity IPOs raised $11.1 billion. Excluding placements of less than $50 million, 39 IPOs were completed raising $8.2 billion, approximately 14% of total IPO activity

---
[13] Alex Brown & Sons, Real Estate Securities, November 24, 1995.
[14] Merrill Lynch, Shopping Center Perspectives, September 13, 1995.
[15] NAREIT.

in the entire securities market for the year. This amount represented more real estate capital than from any other source.

**New REITs Were Different:** Perhaps more significantly, the character of the 1993 IPOs was dramatically different. Virtually all represented vertically integrated real estate operating companies specializing by property type. The new REITs were also significantly larger – ten equity REITs had market capitalization of over $500 million (versus two at the end of 1991), and 40 had capitalization exceeding $200 million (versus ten in 1991). Almost two thirds of new and proposed REITs were structured as Umbrella Operating Partnership REITs (UPREITs), in which the REIT and the original investor each owned an interest in an Operating Partnership (OP), an approach utilized to reduce the tax impact on selling investors.

Most of the 1993 IPOs were internally managed and in many cases, management had significant equity positions, thus minimizing conflicts and enhancing congruency with investors. Most of the management groups had spent their careers specializing in a particular property type and had effectively worked together as a team for many years, including at least one full real estate cycle (Exhibit 4).

**Exhibit 4**
**"Old" vs. "New" REITS**

| Old REITs | New REITs |
|---|---|
| • 1960 - 1992 | • 1992 - 1998 |
| • Passive investments | • Operating company |
| • Externally administered | • Self-administered |
| • Institutional sponsors | • Entrepreneur sponsors |
| • Small mgmt. ownership | • Large mgmt. ownership |
| • Diversified portfolio | • Focused portfolio |
| • Small capital base | • Larger capital base |
| • Little analyst coverage | • More analyst coverage |

At year-end 1993, the REIT market reflected many of the changes occurring at the individual firm level. Total market capitalization of all REITs increased to $31.6 billion. The 30 largest REITs represented $15.1 billion versus $8.6 billion at the beginning of the year.[16]

---

[16] NAREIT.

## Operating as a Public Company II

By the end of 1991, GGC owned 18 regional malls in middle markets throughout the country. Revenue for the year was $103.8 million with NOI of $61.8 million and a cash loss of ($3.6) million.

**The Decision to Go Public (again):** In 1992, GGC had just completed its first project for the IBM investment partnership. On a flight to Seattle to meet with the Frank Russell people, Martin and John discussed trends in the industry.

"With less demand for new malls" Martin said, "we're going to be faced with less need for development. The future is going to go to those firms that can acquire existing centers rather than develop. To do this successfully will require vast amounts of capital – much more than we can raise through investment partnerships."

"What do you think we should do?" John inquired.

Martin replied: "Maybe we should become a public REIT again. Taubman has been able to do it, and we have even more experience operating as a public company."[17]

John, who had spent 10 years learning all aspects of the company's operations, replied, "If we're going to do this, I want to be a part of it."

Martin said, "Is this what you want to do?"

"Yes."

And this was the way it was. Martin and Matthew, who could have "cashed in their chips" at this stage, believed that John was ready to assume greater responsibility in the company they had created and which had been an integral part of their lives for the past 40 years.

Over the next year, John took the lead in moving the firm towards an IPO. In April 1993, the Bucksbaums' reconstruction of GGC culminated in a new General Growth Properties REIT through an IPO of nearly 19 million shares of stock at $22 per share. (See Exhibits 5 & 6 for a breakdown of operating data and a map of property locations; see Appendices B-1, B-2 and B-3 for financial data.)

The Bucksbaums had originally planned to use Merrill Lynch as their underwriter. Merrill had pioneered the new REIT underwritings, but Goldman persisted and finally won the business. General Growth was the first of the new REITs to use Goldman, and this opportunity would prove to

---

[17] A. Alfred Taubman, founder of the Taubman Centers REIT.

be the investment banking firm's opening into the emerging REIT underwriting market.

In reminiscing over the public issue, Matthew and John later recalled, "Investors remember two things: those who made them money and those who lost them money. Any of our original investors in 1970 who held until 1985 received a 24% annual compounded return. We had always made money for our investors and they remembered it." As perhaps a testimony to this view, General Growth came out at the lowest yield of any of the new REIT IPOs to date.[18]

Taxes were also an important issue. Similar to Taubman, the Bucksbaums utilized an UPREIT structure which allowed them to defer taxes until the OP units were converted to shares in General Growth. "In light of our personal tax situation, it was the only way it could have been done," Matthew recalled, "although we certainly did not foresee the later use of OP units as a currency for acquisitions."

**Exhibit 5**
**General Growth Properties Operating Data, 1989-93**

Shopping Centers Owned

Real Estate Assets at Cost ($K)

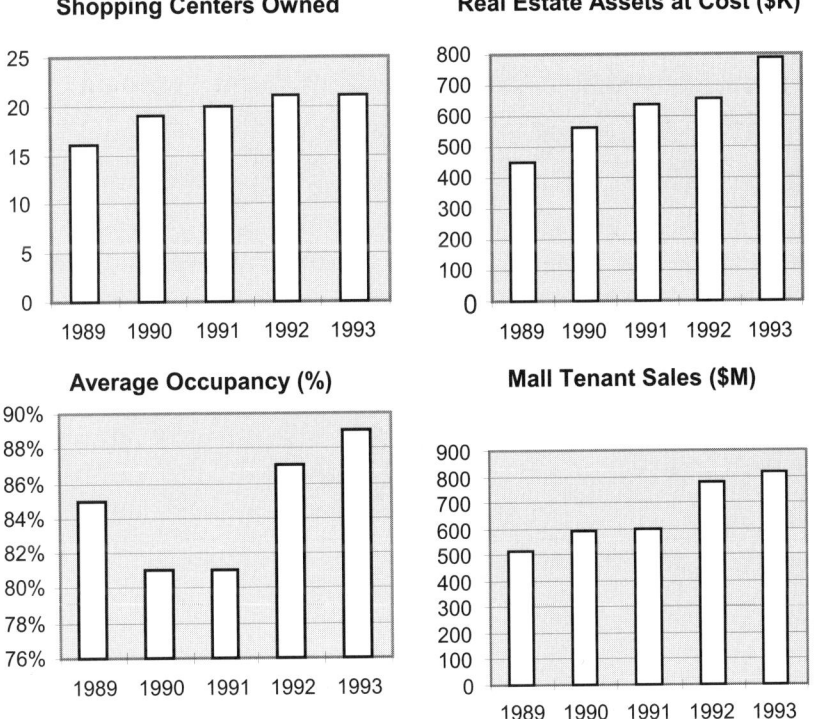

Average Occupancy (%)

Mall Tenant Sales ($M)

Source: General Growth Properties, Inc.

---

[18] General Growth Corporation, Inc.

Not all of the Bucksbaum family's assets were exchanged for REIT shares. In conjunction with the IPO, the Bucksbaums established GGP Limited Partnership (GGP) which controlled 100% of the 21 malls. General Growth owned a majority interest in the GGP Limited Partnership with Martin and Matthew Bucksbaum and a Trust for the Bucksbaum family holding the remaining minority positions.

**CenterMark:** In February, 1994 General Growth acquired a 40% interest in CenterMark Properties, Inc., the regional mall arm of the Prudential Insurance Company (Prudential), which had financed seven of General Growth's malls.

Earlier, Martin had told Frank McDougal of Prudential, "You shouldn't be in the mall business; if you ever want to sell, call me." Prudential had weighed taking the portfolio public but the IPO window was not as attractive as it had been earlier. Recognizing underlying values, General Growth was willing to pay a better return than the public market and ultimately did.

**Exhibit 6
General Growth Properties
Initial Portfolio Sites, 1993**

Source: General Growth Properties, Inc.

Martin was concerned with the size of the transaction in light of the fact that General Growth was a relatively new public company. At the time, a $182 million transaction represented one of the largest acquisitions by a REIT in U.S. history, a deal that immediately added 19 malls and qualitative and geographic diversification to General Growth's portfolio.[19]

In recalling the transaction, John said "We wanted to get in and out quickly. Prudential had invested a lot of money they couldn't get out. If we could enhance value in the portfolio, we could harvest it for our shareholders."

Three years later General Growth sold the CenterMark portfolio for a $108 million profit.

**Homart:** The funds from the CenterMark sale and a secondary offering of 4.5 million shares helped fuel another even larger transaction – a $1.85 billion investment in Homart, an indirect subsidiary of Sears, Roebuck and Co., on December 22, 1995. General Growth purchased 38% of Homart for $200 million, which added an ownership interest in 25 regional malls, two new malls under construction, and several future development sites.

The Homart transaction was widely marketed and attracted considerable interest in the real estate community. Sears, however, wanted certainty of closure and since they had done over 40 deals with the Bucksbaums, knew they could perform.

With the purchase of Homart, the Bucksbaums formed a new management company, General Growth Management, Inc. (GGMI), in which GGP held a 95% equity interest. The remaining 5% of the equity and 100% of GGMI's voting rights were controlled by GGP's senior management. GGMI purchased the Bucksbaums' management company, General Growth Management, and left the Bucksbaums with a substantial interest in both the REIT and its primary property manager.

Several weeks before the announcement of the Homart purchase, Martin Bucksbaum passed away. Martin's position as Chairman and CEO was assumed by his brother Matthew, who had previously held the position of President.

## *Current Trends in Retailing*

**Economic Trends:** By 1997, the best news for retailing continued to come from one of the longest sustained economic cycles in modern U.S. history, which seemed to overpower other more negative changes in the retail outlook.

As a result of high employment, real gains in wages, and a booming stock market, nearly $300 billion in new purchasing power was injected into the

---

[19] The ownership structure was split General Growth: 40%; Westfield: 40%; and Goldman Sachs: 20%.

economy.[20] At the end of 1997, consumer confidence was at its highest level in 10 years.[21] Retail sales for the year crossed the $2.5 trillion mark for the first time (Exhibit 7).

Countervailing this good news were further increases in the level of consumer debt and a sharp increase in personal bankruptcies during the year. It also wasn't clear what impact the economic collapse of Asia would have on retail trends. Lower-cost imports could conceivably whet shopper interest in purchasing more goods as well as fatten the profit margins of U.S. firms with Asian production. On the other hand, a shift to more imported products could adversely impact American jobs and consumer confidence.

**Demographic Trends:** The Baby Boomer generation was 34-50 years old and as it aged, would continue to shift from retail to other types of expenditures such as travel, entertainment, etc. The Baby Bust generation was 22-33 years old and could not be expected to add much to new retail demand. The Echo Boom generation (21 years or younger) could be expected to significantly stimulate retail sales beginning in 2005-2010.

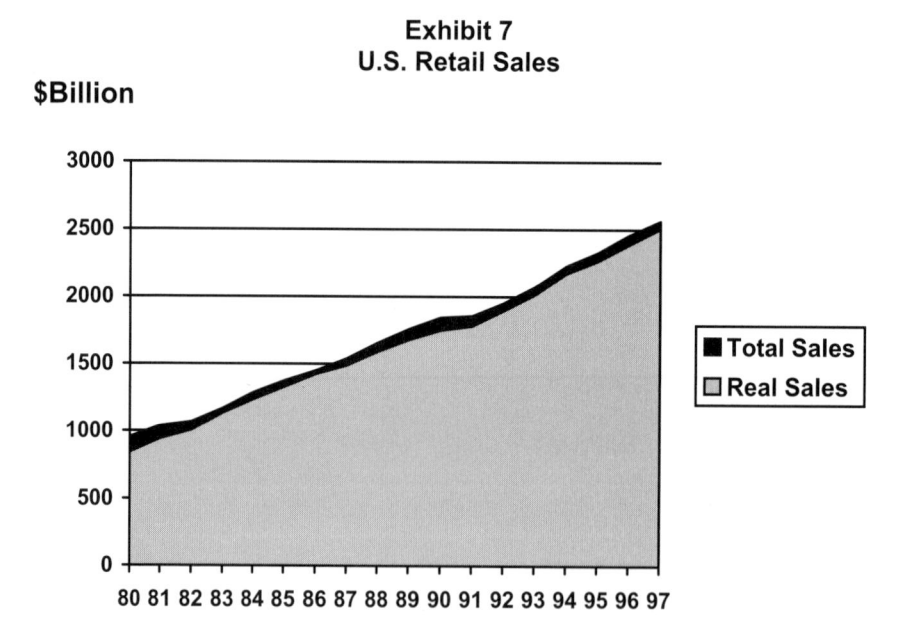

**Exhibit 7**
**U.S. Retail Sales**

Source: U.S. Department of Commerce.

---

[20] Landauer Associates, Inc., Real Estate Market Forecast, 1998.
[21] Prudential Investments, Real Estate Outlook 1998, February 5, 1998.

With a large proportion of new population growth coming from immigration, many retailers were attempting to develop new formats to access these burgeoning markets. Barring changes in legislation, rising immigrant incomes were expected to provide stimulus to retail sales for many years to come.

**Changing Shopping Patterns:** Consumer shopping patterns also continued to change with fewer trips and less spending per trip. The aging of the boomers, as well as the shift to more casual business and entertainment environments, had led to major changes in the apparel industry. Reflecting fundamental changes occurring in the broader society, the "shelf life" of retail formats dropped from 10-15 years to around 5-7 years.[22] Consumers also increasingly wanted to be "entertained" when they shopped.

**Retailers:** In 1997, successful retailers continued to focus on differentiating themselves from the competition by building strong brand image, opening new store formats, and the use of non-shopping center channels of distribution such as airports, highway service outlets, entertainment centers, etc.

Although discount chains such as Bradlees and Caldor suffered the greatest impact of the turmoil in retailing, 1997 seemed to indicate that a more general shake-out was developing. Long time retailers such as Montgomery Ward, Levitz, County Seat, Old America, Wiz Inc, and others filed for bankruptcy. Others, such as Musicland, Grand Union, Shopko, and Service Merchandise received a downgrading of their credit rating.[23]

One of the brighter aspects of the retail industry was the relative stabilization of the department store sector after many years of consolidation. More and more, department stores were demonstrating that they could compete effectively with discount chains and big box retailers.

**New Threat from Technology:** Technology's new threat to retail properties stemmed from its ability to facilitate shopping through non-store channels. The rapid growth in catalogue sales clearly demonstrated that shoppers did not have to be in stores to make purchases. The emergence of TV shopping and e-commerce offered consumers direct access to manufacturers, service companies, and start-up companies with little capital. This potentially explosive link promised to alter the fundamental shopping experience, impacting both traditional real estate shopping venues as well as existing retail firms.

---

[22] Prudential, ibid.
[23] Prudential, op. cit.

## Current Trends in Shopping Center Investment

**Demand and Supply Patterns**: New retail construction was up 2.5% in 1997, further increasing the supply of retail space per capita. Although a large portion of the space was being built to replace obsolete retail formats and locations, the overall mass of retail space could be expected to place a damper on shopping center economics for the next several years.

During the first nine months of 1997, $4.2 billion in new capital flowed into the retail sector for the acquisition of existing properties. The greatest increase in demand was for centers in the 150,000-300,000 SF range. Location continued to be a large factor in property selection, as retailers indicated a continuing willingness to pay for prime locations.[24]

**Shopping Centers**: At the end of 1997, there were 42,874 shopping centers in the U.S., up 2.0% from 1996. The total leasable retail area of these centers was 5.23 billion SF, an increase of 2.5% over 1996. Over 10 million people were employed in shopping centers, a figure representing approximately 8% of non-farm employment.[25]

During 1997, shopping center sales increased 5% to $1,019.3 billion, which represented 40% of total retail sales in the nation. On a square footage basic, however, real growth in shopping center sales was flat, thus continuing the negative pattern of the past decade and reflecting the persisting overhang of excess space (Exhibit 8).

**Exhibit 8**
**The Retail Market**
**Completion Rate vs. Total Employment Growth**

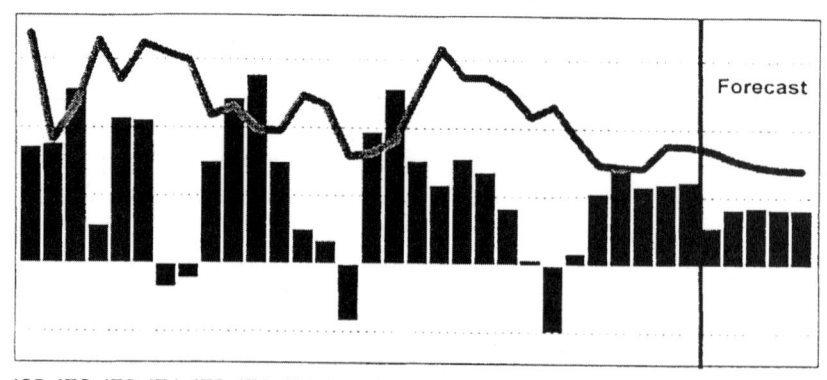

Source: CB Commercial/Torto Wheaton Research

---

[24] Prudential, op. cit.
[25] International Council of Shopping Centers.

**Regional Mall Development:** New regional mall construction continued to be very limited in 1997, thus indicating the demand for other types of formats (e.g., power centers, big boxes, free standing stores, etc.) while continuing department store consolidation made it difficult to attract stabilized anchor tenants. Responding to consumers' desires, many mall owners introduced entertainment formats including movie theater complexes, theme restaurants, food courts, and amusement/recreation areas. Unfortunately, many of these new tenants paid lower rents and often represented higher credit risks.

**Real Estate Yields:** In 1997, yields on retail properties continued to substantially lag other property types in terms of both cash income and property value appreciation. Although income returns appeared to be stabilizing, the retail sector had lost almost 30% of its value since 1990. Going-in cap rates for quality shopping centers increased 190 basis points between 1990 and mid-1997[26] but then turned down as more and more capital was chasing a declining number of investment opportunities (Exhibit 9).

**Exhibit 9**
**Annual Real Growth in U.S. Shopping Center Sales/SF**

Percent

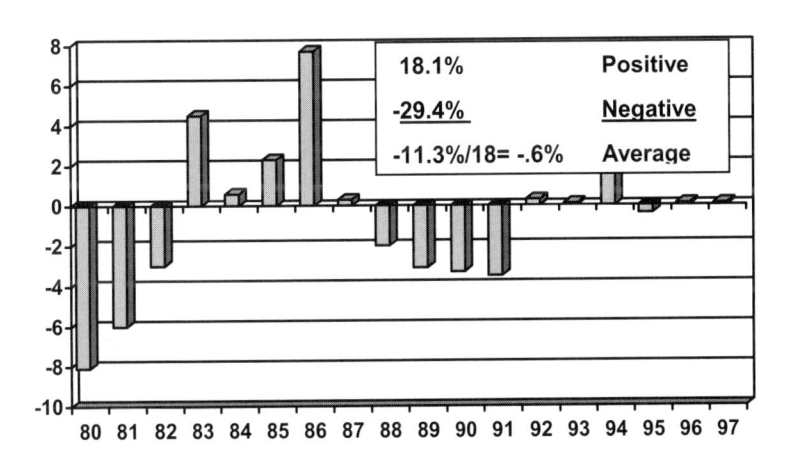

| | | |
|---|---|---|
| 18.1% | | Positive |
| -29.4% | | Negative |
| -11.3%/18= -.6% | | Average |

Source: ICSC, The McMahan Group.

Investors continued to reduce the spread between anticipated cash yields and total return, a trend that reflected an increasingly negative view of the appreciation potential of regional shopping centers (Exhibit 10).

---

[26] Real Estate Research Corporation (see Appendix A-3).

## Exhibit 10
### Regional Mall Investment Criteria

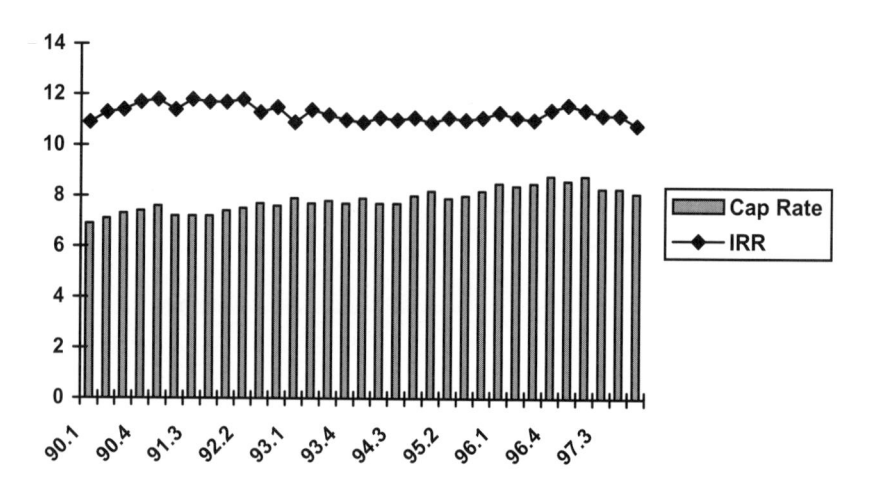

**Percent**

[Bar and line chart showing Cap Rate (bars) and IRR (line) from 90.1 to 97.3. Cap Rate ranges roughly 7–8%, IRR ranges roughly 11–12%.]

Source: Real Estate Research Corporation.

Regionally, the West and Mid-West exhibited the strongest improvement in total return, followed by the East and South where value deterioration was the greatest. In terms of shopping formats, super-regional and regional malls' lag behind other property types indicated vulnerability to changes in retailing as well as continuing high levels of new construction of non-mall projects.

A bright spot in 1997 was the continuing interest of investors in Class A regional malls where premier location and strong management appeared to represent the best opportunity for consistent earnings and long-term growth in asset value. Recognizing this, several cross-merchandising agreements were established during the year between quality malls and credit card issuers. The Taubman Companies and Corporate Property Investors announced a strategic alliance with American Express to provide shopping incentives at 40 shopping centers nationally. Simon DeBartolo Group announced a cash-back cross marketing program with VISA. These and other steps indicated the competitive advantage enjoyed by quality regional malls. Many of these properties were trading at cap rates under 8%.[27]

---

[27] Prudential, op. cit.

## Current Trends in the REIT Industry

By 1997, most successful REITs were fully integrated operating companies rather than the passive conduits envisioned by Congress 38 years earlier. Most were focused by property type and geographical area, although this aspect began changing as larger national firms came onto the scene through mergers and acquisitions. Retail and apartments continued to comprise the major property types, although office, industrial, hotels, and diversified REITs had grown rapidly during the year. Economic scale also became important as larger REITs reduced their cost of capital and spread operating costs over a larger base.

**Valuation:** REIT earnings were typically measured in terms of Funds From Operations (FFO), which is net income (GAAP) plus depreciation and amortization less gain (loss) on sale of investments. Stock prices were generally compared to FFO flows in much the same way as price/earnings ratios are used for non-real estate stocks. More recently, many analysts had begun adjusting FFO for capital expenditures and the impact of floating rate debt. This modification was given the term Adjusted Funds From Operations (AFFO).

REITs were also valued in terms of their premium or discount to Net Asset Value (NAV). Better performing REITs were generally rewarded with premium pricing, a result that reflected the market's perception of greater enterprise value and established the foundation for enhanced future AFFO growth.

Other factors that analysts and investors tracked were "payout ratios" (percent of AFFO paid out as dividends), "total debt to total capitalization;" the proportion of floating debt in the capital structure; management compensation; and the alignment of management's interest with shareholders.

**Enterprise Value:** As a tax-avoidance vehicle, REITs should be expected to trade on the yield of underlying real estate assets less a liquidity discount. By 1997, however, many successful REITs sold for more than their underlying real estate values, thus reflecting a premium for the "enterprise value" inherent in a "going concern." Such a premium reflected the market's belief in management's ability to grow future FFO through market and asset selection, development, refinancing, or restructuring investments (Exhibit 11).[28]

**Pension Fund Investment:** Despite the promise of the new REIT investment format, pension fund interest was slow to develop. Research on early REITs indicated that they performed in a manner similar to small cap stocks, not real estate. This implied that pension funds could not rely on a

---

[28] In many REIT valuation models, enterprise value is represented by ($\Delta g$) or "delta gee."

low or negative correlation with equities to reduce overall portfolio risk. More recent studies challenged this conclusion, maintaining that modern REITs had a higher level of real estate "effect" and could help to improve portfolio risk-adjusted returns, although not to the extent possible through private real estate investment.[29]

**Exhibit 11**
**Regional Mall Investment Anticipated Appreciation Component (IRR - Cap Rate)**

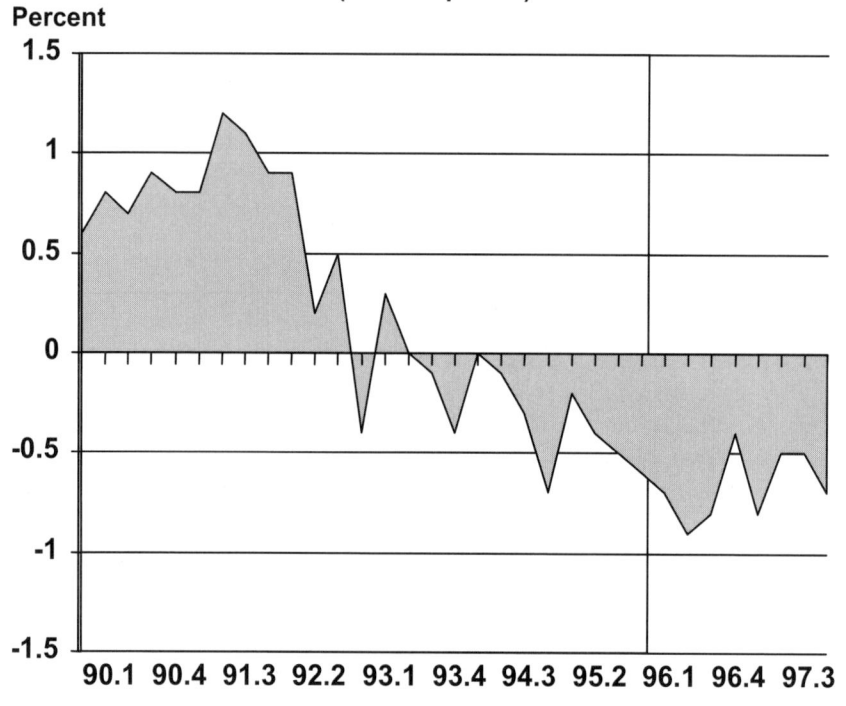

Source: Real Estate Research Corporation.

As a result of these studies, as well as continued growth in the REIT market, pensions' investment in securitized real estate went from virtually nothing in 1989 to over 25% of their total real estate portfolios by 1997.[30]

**REIT Market:** At the end of 1997, there were 210 REITs with a total equity market capitalization of $140.5 billion, almost 9 times the 1992 capitalization

---

[29] For an example, see S. Michael Giliberto and Anne Mengden "REITs and Real Estate: Two Markets Reexamined", Real Estate Research, December 1995.
[30] AEW Capital Management.

when the new REIT era began. Over 80% of these were equity REITs with a total market capitalization of $127.8 billion[31] (Exhibit 12).

Retail comprised the largest component of the market (22%), followed by residential (21%), office (18%), industrial (12%), hotels (8%), and diversified (4%) (Exhibit 13).

**Capital Inflows:** Of the $77.4 billion in new capital that has been raised by REITs since 1993, approximately two thirds were from secondary or "follow on" issues (Exhibit 14).

**Exhibit 12**
**REIT Equity Market Capitalization**

Equity REITs $127.8 billion

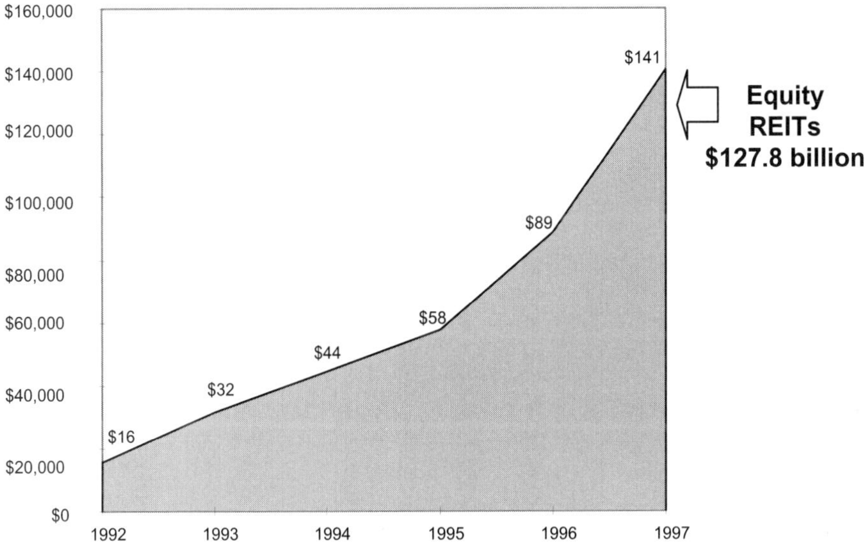

Source: NAREIT.

During 1997, office industrial IPOs represented 54% of the capital raised, followed by mortgage REITs (23%), triple net lease firms (8%), and retail (6%). Secondary offerings comprised almost three fourths of the capital raised for the year, they and were led by office industrial (38%), apartment (18%), retail (14%), and hotel (11%) (Exhibit 15).

---

[31] NAREIT.

**Exhibit 13
REIT Equity Market Cap by Property Type
December 31, 1997**

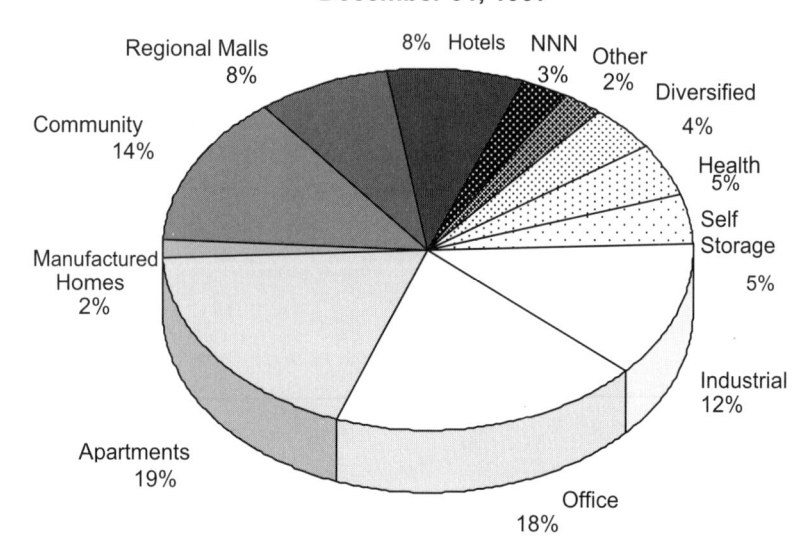

- Regional Malls 8%
- Hotels 8%
- NNN 3%
- Other 2%
- Diversified 4%
- Health 5%
- Self Storage 5%
- Industrial 12%
- Office 18%
- Apartments 19%
- Manufactured Homes 2%
- Community 14%

Source: NAREIT.

**Exhibit 14
REIT IPOs and Secondary Offerings**

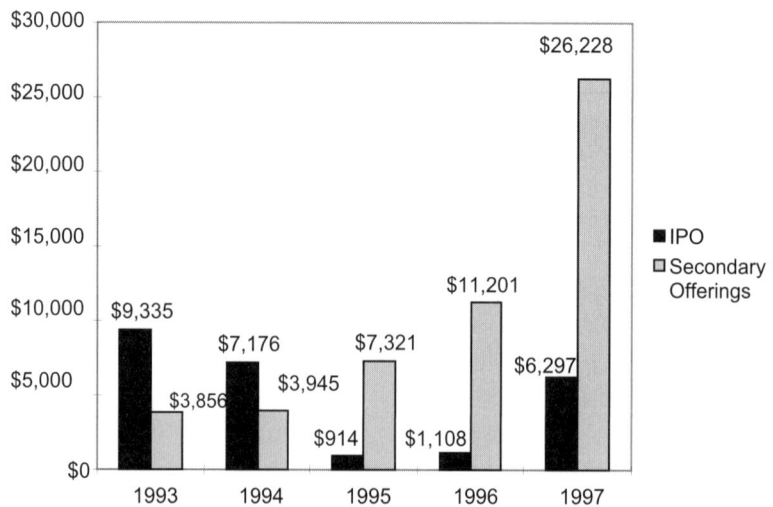

| Year | IPO | Secondary Offerings |
|---|---|---|
| 1993 | $9,335 | $3,856 |
| 1994 | $7,176 | $3,945 |
| 1995 | $914 | $7,321 |
| 1996 | $1,108 | $11,201 |
| 1997 | $6,297 | $26,228 |

Source: NAREIT, Analysis - The McMahan Group

## Exhibit 15
### REIT IPOs and Secondary Offerings, 1997

**Initial Public Offerings**

- Diversified 2%
- Other 6%
- NNN 8%
- Retail 6%
- Mortgage 23%
- Apartment 1%
- Office/Industrial 54%

**Secondary Offerings**

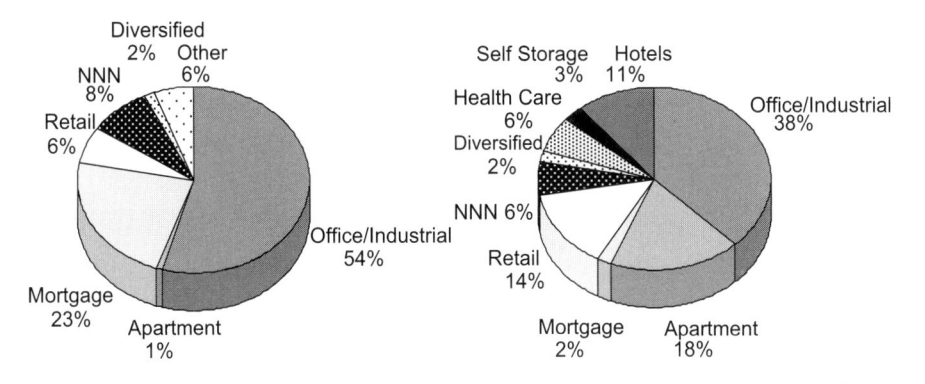

- Self Storage 3%
- Hotels 11%
- Health Care 6%
- Diversified 2%
- NNN 6%
- Retail 14%
- Mortgage 2%
- Apartment 18%
- Office/Industrial 38%

Source: NAREIT; Analysis - The McMahan Group.

**Market Performance:** Between 1995 and 1997, REITs posted a total return of 23.3%, which outperformed the private real estate market (9.29%) but was less than the broader S&P average (31.2%) (Exhibit 16).

Interestingly, 1997 turned out to be a reverse of 1996 in terms of REIT market performance. In 1996, REITs had outperformed the S&P 500 (35.3% vs. 22.7%); in 1997, the S&P turned in a 33.4% return vs. 20.3% for REITs.

During the first four months of 1998, REIT comparative performance was even worse, as equity REITs posted a negative (3.26%) total return vs. an S&P 500 return of 15.10%.[32]

Several reasons were given for this deteriorating situation:

- S&P returns were driven by anticipated increases in company earnings and a wave of new capital from the U.S. and overseas.
- Many U.S. property markets were in or near demand/supply equilibrium.
- Several property types were nearing their cyclical peak.
- Cap rates had fallen, and property prices were rising to the point where future growth in AFFO would be difficult.
- REIT mutual funds experienced shareholder redemptions in 1998 which in turn forced them to sell

---
[32] NAREIT.

REIT shares, a reaction that further depressing the REIT market.

- The Clinton Administration had given notice that it intended to introduce legislation that would reduce the tax preference that REITs enjoyed.[33]

**Exhibit 16**
**Total Annual Return**

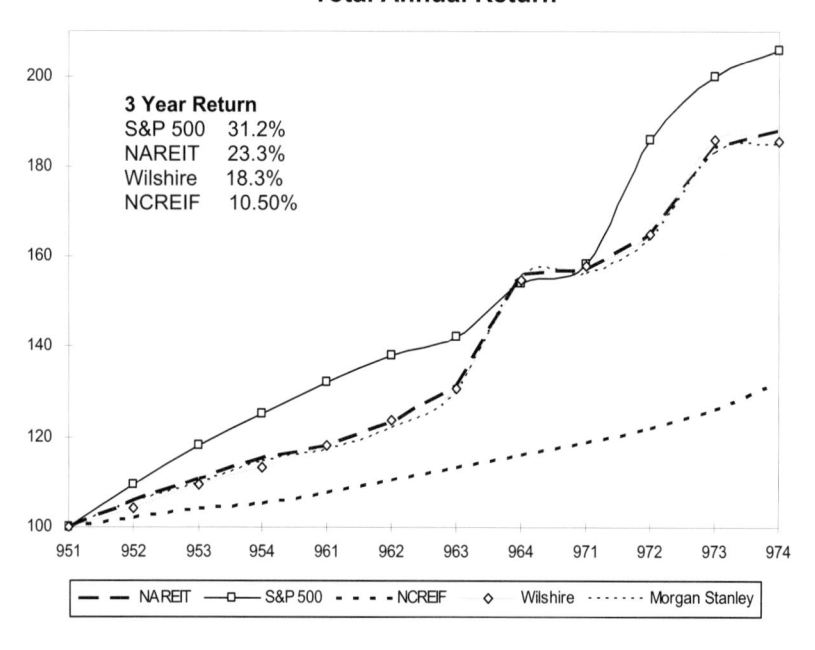

| 3 Year Return | |
|---|---|
| S&P 500 | 31.2% |
| NAREIT | 23.3% |
| Wilshire | 18.3% |
| NCREIF | 10.50% |

Note: Morgan Stanley 3 year return is not available.
Source: NAREIT, NCREIF, S&P 500, Wilshire Associates, Morgan Stanley; Analysis - The McMahan Group.

The downward movement in REIT prices seemed to be disconnected from strong real estate fundamentals; real estate earnings were expected to outpace corporate earnings in 1998. In fact, REIT shares were attractively priced vis-à-vis the broader stock indices in terms of price/earnings ratios and investment yields. With a lower level of volatility, REIT yields were even more attractive on a risk-adjusted basis.

Several analysts voiced concern that the depressed REIT stock prices were not from something that the market was missing but a situation that it had

---

[33] This move was largely in response to lobbying pressure from tax paying real estate corporations who believed that the REIT format provided an unfair advantage.

read all too well – namely that the real estate fundamentals that had driven the growth in REIT shares for almost eight years were now reversing.[34]

Much of this concern was based on the ability of REITs to grow future AFFO and dividends per share, particularly in what appeared to be a maturing property market. In the case of retail REITs for example, an optimistic anticipation of annual total return of 14.4% would be comprised of 7.5% dividend yield and approximately 6.9% of growth-related factors such as same store growth in sales (3.0%), improvement in operating margins (.3%), development and acquisitions (.5%), and capturing related business opportunities (2.0%). A more pessimistic scenario would retain the 7.5% dividend yield but reduce growth related sources of income to 3.8%, which would result in a total return of 11.3%.[35]

All of this was an unsettling scenario for many real estate investors who recalled that changes in REIT share prices had been an accurate predictor of the downturn in the broader real estate market in the 1980s as well as the rebound of the mid-1990s.

**Sector Performance:** Exhibit 17 looks in greater detail at a universe of 96 of the larger REITs, which comprise 94% of total equity capitalization. In 1997, diversified REITs led all sectors in total return (31.8%), followed by office (25.8%), industrial (23.8%), and hotels (23.6%). With the exception of hotels, all of these sectors had higher than average price/AFFO multiples. For the most part, this status reflected more recent IPOs, which analysts believed were positioned earlier in the real estate cycle and therefore had greater future growth potential. Returns from the more traditional sectors – shopping centers, regional malls, and apartments – lagged considerably with below-average multiples.

The industrial sector led in terms of enterprise value (35.1%), followed by office (32.3%), shopping centers (24.5%), diversified (22.4%), regional malls (21.4%), and apartments (17.4%). Hotels traded at a smaller premium (3.5%), thus reflecting extensive consolidation in the sector during the year.

During the first five months of 1998, REIT performance deteriorated as indicated in Exhibit 18. AFFO multiples dropped by 20.1%, which cut enterprise premiums by 68.3%. In terms of Enterprise Value, hotels, office and industrial sectors were hardest hit, followed by malls, apartments, community centers, and diversified REITs (Exhibit 19).

---

[34] J.P. Morgan Investment.
[35] The Penobscot Group, Inc. June, 1998.

## Exhibit 17
### REIT Characteristics by Property Sector
### December 31, 1997

|  | Newer IPO's ||||| Older IPO's ||| Total/Average** |
| --- | --- | --- | --- | --- | --- | --- | --- | --- |
|  | Diversified | Office | Industrial | Hotels | Centers | Malls | Apts. |  |
| Number of Reits | 7 | 14 | 11 | 11 | 17 | 12 | 24 | 96 |
| Equity Market Cap* | $8,021.2 | $31,589.0 | $14,662.6 | $11,612.9 | $11,095.2 | $18,147.9 | $25,028.4 | $120,028.4 |
| Average Size* | $1,145.9 | $2,256.4 | $1,333.0 | $1,055.7 | $552.7 | $1,512.3 | $1,042.9 | $1,251.6 |
| Price/AFFO | 14.8 | 15.2 | 14.4 | 11.8 | 12.2 | 13.1 | 12.8 | 13.9 |
| Enterprise Value | 22.4% | 32.3% | 35.1% | 3.5% | 24.5% | 21.4% | 17.4% | 23.7% |
| Dividend Yield | 5.4% | 4.8% | 5.4% | 6.5% | 7.1% | 6.7% | 6.5% | 5.9% |
| 1997 Price Change | 4.0% | 20.1% | 17.1% | 16.5% | 7.9% | 6.9% | 6.8% | 12.4% |
| 1997 Total Return | 31.8% | 25.8% | 23.8% | 23.6% | 15.5% | 13.9% | 13.5% | 20.4% |

\* Billions
\*\* Weighted by equity Market Capitalization
Source: Realty Stock Review, January 30, 1998; does not include all REITs.

**Industry Challenges:** The downward pressure on REIT prices was indicative of many of the problems the industry faced in the spring of 1998. The declining public real estate market contrasted markedly with the private market, where values were continuing to rise. This made it increasingly difficult for REITs to compete with pension advisors and other investors. The availability of large amounts of low priced mortgage money also gave taxable investors an edge in competing for properties. REITs were competitive primarily in those situations where the use of OP units attracted sellers with negative basis and/or estate planning problems.

**Exhibit 18**
**REIT Characteristics by Property Sector**
**June 10, 1998**

|  | Newer IPO's |  |  |  |  | Older IPO's |  | Total/Average** |
|---|---|---|---|---|---|---|---|---|
|  | Diversified | Office | Industrial | Hotels | Centers | Malls | Apts. |  |
| Number of Reits | 9 | 17 | 12 | 11 | 17 | 12 | 21 | 99 |
| Equity Market Cap* | $8,130.7 | $32,047.4 | $15,506.3 | $18,428.5 | $11,183.7 | $18,060.7 | $26,585.2 | $129,942.5 |
| Average Size* | $803.4 | $1,885.1 | $1,292.2 | $1,675.3 | $1,657.9 | $1,505.1 | $1,266.0 | $1,312.6 |
| Price/AFFO | 12.2 | 12.2 | 11.4 | 8.9 | 10.6 | 11.4 | 11.0 | 11.1 |
| Enterprise Value | 13.7% | 8.3% | 17.4% | -15.4% | 14.4% | 10.7% | 9.8% | 7.5% |
| Dividend Yield | 5.9% | 5.7% | 6.0% | 7.6% | 7.6% | 7.0% | 7.0% | 6.6% |
| May Price Yield | -0.1% | -5.2% | -1.7% | -8.3% | -1.7% | -1.8% | -0.2% | -3.1% |
| 1998 Price Change*** | -4.3% | -10.2% | -8.2% | -13.1% | -4.5% | -2.5% | -4.1% | -7.2% |
| 1998 Total Return*** | -1.8% | -8.8% | -6.4% | -11.0% | -2.2% | -0.2% | -1.3% | -5.0% |

* Billions
** Weighted by equity capitalization
*** Through June 10, 1998
Source: Realty Stock Review, June 15, 1998; does not include all REITs.

There were other challenges. With highly competitive property markets, the lack of attractive investment opportunities was leading some REITs into marginal investments both in terms of physical quality and economic return, thus implying that portfolio risk was increasing without a commensurate increase in return. In some cases, risk levels were also increasing through higher levels of development activity and the use of joint venture arrangements.

**Exhibit 19**
**REIT Property Sectors Percent Change in Enterprise Value**
**First Five Months of 1998**

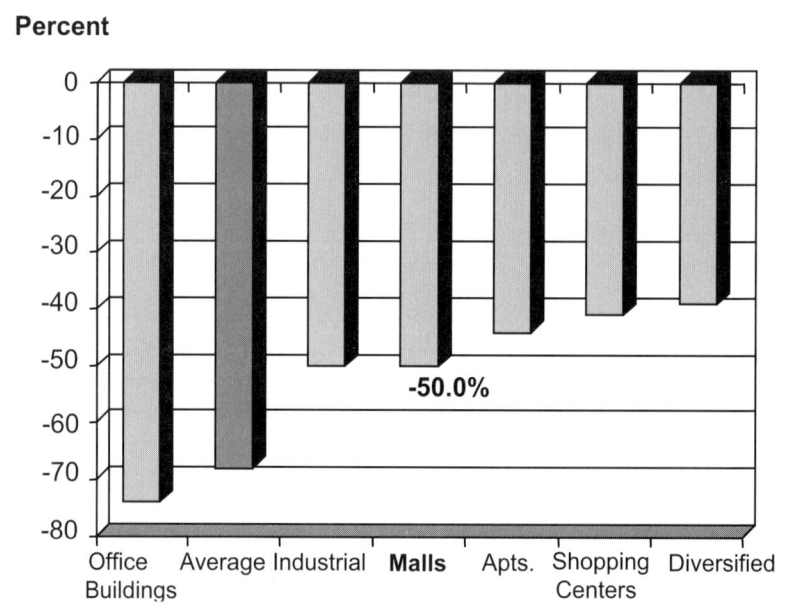

[Bar chart showing Percent change, with values ranging from 0 to -80. Categories: Office Buildings, Average, Industrial, Malls (-50.0%), Apts., Shopping Centers, Diversified]

Source: Realty Stock Review, June 15, 1998; does not include all REITs.

Underwriting risk was being compounded in many cases by an increase in both property and corporate leverage. This move was being driven primarily by historically low interest rates and the fact that REITs had traditionally, by real estate standards, been under-leveraged. To some extent, the analysis of REIT leverage as a percentage of total market capitalization understated the effect of increased leverage on the balance sheet. As a result, several analysts were shifting to greater use of debt coverage and loan-to-value ratios.

Another portfolio factor was causing concern – as a result of the all-consuming emphasis on asset growth, few REIT managers had active core asset disposition programs. This problem was particularly pronounced for REIT sectors such as apartments and retail, which were relatively further along in the real estate cycle.

In addition to portfolio problems, there also were concerns about REIT management. The sheer size and scope of many REITs placed pressure on managers to develop strong organizational as well as real estate skills. Many REITs, however, were slow in developing the policies, procedures, and systems that large businesses had utilized successfully in other industries. For example, few REITs had formalized succession plans providing for an orderly transition in leadership.[36]

In terms of governance, many so-called "independent REIT directors" were in fact very close to management, and it wasn't always clear how good the vaunted REIT governance policies really were, a particular concern to pension fund investors. Finally, many REIT boards and management seemed to lack the vision and courage necessary to reposition their firms for future growth and profitability.

## *General Growth's Situation*

At the end of 1997, General Growth owned, developed, or operated 114 shopping malls located in 38 states. Approximately one half of these centers was owned and one half was managed for others. Through an affiliated partnership, GGP/Homart, the firm also owned 38% of 25 malls totaling approximately 21 million SF. Major anchor tenants included Sears, JC Penny, Target, and Foley's.

Summary financial data for 1997:

|            | 1997    | Compounded Annual Growth |          |         |
|------------|---------|--------|---------|---------|
|            |         | 1 Year | 3 years | 5 years |
| Revenue    | $377.8  | 33.1%  | 33.4%   | 26.0%   |
| Net Income | $ 89.5  | 49.9%  | 84.7%   | 101.0%  |
| EPS        | $ 2.73  | 28.8%  | 63.9%   |         |

Exhibit 20 compares General Growth's operations in 1997 with other regional mall REITs with equity capitalization over $1 billion. General Growth led the group in total return (17.6% vs. an average of 10.5%). Its enterprise premium was also the highest of any of the peer group, and its price multiple was equaled by only one other competitor. A large part of this success was the 12.0% increase in the firm's stock price during the year, the greatest increase of any of the comparable firms.

In the first quarter of 1998, revenue was $121.8 million compared to $99.2 million in the first quarter of 1997. Net operating income was up 22% from $54.6 million to $66.8 million. FFO was up 23%, which marked five full years of consecutive quarterly FFO growth.

---

[36] An exception: in late 1996, Steve Roth, CEO of Vornado Realty Trust hired Michael Fascitelli as his appointed successor.

During the first quarter, General Growth completed construction on three projects totaling 262,000 SF with 2.8 million SF still under construction. The firm also acquired Southwest Plaza and the MEPC portfolio of centers for $871 million. Portfolio occupancy at the end of the quarter was 85.3% and was expected to increase to 87.0% by year end. Same store sales were up 5.5% for the quarter, although leasing spreads were down. Operating margins were flat at 55.8%.

**Exhibit 20**
**Regional Mall REITs (Over $1 Billion)**
**December 31, 1997**

|  | Simon Debarto | Rouse Co. | Gen. Growth | Taubman | Westfield | Macerich | Total/Avg.** |
|---|---|---|---|---|---|---|---|
| Equity Market Cap* | $5,595.2 | $2,299.7 | $1,927.8 | $1,797.9 | $1,319.4 | $1,072.8 | $14,012.8 |
| Price/AFFO*** | 13.7 | 14.3 | 14.9 | 13.4 | 11.3 | 14.9 | 13.8 |
| Enterprise Value | 16.8% | 37.3% | 37.7% | 8.7% | -2.3% | 36.2% | 21.7% |
| Dividend Yield*** | 6.2% | 3.1% | 5.0% | 7.2% | 8.2% | 6.5% | 5.9% |
| 1997 Price Change | 5.4% | 3.1% | 12.0% | 1.0% |  | 9.1% | 5.1% |
| 1997 Total Return | 11.9% | 6.3% | 17.6% | 8.2% |  | 15.9% | 10.5% |
| Debt Coverage | 3.2 | 1.8 | 2.4 | 2.4 | 2.7 | 2.5 | 2.7 |
| AFFO Payout Ration | 84.5% | 43.7% | 74.4% | 96.9% | 92.1% | 96.3% | 79.6% |
| 1998 AFFO Growth | 12.7% | 10.1% | 9.0% | 7.8% | 7.8% | 9.1% | 10.4% |

* Billions
** Weighted by equity Capitalization, price change and total return exclude Western
*** TAs of December 31, 1997
Source: Realty Stock Review, June 30, 1998; does not include all REITs.

On May 15, 1998, General Growth announced the acquisition of six additional centers for $625 million from U.S. Prime Property, Inc., a private real estate investment trust managed by ERE Yarmouth, Inc.

On the development front, construction was almost complete on the firm's 1.2 million SF Iowa City development, which was scheduled to open in July. The project was 100% pre-leased or committed prior to completion, a rare event in regional mall circles. Also somewhat uncommon were first year cash returns, which were expected to be in excess of 12% vs. the more typical 7.5% to 9.0%. Small stores comprised only 17.5% of total space vs. a more normal ratio of 40%.[37]

Exhibit 21 looks at the market performance of the largest regional mall REITs during the first five months of 1998. Exhibit 22 analyzes the percent change in enterprise value. General Growth lost 57.3% of enterprise value during this period.

**Exhibit 21**
**Regional Mall REITs (Over $1 Billion)**
**June 10, 1998**

| | Simon Debardto | Rouse Co. | Gen. Growth | Taubman | Westfield | Macerich | Total/Avg** |
|---|---|---|---|---|---|---|---|
| Equity Market Cap* | $5,626.8 | $2,007.0 | $1,924.4 | $1,878.8 | $1,337.7 | $1,280.0 | $14,054.7 |
| Price/AFFO* | 12.5 | 11.9 | 11.9 | 13.0 | 12.1 | 12.3 | 12.3 |
| Enterprise Value | 19.9% | 9.8% | 16.1% | 10.0% | 0.9% | 12.8% | 14.2% |
| Dividend Yield | 6.2% | 3.7% | 5.3% | 6.7% | 7.7% | 6.9% | 6.0% |
| 1998 YTD Price Change | -1.0% | -8.4% | -2.1% | -7.7% | 7.4% | -7.0% | -0.8% |
| 1998 Total Return | 2.1% | -7.5% | 0.8% | 9.5% | 9.4% | -3.8% | 1.7% |
| Debt Coverage | 3.1 | 2.0 | 2.5 | 2.3 | 2.7 | 2 | 2.6 |
| AFFO Payout Ration | 78.3% | 44.3% | 63.1% | 87.0% | 90.4% | 85.2% | 74.3% |
| 1998 AFFO Growth | 7.9% | 12.4% | 12.0% | 11.3% | 5.4% | 8.5% | 9.4% |

* Billions
** Weighted by equity market capitalization,
Source: Realty Stock Review, June 15, 1998; does not include all REITs.

---

[37] Salomon Smith Barney, May 19, 1998

**Exhibit 22
Regional Mall REITs Percent Change in Enterprise Value
First Five Months of 1998**

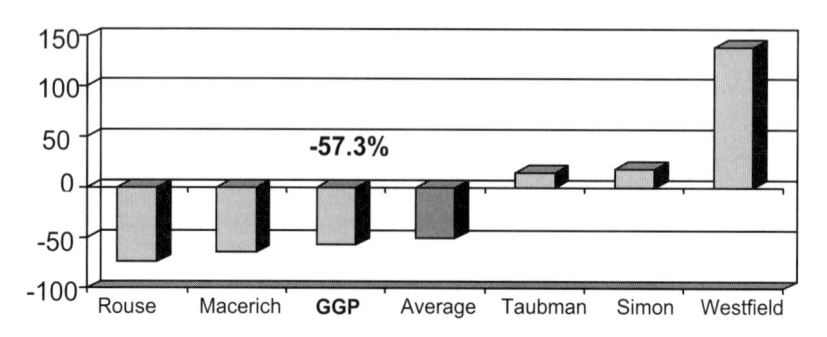

Bar chart showing percent change in enterprise value for: Rouse, Macerich, GGP (-57.3%), Average, Taubman, Simon, Westfield.

Source: Realty Stock Review, June 15, 1998; does not include all REITs.

## Monday Morning Meeting

As John contemplated the next day's meeting, he had conflicting views. On the one hand, there was no question that General Growth was in relatively good shape in what had been a fairly sharp REIT sell-off during the first five months of 1998.

John also knew that retailers were scrambling to find expansion space, particularly in well-located regional malls. The power balance seemed to be shifting once again to landlords, a possible indication of future growth in rents. He was pleased with the market position that General Growth had established within the regional mall sector with a virtual dominance of retailing's middle markets. Recent acquisitions had provided the firm with the large economic base that many analysts believed necessary to produce efficient operations. The Iowa City project had been a real winner and demonstrated that the firm still had the ability to develop as well as acquire. John was also pleased with the quality of the firm's management team and its ability to continue the family's strong entrepreneurial tradition within a public company framework. He was concerned, however, that General Growth had experienced a significant hit on its AFFO multiple in spite of the fact that the firm expected one of the smallest changes in anticipated 1998 AFFO growth. He was also concerned that with the exception of Rouse and Macerich, General Growth had lost more of its enterprise premium in the first five months of 1998 than any of the other members of the peer group.

He knew that a continuing loss of enterprise value would have a "ripple effect" through the entire firm; it would make acquisitions more difficult, increase the firm's cost of capital, and undermine the value of employee stock options.

John worried about the overall state of the real estate market as well. Perhaps analysts were right in viewing the REIT sell-off as a possible precursor to a broader decline in real estate values. There was also the question of how long Congress could be delayed in implementing changes in the tax code that would reduce the competitive position of REITs in the marketplace.

On a broader front, John was uncomfortable with the impact of the Asian collapse on future retail sales. Although consumer confidence was currently high, he knew that any major fall off in employment could directly affect consumer confidence and retail sales. This was compounded by the high consumer debt levels and personal bankruptcies that seemed to be building in the economy.

Finally, John was concerned about the possible impact of an external "shock" to the U.S. economy. While many economists argued that America had entered a "new era" of peace – high economic productivity, low inflation, and a broad public stake in private enterprise – there was increasing concern about the "bubble" that seemed to be forming in the U.S. economy.[38] More and more parallels were being drawn to the decline in the Japanese economy in the early 1990s, a situation which only seemed to be getting worse. In early 1998, Japan also was highly exposed to the Asian economic collapse through country-risk bank lending.

John had recently read an article in Time Magazine indicating that it wasn't just the Japanese banks that were at risk from the problems in Asia. Several large American banks held approximately $10 trillion in derivative positions with Asian firms, some of whom had already defaulted. The credit risk from these derivative positions was, in many cases, substantially in excess of the net worth of many of the banks.[39]

John thought that perhaps General Growth was at another cross roads in which external events would dictate a change in strategic direction. Certainly the company had faced similar situations in the past and thus far, it had made perceptive decisions that refocused it on new and successful paths for its shareholders.

As he got ready to retire for the evening, he knew that tomorrow's meeting would be an interesting and perhaps pivotal one for the Company.

---

[38] The Economist, April 18, 1998.
[39] Time Magazine, May 25, 1998.

## Appendix A-1
## U.S. Shopping Center Statistics

| | Shopping Center Space (Billion SF) | Retail Sales ($B) | Shopping Center Sales ($B) | Center Sales/ Retail Sales | Center Sales per SF (Nominal $) | Center Sales per SF (1994 $) |
|---|---|---|---|---|---|---|
| 1967 | 1.233 | 297 | 57 | 19% | 46.23 | 206.02 |
| 1968 | 1.314 | 329 | 65 | 20% | 49.47 | 213.82 |
| 1969 | 1.407 | 353 | 73 | 21% | 51.88 | 215.23 |
| 1970 | 1.456 | 375 | 82 | 22% | 56.32 | 221.45 |
| 1971 | 1.561 | 414 | 91 | 22% | 58.30 | 216.86 |
| 1972 | 1.650 | 458 | 103 | 22% | 62.42 | 222.43 |
| 1973 | 1.797 | 512 | 120 | 23% | 66.78 | 230.57 |
| 1974 | 1.874 | 542 | 134 | 25% | 71.50 | 232.47 |
| 1975 | 1.972 | 588 | 147 | 25% | 74.54 | 218.34 |
| 1976 | 2.278 | 656 | 177 | 27% | 77.70 | 208.60 |
| 1977 | 2.400 | 772 | 199 | 26% | 82.92 | 210.40 |
| 1978 | 2.498 | 804 | 221 | 27% | 88.47 | 210.79 |
| 1979 | 2.785 | 897 | 272 | 30% | 97.67 | 216.27 |
| 1980 | 2.963 | 956 | 305 | 32% | 102.94 | 204.79 |
| 1981 | 3.101 | 1,038 | 333 | 32% | 107.38 | 188.23 |
| 1982 | 3.239 | 1,069 | 359 | 34% | 110.84 | 176.14 |
| 1983 | 3.324 | 1,170 | 397 | 34% | 119.43 | 178.72 |
| 1984 | 3.376 | 1,287 | 423 | 33% | 125.30 | 181.68 |
| 1985 | 3.466 | 1,375 | 460 | 33% | 132.72 | 184.51 |
| 1986 | 3.520 | 1,450 | 512 | 35% | 145.45 | 195.19 |
| 1987 | 3.724 | 1,541 | 563 | 37% | 151.18 | 199.09 |
| 1988 | 3.950 | 1,656 | 610 | 37% | 154.43 | 196.30 |
| 1989 | 4.210 | 1,759 | 661 | 38% | 157.01 | 191.72 |
| 1990 | 4.390 | 1,845 | 704 | 38% | 160.36 | 186.85 |
| 1991 | 4.550 | 1,856 | 735 | 40% | 161.54 | 178.57 |
| 1992 | 4.650 | 1,952 | 776 | 40% | 166.88 | 177.04 |
| 1993 | 4.770 | 2,074 | 821 | 40% | 172.12 | 177.28 |
| 1994 | 4.860 | 2,230 | 876 | 39% | 180.25 | 180.25 |
| 1995 | 4.970 | 2,329 | 917 | 39% | 184.51 | 179.83 |
| 1996 | 5.100 | 2,461 | 970 | 39% | 190.20 | 180.33 |
| 1997 | 5.230 | 2,566 | 1,019 | 40% | 194.84 | 179.35 |

Source: International Council of Shopping Centers; U.S. Department of Commerce.

## Appendix A-2
## Comparative Returns

| | S&P 500 Index | NAREIT Equity REIT Index | NCREIF Property Index | NCREIF Retail Index |
|---|---|---|---|---|
| 1978 | 6.56% | 10.34% | 16.11% | 10.93% |
| 1979 | 18.44% | 35.86% | 20.46% | 11.24% |
| 1980 | 32.42% | 24.37% | 18.09% | 12.78% |
| 1981 | -4.91% | 6.00% | 16.62% | 11.03% |
| 1982 | 21.59% | 21.60% | 9.43% | 7.02% |
| 1983 | 22.43% | 30.64% | 13.33% | 13.84% |
| 1984 | 6.10% | 20.93% | 13.04% | 16.90% |
| 1985 | 31.57% | 19.10% | 10.11% | 14.40% |
| 1986 | 18.21% | 19.16% | 6.64% | 12.52% |
| 1987 | 5.17% | -3.64% | 5.48% | 12.38% |
| 1988 | 16.50% | 13.49% | 7.04% | 14.94% |
| 1989 | 31.44% | 8.84% | 6.21% | 12.53% |
| 1990 | -3.19% | -15.35% | 1.46% | 5.97% |
| 1991 | 30.55% | 35.70% | -6.08% | -1.85% |
| 1992 | 7.68% | 14.59% | -4.36% | -2.23% |
| 1993 | 10.00% | 19.65% | 0.56% | 4.84% |
| 1994 | 1.33% | 3.17% | 6.85% | 6.01% |
| 1995 | 37.51% | 15.27% | 8.83% | 3.99% |
| 1996 | 22.96% | 35.27% | 10.29% | 4.86% |
| 1997 | 33.36% | 20.26% | 13.74% | 8.39% |

Source: Frank Russell Company; Realty Stock Review; NAREIT; NCREIF.

## Appendix A-3
## Regional Mall Investment Criteria

| Quarterly Period | Going-in Cap | Pre-tax Yield (IRR) | Quarterly Period | Going-in Cap | Pre-tax Yield (IRR) |
|---|---|---|---|---|---|
| 1990-1 | 6.9 | 10.9 | 1994-1 | 7.9 | 10.9 |
| 1990-2 | 7.1 | 11.3 | 1994-2 | 7.7 | 11.1 |
| 1990-3 | 7.3 | 11.4 | 1994-3 | 7.7 | 11.0 |
| 1990-4 | 7.4 | 11.7 | 1994-4 | 8.0 | 11.1 |
| 1991-1 | 7.6 | 11.8 | 1995-1 | 8.2 | 10.9 |
| 1991-2 | 7.2 | 11.4 | 1995-2 | 7.9 | 11.1 |
| 1991-3 | 7.2 | 11.8 | 1995-3 | 8.0 | 11.0 |
| 1991-4 | 7.2 | 11.7 | 1995-4 | 8.2 | 11.1 |
| 1992-1 | 7.4 | 11.7 | 1996-1 | 8.5 | 11.3 |
| 1992-2 | 7.5 | 11.8 | 1996-2 | 8.4 | 11.1 |
| 1992-3 | 7.7 | 11.3 | 1996-3 | 8.5 | 11.0 |
| 1992-4 | 7.6 | 11.5 | 1996-4 | 8.8 | 11.4 |
| 1993-1 | 7.9 | 10.9 | 1997-1 | 8.6 | 11.6 |
| 1993-2 | 7.7 | 11.4 | 1997-2 | 8.8 | 11.4 |
| 1993-3 | 7.8 | 11.2 | 1997-3 | 8.3 | 11.2 |
| 1994-4 | 7.7 | 11.0 | 1997-4 | 8.3 | 11.2 |
|  |  |  | 1998-1 | 8.1 | 10.8 |

Source: Real Estate Research Corporation.

## Appendix B-1
## General Growth Properties, Inc. - Consolidated Balance Sheets

|  | December 31, 1972* | December 31, 1993 | December 31, 1997 | March 31, 1998 |
|---|---|---|---|---|
| **Assets** | | | | |
| Current | | | | |
| Cash | $3,189,103 | $5,554,000 | $25,898,000 | $6,436,000 |
| Investments | | 61,832,000 | | |
| A/R | 2,376,124 | 9,471,000 | 34,849,000 | 35,332,000 |
| Mortgage Notes | 3,761,764 | | | 49,948,000 |
| Total | 9,326,991 | 76,857,000 | 60,747,000 | 91,716,000 |
| Real Estate | 131,375,274 | 683,162,000 | 1,923,956,000 | 1,947,833,000 |
| Other | | | | |
| Escrow deposits | 891,228 | | | |
| Unamortized leasing costs | 1,471,212 | | | |
| Deferred expenses | | 18,362,000 | 42,343,000 | 45,734,000 |
| Prepaid Expenses | | | 9,085,000 | 9,638,000 |
| Note Receivable | | | 61,588,000 | 67,439,000 |
| Other assets | 782,106 | 11,074,000 | | |
| Total | 3,144,546 | 29,436,000 | 113,016,000 | 122,811,000 |
| Total Assets | 143,846,811 | 789,455,000 | 2,097,719,000 | 2,162,360,000 |
| **Liabilities and Equity** | | | | |
| Current | | | | |
| A/P | 2,416,713 | 30,098,000 | 36,540,000 | 40,514,000 |
| A/P Affiliates | | 1,179,000 | | |
| Accrued Taxes | 1,557,846 | | | |
| Accrued interest | 663,378 | | | |
| Notes Payable | | 3,424,000 | 1,275,785,000 | |
| Dividends Payable | | 14,075,000 | 24,421,000 | 25,620,000 |
| Other accrued liabilities | 130,939 | | | |
| Total | 4,768,876 | 48,776,000 | 1,336,746,000 | 66,134,000 |
| Mortgages | 107,851,205 | 450,013,000 | | 1,349,009,000 |
| Total Liabilities | 112,620,081 | 498,789,000 | 1,336,746,000 | 1,415,143,000 |
| Minority Interest in Partnership | | 117,653,000 | 262,468,000 | 256,052,000 |
| Notes | 10,300,000 | | | |
| Equity | 20,926,730 | 173,013,000 | 498,505,000 | 491,165,000 |
| Total Equity | 31,226,730 | 173,013,000 | 498,505,000 | 491,165,000 |
| Total Liabilities & Equity | 143,846,811 | 789,455,000 | 2,097,719,000 | 2,162,360,000 |

*Pro Forma

## Appendix B-2
## General Growth Properties, Inc. - Statement of Operations

| | December 31 1972* | December 31 1993 | December 31 1997 | March 31 1998 | Annualized 1998 |
|---|---|---|---|---|---|
| **Revenue** | | | | | |
| Minimum Rents | | $89,000,000 | $175,830,000 | $50,507,00 | $202,028,000 |
| Tenant Recoveries | | 47,299,000 | 97,291,000 | 25,591,000 | 102,364,000 |
| Percentage Rents | | 4,047,000 | 7,976,000 | 2,433,000 | 9,732,000 |
| Other | | 1,864,000 | 5,577,000 | 930,000 | 3,720,000 |
| Fee Income | | | 4,473,000 | 986,000 | 3,944,000 |
| Total | 11,247,501 | 142,210,000 | 291,147,000 | 80,447,000 | 321,788,000 |
| **Expense** | | | | | |
| Real Estate Taxes | 1,165,167 | 11,417,000 | 20,761,000 | 5,784,000 | 23,136,000 |
| Property Operating | 1,713,069 | 38,402,000 | 79,175,000 | 22,109,000 | 88,436,000 |
| Management Fees | | | 3,308,000 | 875,000 | 3,500,000 |
| Total | 2,878,236 | 49,819,000 | 103,244,000 | 28,768,000 | 115,072,000 |
| **Property Operating Income (NOI)** | 8,369,265 | 92,391,000 | 187,903,000 | 51,679,000 | 206,716,000 |
| General & Administrative | 150,782 | 4,028,000 | 3,408,000 | 1,146,000 | 4,584,000 |
| Unleveraged Cash Flow | 8,218,483 | 88,363,000 | 184,495,000 | 50,533,000 | 202,132,000 |
| Interest (Net) | 3,640,165 | 37,495,000 | 70,252,000 | 17,883,000 | 71,532,000 |
| Leveraged CashFlow | 4,578,318 | 50,868,000 | 114,243,000 | 32,650,000 | 130,600,000 |
| **Non-Cash Charges** | | | | | |
| Depreciation and Amortization | 1,879,433 | 25,377,000 | 48,509,000 | 13,967,000 | 55,868,000 |
| Provision for Doubtful Accounts | | 1,226,000 | 3,025,000 | 608,000 | 2,432,000 |
| Total | 1,879,433 | 26,603,000 | 51,534,000 | 14,575,000 | 58,300,000 |
| **Income Before Affiliates** | 2,698,885 | 24,265,000 | 62,709,000 | 18,075,000 | 72,300,000 |
| **Equity in Affiliates** | | | | | |
| GGP/Homart | | | 16,505,000 | 1,735,000 | 6,940,000 |
| Property JV's | | | 3,033,000 | 1,041,000 | 4,164,000 |
| General Growth Management | | | -194,000 | -7,969,000 | -31,876,000 |
| Total | | | 19,344,000 | -5,193,000 | -20,772,000 |
| Income Allocated to Minority Interest | | -9,823,000 | -49,997,000 | -4,427,000 | -17,708,000 |
| Net Gain on Sales | | | 58,647,000 | | |
| Extraordinary Item | | -1,832,000 | -1,152,000 | | |
| Net Income | 2,698,885 | 12,610,000 | 30,904,000 | 8,455,000 | 33,820,000 |
| Depreciation & Amortization | 1,879,433 | 25,377,000 | 48,509,000 | 13,967,000 | 55,868,000 |
| Net Gain on Sales | | | 58,647,000 | | |
| Total | 1,879,433 | 25,377,000 | 107,156,000 | 13,967,000 | 55,868,000 |
| Funds From Operations (FFO) | 4,578,318 | 37,987,000 | 138,060,000 | 22,422,000 | 89,688,000 |
| Shares Outstanding | 4,907,064 | 22,927,273 | 35,634,977 | 35,936,000 | 143,744,000 |
| FFO Per Share | $0.93 | $1.66 | $3.87 | $0.62 | $2.50 |

Source: Adapted from General Growth Properties, Inc. 1972 Prospectus and subsequent reports. *Pro forma

## Appendix B-3
## General Growth Properties, Inc. - Stock Price

| Date | Stock Price ($) |
| --- | --- |
| December 31, 1993 | 21.500 |
| December 31, 1994 | 22.625 |
| December 31, 1995 | 20.750 |
| December 31, 1996 | 32.250 |
| March 31, 1997 | 31.750 |
| June 31, 1997 | 33.500 |
| September 31, 1997 | 37.000 |
| December 31, 1997 | 36.125 |
| March 31, 1998 | 36.875 |

Source: NAREIT.

## Questions for Discussion

Questions that should be addressed in this case include:

1. What are some of the key trends in retailing that occurred over the last 40 years (1958 – 1998) and how did they affect regional mall development/investment?

2. Describe how General Growth Properties' (GGP) management responded to these trends? What was their business strategy? How well did it work?

3. What trends were occurring in the interface between private and public markets in real estate? How were investor returns affected by these trends?

4. What factors did GGP's management consider in each of their decisions as to whether to operate as a private or public company?

5. What are the advantages and disadvantages of electing REIT status? How does being a public company compound this decision?

6. What are some examples of GGP's handling of business conflicts? Were the investors treated fairly?

7. What are some examples of GGP's successful use of long term business relationships? What role did each play?

8. Discuss the factors impacting the current (1998) REIT market. What is the reason for declining performance of REITs? What are some of the challenges facing REIT management?

9. What are the positive and negative market and company factors influencing GGP in its strategic planning efforts?

10. What are your recommendations regarding GGP's future business strategy?

Please use these questions as a guide and not a format or a reflection of all of the questions that need to be addressed by the case.

# 18

# WESTERN REAL ESTATE ADVISORS [1]

## REIT Roll-Up

Camilla Concilatore raced into the management meeting 25 minutes late, heart pounding and largely out of breath. Just before the meeting, she had placed a call to Tom Razier to ascertain his receptivity to a "roll-up" of Western's clients' assets into a Real Estate Investment Trust (REIT). Tom was the head of real estate investments for the Bloomfield Urban Retirement Plan (BURP), one of Western's largest clients.

Cami had started at Western in 1991 as a real estate acquisition officer and now served as the firm's Director of Portfolio Management. The management meeting was called to finalize strategy for the proposed roll-up, which was tentatively scheduled for closing on October 15, 1997, just three months away. Unfortunately, the news she brought would not be well received.

---

[1] Copyright © 1997 and 2004, John McMahan, all rights reserved.

## Company Background

**Firm's Beginnings:** Western was founded in Los Angeles in 1987 as an investment advisor for pension investor clients. The firm was registered under the Advisor's Act of 1940 and was a fiduciary under ERISA. Western specialized in suburban office and industrial properties located primarily in the Western United States.

Western's founders, Jim Aires and Serge Leosky, were 1981 classmates from a well-known western business school who later worked together as mortgage brokers specializing in loans for office and industrial properties. As a result of their mortgage activities, they became acquainted with several major pension funds and believed that they could develop an investment niche that would provide attractive equity returns to pension investors. To raise the initial $200,000 in equity capital for their new firm, they invested their life savings as well as proceeds from second mortgages on their homes.

**Clients:** Raising pension capital turned out to be harder than they had anticipated. It took over two years to secure their first pension client, who invested $25 million in a separate account.

Although from time-to-time they considered sponsoring pooled funds, they continued to focus on separate accounts and by mid-1997 had attracted 14 pension clients allocating $835 million to the firm for investment purposes. Six of the clients were public pension plans, five were corporate, two were Taft-Hartley, and one was a college endowment fund.

**Investment Strategy:** Western's investment strategy was to concentrate on the rapidly growing suburbs of metropolitan areas in the Western United States where they believed they could secure superior investment returns. They focused on new modern suburban office buildings leased to local (27.3%), regional (39.2%), and national business firms (33.5%).

**Assets:** As of December 31, 1996, the firm had under management approximately $725 million in assets comprising 43 properties located in California (48.3%), Washington (27.1%), Arizona (17.6%), Oregon (5.2%) and Colorado (1.8%). Ninety-three percent (93.0%) of the portfolio's value was in office and R&D buildings, with the remainder in industrial warehouse facilities. The average length of leases in the portfolio was 4.2 years. Approximately 20% of the investments had been developed by Western's staff.

**Investment Performance:** Despite the recession of 1991-1993 and the problems besetting the office sector, the properties had performed relatively well over the past seven years with a 10.3% total annual return, of which 8.2% represented net operating income (NOI).

And things were getting much better. As a result of asset value write downs in the early 1990s and rapidly improving property markets in the West, Western's NOI return for 1996 was 10.3% and was expected to be 11.3% for 1997. Management believed that NOI returns would reach 12% by 1998. Tenant improvements and leasing commissions typically reduced NOI returns by approximately 15% annually.

**Organization:** Western was organized as a corporation with a largely functional/matrix organization. Jim was president and CEO with Serge serving as the Chief Operating Officer. Besides Cami, other officers included Mary Ishade, Chief Financial Officer; Bill Closdeale, Director of Acquisitions' and John Leascom, Director of Asset Management. Property management was performed by independent contractors. Nonfounding officers owned 37% of the company.

**Profitability:** During its early years, Western had lost money but began to enter the black in 1990. Profitability then turned down in 1993, as new capital dried up and clients demanded higher levels of reporting and other services. With new capital flows in late 1995, however, profitability had returned. EBITDA for 1996 was $2.2 million and was expected to increase to $2.6 million in 1997 and $3.1 million in 1998 (See Exhibit 1).

## *Pension Investors*

**Poor Performance:** Although Western had faced problems, they paled in comparison to those experienced by older, larger investment advisory firms. And not without reason – pension investors were upset with real estate returns consistently lower than their securities portfolio, largely as a result of losses of up to 40% in real estate portfolio value. Also a concern was the incredible amount of staff time that real estate investing seemed to require.

**"Agency" Problem:** Many investors believed that a large part of the poor performance record was an inevitable result of the investment advisory delivery system in which the advisor not only initiated the investment but managed it as well. Investors perceived a conflict of interest in this arrangement where no one knew who the investment advisor really worked for. The fact that most advisors did not invest in the properties meant that advisory firms could be making money while their clients, the pension investors, were losing theirs.

**Search for Solutions:** In order to resolve these concerns, pension investors began exploring alternatives. About 30%, mostly the smaller pension plans, decided to get out of real estate altogether. Not wishing to leave real estate, other plans sold their private market assets and invested the proceeds in securitized real estate, primarily REITs. Some of the larger public plans attempted to modify the private market investment process by requiring changes in their investment advisory contracts. They believed that by making certain requirements of their advisors (e.g., dedicated advisor staffs, dedicated reporting, advisor co-investment, etc.), they could capture the major benefits of securitized investing and still enjoy the greater portfolio diversification benefits provided by private market assets.

## Exhibit 1
## Western Real Estate Advisors, Inc.
## Profit and Loss Statement (Unaudited)
## ($Thousand)

|  | 1996 (actual) | 1997 (estimated) | 1998 (forecasted) |
|---|---|---|---|
| **Assets Under Management** | | | |
| BOP | $688 | $725 | $835 |
| Acquisition/Development | 55 | 116 | 165 |
| Dispositions | 18 | 6 | 0 |
| EOP | 725 | 835 | 1,000 |
| **Revenue[1]** | | | |
| Asset Management | 4.713 | 5.226 | 6.675 |
| Acquisition/Development | 0.930 | 1.346 | 1.980 |
| Dispositions | 0.179 | 0.113 | 0.000 |
| Total | 5.82 | 6.69 | 7.80 |
| **Expense** | | | |
| Salaries | 1.88 | 2.01 | 2.20 |
| Fringe Benefits | 0.413 | 0.442 | 0.440 |
| Rent | 0.120 | 0.125 | 0.125 |
| Insurance | 0.028 | 0.030 | 0.050 |
| Travel | 0.541 | 0.615 | 0.800 |
| Promotion | 0.433 | 0.492 | 0.600 |
| Legal | 0.057 | 0.044 | 0.100 |
| Accounting | 0.036 | 0.042 | 0.060 |
| Research | 0.103 | 0.305 | 0.300 |
| Total | 3.61 | 4.10 | 4.68 |
| **EBITDA** | 2.21 | 2.59 | 3.13 |

[1] Western's standard fee structure was .70% annually for asset management; 1.0% for acquisitions; 2.0% for development; and 1.0% for dispositions. Disposition fees often had a portion of cost recovery reflected in them.

## Real Estate Investment Trusts

**Legislation:** The REIT Act of 1960 envisioned a conservative investment vehicle with certain tax avoidance features, which would encourage long term investment in real estate by individual taxable investors.

Although regulations have loosened considerably over the years, REITs still must meet fairly stringent rules if they are to annually maintain their REIT status:

- Have at least 100 shareholders. Five individuals can not own more than 50% of the stock (5/50 rule).[2]
- Seventy-five percent of assets must be in real estate equity, mortgages, REIT shares, or cash.
- Seventy-five percent of income must come from rents or mortgage interest.
- No more than 30% of operating income can come from properties held less than 4 years.[3]
- Ninety-five percent of taxable income must be paid out annually.

In terms of organization, all REITs must be either a corporation or a trust and be managed by a board of directors or trustees. The majority of trustees must be independent of REIT management.

**Early History:** Less than half of the REITs operating in the sixties were self-advised (i.e., internally managed with no external advisor) and even in these cases, management did not participate extensively in stock ownership. There was little market activity and not much coverage from the financial community.

In the late 1960s, Wall Street began shifting the emphasis of REIT Initial Placement Offerings (IPO) from long-term equity investment to short-term mortgage investment, largely in the form of construction loans. Mortgage REITs were the largest single source of capital funding for the 1971-75 real estate "boom," largely borrowing short and lending long in order to arbitrage the yield curve. This bubble collapsed in the mid-seventies and REITs became tarred with a negative image that they would not overcome for 20 years. Not all of this was investor perception – REIT *market values had declined almost 75% from their 1972 highs.*

---

[2] Congress recently passed legislation allowing the IRS to "look through" the pension fund structure and treat plan beneficiaries as individual shareholders. This effectively exempts pension funds from the 5/50 rule.
[3] Current legislation was being considered by Congress which would liberalize or eliminate this provision.

Largely as a result of the debacle of the 1970's, REITs missed the real estate "bubble" of the 1980s. In the subsequent collapse of the real estate markets at the end of the decade, all forms of capital for real estate evaporated. Developers and other owners of real estate found themselves with highly leveraged properties, often built with short-term financing and no source of refinancing. With interest rates falling and real estate yields rising, Wall Street saw an opportunity to arbitrage the private and public markets.

**Birth of the "Modern REIT":** The Kimco offering in late 1991 was the first sign that REITs could play a major role in financing real estate and more importantly, real estate operating companies. During 1991, eight IPO's involving REITs raised $808 million. A similar number were completed in 1992, raising $919 million.

While this was meaningful investment activity, particularly in a capital-starved real estate market, 1993 proved to be a real turning point – 75 equity IPOs raised $11.1 billion. Excluding placements of less than $50 million, 39 IPO's were completed raising $8.2 billion, approximately 14% of total IPO activity in the entire securities market for the year. This represented more capital for real estate than from any other source.

**New REITs Were Different:** Perhaps more significantly, the character of the 1993 IPOs was dramatically different. Virtually all represented real estate operating companies which specialized by property type. The new REITs were also significantly larger – ten equity REITs had market capitalization of over $500 million (versus two at the end of 1991) and 40 had capitalization exceeding $200 million (versus ten in 1991). Almost two thirds of new and proposed REITs were structured as UPREITs, in which the REIT owns an interest in one or more existing partnerships, an approach utilized to reduce the tax impact on selling partners.

Most of the 1993 IPOs were self-administered, and in many cases management had significant equity positions, thus minimizing conflicts and enhancing congruency with investors. Most of the management groups had spent their careers specializing in the particular property type and had effectively worked together as a team for many years, including at least one full real estate cycle (See Exhibit 2).

By the end of 1996, there were 302 REITs with a total market capitalization of $126 billion. Approximately two thirds of these were equity REITs with a total market capitalization of $95 million (See Exhibit 5).

### Exhibit 2
### "Old" vs. "New" REITs

| Old | New |
|---|---|
| 1960 - 1992 | 1992 - 1997 |
| Passive investments | Operating company |
| Externally administered | Self-administered |
| Institutional sponsors | Entrepreneur sponsors |
| Small mgmt ownership | Large mgmt ownership |
| Diversified portfolio | Focused portfolio |
| Small capital base | Larger capital base |
| Little analyst coverage | More analyst coverage |

Today, most successful REITs are fully integrated operating companies rather than the passive conduits envisioned by Congress 37 years earlier. Most are focused by property type and by geographical area, although this condition is changing as larger, national firms come onto the scene. Retail and apartments are still the dominant property type, although office, industrial, and hotels have grown in importance in recent years. Economic scale is also important as larger REITs reduce their cost of capital and spread operating costs over a larger base.

**Market Valuation:** REIT earnings are usually measured in terms of funds from operations (FFO), which is net income (GAAP) plus depreciation and amortization less gain (loss) on sale of investments. Stock prices are generally compared to FFO flows, which are much the same as price/earnings ratios for non-real estate stocks. More recently, many analysts have begun adjusting FFO for capital expenditures and the impact of floating rate debt. This revised measure is termed Adjusted Funds From Operations (AFFO).

REITs are also valued in terms of their premium or discount to Net Asset Value (NAV). Better performing REITs are generally rewarded by premium pricing, reflecting the market's perception of greater enterprise value which should result in enhanced future FFO growth.

Other factors that analysts and investors track are "payout ratios" (percent of distributable income that will be paid out as dividends), total debt to total capitalization ratio (the market doesn't like leverage exceeding 40%); the proportion of floating debt in the capital structure; management compensation; and the alignment of management's interest with those of their shareholders.

## Exhibit 3
## REIT IPOs by Sector

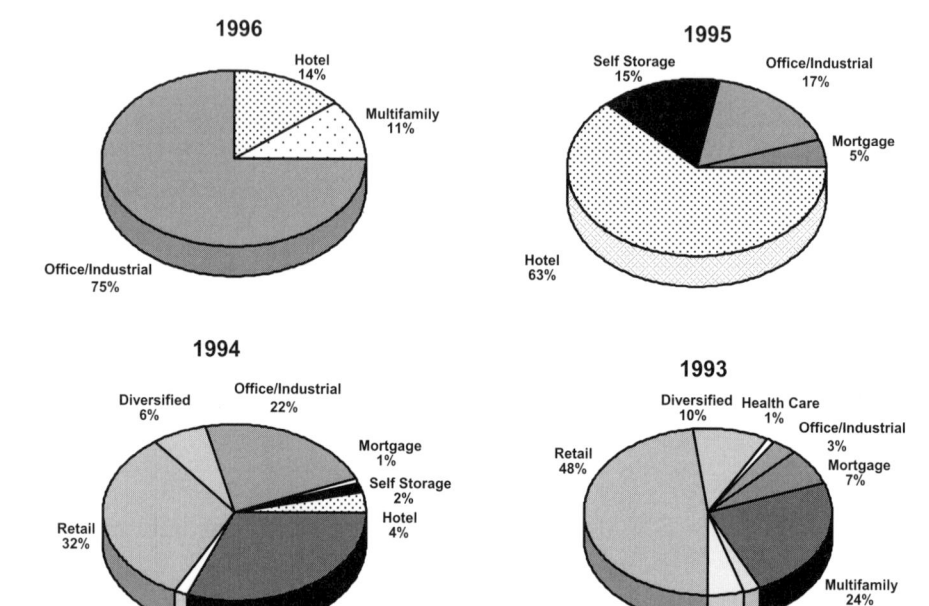

**1996**
- Office/Industrial 75%
- Hotel 14%
- Multifamily 11%

**1995**
- Self Storage 15%
- Office/Industrial 17%
- Mortgage 5%
- Hotel 63%

**1994**
- Diversified 6%
- Office/Industrial 22%
- Mortgage 1%
- Self Storage 2%
- Hotel 4%
- Multifamily 31%
- Health Care 2%
- Retail 32%

**1993**
- Diversified 10%
- Health Care 1%
- Office/Industrial 3%
- Mortgage 7%
- Multifamily 24%
- Golf Course 2%
- Residential 5%
- Retail 48%

Sources: Legg Mason Wood Walker, NAREIT Handbook 1994, 1995.

## Exhibit 4
### IPO and Secondary Equity Offerings

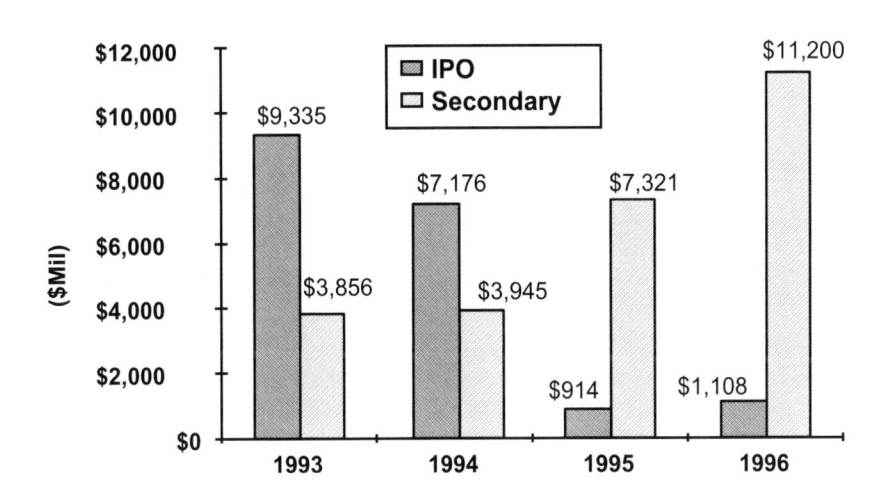

| Year | IPO | Secondary |
|------|-------|-----------|
| 1993 | $9,335 | $3,856 |
| 1994 | $7,176 | $3,945 |
| 1995 | $914 | $7,321 |
| 1996 | $1,108 | $11,200 |

($Mil)

Source: NAREIT

## Exhibit 5
### REIT Total Market Cap

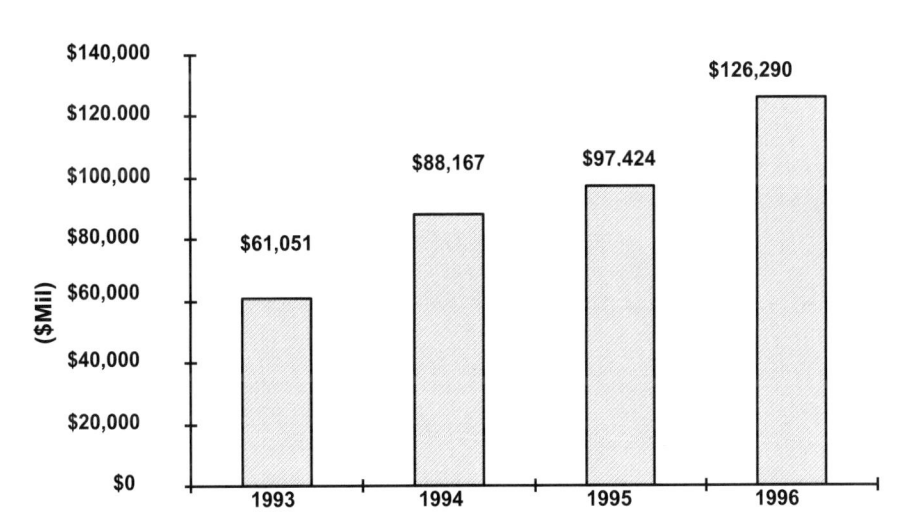

| Year | Amount ($Mil) |
|------|---------------|
| 1993 | $61,051 |
| 1994 | $88,167 |
| 1995 | $97.424 |
| 1996 | $126,290 |

Source: NAREIT. Annual amounts as of 12/31.

**Recent Market Performance:** 1996 turned out to be a good year for REITs with the average share price increasing 22.5 points, thus driving average total returns to over 35%. Office REITs produced the best investment performance, followed by industrial, hotels, apartments, and retail (See Exhibit 6).

**Exhibit 6**
**REIT Returns by Property Type**

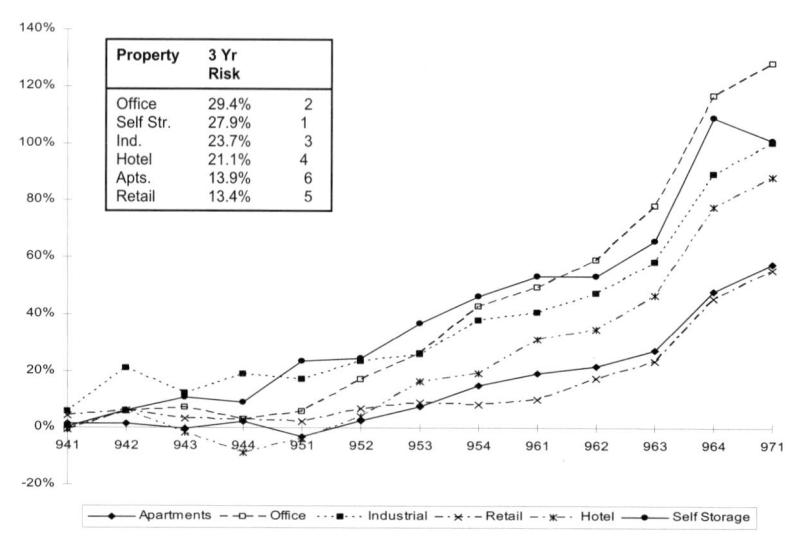

| Property | 3 Yr Risk | |
|----------|-----------|---|
| Office | 29.4% | 2 |
| Self Str. | 27.9% | 1 |
| Ind. | 23.7% | 3 |
| Hotel | 21.1% | 4 |
| Apts. | 13.9% | 6 |
| Retail | 13.4% | 5 |

Note: Risk Adjusted Return ranking calculated using Sharpe ratio methodology.

Source: Data: NAREIT, *Wall Street Journal.* Analysis: The McMahan Group

A large factor driving REIT investment performance was an increase in the price/FFO ratios, which peaked in late 1996. Multiples declined after the first of the year and as of June 30, 1997, averaged 12.4X 1997 FFO. The average dividend yield was 6.5% with an average total return of 15.7% over the prior 12 months. The average premium to NAV was 20.5% (See Exhibit 7).

As indicated in Exhibit 7, office REITs traded at a premium of 26.0% over NAV in mid 1997, second only to industrial REITs (33.9%). The office price-to-earnings multiple of 13.3X was the highest in the industry. Office REITs also traded at a 7.3% premium to other equity REITs, reflecting the belief in the market that they would experience higher levels of future growth.[4]

---

[4] Montgomery Securities.

## Exhibit 7
## REIT Performance by Property Type
## June 30, 1997

|  | Apartments | Regional Malls | Office | Industrial | Shopping Centers | Hotels | Totals/ Average* |
|---|---|---|---|---|---|---|---|
| Equity Market Cap* | $20,493.3 | $15,807.1 | $12,324.4 | $9,590.9 | $9,409.0 | $7,793.9 | $75,418.6 |
| Dividend Yield | 6.8% | 6.7% | 5.5% | 5.8% | 7.5% | 6.8% | 6.5% |
| Multiple | 11.9 | 13.1 | 13.3 | 12.9 | 11.6 | 10.9 | 12.4 |
| Premium to NAV | 15.5% | 16.2% | 26.0% | 33.9% | 17.1% | 21.2% | 20.5% |
| 12 Mo.Total Return | 15.7% | 14.0% | 15.9% | 18.0% | 13.6% | 19.0% | 15.7% |

\* Billions
\*\* Weighted by equity market capitalization

Source: Realty Stock Review, June 30, 1997

**Pension Fund Interest:** Despite the promise of the new REIT investment format, interest from pension funds was slow to develop. Research on early REITs indicated that they performed in a manner similar to small cap stocks, not real estate. This implied that pension funds could not rely on a low or negative correlation with equities to reduce overall portfolio risk. More recent studies challenged this conclusion, maintaining that modern REITs had a higher level of real estate "effect" and could help to improve portfolio risk-adjusted returns, although not to the extent possible through private real estate investment.[5]

As a result of these studies, as well as continued growth in the REIT market, pension investment in securitized real estate went from virtually nothing in 1989 to approximately 25% of their portfolios in 1996 (See Exhibit 8). A recent survey of pension investors indicated that they invest in REITs primarily through separate accounts and mutual funds. As with the broader REIT market, residential and retail are the major property types, followed by office, industrial, and hotels (See Exhibit 9). Other characteristics of the pension securitized real estate portfolio include debt ratio: 33.9%; dividend yield: 6.4%; P/E ratio: 14.2X; and portfolio turnover: 39.0%.[6]

---

[5] As an example, see S. Michael Giliberto and Anne Mengden, "REITs and Real Estate: Two Markets Reexamined", Real Estate Research, December 1995.
[6] Evaluation Associates.

## Exhibit 8
### Pension Investment in Equity Real Estate

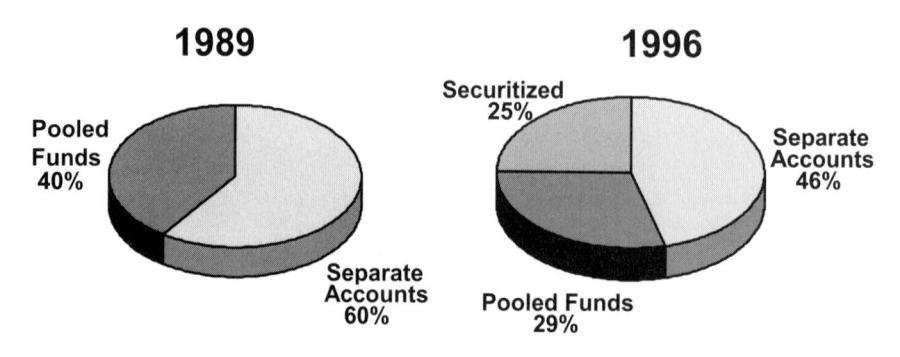

**1989**
- Pooled Funds 40%
- Separate Accounts 60%

**1996**
- Securitized 25%
- Separate Accounts 46%
- Pooled Funds 29%

Source: AEW

## Exhibit 9
### Pension Investment by Property Type, 1996 ($10 Billion)

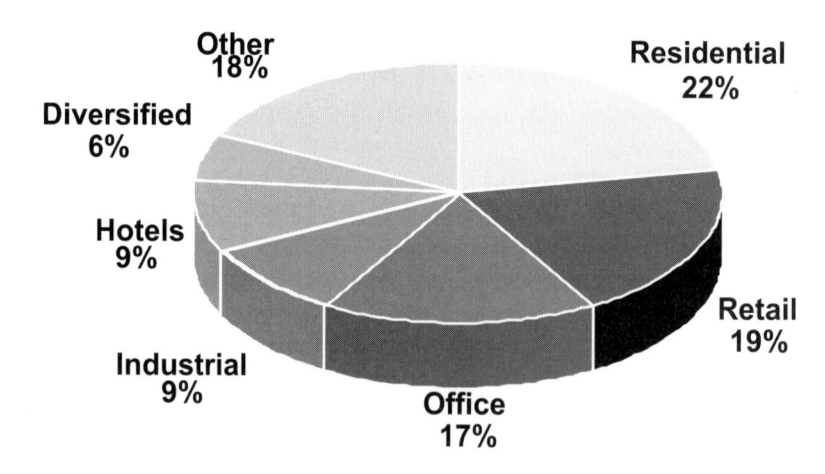

- Other 18%
- Diversified 6%
- Hotels 9%
- Industrial 9%
- Office 17%
- Retail 19%
- Residential 22%

Source: Data: Evaluation Associates. Analysis: The McMahan Group

**Enterprise value:** As a tax-avoidance vehicle, REITs should be expected to trade on the yield of underlying real estate assets less a liquidity discount. Today, however, many successful REITs sell for more than their underlying real estate values, reflecting a premium for the "enterprise value" inherent in a going concern."[7] Such a premium reflects the market's belief in management's

---

[7] In 1997, the premium ranged from 15% to 35% of the value of the underlying assets.

ability to grow future FFO through market and asset selection, development, refinancing, or restructuring investments (See Exhibit 10).

**Problem Areas:** Despite the success of many REITs, the industry faced some formidable problems in mid-1997. The combination of analyst and shareholder pressure on short-term FFO growth and the high payout of annual cash flow forced most REITs to return to the capital markets frequently. With highly competitive property markets, the lack of attractive investment opportunities was leading some REITs into marginal investments, both in terms of physical quality and economic return. Many so-called "independent directors" were in fact very close to management, and it wasn't always clear how good the vaunted REIT governance policies really were. Finally, many REIT boards and management lacked the vision and courage necessary to reposition their firms for future growth and profitability.

**Exhibit 10**
**Real Estate Enterprise Value**

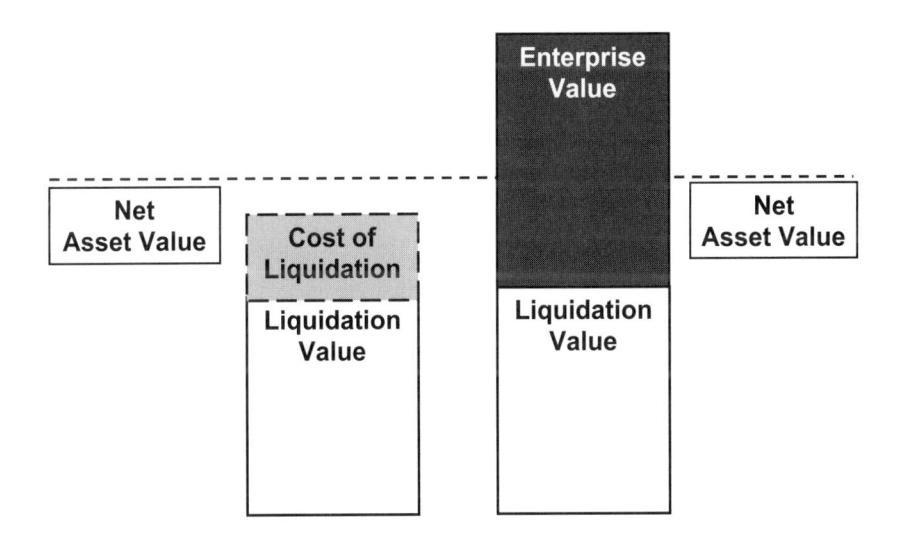

## The Boom in Office Markets

The office sector had been devastated by the real estate depression of 1987-1994 and as a result, was one of the last areas to experience economic recovery. By early 1997, however, America's office building expansion was in high gear, driven by strong growth in office jobs and the lack of new construction over the prior 10 years. In July 1997, office construction was running at a rate of 23 million square feet annually vs. 50 million square feet of annual absorption.[8] Reflecting the strong nature of office demand, almost three fourths of new construction involved build-to-suit facilities where a tenant was already in place.

This surging demand for office space helped to drive down vacancy rates for both downtown and suburban markets. As of March 31, 1997, downtown vacancy rates stood at 13.2%, down from 17.6% at the end of 1992, and suburban rates were 10.6%, down from 19.4% in 1992.[9] With less space on the market, effective rental rates were steadily increasing – up 4.9% in 1995 and 6.8% in 1996.[10]

The nature of office space demand was also changing. As business firms downsized and outsourced their operations, office demand began shifting from large companies to smaller companies, many of which worked for the larger companies. This trend has been accelerated by the application of new technologies which allowed many employees to operate from venues other than the traditional office (e.g., home, hotel, airplane, etc.). Many firms also have experimented with a variety of new ways to organize the work effort including open space design, "hoteling," and the widely reported "virtual" office format. In all cases, the emphasis is on providing the firm with flexibility in dealing with its office requirements.

These shifts in demand have made many older office buildings functionally obsolete. They may be designed for the large company "footprint" where columns and other obstacles make it difficult to reformat space for smaller tenants. More commonly, many older buildings are not designed to adapt to the requirements of modern technology, and retrofitting is expensive if not impossible. Finally, the building may not be functionally obsolete but is in an area where people do not wish to work.

The combination of these and other factors has contributed to suburban locations becoming more attractive to many office users. The suburbs offer lower land costs, facilitating new design and construction, and are located where most people live. In many cities (e.g., Dallas, Denver, San Diego, Tampa, etc.), suburban rents exceed downtown locations.[11]

## *Office REITs Share in the Boom*

Consistent with their position in the real estate cycle, office REITs did not really get going until mid-1996. In the succeeding 12 months, six office REITs went public and a large number were poised in the pipeline, including Equity Office Properties Trust, a multibillion national office REIT which went public

---

[8] Grubb & Ellis.
[9] CB Commercial.
[10] Grubb & Ellis.
[11] National Real Estate Index.

shortly thereafter. The total equity raised by these REITs was $2.2 billion. As of June 27, 1997, the average price had increased 13.7% over the issuing price (See Exhibit 11).

In terms of operations, these new office REITs had a relatively low debt ratio (27.1%), although floating debt was quite high (22.8%). FFO is expected to increase 11.3% over the next 12 months. FFO multiples, however, were expected to decline in 1998 along with lower expectations for the market overall (See Exhibit 12).

### Exhibit 11
### Recent Office REIT IPOs

| Ticker | Company | Market* | IPO Date | Capital Raised** | IPO Price | Price ###### | Percentage Change |
|---|---|---|---|---|---|---|---|
| ARI | Arden Realty Corporation | CA | 10/4/1996 | $377 | $20.00 | $26.00 | 30.0% |
| PP | Prentiss Properties | TX/WI/CA/GA | ####### | 323 | 20.00 | 25.00 | 25.0% |
| KRC | Kilroy Realty Corporation | CA/WA/AZ | 1/29/1997 | 331 | 23.00 | 25.50 | 10.9% |
| CPP | Cornerstone Properties, Inc. | NY/WA/MA/IL | 4/15/1997 | 225 | 14.00 | 15.00 | 7.1% |
| GL | Great Lakes REIT, Inc. | IL/WI/MI | 5/7/1997 | 88 | 15.50 | 16.00 | 3.2% |
| BXP | Boston Properties | MA/DC/CA | 6/18/1997 | 903 | 25.00 | 26.88 | 7.5% |
| Totals/Averages*** | | | | $2,247 | $21.67 | $24.64 | 13.7% |

**In Registration**

| | | | | | | |
|---|---|---|---|---|---|---|
| | Equity Office Properties Trust | | | $345 | $20.00 | |
| | SL Green Realty | | | $186 | $20.00 | |

\* States in order of number of properties
\*\* Millions
\*\*\* Weighted by capital raised.

Source: Montgomery Securities; The McMahan Group

Interestingly, office REITs own only 6% of institutional grade office square footage in major metropolitan areas.[12] Many observers expect this relatively low penetration to lead to a large amount of consolidation activity as managers attempt to add economic scale to their operations through the acquisition of private market portfolios and companies. The improvement in office property values also makes it more attractive to sell companies than it did a few years ago.

---

[12] Montgomery Securities.

## Exhibit 12
### Office REIT Operating Data

| Ticker | Company | Debt/ Mkt. Cap. | Floating Debt | EBITDA/ Interest | FFO/Share 1997 | FFO/Share 1998 | FFO Multiple 1997 | FFO Multiple 1998 |
|---|---|---|---|---|---|---|---|---|
| ARI | Arden Realty Corporation | 23.0% | 100.0% | 5.3% | $2.16 | $2.39 | 12.0 | 10.9 |
| PP | Prentiss Properties | 25.0% | 3.0% | 5.7% | $2.25 | $2.45 | 11.1 | 10.2 |
| KRC | Kilroy Realty Corporation | 18.0% | 13.0% | 4.2% | $1.97 | $2.26 | 12.9 | 11.3 |
| CPP | Cornerstone Properties, Inc. | 32.0% | 4.0% | 2.7% | $1.26 | $1.37 | 11.9 | 10.9 |
| GL | Great Lakes REIT, Inc. | 4.0% | 0.0% | N/A | $1.49 | $1.69 | 10.7 | 9.5 |
| BXP | Boston Properties | 34.0% | 8.0% | N/A | $1.95 | N/A | 13.8 | N/A |
| Average* | | 27.1% | 22.8% | 4.6% | $1.94 | $2.16 | 12.7 | 10.7 |

* Weighted by capital raised.

Source: Montgomery Securities; The McMahan Group

The trend to larger economic units is consistent with and reinforces the need of office tenants for more flexible operating environments and a greater menu of services as a result of downsizing. Many observers believe that ownership and rental of office space will provide a platform to market a wide variety of services to building tenants. Larger companies, the reasoning goes, will have the resources to launch and maintain such platforms and benefit from a broader array of income opportunities.

## The REIT Roll-Up Phenomenon

The exceptional market performance of REITs and the continuing strong IPO market has led many investment advisors and other private market managers to propose programs to "roll-up" their clients' assets into new REITs. To some extent, this is a response to client pressure to create new approaches to real estate investing. As of June 1997, as many as 18 roll-ups were under consideration, although one proposal had been withdrawn as a result of investor pressure (See Exhibit 13).

The term "roll-up" was coined in the early 1990s to describe the process by which general partners of syndicated real estate limited partnerships forced limited partners to convert their partnership interests to stock ownership, often at a steep discount. Noting that the current REIT roll-ups were usually at a premium and that investors had much more influence over the roll-up process, many sponsors prefer to term them "consolidations" or "restructurings."

## Exhibit 13

### Potential IPOs Involving Advisory Firms and/or Their Assets

| Sponsoring Firm | Potential REIT size | Property Type | Current Structure | Status |
|---|---|---|---|---|
| AMB Institutional Realty Advisors, Inc. | $2.5 B | Industrial with some retail | Commingled funds; sep. accts; private REIT | Studying roll-up as one of several options to present to clients. If approved, AMB would launch an IPO of $200-$300M as early as 4Q '97. |
| Cabot Partners | $1 B | Industrial; R&D office | Primarily sep accts; 1 commingled fund | Expects to present plan for preliminary first step by June. Pending investor approval, Cabot would proceed with portfolio valuation this summer. |
| Heitman Capital Management Corporation | $1.6 B (3 REITs) | Industrial; office | 18 commingled funds; co-invested w/ sep accts | Withdrew proposal on May 15. Intends to go forward according to original business plan of each fund. |
| Koll/Bren Realty Advisors | $1.1 B | Industrial; office | 4 opportunistic funds; sep accts | In early June, tabled its plan to consolidate industrial and office properties. Intends to pursue original business plans. |
| MIG Realty Advisors | $1.5 B | Multifamily | Sep accts; 2 priv trusts; priv REIT | Proposing to consolidate into a private REIT this summer that could go public as early as 4Q '97. Investors approved first stage: property appraisals. |
| The Retail Property Trust (RPT) | $5 B | Retail | Private REIT advised by The O'Conner Group | RPT, Richard E. Jacobs Group, Inc., and New England Development may merge. Pending investor approval, the firm could file a REIT IPO by 4Q '97. |
| W.P. Carey & Co., Inc. | $800 M (9 REITs) | Triple net lease; R&D office | 9 investment partnerships | Hired third parties to evaluate exit strategies for the partnerships. |
| Zell/Merrill Lynch Real Estate Opportunity Funds | $2.1 B | Office | Comm funds; private REITs | Filed an initial public offering with the SEC in May. |

Source: Institutional Real Estate Securities, June 1997

Sponsors believe that the new entities formed by the roll-up process will be attractive to investors for several reasons. Most institutional real estate holdings reflect higher quality properties than those traditionally held by REITs. The sizes of the portfolios are often larger than most REITs, in some cases among the largest of their property type. This larger economic scale helps to lower the cost of capital and spread the cost of corporate infrastructure over a larger base, thus leading to higher investment returns. Some advisors also believe that they can bring a better quality of management than the public market has experienced to date.

Critics argue that larger economic scale can also create problems as the pressure to acquire large numbers of assets makes it more difficult to develop a "growth story" and have a significant impact on earnings. Furthermore, not everyone agrees that advisors are better managers of assets, as demonstrated by their disastrous performance in the 1980s. There is also concern that managing a public company is "different" and requires special skills most advisors have not utilized in the past. This perception becomes particularly important if the roll-up process awards a "value premium" to a management team before it has proven itself in the public marketplace.

## The Western Roll-Up Proposal

In order to retain their clients, preserve Western as a viable firm, and monetize the value of their personal equity positions in the firm, Jim and Serge decided in early 1997 to explore the possibility of a roll-up of their clients' assets into a new public entity. They consulted several investment bankers experienced in REIT public offerings and began to develop a plan, which was distributed to clients for comments in early July.

The new entity would be organized as a private REIT, which would continue to acquire and develop properties and go public in 6 to 12 months when it reached approximately $1 billion in assets. If the REIT did not go public within one year, investors could force a registration through a two-thirds affirmative vote. The new REIT would be internally managed and include a new property management group that would be integrated into the overall operation.

In capitalizing the new entity, Western's pension clients would contribute the $725 million in assets currently managed by Western. Western would contribute its management fees (e.g., acquisition, development, asset management, property management, and disposition). Jim and his team would execute three 3-year employment contracts filling similar roles as they had in the advisory firm. Both clients and Western would receive common shares with equal voting rights.

The new REIT would be valued at $750 million, reflecting a value to the management company of approximately $25 million. Both the property values and the value of Western would be confirmed through independent appraisal. When the REIT went public, a fairness opinion would be obtained from the investment banking firm leading the underwriting. Total costs of the public issue were estimated to be approximately $6 million, most of which ultimately would be paid by Western's clients.

The Western portfolio was largely unleveraged. While operating as a private REIT, however, up to 30% of the portfolio's value could be borrowed in order to provide funds to acquire and develop sufficient assets to reach the $1 billion IPO threshold. At this point, a five million share IPO would raise an additional $100 million to be utilized for new acquisitions and development projects. The pension investors would agree not to sell their shares for one year after the IPO (termed a "lock-out"), and management shares could not be sold for 3 years.

The new REIT would have a seven-person board: Jim, Serge, Bill and four independent directors. Western clients could participate in the selection of independent directors if they chose to do so.

A REIT subsidiary would be formed to own and manage assets that clients did not want to place in the new REIT or properties that Western did not choose to include. Up to 15% of Western's portfolio could be owned in the subsidiary, which would also have the right to add private market assets from shareholders in the REIT as well as manage assets for new clients who preferred to own assets directly.

In terms of pricing, most of the investment bankers felt that Western would command a multiple of 12-13X since it was active in the suburban office markets in the Western U.S. where growth prospects continued to be very favorable. The offering would also be attractive since Western had quality assets and strong institutional backing. The management team was also seasoned, having worked together for many years. Their development capabilities also would be attractive to investors in light of the dearth of new office construction.

Jim believed that the roll-up would be a "win-win" situation for Western's clients. The greater liquidity ultimately created by the daily pricing of a public market would provide greater control over investment programs. The stock value would be "accretive" to investors, allowing them to essentially arbitrage the public and private markets and participate in the "enterprise value" of the new firm. Management's interests would be better aligned with those of investors, with a large portion of personal compensation materializing only if investors made money. Finally, the public market process would establish higher levels of scrutiny, disclosure, and governance to help protect the plan sponsor's fiduciary interests.

## *Conversation with Tom Razier*

Cami had begun her client follow-up calls with some of Western's older and smaller clients who were generally pleased with the Firm's performance and with whom they had long-standing relationships. Generally, all of these calls went well.

She had put off talking with BURP and other large clients until she had a better understanding from the earlier calls as to the questions she might receive and the nature of possible client resistance.

Despite these precautions, she was not prepared for Tom's reaction.

He first reminded Cami that the reason BURP was in real estate was to reduce total portfolio risk by investing in an asset class that had low or negative correlation with its stock portfolio. Tom had seen research indicating that REITs had a high positive correlation to stocks and that he could expect little, if any, reduction in portfolio risk from adding REITs.

He also did not like the idea of the private REIT as an interim step. If he were to give up control over his portfolio, he wanted the right to sell his shares if he didn't like the way things progressed. As presently contemplated, the private REIT would be largely illiquid and, when coupled with the one year lock-out, he and other investors would not be able to trade their shares for at least 18 to 24 months. Even then, the size of their holdings would make it difficult to trade large blocks of stock.

Tom contrasted the illiquidity of the roll-up process with the private market where, as a result of intense demand for office properties and little new production, BURP's assets currently could be sold at relatively high prices. He didn't know how long this market frenzy would continue and felt that perhaps the clients would be better served if Western began culling portfolios to capture appreciated values and enhance investor returns.

He also was concerned with the REIT subsidiary that Western was proposing to use to continue managing private assets. Although Tom realized that this proposal was to some degree a means of giving investors more choices, he was concerned with the potential conflict of interest between public and private investors and with the way the arrangement might be viewed by security analysts and non-pension investors. "Isn't one of the attractions of REITs their ability to reduce conflicts by better aligning management and investor interests?" asked Tom.

The valuation of Western also bothered him. He felt that $25 million was too much for a company whose only assets were management contracts, the vast majority of which were cancelable on 30 days notice. As he put it, if he were going to trade hard assets (real estate) for "elevator assets" (people), he would at least expect to receive shares with some form of preferential interest.

Besides, if he wanted to convert his interest to REIT shares, he could trade his assets for the shares of a seasoned REIT that is well regarded in the public market place. He had been approached by several existing office REITs and believed that a workable asset trade could be arranged. Cami mentioned that such an approach would not provide the IPO "pop" in value inherent in the roll-up.

Tom countered that he was somewhat dubious about the true value of the IPO "pop" to the investors. He felt that much of the anticipated increase in value came from leveraging the portfolio and that the increased risk from leveraging had not been adequately considered by Western in its proposed plan. When Cami asked if a lower level of portfolio leverage would ease his concerns, Tom said he didn't think it would make much difference.

Finally, Tom was upset with the relatively short amount of time that he and his Board had been given to make a decision. BURP had been systematically considering its strategy for securitized real estate for some time, and the Western roll-up put them under pressure to make a decision much faster than they desired. Tom felt that they needed more time to analyze their overall portfolio strategy and suggested to Cami that the decision on participating in the roll-up be extended until after the first of the year. He also stated that he felt Western should pay for the major portion of the $6 million in underwriting costs.

Cami finally gathered up her courage and asked Tom if, despite his concerns, he would vote for the roll-up. Tom said that if the proposal was the same as the package he had just reviewed, he would vote no and if asked, would encourage other investors to do the same. He did say, however, that he would consider a revised proposal that addresses his concerns.

In a state of shock, Cami thanked Tom for being candid and said she would get back to him in the next few days.

## *The Management Meeting*

Before Cami had a chance to catch her breath, Jim interrupted the management meeting to ask what had happened in her phone conversation with BURP. As Cami related her conversation, an enveloping cloud of gloom settled over the meeting. When she finished, the mood of the meeting changed abruptly to heated debate as the whole concept of the roll-up was back on the table, and latent wounds reopened.

One group of managers led by Jim wanted to proceed with the roll-up as it had been proposed. Western had generally good relations with its clients and with the exception of BURP, all contacted so far had indicated support. Western's investment banker believed that a successful public issue could be completed once Western had $1 billion in assets in its portfolio.

Jim also expressed concern that Western's assets were "in play" and if they didn't proceed with the roll-up, many of the assets would be picked off by office REITs or other advisors undertaking roll-up programs. Jim was particularly concerned with the ability of REITs to trade assets for common shares or for Operating Partner (OP) units, which could later be converted to REIT shares. Cami was aware of at least four of Western's clients that had been contacted by REIT representatives since news of their roll-up had leaked to the investment community.

In addition, Jim was concerned with the fall-off in private market commitments from pension investors. Western had been in many fewer RFP situations in the last 12 months, and the $110 million in uninvested commitments may be all of the new funds they might receive if they didn't take a dramatic step such as the roll-up program.

A second group of managers wanted to modify the roll-up proposal to make it more attractive to BURP. They argued that since BURP was their largest client ($135 million), its rejection of the roll-up most likely would be viewed as a negative by other investors and perhaps by Wall Street. This group wanted to drop the private REIT interim step and move immediately to a public issue to take advantage of the current strong IPO market. "Who knows what the market will be like in 6 to 12 months?" one of them argued. Several members of this group also were willing to modify management shares to make them subordinate to their clients' position and extend management contracts and "lock out" provisions from 3 to 5 years.

The final and most vocal group wanted to drop the roll-up idea altogether and continue as a private market investment advisor. They believed that the "move" to securitization by pension investors was a more of a temporary "lurch" that would go away with any major drop in the stock market. They were also concerned that their personal compensation would be tied to stock options, which could be worthless in the event of such a market downturn. In terms of operation, they also did not believe that property management should be internalized or that a REIT was a good vehicle for development activities.

After two hours, Jim abruptly announced that they weren't getting anywhere and that they all should go home and "cool off." The management meeting was rescheduled for 10:30 AM the next morning and each of the managers was asked to prepare a memo recommending a course of action for Western with full supporting arguments.

As she left the meeting, Cami wondered what she would recommend and how it would be received by Tom and their other clients. She knew it would be (another) long night.

## Questions for Discussion

Questions that should be addressed in this case include:

1. How would you describe Western's operation? How good is the management team and Western's relationship with its clients?

2. What are BURP's concerns about the asset roll up scheme that Western has proposed? Are they logical and well founded? What risks do BURP and other institutional investors have in the use of the private REIT structure?

3. What alternative courses of action does Western have? Which one should they pursue? Why?

Please use these questions as a guide and a format or a reflection of all of the questions that need to be addressed by the case.

# 19

# HINES INTERESTS LP EMERGING MARKETS REAL ESTATE FUND II[1]

## Global Investing

Hasty Johnson put aside the draft prospectus describing Emerging Markets Real Estate Fund II (Fund) and poured himself another glass of iced tea. Hasty was the Chief Financial Officer of Hines Interests, LP (Hines), a worldwide real estate development and management firm, and was struggling in the summer of 1999 whether or not to recommend proceeding with the Fund.

Fund I had been established in May, 1996 to invest U.S. capital in real estate located in emerging countries. Hines and The TCW Group (TCW) were General Partners in Fund I and would team together for Fund II. Dean Witter Realty Inc. (Dean Witter) was a partner in Fund I but had dropped out from subsequent funds following its merger with Morgan Stanley in early 1997.

Based on their success in raising capital from institutional investors in Fund I, Hasty and his partners intended to market Fund II exclusively to institutional investors. Several of the Hines managing partners, however, feared that marketing and executing Fund II would be difficult due to recent financial crises in Russia and Asia.

---

[1] This case was prepared by John McMahan and Andrew Light in 1999. All material in the case is deemed to be factual except for the circumstances of the management meeting and its consideration of various strategic alternatives added to provide an educational context. Copyright © 1999 and 2004 by John McMahan, all rights reserved.

These partners argued that the world's emerging markets had not recovered sufficiently from the financial turmoil that occurred since the marketing of Fund I. They worried that it would not be easy to place capital under such turbulent conditions. They also believed that new investors would want to know the investment performance of Fund I before they invested in Fund II. As of June, 1999, most of the projects in the earlier fund were not stabilized sufficiently to provide meaningful performance information.

While Hasty would not personally have the final decision on the target investors or the timing of Fund II, he would have considerable influence over the direction that the marketing program would ultimately take. A meeting of the Hines partners was scheduled for July 1st, and Hasty knew he had to come to closure regarding whether to proceed or not and, if they decided to proceed, how to best position the fund in the marketplace.

## *Investment Concept*

Fund I had been based on the concept of capitalizing on unsatisfied demand for high quality real estate space near urban areas in emerging and transitional markets. The goal was to develop, own, manage, lease, operate, and sell Class A real estate projects in order to generate high cash yields and selling prices for the Fund's investors. Fund II was based on the same concept as Fund I and as currently proposed, would be structured and operated largely in the same manner.

**Demand/Supply Imbalance:** Over the last several years, demand for high quality space in emerging markets had increased as many of these nations' economies grew stronger. The World Bank predicted that from 1996 to 2004, developing economies would grow at an average annual rate of 4.8%, which would be a substantially faster pace than the 2.7% rate predicted for wealthier industrialized countries.

Emerging market growth was driven by ongoing economic reforms that promised to streamline trade and investment. These reforms included the privatization of state enterprises, reduction in foreign debt levels, liberalization of trade and foreign investment regulations, and inflation control through improved fiscal and monetary policy.

Despite these strong demand forces, Class A real estate space was in low supply in most emerging markets due to a combination of factors including a lack of capital, lack of construction and design expertise, absence of reliable real estate information, and poor property management.

This imbalance existed across a broad range of property types including residential, retail, industrial, and office. Demand for Class A office space was growing as multinational companies expanded their presence in emerging markets and domestic companies sought to "trade-up" into space with superior ventilation, lighting, and technological capacity.

Demand for well located and efficient industrial space also was growing as trade flows increased. Residential and retail demand was particularly strong among expatriate employees of multinational companies who appreciated and would pay a premium for first class shopping and housing accommodations.

**Limited Capital:** Debt financing for real estate in emerging markets was extremely difficult to obtain, and very few countries had any form of mortgage lending markets. Title insurance was essentially nonexistent in Hines' target markets except in Mexico.

Undercapitalized local developers frequently utilized pre-sales to hedge risk of loss, thus limiting their ability to invest in long-term, quality projects. Chronic inflation led many people to own their own apartments or offices, and widespread "condominium" ownership of individual units within buildings inhibited efficient property management and the formation of real estate service companies. The absence of such companies prevented access to relevant real estate information, a factor that further inhibited real estate development.

**Role of Foreign Direct Investment:** Higher investor confidence in emerging markets was demonstrated by changes in the levels and composition of capital flows. While inflows to emerging debt and equity markets decreased from $107 billion in 1993 to $32 billion in 1995, inflows in the form of foreign direct investment (FDI) rose from $19 billion in 1990 to $106 billion in 1996. From 1996 to 1998, FDI levels remained strong in the countries where Fund I's projects were located.

Because FDI generally consisted of relatively long-term investments, these inflows were less volatile and not as susceptible to rapid capital flight in the event of unforeseen political or economic trouble. During the Mexican peso devaluation of 1994-95, for example, investors' fear of instability in emerging markets led to a significant decline in portfolio investment. In contrast, FDI remained relatively stable.

As one of the Hines managers noted,

> "FDI is a particularly important indicator for us because we pursue a much less volatile investment strategy than most equity investors. The relatively long-term horizon for FDI is similar to the horizon of real estate investments and, most importantly, the commitment term of quality multinational tenants.

Like many real estate investors, large corporations with substantial investments in production systems and human capital frequently elect to ride out short-term economic swings. We believe that stable FDI levels foster growth in demand for quality space in supply-constrained markets and that we should take advantage of this through a well-conceived investment program."

**Focus on Development:** Many Hines managers believed that the supply of space in emerging markets would continue to be constrained and that both Funds I and II (the Funds) were uniquely positioned to capture high levels of market share in target markets. The imbalance of supply and demand suggested high occupancy rates and high rental and sales revenues relative to development costs, which would translate into high returns for investors.

The Funds focused on the development of new real estate but would consider investing in existing properties whose value could be enhanced through renovation and better property management. No more than 25% of the Funds' committed capital could be invested in any single project, and no more that 33% could be invested in any single country, although these figures could be increased to 40% with the approval of the Fund's Advisory Committee. In addition to equity interests, the Funds could invest in debt, leasehold interests, land use rights, or other real estate interests.

Another Hines manager commented:

"In our experience, real estate projects in emerging markets are quite different from those in industrialized countries. In Europe and Japan, for example, land is a larger percentage of a project's cost and deals are often leveraged up to 90% in order to reach hurdle rates. We considered a European fund and backed off because the leverage required to meet returns would have been too risky. In contrast, emerging market projects are more "basic real estate" with little leverage and higher cash-on-cash returns. Russia, for example, is not as bad a market as it sounds because we can earn 20-25% cash-on-cash return and a fallback strategy is to earn your way out. China can be even less risky because a well conceived project can achieve a 25-35% cash-on-cash return.

One might think that construction costs are lower in emerging markets, but that has usually not been the case in our experience. For example, we had to fly a number of our Russian staff to the U.S. for training so that we could be sure they understood top-quality product, techniques, and processes.

Furthermore, our international real estate strategy is substantially different from that of most opportunity funds. Our Funds pursue a fundamental real estate strategy while other funds, particularly those run by investment banks, often focus more on financial arbitrage such as interest rate and return differentials. One of our challenges is that the five year holding period of the fund format may not allow us enough time to sell assets at the top of real estate cycles. Ideally, our projects can be profitably liquidated within five years, but if that is not the case we will have to be ready with alternative strategies. "

## *Organization*

The proposed organization and operation of Fund II was similar to Fund I except as noted below.

**General Partners:** The original partnership between Hines, TCW, and Dean Witter grew out of previous business relationships. Prior to forming Fund I, affiliates of Dean Witter and TCW had teamed together on various international joint ventures including roughly $400 million of direct investment in non-real estate projects in China.

Through this experience, the companies developed contacts with government officials and movers and shakers in China's business community. For example, when a Chinese joint venture partner had a site in Beijing and was looking for a partner with development expertise, Dean Witter invited Hines to review the opportunity. At the time, Hines was seeking international projects in order to meet the increasing space requests of its existing multinational tenants. Although Hines declined to pursue this deal, the company continued to investigate real estate opportunities in China with Dean Witter.

Working together, the two companies concluded that capital was a major entry barrier and decided to explore the concept of an investment fund. The Fund would be targeted toward real estate in China with Dean Witter calling upon its contacts at TCW to assist in capital raising.

TCW reviewed the Chinese opportunities and suggested that a global fund would be easier to market to institutional investors. TCW's reasoning was threefold: 1) the favorable economic conditions in China were also present in a number of other emerging markets; 2) a global fund would enjoy the risk-mitigating benefits of diversification; and 3) a broader opportunity scope would likely identify superior projects.

The partnership was strengthened by the complementary abilities of each of the three entities.

**Hines**: Hines brought expertise in property development and management as well as an understanding of real estate markets in industrialized, transitional, and developing countries. The company's relationships with corporate tenants, built over four decades of operations, offered the General Partner insight into multinationals' space demands and facilitated the marketing of the Fund I's properties.

Hasty commented:

> "We have found that many of our multinational tenants view real estate in emerging markets as a headache. Their companies want to expand into new countries, but there are very few quality places to house their employees and operations. Space is such a problem for them that they are unusually forthright in communicating their needs to us, and they are sometimes willing to pay 700 basis points above U.S. real estate prices in order to make the headache go away."

Hines was a privately owned international real estate firm that had developed more than 400 properties in the United States and abroad. This activity represented more than 100 million square feet of office, mixed-use, industrial, retail, and residential space. Tenants included blue-chip multinational companies such as American Express, Disney, Merrill Lynch, Nippon Life, Hoffman-LaRoche, Pepsi Cola, Proctor & Gamble, and Toyota.

Hines had experience in all phases of real estate development from site selection to completion and was one of the few major U.S. real estate firms to maintain a core focus on development through the real estate bear market of the early 1990s. The company was known for its low employee turnover and close-knit culture. Hines recruited mainly MBAs and emphasized rigorous training with relatively long assignments on major projects. At the time of Fund I's inception, Hines had international development or redevelopment projects underway in Berlin, Mexico City, Prague, Paris, and Frankfurt.

Hines was headquartered in Houston, with offices in Atlanta, Chicago, New York, and San Francisco. The firm also had branch offices in 40 other U.S. cities and in Asia, Europe, Russia, and Mexico.

**TCW:** TCW was a leading institutional asset management firm with over $50 billion under management at the time of the launching of Fund I. TCW brought relationships with key figures in the government, financial, and business sectors of many target countries. TCW also was able to provide in-depth analyses of market trends and identify conditions that were suitable for foreign direct investment. At the time of Fund I's inception, TCW had approximately $11.6 billion in assets under management internationally with $4 billion in emerging markets. In the 12 years prior to forming Fund I, TCW had raised approximately $3 billion for investment in real estate.

**Dean Witter:** Dean Witter Realty brought extensive experience in real estate acquisitions, dispositions, financing, and securitization. The firm was a subsidiary of Dean Witter, Discover & Co., a $9 billion financial services company with approximately $80 billion of assets under management.

From 1982 to 1996, Dean Witter Realty raised approximately $3.2 billion in debt and equity for investment in institutional quality real estate in the U.S. Its affiliates had acquired or developed more than 90 properties. In addition, between 1992 and 1996, an affiliate of Dean Witter had managed 84 public real estate offerings for real estate investment trusts, activity that made it the second largest manager of such offerings in the U.S. The company was particularly strong in designing disposition strategies.

Just as the General Partners were considering a second fund, Dean Witter merged with Morgan Stanley. Morgan Stanley already had several of its own real estate funds, at least two of which were investing overseas. This presented the General Partner with a dilemma: how could Hines and TCW continue to sponsor a fund with a partner that already had its own funds abroad? The conflict of interest ultimately required that Dean Witter drop out of the planning for Fund II and all subsequent funds, although the Dean Witter partners remained with Fund I.

**Limited Partners:** Fund I was actually three parallel funds, each structured as a limited partnership with a distinct group of Limited Partners. Fund IA's sole Limited Partner was a major U.S. corporate pension fund. Fund IB's Limited Partners included other pension investors. Fund IC's Limited Partners were investors other than the Fund IA and IB investors. The General Partners were considering following a similar three-fund structure for Fund II.

The composition of Fund II limited partners was still being discussed by the management team. The current concept was to market Fund II exclusively to U.S. institutional investors.

## *Governance:*

**Investment Committee:** All investments were approved by an investment committee comprised of two individuals from each firm serving as the General Partner. The General Partner had the right to increase or decrease the size of the investment committee.

**Advisory Committee:** The Limited Partners with the five largest capital commitments across all the funds would each appoint a member to an Advisory Committee. The Advisory Committee would approve exceptions to diversification requirements and manage conflicts of interest in operating and financial agreements between the Funds and any affiliates of the General Partner (such as a property management company).

**Cash Distributions:** Cash flow from project investments was distributed as follows:

1) Recovery of all partners' capital contributions plus 10% compound return.
2) Then, "disposition" fees to the General Partners.
3) Then, 60% to Limited and General Partners in proportion to their investments, and 40% to the General Partners until the General Partners had received 20% of all distributions.
4) Then, 80% to the Limited and General Partners in proportion to their investments and 20% to the General Partner.

**Tax Issues:** Investments were structured to maximize after-tax returns.[2] One step was to qualify the Funds as a "venture capital operating company" under ERISA. To the extent possible the General Partner attempted to avoid "unrelated business taxable income." The Funds were structured as partnerships rather than corporations in order to avoid corporate taxes in the U.S. Operating Entities paid income taxes to the country in which they were organized and operated.

In addition, some countries required withholding taxes for distributions paid abroad. Non-tax-exempt U.S. partners were generally entitled to a tax credit against U.S. tax liability on foreign income for any taxes paid to foreign

---

[2] Although tax-exempt in the U.S., pension funds were subject to taxes in other countries.

countries. To the extent possible, the funds were operated in a manner that allowed non-U.S. investors to avoid U.S. income taxes.

The structure of the Funds' investments in an Operating Entity (i.e. equity vs. debt) varied according to how a particular country treated interest payments when computing income tax. Consideration also was given to whether an income tax treaty between the country and the U.S. provided a substantial benefit to utilizing dividends or interest.

**Fundraising:** Fund I was launched in 1996, just over a year after the Mexican peso crisis of December, 1994. While FDI inflows to Mexico remained relatively stable after the crisis, the event made institutional investors wary of the risk and volatility associated with international investments. In addition, many institutional investors had already been made aware of real estate risk due to the large write-offs that many had taken on their U.S. real estate holdings in the early 1990s.

Despite these challenges, the General Partners believed in the fundamental soundness of their investment strategy and forecasted leveraged returns in excess of 20%. Their marketing program was successful and Fund I closed in September 1996 with approximately $410 million in commitments raised over a 15-month period.

## Investment Process

**Country Screening:** In targeting countries for investment, the General Partner sought the following characteristics:

- Potential for high economic growth in the medium term (i.e. five to seven years), particularly growth due to productivity or technological advancements, privatizations, or increased presence of multinational corporations.

- Favorable macroeconomic indicators, particularly a country's ability to service debt. This ability was evaluated based on manageable current account balances, reasonable total debt to GDP ratios, and foreign exchange reserves. A nation's inability to service debt could lead to currency devaluation, exchange rate volatility, inflation, higher interest rates, restricted capital flows, and ultimately, slower economic growth.

- Commitment to free market economic policies including liberal trade rules and prudent regulatory and fiscal measures.

- Increasing FDI, usually an indicator of future capital inflows, economic growth, and increased demand for high quality space.

- Population and demographics with an expanding "middle class" that participated in the political system and government reforms. The General Partner believed that growth of a middle class generally stabilized political and economic conditions, thus fostering foreign investment and economic growth.

- A legal framework that reasonably protected foreign investors.

**Analysis of Real Estate Markets:** In addition to country characteristics, the General Partners screened for general real estate market conditions. Specific factors considered included the system of title or land registration, restrictions on foreign ownership of land, mortgage lending and insurance markets, property transfer fees or restrictions, current leasing markets, and property management sophistication. Property taxes, taxes on sales of properties, and taxes on repatriation of funds would be considered in terms of their impact on expected investment returns.

As one of the Hines partners noted,

> "Once we identified a promising target country, we conducted a more detailed analysis on particular cities and projects. We wanted to be in the prime business areas or in the path of future growth. Urban centers were usually most sought after by multinationals and would produce the greatest demand for high quality space."

Target metropolitan areas were divided into submarkets by prevailing property type or tenant use in order to identify what types of projects would be successful. Land use patterns and trends were analyzed to determine how the city would most likely evolve. Submarkets were evaluated according to key drivers of location preference such as proximity to airports and transportation infrastructure, ease of commute to principal residential areas, security, and availability of retail and entertainment amenities.

The General Partners also evaluated the existing and planned supply of properties. Existing facilities would be examined for their size, functionality, technological capacity, occupancy levels, tenant mix, and aesthetic appeal. The General Partners also reviewed new, potentially competing projects, noting their location, quality, ownership, tenant pre-commitments, and the strength and focus of marketing. The combination of data on existing and planned supply, along with information on prevailing government attitudes toward new development approvals, assisted in defining the supply and demand characteristics of desirable submarkets.

Through interviews with local architects and contractors, the General Partners gathered information on land, construction, and operating costs in addition to collecting limited data on cap rates and comparable sales. Wherever such information was unreliable or unavailable, the General Partners developed estimates by adapting data from similar markets.

Hines also interviewed its existing multinational tenants to better understand the nature of their space needs in terms of property types, preferred ownership structure, or proximity to residential districts.

**Operating Entities and Local Partners:** The General Partners formed project-specific Operating Entities that could enter into joint ventures with local partners. Under such arrangements, Operating Entities would marry the Fund's capital and development expertise with a local partner's familiarity with local issues and business practices and in some cases, with additional capital.

If a local partner were not available, the Operating Entities might contract with individuals with experience in development or management of local real estate projects. In all cases, the General Partners retained a controlling interest in order to oversee and supervise the activities of the local partners.

One of the Hines partners pointed out:

> "Finding a good local partner is always a challenge. The key is to select someone you hold in high regard and who can add value to the project. A local partner might be someone who controls a particular site or has the ability to locate and acquire other development sites. Or, it might be someone who understands the nuances of a country's planning and approval process and has relationships with local contractors, architects, and engineers. It is also a plus if the local partner can help market the property to creditworthy domestic tenants.
>
> In almost every case, we have found that developing and managing cross-cultural business relationships requires two to three times as much executive time and attention as a U.S.

partnership. We look to leverage that time investment and pursue more than one project in the markets that we know and in which we have established trusted partners. In Mexico, we developed trust and confidence in our local partner as a result of several previously successful projects.

Also, corruption has not been as big a problem as some people might imagine. In fact, we have encountered more corruption in Europe than we have in any of our emerging markets."

Operating Entities could be structured as partnerships, corporations, or other entities, depending on U.S. and domestic tax, legal, ERISA, and other considerations. An attempt was made to mitigate currency risk by requesting rental and purchase payments in U.S. dollars. To the extent possible, this would be achieved by attracting multinational companies and creditworthy domestic tenants.

## Fund I Investments

As of April, 1999, Fund I had invested $150 million in five countries. More than 80% of the Fund's tenants to date were multinationals. Descriptions of some of the major projects are discussed below.

### Queretaro Industrial Park:

**Description:** Located 120 miles north of Mexico City, this 730 acre industrial park had over a mile of frontage on both sides of the NAFTA highway, the principal artery for international trade between Mexico, the U.S., and Canada. The park was designed to be one of the most advanced facilities of its kind in Central Mexico, by offering rail access, a cloverleaf overpass exit from the highway, 24-hour security, fiber-optic communications, and waste-water treatment facilities.

**Strategy:** Due to its proximity to Mexico City and well-developed transportation and communication infrastructure, the town of Queretaro was ideally suited for multinational manufacturers and distributors. By providing the best industrial product in a desirable market, the project sought to take advantage of multinationals' increasing trade and commerce. Most of the buildings would be constructed on a build-to-suit basis, but improved land would be sold in order to develop speculative facilities to satisfy immediate demand.

**Progress:** By April 1999, approximately $12 million had been funded for the project, primarily for land acquisition, infrastructure improvements, operating expenses, and construction of multitenant industrial buildings. 100% of one of the buildings had already been leased for five years, and another building was nearing completion. In addition, the Fund had sold or was negotiating to sell almost 91 acres of land.

## *Torre del Angel:*

**Description:** Originally constructed in 1980, this 21-story office building was ideally located in Mexico City's commercial district. When the Fund purchased the building, it included 14 levels of office space, four levels of retail, and five levels of parking. By remodeling the building, the General Partner increased office and parking space, and its reconfiguration of the lobby and retail areas improved ease of access. The remodeling, which was designed by internationally recognized architect, Robert A. M. Stern, also added new mechanical systems and elevators, as well as new interior finishes.

**Strategy**: The Fund purchased and redeveloped the building at 80% of replacement cost. At the time of purchase, there was a shortage of large contiguous blocks of quality office space in Mexico City, so the General Partner redesigned the configuration to better satisfy the particular shortage.

**Progress:** By April 1999, approximately $24 million had been funded for the project, most of which was used for building acquisition, professional fees, demolition costs, structural modifications, and G&A expenses. Structural work on the floor plate extensions and roof had commenced as had marketing of the building to prospective tenants.

## *Guadalajara Industrial Tecnologico:*

**Description:** This industrial park was situated on a 24-acre in-fill site in the heart of Guadalajara, Mexico's industrial sector, less than 1,000 feet from a beltway surrounding the city and near an important north-south access road. When completed, the project would offer almost 700,000 square feet of U.S.-quality industrial warehouse and distribution space in a supply-constrained industrial market.

**Strategy:** The General Partner believed that the project's proximity to Mexico's seven largest electronics manufacturers and easy access to transportation infrastructure would attract a myriad of industry suppliers. Industrial facilities were supply-constrained in Guadalajara and the region's electronics growth created a supply/demand imbalance for desirable industrial space.

**Progress:** By April 1999, approximately $8 million had been funded for the project, most of which was used for land acquisition, professional fees, construction and other project expenses. A major tenant planned to occupy one building by the end of June, and the Fund had outstanding lease proposals for an additional five potential tenants for over 535,000 square feet of space.

## *Panamerica Park:*

**Description:** Panamerica Park was planned for 430,000 square feet of office and high-tech, single and multi-tenant facilities and was on one of the few remaining sites with easy access to the principal freeway in Sao Paolo, Brazil.

The project was located near the Marginal Pinheiros commercial district and its large concentration of multinational headquarters and executive residential areas. In addition, a new Metro commuter train station was under construction approximately 500 yards from the site.

**Strategy:** Flexibility in design was a key to the project's strategy. Office facilities would offer three levels and covered parking, and high tech space would offer delivery access and increased floor-to-ceiling height on the ground floor. The buildings were designed to maximize occupancy efficiency and adaptability for both primary and back office functions. The project was targeted toward tenants desiring a Marginal Pinheiros location but preferring lower occupancy costs than those offered in traditional high rise space.

**Progress:** By April 1999, $16 million in funds had been approved for the project, joint venture documentation with the land owner was complete, and pre-lease negotiations with several major tenants were in progress.

## *Pokrovsky Hills:*

**Description:** The Pokrovsky Hills project was a master planned residential development in Moscow, Russia. Located only 8 miles from the Kremlin, the hilly, 23-acre site was adjacent to the heavily wooded Pokrovskoye Glevobo Park on the way to the Moscow International Airport.

Two hundred fifty-seven town home units were planned in two phases, the first of which would include 103 units for delivery in 1999. All units would come with a balcony, terrace or garden, and would include three to five bedrooms, stucco exteriors, pitched roofs, one or two-car garages, and formal dining rooms.

In addition, the project offered a guarded entrance, walking and cross-country skiing trails, and a layout designed to minimize impact on the natural environment. One key element of the development was a new Anglo-American school adjacent to the property.

**Strategy:** The project targeted the expatriate residential market in Moscow. Expatriates were able to pay high rents and sales prices but faced a low supply of quality residential units. Many of the amenities offered by the project, including the Anglo-American school, were unique and not easily found in Russia.

**Progress:** By April 1999, approximately $50 million had been funded for the project, most of which was used for land acquisition, professional design fees, construction and administrative expenses, and off-site infrastructure improvements. Nearly all of the 103 Phase I units were scheduled for completion in August, 1999, and strong interest had been received from the embassy community. Several leases had already been signed. The Anglo-American school had completed its foundation and had commenced structural construction.

## *Warsaw Opera Center*

**Description:** Located in the heart of Warsaw's Central Business District, this 3.2-acre office project was near the city's Opera House and Saski Park and was within walking distance of the historic Old Town of Warsaw. The project included a central garden surrounded by several interconnected buildings that could be leased or sold individually. The General Partner believed that the project's site was one of the most prestigious office locations in Warsaw and that the development would be a major landmark for the city.

**Strategy:** The General Partner anticipated that high levels of FDI, low labor costs and economic growth would drive multinationals' sustained demand for high quality office space in Warsaw. Supply of such space was limited in Warsaw, although the Partners acknowledged that several new projects in the area might impact rental rates.

**Progress:** By April 1999, approximately $6 million had been funded for the project, most of which was used for land acquisition, professional fees, and legal expenses. Land acquisition was to be finalized at the end of 1999. The Condition of Site Development Permit was validated in April, 1999, the building permit was expected by the end of the year, and the project infrastructure permit had been issued. Final bids were being negotiated with three contractors.

## Beijing Embassy House

**Description:** The Embassy House project was a 32-story residential tower in Beijing with 174 luxury apartments and three levels of underground parking. The project was located on one of the most desirable sites in northeast Beijing, adjacent to the Australian, Canadian, and German embassies and with easy access to the airport, international schools, medical clinics, and Beijing's Central Business District. Amenities included a swimming pool, fitness center, and a business center. Apartment units consisted of two to four-bedroom layouts with 16 penthouse apartments on the top four floors.

**Strategy:** China was emerging as one of the leading growth markets in the world, attracting consistently high levels of FDI. The nation's capital, Beijing, was the major political and commercial center and the location of most multinational firms' China headquarters. Demand for first-class senior expatriate housing was high and the supply of such facilities was constrained by a difficult approval process, lack of developer sophistication, and a scarcity of sites.

**Progress:** By April 1999, approximately $20 million had been funded to the project for demolition expenses, land use fees, professional fees, and administrative expenses. A general contractor had already been selected and subcontractor selection and a construction permit were expected to be finalized by mid-May.

**Other Projects Considered:** In 1996, Fund I considered two projects in the Czech Republic whose potential returns did not justify perceived risk. The Fund also considered a development of single–family homes near Warsaw but turned it down due to concerns related to land assemblage and master planning risk.

## Current Climate for International Real Estate Investment

**World Economic Situation:** Fund II's marketing effort would be challenged by dramatic volatility in global markets since the successful launch of Fund I. During this period, severe currency devaluations in Asia, Russia, and Latin America had led to a worldwide economic crisis. Although the U.S. economy managed to recover within a few months, the economic contraction reduced demand for commodities and hurt commodity-producing countries throughout the world.

The crisis was due to several factors:

- Poor lending practices by financial institutions
- Corruption in business and political communities

- Over-investment in real estate
- Lack of adequate bank regulation
- Lack of "transparency" in financial transactions
- Absence of bankruptcy laws, particularly in Asian countries

When it appeared that several countries would be unable to meet their debt obligations, investors reacted with a large-scale capital flight from risk. This severely impacted stock market performance and real estate returns.

By 1999, however, some good news began to emerge. Asia, Korea, Thailand, Singapore, and Japan appeared to be turning the corner. Through careful economic restructuring, China also seemed to be avoiding economic catastrophe. The major problem areas in Asia appeared to be Hong Kong and Indonesia.

In Latin America, Brazil was experiencing a surprisingly strong recovery from a January currency devaluation. In Mexico, economic growth was expected to slow from the previous year, but healthy political reform promised to reduce corruption in government. In Eastern Europe, the Czech Republic, Hungary, and Poland continued to make progress despite collateral economic damage from the war in Kosovo.

Russia, unfortunately, remained a disaster area. In August, 1998, a devaluation of the ruble and a default on domestic debt devastated the Russian economy. Payment systems broke down, bank accounts were frozen, and credit cards no longer functioned. Within two months, imports fell by 45%.[3]

In the Spring of 1999, Russia's political system, like its economy, appeared on the brink of collapse. President Yeltsin's chronically poor health and his recent dismissal of Prime Minister Primakov created an atmosphere of complete unpredictability. Few political analysts expected many major policy decisions before parliamentary elections in December.

To make matters worse, Russia's political leaders faced conflicting domestic pressures regarding their relationship with the West. On one hand, many Russians felt threatened by and opposed to NATO's actions in Kosovo. On the other, Russian leaders were courting the IMF to approve a $4.5 billion loan.

**Investors' Flight to Quality:** By 1999, the worldwide liquidity crisis had created a major disconnect between financial and "real" economies. The daily financial float was approximately $2 trillion, of which only about 2% represented goods and services.[4] Global financial markets were based on

---

[3] "As Winter Draws In," The Economist, October 24, 1998.

national central banking systems and were not prepared for worldwide movements of capital at the speed of light.

This situation created a severe pressure on liquidity where capital sought the most secure types of investments, which were generally high quality currencies, debt instruments, or equity securities. To some extent, this flight to quality had been responsible for the great boom in certain U.S. blue chip stocks in the first half of 1999.

On the positive side, this situation had created a market in which financial assets were generally overvalued and real assets such as real estate were generally undervalued. Hasty thought that this state of affairs might bode well in the marketing of Fund II.

**Institutional Investors' Perception of Real Estate:** Several of the Hines partners were concerned that the institutional community might not be enthusiastic about international real estate investment *per se*. These partners were particularly alarmed by the results of an institutional investor survey that appeared in the Winter 1998 edition of the *Real Estate Finance Journal*.[5]

The survey polled a number of pension plans and insurance companies over a period of several years. Respondents were asked to rate their perceptions of risk and return on twenty types of investments with varying degrees of risk. The investment categories included AAA corporate bonds, Treasury instruments, commodities, marketable securities, venture capital, and a variety of real estate vehicles. (See Appendix B)

Overall, the survey found that a large majority of respondents believed that real estate had a high degree of risk relative to its expected return. Within real estate, only Commercial Mortgage Backed Securities (CMBS) received a favorable risk/return ranking, and international real estate was consistently rated as one of the worst investments with very high levels of risk relative to expected returns.

Several of the Hines managers believed that the realignment of risk and return expectations on the part of institutional investors might be a positive factor for Fund II if they could be convinced that the new Fund could meet its 20% return hurdle.

As one of the managers noted,

> "When we were raising money for Fund I, very few investors were interested in international real estate, and we really had to work to sell them on the opportunities created by emerging market growth.

---

[4] Dr. Michael A. Goldberg, University of British Columbia.
[5] Elaine Worzala, Emily Zietz, and G. Stacy Sirmans, "What's Wrong with Real Estate?", <u>Real Estate Finance Journal,</u> Winter 1998.

However, due to the success of the opportunity funds over the past few years, many investors began to expect real estate returns in the 17-20% range.

As a result, by August of last year, just before the Russian debacle, we were consistently receiving inquiries from investors who were seeking high returns in international real estate. Although the troubles in Russia and Asia may have scared some of those investors away, there is substantially more capital chasing international real estate deals today than there was when we ramped up Fund I.

For example, we considered but turned away from sponsoring a European fund last year. Our conclusion was that we would have to expose ourselves to too much risk and leverage in order to achieve the returns that our investors would demand.

Several industry observers estimate that there is approximately 7 to 10 billion dollars targeted toward international real estate today. If we were to proceed with Fund II, one of the factors we would have to consider is how quickly we could identify projects and deploy any capital that we raised."

## Partners' Meeting

In preparing for the Hines Partners' meeting, Hasty felt pretty comfortable with the decision to market the fund exclusively to institutional investors. TCW had strong relationships with many of the fund managers and could identify the most promising targets and minimize marketing time. Several funds would be looking to redeploy assets as U.S. equity markets continued to appear overheated. In addition, in April of 1999, a series of large, high profile investments in U.S. REITs seemed to suggest a renewed interest in real estate investments.

A major issue, however, would be the "theme" of Fund II's marketing effort. Hasty recognized that part of the challenge of the "buy low, sell high" formula was having the courage to buy when the market was at the bottom. He also had some concern whether the "bottom" in many target countries had actually been realized.

The General Partners' job would be to convince investors that recent economic difficulties presented unusual values and buying opportunities for smart, experienced real estate professionals. He concluded that opportunity funds had been able to make this pitch successfully, and he saw no reason why they couldn't do the same since they had more depth of international experience and greater financial resources than many opportunity funds.

Prospective investors would have to believe in an investment strategy that was difficult to support quantitatively. Much of the available data, including limited return information from global real estate securities, was generally not positive enough to support the marketing case. Although the General Partners were pleased with the progress of the Fund I projects, none was mature enough to provide stabilized operating results. On the other hand, $7-10 billion had already been allocated to international real estate via opportunity funds with little or no return information. Moreover, in markets such as Russia and Poland, there were few, if any, sources of reliable real estate market information. The General Partners would have to effectively sell the due diligence capabilities of the management team and its joint venture partners.

Although Hasty was concerned about the survey that reported negative perceptions of international real estate investments, he was also aware that Fund II's projected 20% returns were substantially higher than the 13.2% return institutional investors expected from most opportunity funds. The partners would have to convince investors to trust their projections, which raised the question as to whether this level of return would be enough to justify perceived risk.

He also wondered whether they would have to explain how Hines and TCW would fill the void created by the departure of Dean Witter. In particular, Hasty knew he would have to demonstrate that the remaining team would be able to perform the project identification, due diligence, deal negotiation and asset disposition roles that had been Dean Witter's expertise. This would no doubt require the hiring of additional personnel. Another alternative would be to bring in another partner with this expertise, but an additional partner would dilute the equity position of Hines and TCW.

One option that the Hines Partners were considering was to broaden Fund II's investment scope to include an allocation to real estate in industrialized countries. Although this strategy might result in lower returns, it might make the fund more palatable to institutional investors by increasing diversification and allowing the General Partners to deploy capital more rapidly. However, Hasty wondered if institutional investors would prefer a more focused strategy that would allow them to diversify on their own.

Another alternative that Hasty and his partners were considering was to include international real estate securities in Fund II. Europe had well established securitized real estate markets, and recently a number of Asian countries had taken steps to make real estate securities more appealing to foreign investors. For example, Japan now permitted foreign ownership of real estate investment trusts, and in Thailand, similar REIT-like trusts were being utilized. The Government of Singapore was also debating REIT-like vehicles.[6]

The problem with this approach, however, was that it didn't play to Hines' experience in development and to its relationships with multinational corporations. It most likely would require a shift in the lead role from Hines to TCW, which had extensive security fund management.

Although Hasty was comfortable with targeting institutional investors for Fund II, there was by no means unanimous agreement among the partners. In light of the unsettled world markets and the lack of performance data on Fund I, several managers wanted to take a much broader approach and include both U.S. institutions and individuals from other nations as well.

Hasty also wondered if launching Fund II was the best use of his time and that of other Hines staff. Recent global economic volatility and mixed international real estate returns threatened to extend the time it would take to market Fund II. A drawn out marketing road show would require that he spend a great deal of the next year in airports and airplanes. Hasty wondered if his energies could be more profitably applied to U.S. development opportunities, which were much more plentiful than they had been in 1996. He was also aware that Fund II would require several Hines senior executives to commit the majority of several years of their time abroad, which would impose a significant burden on their personal and family lives.

As he began preparing his memorandum for the partners meeting, he knew that he would have to come up with some answers to these fundamental questions before he could recommend proceeding with Fund II.

Hasty found that his thoughts were beginning to center around the enormity of the risks and rewards that were involved for the firm in making the right decision:

> "I'm not convinced that our company can justify pursuing Fund II strictly on financial terms, but strategically it may be a great opportunity for us. We have very little development competition on a global level now, and most major developers are focused on the U.S. These Funds may be our chance to build a first-mover international presence that could establish Hines as the world's premier global development company and be a platform for business for many years to come.
>
> But the risks are very high. We are in many ways "betting the ranch" that we can succeed internationally. Hines has a premier brand name and failure is not an option for us."

---

[6] Lend Lease Investment Research.

## Questions for Discussion

Questions that should be considered in this case include:

1. What are some of the risks associated with international real estate investing and how can these risks be mitigated?
2. Assuming that projected targets can be met, do the returns from international real estate investing compensate for these risks?
3. How does international real estate fit into a pension fund's investment portfolio?
4. How important is the "lack of data" issue?
5. How important is the "local partner" issue?
6. What governance policies and procedures should exist to protect institutional investors?
7. What characteristics should a firm(s) have in order to successfully sponsor an international real estate investment program?
8. What are Hines competitive advantages in marketing Fund II?
9. How should the loss of Dean Witter be handled?
10. Should proposed investments be expanded to include industrialized countries?
11. Should proposed investments be expanded to include securitized real estate investments?
12. Should targeted investors be expanded to include non-tax exempt investors? Non-U.S. institutional investors?
13. How should the lack of performance data on Fund I be handled?
14. What does Hines need to do in terms of organization in order to successfully handle its entry into the international arena?
15. Should Hines proceed with Fund II? If so, what changes, if any, would you make in the proposed program?

Please use these questions as a guide and not a format or a reflection of all of the questions that need to be addressed by the case.

# 20

# PACIFIC APARTMENT TRUST, INC.[1]

## Strategy and Board Governance

In January 2005, Jeremiah Masters ("Jerry"), Chairman of the Board of Pacific Apartment Trust (PAT) sat down at his computer and began sorting through his email, which included several messages from PAT management and individual Directors. The number of emails he received from management and the board had increased dramatically as a result of the tough governance requirements for public companies brought about by the Sarbanes-Oxley Act of 2002 (SOX) and other government and industry regulations.

Over the past two years, the PAT Board and management had struggled with not only the magnitude and breadth of SOX and other regulatory reforms, but with the tremendous increase in time and costs required to ensure compliance.

One of the emails jumped out at him. The message was from Robert Keagle, Chairman of the Audit Committee and Bruce Breadwinner, Chairman of the Compensation, Governance, and Nominating Committee, announcing a joint meeting of the committees on February 16. The purpose of the meeting was to discuss, modify, and adopt PAT's new Corporate Governance Guidelines, which both committees had been working on for several months. (See Appendix A).

The recommendations of the joint committee would then be referred to the full board for approval prior to the finalization of the proxy. The proxy would have to be mailed to the shareholders in early April to be discussed at the annual shareholders meeting on May 12.

---

[1] This case was prepared by John McMahan in 2005. Copyright © John McMahan, 2005, all rights reserved.

Jerry knew it would be a long and difficult meeting, as the Board struggled to successfully culminate what had been a two-year effort by the firm to meet the new requirements.

## HISTORICAL PERSPECTIVE

PAT was a Los Angeles-based corporation which elected annually to be treated as a Real Estate Investment Trust (REIT). Originally formed in the early 1970s, PAT had evolved by 1993 into a $300M national operation, with investments in most major property types. PAT prided itself on consistently maintaining a strong balance sheet and relatively "clean" annual financial statements. Nevertheless, some market analysts continued to label PAT as being "sleepy."

Jerry joined the PAT board in 1993[2] and was given the charge of leading a restructuring of the firm into a modern REIT. The first step was to hire a new CEO experienced in restructuring companies and successfully communicating with public capital markets. After a comprehensive search, the Board hired Fred Marshall (Fred), who had restructured several public companies and had a strong following in the investment community.

In 1994, Jerry and Fred led the Board in considering and adopting a new strategic plan. The basic elements of the Plan called for:

- ❏ Focusing by property type and geography
- ❏ Internalization of property management
- ❏ Creating a development capability as an alternative to property acquisition
- ❏ Entering second- and third-tier markets
- ❏ Additional leveraging of the portfolio

It took several years to implement these initiatives. Some were winners; some were losers. Following is a general summary of events around the implementation of each of these initiatives over the succeeding ten years:

### *Focus by Property Type and Geography*

The first step in the restructuring program was to focus PAT's activities by property type and geography. In order to accomplish this, the Board approved a program to sell $70 million in nonapartment assets and invest the proceeds in new apartment properties.

In order to accelerate its move into the apartment market, PAT also decided to proceed with a secondary offering of 2.25 million shares of common stock.

---

[2] Jerry became Chairman in 1996.

Reflecting the strong financial position of the firm, its decision to restructure, and the generally robust nature of the REIT market, the offering was sold at $38 per share, with a net of $35 per share to the firm (in 1992, the stock price averaged $32 per share).

The secondary offering, coupled with the conversion of outstanding debentures, increased shareholder equity by approximately $150 million. Virtually all of these funds were utilized for the purchase of new apartment properties.

By the end of 1993, PAT's portfolio contained almost 5,000 units, representing approximately 92.9% of total investment value and generating about the same percentage of rental income and FFO. This figure was up from 83.4% in 1992 and 79.5% in 1991.

This expanded investment portfolio required additional management talent. In 1994, PAT merged with Sunshine Real Estate Investment Trust (SUNREIT), which brought with it apartment units, mostly in Southern California, plus some mixed properties which were subsequently liquated. More importantly, SUNREIT had an experienced management team, particularly in the asset management and financial reporting areas, which ultimately filled key positions in the restructured organization.

## *Internalization of Property Management*

By 1994, all but one of competing apartment REITs were self-administered and most were self-managed. Several Board members believed that self-management was an important strategic objective for PAT. Directly managing properties in the portfolio would allow for some of the asset management expense to be spread over a larger base of revenue. Self-management would also provide increased control. Supplies could be purchased over a larger unit base, and the firm's employees would not be distracted by possible conflicts of interest.

One drawback to internal property management, however, was that the quality of outside management had improved dramatically over the last several years, and management fees were now very competitive. Also, if PAT wanted to leave a market, it could do so quickly without having to relocate or liquidate a staff.

The refocus of the firm by property type and geographical area, and the move to internalize property management, were generally viewed as successful. As of the end of 2004, PAT had an internal management staff managing 95 apartment communities containing over 20,000 apartment units.

## Becoming a Developer

Several members of the Board believed that one way to improve performance was to integrate into property development. Several PAT managers and directors had development backgrounds, and at least one of them had said it would not be too difficult to create a development unit that could seek out and build projects from the ground up.

This strategic direction was particularly attractive, since development yields were reported to be 200-300 basis points over investment returns in first-tier markets. It was believed that property development could not only improve yield spreads but would also allow PAT to control the quality of its assets and target design and amenity packages to each segment of its target markets.

Development had its risks, however, particularly in times of economic decline, as developers had discovered in the mid-to-late 1980s. Also, it could take three to five years to obtain the permits needed to secure the entitlement rights required to proceed with construction, and there were no assurances that the entitlements could be ultimately obtained.

The Board also was concerned with the management of the development process and whether it could be integrated successfully into the organization. While several members of the existing staff had development backgrounds, it had been some time since they had actually developed a project. Also, if existing staff were utilized, replacement personnel would have to be hired in the acquisition and asset management groups.

Over the next several years, PAT built an internal development capability to complement its property acquisition program. It was a bumpy road, however, with a significant amount of time and money invested, and no conclusive evidence that the investment had produced the yield spreads anticipated.

By the end of 2004, PAT had a "development pipeline" of over 3,000 units, representing an ultimate property value of over $900 million.

## Entering Second- and Third-Tier Markets

The higher yield spreads available in second- and third-tier markets were based on the assumption of higher risks, since smaller markets were more vulnerable to adverse changes in major employers or industries. There was greater availability of easily entitled land in these markets as well, and they often tended toward higher levels of overbuilding. This could pose a problem if PAT wanted to dispose of an asset at a time when few, if any, buyers were active.

PAT entered several second-tier markets through its acquisition of ABC Residential in 1998 This transaction resulted in PAT owning apartment communities in Tucson, Albuquerque, Las Vegas, and Salt Lake City. The firm began developing and managing projects in each of these cities, and pursuing ABC entitlements to future development in first-tier markets in California, Washington, Colorado, and Arizona.

In 2001X, PAT's management reviewed a research report which analyzed the performance of ten major apartment REITs over a five-year period. The REITs were broken into two groups: one group consisted of five REITs that largely focused on "constrained" markets; the other largely focused on "commodity" markets such as Dallas and Atlanta, and second-tier cities with few barriers to the new production of multifamily units. This analysis indicated that REITs focusing on constrained markets had a 500% higher annual growth rate in "same store" Net Operating Income (NOI) than those involved in commodity markets over the five year period.

As a result of this study and extensive discussions among management and the Board, PAT decided in 2003 to begin withdrawing from these markets and focus on constrained markets, which had been its traditional turf. However, PAT did continue to pursue the entitlement rights located in constrained markets acquired in the ABC transaction.

## *Leveraging the Portfolio:*

A final strategic initiative PAT pursued was leverage. The firm had always had a strong balance sheet, and the 1993 secondary offering had reduced its debt ratio substantially, resulting in room to add new debt. The cost of debt was still relatively low, thus creating a positive yield spread. There was some question, however, as to how long this favorable investment climate might last, with interest rates now moving up for the first time in several years.

If increased leveraging were to be utilized, one question would be what type of debt to assume. One approach would be to obtain a single mortgage for each new or presently unleveraged property. A variation on this approach would be to pool the properties and leverage the pool with a single mortgage. This strategy would most likely require cross-collateralization and cross-defaulting of the properties, as well as securing the ability to release title to individual properties if they were sold. Both of these property-specific alternatives were ultimately rejected by the Board, in part because they would limit PAT's flexibility in terms of future operations.

The approach finally adopted was to borrow in the commercial debt markets through increased bank lines of credit, a new corporate debenture, or a combination of both. This would leave PAT with operating flexibility in terms of its properties but might inhibit future equity issues due to the higher debt levels.

As a result of the success of most of the features of its corporate restructuring program, by 2004 PAT had grown into a $3.5 billion fully integrated REIT, focusing on the ownership and operation of multifamily residential properties located in the rapidly growing markets of Los Angeles, Orange County, San Diego, the Inland Empire (San Bernardino and Riverside Counties), San Francisco Bay Area, Seattle, and Denver.

The PAT properties were generally quality complexes with over 25,000 units with an average size of 920square feet per unit. Overall occupancy at the end of 2004 was 92%. Best of all, PAT had paid a consistent dividend since 1990, and shareholders had enjoyed a total average return (dividends plus share value growth) of over 20% annually.

## AMERICA TURNS TO CORPORATE REFORM

### *Collapse of Enron*

In 2000, ENRON was the firth largest company in the United States, hired the "best and brightest," possessed the most advanced technology, and operated in a state-of-the-art complex in Houston, Texas. What's more, ENRON considered itself a model of modern management, a symbol of the "new economy firm" in which "virtual" assets (technology and people) were more important than hard assets in creating shareholder value.

In late December 2000, Enron was named one of the "100 Best Companies to Work For in America" by *Fortune* magazine, climbing to number 22 from number 24 the prior year. Enron was the highest ranking global energy company on the *Fortune* list.

In reality, as events would subsequently reveal, ENRON was a giant "Ponzi scheme," inflating revenue and profits, which increased the company's stock price and capitalized value, with lucrative executive bonuses tied to this inflated value. This was accomplished by structuring off-balance sheet, non-economic energy deals arranged with partnerships and Special Purpose Entities (SPE's). Projected revenues were then discounted, and the resultant present value recognized in the current period, utilizing the "mark to market" method of accounting.

The increased capitalized value allowed Enron to maintain investment grade credit and continue borrowing from its banks, which received above average interest payments (6.5%-7.0%). As one observer put it, Enron was a "hall of mirrors inside a house of cards." Exhibit 1 indicates the discrepancies between what was reported publicly and what was actually going on.

Unfortunately, ENRON was only the tip of the iceberg, with several large firms involved in similar, if less spectacular, abuses. These included

WorldCom, TYCO, HealthSouth Corporation, and Gemstar-TV Guide International Group Ltd.

**Exhibit 1**
**ENRON by the Numbers**

| Year | Reported Income | Revised Income | True Debt | True Equity |
|------|-----------------|----------------|-----------|-------------|
| 1997 | $105M | $77M | Up $771M | Down $258M |
| 1998 | 733M | 600M | Up 561M | Down 391M |
| 1999 | 893M | 645M | Up 685M | Down 710M |
| 2000 | 979M | 880M | Up 628M | Down 754M |

Source: ENRON/Powers Special Report

During 2001, as the truth about ENRON was finally understood, ENRON's stock price collapsed (Exhibit 2).

**Exhibit 2**

## Enron's stock market collapse

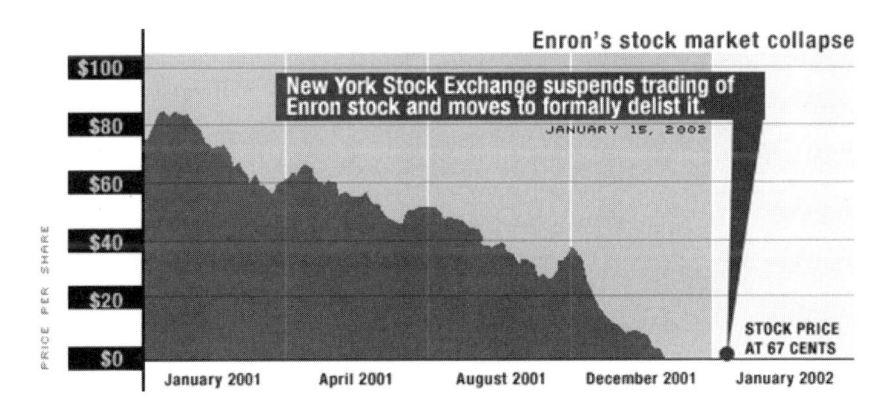

## Where Were the Gatekeepers?

A question many raised following the collapse of Enron was "where were the gatekeepers?" Where were those individuals and firms who were expected to keep this from happening to an American public company. The gatekeepers and their roles in the ENRON disaster included:

**Auditors:** Arthur Andersen shredded documents.

**Lawyers:** Vinson & Elkins and Kirkland & Ellis created SPE legal structure and whitewashed the Board just before collapse;

**Bankers:** JP Morgan, Banc of America, Barclays, Deutsche Bank, Canadian Imperial Bank of Commerce, Merrill Lynch, CS First Boston, and Lehman Brothers made short-term and takeout loans. Some of these bankers also sold SPE units to investors.

**Board of Directors:** The Board waived Enron's Code of Ethics three times in 2000 and 2001 to accommodate management's participation in SPE'S.

Ultimately, it was hard to avoid the logical conclusion that the gatekeepers who were supposed to protect shareholders were in on the conspiracy.

## *The Move to Legislative and Regulatory Reform*

As the public became more outraged at the ENRON and other corporate financial scandals, legislative and regulatory bodies reacted with a broad-based assault on public investment abuse. This resulting reforms included:

- Congress: Sarbanes-Oxley Act of 2002 (SOX)
- NYSE and NSDEC Exchanges: Regulatory reform
- Securities and Exchange Commission (SEC): Regulatory reform
- Selected state reform legislation

As a result of the public outrage and ensuing reforms, public corporations knew by 2003 that they were in for major changes in the way they did business. The major impact was in the following areas:

**Financial Reporting:** SOX required that the Chief Executive Officer (CEO) and the Chief Financial Officer (CFO) be held personally responsible for the ultimate accuracy of corporate financial reporting and have primary responsibility for company reports filed with the SEC. That includes attesting to the "completeness and accuracy" of the information in the reports. The new legislation also called for, written assurances that senior managers had disclosed all serious deficiencies, material weaknesses, or acts of fraud.

**Internal Controls:** SOX mandates an annual written evaluation of internal controls and procedures. In addition, senior managers were required to report quarterly to shareholders as to the effectiveness of the underlying internal controls of the Company, and that information provided the public is "transparent" and fairly presents the company's financial condition, operations, and cash flows. The Independent Auditor must attest to management's assertion of the effectiveness of internal controls and procedures for financial reporting

**Management compensation:** Corporate compensation was restructured to encourage better alignment with shareholders by restricting the utilization of stock options.

**Directors:** The new governance regulations required boards to reorganize in order to gain greater independence from management. The majority of board directors are now required to be "independent." That is, the board must affirmatively determine that each director has no material relationship with the Company. Specifically, governance regulations require that each board member:

- Has not received more than $100,000 annually from the Company in the previous three years.
- Is not affiliated with the Company's auditor.
- Was not previously employed by a firm in which any of the Company's senior executives serve on the Compensation Committee, or which contributes 2% or more of the Company's revenues.

Independent directors were now required to regularly schedule executive sessions without management present.

**Board Committees:** Key standing board committees must be comprised exclusively of independent directors who meet regularly without management present. These committees must have direct access to individual managers, shareholders, and outside advisors.

> Special requirements were designed for the **Audit Committee:** one committee member must qualify as a "financial expert" and the others must qualify as "financially literate."[3] The Audit Committee must directly hire and fire auditors and pre-approve any non-audit services provided by the auditing firm. Directors' fees are the sole remuneration for serving on the Audit Committee.
>
> The **Compensation Committee** also has to meet special requirements: Under the new legislation, this Committee was given the exclusive mandate to establish the corporate goals for CEO compensation and evaluate the CEO's performance against these goals. The Compensation Committee also must recommend to the Board compensation for other senior managers. Finally, this committee must produce an annual report on executive compensation for the proxy statement.

---

[3] The chairman must be an experienced CPA or investment banker; all other members of the Committee must be experienced in reading and understanding corporate financial statements.

The **Governance Committee** is a new standing committee (for most public companies) which must adopt and publicly disclose governance guidelines for the firm.[4] Its responsibilities include establishing director qualifications and responsibilities, directors' access to management and advisors, director compensation, and management succession. This committee also conducts an annual performance evaluation of the Board and provides oversight of the director nominating process.

**Shareholders:** Individual shareholders now are permitted direct access to board committees and must ratify certain key company decisions, including all equity-based executive compensation plans (such as stock options). For those companies listed on the New York Stock Exchange, larger shareholders (those owning more than 5.0% of the shares) also have the ability to directly nominate directors.

**Auditors:** Under SOX, corporate auditing standards also were strengthened to ensure greater independence from management. The Auditor now reports to the board exclusively through the Audit Committee and is responsible for management assertions about internal controls and procedures for financial reporting. The auditing firm must rotate its project manager every five years, and the Company may be required to rotate firms in the future. Should the partner in charge leave the auditing firm, he or she cannot become CFO of the client firm for one year.

**Attorneys:** Corporate attorneys are now held responsible for reporting security law violations, and must so certify in the annual proxy statement.

**Security Firms:** Regulations have been strengthened to prevent misuse of insider data and investor relationships.

**"Whistleblowers":** Employees and outsiders are now protected from recrimination by the firm for "whistle blowing" activities.[5]

As Leon Panetta, the head of the Leon Panetta Institute for Public Policy, has observed, "The purpose of these reforms is to restore the essential trust needed on behalf of the investing public in a strong securities market and a strong economy."

---

[4] Can be a subcommittee of the Compensation Committee.
[5] Public firms must now establish and maintain acceptable methods for monitoring "whistleblower" activity.

# REACTION TO SOX AND OTHER GOVERNANCE REFORMS

## *Public Companies*

In 2004, directors of 1,200 public companies were surveyed by PricewaterhouseCoopers (PWC) and *Corporate Board Member* magazine regarding their reaction to SOX following two years of attempting to implement this and other highly challenging governance reforms.[6]

**General Response:** The response of the Directors surveyed was largely positive. Ninety-one percent (91%) found it easier to hire new Directors, 85% expected the company image would be improved, and almost half (48%) expected the company's stock price to be positively affected.

**Corporate Liability:** When queried about corporate liability, 85% of the Directors responded that the company would be exonerated if it faced shareholder or other litigation. Seventy-one percent (71%) believed that the company wouldn't be sued in the first place, and 62% said that they expected their Directors and Officers (D&O) insurance to cost less as a result of the reforms.

**Director Liability:** When asked about their own personal liability, 68% responded that it had increased, with only 2% believing it had decreased. The remaining 30% believed it was "about the same."

**D&O Insurance:** When asked about the importance of D&O insurance in their decision to serve on a board, almost half (49%) replied "very important." Another 37% indicated it was "somewhat important", while the remaining 14% said it was "unimportant."

When queried further if they would pay personally for the insurance, 79% said "no" and 21% said they would. It's clear that most directors expect companies to have D & O coverage and to pay for it as an ongoing cost of operating a public company.

**SOX Implementation:** When asked if their company was ready to implement the internal controls requirement of SOX (Section 404), 82% of respondent replied "yes" and only 4% replied negatively. The remaining 14% felt they were "not sure yet."

One of the great concerns about SOX and other new governance regulations is the tremendous amount of time that companies have had to spend in putting the reforms in place, not to mention the higher auditing, legal, and other costs related to its implementation. In the PWC survey, however, 44%

---

[6] *What Directors Think,* © 2004 by *Corporate Board Member* magazine.

of the Directors felt that the time and costs were not so great as to adversely impact company financial performance. However, more than a third (36%) believed it was too early to tell.

**Amendments to Legislation:** Despite their overall positive view of the new governance regulations, 77% of Directors surveyed believed that Congress needed to "revisit" SOX to "eliminate some of the unintended consequences" of the Act. Only 4% believed such an action wasn't necessary, with the remaining 19% "not sure yet."

**Future Board Focus:** Exhibit 3 indicates the Directors' responses when queried about where they wanted to direct their focus, now that preparation for the major elements of SOX has been largely completed. Not surprisingly, the majority of Directors surveyed wanted to return to the traditional responsibilities of "strategic planning," "management succession," "analysis of the competition," and "risk management." The tasks they wanted to spend less time on, also not surprisingly, were "compliance issues" and "governance guidelines."

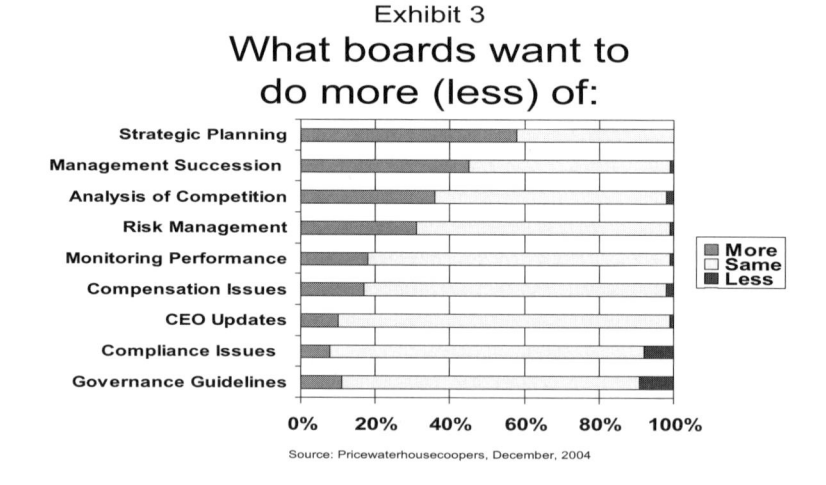

Exhibit 3
**What boards want to do more (less) of:**

Source: Pricewaterhousecoopers, December, 2004

## *Public Real Estate Companies*[7]

**Structural Obstacles to Improved Governance:** Many REITs and other public real estate companies were initially established as closely controlled private companies, with many built-in legal features that made implementing governance standards difficult.

---

[7] Includes REITs, Real Estate Operating Companies (REOCs), publicly traded homebuilders, residential mortgage finance/insurance companies, and hospitality firms.

As an example, the articles of incorporation of many real estate companies established limitations connected to share ownership, as well as stringent anti-takeover measures. Some of these companies went public with a large amount of the assets of the founders remaining in private hands, through various entities established for that purpose (e.g., UPREITs, Special Purpose Entities (SPE's), private partnerships). Many boards also were closely held and controlled by the founders and their friends. Finally, most REITs use unique, non–GAAP accounting and performance measures, such as Funds From Operations (FFO).

**Shareholder Forces for Change:** These structural obstacles were ultimately overcome, in most cases, by the makeup of the shareholder base of most public real estate companies.

As an example, a high percentage of shares are often held by institutions, particularly pension funds. Many companies are listed on the New York Stock Exchange which, in response to corporate fraud and mismanagement, developed new rules permitting large shareholders (those holding over 5%) to nominate their own directors.

And, finally, real estate is the only industry to have dedicated money managers who have a direct stake in how well REITs are governed. Exhibit 4 represents the firm scoring criteria used by one of the largest and most influential public real estate company advisors. Note that virtually all of the criteria are governance-related.

**Exhibit 4**
**Greenstreet Advisors Scorecard**

| | |
|---|---|
| Non-Staggered Board | 20 points |
| Past Conduct/Reputation | 15 |
| Board Investment | 12 |
| Anti-takeover Provisions | 9 |
| Ownership Limits | 9 |
| Insider Veto Rights | 9 |
| Shareholder Rights Plan | 8 |
| Independent Board | 8 |
| Dealings with Management | 6 |
| Investor Tax Basis | 4 |
| | 100 |

Source: Greenstreet Advisors

**Importance of Corporate Governance:** In 2004, Ferguson Partners, a Chicago-based management search and compensation firm, interviewed over 200 public real estate company Directors, CEO's, and institutional investors about governance and compensation issues.[8] On a five-point scale, the respondents ranked corporate governance 4.27, second only to corporate performance (4.51) and ahead of corporate strategy (4.21).

**Ideal Director Characteristics:** In ranking important factors in selecting a new director, the respondents ranked "personal qualities" as being most important (4.96), followed by "time and commitment" (4.61), "public company experience" (4.18) and "prior board experience" (3.82).

Among the "least important" characteristics were "local community member" (2.08), "professors and academic administrators" (2.10), "government contacts" (2.12), and "legal experience" (2.46).

**Optimum Size of Board:** When queried about the optimum size of a public real estate board, 42.0% of respondents said nine was the optimum number; 25% said seven to eight; and 23% believed that ten to eleven directors was the optimum size for a board. Collectively, nine out of ten respondents believe that a public real estate board should have between seven and eleven directors.

**Frequency of Independent Director Meetings:** Sixty four-percent (64.0%) of respondents believed that four meetings per year was the right amount; the next closest responses were two meetings per year (15.0% of respondents) and three (6%).

**Staggered Board Terms:** Despite significant pressure to drop staggered board terms utilized by many public real estate companies, 44.0% of respondents surveyed felt that staggered terms should be retained; 39.0% disagreed (14.0% "strongly" disagreed). Only 17.0% were indifferent on the issue. Director's attitudes towards staggered board terms remains one of the major differences between public real estate directors and the broader spectrum of public company directors as a whole.

**Separation of CEO and Chairman:** There was a much clearer response to a question about the separation of the two top corporate officers, with 50.0% of respondents agreeing they should be different individuals and only 20.0% disagreeing. Thirty percent (30.0%) were indifferent.

**Female Directors:** Fifty-four percent (54%) of the respondents agreed with the statement that a public real estate company "needs a female director on the board," with only 10% disagreeing. Thirty-six percent (36%) were indifferent.

---

[8] Source: FPL Associates LP; Ferguson Partners Ltd., 2004 Board Practices and Compensation Survey.

**Minority Directors:** Respondents were not quite as positive about ethnic minority representation on the board, with 46% agreeing this is important and 12% disagreeing. Forty-two percent (42%) were indifferent.

**Director Term Limits:** Although not a part of the Ferguson survey, one of the major issues faced by most boards is the length of time that a Director should serve. This has become a more critical issue as people live longer and continue to be effective in their later lives. On the other hand, bringing new blood onto the board can be very effective in introducing new backgrounds and perspectives to the board's deliberations.

The most common resolution of this dilemma is to have two criteria: the length of board service and natural age, with the criterion occurring first becoming the deciding factor (for example, 10 years of service or 70 years of age, whichever comes first).

Many observers agree with the terms of service, but using 70 as the age limit is increasingly under pressure, as people live longer. Seventy-five is therefore becoming more and more common.

To illustrate how fast public real estate companies are changing their position on governance issues, a recent ranking by the Institutional Shareholder Service (ISS) ranked real estate as the number one industry in terms of corporate governance!

## *PAT's Joint Committee Meeting*

Jerry turned his attention back to the recent email and the objectives of the upcoming joint committee meeting. An excerpt from Keagle and Breadwinner's email laid out the objectives for the joint meeting:

- ❏ Recommend to the board Corporate Governance Guidelines statement that would be published in the annual proxy statement and on the Company's website (Appendix A). Many of the changes are mandated by SOX but there are some over which we have more discretion and should be discussed more fully. These include:
    - o Director Responsibilities
    - o Director Independence
    - o Size of Board
    - o Election of Directors (elimination of staggered board)
    - o Maximum term of service
    - o Maximum age
    - o Leave of absence
    - o Service on other boards
    - o Frequency of meetings

- o Frequency of meetings
- o Director attendance
- o Attendance of non-directors
- o Agenda
- o Advance receipt of meeting materials
- o Board compensation
- o Selection of new directors
- o Continuing Corporate Governance

❏ In addition, we should also review and discuss the paragraphs on board committees. Although these have already received considerable input from each of the committees, we need to put them into the context of the overall guidelines document. Note that each of these would be linked directly with the Charter for each committee.

❏ We also should discuss some items that are not (at this time) in the guidelines, but which will be important as we proceed with implementation. These include:

- o Female directors
- o Minority directors

After finishing the email, Jerry let out a sigh, turned off his computer, and proceeded to bed. The Joint Committee was in three days and he needed a good night's rest.

**Appendix A**
**Pacific Apartment Trust, Inc.**
**Board Governance Guidelines**

# January 6, 2005
# (Draft)

The Board of Directors ("**Board**") of Pacific Apartment Trust ("**Company**") has adopted the following Corporate Governance Guidelines ("**Guidelines**") to assist the Board in the exercise of its responsibilities and to serve the interests of the Company and its shareholders. These Guidelines should be interpreted in the context of all applicable laws and the Company's Amended and Restated Articles of Incorporation, Amended and Restated Bylaws and other corporate governance documents.

These Guidelines acknowledge the leadership exercised by the Board's standing committees and their chairs and are intended to serve as a flexible framework within which the Board may conduct its business and not as a set of legally binding obligations. The Guidelines are subject to modification from time to time by the Board as the Board may deem appropriate in the best interests of the Company and its shareholders or as required by applicable laws and regulations.

These Guidelines are available on the Company's website and to any shareholder who otherwise requests a copy. This information is also included in the Company's Annual Report to Shareholders.

## *Board of Directors*

**Director Responsibilities:** The business and affairs of the Company are monitored by the Board of Directors as set forth in the Amended and Restated Bylaws and committee charters. Each director is expected to spend the time and effort necessary to properly discharge his or her responsibilities, including, but not limited to, the following:

- Reviewing and, where appropriate, approving the Company's long-term strategy for future operations. Overseeing the conduct of the Company's business in order to evaluate whether the business is being properly managed in conformance with established Company strategic and annual plans.

- Reviewing and, where appropriate, approving major changes in the appropriate auditing and accounting principles and practices to be used in the preparation of the Company's financial statements.

- Reviewing and, where appropriate, approving changes in the Company's Corporate Governance Guidelines, Code of Business Conduct and Ethics, and other Company policies.

- Reviewing and, where appropriate, approving actions to be undertaken by the Company that would result in a material change in the control of the Company, the acquisition or disposition of any businesses or asset material to the Company, or the entry of the Company into any major new line of business and/or new geographical area.

- Regularly evaluating the performance and approving the compensation of the Chief Executive Officer.

- With the input of the Chief Executive Officer, regularly evaluating the performance and compensation of principal senior executives.

- Planning for succession with respect to the position of Chief Executive Officer and monitoring management's succession planning for other key executives.

- Ensuring that the Company's business is conducted with the highest standards of ethical conduct and in conformity with applicable laws and regulations.

**Director Independence:** The Board is comprised of a majority of directors who qualify as independent directors ("**Independent Directors**") under the listing standards of the New York Stock Exchange ("**NYSE**").[9] No more than three (3) management executives who are employed by the Company or who were employed by the Company in the previous three (3) years may serve on the Board at the same time ("**Management Directors**").

The Board will review annually the relationships that each director has with the Company directly or as a partner, stockholder or officer of an organization that has a relationship with the Company. Following such annual review, only those directors who the Board affirmatively determines have no material relationship with the Company will be considered Independent Directors, subject to additional qualifications prescribed under the listing standards of the NYSE. The basis for any determination that a relationship is not material will be published in the Company's annual proxy statement.

---

[9] The NYSE rules distinguish between "nonmanagement" directors and "independent" directors for certain purposes. The NYSE rules provide that "nonmanagement directors" are those who are not company officers and include "directors who are not independent by virtue of a material relationship, former status or family membership, or for any other reason." Thus the group of directors considered "nonmanagement" may differ from the group of directors considered "independent."

**Size:** The Company's Amended and Restated Articles of Incorporation provide that the Board will consist of not less than three (3) or more than fifteen (15) directors, the exact number to be determined from time to time in the manner specified in the Company's Amended and Restated Bylaws. The Board currently has eight (8) directors and believes that this is an appropriate size based on the Company's present circumstances. The Board will periodically review the size of the Board, and determine the number of Directors that is most effective in relation to future operations including facilitating the smooth transition of individual Directors to and from the Board.

**Election of Directors:** The Company's Board is separated into three (3) Classes, designated Class I, Class II and Class III, with each class consisting, as nearly as possible, of one-third of the total number of directors constituting the entire board. One Class of the Board stands for election by the shareholders of the Company each year at the Company's annual meeting, alternating Classes in order that each Class has a three year term of service.

Each year, at prior to the annual meeting, the Board will recommend a slate of directors for the Class standing for election or reelection to fill the positions occupied by directors whose terms expire at that year's annual meeting. In accordance with the Amended and Restated Bylaws of the Company, the Board also will be responsible for filling vacancies or newly-created directorships that may occur between annual meetings of shareholders.

**Maximum Term of Service:** Each Director shall serve for a maximum of four three-year terms or 12 years, whichever comes last and his or her term of service on the PAT Board shall cease at the annual meeting next following the date on which the director's aggregate service first exceeds 12 years. Service shall be based on the total years of active service on the PAT Board exclusively and shall not include service on prior Boards of firms acquired by PAT or leaves of absence from PAT Board duty. The Board may make exceptions to this guideline of no more than one year duration if it deems it necessary to accomplish a smooth transition of new Independent Directors onto the Board.

**Leave of Absence:** Upon request by an individual Director, the Board shall consider and may approve a Leave of Absence from Board duty of up to six (6) months for personal reasons. Directors are limited to one Leave of Absence per term served.

**Maximum Age:** No director shall serve on the Board after his or her 70th birthday, except to complete an existing term, and shall not stand for re-election if unable to serve for a minimum of two years prior to reaching this age. The Board, however, may make exceptions to this standard, as it deems appropriate in the interests of the Company's shareholders.

**Service on Other Boards:** The Board does not believe that its members should be prohibited from serving on boards of other organizations and has not adopted any guidelines limiting such activities, except with respect to members serving on the Audit Committee, as described below.

**Chairman of the Board:** The Board shall elect a Chairman immediately following the annual Shareholder's meeting. The Chairman shall be an Independent Director in good standing.

The Chairman's responsibilities shall include, but not be limited to, the following:

- Serving as leader of the Board of Directors.
- Coordinating the activities of the Independent Directors and Chairs of Standing Committees.
- Facilitating communications between Independent Directors and the management of the Company.
- Mentoring individual Directors and the CEO.
- Approving the agenda for and chairing meetings of the Board, Executive Committee, and Annual Shareholder's Meeting.
- Serving as a member of the Compensation, Nominating and Governance Committee with primary responsibility for the corporate governance activities of the Committee.
- Meeting with the Chair of the Compensation, Nominating and Governance Committee and the Chief Executive Officer to convey the results of the Chief Executive Officer's annual performance evaluations.

In performing the duties described above, the Chairman shall consult with the chairs of the appropriate Board committees.

**Standing Committees:** A major portion of the work of the Board is accomplished through the use of standing committees. These committees are comprised entirely of Independent Directors, with the exception of the Executive Committee, on which the Company's Chief Executive Officer serves. The membership of each committee is approved by the Independent Directors, upon recommendation of the Chairman of the Board and the

Executive Committee. Each committee shall have a minimum of three (3) members.

The current standing committees are:[10]

**Audit Committee:** The Audit Committee provides assistance to the Board in fulfilling its responsibilities to its shareholders relating to the reliability and integrity of the Company's accounting policies, financial reporting, internal audit functions, internal accounting controls, and financial disclosure practices. The Committee has sole responsibility to appoint and terminate the Company's independent auditors and to approve any significant, non-audit relationship with the auditing firm. For more information, see (Link to Audit Committee Charter).

**Compensation, Nominating and Governance Committee:** Responsible for activities of the Board in each of the following areas:

>**Compensation:** Reviews and approves the Company's goals and objectives relevant to compensation, stays informed as to market levels of compensation and, based on evaluations submitted by management and outside consultants, recommends to the Board compensation levels and systems for the Board and the Chief Executive Officer that correspond to the Company's goals and objectives. The committee also produces an annual report on executive compensation for inclusion in the Company's annual proxy statement, in accordance with applicable rules and regulations.
>
>**Nominating:** Recommends to the Board individuals to be nominated as directors and committee members and prepares any disclosure that is or may be required to be included in the Company's annual proxy statement with respect to the selection and evaluation of directors or nominees.
>
>**Governance:** Under the leadership of the Chairman of the Board, responsible for developing, revising, and approving Corporate Governance Guidelines as well as reviewing and recommending revisions to such Guidelines on a regular basis.

For more information, see (Link to Compensation, Nominating, and Governance Charter)

**Real Estate Committee:** The Real Estate Committee is responsible for approving proposed and monitoring existing real estate acquisition, disposition, and development projects owned by the Company.

---

[10] These are general descriptions only. For more detail, see individual committee charters on the PAT website.

**Executive Committee:** The Executive Committee is comprised of the Chairman of the Board and the Chairman of each of the standing Board committees outlined above, plus the Chief Executive Officer. The Board may delegate to the Executive Committee full powers of the Board in the management and affairs of the Company, subject to limitations prescribed by the Board and Maryland law. The Executive Committee also takes an active role in broader Company issues such as strategic planning, the Company's capital structure, and management and Board succession planning.

From time to time, the Board may form a new committee or disband a current committee, depending upon the circumstances. Each committee will perform its duties as assigned by the Board in compliance with the Company's Amended and Restated Bylaws and the committee's charter, if applicable.

**Assignment and Rotation of Committee Members:** Based on recommendations of the Chairman of the Board and confirmed by the Compensation, Nominating, and Governance Committee, the Board appoints committee members and committee chairs according to criteria set forth in the applicable committee charter and such other criteria that the Board determines to be appropriate in light of the responsibilities of each committee. Committee membership and the position of committee chair will not be rotated on a mandatory basis unless the Board determines that rotation is in the best interest of the Company.

**Committee Agenda:** The Chairman of each committee, in consultation with the appropriate members of the committee, will develop the Committee meeting agenda.

**Committee Self-Evaluation:** Following the end of each fiscal year, each committee will review its performance and charter and recommend to the Board any changes it deems necessary.

## Board Meetings

**Frequency of Meetings:** The Board will meet at least four (4) times annually. In addition, special meetings may be called from time to time by the Chairman of the Board, as determined by the needs of the business. It is the responsibility of all Directors to attend scheduled meetings.

**Director Attendance:** A director is expected to spend the time and effort necessary to properly discharge his or her responsibilities. Accordingly, a director is expected to regularly prepare for and attend meetings of the Board and all committees on which the director serves (including separate meetings of Independent Directors), with the understanding that, on occasion, a director may be unable to attend a meeting. A director who is unable to attend a meeting is expected to notify the Chairman of the Board or the Chairman of the appropriate committee in advance of such meeting, and, whenever possible, participate in such meeting via teleconference.

**Attendance of Non-Directors:** The Board encourages the Chairman of the Board, committee chairman, and senior management to invite outside advisors, consultants or other managers of the company from time to time to Board and/or committee meetings in order to:

- Provide additional insight into items being discussed by the Board or committees, which involve expertise that would be of benefit to the Board and Management.
- Make presentations to the Board on matters which involve the manager, advisor or consultant.
- Bring BRE managers with high potential into contact with the Board.

Attendance of non-directors at meetings is fully at the discretion of the Board or Committee Chairman.

**Agenda:** The Chairman of the Board establishes the agenda for each Board meeting with input from committee chairs, senior management, and individual directors.

**Advance Receipt of Meeting Materials:** Information regarding the topics to be considered at a meeting is essential to the Board's understanding of the business and the preparation of the directors for a productive meeting. To the extent feasible, the meeting agenda and any written materials relating to each Board meeting will be distributed to directors sufficiently in advance of each meeting to allow for meaningful review. Directors are expected to have reviewed and be prepared to discuss all materials distributed in advance of any meeting.

**Board Compensation:** Compensation of Independent Directors shall consist of director fees paid in cash, stock options, and other stock-related arrangements. Director fees are the sole form of compensation that members of the Audit Committee may receive from the Company.

The Chief Executive Officer will report once a year to the Compensation, Nominating and Governance Committee regarding the status of the Company's Independent Director Compensation program in relation to other U.S. companies of comparable size and general market of operations. This report will include consideration of both direct and indirect forms of compensation, including any charitable contributions by the Company to organizations in which an Independent Director is involved.

Following a review of the report, the Compensation, Nominating and Governance Committee will recommend any changes in Independent Director compensation to the Board for approval. To the extent required by law or the NYSE listing requirements, changes in Director equity compensation may be subject to shareholder approval.

Management Directors who are employed by the Company will not receive any additional compensation for their Board service.

## Selection of New Directors

**Director Qualification Standards:** The Compensation, Nominating and Governance Committee is responsible for reviewing with the Board annually the appropriate characteristics, skills and experience required for the Board as a whole, and its individual members.

In evaluating the suitability of new candidates and current Board members, the Board shall consider, but is not limited to, the following:

- Fundamental character qualities of intelligence, honesty, good judgment, high ethics and standards of integrity, fairness and responsibility.
- Ability to make independent analytical inquiries.
- General understanding of marketing, finance and other elements relevant to the success of a publicly-traded company in today's business environment.
- General understanding of the Company's business.
- Specific experience to fill needs or requests identified by the Board.
- Service on other boards.
- Educational and professional background.

The Board shall evaluate each individual in the context of the Board as a whole, with the objective of assembling a group that can best perpetuate the success of the business and represent shareholder interests through the exercise of sound judgment using its diversity of experience and backgrounds.

**Stock Ownership:** Each new Board member shall own within three (3) years of joining the Board a number of shares of PAT Common Stock equal to a minimum of $225,000 divided by the share price of the Common Stock at the time the Director joins the Board.

**Conflicts of Interest:** Directors are expected to avoid any action, position or interest that conflicts with the interests of the Company or gives the appearance of a conflict. If an actual or potential conflict of interest develops, the director should immediately report the matter to the Chairman of the Board. Any significant conflict must be resolved or the director should resign. If a director has a personal interest in a matter before the Board, the director will disclose the interest to the Board and not participate in the discussion of or vote on the matter.

**Board Orientation and Continuing Education:** The Company provides new directors with a Director Orientation Program to familiarize them with, among other things, the Company's business, strategic plans, significant financial, accounting and management issues, compliance programs, conflicts policies, Code of Business Conduct and Ethics, Guidelines, principal officers, internal auditors and independent auditors.

The Company will make available to all directors continuing education programs, and each director is expected to participate in one such ISS-accredited program at least every three years, as management or the Board determines desirable.

## *Continuing Corporate Governance*

The Board believes that good corporate governance requires continuing vigilance and oversight if it is to be successful. The following guidelines have been established to assist in accomplishing this objective.

**Independent Directors Access to Company Management:** Independent Directors shall have complete access to Company management in order to ensure that they can ask questions and receive information necessary to perform their duties. Directors should exercise judgment to ensure that their contact with management does not distract managers from their jobs or disturb the business operations of the Company. Such contact, if in writing, should be copied to the Chief Executive Officer.

**Meetings of Nonmanagement and Independent Directors in Executive Session:** Nonmanagement Directors will meet in executive session without management directors or management present at least four (4) times per year. The nonmanagement Directors will review the Company's implementation of and compliance with its Guidelines and consider such matters as they may deem appropriate. If the nonmanagement Directors include directors who are not Independent Directors, the Independent Directors also shall meet at least once a year in executive session.

Depending upon the subject of the meeting, it shall be chaired by either the Chairman of the Board or the Chairman of the standing Committee most involved in the matter being discussed.

**Shareholder access to Nonmanagement Directors:** Shareholders shall have an opportunity to pose written questions to the nonmanagement Directors about the normal operation of the Company and receive a written response.

**Board Access to Independent Advisors:** Board standing Committees may hire independent advisors as set forth in their applicable charters. The Board as a whole will have access to such advisors and such other independent advisors that the Company retains or that the Board considers necessary to discharge its responsibilities.

**Annual Self-Evaluation:** Following the end of each fiscal year, the Compensation, Nominating and Governance Committee will oversee an annual assessment of the Board's performance during the prior year as well as that of individual Board members. The Committee will be responsible for establishing the evaluation criteria and implementing the process for such evaluation, as well as considering other corporate governance principles that may merit consideration by the Board.

The assessment should include a review of any areas in which the Board or management believes the Board can make a better contribution to the governance of the Company as well as a review of the committee structure and an assessment of the Board's compliance with the principles set forth in these Guidelines. The purpose of the review will be to improve the performance of the Board as a unit and that of individual Board members. The Compensation, Nominating and Governance Committee will utilize the results of the Board evaluation process in assessing and determining the characteristics and critical skills required of prospective candidates for election to the Board.

**Annual Review of Chief Executive Officer:** The Compensation, Nominating and Governance Committee, with input from the Chief Executive Officer, will annually establish the performance criteria (including both long-term and short-term goals) to be considered in connection with the Chief Executive Officer's annual performance evaluation.

At the end of each year, the Chief Executive Officer will make a presentation or furnish a written report to the Committee indicating his or her progress against such established performance criteria. Thereafter, the Committee will meet to independently review the performance report. The results of this review and evaluation will be communicated to the Chief Executive Officer by the Committee Chairman.

**Succession Planning:** The Compensation, Nominating and Governance Committee shall work on a periodic basis with the Chief Executive Officer to review, maintain and revise, if necessary, the Company's senior management succession plan, including the position of Chief Executive Officer. The Chief Executive Officer will report annually to the Board on the status of this Plan including a discussion of assessments, leadership development plans and other relevant factors.

## *Questions for Discussion*

Questions that should be considered in this case include.

1. How successful has PAT been in implementing its strategic plan? How would you measure this success?
2. What were the risks that PAT undertook in implementing each successful initiative? Do you believe the risks were justified? To what extent were they mitigated by PAT? How were they mitigated?
3. What have been PAT's strategic failures? What do you believe were the causes of these failures?
4. Match the specific requirements of SOX with specific corporate excesses. Do you think that Congress did a good job in drafting this piece of legislation, in matching the "cure" with the "disease"?
5. What would be your recommendations to the Board regarding each point of the Joint Committee email?
6. Will any of your recommendations require a change in PAT's operating strategy (as discussed above)? What are the positive and negative ramifications of your recommended changes?

Please use these questions as a guide and not a format or a reflection of all of the questions that need to be addressed by the case.